Consultancy, Ministry
and Mission

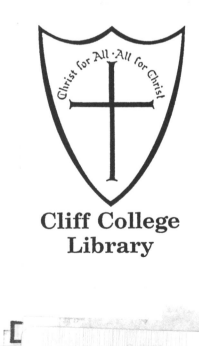

By the same author and published by Burns & Oates

ANALYSIS AND DESIGN
*A Handbook for Practitioners and Consultants in
Church and Community Work*

Consultancy, Ministry and Mission

A Handbook for Practitioners and Work Consultants in Christian Organizations

GEORGE LOVELL

BURNS & OATES

To Dorothy Household, an early
inspirational colleague to whom I owe
much and who would have loved to live and
work on this project
and
to all those who accompanied me in Avec
on the ministry through consultancy pilgrimage
and helped to make this book possible
and to those who still accompany me

First published in 2000 by
BURNS & OATES,
A Continuum Imprint
The Tower Building, 11 York Road, London SE1 7NX
370 Lexington Avenue, New York, NY 11017-6503

ISBN 0 86012 312 X

Typeset by Shelleys The Printers, Sherborne
Printed and bound in Great Britain by
Creative Print and Design,Wales

Contents

PART ONE: PRAXIS AND THEOLOGY OF CONSULTANCY

PART TWO: WORK AND WORKERS

PART THREE:
TOWARDS MAKING CONSULTANCY PROVISION

Extended List of Contents

PART TWO: WORK AND WORKERS

ix

Introduction

CONSULTANCY, AN ESSENTIAL RESOURCE

Consultancy in the Christian context is a means of providing non-directive help on any practical, personal, theoretical or theological aspect of Christian vocation and the work of the Church.
Consultants are not responsible for doing the work. They help those who are without in any way controlling or directing them.[1]

Broadly speaking work consultancy is to reflective practitioners and their work what counselling is to people and their lives.

Consultors are those seeking consultancy help; consultants those offering it.

The Church needs specialist consultancy services but it is essential to its overall effectiveness that leaders, workers and ministers can and do act as consultors and as consultants to each other in the workplace.

Consultancy services will be a commonly accepted and deeply valued characteristic of the work-culture of the third millennium.

The Need for Consultancy Ministry

Generations of people engaged in the work of the church have given outstanding service without consultancy help and many continue to do so. Why then is it now becoming both a perceived and felt need? [2]

Briefly stated I believe it is because of radical changes in the work culture in church and in society. A paradigm shift is occurring in the ways in which people work together. Egalitarian, participative and non-authoritarian working relationships are becoming more widely accepted, in theory if not always in practice. More clergy, religious and laity are using methods from the behavioural sciences. There is a strong movement towards personal and collective responsibility. Appraisal and audit schemes are being introduced. Consequently, for instance, increasingly those who were trained to direct and lead now collaborate, enable and empower. Those schooled to service, maintain and develop established programmes of church, and community work, have now to design and manage new projects and programmes. Those who were trained to follow traditional ways have to think out

1

for themselves how to do things, their motivation for doing them and how to get others to do the same.

Also, there are significant changes in the kind of work undertaken by churches and in the purposes for which it is done. It is now common practice, for instance, for churches, in addition to their traditional activities, to be deeply involved in ecumenical partnerships and in community work. Some churches are engaged in inter-faith projects with genuine altruistic motives: proselytizing has given way to new approaches to mission and evangelism which include dialogue and working together with others for the common good. Consequently ministers and laity who once pursued their ministry with segregated like minded people, now have to relate to and work with people of other denominations, religious and secular cultures and ethnic backgrounds. Considerable interpersonal skills and theological acumen are required to do this with respect for the beliefs of others and the moral and spiritual integrity of all involved.

Alongside these changes, the membership of churches and religious orders is falling, in some cases dramatically. Fewer ministers and religious are available. Many lay leaders and workers find themselves with less time and energy for voluntary work because of the demands made upon them by their jobs and professions. Consequently more is required of retired people especially those who have taken early retirement. Resources are reduced. Logistics and economics mean that organizational changes have to be made. Structures have to be slimmed down. There is less energy and time for reflection and creative thought. At the same time society and human and spiritual needs present new and exciting challenges to the Church. Resources must be used strategically and efficiently if the Church is to seize the enormous opportunities. Lay leaders, deacons, religious and ministers must have every form of help and support that they need.

The Need for Collaborative Reflective Practitioners, Churches and Communities

All this adds up to multi-dimensional changes in the approaches and attitudes of those engaged in contemporary church and community work, in individual, group and organizational behaviour and in the body of knowledge required to work out Christian vocation in the contemporary setting.[3] Combined, these changes make great personal, practical, relational, theoretical and theological demands upon workers. Accepting the practical aspects of these changes without examining the underlying theory and theology makes workers vulnerable because they cannot give adequate reasons for what they are doing. Yet examining the underlying theory and theology openly and critically is a complicated business. It involves exploring other denominations and religions and foraging in many disciplines such as theology, sociology, management and business studies, the study of organizational theory and behaviour, social work and community development studies. Extraordinarily difficult things for busy practitioners to do! Rival claims and contradictory theories can confuse laypeople and specialists alike. No sooner have workers and people got hold of one new idea and concept than it seems to be upstaged by another. Very few people can master even one discipline. Workers often find themselves on the practical and theoretical edges of all this - and they are practitioners, not academics;

they have to decide and act now, not juggle with and speculate about ideas and theories indefinitely.

To be effective and to experience vocational fulfilment in this changing context clergy, religious and laity must reflect, critically, imaginatively and systematically, on their own and with others, on the work, ministry and mission in which they are engaged or contemplating. In short, workers need to be reflective practitioners capable of promoting collaborative reflective groups in churches and communities. For some this is already an established way of life, they are thoroughgoing reflective practitioners; but for many, if not most, it is not.

The Need for Training and Consultancy

Gradually, training is being made available to help clergy and laity to make this radical shift in their work culture, to become collaborative reflective practitioners and to acquire analytical tools which they themselves can use. Experience has proved that, in addition to training, workers now need people who can help them to reflect on their vocation and to examine the nature of their work, think through critical aspects of it, design new action programmes, open up new areas of work and deal with complex problems and emotive issues. Such people - commonly referred to as consultants, enablers or facilitators - need to be readily available at the moment and point of need. As we shall see, over the past thirty years a great deal of effort has gone into providing consultancy help and building up the body of knowledge about the practice theory upon which it is based. Unfortunately consultants are still in short supply as are courses to recruit and train them. *In fact the promotion of reflective practice has outstripped the resources required to sustain and service it.*

Meeting the need for consultants is frustrated by factors other than their shortage. There is considerable confusion about the precise nature of consultancy and the need for it and there is bewilderment about the different forms it takes. It had, for instance, been assumed that the church generally, and appraisal schemes in particular, could readily make use of consultants from the business world. But experience is showing that the transfer of skills from business and industry to the church is more complicated and problematic than was previously thought.[4] Nonetheless, much can be learnt from consultancy theory and practice in these and other domains which will help to develop consultancy services for those engaged in church and community work.

However, consultancy must not be seen as a substitute for long or short courses on the analysis, design and the doing of work with people. Profound learning occurs through consultancy, not least about what needs to be learnt. Consultors are open to it when faced with problems they desperately want to overcome and things they want to achieve. But if such learning is not the gateway to further study then consultors remain undesirably dependent upon the knowledge of the consultant.

Consultancy processes are, in fact, an important feature of the newly emerging work culture and, along with in-service training, are needed to help practitioners enter into it. Increasingly, practitioners need consultants who can help them to develop new work programmes, to tackle the problems as they encounter them, to acquire any skills they require and to integrate into their practice and theory things of value from other disciplines. To do this consultants have to study with practitioners the work in which they are engaged and the possible application of anything they feel might be relevant from their interdisciplinary experience and studies. The integrity and security of workers depend upon such tailor-made consultative processes, without them the contribution of consultants is likely to be just a veneer or add to the worker's confusion. Practitioners need to learn these consultative processes: they are considerable assets to every facet of their working relationships and they add to their security and integrity.

Currently there is a shortage of people skilled to act as consultors and consultants. The need is great as the demand for consultancy services rises sharply. How is it to be met?

A Providential Discovery

A particular form of consultancy has helped me personally to grapple with these changes and opportunities first as a consultor and then as a consultant. I first experienced it as a consultor when, in 1966, I was preparing myself to become the minister of Parchmore Road Methodist Church, Thornton Heath, which had been designated one of ten experimental church, youth and community centres planned for Greater London by the Methodist Church.[5] For four years I had been enthusiastically developing youth and community work in two seriously deprived urban areas in a nearby circuit.[6] It was a new area of ministry with which I was now hopelessly in love. I was married to it but the honeymoon was over! Problems of getting people to accept responsiblity for projects I thought we had agreed upon had beaten me. I knew I would meet such problems in one form or another in Parchmore. I needed help. A wide ranging search for it was successful only when I met Dr T. R. Batten, at that time the Reader in Community Studies in the University of London. I poured out what I wanted to do at Parchmore, the intractable problems I had encountered in my previous attempts at church based open youth and community work and my hopes and fears. He listened intently. He asked questions. His responses showed me that he understood precisely what I was talking about. Within no time we were working things out together, not just talking about them. Words and diagrams were power tools and the papers on which they were written were work sheets of great value. *No one had ever talked to me about my work like that before*. I knew I had stumbled on treasure. I needed and wanted the ways of thinking and working I had just experienced and I was prepared to sell everything to have it for myself. As I write, I experience again the deep feelings of excitement and joy that I had then.

Like all subsequent consultations—and I continued to have them for almost thirty years—this one was significantly but subtly different from anything I had ever experienced before. The process was different, it was an alliance of minds, experience and insights in relation to *my* work, *my* purposes, *my* beliefs and *my* concerns. In contrast, the active giving and the passive receiving of advice, with which I was very familiar, were dowdy and demeaning patronage. The consultations involved meticulous cooperative analysis and the examination of alternative courses of action, but not in an argumentative ór competitive manner: there was no "winner" or "loser" The content was rich, not least because the consultant had a wide knowledge and experience of different ways and means of working with people. It was intense, "structured", and disciplined concentration and yet strangely open and free. It facilitated the development of thought; it enabled us to get to the bottom of things, to face realities and conflicting ideas and views, to keep our feet on the ground whilst dealing with vital theoretical and theological issues; it engendered objectivity and helped to get things into perspective. From his wide repertoire the consultant was selecting first this and then that and testing out with me whether they fitted or were useful or not: those that were not were abandoned undefensively without ceremony whilst those which proved to be suitable were adapted. Concentration on *my* situation and *me as a* worker gave me a confidence and freedom of expression I had never previously known in discussions with people in the academic world.

Not surprisingly, the results and consequences were quite different from those associated with the giving and receiving of advice and arguing cases. I never left such consultancy sessions without feeling challenged, uplifted and encouraged, with insights into what I could and could not do, with a renewed desire and enthusiasm to get on with what I had seen I must do. And I did not feel slavishly bound by what had been decided during a consultation. I was free to work things out as it subsequently appeared right for me to do so in the situation. Always I was urged to subordinate the authority of the consultancy session to that of the working situation. Previously I had not experienced the freedom to explore things privately with the freedom to practise publicly without fear of censure or of losing "friends" if I did not follow the advice I had been given. Both freedoms resulted from the consultant's non-directive approach. Most of the things worked out in these consultations paid high dividends in a wide range of work: sometimes by the direct application of what had been thought out, sometimes through using the same thinking process with others and coming to similar or different conclusions.

Gradually, as my ministry at Parchmore developed, I started to offer to others this kind of consultancy help without naming it, but with much trepidation because I lacked so many of Batten's qualities and abilities. My zealous desire to provide this kind of service compensated to some extent for my lack of skill and ability, at least I like to think so as I recall my first clumsy attempts! Parchmore eventually had a full-time youth worker and a part-time community worker. I acted as "consultant" to them and, in turn, they to me. This arrangement was extended to the voluntary youth and community workers. Sometimes the sessions were formal ones: meeting at an appointed time, sitting around a table with an agreed agenda and objectives and using a blackboard or large sheets of paper upon which to make notes and lists and to draw charts and diagrams. Others were informal and impromptu "sessions": sitting having a cup of coffee and drawing on scraps of paper, or standing by the car before departing for home and constructing diagrams on dusty metal surfaces. The practice was extended to the Sunday School staff; the Sunday School Superintendent (a regular monthly meeting at 4 pm on a Friday in my study on her way home); the Boys' Brigade officers; the Wives' Club, staff and members. These sessions proved to be effective and people began to ask for this still unnamed kind of help. Instinctively they too knew that it was different and valuable. Work consultancy, like pastoral counselling, became a core activity of my ministry. The time-cost-effectiveness of this was enormously high. One hour spent in such a consultation enabled others to achieve much more than they would otherwise have done; it enabled me to have a much deeper and fuller picture of the rapidly expanding work than I could possibly have had otherwise; it enabled both them and me to make more profound contributions to the parts and to the whole. So, I had stumbled upon a way of receiving and giving help on church and community work of which previously I had no notion.

Since those early days Avec* staff developed and used this form of consultancy with some 3,500 people of seven denominations and acted as consultants to numerous individuals, teams and projects. Roughly speaking the staff worked equally with Anglicans, Methodists and Roman Catholics, they worked with laity and almost equally with religious and clergy at all levels of the Church. Most of the people were working in the UK and Eire but they worked extensively with missionaries and led major work consultations in Central and West Africa.[7] All this, which has been thoroughly evaluated internally and externally, confirms my experience of the value of of work consultancy.[8] It enables people to study their own work, receive non-directive assistance, and think out programmes of work which fit them and their situation.

So, over a long period I have been learning about consultancy through receiving and providing it in relation to a wide range of subject matter. At the same time I was a practitioner/trainer in local church and community development work in various settings. For most of this period I was researching all the work in which I was involved through a series of action-research programmes.

Several things emerged from doing these things together. On the one hand I gained a deeper understanding of: different kinds of church and community work and the approaches and methods being used; the contexts in which it had to be done; the essential nature and characteristics of work which promoted human and spiritual development. On the other hand the combined use of the non-directive approach and action research methods led to the development of effective ways of analysing and designing church and community work in the workplace and through consultancy processes.[9] All this helped me to conceptualise work situations, to engage with them and to analyse and design them on my own and with consultors. Gradually, I started to study other people's writings on consultancy and to write about it myself.

This Book

The basic aim of this book is to make a contribution towards meeting the needs for consultancy services in the Church and Christian organizations. It is a handbook for those seriously interested in studying and promoting consultancy and in practising as consultors and consultants and training others to do so. Also, it is useful for those responsible for resourcing and managing church and community work. Therefore, it could make a contribution towards all that is being done to promote reflective practice, equip reflective practitioners, improve the quality and effectiveness of

---

* Avec was a Service Agency for Church and Community Work, from 1976 to 1994. I was the Director from 1976 to 1991. It was an Associated Institution of Roehampton Institute. A critical account of what made and marred this institution is to be found in Lovell, George (1996), *Avec: Agency and Approach* (An Avec Publication).

church and community work and enhance the job satisfaction and creative productivity of those engaged in it. Primary objectives are to:

- spell out the practice theory of consultancy;
- provide information which makes possible a critical assessment of the value of non-directive consultancy to those at work in the church and community;
- help practitioners to be consultors and consultants and to develop their own consultancy practice;
- offer a training resource ;
- provide information about the actual uses which are and can be made of different forms of consultancy services which will help authorities to make them readily available;
- build up a climate of opinion throughout the Church which is more conducive to the provision, funding and use of consultancy.

The Evolution of Three Mental Pictures or Maps

At an early stage in the research and writing programme from which this and other books evolved I found myself confusing and equating analytical and consultancy processes. One of the main reasons for this was that the analysis and design of church and community work form major parts of consultancy. Another reason was that they have approaches and processes in common. Separating them was a disclosure event. It enabled me to see that the nature, practice theory and theology of the one differs significantly from that of the other and that the respective activities were obscured and confused by the overlap and similarities between them. So I set out to write two books, one on analysis and design and the other on consultancy which would clarify both activities and show the relationship between them.

Having published the first book, *Analysis and Design*, and got into this one, other issues which had been rumbling around in my mind for some time surfaced when I was involved in designing a post graduate course on consultancy. I realised that I had been concentrating almost exclusively upon defining the nature of consultancy and the theology upon which it is based and formulating a mental picture of the practice theory that makes it effective. Necessary as this is to the promotion of consultancy, I now saw that two other mental pictures or maps need to be readily available to consultants and consultors. The first of these would depict the *forms and nature of the work* which have to be done to carry out the Christian project in different churches and through them in widely differing socio-religious environments and contexts. The second would depict the *attributes and skills* required of those called and commissioned to do this work. These pictures are constituent parts of my work view.

Previously, I had a much clearer working model in my mind of the practice theory of consultancy than of the nature of the work and the attributes required of workers. I had conceptualised some aspects of the work and the workers required very clearly, especially those associated with non-directive collaborative action. These and other less well thought out ideas emerged in consultancies in various ways but they had not been shaped into rounded models of the essential characteristics of the nature of church and community work and workers. Without such models there was

7

an over-reliance on consultancy praxis. Amongst other things, this meant that conceptually there was an inbuilt bias to work to the actual nature of the work rather than to the actual and the ideal together. The other models act as correctives to this propensity.

But there simply were no overall pictures of the nature of the work and the attributes of workers known to me and those I consulted which would readily facilitate the performance of these functions. Much has been published about the forms of church and community work but I could not find a suitable description of its nature, *i.e.:* its essential characteristics.There are many descriptions of worker's attributes, but none which fitted what I felt was needed. So I took my courage into both hands and did what I now realise consultants and consultors need to do for themselves, I constructed my own. Consequentially, this book includes mental pictures of :

— the practice theory of work and vocational consultancy (Chapters 1 and 2);
— the forms and nature of church and community work (Chapter 6);
— the attributes required of workers (Chapter 7).

These are presented as working pictures or maps, the ones I am currently using. Because they are continually put to work they contain living models which evolve. As I struggle to articulate them, I see them grow and develop into new shapes. They mirror the stage of my development as a consultancy practitioner. So they are not in any way presented as final and perfect.

They are offered to you as aids in formulating your own pictures, maps and models. You may use them as a starting point or as a collection of suggestions to stimulate your own thinking. However this may be, you need pictures and models that you own as yours and with which you feel comfortable and which you can use to good effect.

As the details of the three pictures emerge, ways in which they correlate and correspond become clear. Approach, attitude, belief, purpose, collaborative reflective practice and the non-directive approach, for instance, are common denominators. However, for the purposes of this book the pictures stand side by side, as they normally do when ready to be used comparatively or interactively in analytical or consultative processes. These uses are illustrated in the text generally and in the detailed case study in Chapter Three. The pictures are cross referenced, but not exhaustively so. What has become clear to me through researching and writing this book is that three separate pictures are more useful in reflective analytical and consultative practice than a unitary one.

For our purposes the consultancy practice theory picture is the substantive guide to consultancy processes; those of the nature of the work and the attributes of workers capable of doing it being vital auxiliaries. The picture of the consultancy model helps consultants and consultors to consider realistically, analytically and purposefully the work in which consultors are engaged and the approaches and methods they are using. Consultancy processes are also facilitated through using the pictures and models of the nature of the work and the attributes required of practitioners to compare and contrast the actual in relation to that which is ideally required. This leads to thoroughgoing analysis and design of projects, programmes and problems based on situational realities and theological criteria implicit in the Christian project.

Valuable immediate and long-term returns normally accrue from this form of consultancy because at its very heart are profound learning experiences about the nature of work and the attributes required of workers. Consequently it fashions the work and the workers, consultors and consultants. Consultors invariably find that they have a better understanding of themselves as practitioners and of the work about which they have consulted. This means that, more often than not, they find that they are more effective right away and enjoy greater job satisfaction. Consultors and their colleagues find their confidence grows, morale goes up and new vocational energy is generated. So, the work and workers are in flow. Moreover, what is learnt is not restricted to the specific work situation. Consultors and consultants get a better understanding of the actual and the ideal nature of church and community work, the ways in which it is and should be done, the positive and negative factors in Christian organizations and their communities which enable and prevent their development, the accommodations that have to be made in vocational engagement. At the same time they are learning about ways and means of analysing and designing church and community work and the giving and receiving of consultancy help. Much of this learning occurs whether or not the presenting problems are resolved or not: in fact, there is as much, if not more, potential for learning in failure as in success. The accumulative effect upon consultors is that they are better equipped through the knowledge and skills they gain to do their present work and to do other work in the future.

Also, knowledge and use of the pictures of the nature of the work and workers:

- equip "enablers" and "facilitators" to be church and community work consultants. Without this knowledge they are overly dependent upon the material that consultors produce. They are not equipped to get consultors to take into account other relevant information.
- facilitate the critical, evaluative examination of consultancy practice theory in relation to the essential nature of the work and the attributes of workers. Therefore they can be used to make significant contributions towards the development of Christian models of consultancy practice for church and community work which, in turn, can be examples of good church and community work praxis.
- are a permanent reminder that consultancy praxis evolves from ongoing interactive processes with work and workers: it is not something created in abstraction with a separate life of its own.
- can be used to profile and audit the relationship between the actual and the ideal.This can be done through the continual cross reference of the actual nature of the work associated with a range of programmes and projects and the way in which workers carry them out with those characteristics which make church work and workers what they are intended to be, *i.e.* the quintessence of their true nature.

With hindsight, therefore, three books should have been written on the following subjects and in the following order:

(a) the nature of church and community work and the attributes required of its practitioners

(b) the analysis and design of church and community work

(c) consulting about church and community work.

But, as we have seen, in the messiness of development through trial and error, and reflection and research, that is not how things evolved! *Analysis and Design* which covers (b) with brief reference to (c), emerged first in 1994. It has detailed worked examples of working analytically and constructively on cases, problems, situations and projects. *Telling Experiences* came next in 1996. It illustrates (a), (b) and (c). Now this book deals with (a) and (c)!

Other Parts of The Book

Briefly stated the remainder of the book: illustrates consultancy, describes the forms it can take and discusses common problems; suggests ways in which readers can develop their own models; profiles the uses made of consultancy services and ways of providing them. The structure and details are set out fully in the list of contents.

Emphases and Key Themes

It might be helpful at this stage to note briefly some of the emphases and key themes which are distinctive features of the approach to and the provision of consultancy help in this book. They are as follows.

- *This book is about consultancy processes in church and community work but the approaches and methods could be adapted to any form of purposeful work with people.*
- *Ministry through consultancy is an auxiliary, work centred service to practitioners, churches and organizations provided by specialist consultants and colleagues. It is a way of facilitating creative human involvement in the work of Christ in the Church and the world. It is based on the model of the Church as a working institution and its members as co-workers with Christ.*
  "Work" is a key concept in this book. It helps us to think about the work of Christ and of the Church in ways that, for instance, "ministry" does not, although some prefer to use this term. The notion of work is used to focus on the job of Christian ministry: Consultancy helps people to express and examine work issues, tasks and situations and their feelings about them.
- *Consultancy is an important feature of a newly emerging work culture which is needed to help practitioners and churches to enter into it.*
  Changing aspects of the culture and scope of this work are described earlier in this introduction.
- *Consultancy relationships, processes and purposes require consultants to interact positively and creatively with consultors in a non-directive mode.*
  If the consultor is to own the thinking and the outcome of consultations, this rubric must apply to the consultor's and the consultant's input (of content or procedure or structure). Occasions when consultants have to be directive must not be allowed to compromise the essential non-directivity of their contribution.

- *Seven systemic elements of practice theory and theology form the constituent and systemic parts of the given work and vocational consultancy model.*
  The elements, differentiated and integrated conceptually and practically, are: roles; interpersonal behaviour; working relationships; work-views; thinking together; systemics and logistics; beliefs, values and qualities.
- *Consultancy processes are shown to be profoundly theological because they are incarnational, salvatory, revelatory, resurrectional, creational and sacramental.*
- *Mental pictures of the nature of church and community work and the attributes required of those engaged in it are presented as invaluable aids to working to the actual in relation to the ideal through "work-views".*
  Fourteen essential characteristics of the nature of church and community work are examined in some detail. They form a work map with several frames of reference: attitudinal, relational, situational, vocational, missiological. This, along with a twenty-four factor mental picture of the attributes required of workers, helps consultors and consultants to consider their work in relation to existential and theological realities.
- *Consultancy processes are described, examined and illustrated throughout from the complementary perspectives, abilities, contributions and responsibilities of consultants and consultors.*
  Self-evidently, the effectiveness of consultations depends upon the abilities of both principal parties and not simply upon those of consultants. But, surprisingly, much of the literature concentrates on the skills of consultants and neglects those of consultors. The emphasis here is upon consultants and consultors collaborating in organising, designing and managing consultancy processes and establishing appropriate forms of interpersonal behaviour.
- *This book examines the ways in which consultancy operates through and upon a consultor's work-view interacting with the consultant's.*
  Work-views sum up what consultors know and believe about their work, how they feel about it and how they respond to it. They are not to be equated or confused with the work itself.
- *Consultors and consultants need to develop their own practice theory of work and vocational consultancy and their own mental maps of the nature of church and community work and the attributes required of workers.*
- *Sequential consultations between a consultor and a consultant over an extended period about aspects of their work and their vocation can be very productive: discussions about work and vocation inform and correct each other constructively.*
- *An approach to consultancy is presented which can and needs to be used by external specialists and generalist consultants and by practitioners.*
- *Consultancy needs can be met comprehensively only through the combination of specialist services and by workers giving to and receiving from each other consultancy help in their workplaces.*
  Such internal and external provision alone will meet the need and as it does so it will promote interdependent self-sufficiency in church and community practitioners and organizations, minimise unhealthy dependency on specialist

11

consultants, build up collaborative and reflective relationships throughout the workforce. Progress has been made towards such holistic provision notably through Avec.

- *The design and maintenance of socio-religious institutions which are effective instruments of Christian mission are treated as vital and highly skilled missiological occupations.*

Those who Could find this Book Useful

This book goes into the practical and theoretical detail required by those who wish to learn about the nature of church community work, the attributes required of practitioners and consultancy theory and practice. Also, it explores the theological features of consultancy in order to set it in the praxis of Christian ministry and mission. That makes it a handbook-cum-textbook for those who wish to develop and practise their own consultancy models and to train others to do the same. It is for anyone engaged in any way in the use, organization and provision of consultancy services and especially for:

- ministerial students
- ordained, religious and lay practitioners
- consultors
- consultants
- anyone engaged in appraisal schemes
- those engaged in pastoral management and supervision such as bishops
- those involved in training.

Reading and Using This Book

Having completed Parts I, II and III, I began to wonder whether it would be better to put II first. Was it better, I cogitated, to study the nature of the work and the attributes of workers and then how to consult about it or to study consultancy and then to examine the nature of the work and the workers to which it has to be applied? Eventually I came to the conclusion that the answer depended upon the individual reader. Some may wish to read the book through in an orderly way. Others may enter it through a subject of interest or a particular problem and move backwards and forwards through the text. The material is presented in such a way that it can be readily accessed in many different ways.

Its Nature, Status and Primary Function

T. R. Batten, a keen gardener, developed an extremely good system for making excellent multi-graded compost. The local horticultural society invited him to give a talk about his method. Someone broke into his explanation saying with considerable exasperation, "That is not how it is done!" Batten's reply was sharp and telling, "Undoubtedly there are other ways of doing it, but that is precisely how *I do it* and I was invited here to talk about how *I do it*." That exchange helps me to highlight at the end of this introduction what I am attempting in this book. I describe and examine my approach to consultancy work from the perspectives of being a church and community development worker, consultor and consultant. As I have described earlier; for over thirty years I have been receiving and offering consultancy, on my own and with many colleagues from all denominations. Consequently, at the heart of the book there is an evaluation of the experience of a wide range of consultancy work.

But the book is more than that. Drawing upon wide ranging experience, it puts forward what I *now* consider makes for good practice and discusses the theory and theology upon which it is based. Consequently it is the best statement I can make about the ideas and understanding that will guide the next phase of my work in this field, rather than an attempt to simply describe and/or justify what I did in the past and why I did it.

Some of the things I write about I have learnt directly from my own experience and those with whom I worked. Other things I have learnt from using and adopting other people's ideas and studying their writings. Much of what I have learnt has become an integral part of my own practice theory. Other things I am gradually assimilating. All this I gladly and fully acknowledge. The late James Britton, one time Goldsmith's professor of education, catches the nature of the process I am pointing to:

> The practitioner does not merely apply, he *(sic)* must reformulate from the general starting points supplied by research and arrive at new ends—new not only to him, but new in the sense that they are not part of the research findings, being a discovery of a different order.[10]

Describing the approach in this way facilitates a thorough going critique of it in its own right and in relation to other approaches. That I welcome as part of developmental processes. It follows that, whilst I give some indication of the location of my own approach in the spectrum of approaches, this book is not a typology of consultancy models although it could be used in the construction of one. Readers can use it to locate my approach in relation to their own and that of others.

Presenting the material in this way will, I believe, help to achieve a primary objective to which I am highly committed: *to help consultants to develop their own modes of consultancy, i.e. those which enable them to act ever more effectively themselves both as consultors and consultants.* In other words, I am describing my way so that you can do it your way. Please read the text with this in mind. For some, adopting the approach proffered here may well be a starting point; others may experience the presentation as a foil which stimulates them to articulate their own practice theory and become more committed to tending to its evolution; yet others may find one idea or another useful; and some may expostulate with Batten's critic, "That is not how it is done!" Each and all of these responses could help to achieve my objective, practitioners having a wardrobe of consultancy clothes which fit them. It is highly desirable that all practitioners, organizations and churches should be dedicated to pursuing zealously the development of their own practice theory and drawing out and reflecting upon the theory and theology upon which it is based. Effectiveness and growth depend to some extent upon these activities. Consequently it is important that clergy and laity are taught how to do these things by college tutors, in-service training staff and by consultants. It is a key to good reflective practice.

My hope is that, in one way or another, the book will induce inner and interpersonal dialogues which will enhance all our abilities to act as consultors and consultants. And I pray that it will help to prompt the Church to provide members of its workforce with more and better consultancy services which they deeply need and richly deserve.

These desires and aims point to some of the reasons why I have dared, but not without trepidation, to expose my own practice theory and theology with all its inadequacies to critical scrutiny.

Notes and References: Introduction

1. This statement is an adaptation of definitions by Fritz Steele and Peter Block quoted by Kubr, Milan (1976, Third Edition 1996) *Management Consulting: A Guide to the Profession* (International Labour Office, Geneva) p 3.

2. Lippitt and Lippitt give four reasons for "the growth and development of consultation resources": technological development and its impact on life styles; crisis in human resources and "the under utilization, underdevelopment and misuse of such resources as racial and ethnic minority groups"; undeveloped consulting skills of workers; discretionary time to spend beyond wage-earning activities. *The Consulting Process in Action* (University Associates, Inc 1986) p 2.

3. Kubr *op cit* has interesting chapters on "Consulting and Change" and "Consulting and Culture".

4. Professor Gillian Stamp made this abundantly clear in an article in which she argues that what is required in relation to ordained and episcopal leadership is "a firm rejection of the business model and the creation of a new model which will build on the enfolded and traditional hierarchies, but move towards a relationship with society based on service and example rather than on care and control". "A Church is not a Business", *Crucible* October-December 1983.

5. My six-year ministry at Parchmore was the subject of an unpublished doctoral dissertation: *An Action Research Project to Test the Applicability of the non-Directive Concept in a Church, Youth and Community Centre Setting*. A brief description of this work is given in my Beckley Lecture, *Human and Religious Factors in Church and Community Work* (1982) (A Grail Publication) p 15f and in an Avec publication which I wrote with Catherine Widdicombe *Our Church and Community Development Stories* (May 1987). Garth Rogers , Peter Sharrocks and I have written a book on the ministry at Parchmore from 1966 to 1989: *Parchmore Partnership: George Lovell, Garth Rogers and Peter Sharrocks*, Edited by Malcolm Grundy (1995) (Chester House Publications).

6. See *Human and Religious Factors in Church and Community Work* (p 15) and *Our Church and Community Development Stories* (p 5) on this.

7. An article by Leslie Griffiths on the West Africa Project appeared in the *Epworth Review* Vol.15 No.2 May 1988 p 85-94 entitled "Relationship in Mission". It describes in some detail the consultancy process and the outcome.

8. Avec courses and, when possible, consultations were systematically evaluated by staff and participants. In 1990 MARC Europe undertook an external evaluation of almost all of Avec's work and produced a report: *Viva L'Avec: An Evaluation of Avec's Training Ministry* (MARC Europe Report 1991) pp 188 and Appendices.

9. cf Batten, T. R. and M. (1988) *The Non-Directive Approach* (An Avec Publication)

10. I owe this quotation to an obituary of Professor James Britton by Tony Burgess in *The Guardian*, 3rd March 1994.

LIST OF DISPLAYS

LIST OF FIGURES

CHARTS

Acknowledgements

This book emerges from the enormous privilege of exploring, in depth with thousands of people, critical aspects of the vocational work in which they were engaged over a period of thirty years. My debt to them is enormous and impossible to acknowledge. Also, I am enormously indebted to three groups of people for rich experiences in times of struggle, success and failure in the extensive Avec programme: my close colleagues and especially the late Reg Batten, Michael Bayley, Howard Mellor, Charles New and Catherine Widdicombe; the eighty associates who helped to staff the Avec programme; the Avec Trustees and especially the late Edward Rogers, chair for twelve years. They challenged and helped me to reflect on our raw experiences of consultancy and to give it theoretical and theological shape. From 1992-1996 my research support group gave this process a significant boost: they were Michael Bayley, David Deeks, Leslie Griffiths, Peter Russell, Moira Sleight and Catherine Widdicombe. To all these people I am deeply endebted.

When I retired as the director of Avec in 1991 the Trustees charged me with the responsibility of "harvesting the work of Avec". Pursuing this commission so far has taken nine years of research during my "retirement" and produced four books of which this is the last. This work has in part been financed and funded by: Avec (1991-93); honoraria from The Victoria and Chelsea Methodist Circuit; a Leverhulme Emeritus Fellowship (1993); the late Dr. Reg Batten and Mrs. Madge Batten; a private trust. It is also being promoted by Avec Resources. I am greatly indebted to these sources of financial, practical, moral and spiritual support.

Helping to develop and staff the MA Evangelism course at Cliff College stimulated and enabled me to contextualise my own work in the new and exciting thinking about missiology. For this disclosure experience I am particularly indebted to Kenneth C. Cracknell, Martyn Atkins and Timothy Yates.

My wife, Molly, has lived with the vicissitudes associated with this work and typed and re-typed most of it and checked manuscripts galore. To her I owe an enormous amount. Valerie Tredinnick typed part of the first draft. And various people helped with computerising the text: Sue Gascoigne, Ursula Roberts, Terrie Rees of Tukan. To all these I am deeply grateful.

To Howard Mellor I am deeply thankful. He proffered precisely the kind of help and security I needed at a particularly difficult period in producing this book.

Margaret O'Connor and Catherine Widdicombe have read the whole book in draft. Martyn Atkins read Chapters 6 and 7. Tim Harris and Heather Walton read an early version of these chapters. For the support, encouragement, corrections and suggestions they made I am deeply grateful. The final text is my responsibility not least because those who commented on early drafts have not seen this one!

I thankfully acknowledge permission from the following to quote from their writings or to reproduce figures from their publications: The Rev Professor K. Cracknell; The Revs David G. Deeks, William C. Denning, Diane M. Hare, Kenneth G. Howcroft; Deacon Margaret R. Matta on behalf of the Methodist Diaconal Order; The Rev Dr. Philip R. Meadows; Deacon Jane Middleton; The Rev

Acknowledgements

Charles T. F. New; Real People Press, Utah; Sage Publications Ltd.; Deacon Hilary Smith; University of California Press. I am doubly grateful to The Rev William Denning of Creative Art Network who graciously and generously agreed to his drawing being used on the front cover.

Search Press and Burns & Oates have made enormous contributions to the promotion of my work by producing three key books, the first in 1978. I am particularly grateful to Countess Charlotte de la Bédoyère and to Mr Paul Burns for believing in the value of the work and offering sound publishing advice, practical help and support. Thank you.

PART ONE

PRAXIS AND THEOLOGY OF CONSULTANCY

Introduction

This Part is about a way of helping practitioners, individually and collectively, to be more effective at church and community work without doing their work for them or directing them or supervising them or taking over from them in any way whatsoever. The help is a particular form of non-directive consultancy through reflective engagement with practitioners about their work. Consultations are designed to help people to pursue their vocational aspirations, to do the work in which they are currently engaged and to tackle the problems they are facing. They enable consultors to bring their working world forward into the centre stage of consultancy processes. Indeed, their ability to bring to life their work and their approach to it, is a critical aspect of effective consulting. Consultors are the go-betweens their working and consulting worlds and play key roles in relating them. Consultancy sessions are not ends in themselves. They are subordinate, occasional sub-systems which at best serve and boost consultors and their work systems. They do this through rigorous analytical and reflective processes which interact constructively with all the other ways in which practitioners are thinking about things on their own and with many different people in a range of relationships and contexts. Consultancy processes come full circle when what emerges from consultations generates increasingly more creative thinking in consultors and through them in their working relationships. Providing help in this way avoids consultors submitting themselves to another echelon of control or to others trespassing on their work territory, so it builds up the ability of people to act in their own right as independent and interdependent reflective practitioners. .

Specialist consultants can make important contributions but they simply cannot meet all the consultancy needs. To do that, and to ensure that practitioners are as self-contained and self-reliant as possible, it is necessary that they are able and willing to make do-it-yourself consultancy help readily available to each other in the work place. Fortunately, with some training and a modicum of experience this is possible through the approach to consultancy advocated and described in this book.

This Part has five chapters. The first, is a general introduction to the critical features of the particular approach to work and vocational consultancy central to this book. Chapter Two describes seven elements of the practice theory of this approach. This is an unusually long chapter. To have subdivided it would have partitioned elements which must be held together in praxis. Chapter Three is a worked example of the approach. Chapter Four is about ways and means by which consultants can form their own consultancy models. Chapter Five is about recurring challenges and problems and contains troubleshooting charts for consultors and consultants.

CHAPTER ONE

Consultancy, Consultors and Consultants

This chapter is an attempt to give something of the feel of the non-directive approach to work and vocational consulting as a prelude to, and a preparation for the rest of this Part which plunges into the details of what is involved in practising it. Apart from helping readers to make sense of basics of the practice theory, it will enable them to set the approach in the context of other forms of consultancy and to evaluate for themselves whether it fits in with their way of doing things and is likely to be of use to them.

I The Nature of Consultancy

As already stated, broadly speaking work consultancy is to practitioners and their work what counselling is to people and their lives. Work consultancy is about consultants (those who are consulted) helping consultors (those who are consulting) to think through their work and what they feel about it and helping them to decide what action to take and how to take it. To do this consultors and consultants apply themselves collaboratively to the strenuous activities associated with the analysis and design of the consultor's work. They pool their information and thoughts and work at them assiduously to discover insights and understandings which make sense to both of them and action plans for which consultors accept full responsibility. It is important that consultors do own the action plans and that they feel free to use, modify or abandon them as events subsequent to consultations require. Achieving such free, responsible ownership is of the essence of consultancy. Consultors simply must remain free to act in their own right in whatever way they and those with whom they work see to be best. Emphasizing this is necessary because the autonomy of those involved and implicated in consultancy work can by default be easily and subtly compromised and eroded. Consultors, for instance, can feel they must carry out just what was decided during consultancy sessions; consultants, on the other hand, can feel they want to ensure that what they see to be necessary is done; those with whom consultors work can feel consultants are influencing their situation without being accountable to them. To circumvent these real dangers consultants must avoid any semblance of remote control. They cease to be consultants if they supervise or manage consultors and their work or if they become co-workers through undertaking work that is properly that of consultors. Of necessity, therefore, being and remaining a consultant and avoiding these and other dangers, involves being non-directive in the ways defined earlier by T. R. Batten[1] and considered later. It is the use of this approach that enables consultants and consultors to be vigorously proactive in ways which help consultors and their colleagues to be more creatively active in their own right. It facilitates the bonding of consultants and consultors that is necessary for productive consultancy sessions and forges the freedom consultors need to be independent workers.

Consultancy help of the kind we are considering is offered in all cases through studying with workers work they are doing or contemplating doing. Consultors are active in two main domains: *the private* (in which they, on their own or with others, reflect on their work, think things through, reflect on their feelings and decid what they are going to do and how they are going to do it); the *public* (in which they engage with people in many different forms and modes, formally and informally). The private domain, for instance, might involve planning for a complicated meeting; the public domain, chairing that meeting. The one is at a distance from the public arena, the other is in the midst of it. *In consultancy work, the interaction between consultors and consultants is normally within the private domain. It is a private, off stage activity. A consultancy session is, in fact, an annexe or an extension to the consultor's private work domain.* So, whatever the subject matter, consultors "bring" their public and their private work to consultancy sessions in order that they, together with their consultants, can freely prepare in a safe confidential setting for public work by:

• examining and possibly re-ordering their private thinking and discerning implications for their work;
• considering what action they need to take in the public domain;
• determining how they themselves can translate private thinking into public action;
• considering, analysing and evaluating the effects and consequences of action taken and determining what implications they might have for them, the consultor.

(Consultancy project work and facilitation, as we shall see, differ from consultancy work because, in addition to the private work, consultants are active in the public domain with consultors and those with whom they work.)

By the very nature of things, consultancy is about the inner and outer worlds of workers and those with whom they work and the intricate relationship between them and their environment. These inner and outer worlds are aspects of the indivisible reality of all church and community work.[2] Therefore consultors and consultants must engage with the subjective and the objective dimensions of the consultor's work and of the consultancy processes: on the one hand with such things as belief, purposes, motivation and feelings; and on the other with people (the most significant part of our environment), events and the physical aspects of the working situation.

Work consultancy operates through the complex interplay between consultors and consultants. Thoughts, beliefs and feelings about the consultor's work and ways of approaching it are exchanged and mulled over. Consultors and consultants allow their respective perspectives and their perspectives on each other's perspectives to interact. The art and science of work consultancy is the fusion of these perspectives in processes which produce things within consultors which enable them to do their work more effectively and efficiently than they would otherwise have been able to do and with greater satisfaction. The fusion must occur within the consultors themselves if the energy is to be released in them and subsequently in their work-place. It is most likely to occur when the approach of the consultants is essentially

22

non-directive and when the consultors can handle this approach. Given these conditions,consultations create opportunities for the free association of ideas within the structured context necessary to fusion. Shorter and longer definitions can now be attempted.

Shorter definitions

Consultancy is a mode of critical reflective engagement by consultors and consultants on the consultor's agenda.

Consulting is "any form of providing help on the content, process, or structure of a task or series of tasks, where the consultant is not actually responsible for doing the task itself but is helping those who are".[3]

Non-directive work and vocational consultancy is a complex interplay between consultants and consultors which enhances the ability of consultors themselves to diagnose and do their work to better effect and strengthens their proactive initiatives in relation to reflection and action.[4]

And a longer definition

Consultancy is a process, primarily non-directive, of seeking, giving and receiving help aimed at aiding a person, group, church or organization to achieve their purposes in specific situations and circumstances [5] in ways which express their personalities and beliefs. Analyses and designs are produced through the creative interplay between consultors and consultants (their respective insights, understandings and perspectives) as they focus on consultors as vocational workers and on their work, the what, why and how of what they want to achieve and the circumstances in which they operate. This interplay has a unique and highly valued ethos generated by: the sentience of the methodology; the philosophy, theology and underlying assumptions of the non-directive approach; the nature of the interpersonal and interprofessional working relationships between consultors and consultants. Work consultancy is an aid to the private preparation for working with people for human and spiritual development in church and community. It is a professional service to and a pastoral provision for those engaged in work which is a mode of applied theology.

But as Edgar H. Schein says, "Process consultation", (a similar approach to the one I am describing) "is a difficult concept to describe simply and clearly. It does not lend itself to simple definition or to the giving of a few illustrative examples, because it is more of a philosophy or a set of underlying assumptions about the helping processes that lead the consultant to take a certain kind of attitude towards his *(sic)* relationship with the client".[6] This is what most people who experience the approach feel.

II Consultors and Consultants: Work and Vocation

The effectiveness of consultations is directly related to the ability of the consultors and of the consultants to interact creatively, relevantly and respectfully. To do this they each need the abilities necessary to their role and function and the confidence, freedom and discipline to work to the processes within agreed parameters. It takes two to tango. Some consultations in which I have been engaged as consultor have not achieved their full potential either because I had not the skills required (for instance to describe the situation or problem) or because I lacked courage to question the value of suggestions made by the consultant or because I was unable to deal with my defensive feelings. Notwithstanding these self evident facts, the literature I have read focusses almost exclusively on consultants and what they need to be able to do.[7] The neglect of the consultor's role is also indicated by the fact that, whilst the title consultant is widely used, there is no generally accepted or acceptable word to describe those who consult others. I have chosen to use the word 'consultor' rather than 'consultee' or client even though I have invariably to define it.

Consultants need to be trained, their skills are important. But any hint or suggestion that everything depends upon them is unhelpful and unhealthy. It is unhelpful because it is simply not the case. It can generate dependency. It can suppress the contributions of consultors. It can lead to consultants doing things for consultors which they should do for themselves. It can promote the practice of consultants managing and controlling consultations whereas consultors and consultants together should manage and control them. (Consultors controlling them is equally undesirable.) It is unhealthy because it militates against egalitarian relationships in which there is mutual respect and because it smacks of patronage. Consultants can feel superior and that is very serious in an activity the success of which depends very much upon the humility of consultants and of consultors. *Therefore, as much attention must be given to the abilities and understanding required of consultors as those required of consultants*: the skills, that is, that workers at all levels need to have in order to be able to act as consultors and to use consultants effectively.

One implication of this is that theological colleges would greatly help students by training them in the skills required by consultors and in this way introducing them to the skills required by consultants. (Members of a pre-ordination training course with whom I worked, greatly enhanced their abilities in a few days by practising amongst themselves being consultors to their "bosses" on subject matter of vital importance to both of them . They role played the parts of curates and rectors with a stunning realism!) Such training is necessary for at least two reasons other than those given above: normally they will be consultors before they are consultants; invaluable learning about the consultant's role can be gained from the perspective and experience of being a consultor.

Consultor skills reduce the danger of people becoming the victims of confusing and conflicting advice and will help them to deal with "experts" and their "expert" advice. If a group of clergy I worked with had accepted the advice of "experts" on youth work they would have continued to be locked into a sequence of youth club failures. They did not. They analysed critically the advice they had been given against their experience and decided to do something quite different and to inform the "experts" why their advice was flawed. Twenty years later there is a thriving youth counselling service employing several counsellors.[8]

III Abilities Consultors and Consultants Need

Consultors who understand consultancy processes and what consultants should and should not do are well equipped to consult. They can make their contributions more effectively and economically. They know what they are doing when contracts are made and consultancy boundaries are drawn. They can help consultants to do their job and question and challenge them when they are not. Such knowledge and the associated interpersonal skills give them more responsible control over the consultancy arrangements, reduce the dangers of them going wrong and greatly enhance their potential value. It puts consultants on their mettle! I know this from my long experience of acting as the work consultant to many different groups, the members of which I have helped to develop their consultancy skills through evaluating what we were doing together. Critical mutual awareness of the underlying discipline sharpens up practice quite remarkably.

Some understanding of consultancy can be gained only through evaluated experience of it. Consultants can help workers to acquire the skills consultors need and it is in their best interests to do so. However, even a brief introduction to the what and how of consultancy could add value to and reduce unnecessary costs and the pain of such experiential learning. A brief consultor's manual is needed.

One of the skills consultors need is the ability to get over to consultants as economically as possible the realities of the things about which they wish to consult. As we have noted already these realities have several aspects: the inner personal realities of the consultor's beliefs, purposes, feelings, hopes and fears; the realities of the situation in which the consultor is working; the realities of what the consultor can and cannot do in public and in private and that with which they can and cannot cope intellectually, theologically and emotionally; the realities of the consultor's context and that of the work situation. To be effective, consultors and consultants have to work to these realities and to the possibilities of changing them for the better that are feasible and manageable for the consultor (not the consultant!). When consultors think or feel that consultants have departed from any of these realities, they need the courage and the ability to say so even when they cannot explain rationally their intuitive knowledge that what is being proposed just does not fit or will not work or is something they simply cannot do. Consultors are primarily responsible for earthing consultancies in their realities for no other reason than that they alone can do this. Consultants can ask questions which prompt consultors to describe aspects of their situation and which invite them to check things out against their understanding of reality. Getting consultors to write situational papers is one of the ways in which this can be done. They might get them to reconsider their view of their situation, it often changes as consultations proceed, but consultors alone have the existential knowledge to test things out. Exploring these issues with consultors is a fascinating aspect of the consultant's job, demanding and exciting because of its subtle nuances and complexities. Then, consultants need to be able to check out what consultors say about their realities against the realities with which the consultants are acquainted.

In the final analysis the efficacy of work consultancy depends upon the ability of consultors to use the substance of consultancy to good effect. This involves the transfer of learning from consultancy sessions to the consultor's private and public

25

work places. This can be difficult. Consultants can and should help consultors to do this but they cannot do it for them.[9] (Consultants are sometimes accused of failure when in fact the failure in what follows or does not follow consultancy sessions is the responsibility of consultors or their organisations or maybe no-one's fault!).

All this demands much from consultors. They need many skills and gifts and graces to explore things openly and to avoid being defensive which can be a death sentence on consultancy work. It also demands much from consultants. They need the abilities and skills to help consultors to be consultors and to build up their confidence and abilities as they do so. They can only do this if they are genuinely interested in those who consult them and the work in which they are engaged and able to concentrate upon them single-mindedly. They need to be able to work to the consultor's belief systems. They need to be able to promote and to participate in the kind of interplay between consultors and consultants described earlier. They need to have relevant knowledge about working with people in today's church and community and to be able to get consultors to consider any ideas they might have about ways of doing things without any suggestion of imposing them.

Consultants need to be able to help consultors to work through processes of critical analytical thought [10] which enable them to diagnose the situation in which they find themselves, to explore their feelings and to design action plans which they have reason to believe they themselves can put into effect because they fit them, the ways in which they go about things, their purposes and beliefs and significant features of the working situation. So they have to be able to work with ideas and emotions. Such sequences involve heart and mind and very often traumatic experiences.

Designing people-work-programmes and helping others to do so is a practical craft using technical knowledge about people in religious and secular communities and an art form using creative imagination. Consultors are generally better at analysing and organising than at designing work programmes, not least because significantly much more is written about analysing and organising than about designing.[11]

Consultants must also make sure consultors can draw upon their beliefs when they are analysing and designing. It is imperative that there are active connections between what they believe and what they do: the one must represent and reflect the other. Experiential and applied theology is, therefore, an integral part of consultancy on church and community work. So it is necessary for consultants to be able to reflect theologically and to help others to do the same. Consultants have in fact to help consultors to research, evaluate and design development programmes.

A wide repertoire of skills is required by consultants to do this: the ability to listen and to verbalise; the skill to use questions; the ability to conceptualise and to model, verbally and diagrammatically, work situations, problems and cases in thought forms helpful to the consultors; the ability to find patterns in events that help to understand underlying dynamics; the discipline to work to the pace at which consultors and consultants can think and feel their way through things together.

Ideally consultancy relationships should develop the complementary skills of consultors and consultants so that consultations are mutually affirming and learning experiences which help to release the considerable amount of energy required for the tasks both parties have to do.

IV Features of The Non-directive Consultancy Model

Consultancy approaches and their titles are many and they seem to be on the increase. Comparing and contrasting them is not always easy because there are so many subtle twists and turns in the way in which they converge and diverge. Critical features of the non-directive model advocated in this book are given below to help readers to identify it and compare it with other models. Then in section VI brief descriptions are given of other approaches to help you to locate the model used here and your own in the spectrum of approaches to consultancy. Summarising the features of the approach you use would help you to do this and with the exercise suggested in Chapter Four.

The non-directive consultancy model:

- is pragmatic and theological;
- is essentially non-directive, collegial, egalitarian and collaborative;
- is dialogical, *i.e.:* it is a process facilitated by, and facilitative of, both internal and external dialogues by which people talk with themselves and with each other;[12]
- is a "client centred" approach in that it is orientated to consultors and through them to their work and vocation and the situations in and with which they are engaged;
- is a process which stimulates and facilitates progressive movement from thought to action through successive phases of reflection, evaluation, analysis and design;
- marries the expertise and abilities of consultors (especially their knowledge of themselves and of their situation) with that of consultants (especially their knowledge of ways of analysing and designing and working with people in churches and communities);
- is systemic because it is working with human socio-religious systems;
- engages with objective, subjective and interpersonal dynamics.

A brief statement of what the approach is not further sharpens up its identity. It is not an expert model, a doctor-patient/counsellor-client model, a trouble shooter model, a detective model or a psychodynamic model. Several factors make this model of consultancy possible and necessary.[13]

First, non-directive work and vocational consultancy helps practitioners to work with themselves, others and God. It is one of the ways in which Church workers can fulfil the Christian privilege and obligation to help each other in the work of the Kingdom of God. It enables practitioners to enjoy the privilege of sharing in and making valuable, humble, disinterested contributions to each others' work and vocations. In short, they act as consultancy servants to each other. This breaks down unhelpful competition and jealousy and builds up the spirituality and relationships required of a Christian work-force. The approach in action is reminiscent of the way in which God in general, and the Holy Spirit in particular works with us.

27

Second, as we have seen, practitioners and those with whom they work need to own analyses of their situation and the proposals for development if they are to have the energy and the commitment to take effective action and make things work. This does not necessarily mean that all analyses and designs have to be the original work of consultors, desirable as this might be. They can come from consultants. Whatever their origins consultors need to think them through for themselves. When they do so they will invariably be able to make significant modifications to them. This is the way in which many things happen: people can assess and suggest improvements to things they could not have invented, from socio-religious institutions and services to machines and works of art.

Third, consultors who engage with things in this way are more likely to implement any action plans that emerge. And they will have learnt much about how to deal with similar eventualities. Consultancy is about helping consultors to tackle situations so that they themselves can continue to do so more effectively in the future.

Fourth, from time to time practitioners and churches meet work situations that call for knowledge and experience which they have not got and may not know exists. This happens in relation to projects new to them or problems they do not know how to address. Opportunities would be lost if, before they could take the necessary action, they themselves had to acquire the requisite knowledge or skills through attending courses or doing private research. In circumstances such as these, when practitioners and Churches do want to do as much of the work as they can themselves rather than bring people in to do it for them or where they simply have to be involved in the projects and problems, consultancy can provide significant help. Providing, that is, that the consultants perform two functions: they introduce the consultors to ideas and methods they need in a manner in which consultors can understand and manage them; they get the consultors to think for themselves about the input in relation to their knowledge of their situation and their purposes, beliefs, approaches and temperament.

Fifth, one of the things which makes the approach possible is that consultants from outside of a consultor's working situation can gain from consultors sufficient vicarious knowledge and understanding of a situation to operate effectively without exhaustive and time-consuming study of it or actual participation in it. This is true of situations of which the consultant has no previous direct or indirect experience. To some extent this contradicts the popular belief that only those who have had a common or similar experience can understand "what it is like". Human beings can enter into each other's experiences. This is possible because consultors can provide consultants quite economically with all the information they need to function effectivey. This makes it possible for consultants to work *with* and *through* the mind, experience and knowledge of the consultor. By the same token, it is possible for consultants to contribute, and consultors to use to good effect, relevant aspects of their knowledge and experience to the consultancy process without consultors being thoroughly acquainted with the body of knowledge and experience from which the consultant is drawing. In brief, consultancy processes work because they enable two-way economic and purposeful sharing of information and ideas. Consequently, consultors and their churches can be helped to be more effective immediately without extended training and education. Consultancy really does facilitate interaction between and the interchange of expertise. Basically that is how consultancy works.

Sixth, consultations can help practitioners to discover what help they need when, for instance, they feel vaguely dissatisfied, know something is wrong but do not know what it is.

Seventh, a key function of consultancy is to provide immediate and long-term help in such a way that consultors themselves are equipped to do the things for which they previously needed consultancy help. This may mean helping them to get appropriate training or helping them into the relevant literature.

Eighth, the use of the non-directive approach and systematic methods of analysing and designing by consultants and consultors can have immediate positive effects: it enables people to acquire abilities, knowledge and skills which they did not previously have; it releases creative energy and reduces destructive energy associated with frustration; it contributes to changes in attitudes and working methods from, for instance, authoritarian, directive and competitive ones towards the collegial and collaborative.

V   Other Consultancy Models

A rough and ready classification of consultancy models can be made by distinguishing between the respective importance placed upon the expertise of consultants and consultors, *i.e.:* upon "external" and "internal" expertise. Some models are designed to stimulate and help consultors to contribute their knowledge and use and develop their expertise. The consultant's essential expertise is the ability to do this, to introduce into the process anything of value from her/his body of knowledge and experience and to help consultors to acquire the skills used in doing so. Another group of models are about bringing in consultants with the specialist knowledge and technical expertise which the consultors simply have not got and cannot normally acquire and getting them to apply their skills to the situation. The efficacy of these models depends upon consultants presenting themselves and their contributions in ways that consultors can make good use of them without becoming experts. Overstating the differences to make the distinction, the one aims to develop local internal expertise and the other to use external expertise. Both kinds of models have their appropriate and inappropriate uses.[14]

Nevertheless, to some extent, the distinction is one of emphasis and degree. All consultants need to be able to work with the people and to them and their situation. Most of those who see their essential contribution in getting and helping consultors to work at their own problems, bring knowledge about organizations and communities as well as about analytical and interpersonal processes. A consultancy programme may involve the use of different models of the two kinds through the use of internal or external consultants. For instance, I take into consultancies what I know about the nature of church and community work and development. Consultants, therefore, facilitate and introduce relevant material. (See the discussion about consultants and facilitators in Chapter 8. In some cases consultants do not have any more consultancy skills than their consultors. Their usefulness comes from the

29

opportunities their independence as "outsiders" gives them to be objective and even handed.

What follows are notes of some examples of both kinds of models: the list is indicative rather than comprehensive.

Models Which Emphasize the Uses and Development of the Expertise of Consultors

Systemics are generic to the approaches noted below even though this is not reflected in all the titles and descriptions.

*   *The Process Consultation (PC) Model*
    "Process consultation is a set of activities promoted by the consultant which help clients to perceive, understand and act upon their situation and to work for improvements they wish to see." [15]

*   *Soft Systems Methodology (SSM)*
    This is "an organized way of tackling messy situations in the real world. It is based on systems thinking, which enables it to be highly defined and described, but is flexible in use and broad in scope." The methodology is used to help consultors to take constructive purposeful action in their situations.[16]

*   *Development Consultation and The Use of Systemic Family Therapy in Organizational Consultancy.*
    Several methods are in use. Some derive from the work of a Milan group of therapists and others from the work of the Tavistock Institute.[17]

*   *Collaborative Inquiry: A Postmodern Approach to Organizational Consultation*
    This is a collaborative, collegial, egalitarian and systemic approach to consultation. It is based on a "framework for a partnership in which consultant and client combine expertise to explore their dilemmas and challenges and develop new possibilities for resolving them". Consultants operate from "a non-expert, non-hierarchical position, applying their expertise to the art of creating a dialogical space".[18]

*   *Client Centred Consultancy*
    This originates in client centred counselling. It emphasizes the importance of consultants and their processes being client centred rather than centred on the knowledge and skills of the consultant.[19]

*   *Working With The Energy in Organizations*
    Interesting research is under way into forms of consultancy "based on the idea that organizations can be seen as "flows of energy". This throws much light on all forms of consultancy because they work best when they tap and are vitalised by the energy of consultors and their churches or organizations.[20]

*   *The Non-directive Approach to Work and Vocational Consultancy*
    A form of this is the subject matter of this book.

Models Which Emphasize the Use of the Expertise of Consultants

Some consultancies in this category come under the heading, *"the purchase of expertise models"*. Consultors decide what they need to know and seek consultants who can find or provide the information from established knowledge bases or through surveys or interviews. Then there are consultants who through their expertise get to the bottom of problems and show how they can be solved. One form is the *"doctor-patient"* model. Consultants are invited to check over organizations or to diagnose symptoms and prescribe remedial action. Another form is the *"troubleshooter"* model made famous by Sir John Harvey-Jones. Yet another is the *"detective"* model. Consultants investigate situations in which it is suspected that work programmes and working relationships are being deliberately undermined, wrecked or sabotaged.[21]

Notes and References: Chapter One

1. Batten, T. R. and M. (1988) *The Non Directive Approach* (An Avec Publication).

2. In this section I have adapted some of the ideas shared by Charles Elliott (1987) in *Comfortable Compassion: Poverty, Power and the Church* (Hodder and Stoughton). He argues that tackling problems of poverty and suffering involves "a two-fold process, a dialectical relationship between the outward, material world and the inner spiritual world". p 119.

3. Steele, Fritz (1975) *Consulting for Organisational Change* (Amherst, MA, University of Massachusetts Press) p 3. I owe the quotation to Kubr, Milan (Ed.) (1986, 2nd, revised, edition) *Management Consulting: A Guide to the profession* (International Labour Office, Geneva) p 3. Kubr goes on to say that Peter Block suggests that: "You are consulting any time you are trying to change or improve a situation but have no direct control over the implementation." I feel this definition needs further qualification. "Consultants" could be trying to affect change by persuading or lobbying or even by manipulating.

4. Schein, Edgar H. (1988) *Process Consultation Vol. 1: Its Role in Organizational Development* (Addison-Wesley Publishing Co.) p 11 where he defines process consultation which helped me to formulate my shorter definition.

5. I owe some of the phrasing of this part of the definition to Lippitt, Gordon and Lippitt, Ronald (1986) *The Consulting Process In Action* (University Associates, Inc.) p 1.

6. Schein, Edgar H. (1980) *op cit* p 4f.

7. cf Lippitt & Lippitt *op cit* for instance.

8. The origins of this are described in *Churches and Communities: An Approach to Development in the Local Church* George Lovell and Catherine Widdicombe (Search Press) (1978 reprinted 1986) pp 86ff.

9. cf *Epworth Review* 15:2 May 1988 p 92f for an example of how seriously this point was taken in a West African project.

10. The sequence I use is described in Chapter 2, Element 5 especially the section on "tools, facilitating structures and thinking patterns".

11. cf Lovell, George (1994) *Analysis and Design: A Handbook for Practitioners and Consultants in Church and Community Work* (Burns & Oates) Chapter 6. Edward de Bono shares important insights into designing in *Parallel Thinking: From Socratic to de Bono Thinking* (Viking 1994). Parallel thinking "simply means laying down ideas alongside each other". Then "we design forward from a field of parallel possibilities".

12. The Phraseology of this point I owe in part to an article by Anderson, Harlene & Burney, Paul J. P., 1997, "Collaborative Enquiry: A Postmodern Approach to Organizational Consultancy" in *Human Systems: The Journal of Systemic Consultation and Management,* Volume 7 (2-3): 177-188.

13. Schein, Edgar H. (1988) *op cit* p10f helped me to formulate these points.

14. The Bible Society consultancy model is an example of the use of both process and expert models. cf *Bible Society Transmission* (Spring 1997) where the Rev Barrie Cooke explains the model in an article entitled "Charting a New Course for Your Church". It involves the consultant gathering detailed

information about the communities and churches, presenting profiles and helping churches to reflect on their mission in relation to the profiles and the data they contain. Barrie G. Cooke is making some useful points about the distinctions between different models of consultancy in research of the Bible Society consultancy model for an MPhil at Sheffield University through Cliff College. His distinctions have helped me in this section.

15. See for instance the work of Edgar H. Schein to which reference has already been made. The Rev David Coghlan, S. J., is making interesting contributions to the application of process consultation to the Church in general and to religious orders in particular, cf "In Defence of Process Consultation" an article he contributed to *Leadership and Organizational Development Journal* Vol 9:2 1988. And "Religious Orders and Consultants: Questions and Answers" which he contributed to *Religious Life Review* Vol. 26:128, Sept/Oct 1987.

16. Checkland, Peter and Scholes, Jim (1990) *Soft Systems Methodology in Action* (John Wiley and Sons) quoted from p 5.

17. See chapter 25 of Wynne, Lyman; McDaniel, Susan; & Weber, Timothy (Eds) (1985) *Systems Consultation* by Borwick, Irving "The Family Therapist as Business Consultant" (Guildford); Palazzoli, Mara Selvini *ibid*.

18. cf Anderson & Burney *ibid*.

19. cf Cockman, Peter; Evans, Bill; Reynolds, Peter (1992) *Client Centred Consulting, A Practical Guide for Internal Advisers and Trainers* (McGraw Hill Book Company). I owe this reference to Barrie Cooke.

20. Casemore, Roger; Dyos, Gail; Eden, Angela; Kellner, Kamil; McAuley, John; Moss, Stephen (Eds) (1994) *What Makes Consultancy Work—Understanding the Dynamics* International Consulting Conference 1994 (South Bank University) contribution by Tosey, Paul, "Consultancy as Working With The Energy in Organizations: A Report on Research in Progress" pp 394-405.

21. I am indebted to Schein for some of these distinctions.

CHAPTER TWO

Seven Elements of Practice Theory

Exploring what makes and mars consultancy is endlessly fascinating. Here I do just that in order to discern why it is advisable to do things in this way rather than that. My aim is to get at the practice theory or, as some would describe it, the praxis of consultancy. This is the practical wisdom grounded in consultancy experience, informed and sharpened by theoretical and theological insights, which helps people to be consultors and consultants and which contributes to the continuing development of effective consultancy practice.[1] Critical aspects of consultancy practice theory cluster around one or other of the following seven basic elements.

> Roles
> Interpersonal behaviour
> Working relationships
> Work views
> Thinking together
> Systemics and logistics
> Beliefs, values and ethics

The systemic relationships between the first six are modelled in Figure 2:1. Good practice requires that beliefs, ethics and values, the seventh element, suffuse all aspects of the other six elements. This is modelled in Figure 2:2. An integrated consultative system is in being when good practice in each of the seven elements jells.

These seven elements enable practitioners to keep the whole process and system in focus and perspective as they pursue the many aspects and minutae of good practice. They also provide a check list against which consultors and consultants can readily assess their consultancy strengths and weaknesses in general and evaluate good and bad experiences they may have had.

These elements of consultancy practice theory are compounds. They are formed from three different kinds of human and spiritual qualities and abilities. The first of these is the cluster of *personal attributes*, the being and behaviour that equip people to be consultants and/or consultors. Trustworthiness is an obvious example of this kind of quality. Secondly, there is the *body or bodies of knowledge*, the knowing and understanding which informs consultancy praxis. This can include such things as the ways in which groups churches and communities function, the broad based theory and theology of development, ecclesiastical structures and politics. Thirdly, there is the *technical and practical human relations skills* related to doing and making which are required of consultants and consultors. The ability and skills which, for instance, enable them to think and work together, to analyse and design problems and situations. So the practice theory elements describe what consultors and consultants need *to be*, what they need *to know* and what they need to be able *to do* and the importance of the unitive interplay between *being, knowing and doing*.Not surprisingly the same thing applies to the attributes required of practitioners as Chapter Seven demonstrates.

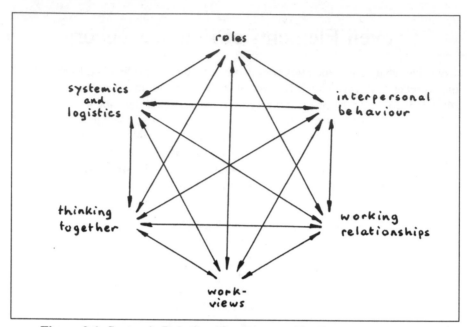

Figure 2:1 Systemic Relationships Between Six Consultancy Elements

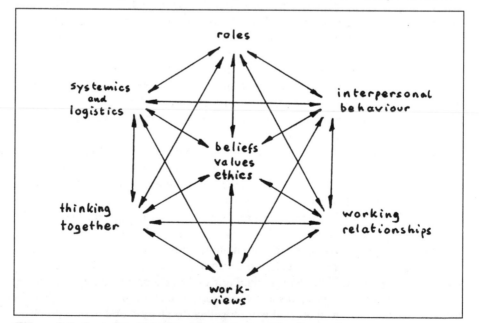

Figure 2:2 Systemic Relationships Between The Seven Consultancy Elements

At the heart of good consultancy practice is the ability of consultants and consultors to build these elements into consultancy systems that *work for them* in relation to what *they are doing*. To do this they have to put aside any ideas that a code of good practice is a simple list of "do's" and "don't's". Work consultancy is not a series of mechanical procedures. It is a creative art, based on the insights of Christianity and the behavioural sciences, which engages with all that is involved in the work of God and people in all the glory and messiness of human and spiritual life in the church and the world.

Consultancy work takes place in many different settings and relationships (cf Chapter 8). Except where otherwise stated, the situation I have in mind whilst writing this chapter is one where consultants and consultors meet privately away from the consultor's work situation. Normally the consultants have not and do not visit the working situation. (The pros and cons of consultants doing so are considered in Chapter 5, section 2.) Consultancy relationships could be between a consultant and a consultor or one or more consultants and a group of consultors or it could be a co-consultancy group led by a consultant. However, much, but not all, of what follows relates to any consultancy relationship however formal or informal, long or short it might be.

Now to a commentary on the seven elements.

ELEMENT ONE: ROLES

In non-directive work and vocational consultancy as defined in Chapter One, the essential role of a consultant is that of an enabler or a facilitator and the role of a consultor is that of an independent practitioner seeking help in thinking through aspects of his/her work without in any way becoming obligated to the consultant. Both are experts and learners. Their roles are complementary. They are fashioned to enable them to be collaborative egalitarian agents of creative reflective engagement on the consultor's work concerns in consultancy session. Their consultancy roles begin and end with consultancy relationships. Consultants and consultors move out of their consultancy roles if consultants become counsellors, supervisors, managers, colleagues or project partners of consultors. As it is all too easy for them to drift into roles such as these, continual role vigilance is essential on all sides. David Campbell describes vividly what can be involved in taking up the role of a consultant in a group:

> Learning to take the systemic "consultant position" is, to a very large degree a case of absorbing an altered picture of the world . . . We can learn some techniques and methods in advance, but it all boils down to assuming a consulting position in the group that summoned us as agents of change. And this requires a special kind of personal daring and a willingness to run risks, as we have placed ourselves in an unpredictable, uncontrolled field—in a web of relations and several assorted versions of a reality we seemingly share . . . When the consultancy role is thus described, we must possess a peculiar mixture of dominance and reservedness, a difficult mixture of waiting and guiding: an ability to be a "non"-person, abandoning personal safety and control of the situation when, at the same time, the client strongly demands our visibility and willingness to act. We have to trust our own perceptions even when they are in conflict with the traditional demands for a successtul consultation. We must be

able to keep quiet and let the process run- often for much longer than might be expected from a traditional consultant with the supposed amount of immediate power of action, suggestions for solutions, and plans of action. As a systemic-based process consultant, I float in a room of not-understanding. I have to listen to what is happening, form my hypotheses, and ask my questions in order to mobilize the participants' own knowledge.[2]

A consultor's substantive role is determined by and located in his/her work situation and role-sets, that is, the complement of roles organized around his/her particular role. The roles adopted in consultancy relationships must enhance these roles: they must not undermine or compromise them in any way. This has profound implications for the attitudes of consultors and consultants towards those with whom consultors work. They need to be positive and respectful.

Taking up appropriate roles[3] is a master key to work and vocational consultancy; it facilitates the process. Consultors and consultants simply have to get into and remain in their respective roles for the duration of sessions and then to exit from them into their other roles. Doing this can be tricky for both of them. Most consultors do not have role models to help them apart from counselling relationships and they are not good guides.[4] Consultancy roles, like the processes, are subtly and significantly different from those with which they may well be confused: expert/non-expert; advice giver/advice receiver; counsellor /client or "counsellee"; doctor/patient; trainer/trainee; supervisor/supervised; manager/managed. Further clarification of appropriate consultancy roles is attempted in this chapter by studying what consultants and consultors have to do and the relationships which enable them to do it. And that takes us to the study of the other elements.

ELEMENT TWO: INTERPERSONAL BEHAVIOUR

Much is required of the interpersonal behaviour between consultants and consultors. It has to establish and sustain consultancy relationships and processes in meetings of equals working interdependently at agreed tasks in consultancies ranging from those between colleagues in their work place to those with specialist work consultants outside of the consultor's work domain. Some consultors and consultants know each other well, meet each other continuously in different settings and their personalities, approaches to work with people, theology and spirituality are compatible. Others are strangers at the outset of the consultations, vary greatly in their natural compatibility, and meet exclusively for formal consultancy sessions, often infrequently.

Relationships between consultors and consultants have to facilitate intense task centred work in a friendly way on things of great importance to consultors when things are going well and when they are going badly.[5] Clearly interpersonal behaviour is a key to every aspect of consultancy. It creates the emotional ambiance and atmosphere. At best it facilitates consultancy processes, at worst it inhibits or prevents them. Effective use of approaches and methods do, of course, produce good vibes but they are no substitute for appropriate forms of behaviour. Moral trust comes before skills and technology.[6]

Critical aspects of behaviour which I consider here are: confidentiality; genuine interest and single minded concentration; empathic relating; controlled emotional involvement; openness and privacy; freedom in interdependence and accountability; respectful and humble engagement. Other aspects are considered in the theological observations in the discussion on Element Seven.

1. Assurance of Confidentiality

Confidentiality and the trust that it engenders are of fundamental importance in all forms of consultancy and not least between people in the same organization. Consultancy work begins when consultors and consultants believe that confidences will be honoured. Sadly, a significant proportion of those with whom I have worked have suffered through breach of confidence in the church.[7] Untold damage has been done through these betrayals. Understandably both consultors and consultants are circumspect. Consultors can breach confidentiality as well as consultants, not least by quoting what consultants said out of context and using it to give authority to what they are saying or by distorting what was said: *e.g.,* "Dr Lovell said that so and so is the cause of our problems and that we should do this and that", when in fact what I said was a tentative summary of our joint analysis and our speculation on possible courses of action. I have experienced this kind of thing many times. Reinstating valued relationships has been costly. Consultors and consultants need to be able to trust each other, not only that confidences will be kept, but that whatever emerges from their exchanges will be used wisely and constructively in ways that further the causes they espouse. Apart from the obvious aspects of confidentiality about which much has been written, one thing needs to be mentioned here. Sometimes it is a breach of confidence to disclose that a person has consulted you—and doing this and declining to tell what transpired can cause people to be suspicious about secret meetings and to speculate wildly in ways that can lead to destructive rumours and gossip. To make consultations confidential it is sometimes necessary not only to agree to honour confidences but to be quite explicit about what that means in specific consultations at the beginning, during and at the end of sessions.

Confidential discussions create a safe house in which people can reflect freely, do their private work and determine what action they must take for the common good. On the other hand they can be used to plan secretly for personal or sectarian interests and against the common good. Secrecy for ulterior motives has no part in the consultancy processes I am considering. Consultants have to be on their guard against being drawn into such arrangements. If and when they begin to appear, they have the responsibility to question and challenge. The justification for critically examining in confidence behaviour that has caused problems, is the sincere intent to discern remedial action rather than to engage in secret censorious gossip. All kinds of things are said, of course, as consultors give vent to pent up anger and frustration in the security of confidential discussions. The challenging task is to avoid collusion and to help consultors to work through their feelings to constructive attitudes and approaches.

2. Paying Attention: Genuine Interest, Singleminded Concentration and Professional Curiosity

Genuine interest, single-minded concentration and professional curiosity are qualities of interpersonal behaviour essential to good consultancy practice. They can be contagious. They are at the heart of consultancy; they constitute its spiritual core; they are the media of powerful creative forces. The degree to which they exist is an index of the quality and potential of any consultancy relationship: skills, procedures and methods are the servants of them, they can never be substitutes for them. Pretending they are present when they are not deceives no one. Feigned interest is soon apprehended no matter how consultants try to veneer and disguise it by acting out the body language signs and symbols of attention. It nullifies any good effects that consultancy might otherwise have and, sadly, increases the mental and spiritual isolation of consultors at times when they desperately need the true alliance of the minds and hearts of other human beings. There is no substitute for "behaving authentically." [8]

Consultants are in a position to offer very much the same thing that, in the following quotation, Professor David Smail says psychotherapists offer.

> The psychotherapist, in fact, offers a commodity available almost nowhere else (not, that is, with any consistency or predictability). Quite regularly, for about an hour at a time you can go to your psychotherapist and be listened to, concentrated upon, thought about, puzzled over, understood, questioned, encouraged. Here is someone who will take an absolutely exclusive interest in you (or so, certainly, it is likely to seem to you), who will attend to and remember even apparently trivial details of your life, who will sympathize with your pain even when gently remonstrating with instances of your intransigence, who will blame you for nothing and demand nothing from you, fob you off with no superficial or impossible advice, but open the way for you to tackle the difficulties in your life. Put like this, surely, it is not hard to see the attraction of psychotherapy nor to understand its popularity, and scarcely necessary to invent for it any spuriously technical justification. The more therapists' interest and concern is genuine (as opposed to the rather coldly distant professional posture which some earlier psychotherapists took to be proper), the more they appear as real, recognizable people, the more they are likely to be trusted, and the more effective their influence—just as loving, and lovable, parents will have more influence over children than punitive, forbidding, or indifferent ones. Just such inferences as these are to be drawn from research revealing the "non-specific" factors in psychotherapy. [9]

I value this quotation because it expresses much of my consultancy experience. (I had used the phrase "genuine interest, single minded concentration and professional curiosity" long before I read this paragraph by Smail.) To my surprise I discovered that during consultancy sessions of anything from one to two hours I rarely think of anything except consultors and their work and things which they evoke. Doing this is deeply satisfying and engenders feelings of peace *(shalom)* and fulfilment. Such absorption is pregnant with creativity when it is shared by consultors and consultants. They discover things they didn't know they knew, they have penetrating insights into their work and gain new ideas which enable them to make quantum leaps in understanding. The "listening" associated with this attention has the power to draw things from the depths of our experience, memory and consciousness. It is, of course, not without some strain. E. R. Ackerley in a personal memoir to E. M. Forster expressed this very effectively:

When I was alone with him and his unselfconscious listening attention was turned upon me—attention which I felt was hearing not only the things said but the motive in saying it—I experienced a sense of strain, as though more and more were expected of me than I believed myself to contain. To be really listened to is a very serious matter.[10]

And Roger Graef after speaking of the "stillness of his presence as a listener" said this of the oral historian Tony Parker:

The power of his silence created a vacuum which invited others to fill it. But he had not switched off: the quality of his attention made it clear he was taking in every word.[11]

These accounts resonate with my experience of being listened to by T. R. Batten, I would simply add that because it is a serious matter it is also a creative one. Sadly in the early days of my consultancy experience most consultors said that they had not been listened to in this way in relation to their work.[12]

Listening like this is an inner activity and attitude. It involves giving oneself to the other(s). It is considerably helped by practical arrangements which prevent unwanted interruptions of any kind. Whenever possible I make such arrangements and when I cannot I discuss with consultors interruptions that might occur and how we could minimise their possible adverse effects upon our concentration. Besides providing conditions for concentration such arrangements are a sign of the seriousness of the exercise and the value placed upon concentrated attention. This is so different from interviews punctuated by telephone calls and other people popping in without apology. Sometimes people seem to exult in this because they think it indicates just how busy and important they, not the consultor, are.

People can enhance their capacity for this kind of concentration through practising it. I have seen it happen time without number in co-consultancy groups of six practitioners with an experienced work consultant. There were two ground rules: concentration on one practitioner and his/her situation at a time; no anecdotes! The ability to concentrate on the other increases dramatically after two or three consultancy sessions. Concentration is self-generating from genuine interest in and curiosity about, the work of others in a similar field, the way in which they go about things and as to whether they are facing similar problems to you and, if so, how they tackle them. Interest and concentration rise sharply in co-consultancy sessions when people realise, as they invariably do, that they learn much that is of relevance to them and to their work by studying the work of another: the more deeply they go into the thinking and experience of another, and the longer they delay reading off the implications, the more they learn.

"Attention" plays an important role in consultancy as Simone Weil has shown it does in study of any kind, in prayers and in the love of neighbour and God.[13] There are further references to attention in the discussion about Element Seven, cf p 131-132.

Consultors too need these qualities. Getting them to concentrate on things of vital importance in sufficient depth and over long enough periods for them to break through barriers and discover ways forward, can be one of the most important things that is achieved through consultations. It is very frustrating when you fail to galvanise a consultor's interest in what you feel to be of critical importance and when they are grass hopping from one thing to another when it is necessary to focus on one thing at a time.

3.   Empathic Relating

Consultants need to relate to consultors with warmth, empathy, genuiness, rigour and love [14] not, as Smail noted, with austerity and supposedly cold clinical correctness. This way of relating is human and Christian, epitomising how people should relate. Consultancies are experiential expressions of the kind of working relationship which consultors frequently need to have with and between those with whom they work and live.

Empathic relationships can and do, in fact, foster and facilitate disciplined thinking, rigorous analysis and a businesslike approach. Also, they give consultants and consultors access to each other's subjective worlds in which, says David Smail, "We conduct our relations with each other, register and react to the impressions we give and receive, administer and respond to offers of love or threats of annihilation".[15] Our "intuitive sensitivity" says Smail, gives us access to these inner worlds with their "immediate knowledge of interpersonal 'truth'".[16] Intuitive sensitivity is not, of course, infallible [17] but it provides some of the insights and understandings vitally important to consultancy processes.

Watts and Williams came to a similar conclusion through considering "empathic knowing".[18] "The classical concept of empathy", they say, "involves vicarious emotional experience. Sharing the emotions of another person, and seeing things from their point of view, are two intertwined aspects of empathy that facilitate each other". They submit that there are two alternative modes of perceiving other people, the analytical and the non-analytical. "Empathy involves the latter, and is thus a form of intuitive cognition".[19]

Empathic relating and knowing enable consultors and consultants to explore analytically deeper subjective substratas of a consultor's approach to work and vocation. [20] What is involved in empathic relating is further developed in the discussion of Element Four, interaction of perspectives. Theological implications are discussed in relation to Element Seven.

4.   Controlled Emotional Involvement

Notwithstanding all that has been said in the previous section, effective empathic relating in consultancy work involves controlled emotional involvement. To get caught up with or carried away by a consultor's positive or negative feelings can skew consultancy processes. One of the many ways in which this can happen is through consultants giving vent to their feelings during consultancy sessions when they are incensed by the deplorable way in which they believe their consultors have been treated and disturbed by the distress caused to them. When I have done this I have discovered that whatever the expression of my feelings might have done for me it has had serious adverse effects upon the consultancy process. Taking the consultor's side in such an unqualified and undisciplined emotional manner compromises my ability to help the consultor to think about the events from the perspectives of any others who were involved or implicated. Also, adding my feelings to the consultor's has heightened the emotional temperature. The effect has been to generate heat without illuminating the situation. Thinking in a measured way was much more difficult for consultor and consultant. Emotional indulgence had compromised intellectual activity. Controlled emotional involvement is essential. What that means in these circumstances is working through our own feelings and thoughts in order that we are free to work with consultors on their feelings and thoughts. That is quite different from working together on their feeling and ours. Empathising with the consultor's feelings is essential but this does not necessarily involve sharing all we feel and think.

Take one more example. Problems arise when consultants get increasingly more excited about an idea than their consultors and express it enthusiastically. Consultors can be marginalised from the idea, the discussion, the enthusiasm and the consultant. They can feel that the idea is now owned by the consultant more than it is by them.[21] The dynamics can be confusing because consultancy is about helping consultors to develop ideas which they own and about which they are enthusiastic. In effect, the result of the consultant's over reaction militates against consultancy purposes. Given that consultants are genuinely enthusiastic about a consultor's project, and that is potentially an advantage, they need to express their feelings in ways that they give support to consultors and build up their responsible affective ownership without in any way appearing to take over. That too requires controlled emotional involvement.

Experiences of these kind of phenomena are not restricted to consultancy work. People experience them in all kinds of relationships and settings.

Of itself, awareness of the dangers of these kinds of emotional involvement enables consultants and consultors to guard against them. What I have also found is that consultants and consultors can help to control their emotional involvement by:

- *establishing what kind of a person they are emotionally;* (See the section on "accepting, knowing and trusting yourself as an instrument of engagement and analysis" in Chapter Seven and especially notes 65 and 66, which describe practicable ways of getting a better understanding of the ways in which we behave emotionally.)

- *reflecting on and mapping out critical aspects of positive and negative affective involvement and engagement with each other and the work they are considering;*

- *evaluating their emotional performance in relation to purpose and beliefs and drawing out the implications for their consultancy practice theory.* (Records of positive and negative consultancy experiences and a consultancy diary can help to do this.)

5. Openness and Privacy

Even when they are desperate for help, consultors risk sharing things which are personal and important to them only when they are confident that they will be treated with respect. When they do share these things with consultants in order to get the help they need, consultors and consultants need to feel that the consultation has been a wholesome experience, that precious areas of privacy remain inviolate, that confidences will be kept, that they have discussed others in an honourable way.

Otherwise they can feel sullied. A recurring struggle in consultancy sessions is to find ways of examining realistically, without feeling pseudo guilt, what action to take about the attitudes and behaviour of people, colleagues and friends, which are causing problems. Consultors can find it very difficult to do this. The most sensitive and honourable are inclined to withdraw from doing so because they feel they are betraying people they love, gossiping about them, "pulling them to pieces", "talking about them behind their backs", "destroying their reputation". When this situation arises it helps, I find, to consider openly these kinds of feelings in relation to the purpose of the discussion. It is justifiable to talk openly and honestly providing that the exchanges about other people are constructive rather than destructive, that is, that the purpose is to discern action likely to be for their good and that of everyone else. Such discussions help to orientate consultants and consultors towards thinking positively about problematic relationships. They avoid polite pretence and backbiting—both of which have no constructive place in consultancy relationships.

To do these things, consultants and consultors have to facilitate, through their interpersonal behaviour, openness which respects privacy boundaries. Consultors need to be disciplined, economical and purposeful in their sharing. Consultants have to guard themselves against asking intrusive questions and making hypercritical comments. When consultors are getting carried away in a manner which they may later regret, consultants need to hold them back in order to give them an opportunity to reconsider whether or not they should continue.

6. ⟨ Securing the Freedom of Consultors to be Their Own Person in Interdependent Relationships (cf the section in Chapter Six on the creative engagement with the nature and operation of freedom.)

Consultors seek consultancy help because they feel unable to do their job to their own satisfaction from their own resources. Consultations are most effective when they enable consultors to do their job to their satisfaction from their own resources; they are least effective when consultors become unhealthily dependent upon consultants and their services in ways which impair or compromise their ability to be their own person in interdependent relationships and to enable others to be so. Effective consultations bring out the rich qualities of human and spiritual interdependence and the joy of living and working with people for development. Interdependency is vital to achieving consultancy aims not least because it is a paradigm of all working relationships.

Paradoxically, the dangers of dependency are in some ways greatest when consultations produce telling insights and workable ideas. Consultors can experience subtle and debilitating personal and relational problems associated with dependency and autonomy. For instance, knowing that consultations will improve their analyses and designs they can feel less secure in their own judgements and hesitant to act without consultancy guidance. Again, they can feel bound by, or even psychologically trapped, by suggestions made in consultancy sessions: for example, consultors can feel compelled to carry through plans made with consultants about which they are increasingly uneasy for one reason or another.

Consultancy relationships in which problems of this kind are present but not tackled can undermine the confidence of consultors and impair their ability to get on with their work. Fundamental damage of this kind caused to consultors is an unacceptable price to pay for any help they might get on specific work situations from processes which cause and mask the unwanted side effects associated with obtaining it. Dependency prevents the realisation of one of the fundamental objectives of consultations, viz, to assist consultors themselves to gain the confidence and the abilities that they need to be able analyse, design and do their work in their own way and in their own situation. Sessions, therefore, must help consultors to be their own person within all their working relationships including consultancy ones. Being their own person is not to be equated with being autonomous or independent. Working with people is of necessity an interdependent activity with its components of dependency and independency which, at best change dynamically according to roles, functions, relationships and situations. (When roles and relationships are fixed hierarchically the flexibility necessary for human well-being and development is reduced.)

Taking all this into account is easier said than done. Many things in human nature and the ways in which people normally relate in church and society militate against achieving such relationships. It is all too easy and natural, for instance, for consultants to trespass upon the inner freedom that consultors need in order to be creative workers and to collude with them in forming unhealthy dependent relationships around their felt need for consultancy help. It feeds the consultant's ego. Consultors can misuse consultants by getting them to do things for them that they can and should do for themselves. Clearly, both consultors and consultants have parts to play in tackling these problems. What kind of interpersonal behaviour helps to avoid and deal with the difficulties noted and to free consultors to be workers in their own right? That is what we now consider.

(a) Consultants need to be non-directive and consultors must want to be "their own person"

Non-directive[22] behaviour directs people's attention towards the need to do their own thinking and to be their own person and enables them to do the one and become the other. Discussions between consultants and consultors about the nature, use and relevance of this approach in their consultancy relationship, therefore, opens out on the issues raised above and agreement about how to deal with the dangers. It is natural to do this in making consultancy relationships because, to be true to the non-directive approach and for it to be most effective, its use needs to be negotiated and agreed: imposing it can be a denial of its nature and a missed opportunity. For the form of consultancy we are considering to be effective, consultors must want to do their own thinking, albeit with help. And this flows from an inner desire to be their own person. If, on the contrary, they want to be directed—and such discussions would reveal this and lead to participants assessing its advisability which of itself is a consultancy service—then the danger of entering an abortive consultancy relationship would be avoided.

Consultants too need to be their own person, otherwise they do not contribute all that they might. The non-directive approach allows consultants to make strong

43

inputs and challenges because it enables consultors to examine critically whatever is contributed in relation to what they want to do, what they can do and who and what they are.

(b) Consultors and consultants need to play their respective parts in ensuring that consultors remain true to themselves and their abilities

The following poem needs to be the heartfelt cry of all consultors. It helps them to assess consultants' contributions and to correct them. It alerts consultants to their solemn responsibility to help consultors to be themselves and to do things in their own way—not simply to be themselves as they are but the best selves that they can be through consultancy help.

> I am not you—
> but you will not
> give me a chance
> will not let me be *me*.
>
> 'If I were you'—
> but you know
> I am not you
> Yet you will not
> let me be *me*.

> You meddle, interfere
> in my affairs
> as if they were yours
> and you were me.
>
> You are unfair, unwise,
> foolish to think
> that I can be you,
> talk, act
> and think like you.

> God made me *me*.
> He made you *you*
> Let me be *me*
> For God's sake.[23]

The inner orientation and commitment on the part of both consultors and consultants to "me being me" and "you being you" are effective agents in achieving self-definition. They allow all parties to present and use their real selves. Simple but effective practices, however, help. For instance asking consultors how they would do things; checking out whether they could do such and such in the way suggested—"is this you"?—or would some other way be better for them; getting them (rather than the consultants) to summarise the action they propose to take and what they are getting/learning from a discussion. Other things also help: consultants, for instance, continually assessing what they must do *with* consultors, what they must do for them and what they must leave them to do *for themselves and with other* people (cf Chapter 7:I, 5 for more on this point). Getting that equation right is of vital importance and the terms of it are not constant. Putting this into practice involves, inter-alia, doing only that work with consultors which enables and frees them to work things out themselves privately and with others. Anything that takes away that freedom must be rigorously avoided. Questions such as the following can help, "Have we done enough on this for you to take it forward yourself?" "Can we leave this now or is there more we need to do?" "Do we need to do any more here and now?" This is sound educational practice which enhances their autonomy—and it is economical in consultancy time. Similarly, consultors, in order to make sure that consultants work at that which they would find most difficult to work on by themselves, can say things such as: "I think I can do that myself, but this I would like to consider with you". "I think we have done enough on that now for me to follow it through. Thank you." All of these things help consultors to be increasingly more in control and for them to be their own person in interdependency.

These processes of enabling consultors to be their most effective selves and to do things in their own way are consummated through consultors being mandated to work to the realities of their situation as it unfolds after a consultation. (This is quite different from working to the consultation in the working situation as we will see.) Mandating can be initiated by either consultant or consultor. Consultors do so by saying things such as: "I understand that my responsibility now is to work these ideas out with people in my situation and to modify them to fit anything that might arise which we have not considered". Consultants need to discover whether consultors have the confidence to take the next steps on their own and whether they feel free to do whatever seems appropriate to them *in situ* whether that accords with conclusions reached in the consultation or not. And, should they have doubts, to work at them until they have made the transition from being a consultor working with a consultant on their situation to being a practitioner working on their own and with others in the situation. Consultors simply have to leave the consultant behind: they can be tempted to try to take the consultant's mind set with them. Evidence of this is to be found in questions such as, "I wonder what my consultant, John Blower, would suggest I do in this situation?" The transition involves making the switch *from* thinking about the situation in a consultancy session to thinking about the consultancy session in the work situation. And that involves knowing when to hold to what was worked out in the consultancy session and when to let it go—and the freedom, courage, humility and common sense to do so! And all this is most likely to occur when consultors are using the thinking processes induced by consultations and not simply their products.

Consultants too have to let go, to withdraw and wait, in ways discussed later (cf p 122). Concepts and models devised by Professor Gillian Stamp are most helpful in conceptualising what these processes are all about. First of all they are about "trusting": about helping consultors to trust their own judgement and freeing them to do so and about consultants entrusting consultors with the substance and outcome of consultations. Second, they are about helping consultors to exercise their discretion. "Discretion", says Stamp, "is the expression of the self in judgement and action . . .". and, "the exercise of discretion is the part of work in which the person is responsible for making choices".[24]

When consultors have the autonomy they need, consultants are more likely to have the autonomy that they need, and consultors and consultants are able to relate in a relationship of creative freedom in which neither seeks to dominate the other. Such behaviour is properly Christian and properly non-directive.

7. The Need for Consultants and Consultors to be Respectful and Humble in Creative Reflective Engagement

Consultants are allowed the great privilege of a guided tour of work that is a person's personal God-given vocation: they tread on holy ground; they need to take off their shoes in respect. Consultants are least likely to be helpful if they are not judgemental or aggressive or assertive in relation to other people's work. Such attitudes can engender defensiveness and that spells death in consultancy work. Consultants are likely to be of most help if they respond in humility, with respect and appropriate deference to the authority and autonomy of consultors and the unique way in which they see and experience things. Then they can affirm and comfort; they can be forthright, direct, open, honest, specific, rigorously analytic and clear; they can raise questions of concern and be open about things they see to have potential for good or ill; they can make judgements, assess things and challenge without being judgemental. They do not allow acts of affirmation to veneer concerns. They encourage and help people to get to the heart of things even when this is painful. But judgemental, aggressive or assertive they must not be, these are the things which destroy or mar consultancy work. They must be humble before the sanctity of workers and their work, tentative in their submissions, non-directive in their approach. This calls for sensitivity, compassion, understanding and humanity.

Freedom without accountability is in danger of becoming licence. Mutual understanding and trust is built up when consultors and consultants voluntarily give to each other explanations for actions they have taken related to the consultancy relationship. Such explanations must be offered and received in an egalitarian relationship, not in a supervisory or didactic one.

Together these seven aspects of interpersonal behaviour build up mutual trust that creates the environment necessary for effective consultancy. They greatly help consultors to experience consultants as a "non-anxious presence" [25] and that reduces their anxiety and helps them to be freely open to the rigours of consultations which can make heavy demands upon them intellectually, emotionally and spiritually.

ELEMENT THREE: WORKING RELATIONSHIPS

Working relationships are task oriented. Practitioners have many such relationships. When they enter into consultancy arrangements, essentially working relationships, new relational dimensions are added to those in which they are already engaged. Figure 2:3 illustrates some basic working relationships and those added by consultancies. With reference to these relationships, four of the many conditions which make for effective consultancies are:

- consultors and consultants relating together constructively;
- consultors being able to live with and handle, interiorly and exteriorly, their local and consultancy working relationships and the interaction between them; (cf the discussion about "openness and privacy", pp 41-42);
- the acceptance of consultants and consultancy arrangements by all those who know about them in the consultor's working domain;
- the absence of negative attitudes, feelings and actions from those with whom consultors work towards consultants and consultancy arrangements.

These conditions variously relate to the consultancy sub-system and the organizational system(s) upon and within which it has to operate. Many things which establish and maintain these conditions and those which undermine them are considered in this book. In this section we consider the part played by the form of consultancy adopted and essentials in the working relationships between consultors, those with whom they work and live, consultants and supervisors.

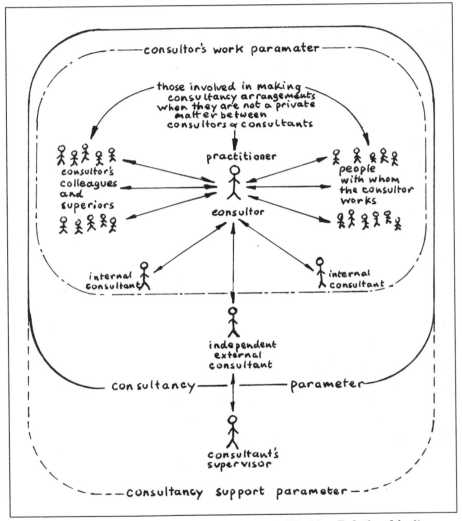

Figure 2:3 Consultors' and Consultants' Working Relationships[26]

1. Forms of Relationships Between Consultors, Those With Whom They Work and Consultants

A common consultancy arrangement is one between a consultor, say a minister, and a consultant. This basic consultancy unit can take many forms and relational shapes. It can, for instance be:

— an exclusive, private and confidential relationship between the consultor and the consultant;

— known about in confidence by the key officers in the consultor's organization and /or church;

— known about openly by all and sundry;

— backed officially and possibly contracted and paid for by the consultor's organization or church.

Another common form is a consultancy arrangement between a group, team, church and a consultant variously mediated through meetings of all concerned with the consultant and/or through their representatives acting as consultors. This consultancy unit also can take many relational shapes.

No one consultancy relationship is always right. The art is to choose the one which is most likely to create the conditions necessary for effective consultancy in relation to the consultor, the people with whom s/he is working and the particular circumstance of their situation.

As was noted earlier whatever arrangements are made it is an advantage if all who know about the consultancy in the working situation are positive towards it. Suspicion, for instance, that an outsider, albeit a non-directive consultant, is influencing or controlling local affairs can have adverse effects which outweigh the potential value of the consultancy. Similarly, people can feel very uncomfortable about private conversations taking place about them and their work. If potential consultors do not see any way of getting local agreement and receiving good will for a consultancy they have several choices: drop the idea of going for consultancy help until they can get local support for it; go for it privately and confidentially and risk people finding out; discuss their dilemma with those who are their pastor managers providing they respect confidences or will be sympathetic and trustworthy. Sadly, it is often the case that those in greatest need of consultancy help are most likely to encounter local difficulties over the arrangement. Often they will need ready recourse to confidential consultancy help to think constructively about the help required, the forms that it might take and possible ways of getting backing for it. Various factors indicate that open consultancy arrangements of one kind or another are possible. Openness is likely to produce good effects when:

• a consultor's local interpersonal behaviour is valued and s/he is respected and trusted;

• it is known that consultors are sincere and positive about their work and are known to have good will for and to be respectful towards those with whom they work;

• consultants are known and trusted;

• the consultant is non-directive and the nature of this approach is generally understood;

• the benefits of consultations are experienced not only by consultors, but by those with whom they work through consultors sharing the insights they receive and through developments that are valued locally and are attributed to the consultancy;

- a consultancy is seen by all concerned to be an integral part of a developmental programme.

These conditional factors can be used to determine whether the form of consultancy should be an open or private one. They can also be used to determine precisely what changes are required to create circumstances more conducive to consultancy help being generally acceptable and to decide what action to take to promote the changes.

In many circumstances the private consultancy mode is the only viable form. Of itself, the fact that it is not generally known about does not necessarily make it a lesser good. Much study, training, preparation and research is a private occupation undertaken without any other person's permission or knowledge. Such a consultancy arrangement gives a consultor freedom to explore any and every aspect of their thinking and situation without let or hindrance. Critical analytical thought requires such freedom. The morality of the action is determined by purpose and intention.

2. Consultors' and Consultants' Responsibilities

This section points to essentials of the working relationship between consultors and consultants through identifying their functions and responsibilities. To sharpen up the nature of the relationship most points are made in summary form. In some ways it is a check list of much that is said elsewhere in the book. Theological functions and responsibilities are discussed in the section on Element Seven.

Overall responsibilities: As we have seen, consultors are and must remain responsible for their work and for what they do or do not do about the outcome of consultations. Consultants have primary, but not exclusive, responsibility for the consultancy processes. Put in another way, consultors have substantive responsibility for their work, consultants for the consultations. They share responsibility for forming and maintaining working relationships which enable them to discharge their respective roles and functions to good effect.

Joint functions and responsibilities: Consultors and consultants are jointly responsible for the consultancy relationship and particularly for the following functions:

- defining and negotiating the scope and boundaries of the consultancy relationship
- making honest contracts, committing themselves to them and making them work
- seeing that the consultancy relationship is consistent with their respective beliefs and purposes and those of the organizations they serve
- for agreeing ways of working together and making them work
- for raising any difficulties encountered in and by the consultancy and working out their implications.

Consultors' functions and responsibilities: Consultors are responsible for:

- producing relevant information and being as honest and open as possible
- ensuring that the work done reflects the reality of the working situation

- working out the implications of the consultancy
- helping consultants to be as effective as possible and to become better consultants
- their own learning and working out its implications.

Consultants' responsibilities: Consultants are responsible for:
- introducing effective consultancy processes
- seeing that respective and joint responsibilities of consultants and consultors are clarified and agreed
- making realistic assessments of what can be achieved in the time available so that unrealistic expectations are not aroused
- working to the consultor and her/his purposes, priorities, beliefs and situation
- helping consultors to be effective consultors
- building up the confidence of the consultor
- ensuring that, whenever possible/necessary, the consultor has got the agreement and understanding about the consultancy of any with whom he or she is working so that the consultancy is seen for what it is and not as a threat
- enhancing the relationships between consultors and those with whom they work
- their own learning and its implications. (One person said at the end of a course on consultancy, "The most startling thing I have learnt here is the willingness of the consultant to be changed by the process".)

3. Consultants, Those Whom They Consult About Their Consultancy Practice and Their "Supervisors"

Consultants, especially those working on their own with individuals or groups, frequently need help just as consultors need it. Consultancy subject matter is always of great importance to consultors. They are seeking help because they are stuck or stumped by human relations or their failure to overcome problems or to convert plans into projects. Invariably much is at stake. As would be expected, consultants grapple with questions such as: is our analysis correct? Have we missed something of importance? Why am I uneasy about the suggestions that seem so logical? Sometimes it is possible for them to pursue the questions to a satisfactory conclusion. When they remain hauntingly unanswered a second opinion is welcome. Sometimes they can get help through ad hoc consultations with someone with consultancy experience or from someone with the appropriate expertise if the problem is a technical one. To be effective, the nature of these consultations on consultancy must be the same as those on church and community work. The same rubrics apply. Sometimes they can legitimately take place without the permission of the consultor especially if the issues can be discussed anonymously without betrayal of confidences. At others times the permission of consultors must be sought if it is not a part of the initial contract. Consultors can gain considerable advantages from such an arrangement but it can create problems. The relationship is similar to the relationship between consultors, those with whom they work and consultants (cf Figure 2:3).

I have sought help in this way extensively. It assists with immediate problems and contributes to the development of consultancy practice theory. It unearths faulty practice of which you are unaware. Consultancy "supervision" is a way of doing that. Supervision, in this case the practice of consulting about consulting, models consultancy practice theory. It enables consultants to develop their skills through systematically and continuously examining and reflecting upon consultancy work in which they are or have been engaged with a supervisor.[27]

If the supervisor has been present at the consultancy session or viewing it from an observation post behind a one way mirror, the discussion is based on the consultor's and supervisor's experiences of the session. If not, as is generally the case, supervision is based upon the consultant's description of consultancy sessions along with any other evidence or video recordings. Learning occurs through analysing sessions, role playing critical exchanges, exploring suggestions about alternative ways of proceeding, instruction, through the interaction between consultant and supervisor when it reflects good consultancy practice and when it does not! Supervisors act as guides, instructors and teachers but not as directors. As they accompany consultants in these capacities they offer models, support and encouragement to consultants.

An effective form of supervision was practised by the Avec staff. Consultants were appointed to courses which studied the participants' work through co-consultancy groups. They attended key staff meetings but not the course sessions. They read documents. The staff described to the consultant what they had done, why and with what results. Course consultants acted as supervisor-facilitators in these discussions. Their role was made known to all participants from the outset (cf the section on "Consultancy Courses" in Chapter Eight).

Members of consultancy teams can offer each other supervisory services. They can for instance, in turn, take observer roles in each other's sessions and later discuss what they observe. In Chapter Eight (the section referred to above) there is a description of the application of these procedures in co-consultancy groups.

ELEMENT FOUR: WORK-VIEWS

Fundamentally, work and vocational consultancy operates through and upon the ways in which consultors see, think and feel about themselves as practitioners, their vocation, their work the Church and the world: that is, through what we will call their "work- views". The following well known phenomena make this possible and necessary.

- The way in which practitioners see things is a primary determining factor in the ways in which they present and deploy themselves and in how effective they are.

- Practitioners' perspectives, normally permeable, are open to outer as well as inner influences. (Consultors can change their perspectives: they can tell themselves new and radically different stories about themselves and their world; they can convert and be converted; they can be influenced to change by others and various kinds of perturbations;[28] they can adopt and adapt alternative stories consultants tell them about themselves and their circumstances.)

51

- It is possible for people to engage conceptually and creatively with each other's inner and outer realities because it is possible for them to understand sufficiently well what the other thinks and feels and to know that they understand and are understood or not as the case may be, *i.e.:* it is possible for them to "stand in each other's shoes" and "to see things through each other's eyes".

- Practitioners can engage actively in reflecting upon and creating their "reality".[29]

The first two of these phenomena are generally accepted. Doubts or reservations are often expressed about the third. Sometimes people say that it is impossible for other people to understand them when what they actually mean is that it is not possible for them to describe their thoughts and feelings. More commonly people say that only those who have had similar experiences to theirs can understand what they are going through. This assumption confuses and mistakenly equates the ability to enter into the experience of another with having had a similar experience. People can emphathize without having had the same experience. People can have similar experiences without being able to empathize; they can misread the experience of another person by assuming that they understand it through reading off what happened to them .

In this section we examine how consultancy operates through these phenomena by stimulating and helping consultors of their own free will to examine and, when necessary, to change their inner orientation to themselves as workers and to their work and how they intend to go about it. Basically it does so through the interaction of the "work-views" of consultors, which are the aspects of consciousness of primary importance in consultations, and of consultants. This term was suggested to me by one used in sociology and philosophy, world-view *(weltanschauung)*, and an article by Philip Meadows.[30] Meadows suggests that, "put simply, a world-view may be likened to a pair of spectacles through which we both see and read the world in which we live". Similarly, work-views enable us to see, read and to find our way around the complexities of vocational work in the Church and in society. More precisely, a work-view is an inner function of human cognition which sums up and models what we know and believe about our work generally and specifically, and how we evaluate it emotionally and respond to it volitionally.[31] Work-views are in part formed by, and in turn, are used to form aspects of the world of church and community work. (See Figure 2:4) In various ways our work-view sums up, conceptualizes, represents and models:

- what we believe about the nature of our work, *i.e.:* it can have a *theological, philosophical* and *spiritual* content;

- what we know, understand and think about it , *i.e.:* it can have a *cognitive* content;

- how we feel about it and evaluate it emotionally, *i.e.:* it can have an *affective* content;

- how we respond to it volitionally, *i.e.:* it can have a *vocational* content;

- what we know, think, believe and feel about the actualities and realities of church and community work in general and that in which we are engaged in particular, *i.e.:* it can have *existential* content.

The content of work-views, therefore, is both general and specific and represents aspects of the actual and the ideal. On the one hand, for instance, they contain mental pictures of the forms of work and its nature and the attributes of workers of the kind described in Chapters Six and Seven. Aspects of these pictures are often fixed reference points over long periods of time. They give direction, thrust and stability to practitioners and their work. On the other hand, they contain views of specific situations, projects, problems. Continually, reflective practitioners find new information is being introduced into their work-views through processes of applying and assimilating. Some of it fits neatly into place. But some of it, because it is not a fit, challenges and confuses. Work-views themselves, therefore, require attention if they are to facilitate the development of practitioners and their work and this is often achieved through consultancy. Ideally there is continual interaction between the different parts of a work-view. In fact a work-view should be the crucible of development not a static group of mental pictures.

Work-views are formed in many different ways, actively and passively, through study, research, personal and spiritual experiences, the experience of others, observation, osmosis and from direct and indirect experiences of particular situations and church and community work in general. They draw upon a multiplicity of diverse sources such as recognised bodies of knowledge associated with such disciplines as biblical studies, the social and behavioural sciences, theology. Then there is the practitioner's personal sources which draw upon self-knowledge, their general and spiritual experience and their stance (attitudes, approaches, prejudices etc, vocational commitments). Other sources are: tradition; general and specific information about religious institutions and church and community work; practice theory; factual and topographical information; religious, spiritual , moral and aesthetic insights and judgements; personal theories, hunches, common sense observations, impressions, hearsay and prejudices; empathic understandings of the experience of others.This list, by no means comprehensive,

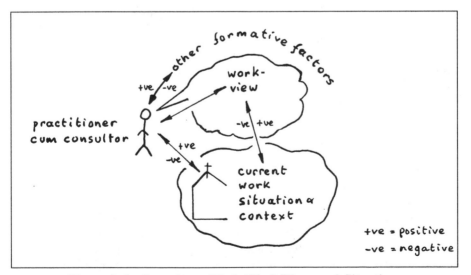

Figure 2:4 : Consultors: Their Work Views and Situations

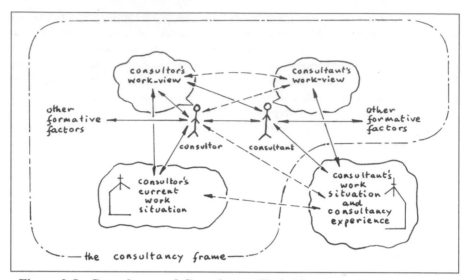

Figure 2:5: Consultors and Consultants: Their Work-Views and Situations

indicates that different kinds of data are woven into the work-views. The permutations and variations of these variables are infinite. No one work-view is exactly the same as another, And that is one of the things that makes consultancy work endlessly fascinating and for ever full of surprises. Reflecting on them and reorganising them is, of itself a form of work, very hard work at times even when it is exciting. The inner realities represented by work-views must be differentiated from the outer realities to which they refer and relate.

During consultancy sessions different facets of the consultor's work-view come to the fore. Generally speaking it is an admixture of what they think and feel about specific situations and about the work in general. This mixture can be seen in the outlines for consultancy briefing papers in Appendix I. As consultants concentrate on the consultor's work-view. aspects of their own work-view come into their minds and induce interactive processes which are described later.

The resulting interplay of consultors' and consultants' work-views must be directed towards consultors and their work-views. Any effect upon consultants and their work-views is incidental but, of course, not unimportant to them and sometimes to consultations. Aspects of this are illustrated in Figure 2:5.

The aim is to help consultors to sort out their feelings and thoughts so that they are more adequately equipped and in the best possible frame of mind to pursue their purpose in their work situation and its environment. To do this they have to reflect critically on their work-views and revise them in relation to their work in general or aspects of it in particular and any other relevant information.

All this means that consultors and consultants engage conceptually with work situations without being in direct personal encounter with them and the other people involved in them. Consultors simply cannot bring their work situations with them no matter how well they describe them and bring them to life through descriptions or anecdotes or pictures or video films. They can only bring themselves and their work views and possibly, at second hand, work-views of people with whom they work. Consultants can visit consultors' work situations. In some instances this can illuminate or challenge aspects of a consultor's work-view. But in other instances consultants can become preoccupied with their own limited view of the situation and fail to give proper attention to the consultor's view of it. Such a deflection of perspective can undermine consultancy processes. (See pp 28 and 35 and Chapter 5, Section 2 for a further discussion of this.)

Working to consultors and their work-views means that consultants operate through direct encounter and dialogue with one side of many sided stories. This is so even when they know of other sides. The situation is moderated when working with a team or a group but even then consultants are working to the work-views of individual members, the interaction between them and, where there is consensus, their collective work-view. Rarely are they in direct contact with more than a few of those critically involved in the complex interpersonal relationships in a working situation.

Clearly the limitations and dangers in this approach present considerable challenges. First we explore ways in which consultors and consultants can ameliorate the limitations and avoid some of the dangers and then reflect on the practice of consulting through work-views.

1.   Aids to Working to Consultors and Their Work-Views

The things which help and hinder consultancies being effective are discussed under seven headings.

(a)   Working to consultors and their work-views faithfully

Effectiveness depends upon consultants, and ideally consultors, understanding the nature of the process, its limitations and dangers and being faithful to the underlying principles and the distinctions made in the introduction to this section. Work-views must not be equated with the consultor as a worker. Nor must they be confused with the work itself. Their true nature must be respected. Some aspects will normally appear fixed, others in flux; some will be in harmony, others not; some will be distinct, others will overlay each other and merge with the general view.

Again, as we have noted, the primary consultancy focus must not be allowed to drift from the consultor's to the consultant's work-view. This can occur all to easily when, for instance, it appears that the consultant has a better conceptual grasp on the situation under consideration or the field in general than does the consultor. To plan to his/her conceptual view may cause both consultor and consultant to miss critical nuances in the consultor's view not represented in the consultant's. And that could mean that the action plans simply will not work. Whilst the consultant's view must not be substituted for the consultor's, it must not be ignored. It must be used purposefully as a foil to explore, to develop and, if necessary, to refine the consultor's view.

(b)   Realistic approaches to the nature and use of work-views

Work-views are attempts at expressing critical aspects of the complex inner and outer human and spiritual worlds of consultors and the intricate interplay between them. Aspects of them can be presented verbally or through written statements such as position papers (cf p 87 and Appendix I). Composing representative statements and pictures of complex work situations and working relationships is a demanding task requiring courage and skill. Invariably people feel some degree of dissatisfaction with their attempts and frustration at their inability to communicate elusive aspects of their situation and thoughts about it as they experience them. Consequently an important aspect of consultancy practice is the correcting and editing of work-view presentations, verbal and written, through dialogue and questioning and by consultants checking out work-views by reflecting back to consultors the picture they are receiving.

Work-view presentations can be distorted by factors other than the difficulties of those who know situations intimately portraying them to those who do not know them. Consultors, for instance, can deceive themselves and they do have blind spots. Proximity to or distance from emotionally charged events, of a positive or negative kind, colour the presentation. Hurt can distort. Events in other aspects of a consultor's life can and do influence, for better or worse, how consultors feel about their work in ways that can be difficult to discern. Then again, quite frequently critical aspects of a situation are left unmentioned until the analysis reveals that that which was considered of no importance is in fact a vital factor.

Work-views have substantive and continuing core characteristics. But this does not mean that the practitioner's consciousness of them is unchanging. Conceptually and emotionally it changes as circumstances, moods and events accentuate some features and depress others. Consequently, descriptions of work situations at any moment of time represent the effect of the interplay of critical interior and exterior contextual factors upon core work-view characteristics. Work or position papers are, therefore, cross sectional views of long-term core values and features of conditioning factors currently operative: in fact, long- and short-term work-views are in play together. Rarely, if ever, do descriptions give comprehensive pictures of work-views. David Smail, a clinical psychologist, casts some light on this aspect of the nature of work-views. He has come to the following conclusion, "For every day purposes it seems that reality *is* the best description I am able to give myself of it".[32] To demonstrate this he invites us to consider an occasion when something happened which constituted a painful blow to our pride and threatened our peace of mind. Then he says:

> The chances are that in the course of the hours following this event you reconstructed it "in your mind" several times (*i.e.:* told yourself several alternative explanatory versions of it) until you settled on a version which seemed best to account for the facts. The chances are, too, that the version which best accounted for the facts was also one which left least injury to your self-esteem.[33]

This rings true for me. I have done this as a consultor. I have seen countless others do it in all kinds of consultancy relationships. And, when my self-esteem has been reinforced as consultations have proceeded, I have been able to bring out more things which reflect badly upon me without losing face and to modify my work-view to take them into account. I have seen others engage in this same kind of progressive revelation which follows close behind affirmation. Such experiences can have two effects upon consultants and consultors: it can make them less judgemental; it can stimulate them to explore more deeply and creatively inner and outer realities and the interplay between them.

Work-views, therefore, are created by several interrelated variables not one. They represent something of each variable—consultor, beliefs, work, relationships, context, events, vocation—and the form which they take at a given period of time. They are projections of socio-religious systems and need to be understood, interpreted and used as such: they do not represent the independent reality of one variable, be it the consultor or the work. Multi-factor, not mono-factor analysis is required because work-views represent systemic realities. Much of what follows helps consultants and consultors to do just that.

(c)   *Respectful and critical approaches to consultors' work-views*

Consultors need to know that consultants understand and respect them and their work-views. Non-judgemental initial acceptance is required to establish trust and to learn about the ins and outs of another person's work-view. The presenting work-view forms the base line for consultancy processes, the point from which consultants must start with consultors if they are to work together. Effective consultancy depends upon this. Equally, it depends upon an approach which pursues any questions or unease consultants might have about the work-view as a whole or any aspect of it. During the early stages of entering into the consultor's work-view such questions often have to be held in suspended animation. Noting them, mentally or on paper, can help to do this. Some of the points will be answered. Those that remain unanswered need to be pursued as trust, process and opportunity permit.

Generally speaking I have found work-views as presented convincing. For the main part they speak of and echo realities with which I can identify. The stronger the identification the more difficult it can be to maintain the distance and the emotional independence to be analytical and to avoid taking the consultor's side. So it is good practice to ask oneself habitually, "Does the picture of the situation as depicted by the consultor and perceived by me seem to be sufficiently representative of the reality? Does it provide reliable data for the consultancy process? If the answer is in the positive, fine, but it is advisable to return to the question at critical consultancy stages. If it is in the negative then it becomes the substantive consultancy issue until it is resolved. The ways in which this might be done are dependent upon the nature of the unease and the working relationships between consultors and consultants. Some of the many possibilities are:

- To ask consultors how they would describe the mood and context in which they wrote the notes on their work-view and/or are presenting it. And, as necessary and possible, to pursue any implications of their response with them in order to establish the veracity of their presentation.

- To explore with consultors their experiences by asking them to clarify, explain, illustrate what they mean by statements they have made about events and feelings.

- To ask consultors how they would demonstrate, prove, explain an aspect which does not ring true to the consultant.

57

- To ask consultors whether they feel their description/explanation represents their experiences of situations or events. Then, if the answer is in the negative, to try to tease out with them a description/explanation which gets nearer to the experience.

- To ask consultors if they have always seen things in the way they have described them. If they have not, then explore critically with how they came to feel and think differently.

- To ask consultors whether others see things as they do and explore any differences or significant points that emerge.

- To ask consultors how they think specific representative people in their situation (not people in general) would respond or react to their work-view and explore what emerges. (cf pp 65-66 and Display 2:1)

- For consultants to share with consultors difficulties they are having in getting in touch conceptually and affectively with the realities which the work-views purport to represent.

- To ask permission to see any documentation independent of the consultor which confirms critical aspects of his/her work-view.

Various other methods which help to work realistically with work-views are to be found in the suggestions in the next four sub-sections about getting inside the consultor's work-view, negotiating the interplay of work-views, practising circularity and the interaction between observer and observed

(d) Ability to get into consultor's work-view

The need to get into consultors' work-views without trespassing upon their privacy is self-evident. The efficacy of methods of entry depend upon the nature of the consultant's desire, attitude, intention and approach. Consultants must really want to get into the work-views of consultors and to know how they see things and feel about them. Genuine altruistic interest and the deep desire to understand, of themselves, open windows and doors by which consultants may look at and enter into the consultor's work-view. They create very different feelings and responses from those generated by a matter of fact approach to getting the necessary information no matter how professional it is. The most effective approach is achieved through the combination of the following characteristics:

— genuine interest which can be cultivated but not feigned;

— accepting, patient, disciplined, reflective, sensitive and critical approaches to consultors and their work-views;

— a graceful, accepting and respectful approach to knowing and not knowing; (cf p 40 and Display 7:5)

— skills such as listening, questioning and conceptualising which can be learnt and polished through practice.

This is a formula for empathic relating (cf p 40) which is crucial to creative reflective engagement (cf Chapters 6 and 7). Two conceptual aids to applying it are discussed here, role-taking and virtual insidership .

Role-taking.[34] Imaginatively taking the roles of others is one way of entering into their work-views. Role-taking is a conceptual form of role play: imagining one's way into the roles of another and noting the inner spontaneous reactions evoked. It helps consultants to deepen their subjective understanding by getting the feel of what it is like to be in the consultor's role and role-sets.[35] Role-taking can be an important aspect of participant observation (discussed in Chapter 7).The form of role-taking which is most helpful to consultants is that which seeks to understand a consultor's role in a particular work situation. This can involve reflexive role-taking by, for instance, trying to discover how the consultor might appear to others or how the consultant might appear to the consultor and vice versa. (The use and misuse of reflexive role-taking in consultations is considered later.) However, non-reflexive role-taking is required for the consultancy objective of entering into a consultor's work-view.

"Virtual insidership" is another approach to understanding the process of getting into the work-views of consultors. I am drawing upon the development of this conceptual device by Philip Meadows, a Methodist minister with a master's degree in multimedia and artificial intelligence. One of the ways in which he has pursued his interest in the dialogue between computing and theology is through examining the use of virtual insidership in inter-religious dialogue.[36] What I attempt here is an application of his approach to the processes of entering into a consultor's work-view. In this concept consultants are seen as *outsiders*, consultors are *insiders*. A consultant, an outsider, attempts to gain an understanding which matches as closely as possible the consultor's understanding, an insider's view, whilst remaining an insider to his/her own work-view. Consultants are, in fact, outsiders seeking empathic insidership. *Virtual insidership* is a metaphor which helps to explore and understand this process. It draws upon a method developed by computer scientists which generates a three-dimensional virtual world which gives people a sense of "really being there". Consultants who make the empathic journey become *virtual consultors*. The virtual reality of the consultor's work view is constructed through the joint activities of the consultor and the consultant. The consultor shares, describes, projects, illustrates, explains and demonstrates ideas, situations, events, emotions, beliefs, hypotheses. Consultants discipline themselves to learn the consultor's language, to listen, question, imagine, immerse themselves in the consultor's situation, feelings and ideas and check out the way they are beginning to see things through the consultor's eyes. Consultors and consultants engage in dialogue until they have pieced together what is for both of them is a virtual reality which is a reliable basis for the work they need to do together. This is represented diagrammatically in Figure 2:6. Note, there is a sense in which the description and profile of the consultor's work-view used to facilitate the consultancy dialogue is a virtual reality for the consultor as well as for the consultant because it is "approximate, nearly-but-not-quite the same" as the consultor's reality. It is "really-but-not-fully" or" similar—yet different". Consultants and consultors approach it from different points of being. Nevertheless for both of them it "approximately corresponds to the 'fullness' of that to which it refers".[37] Consequently it is near enough to act as a basis for effective consultations.[38]

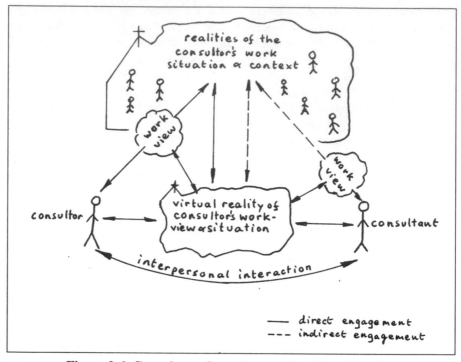

**Figure 2:6 Consultant, Consultor and the Virtual Reality
of the Consultor's Work-View which they Construct and Use** [39]

Getting inside a consultor's work-view is not a discrete phase in a consultancy. During the initial stages it will normally be a major pre-occupation along with establishing working relationships. But it is not a task which is neatly packaged at the beginning of a consultancy. At various stages the dialogue will reveal further aspects of the consultor's work-view—sometimes things which come as new and fresh to the consultor as to the consultant. Consequently, there may well be points at which it is necessary to concentrate exclusively on the re-shaping of the consultor's work-view in the light of new insights, perspectives and patterns of thought. Indeed, there is a continuing pre-occupation with the consultor's work-view because, as was said at the beginning of the discussion about this element of practice theory, the consultor's work-view is a determining factor in his/her vocational performance.

(e)   The ability to negotiate, manage and use creatively the interplay of work-views through the interaction of perceptions

Consultants are unlikely to have their own work-views in mind whilst concentrating on getting a thorough understanding of their consultors' work-views. But it is in play at some level of consciousness, it is never out of action. Indeed, consultancy processes are promoted through the creative interplay between similar and dissimilar aspects of the consultor's and consultant's work-views because of their importance and relevance to the consultancy dialogue. Occasionally this may involve comparing and contrasting the consultor's and consultant's work-views in toto. For the main part, the interaction is between the perceptions and perspectives of consultors and consultants.

The interaction of perspectives and perceptions in consultancy dialogues (and, of course, in any other form of human encounter) is incredibly complex. A wide range of sophisticated mental skills combined with emotional discipline are required to negotiate and manage them. The natural and acquired abilities to do this are amazingly widespread in the population at large. This phenomenon means that consultancy services are readily accessible to people with no previous experience of them. The complexity is demonstrated by differentiating some of the perceptions that come into play during consultancy sessions. A selection is described below and referenced as perception 1, 2, etc. (p 1, p 2, etc.) for ease of reference in the figures. Then, the value of being aware during consultations of the perception in play is discussed.

Consultants are variously aware of and concentrating and working upon the following perceptions:

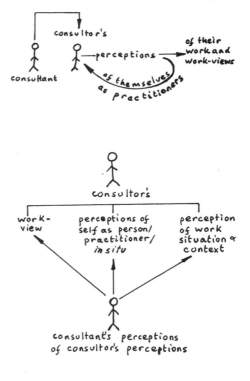

Perception 1: Consultants focussing upon the consultor's perceptions of his/her work-view and of themselves as practitioners.

Perception 2: Consultants focussing on their own perceptions of the consultor's perceptions of
— themselves as a practitioner and person
— his/her purposes, beliefs, approaches, etc.
— his/her work-view and situation
— self *in situ*
(They might for instance be thinking, "What are the implications of the positive/negative thoughts and feelings I have about the consultor's perceptions, the consultor as a person etc.?")

61

Perception 3: Consultants focussing on the consultor's perceptions of their, the consultant's, perceptions.

(*e.g.:* "How do I think/feel s/he is seeing me?" "It seems s/he is reacting negatively to how I see things". "Do we need to discuss what s/he is thinking and feeling about my ideas? How could I raise the subject?")

Perception 4: Consultors focussing upon their own perceptions of their work and on themselves as a practitioner.

Perception 5: Consultors focussing upon the consultant and upon his/her work-view and perceptions.

(*e.g.:* "I like the way s/he is approaching this project but I am uneasy about his/her view of things but I cannot say why. What on earth can I/should I do about this?")

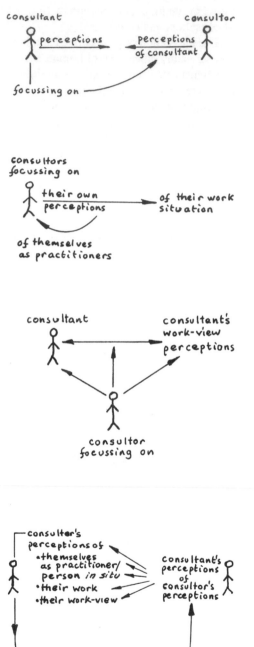

Perception 6: Consultors focussing on the consultant's perceptions of:
— their perceptions of themselves as a practitioner
— themselves as a person
— their work-views
— their situation
— themselves *in situ*.

(*e.g.:* "What does that mean about what s/he thinks or feels about my perceptions and my situation and me as a person? I would like to know but is it wise to ask? Can I handle the truth, be it good or bad?")

Perception 7: Consultors focussing upon their perception of the consultant and his/her perceptions.
(*e.g.:* "Is my judgement of her/his analysis and proposals impaired by my respect for his/her experience and wisdom?")

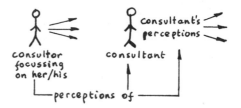

Perceptions can interact positively or negatively or neutrally. They are variously shared and owned. When lecturing about this I illustrate the different perceptions by building up diagrams of the kind presented above and in Figure 2:7. A typical initial response to a presentation of this analysis of perceptions is that whilst it explicates features of common experience, it is too cumbersome a conceptual construct to be used in consultancy sessions especially when the exchanges are intense and rapid. Subsequently, however, some who have made this kind of response say that, to their surprise, they have found it a useful reflective device when they were participating as consultors and consultants. They had become more aware of the perceptions and perspectives active at a particular stage, better able to use them constructively and freer to move from one perception to another as purpose and situation required it. Also, they found that, as consultors and consultants, they were better able to understand the consultancy dynamic and to evaluate the status, significance and meaning of their observations, feelings, thoughts and the contributions made by others. All of this is true to my experience.

At times they found it, as I have, extremely helpful to make explicit the perspective(s) around which the dialogue revolved. For example, a consultor might say to a consultant, "It seems that we have now turned from how I see the root of this problem to the way in which you are approaching and tackling it". Such interventions can prevent the kind of cross-purpose conversation that occurs when contributions are coming first from this and then from that perception and perspective in a confused and confusing manner. That kind of interaction can confound, depress, de-energise and bring consultations to a grinding halt. As well as preventing difficulties, the constructive use of the awareness of perspectives facilitates all round thinking participation in contradistinction to talking participation which may or may not be thinking participation—and that is at the heart of the consultancy process.[40]

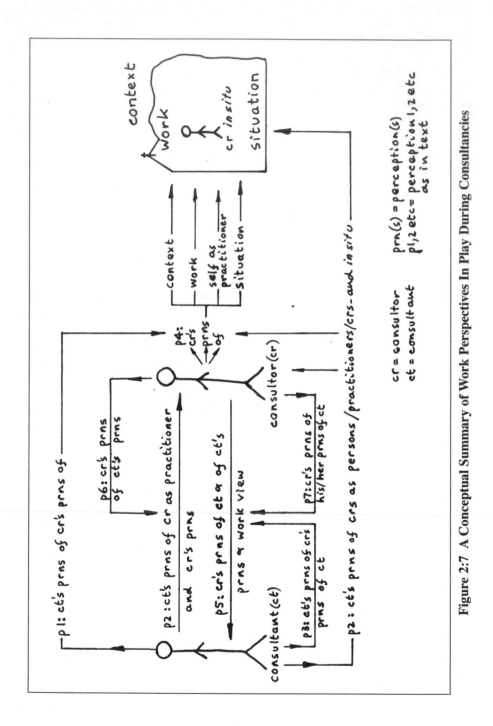

Figure 2:7 A Conceptual Summary of Work Perspectives In Play During Consultancies

One of the things of particular value about this kind of awareness, a particular form of reflexive role taking, is that it enables consultors and consultants to develop and build upon each other's contributions and thoughts collaboratively: analyses are fine tuned; ideas emerge and grow; designs evolve and are embroidered; consultors and consultants are engrossed and work as one. Animated experiences of this kind are high moments of consultancy creativity. They are precious and productive moments. They can appear to be spontaneous mental combustion caused by a fortuitous combination of events and circumstances. And to some extent they are. By definition, it is not possible to devise, hatch or engineer such events: they contain elements of surprise. But people can prepare themselves to make the most of the events when they arise and they can organize meeting points where they are most likely to happen. That is what this book is about — the attitudes, approaches, methods, preparation and action which are most likely to facilitate creative interaction between consultors and consultants in all kinds of circumstances, formal and informal, and in relation to a wide range of issues.

(f) Practising "Circularity"

Dependent upon the way in which you look at it, one of the limitations or challenges of consultations with individuals is that consultants are in dialogue with only one side of many sided stories. Remembering this and taking it into account is of itself an antidote. Some of the disadvantages can be overcome by using an adaptation of a practice common to systemic family therapy which is rather misleadingly called "circularity". It is a process used in sessions with families to get a picture of the systemic relationships between all the members. An example given by Mara Selvini Palazzoli to illustrate the process is from the first therapy session with a family with an anorexic son, Marcello.[41]

Therapist (to sister Ornella): When your mother tries to get Marcello to eat and he refuses the food, what does you father do?

Ornella: For a while he holds himself back, but after a while he gets mad and starts yelling.

Ther.: At whom?

Ornella: At Marcello.

Ther.: And when he yells at Marcello, what does your mother do?

Ornella: She gets mad at Daddy. She says that he's ruining everything, that he doesn't have any patience, that he's just making everything worse.

Ther. (to father): And while all this is going on, what does Ornella do?

Father (smiling at his daughter with open admiration): She just goes on eating as if nothing is happening!

Brief as this extract is, it shows how the therapist gradually teased out the dynamics of the systemic interaction between members of the family. Insights into the interactions between individuals and groups can be obtained by using an adaptation of this method to get a consultor to trace out the pattern of actions and reactions and of initiatives and responses between the people involved. "What did they say when you made that proposal?" "How did others react to their response?"

etc. The method can also be used to get people speculating privately about the probable responses of others to their work perspective. Display 2:1 describes such an application.

A variation of this method is to make imaginative mental and affective attempts at taking the part or playing the role of other key participants whilst consultors are describing events. In this way consultants can get some idea of what might be happening to those located elsewhere in the story and the system. Consultors can be encouraged to engage in the same kind of exercise especially when there is an impasse in thinking things out. Such exercises generally shed light that does not always come through other forms of analysis. The method can also be used to good effect to test out possible ways of approaching individuals and groups.

Notwithstanding, it is of the essence of human life that the ways in which people respond cannot be determined precisely by calculation or by the most sensitive and perceptive role play. Even people we know well and whose responses we think we can predict continually surprise us by what they actually say and do. Nonetheless, much of value can be learnt about the possible range of responses. Any attempt to look at things from the position of others and through their eyes can be useful. It stimulates consultors and consultants to look at human systems from other perspectives in addition to their own and those of consultors. Consequently imaginative exercises of this kind are charged with creative potential.

By way of preparation for a co-consultancy course participants were required to write a position paper describing their work-view and situation from their own perspective using an outline similar to the one given in Appendix I. As an addendum to their paper, participants were invited to consider the perspectives of others by trying to imagine how they might respond to what they had written. The instructions given were:

This part is an exercise in imagination, of putting yourself in other people's shoes. It gives you the opportunity to articulate your picture of the answers they might give.

For this part we invite you to think of two or three people in your church or institution. Describe who they are and their place in your church or institution, and why you have chosen them.

Imagine you are engaged in discussion with them about the issues you have listed for consideration.

What do you think they would say about the subject matter and what would they say about considerations raised?

We suggest you do not discuss this with the people concerned, but keep this to yourself for the time being.

Finally, describe what you experienced whilst writing this part.

The results were fascinating. Most found the exercise difficult; surprisingly, a few found it impossible. For some it proved to be a transforming experience—they radically revised their views of themselves and their perspectives and their attitude to, and understanding of the people they had "used" for the exercise. One person said that he realised that up to that point he had been so pre-occupied with what he thought about his ideas that he did not listen to what others said about them or to the ideas they had. Another "heard" for the first time what the laity had been saying to him for a year or more about plans he had.

**Display 2:1 Stimulating Imaginative Speculation by Consultors
About Possible Responses of Those With Whom They Work
To Their Perspectives On Their Situation**

(g) *Recognising and respecting potential limitations*

To a greater or lesser extent all of us are the victims of self-deception, we are capable of "kidding ourselves" (cf Display 2:2). Consultants and consultors need to be mindful of the possibility of dysfunctional self-deception, especially when presentations seem to be very convincing. Self-deception is no foundation for constructive analysis and design.

As a general rule, then, we assume that if a person gives us an account of his actions which he *(sic)* sincerely believes to be the case (*i.e.:* he is not lying) this is the best guide we have as to the true state of affairs. It is the prevalence of this myth which makes possible the phenomenon of self-deception. That people are capable of "kidding themselves" is of course something widely acknowledged in our culture, though I suspect that this possibility is considered only in relatively rare and fairly superficial cases; what we do not recognize, I think, is that self-deception is the characteristic mode of existence in this society, nor that it is the combination of self-deception and our excessive over-valuation of words which maintain the objectifying structures of our culture.

To say that people deceive themselves is not to question the sincerity of their utterances—the element of dishonesty in self-deception exists more at the level of experience than at that of words. Indeed, dishonesty may not itself be the best concept to invoke in this context: on the whole, people deceive themselves through lack of courage rather than lack of honesty, or even simply through lack of clarity about the predicament in which they find themselves—one may deceive oneself because one lacks the courage to face the implications of one's experience, or simply because that experience is so confused and puzzling that one opts for a relatively non-threatening interpretation of it. But in either case there is no doubt that people believe the stories they tell themselves.

**Display 2:2 Self-deception and the Stories People Tell Themselves:
An Extract from David Smail**[42]

Self-deception can take many forms in church and community work. There is a propensity, for instance, to focus on laudable vocational purposes and intentions in planning and evaluating and to edit out those related to meeting personal needs. Clearly this leads to distortions in self-perception, planning, working and evaluating. Identifying what needs to be avoided, noxiants, is a manageable way of bringing into play some of the complexities of mixed motivation, a normative condition, and treating them seriously as an integral part of the human situation. Another area in which self-deception occurs is in a practitioner's understanding of his/her performance in interpersonal working relationships. If s/he has got it wrong then s/he is likely to misappropriate responsibility. The case study method is a most effective way of identifying the many ways in which we can deceive ourselves about the nature of our action and culpability. (The method is discussed later cf pp 79-80.)

For the most part approaching and using work-views in the vigilant way described above helps consultors and consultants to become aware of, and to counter self-deception by bringing it under some measure of affective and intellectual control. Information is gained by which to correct, edit, modify and develop perception and perspectives. Occasionally, however, I have experienced consultancies in which any progress has been prevented through my inability or lack of courage to get a consultor to consider the real possibility of his/her self-deception. Such encounters, I hesitate to call them consultancies, have devoured enormous amounts of energy and time to no apparent good effect and generated all round frustration. In some instances, it appears—and feels—as though consultors are conjuring up pictures of their situation from data quite inaccessible to the consultant in order to invalidate successive analyses and designs each of which took account of the reasons given for the rejection of the previous one. Things do not add up or make sense. Suspicion that consultors are deceiving themselves and, possibly by default rather than design, trying to deceive their consultant is inescapable. Certainly everyone and everything are being confused. Consultations with these dynamics are something of a black hole experience.[43]

At an early stage such consultancies can seem so plausible that they make consultants feel that the problem is in their lack of skill. Once consultants are engaged with the consultancy their desire to find solutions and their professional pride can make them prisoners to the successive inconclusive cycles of interaction. Possibly the consultations serve other ends for consultors than those of finding ways forward. For instance, consultors may be using, probably unconsciously, consultations to demonstrate to all and sundry that their situations are beyond redemption, that there is no way that they themselves could be expected to improve them when even professional consultants cannot find a way forward. The situations must be beyond redemption and so they, the consultors, cannot be held in any way responsible for the failure. In such situations consultors are deceiving themselves and the consultants about their motivation and aims for the consultations. The consultor's unacknowledged desire for vindication is at the heart of the consultancy impasse. Their determination to prove the situation to be impossible is in dysfunctional conflict with the consultant's determination to find a way forward!

In some cases I have made limited progress by raising with consultors what I felt was happening. In others I have done so by examining in detail with them procedures they said did not or would not work. In yet other cases, they have had the grace to acknowledge at a much later date that they had put into effective practice ideas they had previously dismissed out of hand. But a small hard core of cases soundly beat me. I keep a weather eye open for such possibilities in order to conserve my energy for more profitable consultancies. But identifying them at an early stage is problematic and the danger of withdrawing when you should not is always present. I become uneasy when: suggestions about well-tested methods are rejected out of hand; consultors simply do not try to understand what I am saying; there is the slightest evidence that consultors are seeking my support for views they hold about the impossibility of the situation; consultors are defensive when approached in a thorough-going, non-directive and respectful manner.

Yet another kind of situation can arise, but only rarely in my experience, when a consultor's view of a situation appears to the consultant to be incredible. In one way or another it simply does not touch reality as experienced by the consultant. If, after careful questioning, the consultant concludes that the work-view does not recognisably represent a reality other, that is, than the one that is in the consultor's mind and feelings, there is no starting point for the consultancy processes we are considering. If the consultor is deluded or fantasizing, then, whatever the meaning of the story, the consultor needs other kinds of professional help from a counsellor or psychiatrist. Then the consultant's job is to point the consultor to more appropriate forms of help through what could be described as first aid pastoral-cum-work counselling. Drifting across the boundaries between consultancy and clinical psychology can be dangerous. (see section 7 of Chapter 5 for a discussion about the interplay between consultancy and counselling.)

The need for any kind of specialist help that the consultant does not have marks out other boundaries of the limitation of the method. In one consultancy with a missionary on furlough from a post in Africa little progress was made until, at my suggestion, the consultor sought the advice of a social psychologist. Action plans were then made using the insights gained. Upon her return to Africa the action programme we devised worked admirably. The specialist and technical help that might be required varies enormously. Consultants may have to help consultors to define the help required, to obtain it, to interpret it and to determine how to apply and use it.

2. Reflective Notes on the Work-View Approach to Consultancy

Having examined the nature of work-views and some of the things involved in their use in consultancy practice we can now consider the reasons for, and the wisdom of investing heavily in this approach to consultancy.

The approach is essential to self-development. There is no viable alternative to work-view based consultancy when practitioners want and need help which will enable them themselves to do their own work more effectively. Similarly, those who wish to promote holistic human and environmental developmental programmes simply must engage with people and their work and work-views: they must not ignore or bypass or take them for granted or try to impose changes upon them.

Opportunities to pursue this approach present themselves naturally and frequently. An infinite number of opportunities to influence vocational ministry and church and community work through this approach are presented by practitioners and religious institutions when they seek help.

Work-views are reliable guides because they represent comprehensively the theological and existential features underlying the activities of practitioners. Rightly, sociologists would describe work-views as we have described them, as an admixture of "hard" and "soft" data varying in quality. What is important, however, is that they enable all concerned to get as close as possible to the idiosyncratic characteristics of the ways in which consultors (and consultants) think and feel about themselves as practitioners and about their work. And, as no one work-view is exactly the same as another, that is vital to building on the bedrock of human reality.

Work-views facilitate a multi-factor approach needed for holistic development. At their best, work-views are an operational synthesis of many aspects of the nature of a vocational approach to church and community work. This means that they facilitate a multi-factor approach which avoids the limitations and dangers of working to one or two factors such as purpose or belief or approach. Consequently they are profound but complex instruments of development.

Practitioners can access their work-views and scrutinize them with others. Practitioners can of course fail or refuse to do this. But the fact that they can and do access and submit their work-views to others openly and undefensively makes this approach to consultancy possible. Examining, researching and interpreting work-views can be difficult and complicated as we have seen and human fallibility is ever present. So their analysis cannot be an exact science: but that does not mean that they cannot be subjects of critical scrutiny. They can and must be. Given the time that can normally be spent on describing work-views, the best that can be expected is a working model. A perfect description is unlikely. To achieve the desired result, consultors must be openly forthright; consultants must be thoroughly non-directive in relation to the substance of the consultor's work-view to avoid veneering it with his/her own ideas; both must persist with the processes of clarification until they are satisfied that they have an acceptable definition. Position papers of the kind outlined in Appendix I help towards this process.

Work-views will be most useful if they are based upon astute assessments of the reliability and unreliability of the data used. Doing this involves hard thinking using all our critical faculties and drawing upon intuition, imagination, empathic insight and the common touch. Analyses which proceed from the unquestioning acceptance of the data upon which the work-view is based can be grotesquely skewed away from reality and produce action plans which at best are impracticable and at worst dangerous because they can be implemented. Testing out plans for purposeful feasibility with consultors is one of the ways of unearthing the unreliability of the data on which diagnoses and designs were based and correcting work-views. Thus, the effective use of work-views as the medium of consultancy is an important part of the craft of human and spiritual purposeful action. It draws upon a wide practice theory base. The use of work-views lends itself to the rigours of the behavioural sciences even though it is not based on an exact science. Further, research into the anatomy of work-views could greatly help in shaping, articulating, examining, using and refining them.

Periodically practitioners need help to give their work-views the attention they need. Healthy vocational development and the evolution of good practice require that, from time to time, work- and world-views need revamping or revising or adjusting. Otherwise they become instruments of undesirable action or they prevent or pervert change for the better. *In fact, work-views are important subjects as well as objects of developmental programmes.* They are also important data banks containing practice theory memories, reference points and a repertoire of working and theological models. They are formed, shaped, structured, converted within people by their responses to, or the effects of, all kinds of stimuli, variously personal and impersonal, which are experienced through the mass media, educational and developmental programmes, personal and religious experiences, secular and religious institutions, spiritual and charismatic figures. As we have seen handling all these influences responsibly is a complicated business. Not surprisingly, therefore, those seeking consultancy help generally need face to face assistance in articulating and sorting out their work-views so that they are the best possible instruments of their vocational aspirations in the realities in which they pursue them.

Experience suggests that a good way of meeting this need is by reviewing work-views contextually rather than abstractly and generally. That is, by exploring the dialectic between a practitioner's work-view and his/her work situation in order to determine any implications for both entities and the relationships between them. From time to time practitioners need consultancy help and moral support to discern and determine any changes that they might need and want to make which can vary from fine tuning to transformational change. They might also need help in determining how to implement changes. Progress in meeting this need is a multiplier because it enables practitioners themselves to be more effective *and* to help individuals and groups to work at things in similar ways.

Getting people involved in creative contextual reflective engagement with their work-views is, therefore, essential to qualitative human and spiritual development. Doing so through one-to-one and small group consultancies and assessment programmes is a costly necessity, not an expensive luxury. It needs to be a part of the missiological economy through budgeting and planning. Without it much of the potential value of research findings, development programmes and projects and mission strategies will simply not be realised. Put another way, work-views are an unavoidable critical factor in any serious approach to human betterment. Their definitive formation is an inner human and spiritual activity, with which occasionally practitioners in church and community work need the collaborative assistance and support of non-directive consultants.

The approach has the potential and power to extend and deepen the work-views of consultors and consultants. Several things invariably happen when one person explores his/her work-view with another person. Consultors gain a better understanding of their work-view. Through the privilege of being allowed access to the inner mysteries of another person's work-view, the consultant's work-view is variously confirmed, extended, challenged, revised. And, paradoxically, the more that consultants give themselves to the study of the consultor's work-view the more open consultors become to in-depth exploration of other people's work-views, including the consultant's and to new ideas. This effect is particularly noticeable where there are significant differences between those involved. So, by helping consultors, new understandings and relationships evolve.

The efficacy of the method is proven. There is an abundance of evidence that working with consultors in these ways is an effective and efficient way of improving their performance, enhancing their abilities, extending their knowledge and understanding and enabling them to gain job satisfaction. The evidence is to be found in carefully evaluated consultancy experience of a wide range of secular and religious consultancy services referred to in various parts of the book. It follows that an understanding of the nature of work-views and the ability to use them critically and creatively help to equip clergy and laity to be: consultors and consultants; reflective and collaborative practitioners (see Chapters 6 and 7); participant observers (see Chapter 7); analytical instruments (see Chapter 7).

The proper use of work-views necessitates and facilitates taking seriously other relevant thinking, perspectives and analyses.

ELEMENT FIVE: THINKING TOGETHER

A. N. Whitehead said that "Organised thought is the basis of organised action" and that "Science is the organisation of thought . . . a river with two sources, the practical source and the theoretical source".[44] This section is about some things which help or hinder people from being able to organise their thoughts about church and community work in ways which lead to organised action. It describes aspects of the practice theory of promoting creative thinking: it does not purport in any way to be an exposition of the psychology of thinking.

Collaborative thinking on anything from concepts to feelings is of the essence of consultancy processes. Consultors engage consultants primarily to help them to think through things which they have not been able to work out on their own or with others. To do this, a temporary alliance of minds is formed to promote the free flow of constructive thought which, hopefully, reveals to the consultor ways forward. As they work on immediate concerns consultants also aim to help consultors to extend their thinking capabilities and their abilities to help people to think on their own and with others.

1.   Four Approaches

Roughly speaking, consultants proffer help in four ways: they think things out *for* consultors; they accompany consultors as they themselves think things out; they stimulate and help consultors to think; they think things out *with* consultors. Here we note the differences in these approaches and consider their uses.

(a)   Thinking things out for consultors alongside them. One way in which a consultant can help is by taking the lead in thinking and working something out for a consultor in such a way that s/he can follow the process step by step, make contributions, check what emerges and assess anything that emerges for feasibility and acceptability. The consultant thinks aloud; the consultor accompanies. This method is appropriate when, for example, a consultor simply cannot think out how to prepare for and run an important meeting or event either because they simply do not know how to do so or because they have not got the time and/or the energy to do so and/or because the thought of the event renders them emotionally and intellectually unable to face the task. When I have used this method in such circumstances I have invariably found that consultors relax, find reserves of energy, and become increasingly more active in the process—sometimes to the point that we are working with each other or they take over. They needed a start. The method is also appropriate in cases where people simply have no experience of designing, say, a project or a research programme. In the first instance they participate by following the process.

(b)   Accompanying consultors as they think things out. A second way, the obverse of the first, is that the consultant accompanies a consultor as s/he thinks through something or other in their own way. The consultant's presence stimulates the consultor to think and provides moral support. The consultor thinks aloud; the consultant affirms, follows, accompanies. S/he helps the consultor's thinking processes in any way that s/he can. But s/he is working to the consultor's ways and means of thinking things through. More often than not during consultancy sessions over a period of thirty years with T. R. Batten I sat on the same chair in his study. Simply to sit there was often all I needed to think about things which in other circumstances I would shy away from. Batten and his study were for me a presence and a place which stimulated creative thought. Frequently he followed, challenged,

developed my line of thought. But he also contributed alternative thought patterns and processes which took us into the third and fourth approaches where we spent most of our time.

(c) . Promoting, stimulating and facilitating consultors to think. In this mode consultants are primarily the originating and/or the facilitating agents of thought in consultors. They seek to get consultors to think about things which they are either not thinking about or not doing so productively. Their aim is to engender creative thinking processes in others, not to transfer patterns of thought or ideas. this can variously involve consultants getting consultors to think:

— about something they have not previously considered which is potentially of importance to their work and vocation;

— again and possibly revise their ideas about this or that;

— about something they need and want to think about but so far have failed to make much progress;

— about things they need to think about but do not want to do so;

— their way through emotional and intellectual blockages.

(d) Thinking things out with consultors. A fourth way is for the consultor and consultant to think through things together. They decide what they are going to think about and how they are going to do so. Consultors give a lead in relation to the substance and, more often than not, consultants give a lead in relation to the approach and method and new material.

Each of these approaches has a place in consultancy. One is not necessarily better or worse than the others. As we have seen each is more or less appropriate to a given relationship task, and situation. All four can be used in quick succession even in short consultancy sessions. Consultors and consultants need to be able to alight quickly upon the apposite approach with which to start and to pick up the clues which indicate when it is advisable to move from one approach to another and to do so freely and naturally. It is vitally important, for instance, to give consultors their head as it were, when spontaneously they break excitedly into a line of thought after a period of groping with the consultant for a lead on a problem. Consultants simply must move with them into the second approach. Whilst all the approaches have their uses, the third and the fourth—promoting and facilitating consultors to think and thinking with them—are the ones basic to the mode of consultancy developed in this book. Indeed, it could be argued, that the first and second approaches are allies to the third and fourth.

2.   Technical Aids to Analytical Thinking

The aids to thinking discussed here are relevant in different ways to each of the modes of thinking described in the previous section. Consultants and/or consultors can take the lead in using them.

(a) Conceptualising and formatting consultancy subject matter. Consultancy subject matter is an extraction from complex situations, relationships and events with positive or negative emotional overtones presented from the consultor's

perspective. To describe the situation as economically as possible consultors have to select essentials. Understandably the initial presentation can be somewhat ragged; ends need to be tied up. Constructive thinking involves getting an agreed understanding or conceptual picture of what the consultor wishes to consider. Diagrams help to do this concisely. They quickly reveal distortions and misunderstandings in ways in which they can be corrected without hesitation and loss of face.

Then it is necessary to format the subject matter in a way which lends itself most readily to constructive thought. A simple example illustrates this procedure. A consultor sought help because he was experiencing difficulties in working with people from the church of which he was minister, a community activists' group of which he was chairman and the council which he served as the mayor's chaplain. His difficulties related to conflicts of role and interest, frequently, he said, he felt he was "piggy in the middle." It became clear that different kinds of difficulties were experienced in different settings: meetings attended by representatives of all three groups and which he chaired; working with the groups separately, variously on their own and on neutral ground; formal and informal discussions and encounters with individuals. Formatting the information in relation to each of the settings was the prelude to thoughtful exchanges about the things he should/should not be and do.

Consultancy subject matter can be formatted in many different ways. Much of it can be formatted as either a case or a problem or a situation or a project. In fact these four natural categories are widely used by practitioners to talk and think about their work. The most useful way of formatting a case, a sequence of events which concluded in unresolved difficulties, is as a story told from the consultor's perspective. It starts with an objective and ends with an assessment. Specific and general problems are formatted by defining and describing them. (cf Display 2:3) Material about situations can be formatted by constructing position papers and situational profiles to outlines such as the ones presented in Appendix I. Projects are formatted by setting out: the origin and purpose of the project; any available information about the design criteria; possibilities and difficulties foreseen and action already taken in relation to them; the consultancy help that is sought and why. These ways of formatting are examples of the many possible adaptations of the generic thinking structure described in section (g).

(b) **Diagnostic Reading of Consultancy Subject Matter.** *Diagnostic reading* is a phrase used by Gareth Morgan in an impressive book on organizations. He uses the word "diagnostic" not in the medical sense of attempting to identify diseases (or, in the case of organizations, problems) but in the old Greek sense of attempting to discern the character of a situation. Morgan claims that "any realistic approach to organizational analysis must start from the premise that organizations can be many things at the same time".[45] Revealing diagnostic readings can be obtained by using different metaphors or images to "read" situations and to highlight key aspects of them. This facilitates the reading of "the same situation from multi perspectives in a critical and informed way".[46] He uses a range of images of organizations as aids to diagnostic reading: organizations as machines; organizations as organisms; organizations as brains; organizations as cultures; organizations as political systems;

74

organizations as psychic prisons; organizations as flux and transformation; organizations as instruments of domination. He claims:

> As our experience in this diagnostic process develops, so does our skill. As we
> . . . learn how a particular image leads us to a way of thinking about the subject
> under study, the process becomes a very natural ability. Indeed, it becomes part
> of the intuitive process through which we judge the character of organizational
> life.[47]

Diagnostic reading through using images of organizations, models of the church and concepts of community is a way of stimulating new trains of thought through a form of lateral thinking. Frequently, for instance, as I have listened to a consultor describing a situation in which s/he feels trapped, the image of an organization as a psychic prison has come to mind and proved to be a powerful aid to analytical thought. An example of diagnostic reading through images is to be found in some work by the Revd Diane Hare. She discerned an unusual range of twenty two models of church which enabled her to think about the ways in which people in ex- mining villages in South Wales saw local Methodist churches, the ministers and themselves as members. The chart she compiled is a remarkable example of getting at the complex character of the chapel communities and the nature of local folk religion. (It is reproduced in reference 80 of Chapter Six.) Gradually, through using these models as diagnostic tools, she began to collect clues to new ways of tackling problems which had previously baffled her and blocked her ministry. Overviews of the field of work similar to those presented in Part Two are other invaluable aids to the diagnostic reading of working situations ranging from the local to the international.

Both consultants and consultors need to be involved in diagnostic reading of situations which involves "listening" to and having a "dialogue" with situations. Indeed, one of the consultant's primary tasks is to help consultors to develop their ability to do these things in consultancy sessions and in their day to day work. These ideas are developed further in Chapter Seven in discussions about the attributes required of practitioners.

(c) Identifying Systemic Hypotheses.[48] Diagnostic reading can frequently help to identify systemic hypotheses, *i.e.:* hypotheses which relate to human systems and the functional, structural and affective relationships between their parts. To search for these hypotheses people have to think hard and deep; once formulated they are thought provoking tools.

(d) Contextualising: Comparing the Specific with the General. So far the emphasis has been upon studying, examining and reflecting upon the consultancy subject matter itself in relation to itself. Thinking about specifics in this way is utterly essential. New light can be cast upon specific situations by thinking about them in relation to the generality of which they are a particular example. This is where Part Two comes into its own. It can be used as a contextual map of church and community work to identify, define and locate the form and nature of the situation and issues under consideration and the consultor's approach to it. As a foil it can bring into sharper relief characteristics of the situation and reveal things that are missing or neglected.

These dialectical and cross referencing processes can generate creative thinking about the specific and the general and the relationship between them. They will do so in direct proportion to the clarity of the conceptual pictures of them both. Comparing a clear picture of the consultor's situation with a blurred one of the generality of church and community work can adversely affect the thinking about both—as indeed can a clear picture of the general and a blurred one of the specific. Consultants simply must be students of the relevant field(s) of work and encourage consultors to be so. They need to be able to penetrate the outer forms of work and practice to get at their essential nature deep in the heart of things. This is no easy task as I found whilst writing Part Two. But it is necessary because, whilst the outer forms can be instructive, the deeper insights necessary to creative consultancy come from studying the nature of the work and its impact on the forms. Chapter Six makes this absolutely clear in relation to the nature and properties of work whilst Chapter Seven does so in relation to characteristics required of creative practitioners. The ability to do this kind of thinking makes process facilitators into church and community work and vocation consultants (see Chapter 8).

(e)   Introducing Consultors to Relevant New Material. Consultations open out on to a vast amount of subject matter potentially relevant to a consultor's situation—contextual factors, approaches and methods and subject matter from pastoral theology and the behavioural sciences. One of the consultant's tasks is to get into play relevant information which is not being taken into account, some of which will be new to the consultor. The skill is to introduce it in a form which enables consultors and consultants together to work at it constructively there and then. Some, if not much of this material, will come from the consultant's work-view. Chapters Six and Seven show that this will be about what practitioners need *to be* and/or *to know* and/or *to do* in order to operate effectively. This is quite a different procedure from the extended and systematic study, through courses of one kind and another, of subjects prior to application. High risk factors can be associated with consultors using ideas and methods without extended study of the field or discipline in which they evolved. It makes consultants and consultors vulnerable. Therefore skill, discernment, discipline and judgement are required to select subject matter, to introduce it succinctly and to find ways of working at it realistically in a limited period of time. Doing this, and coping with the frustration of not being able to pursue subjects in detail, can be energy consuming. The material introduced is more likely to be apposite when consultants concentrate on the consultor, their reference points and their situation than when they focus on pre-determined input. When I do concentrate on consultors, relevant material generally flows into my consciousness, the selection of it just seems to happen unconsciously. The shortest possible statement of it is required to start a dialogue with the consultor about it and its relevance: "I think Kurt Lewin's concept of high and low equilibrium would help us to understand this situation. If you are not acquainted with it, may I explain what it is and then together we can see whether it is relevant?"

(f)   Using Recent Research Findings and Research Methods. What is true of generally accepted knowledge discussed in section (e) applies to more recent research findings. Consultancies have considerable potential for two-way flow between research and work praxis and between researchers and practitioners. They

provide significant inlets to the workaday world for the findings of any form of relevant research. This is effected through several features of consultations. Core activities of analysis and design take consultors and consultants, experientially and conceptually, into close proximity to the basic characteristics of the consultor at work and to his/her work situation. The mode and mood of the engagement make consultors expectant and open to what is to them new and even radical thinking: they have withdrawn from physical involvement in their situation and willingly entered into processes of critical reflection in order to take different and possibly daring initiatives. Consultors and consultants are, therefore, in sound positions from which to assess the potential of research findings for consultors and their work. They can, for instance, through analytical thought, test out the research findings in relation to their own explanation and interpretations of phenomena with which they are dealing. They can speculate about hypotheses and proposed solutions and whether they fit the consultor and his/her circumstances; they can write the findings into project designs; they can learn how to organise their own action and survey research programmes to test out research findings which seem to hold potential but about which they have some reservations. In these and other ways, consultors and consultants can take other people's research into the ambit of their thinking and, if it proves useful, embody it through applying it. A fuller understanding of research approaches and methods will help them to do this more circumspectly. So much for the inflow; the contraflow is from work situations via practitioners engaged in analysis and design through consultancy processes to researchers and their research. Flow in this direction enables those engaged in reflective practice to provide researchers with all kinds of information including the usefulness of their consultancy experiences. Thus consultors and consultants engage in qualitative research.

There are yet other aspects to all this. Practitioner-consultors can not only use and test other people's research, they can be researchers in their own right as they work, analyse and design. As we will see later, they can be disciplined "participant observers", variously active and passive, of the phenomena they are experiencing and examining, the process by which they are doing so and of the action to implement plans and projects they have helped to create. This means that they are instruments of research (see other references to research).

Again, their analytical thinking may well take them to the point where they cannot make any further progress without getting information which they can only obtain through exploring their own experience in this way. To make progress with the design of projects and developmental programmes they may need information that can be obtained only through engaging in or commission research.

Intermission: Two Notes Reflecting on the Nature of the Processes Underlying the Approaches to Thinking throughout this Section

1. Concentrating on the given specifics of a consultor and her/his situation can be described as "single loop learning" because it operates in relation to consultors, their situation and their operating norms. Introducing material new to consultors causes them to take a "double look" at their situation and their approach to it and their operating norms. That is referred to as "double loop

learning" (see reference 57 of Chapter 7). It stimulates new thinking. That is the process proposed in (d), (e) and (f) and to a lesser extent in (b) and (c). The material in Part Two can be used to facilitate both forms of learning.

2. Consultors and consultants who are analysing, designing and evaluating in the ways discussed above are variously engaged in complementary processes. They are working deductively, i.e. from their understanding of things to their application in their particular situation. They are also working inductively, i.e. from their particular situation and experience to the general. These processes complement each other in the analytical design and evaluative activities of reflective practitioners. A model by A. W. Ghent which helps to conceptualise this is reproduced here, see Figure 2:8.[49]

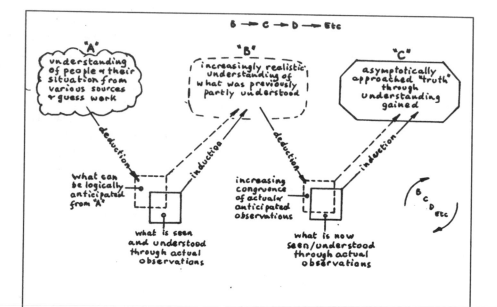

Notes

- Deductive: working from the general to the particular.

- Inductive: working from the particular to the general.

- Both deductive and inductive are experientially based.

- The deductive and inductive processes are variously effected by different research and working methods.

- Asymptotically: a line which continually approaches a given curve but does not meet it within finite distance (SOED).

- The dotted lines have been put alongside the 'induction lines' because it seems that 'B' results from a comparative analysis of the two squares representing what is anticipated and what is observed.

- This model shows the dangers of absolutising.

Figure 2:8 Deductive and Inductive Processes

(g)   Tools, Facilitating Structures and Thinking Patterns. Basic tools are words, diagrams, questions and hypotheses. These are illustrated and discussed fully in Analysis and Design, the companion volume to this book.[50] Facilitating structures are sequences of questions or tasks designed to help people to discuss things effectively and efficiently. Those in common use are legion. Structures which I use to study cases and problems are presented in Display 2:3. They, along with many others that I use, are particular applications and adaptations of a basic schema that can be formatted in many different ways to aid the analysis of all kinds of situations and their contexts and the design of widely differing projects and work programmes. (see Figure 2:9) Central to the schema are the following eight stages in creative and imaginative thought.[51]

Stage 1   Depicting situations, backgrounds, contexts and how consultors see and feel about them.

Stage 2   Depicting things as consultors would like them to be.

Stage 3   Establishing points of reference such as purposes.

Stage 4   Conceptualizing, analysing, diagnosing, forming hypotheses and synthesizing.

Stage 5   Drawing up development agendas.

Stage 6   Designing work programmes and means of evaluating them.

Stage 7   Planning ways of putting designs to work and of evaluating them.

Stage 8   Deciding, contracting and commissioning.

Roughly speaking stages 1 to 4 are studying things as they are; stage 5 is defining what needs to be done; stages 6 to 8 are working out how to do things.

During the first three stages and part of the fourth the emphasis is upon consultants getting into the consultor's mind, feelings, work-view and situation through seeing them through his/her eyes and standing in her/his shoes. Then the fourth stage, analysing and synthesizing, opens out into the sharing and the interaction of perceptions, the introduction of material by the consultant and mental and spiritual collaboration in making a diagnosis and a synthesis with which the consultor identifies and really owns. So we are back to how the consultor sees things and feels about them. At all stages their perceptions and perspectives are determinative.

Stages five to eight, mark a radical change of activity from taking things apart to planning and making things, from analysis to design. During these stages all kinds of ideas and suggestions are likely to emerge. Those selected must fit the situation, the people and the consultor if they are to work and achieve developmental purposes. So the process starts and finishes with what consultors think and how they feel: it is their situation, work, vocation; they are the bridge between the consultation and situational realities; effectiveness is related to whether or not they can and do act out of their own personal understanding and conviction.

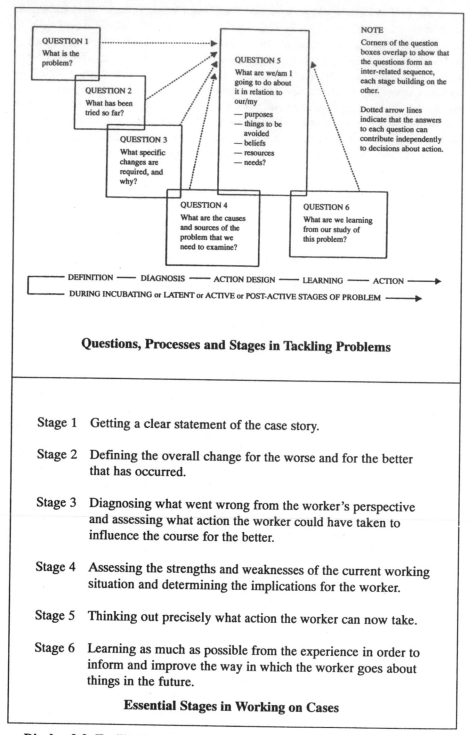

Questions, Processes and Stages in Tackling Problems

Stage 1   Getting a clear statement of the case story.

Stage 2   Defining the overall change for the worse and for the better that has occurred.

Stage 3   Diagnosing what went wrong from the worker's perspective and assessing what action the worker could have taken to influence the course for the better.

Stage 4   Assessing the strengths and weaknesses of the current working situation and determining the implications for the worker.

Stage 5   Thinking out precisely what action the worker can now take.

Stage 6   Learning as much as possible from the experience in order to inform and improve the way in which the worker goes about things in the future.

Essential Stages in Working on Cases

Display 2:3 Facilitating Structures for the Study of Cases and Problems

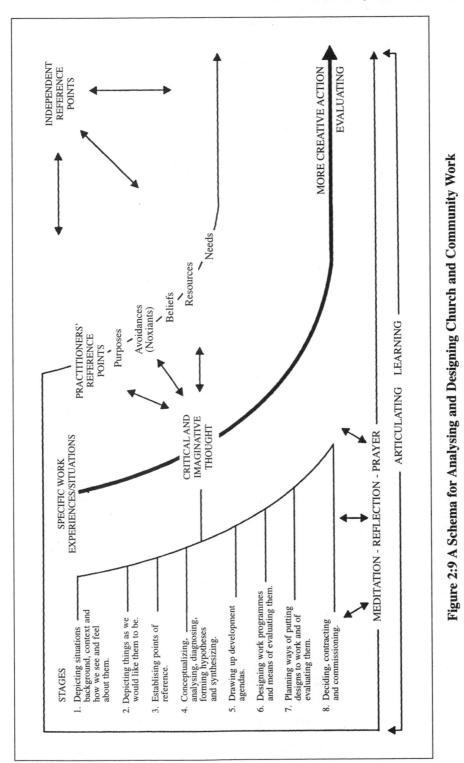

Figure 2:9 A Schema for Analysing and Designing Church and Community Work

INDEPENDENT
REFERENCE
POINTS

PRACTITIONERS'
REFERENCE
POINTS

Purposes

Avoidances
(Noxiants)

Beliefs

Resources

Needs

SPECIFIC WORK
EXPERIENCES/SITUATIONS

CRITICAL AND
IMAGINATIVE
THOUGHT

MORE CREATIVE ACTION

EVALUATING

ARTICULATING   LEARNING

MEDITATION - REFLECTION - PRAYER

STAGES

1. Depicting situations
   background, context and
   how we see and feel
   about them.

2. Depicting things as we
   would like them to be.

3. Establishing points of
   reference.

4. Conceptualizing,
   analysing, diagnosing,
   forming hypotheses
   and synthesizing.

5. Drawing up development
   agendas.

6. Designing work programmes
   and means of evaluating them.

7. Planning ways of putting
   designs to work and of
   evaluating them.

8. Deciding, contracting
   and commissioning.

Clearly, there is a logic in the order of the thinking stages, but the sequence of tackling them is not invariable. Stages 2 and 3 could well precede Stage 1. Sometimes an examination of a situation or problem starts with what people are planning to do next, *i.e.:* with Stages 6, 7 and 8 or in the evaluation of a programme of work. Wherever a start is made, some of the steps can be done adequately only when the others have been worked on: 2, for instance, can be informed by 4 and 6 and 7, dependent upon what people are prepared to do, and that comes out clearly in 8. In practice, each stage facilitates and refines the others, and stage 3, points of reference , is a guide to them all. It is good practice to summarize what is emerging in order to revise earlier thoughts in the light of later insights.

These thinking stages are especially helpful when we are overwhelmed by complex situations and issues, when we are daunted by the task, when our feelings tend to inhibit rational thought, when we feel it is not possible for us to think our way to a good conclusion and when we are so eager to get on with things that we do not want to stop and think.

The schema, represented diagrammatically in Figure 2:9, is important to consultancy for many reasons. First, it models critical features of the processes of shaping patterns of thought and feelings about work situations and human and spiritual development programmes. It is, therefore, an aid to the processes of construction, de-construction and re-construction of thought patterns. Second, it helps to give mental and procedural order to the existential processes of analysis and design which can be anything but orderly and tidy. Third, it helps consultors and consultants to keep in touch with subjective, objective and spiritual realities and to interrelate these domains of experience. What follows are explanatory notes on some of the stages and aspects of the schema which may not be self-evident.

The action thrust. Maintaining the thrust through the stages of critical and imaginative thought to more creative action is vitally important because, for instance, it reduces the danger of action without due thought and thought without the action which should accompany it.

Consultor's reference points. Reference points are important for reflecting, planning and evaluating. Stage 3 shows that formulating and checking them is an integral part of the consultancy process. They are set alongside the thinking processes, as well as within them, so that they are more likely to be used in relation to each and all aspects of analysis and design and revised in the light of developments—they are all too easily formulated, polished, revered and forgotten in the cross currents of thought and feeling.

Independent reference points. Consultors create a context within which they are going to think and work by constructing their own reference points. A danger of this is that consultors can be locked into their own closed thinking circuits. Using independent reference points, such as organizational mission statements, helps them to avoid this and to engage with the issues at the interface between their thinking and activity and that of others and especially that of their denomination.

Beliefs. Articulating beliefs enables consultors to get in touch with them, to examine them critically, to modify them and to use them habitually as reference points. Amongst other things, this enables them to pursue concurrently vital aspects of mission which ideally go together: the articulation of faith; work for human and spiritual betterment; the communication of faith through the body language of action programmes; the sharing of beliefs and faith and dialogue about them; the development of personal and spiritual relationships.

Purposes and things to avoid (noxiants). Thought is much more likely to be profound, and action to be effective, when it is related to what we want to achieve (purposes and objectives) *and* to what we want to avoid (noxiants).

Development agendas comprise those things which need to be done to pursue the implications of the analysis.

Designing is working out ways in which things work or will work or are meant to work. Designs are models which show the causal connections between people's tasks, working relationships, the secular and religious organizations with which they are engaged and connections by which desired ends can be achieved. Designing, a demanding but deeply satisfying activity which pays high dividends, is one of the most neglected aspects of all forms of church and community work.

Facilitating structures such as the schema we are considering can be used as private or public aids, they can be followed consciously and deliberately stage by stage; they can become so ingrained in the way individuals, groups and organizations tackle things that they come into play automatically. For the most part they are hidden mechanisms in the consultancy activities to which they give shape, form and movement as does the skeletal structure to the human body. They are most effective when they cause the consultancy processes to flow with grace and rhythm which feels natural and good to all participants. For this to happen consultors as well as consultants have to feel comfortable with them as aids to thinking. On occasions this can happen when they are entirely new to consultors and consultants use them naturally, rhythmically and effectively without explaining or negotiating them. At other times it is necessary to explain procedures and test them for acceptability. However this might be, unobtrusive flexible infrastructures must be there to help to shape and form the substance of the consultation.

(h)   Thinking in Different Emotional States. So far the affective dimension has been somewhat neglected in the emphasis upon what needs to be thought about and ways of doing so. To my surprise I can find few references in the literature to this aspect of consultancy. Creative thinking is variously and complexly enabled and disenabled by positive and negative feelings and emotions and by affections and disaffections. Sometimes consultors express their feelings fiercely, at other times they bottle them up. Their emotional state can range from bubbling excitement to a feeling of emptiness or deadness, as can that of the consultant. Their feelings influence to a greater or lesser extent, the ability of consultors and consultants to think at all and to do so constructively. But feelings do not simply countervail against thoughts and vice versa. Thinking is an emotional as well as a cerebral activity. Indeed, feelings of one kind or another associated with such things as compassion, interest and curiosity and sheer necessity, motivate people to think. It is because I feel very deeply about practitioners who need consultancy help, that I struggle to put my thoughts on paper.

Consulting itself is a profoundly sentient activity. Some of the deepest and most important feelings, emotions and sentiments about the human and the spiritual are encountered in consultations. There are several sources of this affective content. Direct sources are: the consultors; the people with whom they live and work; the things about which they are concerned; consultants and the responses they make. Indirect sources are any other people or circumstances which have significant effects upon consultors and consultants. Family events, celebrations or problems could, for instance, distract consultors and consultants and put them in a good or a bad mood.

Consultants can experience all kinds of emotions in relation to the consultor and the consultations such as: admiration or envy or jealousy of the consultor and his/her abilities and opportunities; a sense of privilege at being allowed to contribute to another person's vocational work; a deep desire to help; feelings of inadequacy; apprehension that s/he will not be able to help. Consultors also have all kinds of feelings: elation; excitement/apprehension about and thankfulness for the opportunity to share concerns in confidence; relief; good and/or bad feelings about their work; unhappiness, anxiety, dread, fear, panic; desperate hope that the consultation will help them and/or fear that it will not; unease about talking about people they respect and love; admiration or veneration, envy or jealousy of the consultant. Then there is the emotional ambience of the working situation under consideration which is of critical importance.

These various feelings and emotions congregate to create the sentience of consultations. Consultors and consultants, separately and together have to manage the affective milieu in which they find themselves. In some instances the consultor's feelings, always to be taken seriously, are the critical factor. Inevitably these feelings become part of the substantive subject matter—whatever their sources might be, primary or secondary—because they influence and affect, positively or negatively, the consultor's ability to be an effective practitioner. Invariably, the opportunity to give free expression to their feelings in a safe environment is cathartic. Sometimes that is all that is required. On other occasions it is a prelude to a pastoral and/or analytical conversation about the feelings in relation to the consultor and his/her work and vocation: consultancy is a pastoral office as well as a professional service. Rational discussion of feelings can be productive. In most cases a combination of pastoral and professional approaches enables consultors to deal with their feelings and to get into the frame of mind they need to be in. When it appears they need more than this kind of help and first aid counselling, it is up to the consultant to discuss this possibility with them.

Generalising about cause and effect of feelings and the ideal emotional state for reflective practice is unhelpful. Different people make different emotional responses to similar circumstances. For instance, pressure, high drama, conflict and tension associated with deadlines make some people think clearly but cause others to freeze and panic. Difficulties and problems depress some people and stimulate others. But guidance about dealing with feelings and emotions is needed. It is proffered here in the following responses to the question, "What can consultants do towards creating sentient conditions conducive to good thinking?"

- Consultants can provide and create the personal and environmental conditions for consultancy sessions which are emotionally neutral to consultor and consultant. That is, an emotional refuge or safe house in which they are free from unrelated and unhelpful emotional interventions and distractions. For instance, good or bad news conveyed by telephone or someone bringing in messages can add an unhelpful emotional layer to the session.

- Consultants can control their own affective state in order to concentrate upon the consultor's emotions and feelings and those associated with the situation. Their feelings must not obtrude unhelpfully.

- Consultants can accept the consultor's emotional state non-judgementally and non-indulgently. They can seek to quieten disturbing feelings but avoid any suggestion that they should not have been expressed or that they are not relevant to a technical discussion. On the contrary they can say and show that it is acceptable and necessary to show feelings and that it is possible and essential in some circumstances to examine them in the same way as other things are examined. Doing this can be an important part of analysing and designing. *Emotions and feelings are proper consultancy subject matter which can be important objects of critical creative thinking.*

- Consultants can address what is causing emotional dissonance: "The emotional content of a task oriented job related problem is dealt with indirectly as help and relief is provided directly to the work dilemma." [52]

- Consultants can discuss with consultors how to take feelings into account. They can enquire about them especially when they are not expressed verbally or non-verbally in any clear way.

- Consultants can empathise without making it more difficult for consultors to handle their feelings. Consultants must avoid adding their feelings to those of the consultor's (cf pp 40-41). For instance, a consultant may feel incensed at the way the consultor has been treated. Empathise s/he must, but to give free expression to his/her anger means that the consultor has to cope with the consultant's emotions as well as his/her own; attention focuses upon, the consultant's feelings when it should concentrate on the consultor's; the consultant's feelings become a rogue factor in the analysis and design.

- Consultants can learn as much as possible about the way in which feelings affect the consultor's ability to think creatively and how s/he manages her/his emotional responses. This can be done in two ways: by observing how the consultor in fact copes with feelings during consultancy sessions; through discussions with the consultor. The latter is not always possible. Whatever information is available is used by the consultant, hopefully in collaboration with the consultor, to create optimum conditions and to facilitate constructive thought about things which generate considerable emotion. Consultancy sessions become a place in which consultors, and consultants, can learn how to deal with emotion when thinking privately and publicly in other situations.

- Consultants can engender different thinking moods and modes. This is considered in the next section.

No matter how helpful consultants might be, sharing and examining their feelings can be demanding and traumatic for consultors. Given that they are convinced that it is important to consider emotions and feelings and that it is safe to do so, there are things consultors can do towards getting them taken into proper account. They can make sure that the consultant really understands them, accepts their significance, addresses them and takes their implications seriously. The danger of feelings being expressed and accepted sympathetically and then ignored must be avoided: they may have to be put on hold whilst some things are thought through but account must be taken of them in any creative thinking. This will involve consultors in expressing and describing their feelings and their effects in ways which promote constructive thought rather than quash it. Consultors must do all they can to manage their affective involvement. Emotional self-indulgence must be avoided. When consultants are acting as suggested above they need to cooperate with them; when they are not consultors can use the points to suggest ways in which they could be more helpful.

(i)   Using Different Thinking Moods and Modes. Thinking things through in consultancy sessions involves different but complementary activities. ***Analysing and designing*** are in the active mood and mode of thoughtful being and doing. This kind of thinking involves the disciplined application of mind and heart to the job of exploring, questioning and working things out systematically. It is carried out in various ways through logical dialogues informed by intuitions and hunches; by forming and testing hypotheses; by submitting the product of the imagination to critical scrutiny. ***Meditating and reflecting*** are in quite different moods and modes, relaxed rather than active. They involve concentrating and waiting upon things expectantly, mulling things over and cogitating, "listening" to what they might say, pursuing thoughts that arise. ***Prayer*** is a listening to and a dialogue with God. ***Meditation, reflection and prayer*** are activities which allow the free wheeling association of mind and heart with all that is happening in the widest possible context. ***Formulating learning*** is in a reflective, reflexive, searching, active, disciplined mood and mode. It involves standing back from things, looking for connections, surveying and scanning for anything that might emerge and finding ways of expressing it accurately. ***Doing theology*** is variously in the active and reflective moods and modes. Applied or practical theology is actively putting beliefs into practice. Experiential theology is reflecting on events. Emergent theology is discovering God working in situations.

These different thoughtful activities range from "direct thinking" to what Koestler calls "thinking aside".[53] They draw and feed upon one another. Working at things systematically and praying about them in a consultancy context of pastoral care integrates them, creates a spirituality of its own, generates and releases energy and enables consultors to work more creatively for human and spiritual development.

Sometimes the movement from one mood and mode of thinking to another occurs quite naturally. When that happens it has to be recognised, accepted, respected and used. It happens, for instance, when conversation gives way to a comfortable quietness in which participants are quite clearly thinking deeply. An analytical consultancy conversation merges into a meditative silence. At other times it has to be effected. One of the skills of the art of consultancy is to discern which approach to suggest and when: a structured analytical approach; a meditative reflective period to mull over what has emerged; a time of prayer or to use St Ingatius of Loyola's expressive phrase, "a colloquy with the Lord". Simple questions or statements can cause a movement of mood and mode: "Can we take a moment to catch up with our own thoughts and feelings?" "I feel the need to reflect/ meditate on that for a moment, may we?".

(j) Drawing and Writing. Drawing, speaking and writing are means of communicating what has evolved from thought, of getting others thinking and of promoting debate and dialogue. Equally the very acts of drawing, talking and writing are means of thinking—of engendering and refining thinking processes and generating new thought. Self-evidently, talking is vital to consultancy. It is the medium by which consultors and consultants think aloud separately and together. What each of them says must express as clearly as possible what they are seeing, thinking and feeling in its clarity and confusion in order that they can think aloud together. Here we concentrate upon the ways in which writing and drawing promote and extend thought in consultancy.

Writing can make contributions at different stages of the consultancy process. Already it has been shown that, when consultors can write notes on the work about which they want to consult, it is invariably helpful. It causes consultors to think, orientates consultants and facilitates preparation. Sometimes, however, emotions or a block to writing or lack of time mean that they simply cannot write anything. They simply want and need to talk. Currently I am involved in consultancy with two people. By common agreement, substantial position papers prepared for the first session proved to be indispensable whereas they could not bring themselves to, or find the time to write papers for the second session.

Emphasizing that it is working notes that are required not polished essays, helps consultors to put pen to paper. The scope of the notes requested varies enormously and must fit consultors and their circumstances. I simply ask some people to drop me a line confirming the arrangements and indicating: why they want a consultancy session, what they want to discuss and what they hope to get out of it; how they feel about their work and how things are going. More often than not this low key approach produces a short, often hand written, letter packed with punchy information and insights. Those who write such letters benefit from the exercise and say so. This approach proves to be useful when a more formal request for a briefing paper would have been threatening. At the other end of the scale position papers covering a range of stated topics can be requested. (Appendix I) Those who attended Avec work and theory consultancy courses had to produce "work papers" similar to those suggested in Appendix I. For most of them it was the first time they had produced a technical paper on themselves as a practitioner and their work. (On the basis of the MARC Europe evaluation of Avec's work most of them were in mid-career: 15% under 40; 62% 40-59; 23 % 60 or over.) [54] Most people struggled over writing these papers even though they were well used to writing academic essays and reports, lectures and sermons and were provided with a suggested outline—but they invariably found that it had been a most valuable learning experience. It had really made them think, enabled them to reflect on their work and themselves and find a vocabulary for a creative dialogue with others about their situation and thinking.

Writing things down is also useful during consultancy sessions. When working with small consultancy groups (5 - 8 people) I use newsprint to draw diagrams, note principal points and to summarise a discussion. When working with one or two consultors I do the same, but on sheets of A4 paper. A sample is reproduced in Display 2:4. This makes many useful contributions to the consultancy process:

- it provides a shared focus for the discussion;

- it creates time in which to think again about the points made and therefore it is a check on things; (I frequently find consultors correct things when they are written down or put in diagrammatic form, which they did not when they were spoken.)

- it helps consultors relax and give themselves more fully to the process (they often take over the pen) because they know that they are not losing anything by not keeping their own notes; (Frequently they ask for things to be written down.)

- there is a shared reference point for and note of the session (consultors invariably ask for a copy) which consultors and consultants can gloss as they require for their own record purposes;

- these notes are an admirable way of recalling sessions.

Consequently, the writing and drawing, which at first seems to slow down the consultancy process, does in fact add considerably to the effective and efficient use of time. The work sheets become records which consultors can and do go over with others and use to do further thinking and planning. In a consultancy group, members might be asked to make notes for each other. Establishing the understanding that without ceremony anyone can instruct the note taker to write something down makes the service more useful.

Consultants can learn much about consultancy if they follow consultancy sessions through by writing structured accounts and records of them which describe and reflect analytically upon: the subject matter; positive and negative aspects of the pattern of interaction; the processes and the outcome.[55] This is one of the principal ways in which I have learnt about consultancy and working with people. Similarly, consultors can add value to the consultations and learn much about themselves as practitioners, their work and consultancy by writing records. In writing about the consultancy subject matter they are likely to gain further insights. They could find it helpful to describe and reflect upon what s/he now considers to be: the principal features of the work situation; the processes which promote and those which prevent development; the key issues, major opportunities and main problems; the development plan; the action choices, the decisions to be made and the balance of advantage. Reflective writing before and after consultancy sessions promotes reflective "talking work". Consultors and consultants are all the poorer when they neglect to do this.

There are, however, times when, as Arthur Koestler argued so cogently, "we have to get away from speech in order to think clearly"[56] and that is when drawing comes into its own and brings in the right side of the brain.[57] Drawing, diagrams and models and constructing critical paths and flow charts make important contributions

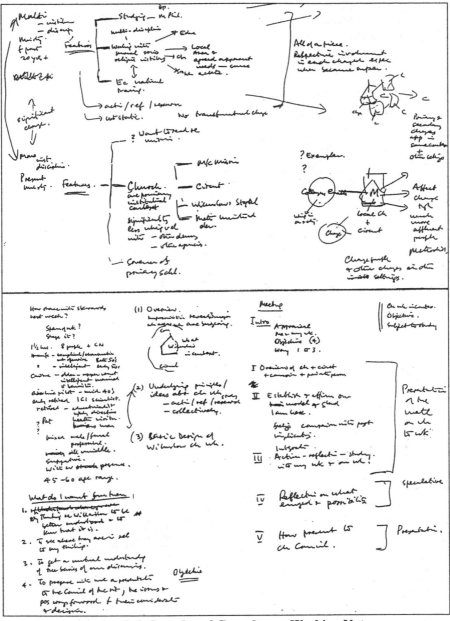

Display 2:4 Samples of Consultancy Working Notes

to analysing and designing.[58] I use these methods extensively. This book is illustrated by them and exemplifies their use in consultancy sessions. Sketching also can be used to great advantage as can be seen from Display 2:5.[59] Most people find drawings useful even if they themselves are not in the habit of using them. Subsequently a large percentage of consultors do start to draw their own diagrams and show considerable skill in doing so. For the majority they open up new exciting worlds of thought because they are powerful thinking tools.

89

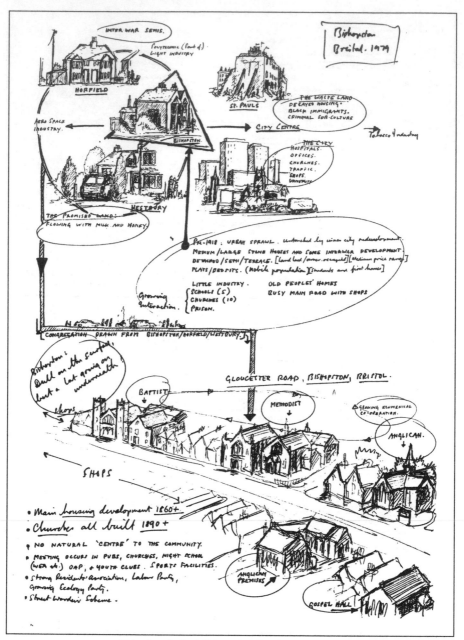

Display 2:5 A Pictorial Position Paper

Diagrams and diagrammatic models are line drawings showing the parts of things or how they work. They select, simplify and exaggerate aspects of reality seen to be significant for the purposes in hand and play down those that are not. Some diagrams picture things, map or plot them out. Diagrammatic models, particularly disclosure models, reveal something of the inner structure and essential shape of things; they disclose the connections between variables and processes of cause and effect; they show how things do or could or should fit together and function. Examples are to be found in this book. Diagrams and models are useful because they enable us to talk about things that are difficult or impossible to describe.[60] Once constructed, they are invaluable aids to the consultancy process. Consultants and consultors can identify unmistakably things to which they are referring by pointing to them. Making points verbally without recourse to diagrams can be very difficult and takes much more time and effort. Consultors have made blobs on a piece of paper to help them to explain complex patterns of interaction between people. As they explained what each person did they pointed at "their" blob and indicated the interpersonal dynamic by pointing at the blob representing the next person. The description took less time and was more intelligible! Ideas flow freely. They use the side of the brain that thinks in pictures rather than words. Diagrams are particularly useful for conceptualizing, analysing and designing projects and programmes and explaining them. But they do have their limitations: they are approximate; they are not comprehensive statements of realities; some of them do not travel well— diagrams which promoted exciting discussion when reproduced in another context appear lifeless because that which was experienced as the diagram was built up stage by stage is not communicated by the final drawing.

3.   Interpersonal Aids to Interactive Thinking

I have used this heading to differentiate these aids from technical ones.

(a)   Consultors and consultants need to understand and work to each other's modes of thinking. Amongst other things, the quality of the interaction between consultants and consultors depends upon them understanding and being open to each other's ways of thinking which may differ considerably. During consultancy sessions they may use each other's methods or work together in ways new to one or other of them. Sometimes consultants use methods without discussing them and then test them out for acceptability. At other times they must be tested out for acceptability at the outset of a piece of work and then as it proceeds when the consultor has experience of the approaches simple questions help: "Is this a way of working which is acceptable to you?" "Are you comfortable with this way of thinking things through?"

Forthright presentations of methods is in order but they must be tested out non-directively. Collaborative approaches of this kind help consultors and consultants to find the best methods and enable them to learn about each others' approaches and methods and facilitate creative interactive thinking. Consultors may or may not use the consultant's methods beyond the consultancy sessions. That is another question. Finding a mutually acceptable modus operandi is the prior question, assessing its wider application is another which is discussed later.

(b)   The thinking between consultors and consultants needs to be first open, collaborative, flexible and imaginative and then focused. Thinking of this kind is the life blood of consultancy processes. Because they are private and confidential, consultations provide opportunities to think in the most adventurous ways and to pursue any and every idea including the most outrageous ones. Open, tentative and

uninhibited thinking can be very creative. This is most likely to happen when the different thinking roles and functions that consultors and consultants perform and their respective abilities are seen to be complementary and used collaboratively. Attitudes or actions that lead to dominance or deference or paternalism in either party, inhibit open and free thought in consultors and consultants and between them. Defensiveness breaks down and ultimately destroys consultancy processes.

Consultations, however, are not "open ended". They are open in exploration in order to focus down on specific action programmes. Periodic strategically timed summaries help the process of gathering together wide ranging, complex, open discussions and giving them coherence and direction. Summaries can enable no less than four things to happen. First, they recall the essentials and reveal where consultants and consultors have got to in their thinking. (Sometimes it is better for the consultant to make the summary and for the consultor to supplement and amend it. But, whenever possible it is advisable for consultors to do it and for consultants to add their contributions as it enables them to shape and own what is emerging and it reveals how they are thinking. When acting as a consultant, I have to hold myself back from making summaries because I invariably find it is a way of developing the thought as well as synthesising it—and I love doing it and showing how it can be done!) Second, summaries enable corrections to be made and any afterthoughts sidelined by the flow of the discussion to be gathered in. Third, they provide opportunities for consultors and consultants to take hold of the discussion and to make conscious decisions about the direction in which they want to take it and thus they avoid unhelpful drift. Fourth, they facilitate editing. They enable earlier points to be re-shaped and re-stated in the light of later ones; they enable consultors and consultants to organize and re-organize what has emerged in different conceptual patterns by establishing clusters of ideas and the connections between them. Summarising, therefore, can give a major forward thrust to consultancy sessions by putting things together in more meaningful, useful and productive forms. People give themselves much more freely and confidently to open wide-ranging discussions when they know from past experience that it will be garnered in a summary and that they can make or request one if they wish. Summarising is a very useful tool of interactive thinking.

(c)   Critical factors in collaborative thinking are the manner and mechanics of verbal and non-verbal communications between consultors and consultants and their interpersonal engagement. Ideas, insights and concepts which open up new possibilities for consultors are primary sources of creative and inspirational thinking in consultancy sessions. That is true but not the whole truth. The manner and mechanics of verbal and non-verbal communications between consultors and consultants and their interpersonal and behavioural engagement have considerable influence upon the way in which thinking does or does not develop. What is required is that the thinking of one participant is forwarded by the content of the other person's contribution, by the way in which it is made and the manner and mechanics of their interaction. This can happen through ideas complementing one another and jelling or through challenges or in many other ways. One contribution builds upon/leads to another: it is as though one thought cog engages with another. The forward thrust is exciting and satisfying. Here we consider things which help and things which hinder the creative dynamics of interactive thought.

Rate of Thinking, Reactive Speed and Tempo of Interaction. For the interaction between consultants and consultors to be effective, in relation to any kind of content, the speed and tempo of the exchanges between them have to fit the rate at which consultors can think creatively, rather than at that which consultants can: consultants have to work to the pace of consultors. If the natural rate of the consultant's thinking is faster than that of the consultor's, s/he has simply got to contain herself/himself in patience and manage any frustration s/he might experience. When I am in such a situation, I try to ensure that consultors have the thinking space they need. I simply sit, wait and think. At other times I might ask them if they need time to reflect. Or I might ask if we are going too quickly or need to go back over things. Often I write things down that I want to raise—it reduces the desire to verbalise them at that moment and means that I do not have to fumble in my mind for them later.

Notwithstanding, there are times when I have got so interested in and excited by ideas that I have left consultors behind when they are not having the same effect on them. This is not good if, as we have seen, consultors feel out of it and that their work has been taken over, intellectually and emotionally possessed, by the consultant. In other circumstances, however, it can be a trail blazing way of thinking out an idea *for* consultors when they glimmer the idea to be helpful and, whilst they cannot keep up they know that there will be an opportunity later to go over at their own speed what is emerging. Frequently consultors have said, "Go on, don't stop in full flow. I will catch up. I want to see where this idea could take us".

The shoe can be, and often is on the other foot: the consultant cannot keep up! Things can be much more difficult for me when I am acting as consultant to someone who thinks much more quickly that I do and is much cleverer than I am. S/he can intimidate me especially when the amount of information and number of ideas I have to try to get my mind round is vast and complicated. I am afraid that I will be left behind or that reducing the rate of thinking so that I can keep up, will create a speed of interaction too slow to generate creative thought in the consultor and that I will frustrate or bore him/her to the extent that consultations become of little or no value. In such relationships I ask consultors to go back over things as I summarise concepts and ideas to make sure I have got hold of them. I ask for thinking time—in sessions and if necessary between sessions. I ask for prior notice of subjects and background material to study beforehand. When this is not possible the face to face briefing during sessions is most useful when it has been prepared carefully. Consultors can help consultants by providing them with copies of their notes or diagrams or other briefing papers and working through them with them. Consultants have more time to absorb the material because they do not have to take notes and can annotate the papers as an aid to the consultancy process. Sometimes I discuss the rate of interaction and effects upon each of us. Not infrequently, however, making consultors think more slowly or getting them to explain complicated ideas in simple language and then reflecting back and modelling what I am hearing and seeing is very profitable to them. They see new things or old things in a new light which primes consultancy processes. In fact as they tell their story to the consultant they are telling it to themselves.[61] Also, consultors can learn a lot from the consultancy relationship about how they can work with people who think more slowly than they do. In spite of my feelings, which are real, rarely does the interaction become an irritant and cause the consultancy relationship to be concluded, at least not to my knowledge!

Thus, three of the critical factors are: the respective rates at which consultors and consultants can think, the speed at which they interact and their ability to adapt to each other. People's capacities to do this kind of collaborative thinking are not fixed, neither quantatively nor qualitatively. They vary with mood, circumstance, subject matter, the personnel involved and their reactions and responses. Sometimes and in relation to certain things consultors can think more quickly than consultants. In relation to other things the situation might well be reversed. Consultants and consultors have separate and joint responsibilities for creating the circumstances which maximise the use of their capacities and for doing all that they can to develop them.

Modes and Methods of Interaction. There can be significant differences between consultors and consultants in relation to their methods of interpersonal interaction:

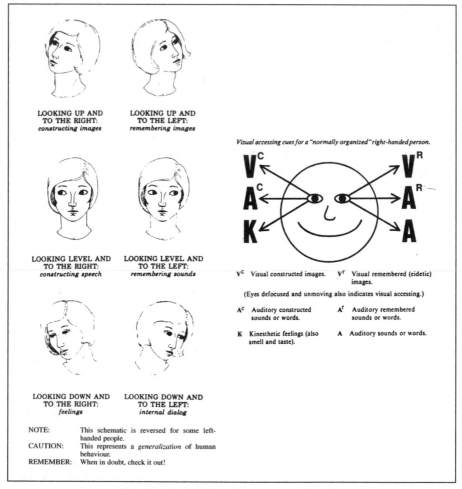

LOOKING UP AND TO THE RIGHT: *constructing images*

LOOKING UP AND TO THE LEFT: *remembering images*

Visual accessing cues for a "normally organized" right-handed person.

LOOKING LEVEL AND TO THE RIGHT: *constructing speech*

LOOKING LEVEL AND TO THE LEFT: *remembering sounds*

LOOKING DOWN AND TO THE RIGHT: *feelings*

LOOKING DOWN AND TO THE LEFT: *internal dialog*

V^c Visual constructed images. V^r Visual remembered (eidetic) images.

(Eyes defocused and unmoving also indicates visual accessing.)

A^c Auditory constructed sounds or words. A^r Auditory remembered sounds or words.

K Kinesthetic feelings (also smell and taste).   A Auditory sounds or words.

NOTE: This schematic is reversed for some left-handed people.
CAUTION: This represents a *generalization* of human behaviour.
REMEMBER: When in doubt, check it out!

Display 2:6 "Visual Accessing Cues" [62]

the amount of speech time that they require to express themselves; the rate at which they speak, speed and tempo; the length of the interval before replying; the rapidity with which ideas are produced and assimilated; the speed of switching from one idea to another; the different forms of mental activity in which they engage and the manner and rate in which they change from one to the other as indicated, for instance, by the movement of the eyes as illustrated in Display 2:6; facial expressions and other forms of body language; eye contact; the rate of change of mood and temper.[63] Not only do these things vary from person to person but they also vary in the same person from situation to situation and during the course of consultancy sessions. For consultations to be effective consultors and consultants have to handle these factors. Understanding, mutual acceptance and patience are required. Consultors and consultants have to facilitate interactive meshing of contributions and the manner in which they are made. This sequence of utterances, interpersonal behaviour, tempo and time sharing need to be acceptable and conducive to all participants. This happens in many different ways.

Consecutive and Overlapping Speech. Consultors and consultants can make their contributions in an orderly sequential pattern or they can overlap or overlay each other's contribution. Cutting in can be particularly problematic in co-consultancy groups when people are not allowed to finish off what they are saying and two or three people are actively vying for speaking time and consequently not listening as they should. My own propensities towards orderliness in exchanges reinforced by my commitment to the non-directive approach, incline me to think that consultations are most effective when people speak in turn, neither interrupting the other. Cutting in before someone has finished can irritate me not least because people are not respected and therefore can feel put down and because valuable points are often drowned and lost. But then I recall some of the most creative moments have occurred when consultants and consultors are speaking at the same time, overlapping each other as they endorse or develop what the other has said. This can be quite exciting in dyads or in groups. Whilst more orderly exchanges are needed to organize the ideas that have emerged, stopping the exchanges prematurely for the sake of good order can be verbal vandalism. Then again, long uninterrupted speeches can inhibit the flow of ideas and kill dead the consultancy process. So much so that when someone is acting as a consultor in a group I seek prior permission privately to interrupt them in public if I think s/he is going on too long. But then, yet again, more often than not, listening to people for 20 or 30 minutes, interrupting only for clarification, as I frequently do at the outset of a session, can pay high dividends. For one thing it allows consultors to articulate their thoughts and feelings in ways that show connections and disconnections, the story lines, gaps in their thinking and the ways in which they think. Sharing of this kind contributes much to the quality of the consultancy relationship and to interactive thinking. Diagrams, as we have seen, help to increase the rate of exchange because a lot can be communicated through them in a short space of time and additional points can be made quickly by pointing to this and that or by adding additional lines, circles or arrowheads. One thing that emerges is that it is impossible to generalise. Consultants need to be able to live and work with many forms of interaction, some of which irritate them! What matters in the end is that there is significant development of thought. This is not to be confused or equated with orderly sequential interaction. It can be generated by untidy and messy interaction.

Some Guidelines. Even though there are so many variables and different patterns of interactive creative thought, I venture some guidelines for consultors and consultants.

- Sensitivity to thinking processes is required throughout.

- Consultors must be heard out and consultants must take seriously what they say and feel and demonstrate that they are doing so. Otherwise, consultors will opt out or make their points over and again ever more insistently and/or or disown "solutions".

- Consultors and consultants must allow each other to think unilaterally when they need to; equally they must not become so excited and preoccupied by their own thinking that they override or leave others behind.

- The uniqueness of the mode of interactive thinking natural to each party to a consultancy must be respected.

- Making eye contact at key moments is of vital importance: it is worth hunting for or inviting it when it is not readily given, because the eyes reveal much of the truth about what people are thinking or feeling. Reading eye movements can be illuminating (cf Display 2:6).

- Consultants and consultors need to be able to regulate the intensity and tempo of their interactive thinking as circumstances require. To do this, inter-alia, they need to be able to stand back from each other to reflect and evaluate each other's thinking as well as to get into close engagement.

- Consultors must remain in control of their own situation and therefore of their own thinking about it.

- Consultors and consultants need to express relevant thoughts and feelings economically: but intellectual economy must not be gained at the expense of satisfying affective needs to spell things out in detail and go over some experiences and details time and again.

- Competing for speaking time is unhelpful.

- Learning together is important. (See section 5.)

4.   Hindrances to Thinking

When the technical and personal aids discussed in sections 1 to 3 are properly deployed, the triangulation between the complexity of the subject matter, those doing the thinking and the effective use of aids to creative thought promotes all round development: the work improves; the thinkers become better thinkers and therefore better reflective practitioners; aids are tested, owned and improved. Appropriate technical and personal aid pays high dividends. They enable, heal and promote growth. When they are not used well, the effect is quite the opposite. The triangulation undermines the work, the thinkers and their confidence in the tools. The thinkers feel bad, lose confidence and their belief in themselves, become depressed, apprehensive and intimidated by challenges of the same kind. Or they can become defensive or place the blame elsewhere. All undesirable outcomes. Serious attention must to be given to the potential hindrances to creative thinking in consultancy sessions which are implicit and explicit in what has already been said in the preceding sections. Briefly stated consultants can hinder thinking processes by: using inappropriate approaches (cf section 1); being ignorant of one or more of the technical aids to thinking or using them unskillfully or ineptly (cf section 2); being clumsy or gauche in their attempts to promote interactive thinking (cf section 3). Consultors can hinder them by their inability: to make the responses to the approaches required of them; to play their part in the use of the technical aids; to engage adequately in the interpersonal relationships which make interactive thinking possible.

Lack of skill apart, the consultors and consultants can hinder thinking through their attitudes. For instance, consultants can be hindered from constructive thinking when they decide that the consultors with whom they are working simply cannot or will not think about this or that. Such feelings can cause consultants, consciously or unconsciously, to write consultors out of the thinking processes and conclude that their only option is to think *for* them. Everything changes if the consultant's approach and attitudes are quite different: "So far I have not been able to get the consultor to think about that nor to help him/her to think through the other matter". Consultants in this frame of mind challenge themselves to find ways of getting people to think. Such an approach refuses to write off consultors. It indicates the consultant's responsibilities and describes his/her problem in relation to the consultor's problem. It humbles the consultant and respects the consultor. Whereas the first approach exonerates the consultant of responsibility by denouncing the consultor. Clearly the first attitude is a hindrance and the second a stimulating challenge.

People block themselves off from critical thinking and consultancy services in several ways. One way is through ill-formed ideas they might have about its value. "It is interesting to think about things beforehand but much of it is a waste of time because things are so different when you get to the action". Another way is through their fear of the consequences of thinking deeply about situations: consultors and consultants might be seen in a bad light; they might not be able to handle what is revealed when the "lid is taken off" a situation.

Some consultors find it hard and painful to think seriously and deeply about things because they have been hurt and injured by various experiences. Some have come to doubt their own intellectual abilities and to believe that they are unable to think because of bad experiences they have had of educational exercises and systems, and through being told repeatedly that they are unintelligent and unable to think. They are wounded thinkers.

Helping people with these fears and learning difficulties is a pastoral office as well as a consultancy function. Progress can be made by talking through the difficulties. Giving them good experiences of thinking their way through work issues and problems can be therapeutic if it shows them that they can think and helps them to acquire the skills and self-confidence to do so on their own and with others. But the development of the skills required and the confidence to use them must go together. It is important to avoid the sort of encouragement that leads people to become over-confident before they realise the depth of the skills they need to acquire.

5. Learning Together about Thinking

Consultations are most productive when learning occurs about: consultors and their work; things which enable the consultors to work to better effect in the immediate future; ways and means by which consultors can think more clearly and constructively about themselves as vocational practitioners and about their church and community work. Combined, these forms of learning develop the abilities of consultors to be independent practitioners and consultants to be consultants. Here we concentrate on learning about thinking. The learning potential of consultations is enormous for consultors and consultants because every consultancy exercise provides opportunities: to test thinking methods experientially; to learn how to improve one's ability to think for oneself and for, with and alongside others; to stimulate other people's thinking and to be stimulated by it; to help others to think in formal and informal situations; to get help with one's own thinking.

Experiences of the four approaches, described in section one, present different learning opportunities. Accompanying consultors as they think things out, the third method, is a direct experience of the consultor's own way of thinking. Whereas the other approaches, stimulating and helping consultors to think and thinking things out *for* and *with* them, are predominantly experiences of the way in which consultants work at things. These opportunities to build up personal practice theory are invaluable.

Some of the learning will occur through processes of osmosis. Many consultors and most consultants are keen to discuss what is being learnt. They can do so by drawing out the learning, reflecting upon it and thinking out the implications for them in different contexts. Consultants have twin responsibilities: to understand the thinking processes and procedures themselves and to help consultors to understand them. Consultors also have twin responsibilities: to learn about the processes and procedures and to help consultants to do so. They can do these things by, for instance, indicating to each other what helps and what hinders and by evaluating sessions and their respective performances. This deepens their mutual understanding of both their roles and enhances their ability to perform them; it increases the potential of their sessions; it helps to make them equal consultancy partners and reflective practitioners. The ways in which they learn from each other will vary considerably. Sometimes it will be through consultants spelling out the what and why of the procedures they propose to use to see if they are acceptable. At other times, it will come through consultors or consultants raising questions or making suggestions about consultancy procedures. Yet more will emerge from evaluting consultancy sessions.

Even so, some consultors have no particular desire or intention of developing their ability to think more rigorously or differently—possibly because they see themselves as activists rather than thinkers, or because they do not feel they have the ability, the time or the intellectual, emotional energy required. They tend to approach consultations in a utilitarian way. They buy in a thinking service as and when required in much the same way as they would employ architects. They neither desire nor intend to learn to do for themselves what they can employ consultants to do for them. They find the kind of approaches to thinking described above very helpful when someone else is deploying them. They enter into the process and procedures with alacrity and find their thinking powers released and stretched. But they take no direct action to learn the skills, although undoubtedly something of the methods used rubs off. Whilst this approach is sometimes appropriate, there is a danger that they use consultants when they should be doing their own thinking. Consultants may have to try to get them to consider this. But from time to time, a desire to enhance their own thinking abilities surfaces when they begin to see that the methods they are experiencing could be useful to them and glimmer ways in which they could adapt them to their way of working.

When considering the implications for consultors of the thinking methods used in consultancy sessions it is essential to do so in relation to the ways in which it is natural and habitual for them to think and work things out. A propensity to neglect this side of the equation has many dangers. It is dismissive of the consultor's ways of thinking; it is tantamount to suggesting that the consultant's way is superior to that of the consultor's and that s/he ought to use it; it leaves consultors to work out on their own tricky and critical questions about the adoption or adaptation, assimilation and deployment of methods new to them; consequently the chances of consultors getting it wrong and suffering for it are increased. Some of these possibilities are dangerous, unacceptable distortions of a responsible and realistic approach. Learning about the ways in which a consultor thinks is utterly essential to the development of their practice theory. Almost by chance I came across a telling case of this when, as part of the research for a book, I was interviewing Charles New, a Methodist minister about his experiences of the way of working with people advocated in this book. A note I wrote on it which received his approval prior to publication is reproduced here because it illustrates points being made about thinking processes.

A member of my research group said that people like Charles have "learnt the skill and forgotten the theory". There is some truth in that. Much of it had become so much second nature to him after twenty three years of practising and teaching the approach that he took it for granted. From what he said about the approach being a "way of life" it appears that theory, theology and methods have been fused within him indissolubly into a praxis nucleus. So, when I asked him if he consciously referred to basic theory and theological principles when deciding what action to take he was nonplussed. It seems that he does not. He focuses and concentrates on situations as they arise. Reflecting on this, it would seem that for Charles the basic dynamic is between situations and the way of life nucleus well-formed within him: it is not within him between his theory, theology and practice and the situation; it is not between his theory and/or his theology and/or his practice and the situation.

An ill-formed working assumption led me to question him sharply about this. The assumption was that continuous conscious interplay between theory, theology and practice should be normative and that it enhances the performance of practitioners. But that is to give it a clarity it did not have at the time. It did not seem to work like that for Charles New. To repeat myself, the interplay which normally led to action was between the way of life nucleus and situations. So far his experience has validated and modified his nucleus but not challenged it radically. Progressive development of these nuclei involves periodically scrutinising them. Exposing them to concepts and practices at variance to them is one way of engendering creative reflection.

A fuller understanding is desirable of the ways in which we and others build up the theoretical and theological bases from which we act and the ways in which we put them into practice. It helps us to develop as practitioners, to understand ourselves and others and thus to work together more effectively. Gaining such understanding is difficult. There are so many variations and permutations. Much eludes us because the processes flow into and out of our unconscious and conscious minds complexly and mysteriously. Much can be achieved through awareness and open-minded observation of the processes within oneself and others. But more research is needed.

Frequently people on (work and theory) courses said they wanted to work from examples to theory because they found "theory" difficult. More often than not others on the same course were happier to work from a theoretical base! For some time I felt I was failing the first group by not working in the way most natural to them even though most of the things we did emerged from careful study of the actualities of their work and situations. I bent over backwards to accommodate them. But I began to see that I was colluding with them to their disadvantage and mine. I was helping them to do better what they could already do satisfactorily and allowing them to neglect what they were not good at. And they, like me, had to work with people who varied in their abilities to work from theory to practice and vice versa. So I actively sought opportunities to discuss with them different ways of learning through theory, practice and experience, to explore with them where they were strong and weak and to consider with them the advantages of them overcoming their weaknesses.[64]

Both of us learnt new things about Charles' way of thinking and reflecting. What emerged is invaluable to us in our ongoing working relationship and in any discussions about the development of his approach. It is with chagrin that I say that we had worked together closely for twenty five years before this emerged. But I am glad that it has!

Some people think about one thing as they are going about other things; some appear to think only when they focus on a topic. Some people's unconscious is prolific, other's seem to be much less so. Some people think better in dialogue with others than they do on paper, for others it is quite the opposite. Some people think logically and systematically, others have a butterfly mind. The differences are endless. Each characteristic has its advantages and disadvantages. Abilities can be improved by strengthening weaknesses and reinforcing strengths. Determining which to attend to is important.

New methods need to become natural to those who use them. Assimilation is important. The difficulties of assimilating things and the dangers of using them without doing so, are directly proportional to the degree to which they are new and foreign and therefore challenging and disturbing to practitioners and their working situations. Explaining and negotiating the transition with colleagues and people can be a great help.[65]

Significant changes can be made quite naturally. This is true of a change to habitually asking unloaded questions. Some of those who have done this have told me that after a while people say to them, "Recently you have been much better at getting us thinking and helping us to work things out. I sense you are doing something differently. What is it?" That is an excellent basis for development.

ELEMENT SIX: SYSTEMICS AND LOGISTICS

Each element of the practice theory discussed in this chapter makes its own distinctive contribution towards the formulation of the character of consultancy relationships, the unfolding of consultancy processes and the ethos of consultancy sessions. That is illustrated in Figure 2:10.

The especial contribution of the action associated with this sixth element is twofold. It helps consultors to move from their workplaces into consultancy sessions and to return to them. This is done by creating consultancy opportunities which fit the circumstances, structures and rhythms of the consultor's workaday

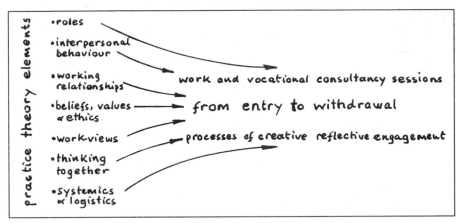

Figure 2:10 Practice Theory and Consultancy Processes

situation. That is illustrated in Figure 2:11. Secondly, it creates systemic frameworks within which consultancy relationships can operate effectively and efficiently. These things are achieved by: establishing contractual understandings related to making, maintaining and concluding consultancies; attending to the logistics;

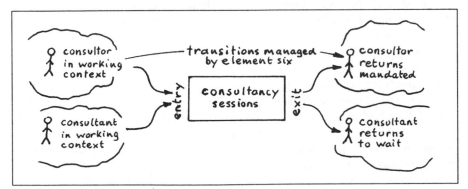

Figure 2:11 Management of Work Consultancy Transitions

arranging consultancy occasions and events; creating spaces for consultancy work; providing opportunities to earth and incarnate consultancy processes. This is illustrated in Figure 2:12. Exploring consultancy possibilities and making the initial arrangements is often the consultor's first impression and experience of the approaches and methods associated with this form of consultancy. It is, therefore, important that essentials of the approach to consultancy are communicated through the initial discussions related to systemics and logistics.

1. Forming Consultancy Systems

Whether consultors and consultants are aware of it or not, they form consultancy systems with a short or a long life span—anything from a brief one-off session to twenty five years or more of frequent sessions. These consultancy arrangements are

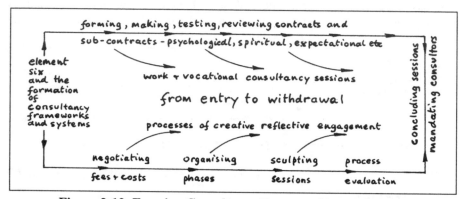

Figure 2:12 Forming Consultancy Frameworks and Systems

temporary or permanent sub-systems to the consultor's personal and vocational systems and the other ones within which s/he lives and works. To be effective, consultancy systems must provide the degree of autonomy consultors and consultants need for them to perform independent and lateral thinking functions essential to the work that they have to do. Relevant contextual factors must, of course, be taken into proper account. But as consultors and consultants analyse and design they must be able to rise above these factors and their thinking must be free from extraneous control or direction. Ideally the consultancy arrangements will be acceptable to all members of the consultor's organization who are involved in them or know of them. Difficulties can be encountered in meeting these conditions in both external and internal consultancies, *i.e.:* when consultants and consultors are members of the same church or organizations.

As we have seen, consultancies simply have to be private and confidential arrangements between consultors and consultants when significant others would be against them and reject or block anything that might flow from them, no matter how potentially useful it might be. In such arrangements, the consultancy system affects the consultor's system which, in turn, affects the systems in which s/he is engaged without revealing his/her sources of change. (See pp 47-49 for a discussion about private vs public consultancies.)

Considerable advantages accrue when it is possible for the arrangements to be public knowledge either to key figures or to members of the organization generally.

Then it is possible to sustain and secure consultancies in various ways by contracts between: consultors and consultants; consultors, those with whom they work and their organization; the consultor's organization and the consultant, especially if they are paying the fees involved. Consequently, more people are able to feed into and learn directly from sessions: as the consultancy is an accepted and supported sub-system, it is more likely to exert more influence through interacting with more people and its findings are more likely to be taken seriously and used.

In the final analysis efficacy is the primary arbiter of the acceptability of consultancies and the value consultors and their organizations place upon them. When organizations are involved in the negotiations leading to the setting up of a consultancy, critical factors can be: the severity of felt need and the degree of the desperation to find help; the confidence in the consultor and whether or not s/he is in good standing and favour; the degree of trust and confidence in the would-be consultant either through knowing her/him or through valued recommendations; tradition; costs; desire to keep control and fear of losing it; pride and apprehension about losing face through consultants learning about difficulties and failures. Another critical factor related to all kinds of consultancies has to do with the natural working rhythms, the diaries and the programme timetables of consultors and their churches and organizations. Consultancy systems must accept, respect and harmonise with them, and then, as proves to be necessary, help consultors, and through them their organizations, to work with them. Amongst other things this involves understanding natural biological, personal and institutional rhythms and habits and the ways in which these attributes are genetically, psychologically, sociologically and ecclesiastically underpinned. *The Metronomic Society* by Michael Young [66] greatly helped me to understand these dimensions and to work to them. The book is about time—how we experience it, how we think about it, how it rules us. Young examines how two complementary notions of time operate in society today: the cyclical with its emphasis on recurrences and continuity; the linear with its emphasis on development and progression.

All too easily creative rhythms can be upset by the imposition of timetables and deadlines. This has many implications for consultancy in particular and church and community work in general. Plans for development, for instance, are systems of intervention. They need to be in tune with the rhythms and timetables of practitioners and organizations and indicate a tempo to which people can realistically be expected to work. Similarly, practical arrangements for consultancy sessions must respect these factors. Ideally they must be timed and arranged so that they fit strategically into the work rhythms and timetables of consultors and their organizations. For instance, to avoid hasty or precipitous or even irascible action, consultors need to have the time and space to feel their way through, mull over and assimilate what emerged from consultations before acting upon it in public. Simple questions can raise these issues: "How does this fit into your timetables and those of your church?" "Does this give you the time you need to mull things over and consult before going public?" Three of the reasons why consultations with Batten were effective were that he took personal and situational rhythms and timetables seriously, he thought in the long as well as short term and, as he was almost always available even at short notice for consultations, he was able to work to our rhythms and timetables.

2. Phases and Sequences

Consultancies vary enormously in length, the amount of organization and planning required and in the way in which they happen. At one end of the scale there are short spontaneous events. They can evolve from what starts as a casual conversation over a meal or on a car journey or at a conference. At the other end of the scale there are carefully negotiated consultancies, briefed by position papers and involving formal sessions over an agreed period of time. They all have interrelated sequences which contribute phases in the process. Listing the full range of sequences paves the way for observations about their uses in various kinds of consultancies.[67]

(a) Entry: forming relationships, engaging in initial discussions, identifying the consultancy agenda, making arrangements to work on it and beginning to form working relationships.

(b) Orientation and preparation by both consultors and consultants for working on the consultancy agenda.

(c) Working together on the consultancy agenda through the various analytical and interactive processes and determining next steps.

(d) Reflecting on the consultancy, assimilating what emerged, taking action or processing feedback.

(e) Repeating (b) to (d) for any subsequent consultancy sessions and renewing or revising contracts, relationships and arrangements.

(f) Concluding the consultancy.

(g) Withdrawing and waiting in ways which make it possible to return if necessary.

As presented, (a), (c), (e) (f) and possibly (d) represent interaction between consultors and consultants through correspondence or telephone conversations or face to face meetings over varying periods of time, whilst (b) and possibly (d) represent private work undertaken by consultors and consultants. In some situations the overall programme of sessions and preparation might be sketched out and be a part of the contract. In others the programme will evolve. Then again (a), (c) and (f) can be concertinaed into a single consultancy event, planned or spontaneous, which can be as short in duration as twenty minutes. Generally speaking in such situations the discussion moves from identifying the subject matter to the conclusion without any overt reference to procedure. Consultants use mental constructs of sequences to help them to structure the session constructively. Formally arranged one-off consultancy sessions average out at one and a half hours but they can be as short as an hour and as long as three hours. Sometimes the sequences are made overt and consultors and consultants collaborate in managing them. At other times they are used by consultants as a guide.

Consultancy sessions take place in all kinds of settings and situations and the degree of formality varies considerably. For the main part they involve face to face discussions but consultations can also be conducted through telephone calls, correspondence, tapes, faxes, the internet and e-mail or through a combination of these methods.

The impression is easily gained from the list of sequences, that consultancy processes are or must be orderly and formal. They are not and they need not be so. Phases and sequences overlap. Structuring and re-structuring thought forms and re-visiting analyses and hypotheses are all part of the process which is systemic rather than linear. Contracts and working arrangements have to be re-negotiated. The attitude and approach to and the use of structures must allow these kinds of things to be done naturally as required. Doctrinaire adherence to procedures of any kind is a potential threat to the creative value of a facilitative structure no matter how finely tuned it might be. Notwithstanding, some things should precede others and it is of the essence of the consultancy process to discover ways and means of shaping, ordering, structuring and handling the purposeful exploration of complex subject matter, some of which has emotional connotations.

From start to finish, promoting and pursuing these consultancy sequences involves consultors and consultants entering into and remaining in appropriate roles *(Element One)*, engaging in apposite interpersonal behaviour *(Element Two)*, establishing and maintaining functionally effective working relationships *(Element Three)*, using work-views *(Element Four)*, thinking together *(Element Five)*, attending to the systems and logistics *(Element Six)* and being true to beliefs, values and ethics *(Element Seven)*. When this happens the creative consultancy processes pulsate through the phases and sequences and into the consultor's vocational life and work.

3. Sculpting sessions

Consultancy work is a fascinating and challenging art form because there are so many things to bring into creative unison in a comparatively short time. Consultancy systems depend upon sessions being entities of helpfulness complete in themselves which form building blocks in a sequential series. To do this in a session requires disciplined artistry which treats each session as a unique event with its own content, mood, rhythm and shape. Sculpting sessions is at the heart of consultancy art. Much has been said already about ways of doing this, here we concentrate on three factors: time and timing; economic information sharing; energy flow.

(a) Time and timing. A recurring thought in the approach to sessions is, how on earth can we work through the processes with the care required in such a short time? The thought of all that is involved can induce feelings of panic. The length of time over which most people can normally maintain the required level of concentration is between $1^1/4$ - 2 hours. There are many desirable effects of concentrated thinking within agreed time boundaries: consultors and consultants are galvanized into intensive, concentrated, creative activity; more often than not mutually accepted tasks for the session are completed; time is treated as the precious commodity that it is and used economically and effectively; consultors are less likely to be defensive (the great time waster); self-discipline increases; adrenelin and energy flows;

concentration becomes part of the work and consultancy culture; a real sense of occasion is engendered.

There is enormous variation in the time required for each of the phases. Dividing the time arbitrarily can frustrate the process. Few generalisations are of any value. One or two things guide me. The speed at which one can proceed with any of the phases is closely related to the degree of thoroughgoing concentration given to the previous phase. Careful attention is a consultancy accelerator. Time and again consultors have said, "I would not have believed that we could have achieved so much in the last twenty minutes. We gave so much time to the first part of the session". In all cases they have agreed that it was because we did not hurry in the early stages that we were able to move quickly and profoundly in the later stages. Listening carefully to consultors and hearing them out during the initial stages invariably pays high dividends. It signals acceptance, affirmation and the desire and intention to understand and to work at things in depth. It gives some idea of the consultor's pace, the complexity of the issues and the consultancy time which is likely to be needed. Consultors relax and give themselves to the process. Consultants have time to think and think again, to formulate and re-formulate hypotheses and to decide how to respond. Consequently, whilst this can easily, and quite often does, take a quarter to a third of a session and in some cases longer, consultors and consultants are better poised to use the remaining time wisely. Time skimping especially during the initial phases, on the other hand, is time consuming and time wasting. As we have seen when this happens consultors are inclined to engage perfunctorily *or* they will repeatedly go back to the beginnings until they get over what they were prevented from communicating *or* they might invalidate suggestions by referring to points they were "prevented" from making. Sound work at each stage is essential. Panicking and yielding to the urge to move on must be resisted. If at any stage I sense that we have not the time to complete the tasks we set out to do, I discuss the situation with the consultor or consultant, as the case may be, so that together we can decide what to do—for instance to complete the analysis and brain storm on what action could be taken and to retain time to decide next steps.

(b)   *Economic information sharing.* Economic information sharing is a key to the effective and efficient use of consultancy time. This is one of the things which is easier said than done. Interest and curiosity can lead us to give and gather information not necessary to the consultancy task. Determining in advance precisely what is and what is not relevant information is difficult if not impossible. An aside late in a consultancy has often been the vital clue. There are narrow lines between too much and too little information, between relevant and irrelevant information. Several things help me to economise, apart, that is, from mastering briefing papers and thorough preparation. I continuously remind myself that I need only the information necessary to do the consultancy job and ask myself questions such as: "What do I need to know to do this job?" "Interesting as it might be, do I need to know this now?" "Have I got all the information we need?" "Does anything else appear to be directly, vaguely or obscurely relevant?" I know I need more information when I cannot make sense of what has happened. I suspect something which could be important is being held back when consultors skirt around a subject

or refer to it vaguely or are defensive about it. I find security and comfort in a recurring experience: when we get near to the nub of something, consultors invariably see the relevance of things that they had not even thought to mention.

Consultors can help enormously by preparing and making their presentations as succinctly as possible. I encourage them to do so whilst remaining aware of what was said earlier about consultors being given opportunities to say what is on their mind and that not all key information is recognised as such at an early stage in a consultation. Consultants can make inverventions which help consultors to economise in their presentation. For instance, asking what happened next encourages consultors to keep to the central story line and to move to the next part more quickly. Again, when consultants ask how much of the detail that is emerging they need to know, consultors are stimulated to edit and prune the information more purposefully. To achieve this, interventions must not appear to criticise their presentation or to rebuke them for being too long-winded or to indicate impatience or, worse, boredom. When any of these things happen consultors can find it very difficult to share their thoughts: fluency and free flow are reduced by lack of confidence and poise. Prompting statements or questions are a useful way of intervening: "This is very interesting but I am not sure that I am getting my mind around all the information. Do I need to? What do you think I need to know?" Another way is to stop the flow and summarize what has been said and possibly list the main points on a piece of paper visible to all, or draw a diagram. Invariably an effect of such an intervention is that the consultors makes the remainder of their input much more succinctly. They tend to emulate the consultant, add to lists and build on diagrams.

Consultants give a lead by making their inputs as economically as possible. They need to avoid anecdotes and pursuing things of interest to them which are not relevant to the consultancy. Preoccupation with verbal economy for economy's sake that leads to hurrying consultors along, however, is likely to be counter-productive.

(c) Energy and energising. This section focuses on the practicalities of the ebb and flow of energy in consultancy session. (See also the Troubleshooting Charts in Chapter Five on "Power Failure: Consultancy Energy Loss".) Consultations require considerable amounts of emotional, intellectual, moral and spiritual energy. People well used to engaging in serious study and thinking have said that they were surprised to find that consultations about their work tired them more than any other intellectual exercises that they had done. Four of the possible reasons for this are: they are not used to thinking about their work so analytically, revealingly and intensively; they are personally involved and implicated because they are the subject of the analysis as well as an instrument of it; they are examining things of great complexity which are very important to them; consultancy exercises can lead to tricky and risky action with people, not simply academic speculation. These attributes make consultancy sessions into occasions and events which, like games or examinations, cause the adrenalin to flow and draw out of people resources that they did not know they had. Nonetheless, as consultancy sessions proceed the energy flow is variable and unpredictable. Sometimes there is a steady flow and a gradual rise in energy levels. At other times it surges and recedes, sometimes rhythmically,

at other times erratically. Consultants and consultors can feel full of energy one moment and exhausted the next.

Energy is required in order that: consultors and consultants are empowered during consultations to do whatever tasks they have to do; subsequently consultors and those with whom they work, are empowered to do whatever they need and have to do. For these things to happen the energy called forth must be "power actively and effectively exerted", to quote the Shorter Oxford English Dictionary. Here we note some things which experience has shown facilitate creative energy to flow and to be used purposefully.

Facilitating processes and relationships. Energy is generated, released and used constructively in consultors and consultants when they feel they are getting somewhere or when they see possibilities of doing so especially in relation to stubborn problems and things of great importance. Time without number I have come to life, and seen consultors do so, when a promising way of tackling things is discovered. Consultors and consultants are energised and empowered whenever the interactive analytical and consultancy processes described in this chapter act effectively upon their work and vocational concerns. This does not necessarily mean that the processes flow smoothly like a well tuned engine; they are anything but mechanical and predictable. Enormous amounts of energy are required, for instance, to stay with a problem when the analytical procedures appear to have stalled or be stymied and one approach after another has to be tried persistently from different angles.

Relaxed concentration on the task. Energy flows in relaxed concentration. C. G. Harding quotes a sport's commentator remarking of a famous fast bowler in a test match, "He is not yet giving of his best; he is not yet relaxed." [68] Relaxed concentration allows the mind to work freely, tense concentration can prevent it from doing so. Relaxed concentration can be be prevented by vocational or personal crises, feelings of frustration, hopelessness, powerlessness and of not getting anywhere; by intellectual, moral and spiritual confusion; by the challenge of the task being either too great or too small. Consultancy processes, on the other hand, can induce relaxed concentration and this enables consultors and consultants to energise each other and draw upon each other's energy. Sometimes the energy required is released from the beginning of the consultative interaction. Everything is right, personal chemistry included. On other occasions my heart sinks as the thought forms, "This one is beyond you". Thinking processes seem to freeze up and panic and despair are not far away when my contributions fail to help a consultor. These are most unpleasant experiences. Considerable resources are required to stem and reverse the ebbing away of energy. Generally speaking I relax and energy returns when I turn from my preoccupation with my feelings and my fear of failing the consultor, myself and those I represent and get back to the processes and the tasks in hand. Three questions often help me to do that:

In what ways and why is the consultor's situations presenting difficulties?
In what ways and why is the consultor experiencing difficulties?
In what ways and why am I, the consultant, experiencing difficulties?

Pursuing these questions can lead to renewed creative reflective engagement with the subject matter and takes me away from wallowing in the intimidation and feeling sorry for myself. I am re-energised by the professional challenge. I feel stretched as I search for ways forward with the consultor and the processes start to function. But—it does not always work! A mirror image experience occurs when consultors reluctantly conclude that the consultant is not going to be able to help them. Their interest and energy plummets. Again, if the situation can be redeemed, it is through trying out one or other of the approaches associated with the basic process.

Awareness of energy sources. Awareness, understanding and acceptance of relevant energy sources in the consultor's work situation enable consultants and consultors to work with the available energy. It can, for instance, be located in the consultor, s/he is the power driving a project or scheme. Or it may be located in other people or in the consultor's organization rather than in the consultor. Possibly the consultant has more energy for a project than the consultor. The primary source may be in beliefs, values, purposes, concepts etc. Mapping the energy distribution is an important part of the profile of any working situation. It facilitates realistic analysis and design. The questions in Displays 2:7 and 8 on "energy auditing and profiling" can help consultors and consultants get a better understanding of energy resources and distribution in a working environment.

Noting and exploring the consultor's energy levels in consultancy sessions. Noting the kind of energy consultors appear to have for different facets of their work and the processes of analysis and design can lead to more profound consultancy interaction. Energy levels, for instance, indicate interest, concern, fear, intimidation, enthusiasm, commitment or lack of it. As it is difficult to feign energy you do not have, the amount of energy in use can be an invaluable aid to diagnosis. For example, raising the subject of energy flow in the following way with a consultor can open up deeper levels of profitable conversation: "You seemed to have a lot of energy when we were discussing what you hope to achieve through the new outreach project but not very much when we were considering how to get the church council more committed to it. Do you feel that you have less energy for that?" If they say they have, considering why could be revealing. Normally such interventions lead to discussions about areas of primary and secondary interest, priorities, problems and how to find energy for what appear to be chores. Occasionally it reveals that the scale of challenge experienced by the consultor is too high or too low. Both extremes de-energise practitioners by taking him/her out of the work and energy flow associated with the state of well-being as described by Professor Gillian Stamp.[69] Exhaustion, burn-out and breakdown occurs when consultors are stimulated to effort which involves a critical deficit balance between the output and renewal of energy levels.[70] Clearly, questions related to energy and power also need to be considered in relation to the consultor's transition from consulting to working out the implications in their work place.

Energy auditing and profiling. Consultors and consultants can increase their effectiveness through using the questions in Displays 2:7 and 8 to audit and profile energy levels and flow in: themselves; their work situations generally; working relationships with individuals and groups; consultancy relationships and sessions.

From where and in what ways do you find the emotional, intellectual, moral and spiritual energy for your work and/or for consultancy sessions?

How do you draw upon them?

What is the present quality of your energy here and now?

What does "energy" mean to you?

What metaphors and concepts do you use to think about it?[71]

Do you experience positive/negative surges of energy?
> When?
> What causes them?
> What good and bad effects do they have upon you and others?

What consumes most energy? Why?

What saps your energy and vitality?

What galvanises you?

What renews your energy? How?

What restricts/blocks your energy flow? Why?

What are the implications of your observations for you?

**Display 2:7 Questions Which Help Individuals and Groups
to Make An Audit of Their Energy**

Whom or what are the main sources of emotional, intellectual, moral and spiritual work energy in your working situation/church/organization?
> How do individuals and groups draw upon them?
> What is the present quality of this energy?
> How is it renewed and developed?
> What importance do people attach to it?

What metaphors and concepts do the people use to discuss their energy and that of the organization/church?

Are there positive/negative surges of energy?
> When?
> What causes them?
> What good and bad effect do they have?

What consumes most energy? why? when?

What saps energy and vitality in your situation/church/organization?

What restricts energy flow? How? Why? When?

What galvanises people collectively?

What are the implications of your observations for you?

**Display 2:8 Questions Which Help to Make Energy Audits or Maps
or Profiles of Work Situations**

Questions in both displays can be used by individuals or groups to stimulate reflection. A complementary way of exploring the issues, is by people keeping an "energy diary or journal" in which they note, with or without reflective comment, anything that happens to them and/or to their church/organization energy-wise. Then they can use the questions to help them explore and to reflect on the recorded information and the recollected experiences, privately or in groups.

Using the available energy to empower consultors. Sometimes consultors have the required creative energy. At other times it is with the consultant. When the latter applies, consultants may have to think things out for consultors alongside them. But this must be done in such ways that the consultor is empowered and not overpowered or disempowered.

Testing the energy thrust before going with the flow. Sources of human and spiritual energy empower people and give direction to their being and doing. Consequently they can play a major part, often untested, in determining the thrust of analytical processes. Spontaneously available energy left to its own momentum can be dangerous. It is judicous to check whether the direction of the energy flow runs along the lines which lead to purposeful creativity. If it does, then consultors and consultants are in the happy position of being able "to go with flow". If it does not, then ways and means have to be found of re-directing the flow or, if this is not possible, tapping into different sources of energy. Making such changes can be tricky because, as noted earlier, energy is closely associated with motivation and interest. A major danger is that one channel is blocked off whilst efforts to open more appropriate ones fail. One of the problems consultors raise is how to direct the energy of groups towards something which is more worthy or closer to the objectives of the church or organization.

Working in sessions for the energy required beyond them. Energised sessions are effective when they result in equipped and energised consultors in their work places, they are not ends in themselves. The memory of the best of them may well continue to be an inspiration well into the future. But consultors cannot live for long off the energy generated in the sessions. They themselves need to be able to use, in their work place with other people, the processes that energised them in consultancy sessions in order to continue and extend the human and spiritual energisation of people in vocational work in the church and in the community. This must be a key objective. Consultancy sessions then become exemplary models for the work in general. Something like this happened to Howard Mellor, now Principal of Cliff College, whilst he was a circuit minister. On a consultancy course he got excited about the idea of working to purposes and beliefs. Let him tell what happened.

> Now there happened to be a stewards' meeting in the middle of the Avec course. I said to them, "I want to tell you about something that is happening to me, something I've learned". I talked about working to beliefs and to overall purposes and of determining objectives which helped you to work step by step towards purposes and to put your beliefs into practice. We discussed what objectives we would need to decide on and how we'd go about determining what were our beliefs and purpose for Methodism in Addiscombe. Well, it was like lighting touch paper, the meeting was dynamic. It went on for hours, nobody wanted it to finish. The following

Sunday lots of people had heard that there had been a dynamic discussion in the stewards' meeting. They were very excited and wanted to know all about it. I thought to myself, this way of working is really such a simple way and yet a preferred way of looking at things. It is quite obvious, except that you never think about it.[72]

To work for empowerment of this kind, can involve addressing, directly or indirectly, with consultors the issues raised above about energy and empowerment. In particular it is necessary to consider with consultors what will energise and empower them and those with whom they work and to test out whether what is emerging from consultancies is likely to do so. If they do not think that the ideas and methods are likely to do so, then, it is back to the drawing board!

4. Contracts and Contracting [73]

Effective consultancy depends upon realistic contracting between consultors and consultants and, in some instances, between them and third parties. Consultancy contracts that help are understandings freely accepted by all parties which set out the essentials of the working relationship between consultors and consultants and their respective functions and responsibilities. Such agreements may be verbal or written and they may or may not be referred to as contracts, although it is now common practice to do so. A work consultancy contract is, in fact, a mutual, sincere commitment which gives consultors and consultants a framework within which to pursue together their separate and joint purposes related to some specific aspect of the consultor's work and/or vocation. It epitomises the living bonds of understanding and aspects of the practice theory to be employed. Contracts are formed by concentrating on those aspects of critical importance to specific consultancy relationships: the casuistry of negotiating every feature would legalise any consultancy relationship to death. Important items in contract making are considered here:

> Sub-contracts
> Fees and costs
> Explicit and implicit contracts
> Forming and testing contracts
> Discerning lack of potential
> Representative types of contractual arrangements
> Coalitions and alliances
> Reviewing and renewing contracts
> Check lists

(a) *Sub-contracts.* Work consultancy contracts comprise four "how and why" sub-contracts: psychological and spiritual; expectational; praxis; logistical. I use the term *psychological and spiritual sub-contracts*[74] to refer to those personal and rather mystical ties which bind together people in a common enterprise, in this case to study the consultor's work. These ties are related to such things as beliefs, vocation, attitude, approach and other personal factors. Each factor can help or hinder consultancy bonding. These contracts can be assumed or they can be articulated: "I am glad that we are working together in this way and on these things". "Because of our shared interests/beliefs/approaches/ . . . I feel confident that we will be able to

examine these issues together". "I feel we are on the same wavelength". "I feel our approaches/beliefs/values/attitudes jell". "We are quite different people, do you think we have enough in common to form a consultancy partnership?" In some cases it is advisable to discuss this aspect openly.

Expectational sub-contracts relate to the expectations of consultors, consultants and other interested parties. They are about what consultants can reasonably expect to offer and provide and what consultors and their people need, want and hope to get out of the consultancy. Equally they are about the effort they expect they will have to put in before, during and after sessions in order to get those returns. So they are about outcome and income expectations, effort required and respective obligations. Important nuances of consultors' expectations which may not emerge in discussing them directly can be discovered through questions such as, "What will have to change in you and your situation for you to be able to say that our consultations have been worthwhile?"

Praxis sub-contracts are about work and consultancy processes and the ideas, theories theological concepts on which they are based. How much of this can or needs to be discussed and the terminology used varies enormously from consultor to consultor. Aspects of it are most easily discerned experientially.

Responsibility sub-contracts are about the respective and mutual responsibilities of consultors and consultants.

Practical sub-contracts are about such things as confidentiality, time required, deciding when and where to meet, evaluating the work done, re-negotiating contracts, terminating relationships and costs.

These sub-contracts variously relate to the other practice theory elements. The psychological and spiritual contracts relate particularly to Elements 1 and 7; the praxis contract to Elements 1, 4 and 5; the responsibility contract to Elements 1, 2, 3 and 5; the practical contract to Elements 2 and 3. No one of these sub-contracts can be a substitute for any of the others. For example, careful attention must be given to the praxis side of the contract in relationships where consultors and consultants are spiritually close and methodologically different, and to fees where their personal relationship makes it embarrassing to talk about money.

(b) Fees and Costs. Freelance consultants and consultancy agencies have to decide whether or not they are going to charge fees and if so how they will calculate them and what their rates will be. Useful information about the ways in which this has been done is available.[75]

Charging fees of this kind is much more acceptable in the Church now than it was. Only a few years ago Churches were not accustomed to buying in such services, it went against their culture and the theological grain. Things have changed with the spread of the service contract culture. But, as the tradition of providing help and advice free of charge is still strong in the church, many people can still feel uncomfortable about paying for consultancy services. And those accustomed to receiving a stipend from the church so that they could minister freely to anyone and everyone, can find negotiating fees for their services embarrassing. However, putting consultancy services on a businesslike footing has some significant advantages. It gives indicative cost value to consultancy service through using a currency people understand. People are inclined to take more seriously that for which they have to pay cash, and even the most dedicated and conscientious consultants tend to take more seriously that for which they are paid: payment enhances accountability. Another advantage is that paying consultants helps consultors to be consultors and to retain control of the services they receive and of their own work: it makes it more difficult for them to adopt the role of an employee or colleague towards the consultant or to be treated as such. The danger of patronage is reduced: consultors are employing the consultant, s/he is not doing them a favour freely. Again, financial commitments are the common currency of contracts, it seals them and the obligations that go with them. Also, it provides funds which give consultants their independence and enable them and their agencies to provide, research and develop the services which are increasingly required.

Experience and aspects of consultancy practice theory have shown that some of these relational advantages can be achieved without the exchange of money. Much depends upon attitude and theology as will become clear in the discussion about Element Seven. Nonetheless advantages of charging fees are real ones: consultancy fees should not be seen as a rationalization of the need to pay and to be paid in the contemporary culture.

There are however, major disadvantages to fee-based consultancy services. Some practitioners and churches, including those most acutely in need of consultancy services, simply cannot afford to pay for them and others are not prepared to do so. Financial considerations hold up and block the development of essential services. A danger is that consultancy comes to be seen as an expensive luxury for those "who are into that kind of thing", whereas it is a necessity which can save large sums of money from being wasted through, for instance, making expensive projects far more effective. Other serious disadvantages occur when church authorities fail to create a climate of opinion favourable to a fee based service economy or decline to arrange for the services to be available freely or at modest charges well within the range of the most needy. In such circumstances those convinced about the importance of consultancy services and committed to doing all they can to provide them, even though they do not have access to the financial resources required, have to struggle on several fronts. They, themselves, have to find the money to make available the consultancy help needed to do the work of the church.[76] They have to learn the necessary skills. They have to try to change the work culture of the Church to be more amenable to consultancy provision. All this they do generally out of love, dedication and loyalty. By design or default, the Church has a propensity to trespass upon vocational commitment. Generally speaking, funds made available for further training and consultancy are pitifully inadequate. It is vitally important that Church authorities make more adequate provision for consultancy services. Otherwise, the relational discomfort experienced will impede the development and use of consultancy services.

Any fees and costs to be charged should be negotiated at the outset of the consultancy. If there are to be no charges, this too needs to be clarified at the outset. Both possibilities have implications for contract making, they are important parts of it and of the consultancy relationships. Money, or the lack of it or confusion about it, simply must not be allowed to come between consultants and consultors.

(c)   Explicit and Implicit Contracts. Considerable emphasis tends to be placed upon making contracts overtly very early in a working relationship so that consultors and consultants know where they stand from the outset. There is good sense in this provided that the contract includes a commitment to re-negotiating it should experience show this to be necessary. However, working out contracts in a business-like manner before getting into the consultancy work itself is not the only way in which contracts are made. Good contracts are formed and forged through the giving and receiving of genuine consultancy help over a period of time. Some of these arrangements can be strengthened through formalising the contract by making explicit what was formerly implicit. Other equally productive relationships could be put at risk by attempts to formalise them. Discussions I had with a Sunday School Superintendent in a church of which I was minister, for instance, were consultations in everything but name, and we adhered rigorously to an unstated contract. To have named the arrangements as a contract could have adversely affected the relationship we enjoyed. Whether or not to formalise contracts which have gradually evolved is a matter of discernment and judgement. Generally speaking consultancies that are working perfectly well should not be tampered with simply to bring them into line with standard procedures.

Effective consultancy contracts take many different forms and are made in all kinds of ways by consultors and consultants doing things together and discussing in prospect and retrospect their working relationships. Some are intuitively discerned, understood and accepted without being articulated. This is especially true of those that evolve and those that just happen spontaneously. Others are negotiated and formalised between the parties concerned in one way or another.

The time and effort required to make and maintain contracts varies enormously. Those who have experience of consultancy or who know and trust each others' ways of working can make good contracts quite quickly. In such instances it can take longer to describe the process than to do it. Whereas it takes more effort and more time to make contracts when consultants and consultors do not know each other and when consultors have no previous experience of the form of consultancy on offer.

(d)   Forming and Testing Contracts. Open exploration of the proposed consultancy subject matter provides information which helps consultants and consultors to assess the value, feasibility and desirability of forming a consultancy relationship. So, for consultors this can be an experiential introduction to consultancy processes, roles, interpersonal behaviour and working relationships. So, without ceremony and a minimum of introduction, whether I am a would-be consultor or consultant, I am inclined to get to work on the subject matter until we have broken through to some mutual understanding about the issues—or come to a desultory impasse. Whatever happens it indicates whether or not it is possible to make the sub-contracts necessary for realistic contracts. One of the suggestions that I make to people seeking a long-term consultant is that they have one-off consultations on specific issues, possibly with different consultants, until they know from experience the kind of consultancy relationships that would work for them.

A whole range of questions that consultors and consultants can ask themselves help them to assess the potential of a proposed consultancy arrangement: Are our personalities, beliefs, spirituality, approaches, purposes etc. sufficiently compatible? Do we jell/get on with each other/hit it off? Do I feel I can trust him/her? Will s/he respect and trust me? Do I feel comfortable and free in her/his presence and able to be open and think? Such questions test the psychological, spiritual and praxis sub-contracts. Some questions which help consultors to assess expectational, praxis and practical sub-contracts are: Does s/he understand my situation and what I am about/saying/thinking/feeling/wanting? Will s/he be able to help me work things out? Does s/he have patience, concentration, time? Does s/he have the relevant experience? (Relevant consultancy experience is not necessarily similar to field work experience, it could be quite different.) In relation to these sub-contracts, consultants have to assess whether they have the ability, experience, patience, time and will to provide the necessary help.

(e) **Discerning Lack of Potential.** Discriminating between consultancy relationships which have potential and those which do not is of considerable importance to both consultants and consultors. Those which do not work devour time and nervous energy in ever increasing amounts for every decreasing returns (cf pp 67-68 reference 43). When I am unsure I tend to focus on things which indicate that a consultancy arrangement is unlikely to work. Some of those which signal an amber or red light for me are:

• people who block all the suggestions I make by saying that they have tried them and found that they do not work but do not convince me that they have tried them and /or that they understand significant nuances of the methods suggested;

• people who blame problems on everyone and everything rather than themselves and who seem unaware of the limits of their competence;

• people who do not identify with the people with whom they work and who denigrate them ("They haven't an idea between them", "No one can do anything with them", "They can't think" — note not, "I have not yet been able to help them to think about so and so");

• hints that would-be consultors are entirely committed to getting their own way and are looking for a "consultant" to help them to do so in a particularly resistant situation, *i.e.:* indicators that they are directive or authoritarian or even autocratic and that they appear impervious to the non-directive approach;

• evidence and hunches that I will be involved in and/or "used" for things which are contrary to my beliefs and purposes (cf (g));

• suggestions that they want readily available solutions, a "quick fix" as it were, and are not prepared to do the thinking that is self-evidently required.

None of these are infallible indicators—indeed they could point to consultancy challenges—but when two or three combine and the "chemistry" of the relationship doesn't seem right the omens are not good. Then, a consultant may decide not accept a request for consultancy and feel that it is not possible to discuss with the would-be consultor his/her reasons for declining. In other circumstances s/he may be able to decline and discuss. Open discussions in an atmosphere of mutual care could be educative and developmental for consultors and consultants and could even lead to clearing the ground for a consultancy arrangement.

(f)   Representative Types of Contractual Arrangements. Four representative types of the wide range of contractual arrangements common in work consultancy are described briefly in this section. The first is a private consultancy arrangement between a consultor and a consultant. This is a similar activity to that in which a consultor seeks to be a better practitioner and to find ways of doing things through studying and researching. As already noted, the consultancy simply has to be private and confidential when people would be highly suspicious and resentful at the thought of *their* minister discussing *them* and *their* affairs privately with an outsider who has the power to influence and is beyond their control. Generating such feelings makes the situation even more difficult at a time when the minister is in need of consultancy help. Overcoming the feelings, getting people to understand the truly non-directive nature of the consultancy and to accept the need for it, could be a tricky piece of development work which the minister simply could not undertake without consultancy help and support. In these circumstances, therefore, letting people know about a consultancy is counterproductive, it creates more problems than it solves.

A second kind of arrangement is one between consultors and consultants which is known to and/or supported by and/or funded by the consultor's church or organization. Various people might be involved in making the arrangements: those in the local church; colleagues; pastoral managers; those responsible for training and development of staff. Having made the arrangements they could treat the consultations as a private matter between the consultor and the consultant. Or they could be more directly involved and that takes us to a third kind of arrangement in which the people are more actively involved. They could, for instance, help the consultor to prepare for consultations and to consider what emerged. In such arrangements it is important to establish precisely who is/are the consultor/s. Is it the practitioner who alone has access to the consultant? Such arrangements can work but only with care. For several years I was one of two full-time workers in a team with three part-time workers.[77] The team members decided what they wanted to consult the consultant about and mandated the two full-time members to meet him. What emerged was then considered by the team. Essentially team members were the consultors The two workers were the consultancy go-betweens for two basic reasons: they were more readily available; to avoid the danger of the consultant being seen as the team leader. Committees and councils could have similar arrangements. Whatever the arrangements, if unwanted complications are to be avoided, *all concerned must be clear about who are the parties to the consultancy, their roles and functions, the nature of the consultancy relationship and the commitments they have made.*

A fourth kind of arrangement is one in which the consultancy contract is with a group or a team or a church or an organization. The contract could take many forms: it could, for instance, involve a series of work consultancy sessions over a short or long period or it could relate to an event such as a conference or a chapter (cf Chapter Three). Contracting with all those who will be involved in the consultancy can be tricky. In relation to some consultancies such as conferences the contract has to be arranged beforehand through intermediaries. Even if those involved have been consulted, the contract is ratified before most of them first meet the consultant(s). Within the overall commitment to the contract that of individuals can vary considerably. Some may well go along with it out of loyalty to the others but with little conviction or enthusiasm. Others may be against it.

In the first kind of arrangement, consultancy contracts are entirely between consultors and consultants. In the second and third arrangements, the substantive contracts are again between consultors and consultants. But this time they are coupled with contracts between consultors and various members of their organization and with contracts between those members and the consultant. In the fourth, the substantive contracts are with an organizational entity. Within that arrangement there may be sub-contracts with individuals and groups as in the second and third arrangements. Maintaining consultancy boundaries is important in each case. Parties to any of the arrangements will, of course, be at pains to honour any moral or statutory or ecclesiastical obligations they may have.

(g)   Coalitions and Alliances. In consultancies with groups, teams, churches and organizations, *i.e.:* the fourth type, potentially debilitating complications can arise. It is common practice, as noted earlier, for two or three people, generally leaders, to carry out the initial negotiations with consultants on behalf of their group or organization.[78] One of the dangers of this practice is that, even when such discussions are quickly followed by thorough-going contracting with the group or organization there is, in the nature of things, psycho/spiritual and expectational, off the record, contract bonding between those involved in the initial negotiations. This bonding can be particularly dangerous when consultants allow themselves to be associated with covert purposes of the initial negotiators through, for example, appearing to accept through failing to challenge statements such as, "What we really want you to do is to get them to accept our new programme and change their ways of doing things". Or they might suggest that they want help in dealing with "problem people". These are attempts to form covert expectational sub-contracts.[79] Such overtures are invitations to act with them against others in what is referred to by some as a "denied coalition". They are described as "denied" because they will not be owned publicly by those who offer them. Consultants must avoid the seductive powers of these overtures. Taking sides in this way prevents them from working independently and in an open alliance with all concerned on things about which people are differently concerned. Pallazzoli says, "Jay Haley in his earlier thinking . . . brilliantly distinguishes between open alliances for (something) and denied coalitions against (somebody). The latter he labelled "perverse triangles".[80] Similar problems can occur when a consultant is engaged with different individuals and groups in the same organization. They can also occur when a sub-group has been formed from a large consultancy group to organize consultancy events.

Countering denied coalitions can be tricky. Understanding their nature and the dangers associated with them helps consultants to be vigilant and to identify them when first they begin to appear, and that is important. Making suggestions about the action to take when incidents arise is difficult because so much depends upon interpersonal skills and behaviour and the quality of the relationships between those involved. However, some suggestions can be made.[81] The possibility of becoming ensnared in denied coalitions is reduced :

- by pre-emptive action;
- by declining, not opposing, coalitions and converting them into alliances;
- by helping potential consultors to see the importance in developmental work of avoiding coalitions and promoting alliances;
- by proposing alliances;
- by ensuring that the substance of discussions and negotiations with individuals and subgroups can be and where necessary are shared with other members of the consultancy group.

These suggestions are best seen as an interrelated, overlapping cluster of possible lines of action, variously possible and effective, rather than a series of steps. At an early stage in the exploratory discussions in situations where consultants feel consultors might suggest a coalition, they can emphasize the importance of alliances being formed and the dangers of coalitions. When they are not pointed, explanations of this kind can be preventive and educative and encourage the search for alliances which supplants the pursuit of coalitions. Frustratingly the expression of alliances, however, can suppress coalitions rather than lead to their rejection with the consequence that they become less accessible and their adverse effects can be even more subtle. Sensitivity and a lightness of touch are required. For instance, a judgemental attack on coalitions combined with unqualified praise for alliances can have all kinds of unintended, undesirable effects: it can, for instance, cause those who deal in coalitions to feel defensive or counter attack; it can impede the development of the relationships needed; in some circumstances it can be experienced as a coalition against a coalition.

Once coalitions have been articulated by consultors they must be tackled. To allow them to pass without comment can be interpreted as acquiescence. That is bad news for contract formation. But what can you do or say without evoking negative personal responses and appearing superior? It all depends on the personalities involved, relationships and circumstances. That is not a cop-out. There simply is no right or wrong approach: there is only action which is effective and that which is ineffective. One possibility is to try openly to get consultors to convert coalitions into alliances: it must not be done covertly or by deception. So a consultant might explore with the would be consultors the possibility of them genuinely changing their intention *from* "What we really want you to do is to get them to accept our new programme and change their ways of doing things" *to* "The purpose is to get the new programme seriously and critically considered along with the possibilities of adopting or adapting it". Exploring such a change—and it may be what they really need and want to do but do not know how to do it—involves *inter alia*: starting where they are and finding the courage and questions to ask them how and why they have come to see that this is what they must do; how they feel about getting people to do things against their will through persuasion, manipulation and "selling" things to them; considering directive and non-directive approaches and which is the more appropriate in the given circumstances and in relation to their purposes; determining what kind of action they wish to take; reconsidering whether the consultant is the person for them and the job to be done and whether the consultant feels s/he could work with the consultors. The consultant should not facilitate a coalition, but s/he can enter into an alliance. The order of decision making is important. Decisions by the consultors about their intentions and approaches must precede and as far as possible be independent of those related to decisions about a consultancy contract. If they are intent upon a persuasive exercise, a non-directive consultant will be an embarrassment and a hindrance to them. If, on the other hand, they genuinely want to pursue a course similar to the revised formulation suggested above, they need a non-directive consultant/facilitator!

Of themselves, therefore, discussions of this kind are educative and developmental consultancy exercises whether they lead to the consultors changing their approach or to them contracting or not. They can be amicable and exciting if they are an open exploration of the pros and cons of alternative approaches and methods through which consultors become convinced which approach has the balance of advantages for them. Consultants must facilitate the examination of the approaches and, no matter how much s/he personally favours one against the other, s/he must not try to persuade. *Non-directive thorough-going exploratory action is an antidote to denied coalitions.*

(h)   Reviewing and Renewing Contracts. As contracts evolve with the consultancy process, earlier agreements can be outgrown. Some modifications just happen, others need to be considered and negotiated. It is easier to raise difficulties if there is an understanding in the initial contract that it is right and necessary to do so if things are not satisfactory. Checking things out periodically is advisable. This can be done with a light touch, "Is the way we are going about things all right or do we need to reconsider the arrangements?"

(i)   Check Lists. By now it is abundantly clear that contract making is a sensitive interpersonal activity that explores the detail to get at the fundamentals of an agreement that will enable and sustain everyone concerned as they attempt to do the work that needs to be done. Consultors and consultants are best equipped for this activity when they are able to give themselves to the nuances of each consultancy relationship because they have assimilated the basics of contracting. For them, contracting is a human event, not a standard procedure to be got through perfunctorily. Nonetheless check lists and guidelines can be useful. I offer the following.[82]

- Set the tone for the relationship early: you can contract for behaviour but not for feelings.

- Contracts must vary to fit people, situations and circumstances. Some are private, others are public.

- Contracts must be made between consultors and consultants and with all significant others in the consultancy frame.

- Implicit contracts can be appropriate forms of contracting.

- Make contracts explicit and write them down whenever advisable and possible.

- Contracts and sub-contracts are made in stages. Think and feel your way into them. Get things as clear as possible at a given stage and wait and watch for the next stage for clarification. "Entry contracting" is followed by "working contracting" in relation to each and all of the four sub-contracts.

- Responsibility for any sustainable contracted relationship must be accepted by all parties, so contracts must :
    — be freely entered into;
    — be tested for commitment;
    — represent negotiated agreements.
- You cannot get something for nothing, so find out whether all parties are able and prepared to give what is required.
- You should not: ask for something that the other person does not have to give; make or accept promises that you have any reason to think cannot be kept.
- Get the finances clear.
- Keep a weather eye open for consultancies which lack creative potential and for coalitions.
- Good contracts require faith and trust and often accidental good fortune.
- Contracts are often broken by default not design.
- Check contracts for acceptability from time to time as the consultancy proceeds.
- Contracts need to be re-negotiable.

5. Process Evaluation

Consultancy processes can be evaluated in relation to the following interrelated objectives:
    — to help consultors to be better reflective practitioners and to do their work more effectively;
    — to make the best possible use of the limited time available for consultations;
    — to help consultors and consultants to learn as much as possible about consultancy;
    — to enhance their abilities as consultors and consultants.

Evaluations can be made in many ways. Consultors and consultants can come to an understanding that, should things start to go wrong, they will say so without ceremony and without beating about the bush. Early warnings save time, avoid frustration and enable an immediate assessment of what is happening. They could agree, that, periodically they will check whether the way in which things are being done is acceptable by, for example, asking, "Is this way of working all right?" If the answer is yes or simply a nod, confidence to go on is gained with a minimum of interruption to the process. If no, then there is the possibility for an on the spot evaluation. Specific evaluations can be supplemented by general and possibly more formal evaluations of a session or a series of sessions. Agreement about process evaluation can be part of the initial contract.

6. Concluding Sessions and the Mandating of Consultors

Much has already been said about the importance of consultors remaining true to themselves and their abilities. Consultors must be free to pursue their work with other people in the light of the sessions and exigencies they encounter upon returning to their situations. Consultants must always help consultors to secure that freedom.

Discerning the right moment to conclude consultancy sessions is an important part of the process. This is partly a matter of the proper use of time but it is also related to the ability of a consultor to continue the process on her/his own. Sufficient work must have been done for the consultor to feel confident that s/he can use the ideas that have emerged. If too much work has been done, consultors, for instance, may feel that the ideas are not their own and fear that they cannot make them work with the result that their confidence could be undermined. In that event, attempts must be made to restore their confidence. Consultors simply must have the freedom to work things out for themselves by themselves and with their colleagues. Anything that takes away that freedom must be rigorously avoided. The stopping point is therefore to be determined not simply by considerations of time and energy but by satisfactory answers to such questions as:

- Has the consultor got sufficient help, the confidence and the will to continue the process on her/his own?
- Is the consultor ready to move on?
- Has the consultant confidence that the consultor can now continue, and is s/he thereby giving her/his confidence?
- Is s/he autonomous, and therefore free to do what seems to her/him appropriate with the ideas worked out together by consultor and consultant? Has the consultant ensured that s/he has that freedom?
- Has s/he made the ideas her own, so that s/he can share them and work on them with colleagues? [83]

At the end of consultancy sessions it is important that consultors and consultants know precisely what, if anything, their future commitments are in relation to each other and the ideas they have worked out. Consultants, as we have seen, must withdraw and wait in patience. This includes mutual understanding about any contacts between sessions and the kind of initiatives they can normally make towards each other in relation to things like afterthoughts or supplementary considerations. Again, summarising what has been done and said helps to determine the next steps.

ELEMENT SEVEN: BELIEFS, ETHICS, VALUES AND QUALITIES

Whichever way it is viewed, the theory and practice consultancy is shot through with theology. Consultancy processes and consultations are formed or influenced or affected in one way or another by the beliefs, ethics and values of the participants. These attributes are at the systemic centre of all elements of consultancy practice theory as Figure 2:2, illustrates. Inescapably and inevitably, because they are intrinsic and generative features, they make determinative contributions to the quality and efficacy of the consultancy services. Consequently, consultancy is a moral and, in our case, a religious activity as well as a technical one. This can be seen through the influence of beliefs, ethics and values which are explicit and implicit in what has already been written about the other practice theory elements. Therefore, in one sense this section is an extraction of the theology of consultancy from its practice theory. That is why it appears at the end of the chapter not as a theological addition to justify consultancy but as an attempt at theological disclosure.

One of our theological objectives is to explore the ways in which beliefs, values and ethics can be and often are powerful creative forces in consultancy. The nature of this objective is well illustrated by quotations from Professor John Hull. "Ideologies have a dynamic quality. They are not merely static belief-systems but are power filled, charged with emotion and effective in activating people." "Therefore", he says "ideologies have a mobilizing as well as a justifying character".[84] Another objective is to help consultants and consultors to be more aware of the shadowy downsides of heavy ideological and theological commitment and to handle them better. To quote Hull again, "Ideologies operate not in front of our eyes but from behind our backs".[85] And he points out that ideology also has a falsifying character. "This lies partly in the way in which the codification of the ideology necessarily wipes out critical distinctions, smooths over problems and so distorts the original events, and partly in the fact that all of this is done without our realization".[86] Ideology, therefore, can be used to generate processes which give self-protective and self-indulgent comfort. Avoiding such processes, which are akin to "group think", is a key function of consultancy. These objectives are pursued by exploring the ways in which beliefs, values and theological concepts are expressed and experienced in:

> the theological orientation to consultancy
> the consultancy subject matter
> the working relationships between participants
> consultancy processes
> theological outcomes
> the qualities of consultants
> an inclusive theological model
> codes of good practice for consultors and consultants.

1.   Theological Orientation and Stance

There are as many belief systems in play in consultancies as there are participants: some will be implicit and assumed whilst others will be quite explicit; some will be similar and others will differ, some greatly. The purposes of consultancy processes require that the consultor's beliefs, ethics and values must be a primary but not the only focus of attention in analysis and design. As core beliefs, ethics and values are generally constant over long periods of time they are reliable reference points. Interaction with other belief systems, including those of consultants, can help consultors to examine and develop or revise their beliefs. And that can, in some circumstances, be an important part of the consultancy process. In fact, to borrow another of John Hull's phrases, consultancy educates "from faith to faith".[87]

A consultant must work to his/her beliefs as well as to those of the consultor and to the interaction between them. Working to his/her own beliefs gives integrity to the consultant; working to the consultor's beliefs and any dissonance between their systems gives integrity to consultancy practice; working to the beliefs of all those in the consultancy frame promotes theologically inclusive thinking and planning.

Underlying this approach are various theological purposes and principles. There is a commitment to theological pluralism and tolerance and socio-religious inclusivism. This stance enables consultors and consultants to accept each other in active consultancy engagement without necessarily endorsing every aspect of each others' beliefs. And at the same time, it enables all participants to be true to and respectful of all the beliefs and values represented and considered in consultations. It proscribes consultants trying to impose their beliefs and values upon consultors and vice versa. It creates the relationships and conditions within which consultants and consultors can collaborate in critical, creative reflective action on the consultor's beliefs, ethics and values and their implications. Without this kind of acceptance, which resonates with the doctrine of justification by faith,* non-directive consultancy is not possible.

So, consultors and consultants can and will work with people whose beliefs and religious practices differ significantly from theirs. To do this they must be ideologically sensitive and theologically multi-lingual—or able and willing to learn the basics of other languages. This is a vital part of the theological approach to consultancy but, as was established earlier, it does not mean that anything goes. Beliefs and values of consultors and consultants work out the dimensions and the boundaries of the broad church of consultancy practice.

2.   Subject Matter

Consultors and their work, the subjects and objects of consultations, are theological entities shaped and formed vocationally whatever else they might be. Even a cursory glance at the list of contents of Part Two illuminates the truth of this statement. Consultors themselves, therefore, are a profound theological presence

---

*Somewhat confusingly justification by grace through faith is about restoring relationships rather than making people just. Norman H. Snaith in "Just, Justify, Justification" in *A Theological Word Book of the Bible*, Ed. A. Richardson (London: SCM Press, 1950), says, "The verb *dikaioo* (justify) does not mean 'to make just', and indeed is not so much an ethical word as a word which belongs to the vocabulary of salvation. On man's *(sic)* part, the essential condition for justification is faith in Christ. This involves a complete trust in him. . . . On this condition every repentant sinner is brought by God into fellowship with him. This is the working of his grace, the undeserved favour with which God welcomes all who truly turn to him. . . . Justification is the first step in the process of salvation, that first reconciliation to God which is the beginning of a steady growth in grace and the knowledge of God (II Peter 3:18)." "Justification is that immediate getting-right with God which God himself accomplishes by his grace when a man has faith." *op cit.* p 119.

D. E. Jenkins, writing on "The Christian Counsellor" in *Living with Questions* (1969) says, "The aim of the Christian counsellor is to help people be themselves. . . . It is the practice of openness based on justification by faith". Kenneth Leech, to whom I owe the quotation, comments, "The counsellor knows that his *(sic)* own ability to be himself depends on God's acceptance of him. . . . He is then released to be an instrument of God's acceptance . . . to others. The Christian counsellor does not seek to dominate or dictate, but to be an enabler, enabling the individual to become open to the activity of the Spirit, and to become more truly human. Clearly there is a very close link between such a view of counselling and the traditional Christian ministry of the cure of souls". *Soul Friendship*: A Study of Spirituality (Sheldon Press, 1977, seventh impression 1985) p 99.

representing, as they do, their own belief and value systems and those of the people with whom they work which they bring into the consultancy process. These are important aspects of the theological content and nature of this form of consultancy.

Consultants too are a theological presence representing their own beliefs and value systems and inserting them into the consultancy process but in a subtly and significantly different way. Consultants and their beliefs are foils, catalysts, independent reference points, stimulants to double loop learning and reminders of essential subject matter of the Christian project. Their functions determine their status which is that of a servant to the process. Consultants must bring their beliefs and values into play alongside those of consultors whenever they can use them to perform the functions described. Their functions performed they are withdrawn into the background so that the focus remains on the consultors and their work. They do not perform their functions if they become a permanent, rather than a temporary, centre of attention and if they are seen to be *the* ideal theological/ideological model to be slavishly and unthinkingly adopted or copied. (My values and commitments are described in various parts of this book.)

When the consultor's and consultant's beliefs and values are being used in these ways consultations are experiences which can have many different effects upon consultors. They can affirm or re-activate their own beliefs and commitments. Or they can challenge them and those common to people in their work place or church. Or, again they can induct consultants and consultors into moral or spiritual aspects and dimensions of which they had not previously been aware. Over and again this has happened to me and I have seen it happen to consultors during their first experience of the non-directive approach to consultancy. Their excitement and joy is a precious memory. Invariably, they wanted to tell others about what had happened but were at a loss to know how to do so because, they said, "You have to experience it to understand and believe it".

3.   Working Relationships

At the very heart of consultancy partnership relationships there is an alliance between consultors and consultants which enables them to concentrate all their resources upon aspects of the consultor's work in order that consultors may pursue *their* vocation more effectively and with deeper satisfaction. The effectiveness of these alliances depends upon the quality of the giving and receiving in consultancy relationships. Consultors have to share with consultants things which are very important to them and sometimes personal. To get the help they seek they have to talk of their successes and their failures, their strengths and their weaknesses. Opening themselves up to another person in this way is a profound and daring form of giving, requiring moral courage and involving considerable risk especially if the consultor is short on self-esteem and confidence. The way in which consultants receive what consultors give to them of themselves determines and affects the relationship and the efficacy of the consultancy processes. This has been worked out in considerable detail in this chapter. Consultants have to give themselves, their knowledge and their expertise to consultors freely and share their concerns in a disinsterested and disciplined manner. They have to give all that they possibly can to help the consultor to live out their vocation in all its fulness. Their concern must be about the success and well-being of the other and the Christian enterprise, not of themselves. This is no small undertaking even though profound self-giving is returned with interest to all parties. This kind of self-giving, quite different from the giving of advice and the sharing of know-how although they may be included, requires considerable spiritual resources as well as technical skills. Consultors, for their part, have to be receptive to the consultant's self-giving. That does not mean that they have to accept unquestioningly the content of what is offered: accepting the consultant is not to be confused with accepting everything s/he says. Complementary giving and receiving in non-directive consultancy is the relational catalyst to the dynamic of analysis and design. A process in which the participants make demands upon one another, challenge each other, support one another, cry *eureka* together and grow in grace as they do so. The cost can be high. Considerable human and spiritual resources are required. Consultors, for instance, can find it difficult to receive things of great value without feeling obligated or losing self-confidence and self-esteem. Consultants can find it difficult to contribute significantly, unreservedly and privately without public recognition to the outstanding success of someone in the same field. But those are the kind of things consultors and consultants have to do. Skills apart, they need the resources of the Christian gospel and the ministries of the Church to do them.

Effective consultations and personal development involves "finding a balance between making demands on other people, and recognising their demands on oneself", and between demands and support.[88] "The religious person", suggest Watts and Williams, "has something analogous to a role relationship with God. There is a common task (of the redemption of the world and of himself) on which the religious person is engaged with God, and his sense of himself will be based in part on his experience of this role relationship. . . . The vocational role relationship with God seems to conform to this general pattern of providing a balance between demands and supports. . . . God is experienced by the religious person as someone who understands him perfectly and supports him constantly, but also as someone who makes considerable demands on him".[89]

Thus, the efficacy of consultancy is directly related to the quality of the relationship which in turn depends upon the quality of the support, the giving and the receiving. Much is said elsewhere in this book about ways and means of forming these relationships, drawing boundaries around them and working within them. One of the many contributions that Christianity makes to the forming of these relationships is that it provides perfect models of the giving of self and the receiving of others. Critical features of this model can be seen clearly in the ways in which God, Jesus and the Holy Spirit give themselves and their resources freely and without condescension, pomp, fuss or ceremony. Each member of this Trinitarian God comes with great humility. They do not impose themselves: they allow us to ignore and exclude them, and we do. They come to engage with us, to confront and challenge, but they display great respect for all people and reverence for life. They come to accompany us, not to take us over. Omnipotent as they are, they depend upon human responses to their overtures to form loving and creative relationships. The incarnation and crucifixion of Jesus show the sacrificial self-giving measures they take to establish the divine-human relationships necessary to their purposes.

Almost unbelievably God gives himself to us and receives us and wants to be received by us and desires that we give ourselves to the interdependent relationships central to the Kingdom.

The very manner in which God comes to us and receives us in Jesus Christ and the Holy Spirit, enables us to enter into the divine-human relationships so wonderfully on offer. God's unconditional acceptance through justification by faith is an archway into relationships real and rich because they take us into a vocational partnership with Christ in which we are taken seriously, affirmed, judged, refuted, challenged and commissioned. New perspectives on life and ultimate realities are revealed in the intimacy of the new relationship. Thus entering into and living within a relationship with God is an incredible learning experience about all aspects of our being and doing.

Through reflecting upon these experiences, relational models can be constructed which help us in forming relationships of any kind, including those required for consultancy. As we shall see in Part Two, in all our relationships there is a knock-on effect from those with God through Christ and the Holy Spirit because they are all interconnected systemically.

But, given the complexities of living and working creatively with all kinds of people, we need more than even the best exemplary models. All kinds of help are available from many sources, such as people in general, the ministry of Christians and the Church, the social and behavioural sciences. I believe that God's influence is experienced through all these aids to relationships. But, there is more. My conviction and experience is that the mediatorial ministry of Christ is a way in which God makes vital contributions to every aspect of our relating. Jesus Christ is, I believe, actively engaged in trying to improve all human relationships. Quite early in my ministry I got hold of the idea from the writings of Dietrich Bonhoeffer that Jesus Christ is *the Mediator* not only between people and God but between people and between them and their realities.[90]

This came as a revelation to me. It helped me to see that relating to people and the physical world in and through Christ lead to a quite different experience from that of doing so without recourse to his mediating ministry. Something very significant is added to the quality of my relational involvement, generally and in consultations, when I approach and see people and their context in and through Christ.[91] At best, the attitudes and actions of consultors and consultants work in concert with Christ's mediatorial activity. Undoubtedly we are facilitated by it. Christ, the Mediator, creates, a relational context in which we can operate. And, therefore, it may not be too presumptive to say that, in turn we can help to create a relational context for consultancy.

Whilst certain mediatorial and go-between functions are unique to Christ, they model the counterpart functions so central to helping consultors to relate ever more effectively to themselves, those with whom they work and their context.

Knowing that Jesus is involved as a mediator in consultancies and in all that happens to consultors subsequently is very important to me. It means that consultors and I are in a working partnership with God through Christ and the Holy Spirit, whether it is openly acknowledged or not. Being in such a partnership draws more out of me because, as Jesus does not normally take over, it certainly does not allow

127

me to relax. As this means that everything does not depend upon consultors and me, it helps me to cope with my anxiety. What I also value is the depth of Jesus' penetration. He always gets to the root of the matter and enables others to do so. The insights brought to the task through Jesus' teaching and spirit are quite incredible. They emerge in all kinds of ways not least in the reflective and meditative aspects of consultancy.

When we are examining the consultative process, the focus is upon the interaction between consultors and consultants. When we are studying the subject matter of consultations the focus is upon the consultor's relational involvement in his/her church, agency, community. There is however another important dimension of which I became much more aware through making an eight-day individually guided retreat at St Beuno's after an extended analysis of my work and vocation.[92] Once or twice each day the person appointed to be my guide or spiritual director, a Jesuit priest, visited me in my room for about half an hour. He listened most attentively to anything I wished to share. Generally, but not always, he commented on what he thought was the nature of my experience. But he did not discuss or analyse with me the substance of my experience. Then he gave me biblical texts or passages as subjects for prayer and meditation in relation to the things I had raised. Stage by stage he described to me the aspects of Ignatius' exercises to which he was directing me, he discussed with me methods of praying and from time to time gave me very useful handouts. Then, having dealt with my practical problems he left me to my prayer and meditation. Initially I was bemused by the method. Gradually I saw how it differed from anything I had previously experienced. My guide was, in fact, preparing and equipping me for a prayerful encounter, as he put it, with the Lord. At the heart of this prayer was a dialogue with Jesus, what Ignatius called a "colloquy". This is significantly and subtly different from work consultancy which is my metier. Consultants, as we have seen, work *with* people, albeit in the presence of God, in an intensive way on the things interesting and concerning them in order that they are better able to work at them on their own, with God and with others. My guide quite deliberately avoided becoming a spiritual consultant or counsellor to me, except on methods of prayer, and he told me so. His job was to get me considering things with the Lord, in the way I would with a soul friend, consultant or counsellor. It worked for me in an amazing way. My guide was, in fact, a facilitator of spiritual colloquy. I was continuously surprised at just how apposite the texts or passages proved to be although I was concerned that they were often used out of context. Following Ignatius, he concentrated on passages which described events such as Jesus washing the disciples' feet, rather than on parables.

This experience helped me to see that consultants must also help people to have colloquys. They certainly must avoid intruding into and trespassing upon personal dialogues with Jesus. This is an important dimension of the spirituality of consultancy. Consultations are carried out in the context of the personal relationships that consultors and consultants have with God. For many people it is these relationships, rather than beliefs, that are the quintessence of life and religion (cf Chapter 6:I, 2).[93]

An inescapable conclusion of this exploration of relationships is that the kind of consultancy we are considering is a form of ministry through which technical and pastoral services are offered holistically to consultors and through them to their constituencies. This throws further light upon consultancy as a pastoral office designed to provide assistance and support to those engaged in ministry and mission.

Relationships between consultors and consultants can run deep. Bonding occurs as they tackle vitally important tasks together at critical points in the consultor's life. Consultants can become so interested that they wish their involvement could be extended beyond the consultancy boundaries into the work place alongside consultors. The danger of interference is always present. Consultors can become dependent upon consultants and inclined to stray into a co-worker relationship. Such feelings can add to the difficulties of securing the freedom of consultors to be their own person in interdependent relationships discussed earlier. Placing high value upon the consultor's freedom in the way in which God does, is a powerful antidote to these difficulties. The stronger consultors and consultants believe this, the more likely they are to be committed to the action which helps consultors to be their own person. But there is an optimum strength to these beliefs: too weak and they all too easily become dependent; too fierce and they are unable to enter into the exciting but risky depths of consultancy relationships.

4. Consultancy Processes

This section offers a theological commentary on the nature of the consultancy processes already described in terms of procedures and interpersonal dynamics. Interestingly, observations on the theological nature of the processes fall naturally under basic Christian doctrines related to incarnation, redemption, revelation, resurrection, creation and the sacraments.

(a) Consultancy processes are incarnational. Consultancy processes are incarnational because they ensure that theology is done with particular practitioners within specific situations. They are about human and divine activities in particular places and their interpretation, meaning and implications. They are contemporary with events concerned with what is happening and with, when, how and why it is happening. Sequences of events, their causes and effect are explored through action-reflection/research procedures.[94] The processes are also incarnational because they help consultors to work out the implications of the gospel and their beliefs and their theological objectives and commitments in and through their vocational activity and the work and situation in which they are engaged. Then, as things proceed, consultants help consultors to reflect on what happens and to evaluate it theologically.

(b) Consultancy processes are salvatory. Consultancy processes are salvatory when, for instance, they assist consultors to remain true to their vocations and save them, as they frequently do, from creating unnecessary problems for themselves and for others and when they help them to see their ways through difficult situations. Such help may derive from technical expertise and/or spiritual and theological resources. However, valuable as this might be, additional help is required to enable us to cope with our inability to deal conclusively with the dilemma that no matter

how hard and well we work we cannot do everything perfectly nor can we finish the work which is endless. Dean Jacobson put it well:

> It is not thy duty to complete the task
> but neither art thou free to desist from it.[95]

Even when we finish our work, the sense of incompleteness remains. Work with people in church and community can be exciting, joyful, very rewarding and deeply satisfying. On the other hand it can be painful, hurtful, disillusioning and bitterly disappointing. In 1974 Dr T. R. Batten, towards the end of his long working life, wrote:

> As I look back over my years of research, study and field work, my overall feeling is one of sadness that so much community development effort has, on the whole, resulted in relatively so little actual betterment and more especially for the poor and under-privileged people who need betterment most. What concerns me is that the well-intentioned efforts of so many planners, administrators and field workers who really want to promote betterment have on the whole, so often fallen so far short of realising their full potential.[96]

Many of us share his feelings. David Deeks puts the case and a basic question: "All our work is distorted by sin and evil. So our work is hardly ever as satisfying as we expect it to be, nor as effective. And it is certainly not free of self-interest and self-aggrandisement. Where, in God's mercy, do we have access to the redemption of our work and our feelings about our work?" He answers his own question in the following way:

> The church is a provisional (and flawed) bearer and focus of what God is achieving and revealing, through divine love, in the nurturing of authentic human community. It exists in the contexts of many other, different and distinctive communities which God has also brought into being. The distinctive contribution of the church, related to all other human communities in a process of giving and receiving, is to guard, reflect upon and transmit:
>
> - the reality of ultimate dependence of all our human striving on the infinitely gracious, though absolutely incomprehensible, Mystery at the origin of all things;
>
> - the good news that what needs to be done for us has in fact been done for us in Christ's saving work, in order that we may be free to work with and for one another in the struggles for justice and peace, freedom and wholeness. When church and community development take place, the body of Christ is constituted. This is enabled by the gracious work of God which flows from the risen and ascended Saviour.
>
> - the conviction that in the face of evil and death and life's disappointments and tragedies, it is good and right to hope in God.[97]

Something that Peter Selby said in a remarkable lecture entitled, "Saved by Hope",[98] delivered in Belfast during the height of the Irish "Troubles" develops Deeks' final point. Selby's opening sentence was, "At the centre of Christian faith is a tradition of repeated intractable and radical disappointment".Then he says that it is

> the character of that tradition of disappointed hope, and hope in disappointment, which have made us as a church who we are and which permeate our beliefs, our

life together, our stories and our practice when we are true to our central purpose. To be the bearers of that tradition of hope purified by successive examples of tragic disappointment, is what the church has been saved for. . . .If we are saved through hope it is because what hope saves us from is the unintelligibility of our past and meaningless in the present.[99]

My experience is that, consultancy processes can help consultors to make salvific connections between their work and that of Christ. Selby talks about "the salvific link between what has happened, what has failed to happen and what we long to happen".[100] Such links make sense of radical disappointment, *i.e.:* "that which on the face of it is disproof of salvation".[101]

(c) Consultancy processes are revelatory. In a chapter in a fairly recent book on consultancy, W. Gordon Lawrence explores the following working hypothesis about the change in the mind set consultants bring to their work: *within the practice of consultancy there is occurring the beginnings of a paradigm shift from the politics of salvation to the politics of revelation.*[102] (Lawrence's italics.) This statement brought me up with a start. Reading it was a moment of disclosure even though at first I did not understand the use of the word "politics" in this context. It is, "the sense of 'influence' of one person or party over another". In a word and a moment I had a concept which interpreted some of the most precious and rewarding moments of my consultancy experience. They are those occasions when consultors and/or consultants have a disclosure experience. Insights and understandings suddenly emerge which illuminate a situation, crack open a problem, show the way forward. They are revelations. They do not supplant or contradict the salvific processes described in the previous section. Indeed revelation is often experienced as a saving event: not as being given solutions but as finding them; not as being saved but as discovering salvation; not as being told the way but as seeing and knowing it. Revelations of this kind seem to emerge from the totality of our experience through things coming and fitting together, sliding into place. There is generally something of a mystery about how it happens accompanied by a sense which is a form of knowing that, beyond the identifiable factors which led to a disclosure, there is an elusive dimension variously referred to as providence, the hand of God, the leading of the Spirit.

Revelations, or disclosures, occur in all kinds of circumstances and ways and at the most unexpected times and places. In my experience, there is no given sequence of thought or analytical procedures which step by step automatically and invariably lead to disclosures. They can come through hard thinking or through the "middle way of religious knowing" (cf Chapter 7:III, 5) or through expectation, openness to the guidance of the Holy Spirit who "leads us into all truth". Marion Milner, for instance, found that disclosures came through what she described as "wide attention", "an act of wide focus", by which she "could see the whole all at the same time".[103] When in this mode of attention she "simply stood and waited".[104] (Milner distinguished between wide and narrow attention. Narrow attention she saw as an automatic way of seeing things, "the kind of attention which my mind gave to everyday affairs when it was left to itself". The book from which these quotations are taken, *A Life of One's Own*,[105] is a remarkable account of the discovery, use and uses of wide attention.) But this is simply one of the countless approaches to reflection and meditation which help to create dispositions, attitudes and frames of mind conducive to seeing things differently, in a new light and having unexpected insights.

(d) ***Consultancy processes are resurrectional.*** One of the claims that H. A. Williams makes in *True Resurrection* is that, "Resurrection occurs to us as we are, and its coming is generally quiet and unobtrusive and we may hardly be aware of its creative power".[106] One of the examples he gives to illustrate this claim is:

> An artist, at first only painfully aware of an utter emptiness and impotence, finds his imagination gradually stirred into life and discovers a vision which takes control of him and which he feels not only able but compelled to express. That is resurrection.[107]

Consultancy processes are resurrectional because repeatedly and regularly they induce experiences of this kind. Consultors come to life when they see ways forward in situations in which previously they simply did not know what to do or in which direction to turn: they are raised to a new lease of working life. There are, of course, dangers in using the word to describe such experiences which are of a different order from the unique event of *the* resurrection of Christ. But experiences of finding new vocational life, common in consultancies, is part of our resurrection in the here and now which is a trailer to our resurrection in the there and then beyond death.

(e) ***Consultancy processes are creational.*** Basically consultancy is about getting people to think and work out for themselves how they can make their best contributions to human and spiritual well-being and development. The processes of reflection, analysis and design are creative: they move inwards so that they are located deep in the creativity of consultors and outwards through them to be creative in the lives of people and their institutions in churches and communities.[108] At best the processes are infused by the creativity of Christ and are an integral part of the new creation.

(f) ***Consultancy processes are sacramental.*** Many people with whom I have shared co-consultancy group work sessions have said that the atmosphere and feel of the sessions has been reminiscent for them of acts of worship and especially of the eucharist. Some talked of them as experiences of the "sacrament of work" because they evoked feelings similar to those they experienced in the eucharist. Attempts to identify just what generated such feelings were never entirely satisfactory. Some attributed it to the privilege and intimacy of entering deeply into the vocational work of others, and doing so with great respect by treating it as holy ground, no matter how analytical or critical the consultancy process might be. Others attributed it to making and keeping contracts which they felt to be an extension of their covenant relationship with God and a particular application of their religious commitment. Yet others felt that the quality of acceptance was related to the processes of "justification by faith". Some felt that going down into the depths of human predicaments, struggling with conflicts and rising above them were sacramental paradigms of crucifixion and resurrection. All were agreed that the particular and precious spirituality was an outworking of the non-directive approach so much at the heart of these consultancy processes.

What significance can be attached to these experiences? Too many of us have had this experience for it to be dismissed as spiritual exaggeration or sentimentalism. The unfolding and representation through words and diagrams of essentials of the consultor's situational and vocational realities in consultancy sessions can be seen as "an outward and visible sign of an inward and spiritual grace". And that is a description of a sacrament, a sacramental presentation of work and vocation.

For a Christian, consultancy is a life-giving conversation of a reflective kind between people about what one or more of them believes God has called them to do, about their vocation. It is, therefore, an extension of a prayerful "conversation", a colloquy with, or a communication from God. It is a working out with consultors in specific terms what it means for them to be obedient to their call in concrete situations. As they engage with the consultor's vocation, consultants are entering into and following through their call from God, their conversation with Him or communication from Him. Outwardly, therefore, consultancy is a conversation about conversations with God. To be credible and effective it must be true to these human-divine encounters. Inwardly, for both consultors and consultants, it is a continuing vocational conversation with self and with God, an act of communion, as Brueggemann puts it, "A conversation of two well-spoken voices".[109]

One of the things that stands out from this section is the comprehensive theological nature of consultancy processes. Conceptually and pragmatically consultancy processes relate closely to the principal Christian doctrines. That alone gives consultancy a secure place in pastoral theology and missiological practice.

5. Theological Outcomes

Many of the desired outcomes of consultancies have already been described and others are discussed later. Here we concentrate on highly desirable theological outcomes. In the following quotation John Hull draws attention to the difficulty of bringing beliefs into focus and play.

Alfred Schutz pointed out that people's ability to speak clearly about their ideas and feelings and beliefs decreases as these become more important, more central to the inner life. It is rather like the sense of sight. If a picture is too far away, you can't see the details, but if it is too close then, once again, the details are lost. There is an optimum distance for clarity of definition, and this seems to apply not only to our sight but to our beliefs as well. People find it more difficult to define the exact nature of their most intimate experience of being loved, or to know exactly what nationality really means to them, or to describe the characteristics of being the age they are, or to tell you exactly what the physical experience of walking is like. Things of this kind are so natural to us, so deep within us, so much part of our taken-for-granted sense of day by day reality that we never stop to reflect upon them, and find it extremely difficult to know quite what to say when asked. . . . Not only are the inward aspects of our deeper life and sense of identity not easily available for our descriptions, but we seem to be less curious about them. Because they are the unexamined verities of life, they do not attract our attention as being debatable. We are curious about the things we see; only in cases of eye disease or failure of sight do we become aware of the eye itself as the organ of vision.

The same is true of religious faith. It is remarkable how little curiosity people show about the religious faith not only of others but of their own tradition. . . .

This lack of curiosity about the things to which we are most profoundly committed seems to be defensive, in the sense that it would be painful and unsettling to question the things which are the source and ground for the rest of our life and its activities.

The basis of thought does not normally or easily become an object of thought. That which shapes our emotions is not in itself experienced as being one emotion among others. The ground of our being is not an aspect of our daily experience of becoming, an aspect concerning which we can take thought.[110]

"An optimum distance for clarity of definition", is a facilitative phrase; it points to a realistic objective. Such a distance is fixed by emotional, conceptual, spiritual and faith co-ordinates. Each of these can bring beliefs and experience into focus or blur them. What emerges from the previous section is that the consultancy processes converge naturally with the theological processes associated with revelation and redemption. This convergence brings into focus that which is discerned through the eye of faith with that seen through the eye of reason. Consultancy sessions help to focus the eye of reason through the analytical processes described earlier. They also help to focus the eye of faith with that of reason by stimulating and helping consultors and consultants:

- to develop those attributes in themselves by which they are
  - in touch with their own beliefs and able to examine them critically
  - able to understand and empathize with the beliefs of others
  - able to discuss beliefs with those with different beliefs
  - able to modify and change their beliefs as they see the need to do so
  - able, separately and together, to put their beliefs into practice;

- to use their beliefs habitually as primary reference points in analysing, designing, planning, programming, carrying out and evaluating their work and dealing creatively with positive and negative theological feedback;

- to deepen their understanding and experience of being co-workers with Jesus;

- to reflect theologically on their work and experience and to promote this practice among others;

- to enhance their ability, and that of others, to work for human and spiritual development with people whose beliefs differ significantly from theirs and to explore those differences with them.

Progress in these theological activities has far-reaching effects. Amongst other things it:

- helps individuals and groups to be theologically firm and flexible rather than theologically shapeless or rigid;

- enhances the quality of work and the satisfaction that people have in doing it with all that that can mean for worship;

- promotes theological growth and conversion(s) of individuals, churches, groups and communities and enables people to keep up theologically with their experience;

- introduces theology and biblical principles into social and community work in a natural and wholesome manner and makes explicit that which is intrinsic to it;

- enables individuals and collectives to communicate their beliefs more clearly and convincingly through the "body language" of action programmes;

- helps to infuse contemporary pluralism with new life and theological vigour through enabling people with different beliefs to work and dialogue more purposefully and with integrity to their convictions;

- makes clear that theology is as much about the way you work at and use your beliefs as it is about what you believe and why you believe it;

- encourages more people to "use" their beliefs in their work and to theologize about the outcome.

6.   Qualities, Gifts and Graces Required of Consultants

Every aspect of consultancy goes back to the people involved in them and the human and moral, ideological and spiritual sources to which they refer and relate and upon which they draw. Broadly speaking consultants and consultors have overlapping complementary responsibilities. Consultants have to ensure that their beliefs and values are expressed in consultancy relationships and processes, seriously considered in relation to the subject matter and reflected in the product. But, as we have already seen, consultants may challenge consultors but they must not try to impose their beliefs and values upon them. To override consultors' beliefs and values in designing and planning can mean that the outcome is not owned nor ownable by consultors. For their part, consultors have to ensure that the consultancy processes are conducive to their beliefs and values and that they are properly respected. Whilst they need to be open to considering beliefs and values which differ from their own, they must ensure that analyses, designs and action plans are based upon their own beliefs, values, commitments and abilities. To do these things and to engage in patient, critical, collaborative theological reflection, consultors and consultants must respect each others' beliefs and values.

This section focuses on the qualities, gifts and graces required of consultants with some reference to knowledge and skills. (Readers could find it interesting to compare these characteristics with the attributes, knowledge and skills required of practitioners which are described in Chapter Seven.) In the first part, (a), they are listed summarily. The list is presented with some hesitation because it constitutes a counsel of perfection to which I assiduously aspire but continually fall short of some aspects more than others. Part (b) has notes on some of the things which help to acquire or develop the qualities in (a). Emphasizing that these qualities are required by consultants is not in any way intended to suggest either that they are their exclusive preserve or to compromise what has been said about the contributions consultors can and ideally should make to consultations. Undoubtedly, those who possess them will be more effective consultors and practitioners of church and community work. The emphasis stresses two things. First, the qualities are required of consultants in order that they may not necessarily be required of consultors. Consultants who have them or aspire to them, make consultancy accessible and safe to anyone regardless of their qualities or capacities. Second, consultants have opportunities, and the responsibility to introduce consultors to these qualities experientially and to help those who wish to do so, to acquire and develop them.

(a) ***Qualities Required of Consultants.***[111] In this section eight primary qualities of consultants are identified and attributes associated with them are noted in summary form.

Consultants need a capacity for altruistic behaviour in relation to the Church and its workers. Amongst other things this involves them :

— being committed to resourcing the Church through its practitioners;

— having a disposition towards pursuing their vocation through those of others;

— having a genuine desire to help others to do their work and fulfil their vocation;

— in contributing all they can to the well-being, professional development and personal and spiritual growth of consultors and, through them all those with whom they work;

— having the ability to contribute generously, continuously and privately to the acclaimed success of others with minimal public recognition;

— having the ability to demonstrate commitment to and concern for others and provide developmental help in an acceptable manner;

— having the capacity to glory and rejoice in others and their achievements.

Consultants need a measure of intellectual ability and emotional and spiritual maturity. Amongst other things this involves them:

— being self-confident and humble and able to gain trust and respect;

— being genuinely interested in and curious about the views of others;

— having the ability to engage in deductive processes (from the general to the particular) and in inductive processes (from the particular to the general);

— being able to gather, select and evaluate facts and to synthesize and generalize;

— having a capacity for independent, imaginative, original and creative thought;

— having good judgement;

— having consistency and stability of belief and behaviour within the dynamic of their own development;

— being reliable, reasonable, responsible and courageous;

— being flexible and adaptable;

— being self-controlled, disciplined, calm, composed and poised;

— having the ability to withstand tensions and pressures, to live with frustrations, ambiguities and uncertainties and to think and act independently;

— being imperturbable and having sang-froid.

Consultants need to be able to understand people and work with them. Amongst other things this involves them:

— being available, approachable, accessible, courteous, well mannered and easy to get alongside and to get on with;

— having the ability to learn quickly from people, to conceptualise their situations and to present what they see in illuminating ways;

— having respect and tolerance for other people and their beliefs;

— having a facility for anticipating and evaluating human and spiritual reactions and responses;

— being trustworthy and just;

— having a facility for empathic relating.

Consultants need to be able to communicate, challenge, motivate and support. Amongst other things this involves them having the:

— ability to listen, "see" and to "hear" what is being communicated verbally and non-verbally;

— facility for oral, diagrammatic, written and non-verbal communication;

— aptitude for collaborative learning along with the ability to stimulate learning and to teach and to train;

— ability to get people to understand what has previously beaten them and to get them to consider that which they are prone to reject.

Consultants need energy and initiative and the ability to use it constructively. Amongst other things this means that they will:

— be mentally and spiritually vigorous in all modes of action including that which is non-directive;

— be ambitious for the human and spiritual well-being of all people;

— have a healthy degree of self-confidence informed and strengthened by knowledge and acceptance of their limitations;

— have physical, mental and spiritual health to sustain them and their work.

Consultants need to have human and spiritual integrity. Amongst other things this means they will:

— be honest and dependable;

— have courage, loyalty and perseverance;

— know themselves and their competencies and limitations;

— have the capacity to handle success and genuine appreciation without being conceited;

— be able to admit mistakes and to cope with and learn from failure;

— be ambitious for and committed to the Christian project and desire to make their best contribution to it;

— respect people and their confidences and their "no-go areas";

— be able to enter into the private lives of others courteously, respectfully and with a sense of privilege and awe;

— avoid voyeurism.

Consultants need theological understanding, ability and nous. Amongst other things this means they will:

— be able to explore their own beliefs and doubts openly, rigorously, critically, undefensively and constructively;

— have the facility to learn and to use the theological and ecclesial languages of their consultors;

— have the ability to help others to explore their beliefs and doubts openly, rigorously, critically, undefensively and constructively;

— have the ability to provide a pastoral context for critical practical, theoretical and theological enquiry;

— have the ability to keep their theological feet on the practical ground upon which consultors have to work.

Consultants need the capacity to love consultors and especially those who are significantly different and those who are tiresome and trying.

(b) Notes on Some Things Involved in the Development of the Qualities Required of Consultants:

On the need for energetic non-directivity. To be effective, non-directivity must be deeply rooted in the core of a consultant's being, beliefs and values. Commitment of this kind generates and releases the energy necessary to pursue this approach which, contrary to common belief, requires of non-directive consultants enormous amounts of physical, emotional, mental and spiritual resources.They have to be vigorous in order to be non-directive. This corrects common misunderstandings that people have to be vigorous to be directive and passive or laissez-faire or relaxed or laid-back to be non-directive. Thinking and deciding for yourself takes a lot of energy; helping others to think and decide for themselves can take even more. Again, this illustrates that beliefs and values are power generating agents at the heart of consultancy practice.

On the capacity to love. Consultants are most likely to be effective if they give themselves in love to the advancement of others, their work, their ministries, their vocations. It is natural to do this for people to whom we are attracted; it can be hard to do it for those we do not particularly like and especially those we envy. Necessary as it is, technical know-how cannot be substituted for love but professionalism can help to compensate for lack of love. To find and retain the love that they need for life in general and this work in particular, Christians will draw deeply upon the love they experience through living the Christian faith and through personal devotions, biblical and theological studies and through the ministry, worship and fellowship of the Church. What they will need and receive will vary enormously, as will the ways in which they get it.

One of the many things that prevent us from loving people is the tempting desire to "control" people.[112] God comes to us in ways that reject control mechanisms. Jesus demonstrates what this meant through his temptations.[113] As co-workers of Christ we are bound to follow his example. Subtle opportunities to control others occur, for instance, when consultors are finding consultants' contributions enormously helpful and when they have propensity to become dependent upon consultants. Reasoning out what is for the good of consultors and consultants and what advances their purposes, may go some way to deal with the desire and temptation to control. But a more effective antidote is the challenge of the nature of love revealed supremely in Christ. The following quotations from W. H. Vanstone[114] about loving the other is pertinent:

> When one who professes to love is wholly in control of the object of his *(sic)* love, then the falsity of love is exposed. Love is activity for the sake of an other: and where the object of love is wholly under the control of the one who loves, that object is no longer an other. It is a part or extension of the professed lover . . .[115]

> Where the object of love is truly an *other* the activity of love is always precarious . . . [it] contains no assurance or certainty of completion: much may be expended and little achieved. The progress of love must always be by tentative and precarious steps: and each step that is taken, whether it "succeeds" or "fails", becomes the basis for the next, and equally precarious, step which must follow. Love proceeds by no assured programme. . . . [116]

> The precariousness of love is experienced, subjectively, in the tense passivity of "waiting". For the completion of its endeavour as triumph or as tragedy, love must wait . . . It is important to see that that for which the lover. . . waits is not some gain or goal which might have been attained by different means, or as some "reward" for his devoted activity. The "reward" for which he waits is nothing less than the completion of his own activity - the response of receiving which is the completion of his activity of giving. For this the lover . . . must wait: and the necessity of waiting brings home to him the precariousness of his love's endeavour - its lack of final control over that situation which it has itself created. Where control is complete and exercised in complete assurance, the falsity of love is exposed.[117]

On the capacity to work privately without public recognition. Consultancy is a private affair. Consultants give themselves to the work and ministry of others. Their work is normally hidden and therefore unrecognised, they are back room workers. There are occasions when to mention that there has been a consultation is to breach confidentiality and to compromise consultors and consultants and their work. This means that consultants do not normally have the impetus, reinforcement, support and encouragement that would come from the public appreciation and recognition of their ministry and its value. All of which is generally enjoyed by their consultors. For the main part, they have to manage without it. This means that they have to rely heavily upon the private acknowledgement by consultors of the value of consultancies, upon their own assessment of the importance of what they are doing and upon seeing this work as their vocation, *i.e.:* what God would have them do. I find great joy and fulfilment in consultancy work although it can stretch me to the limits of my resources. Private recognition of value is all that consultants generally need to sustain them. From my experience, however, I know that there are times when genuine public recognition of one kind or another is craved for and when received is worth its weight in gold. But it must be genuine and freely given, it must not be sought. An unsolicited word of appreciation about a consultancy session, possibly years afterwards, gives the spiritual fillip to continue. Consultants, therefore, need the self-possession which enables them to draw upon the inner spiritual rewards for long periods and wait in patience for evidence of the efficacy of sessions and, possibly, outer recognition. As consultancy is, therefore, an occupation sustained over long periods by inner personal gratification, private rewards and deferred satisfaction, consultants must have access to spiritual resources to meet their psycho-spiritual needs.

On the ability to work with tension.[118] There is a sense in which consultancy sessions are "tension workshops". They are used extensively to work at the positive and negative tensions which consultors are experiencing. Tensions, for instance, which are engendered by what is and what is desired and the problems that persistently keep them apart and tensions which exist between people with conflicting ambitions, personalities and theology.[119] It is tension that makes people act constructively and destructively and the reduction of tension through creativity that produces satisfaction.[120] Sessions provide opportunities for the free expression of tension and feelings about them in a safe environment. This means that consultants and consultors have shared experiences of working on some of the raw material of tension that takes them beyond a description of it. Of themselves such experiences can help consultors to handle it to better advantage in their situation.

Consultors bring to sessions tensions varying greatly in intensity and positive and negative potential. They may well be working conceptually and emotionally at some of these whilst being only partially aware of others. Sometimes consultors share what they feel about tensions they are experiencing. At other times the possibility or probability of there being tensions that need attention is apparent, but consultors do not refer to them and may be avoiding them. They could be only partially aware of them or unable to articulate them or apprehensive about what might emerge from opening them up for rigorous analysis. When this happens consultants have to judge whether or not they should attempt to get the tensions considered overtly. And, if they think they should, how should they do so? How forceful should they be? How much of the tension should they seek to bring to life in the session? How much tension can the particular consultors and consultants cope with? Although there are occasions when consultants have to make unilateral decisions, in response to these questions, generally speaking it is advisable to discuss whether consultors wish to identify and examine any tensions they are experiencing and, if so, do they feel able to do so. This opens up talks about talks through a general discussion about handling tension.

Such an approach is sensibly circumspect. It provides opportunities to do several things: to examine any limitations or fears that consultors and/or consultants might have about tackling the tensions; to consider any doubts either of them might have about their competence to do so; to search for ways in which they might consider the tensions and how they would deal with any difficulties that might arise; then, and then only, to decide whether or not they are going to expose themselves to an examination of the tensions. Sensitive and gradualistic approaches of this kind invariably pay dividends. At best working through these various stages, which need not be a long drawn out process, reduces consultancy process tension by legitimising and enforcing the consultor's power to control what is considered. In turn this conserves and frees more psychological and emotional energy for the work of exploring and of analysing the tensions the consultor is experiencing and the ways in which s/he is experiencing them personally and privately, in the work place and in the dynamic of the consultation.

There is, of course, another possibility: the apparent lack of creative tension in the consultor's relationship with his/her ministry and work: the springs that give life to their vocation seem dead. Of itself, this can generate a depressing tension. The above considerations are applicable to this situation.

As the examination of tension is an important part of consultancy work, consultants and consultors need the psychological and spiritual resources and the technical skills to handle constructively, separately and together, its inner personal dynamic and its outward manifestation and implications. The technical skills have been discussed earlier. Many of the qualities required are those listed at the beginning of this section.

On the ability to do theology. Inescapably consultors and consultants engage in pastoral theology which David Deeks defines as *"an interdisciplinary study which, in order to understand pastoral actions, reflects on the relationships between pastoral work and the human sciences."*[121] So, consultants require abilities in the behavioural sciences *and* in academic and applied biblical studies and theology. They have to work with human, religious and spiritual subject matter, relationships and processes (cf sections 2, 3 and 4 above and Part Two). In one way or another, consultants engage in the following primary theological tasks.

* Consultants help consultors: to correlate the divine and human projects for human and spiritual well-being; to show how the one complements the other; to illuminate ways in which the human project is perfected in and through the divine project. Thus consultancy helps to meet the need:

> to relate faith to work;
> for an antidote to sin;
> to compensate for human incompetence;
> to sustain spiritual morale;
> to stir up the divine and human imperatives;
> to see church and community work in the context of the work of Christ.

Discharging these theological responsibilities involves considering three kinds of theology and the interaction between them:

> *public theology* which is what we say we believe, our public self;
> *head theology* which is what we believe we believe, our thinking self;
> *visceral theology* which is what we show we believe through
> our life-style, value system and commitments, our feeling self.[122]

Consultors and consultants bring these three theological selves to anything they do. Many of those to whom I have acted as consultant have found these concepts revealing but experienced some problems in trying to get in touch with their visceral theology, their "gut" beliefs, and that of the people in their situation. Doing so can reveal significant differences between public, head and visceral theologies. This can help to understand the nature of theological dissonance, confusion and conflict within and between people and sometimes to resolve it creatively. It can show, for instance, that the conflict results from exchanges in which some people are drawing upon head theology whilst others are drawing upon visceral theology.

- Consultants must do all that they can to prepare, encourage and help consultors themselves to think through theological cycles - articulating beliefs, putting them into practice, reflecting on theological feedback, working out the implications for faith and action - and to offer moral and spiritual support to them as they do so.

- Consultants have responsibilities to help consultors to find appropriate ways and means of doing theology with the people with whom they are engaged.

- Consultants have a cluster of functions and responsibilities when there are differences in belief and theology between them and their consultors. They have to work to the consultor's theology without compromising their own theological stance and integrity. If consultants or consultors feel that they are compromising themselves or being compromised, they need to address the problem. The ways in which they do this could be an object lesson for both of them about the way to cope with those working relationships that would take them beyond the limits of theological pluralism that is acceptable to them.

- Consultants have responsibilities to help consultors to be open to the grace of God and the work of the Spirit, that is, to perform what are variously understood as pastoral, ministerial, prophetic and priestly functions. Doing this is a corollary to and not a substitute for helping consultors to be open to the use of analytical processes and the insights, approaches and methods of the social and behavioural sciences. When they are able to perform these functions human reason and divine revelation inform and complement each other.

- Consultants need to help consultors to work to reality by getting them to take seriously into account that human situations are alloys of grace, sin and evil.

Generally speaking, the ability to engage in this kind of theological activity as an integral part of work consultancy depends upon consultors and consultants being able to explore creatively the theological content of the consultor's experience. Academic theological and biblical knowledge are valuable and help to identify relevant theological issues and questions and also helps consultants to introduce relevant material. Important as the imparting of information and knowledge might be, it must not become a substitute for the basic aim, to get consultors to think theologically for themselves. Doing their own theological thinking in the ways already described, enables consultants, and through them, consultors to:

— get in touch with their own beliefs, examine them critically, and use them in analysing, designing planning, progamming, carrying out and evaluating their work and dealing creatively with positive and negative theological feedback and to help others to do the same;

— empathise with the beliefs of others;

— dialogue and work purposefully and creatively with those whose beliefs differ significantly from theirs and to reflect theologically on the outcome;

— live and work so that their relationships with God, themselves and others are all of a piece.

142

Doing these things calls for the range of personal, technical and social skills and pastoral and spiritual qualities already discussed.

7. An Inclusive Theological Model

A creation model is the theological concept which best serves me in relation to consultancy and church and community development work. A creation model, that is, within which there is continuous regeneration, re-creation, revelation and resurrection through the salvific work of Christ and the ministry of the Holy Spirit. A model in which all the processes are consumated at the end of time in the parousia. This model gives a theological framework for every aspect of this seventh element of practice theory.

8. Codes of Good Practice [123]

Throughout this book the ins and outs of good practice for consultors and consultants have been pursued in considerable detail. At this point it could be helpful to pinpoint those things which are key to effective consultancy practice. That is what is attempted here. It is intended as a focus and a reminder of the detailed discussion of consultancy practice theory, not a summary of it. Milan Kubr in an introduction to his formulation of ten commandments for management consultants says that they summarise in telegraphic form the critical points of which they need to be aware. [124]

A Code for Consultors. First of all, we look at what constitutes a code of good practice for consultors. [125]

- Learn about consulting and consultants.
- Be clear about your consultancy agenda, your objectives and critical features of your working situation.
- Choose your consultant carefully to match you and your criteria.
- Be clear about the nature of the consultancy contract and any cost that might be involved.
- Be an open active, egalitarian partner in control of your agenda.
- Safeguard areas of confidentiality and privacy.
- Ensure that anything that emerges fits you, your beliefs and morals and your situation.
- Monitor progress or lack of it.
- Evaluate results and your performance as a consultor and that of the consultant.
- Do not become dependent or feel under an obligation even when you are indebted.
- Do all you can to ensure that consultants in their dealings with you honour codes of good professional practice.

These points indicate what is involved in working with consultants and the qualities to which consultors should aspire. They are a basis for those starting in consultancy and from which consultors and their organizations could develop their own code and policy. A profile of consultors derived from this list would show them to have a cluster of attributes: they would be their own person; they would be committed to self-development, self-determination, self-direction; they would have the self-confidence and self-assurance to receive help from others, from a position of strength or vulnerability, with dignity and without compromising their autonomy; they would be committed and able to work with other people collaboratively as equals in interdependent relationships; they would be humbly aware of their strengths; they would also be aware of their weaknesses and limitations by way of self-understanding and acceptance not self-denigration. In short good consultors are confident clients or customers seeking technical and pastoral help in a dignified and professional manner; they are not supplicants looking for help in relation to their failures. They are Christian workers inviting others to share as equals in their vocational enterprise. And that is an enormous privilege! Clearly, the degree to which consultors will have these desirable personal qualities will vary considerably. Possessing them is not a prerequisite of receiving consultancy help. On the contrary the more they lack them the more they need consultancy help of the kind described in this book because these qualities are amongst the highly valued products of consultancy services.

A Code for Consultants.[126] A code of good professional conduct for consultants in church and community work will include the following elements.

- Consultants will do all they can to help consultors to be effective consultors and to honour codes of good professional conduct.

- Consultants will seek to maintain standards consonant with the Christian faith and ethic: they will treat consultors with justice, courtesy and respect.

- Consultants will act in the interests of consultors and the nature and mission of the Christian Church.

- Consultants will behave in a self-disciplined and self-controlled manner.

- Consultants will maintain independence of thought and action, objectivity and their integrity within the intimacy of creative reflective engagement with consultors.

- Consultants will act only within the limits of their personal and professional competence and, as necessary, they will make those limits known to consultors: they will not, therefore, accept work for which they are not qualified or do not have the resources or which will involve them in a conflict of interests or working relationships; they will explore with consultors anything which limits their ability to help them or impairs their independence, objectivity or integrity.

- Consultants will not enter into any arrangements which will compromise their ability to honour their contract to consultors or which will detract from their impartiality.

- Consultants will agree with consultors in advance: those who are parties to the consultancy contract; the nature of the contract; the terms of remuneration; the acceptable use of consultancy supervisors and resource people.

- Consultants will establish with consultors areas of confidentiality and maintain them: they will *not* disclose, or permit to be disclosed, confidential information concerning consultors; they will not use information gained through consultancies for any purposes or in any ways likely to have adverse effects upon consultors and their interests.

- Consultants will respect the privacy of consultors and their no-go areas; they will avoid inquisitiveness, idle curiosity, prurience and voyeurism.

- Consultants, by attending to the idiosyncrasies of consultors and the specifics of their situations, aim to establish ways forward which are realistic, practicable, clearly understood by consultors and within their capacities and resources: they do not deal in standardised, "off-the-peg", programmes and solutions.

- Consultants will establish with consultors how they will negotiate any changes in the objectives or scope of, or approach to the consultancy, deal with any difficulties that might arise and review or evaluate consultancy processes and programmes.

- Consultants will do all they can to preserve the freedom of consultors to be independent and interdependent, reflective, collaborative practitioners.

Consultants who follow this code give themselves wholeheartedly to the well-being of consultors in relation to the Christian project. They enter deeply into their vocational life and work whilst maintaining the independence and objectivity which enable them to pursue critical questions and issues with consultors. In the closest of consultancy relationships they remain their own person.

GETTING IT TOGETHER

Consultancy relationships and sessions work well when all seven elements interact harmoniously and are integrated systemically. In this extended chapter they have been taken apart in order to show how they work and relate to each other. The aim is to help consultors and consultants to understand the key elements of practice theory; to build up their facility in using them and bringing them together creatively; to research and develop their own practice theory. Effective practice involves bringing the elements together in holistic approaches, relationships and processes to fit consultants and consultors and their consultancy needs. Synthesizing the parts so that the joints are not apparent is both an art and science. Creativity evolves from using the approaches and methods and by building up systemic connections by habitually relating the part to the whole and the whole to the parts. These processes produce a seamless approach to consultancy which is effective, elegant and aesthetic.

Combined, these seven elements of practice theory generate the spirituality of consultancy. Spirituality, a concept much in use now by people in religious and secular organizations, is defined by Dr Gordon Wakefield as "a word which has come much into vogue to describe those attitudes, beliefs and practices which animate people's lives and help them to reach out towards super-sensible realities".[127] This definition helps me to distinguish inter-related aspects of spirituality: the things that generate it (beliefs, attitudes and practices); its affective content within individuals and groups (the "core spirituality"); the feelings, ethos, atmosphere that it engenders (the "projected spirituality"); and those things that it facilitates within, between and through people. The first and fourth of these are comparatively easily described; the second and third are directly communicated to the senses but elusive to description. Thus understood, "spirituality" points to the essential substance of Christian life and living, not to something vague, amorphous and "religious".

At the heart of the spirituality that characterizes work and vocational consultancy are the beliefs, practices and attitudes that enable people in all kinds of situations and circumstances to initiate and sustain imaginative critical thought and action relevant to the complexities of contemporary society. These processes of thought and action engender an ethos and an atmosphere in which people feel they matter and know instinctively that they and their interests are being taken seriously. It is an atmosphere in which they feel equal and enjoy equality of opportunity and participation, and in which they know with deep personal assurance that they are significant. It is an environment within which people know that they are accepted for what they are, non-judgementally and without patronage or condescension. The freedom to think, to think aloud and to think again is the air they breathe freely.

Such an ethos encourages all forms of exploration and the facing up to differences; it discourages argumentation, rhetoric and debate; it is therefore unitive rather than divisive. It is characterized by receptivity, affective as well as intellectual responses, waiting or attentiveness and the acceptance of pain as intrinsic to the bringing forth of life.[128] It constrains people to stop and think, stimulates them to go and act and deters them from being quietists or activists. It is a spirituality of being *and* doing. The atmosphere is that which goes with reflective, creative activity — people discovering and learning together and from each other how to do or to make something of importance to them and to their God. It is the ethos of healthy people at work, rather than sick people at therapy. It is a learning atmosphere. It is my hope that readers will have felt some of these things as they have read the description of the processes in this chapter.

Notes and References: Chapter Two

1.   I have found an article by Philip Bryers very helpful , "The Development of Practice Theory in Community Work", *Community Development Journal* Volume 14 No.3, October 19979, pp 192-199. Following Roger Evans, in "Some Implications of an Integrated Model of Social Work for Theory and Practice", *British Journal of Social Work*, Volume 6 No.2, 1976, he distinguishes between *practice theory* based on experience and the *theory of practice* which is derived from a social scientific knowledge base. For Bryers practice theories are common sense or home-made theories, which practitioners carry in their heads and which are implicit in their day-to-day activities. Later he quotes an Association of Community Workers' paper *Knowledge and Skills for Community Work* (1975): "What we are arriving at here is the practical wisdom of experienced practioners who are used to dealing with people in a variety of situations, but a *practical wisdom which is sharpened by appropriate theory about human nature.*" (p 16) This is nearer to what I mean in this chapter by practice theory. I have adopted some of the phraseology.

2.   Campbell, David (1995) *Learning Consultation: A Systemic Framework* (Karnak Books) p 72f.

3.   This phrase is not to be confused with "role-taking" which has a technical meaning in role theory. See the discussion on Element Four and reference 34.

4.   After only one consultancy session Rosemary Mellor saw that there was something quite distinctive about the roles of consultors and consultants but found it difficult to pin it down. The nearest she got was: "It isn't a doctor/or counsellor/patient model. It's people coming together to deal with, look at things". Earlier she said it was coming "together in equality". cf Lovell, George (1996) (ed) *Telling Experiences: Stories About A Transforming Way of Working With People* (Chester House Publications) pp 154 and 153.

5.   Argyle and Henderson suggest that relationships can be placed along dimensions such as:

intense - superficial
friendly - hostile
equal   - unequal
task   - social

Effective consultancy relationships tend towards the left of these spectrums. cf Argyle, Michael and Henderson, Monika (1985) *The Anatomy of Relationships and the Rules and Skills Needed to Manage Them Successfully* (Heinemann) p 5.

6.   cf *Association of Community Workers Talking Point* No. 122 April 1991.

7.   The situation was considered so serious in 1980 that The Methodist Publishing House at the direction of Conference sent to all ministers an offprint of a Conference Report, *Confidentiality in Pastoral Care*, urging them to keep confidences.

8.   Kubr , Milan (ed), (1996 Third revised edition) *Management Consulting: A Guide to the Profession* (International Labour Office, Geneva).

9.   Smail, David (1984) *Illusion and Reality: The Meaning of Anxiety* (J. M. Dent and Sons Ltd) p 141f.

10.   *The Observer*, 14th June 1970.

11.   *The Guardian*, 5th October, 1996.

12.   Leslie Griffiths said, for instance, of a consultancy experience, "Certainly nobody had listened to me for that long ever about my work" see Lovell, George (ed) (1995) *Telling Experiences* p 19.

13.   Simone Weil does this in *Waiting on God* (London, Routledge and Kegan Paul, 1951). I was introduced to her thinking on "attention" by Watts, Fraser & Williams Mark (1988) *The Psychology of Religious Knowing* cf pp 62, 70, 71, 79 *et al.*

14.   Smail, David (1984) *op cit* p 135 quotes the first three terms, which he says are attributable to Carl Rogers.

15.   *Ibid* p 34.

16.   *Ibid* p 35.

17.   *Ibid* p 37.

18.   Watts, Fraser and Williams, Mark (1988) *The Psychology of Religious Knowing* pp 63f.

19.   *Ibid* p 63.

20.   cf Smail, David (1984) *op cit* p 59.

21.   An experience of this kind that I had is described briefly in *Telling Experiences* p 176 cf viii and ix.

22.   I first used and developed these ideas in my work at Parchmore Methodist Church, Youth and Community Centre. I describe just how I did it in my doctoral thesis, *An Action Research Project to Test the Applicability of the Non-Directive Concept in a Church, Youth and Community Centre Setting.* (A thesis submitted for the Degree of Doctor of Philosophy in the Institute of Education, Faculty of Arts, University of London, 1973) and more briefly in *The Parchmore Partnership*, Malcolm Grundy (ed) (1995) Chester House Publications.

23.   Nolen, Barbara (ed) (1972/74) *Voices of Africa: Stories by Wole Sovinka Chinua Achebe and Other Famous Writers* (Fontana).

24.   The quotations are from notes by Gillian Stamp and a paper *Well-Being and Stress at Work* (September 1988) (Brunel Institute of Organisation and Social Studies). cf Nelson, John (ed) (1996)

Management and Ministry—appreciating contemporary issues (The CanterburyPress) pp 54-56. Also cf Jacques, Elliott (1976) *A General Theory of Bureaucracy* (Heinemann) pp 100ff and 123f.

25.   I owe the phrase to Friedman, Edwin H. (1985) *Generation to Generation Family Process in Church and Synagogue* (The Guilford Press) pp 208ff.

26.   Figure 8:1 in *Analysis and Design* p 195 gives a fuller picture of the private and public work domains and the relationships associated with them.

27.   There is a helpful article on "Supervision, Pastoral" by John P. Millar in Cambell, Alastair V. (1978) *A Dictionary of Pastoral Care* (SPCK) p 272f. There are interesting notes about supervision and learning about consultancy in Campbell, David (1995) *Learning Consultation: A Systemic Framework* (Karnak Books) pp 18, 54, 55, 67, 88, 91.

28.   Theories about the nature of the interaction which causes change in living systems are many. The work of Humberto R Maturana indicates the complexity of the processes. cf Maturana, Humberto R. and Varela, Francisco J. (1928/72) *Autopoiesis and Cognition : The Realization of the Living* (D. Reidel Publishing Company). They examine living systems as autopoietic machines which do not have inputs or outputs but which "can be perturbed by independent events and undergo structural changes which compensate these perturbations" p 81. See Morgan, Gareth (1986) *Images of Organizations* (Sage Publications) for a summary of Maturana and Varela's work under the title of "Autopoiesis: the logic of self-producing systems" (pp 235-240).

29.   Bateson, Gregory (1972) *Steps to an Ecology of Mind* (Ballantine Books, New York) says: " . . . we create the world that we perceive, not because there is no reality outside our heads . . . but because we select and edit the reality we see to conform to our beliefs about the sort of world we live in". p vii cf p 136 *et al.*

30.   I got the idea after reading an article by The Rev Dr. Philip Meadows, "Virtual Insidership: Interreligious Dialogue and the limits of Understanding" in *Discernment : An Ecumenical Journal of Inter-Religious Encounter* Editor Clinton Bennet (Published by The Churches' Commission for Inter Faith Relations in association with The School of Theology, Westminster College, Oxford) New Series Vol 3:2, 1996 pp 29-41. In this article he uses the idea of a world-view to explore "virtual insidership". The influence of the article on my thinking is apparent at several places in this section.

31.   Some of the phraseology I have used draws upon the definition of a world-view quoted by Philip Meadows from the *Dictionary of Philosophy*. Subsequently I have found James F. Hopewell (1988) *Congregation: Stories and Structures* (SCM Press) is very helpful on the nature, function and understanding of world-views in relation to Christian ministry.

32.   Smail, David (1984) *Illusion and Reality* p 64.

33.   *op cit* p 64.

34.   Broadly speaking there are two approaches to role theory, those associated with symbolic interactionism and those associated with functionalism. The first sees role-taking as a form of role-making; the second sees roles as essentially prescribed. cf. Abercrombie, Nicholas, Hill, Stephen and Turner, S. Bryan (1984) *The Penguin Dictionary of Sociology* (Penguin Books) pp 180ff; Mitchell, G. Duncan (ed) (1968, 1970) *A Dictionary of Sociology* (Routlege & Kegan Paul) pp 148ff.

35.   cf. Campbell, Alastair V. (ed) (1987) *A Dictionary of Pastoral Care* (New Library of Pastoral Care, SPCK) pp 241 for a note by Lawrence Reading on role play.

36.   Meadows, Philip *op ci*t see reference 27. I draw upon the terms and concepts he uses.

37.   *op cit* p.33.

38.   There is an interesting discussion in Meadows' article about a claim by Ross Reat that all the world's religions "share to some degree . . . the conviction that true understanding is tantamount to conversion". That is, in order to see the world like a Hindu, for example, one must actually become a Hindu. In the light of this, Reat considers the possibility and importance of becoming a "temporary convert". This is reminiscent of Paul's approach of "becoming all things to all people" cf 1 Corinthians 9:22 and p 138). Meadows feels, as I do, that it is possible to become sufficiently proficient in the language of another world-view without being committed to it. Similarly, consultants can become proficient in the consultor's work-view without being committed to his/her work-view. *op cit* cf pp31f. The differences are, as we shall see, the basis for creative dialogue and dialectic exchanges between people with significantally different world-views .

39.   This diagram is modelled on the ones presented by Meadows in the article referred to in ref. 32 cf pp 33 and 34.

40.   Batten, T. R. (1962) *Training for Community Development : A Critical Study of Method* (Oxford University Press) discusses the importance of getting "thinking participation" and the danger of equating it with talking participation.

41.   Salvini, Mara Palazzoli *et al* "Hypothesizing—Circularity—Neutrality : Three Guidelines for the Conductor of the Session" an article in *Family Process*, March 1980 Vol.19 No.1.

42.   Smail, David (1984) *op cit* p 68.

43.   I have been involved in several consultancies where this has happened. One is reported in Lovell, George, and Widdicombe, Catherine (1978) *Churches and Communities: An Approach to Development in the Local Church* (Search Press) pp 115-123. The consultancy team put an enormous amount of time and energy into the project but nothing was achieved. No convincing explanation was given for the lack of progress nor for dogmatic claims that plans drawn up with great care with consultors and tested with them for acceptability, feasibility and practicability, proved in the event to be either unworkable or simple failed. Reasons, or more accurately, excuses, for their failure were always unconvincing. There was always something that they said we "did not understand". Try as we might, a sense of dealing with understandable realities evaded us.

44.   Whitehead, A. N. (1932, sixth impression 1962) *The Aims of Education and Other Essays* (London, Ernest Benn Limited) pp 153 and 154.

45.   Morgan, Gareth (1986) *Images of Organizations* p 321.

46.   *op cit* p 322.

47.   *op cit* pp 329, see also p 328. Morgan gives an example of diagnostic reading, "The Multicom Case", pp 322-331.

48.   Lovell, George (1994) *Analysis and Design* (Burns & Oates) pp 188f and 78, 91 and 191.

49.   This model is slightly adapted from one presented by A. W. Ghent in "The Logic of Experimental Design", *Bioscience*, 16:17-22, 1966 as quoted by Bill McKelvey in *Organizational Systematics: Taxonomy, Evolution and Classification* (University of California Press 1982) p 19.

50.   cf. *Analysis and Design* Chapter 7, Basic Equipment pp 175-191 and other references in the index.

51.   These facilitating structures are illustrated and discussed in detail in Part One of *Analysis and Design*, pp 29-106; the schema and its stages in Chapter 5; designing in Chapter 6. Examples and case studies have been produced by the Battens. *The Human Factor in Community Work* contains cases set overseas but they are pertinent to work with people in any country. See also: *Training for Community Development* pp 39-40 and 113-120; *The Non-Directive Approach in Group and Community Work* (London, OUP, 1968), pp 96-100; *The Human Factor in Youth Work*, (London,OUP, 1979), is relevant to work with other age groups. In one way or another these cases are highly relevant to the work of the ministry. Further, the classification of the cases and the conclusions the Battens draw are relevant to anyone working with people. Unfortunately the first three of these books are out of print but they can generally be obtained from libraries.

52.   Caplan, Gerald and Killilea, Marie (eds) (1976) *Support Systems and Mutual Help: Multidisciplinary Exploration* (Grune and Stratton) p 268.

53.   Koestler, Arthur (1964) *The Act of Creation* (Hutchinson of London) Chapter VII.

54.   *MARC Europe Survey of Avec Training and Consultancy Services: Notes and Presentation and Discussion of the Report* January 1991 p 2. see *Avec: Agency and Approach* p 158.

55.   There is a fuller description of records and record making in *Analysis and Design* pp 178ff and in Widdicombe, Catherine, (2000) *Meetings That Work* (The Lutterworth Press) see indexed references to records, note-taker, journalling and Progoff.

56.   Koestler, Arthur (1964) *The Act of Creation* contains a chapter entitled, "Thinking Aside : Limits of Logic". He quotes Souriau's famous phrase "to invent you must think aside". p 145.

57.   cf *Analysis and Design* pp 183f and 190f. I developed the ideas in *Diagrammatic Modelling: An aid to theological reflection in church and community development work*,(An Avec Publication, 1980) Dr Hans-Ruedi Weber gives an extremely helpful description of the respective functions of the left or right hemispheres of the brain in an article entitled "Thinking Images". cf an article by Margaret Dewey in the series *Thinking Mission*, No. 39 (Summer 1983) issued by the United Society for the Propogation of the Gospel. The article first appeared in the July 1982 *Ecumenical Review* under the title "Interpreting Biblical Images". For further discussion of this phenomena see *The Intelligent Eye* by R. L. Gregory (London, Weidenfeld and Nicolson, 1979); *Drawing on the Right Side of the Brain: How to unlock your hidden artistic talent* by Betty Edwards (London, Fontana/Collins, 1979); *The Right Brain: A new understanding of the unconscious mind and its creative powers* by Thomas R Blakeslee (London: Macmillan Press, 1980); *Writing the Natural Way* by Gabriele Lusser Rico (Los Angeles: J. P. Tarcher) 1983.

58.   cf *Analysis and Design* pp 179-184.

59.   This was submitted as a pictorial summary of a position paper to a small group on work consultancy in 1979 by the Revd. William C. Denning who is now the Director of Creative Art Network which promotes theological reflection through all forms of artistic activities.

60.   cf *Analysis and Design* pp 180f.

61.   Caplan, Gerald & Killilea, Marie (eds) (1976) *Support Systems and Mutual Help: Multidisciplinary Exploration* (Grune and Stratton) p 267.

62.   cf Bandler, Richard and Grinder, John (1979) (Edited by Andreas, Steve, formerly John O. Stevens) *Frogs into Princes : Neuro Linguistic Programming* (Real People Press) pp 25-27 and Lewis, Byron A. and Pucelik, R. Frank (1982) *Magic Demystified: A Pragmatic Guide to Communication and Change* (Metamorphous Press) pp 121-122.

63.   I got the idea for some of these distinctions from Argyle, Michael, (1967) *The Psychology of Interpersonal Behaviour* (Penguin Books). In a section entitled "Social Techniques and Social Interaction" he suggests that, "Synchronization" is necessarily along a number of different dimensions for smooth and motivationally satisfying interaction to take place: 1. Amount of speech . . . 2. The speed or tempo of interaction . . . 3. Dominance . . . 4. Intimacy . . . 5. Co-operation and competition . . . 6. Emotional tone . . . 7. Task, topic and procedure. cf pp 51-54.

64.   Lovell, George, (1996) *Telling Experiences* pp 40-41.

65.   Brian Woodcock tells how many years of ministry were marred because he did not assimilate new methods before practising them. See Lovell, George (ed) (1996) *Telling Experiences* pp 163f and 177.

66.   Young, Michael (1988) *The Metronomic Society: Natural Rhythms and Human Timetables* (Thames and Hudson, ISBN 0-500-01443-4).

67.   Various ways of defining the phases /stages are used. Lippitt, Gordon and Lippitt, Ronald (1986, 2nd edition) *The Consulting Process in Action* (University Associates Inc) offers the following: 1. engaging in initial contact and entry; 2. formulating a contract and establishing a helping relationship; 3. identifying problems through diagnostic analysis; 4. setting goals and planning for action; 5. taking action and cycling feedback; and 6. completing the contract (continuity, support and termination) p 11. Kubr, Milan (1976, third edition 1996) *Management Consultancy* uses the following classification: entry; diagnosis; action planning; implementation; termination. (cf Part II pp 141-247).

68.   Harding, Rev C. G. (undated) *The Problem of Stress* (A booklet published by The Relaxation Society, Churches' Council for Healing and Health) p 10.

69.   Stamp, Gillian (1988) *Well-Being and Stress at Work* (Brunel Institute of Organisation and Social Studies) pp 3ff—following McGrath (1970), Csikszentmihalyi (1975), Bailey (1988), Handy (1988) and Bonn (1988)—says that a person feels stressed "when what there is to do either out-strips or fails to challenge what the person feels s/he is capable of doing". The graphs in this paper are very telling. A band of well-being, flow and effectiveness set at 45 degrees is the central feature. The triangle above represents the situation in which there is too much to do. The stress here is marked by anxiety, worry, perplexity, indecisiveness, hasty or inappropriate decisions. The triangle below represents the situation in which there is too little to do. The stress here is marked by frustration, boredom, anxiety, vacillation, automatic solutions, lack of serious thought.

70.   It is informative to compare the graphs used by Gillian Stamp with Yerkes-Dodson Law represented by a hump backed graph produced by plotting performance against arousal (stimulation and effort). Once past the optimum working level increasingly more effort produces less performance output. Energy is not renewed as readily and those working at this level progressively experience fatigue, exhaustion, ill health, break-down and burn-out. This has been used by Consultant Cardiologist Peter Nixon at Charing Cross Hospital. cf Horsman, Sarah (1987) *Living with Stress: Understanding and Managing Stress—A Guide For Christian Ministers* (Project Paper, produced privately).

71.   Some of the questions in this and the next section were suggested to me by a paper by Dr Paul Tosey, "Consultancies as "Working with the Energy' in Organizations: A Report on Research in Progress" Published in *What Makes Consultancy Work—Understanding the dynamics:International Consultancy Conference* 1994 Edited by Roger Casemore *et al* (South Bank University Press 1994) pp 394-405.

72.   cf Lovell, George (1996) (ed) *Telling Experiences* p 45.

73.   There is much useful information about contracting in Kubr, Milan (see Ref. 70) and other standard texts on consultancy, see the bibliography.

74.   Edgar H Schein (1988) *Process Consultation Volume I: Its Role in Organisational Development* says:

> There are two aspects to the contract : (1) the formal decision as to how much time will be devoted to the consultation, what general services will be performed, and the form and amount of payment that will be used; and (2) the informal "psychological contract" that involves the client's implicit (and sometimes explicit) expectations of what he will gain from the relationship as well as what he will give to the relationship, what obligations he takes on, and what he expects to gain from it. It is important for both client and consultant to explore as many aspects of the contract as possible provided there is mutual understanding of what is meant. Sometimes this requires delaying the discussion until the client has experienced PC (Process Consultation). (p 126).

It was from this that I got the idea of thinking about aspects of contracts but the classification is my own. I use psychological contract in a different way from Schein.

75.   cf Kubr, Milan *Management Consulting* Chapter 26 cf Chapter 23. Lovell, George (1996) *Avec: Agency and Approach* is a case study of the things which made and marred a small ecumenical agency that actually provided training and consultancy services from 1976-1994 for thousands of people from seven denominations working at all levels in Britain, Ireland, Africa and some fifteen other countries. It covers the period 1976-1991. The aim was for the agency to be self-supporting from fees received. In the event it was possible to raise only 60% of the costs through fees. Details are given about the financing of this agency and raising money through fees cf. pp 73ff and 101ff.

76.   Avec Trustees and Staff had to do this see previous reference.

77.   Lovell, George and Widdicombe, Catherine (1978 Reprinted 1986) *Churches and Communities op cit* p 209.

78.   For case studies of the difficulties which can arise and possible ways of dealing with them see: Palazzoli, Mara Selvini; Anolli, Luigi; Di Blasio, Paola; Giossi, Lucia; Pisano, Innocenzo; Ricci, Carlos; Sacchi, Marica; Ugazio, Valeria (1986) *The Hidden Games of Organizations* Pantheon Books, (New York) particularly the four cases in Part One pp 1-109. Also Bradford, Leland P. (1980) *Making Meetings Work: A Guide for Leaders and Group Members* (University Associates) particularly Chapter 9 pp 66-76.

79.   cf Schein, Edgar H. (1988) *op cit* (see reference 70) p 127.

80.   cf Palazzoli, Mara Selvini (1984) "Behind the scenes of the organization: some guide lines for the expert in human relations" *Journal of Family Therapy* 6: 299-307 see pp 303ff. cf also Palazzoli, Mara Selvini *et al* (1980) *op cit* has an excellent chapter on "Denied Coalitions", pp 149-155.

81.   cf Palazzoli, Mara Selvini (1986) pp 149ff and 154f.

82.   In this list I have drawn upon a chapter entitled "The Contracting Process" by Brian McEvoy in Casemore, Roger, Dyos Gail, Eden Angela, Kellner, Kamil, McAuley, John, Moss Stephen (eds) (1994) *What Makes Consultancy Work: Understanding the Dynamics: International Consulting Conference, 1994* (South Bank University Press) pp100-109. His list of "Contracting Guidelines" draws upon the work of Clare and Mike Reikev and he refers to Block, Peter (1981) *Flawless Consulting and a Guide to Getting Your Expertise Used* (Learning Concepts, Distributed by University Associates Inc.).

83.   In this paragraph I have drawn on an unpublished paper: Russell, W. Peter and Lovell, George (1988) *Furlough Work Study* p 18. This paper is a description and examination of the work consultancy processes used on courses for missionaries on furlough, which were run by Avec in collaboration with the Methodist Church Overseas Division from 1976 to 1993.

84.   Hull, John (1985) *What Prevents Christian Adults from Learning?* (SCM Press) p 64.

85.   *op cit* p 67.

86.   *op cit* p 66.

87.   I cannot locate the quotation but cf *op cit* p 75f.

88.   Watts, Fraser and Williams, Mark (1988) *The Psychology of Religious Knowing* (Cambridge University Press) p 104.

89.   *op cit* p 104f.

90.   cf Bonhoeffer, Dietrich (1937) *The Cost of Discipleship* (SCM, Abridged translation first published October 1948, reprinted August 1956) Chapter 4 and particularly pp 79f. Whilst Bonhoeffer's mediatorial concept has helped me enormously over many years, I have some difficulty with what he said about: Jesus "standing between us and God . . . and all other men *(sic)*" with the consequence that we have no "direct relation to the world" or loved ones or neighbours. He says "our relation to the world has been built on an illusion". My responses are severalfold. Part of me reacts against them. I feel that I am in a direct relation with people and the world and I want to be. Bonhoeffer says that that is an indication of opposition to Christ. Then again I know I relate better when I do so through Christ but I do not always do so. That is an indication that my discipleship is wanting. Part of me feels I am missing something of what Bonhoeffer sees to be the all inclusive nature of Christ's mediation and the consistency and permanence of its operation.

91.   Later I was helped to see more clearly that the Holy Spirit too has a mediatorial role in effecting the Christian mission through a book by John V. Taylor, (1972) *The Go-Between God, The Holy Spirit and the Christian Mission* (SCM Press).

92.   I described this retreat in an article in the *Epworth Review* (Vol. 21:3 September 1994) entitled "An Experience of the Ignatian Exercises".

93.   cf *Analysis and Design* pp 234ff.

94.   cf any standard text book on research methods and *Analysis and Design* pp 219, 226, 287f, 288-90.

95.   Jacobson, Dean (1966) *The Beginners* (Penguin) p 6 a quotation from *The Ethics of the Fathers*.

96.   Batten, T. R. "The Major Issues and Future Direction of Community Development" in the *Community Development Journal* (Vol. 9/2, April 1974) p 96.

97.   From a letter I received from The Revd David Deeks about the theology of work consultancy, 10 July 1992.

98.   From the typescript of a lecture given by The Rt Revd Professor Peter Selby to a Conference in Belfast on 10 April 1986 entitled *Saved Through Hope* cf pp 1 and 2.

99.   *op cit* p 2.

100.   *op cit* p 4 Hasler, Joe (1992) *Becoming Human Together: Theology in the Planning of Community Development* (Diocese of Bristol, Association of Priority Area Parishes 1987-1992) does make some connections by reflecting on the theology of hope, liberation and process in relation to community development.

101.   Selby *op cit* p 17.

102.   This quotation comes from an article entitled "The Politics of Salvation and Revelation in the Practice of Consultancy" in Casemore, Roger *et al* (1994) *What Makes Consultancy Work— Understanding the Dynamics* p 87.

103.   Field, Joanna (Marion Milner) (1934, 1986) *A Life of One's Own* (Virago) p 108.

104.   *Ibid* p 107.

105.   *op cit* cf Chapter VII and particularly 105ff.

106.   Williams, H. A. (1972) *True Resurrection* (Mitchell Beazley, London) p 10.

107.   *Ibid* p 10.

108.   Eric Fromm differentiates between non-alienated activity which gives life to persons and things and alienated activity which is done at a dysfunctional distance from the creative centres of human beings. cf *To Have or To Be* (London: Jonathan Cape, 1978) pp 90ff.

109.   This imagery came to me after reading Brueggemann, Walter (1980) *Finally Comes The Poet: Daring Speech for Proclamation* (Fortress Press Minneapolis) and especially a section headed, "A Conversation of two Well-Spoken Voices" pp 74ff.

110.   Hull, John (1985) *What Prevents Christian Adults from Learning?* pp 54f.

111.   In this section I have drawn heavily upon Kubr, Milan (1976 third edition 1996) *Management Consulting* Chapter 32 pp 665ff and especially upon Box 32:1 on p 669.

112.   There is a most helpful chapter on control by John Habgood entitled "Church and Risk (1)" in Holloway, Richard (1990) *The Divine Risk* Darton, Longman and Todd, London) pp 24ff. See also *Analysis and Design*, pp 253-259.

113.   cf Matthew 4: 1-10; Luke 4:1-13.

114.   Vanstone, W. H. (1977) *Love's Endeavour, Love's Expense* (Darton, Longman and Todd). I was well acquainted with this book but I had not made this application until I read a paper on the *Theology of Community Work: Some Notes* by The Revd Dr Michael Bayley (April 1990). I am indebted to him for this reference.

115.   *op cit* p 45.

116.   *op cit* p 46.

117.   *op cit* pp 49f.

118.   cf Williams, H. A. (1976) *Tensions : Necessary Conflicts in Life and Love* (Mitchell, Beazley, London).

119.   The relationship between theology and personality was explored in an interesting series of articles in the *Epworth Review* from 1981 to 1984 by: George, A. Raymond (Vol 8/1), Lake, Frank (Vol 8/1), Rowland, Christopher (Vol 8/2), Kent, John (Vol 8/3), English, Donald (Vol 9/1), Rack, Henry (Vol 9/3), Wood, A, Skevington (Vol 10/1), Hepburn, Ronald (Vol 10/2), Longley, Clifford (Vol 11/1), Dillistone, F. W. (Vol 11/2).

120.   Batten, T. R. (1957) *Communities and Their Development* (Oxford University Press, fifth impression 1965) has a remarkable section in his final chapter on two of a community development worker's functions: to increase tension and to reduce it with satisfaction. He underlines the importance of doing the former only when it is possible to do the latter! cf pp 228ff.

121.   cf Deeks, David (1986) "Some Recent Work on Pastoral Theology" *Epworth Review* p 88. He notes later that "pastoral care is now seen to involve participation in our understanding of at least the following corporate dimensions of our existence: human groups of all sizes; professions and institutions; politics and social work". He also quotes the introduction of the SPCK "New Library of Pastoral Care" edited by D Blows: "Today it is perhaps the secular helping professions of social work, counselling and psychotherapy and community development which have particular contributions to make to the pastor in his work" (p 90). Deeks sees church and community development to be one of the dimensions of pastoral theology.

122.   Rahtjen, Bruce D, with Kramer, Bryce and Mitchell, Ken (1977) *A Workbook in Experiential Theology* (A Publication of Associates in Experiential Theology inc.).

123.   Again I have drawn in this section on Milan Kubr (cf ref 109) cf Appendices 1 (pp 721-727) and 3 (pp 735-743).

124.   *Ibid* p 721.

125.   I have adapted Kubr's list cf pp 721ff.

126.   Again I have culled points from Kubr, recast them and added my own.

127.   Wakefield, Gordon S. (ed) *A Dictionary of Spirituality* (London: SCM Press third impression, 1986). Article on spirituality p 361. This approach is modelled in *Analysis and Design* pp 278ff.

128. I am drawing here on an article by Professor Nancy C. Ring entitled "Feminine Spirituality" in Wakefield's *A Dictionary of Spirituality*.

CHAPTER THREE

A Worked Example[1]

This worked example describes a consultancy project about individual and collective vocations in the Methodist Diaconal Order (MDO). (See pp 257-260 and 325-326 for discussions on vocation.) It spanned three years, 1992-1995. Extensive records were kept. A comprehensive evaluation was made by the participants. A detailed account of the consultancy processes was published in 1996. This means that a reliable case history can be produced which illustrates aspects of the consultancy processes and procedures described in this book. In this case the consultant acted as a consultant, co-consultant and facilitator to an organization through working with small and large groups. Members of the Order acquired facilitative and co-consultancy skills in order to get people thinking as widely and deeply as possible—including those whose beliefs and ideas differed significantly from their own. Substantial private preparation was necessary for the public events. The design and structuring of the project evolved through tailoring the initial plan to cope with contingencies.

Consultations were held in several settings. Facilitating team meetings were held in the lounge of the Order's House in Birmingham. The seven members sat in a circle in comfortable seats around lounge coffee tables covered by large sheets of paper on which diagrams and charts were drawn and then pinned on the walls. The meetings started around 11.00 am and concluded about 4.00 pm, the team having lunched together. The "service team", the consultant, Jane Middleton and Hilary Smith, met for the same length of time either in an office in London or the consultant's study. These arrangements facilitated the work and bonded the members of the team as an effective working unit. Convocation (the annual meeting of all the members of the Order including those in training and those retired) took place in the Swanwick Conference Centre, Derbyshire.

I Background: The Emergence of the Methodist Diaconal Order

For over one hundred years within the life of the Methodist Church there have been those who have been called to and exercised full-time diaconal ministry. For most of this period women exercised their ministry through the Wesley Deaconess Order (WDO). In 1978 it was decided to cease recruiting. This was a difficult decision because the WDO had an important place within the life of the Church. Members found this very painful: they could only look forward to the slow and inevitable death of the Order. Amongst the complex reasons for this decision were: the changing role of women in society; the acceptance of women within the presbyteral ministry; the decline in the number of candidates. Eight years later the Methodist Conference, the legislating body of the Methodist Church, decided that the Order should reopen and took the radical step of suggesting that men as well as women could offer as candidates.[2] It became known as the Methodist Diaconal Order.

The events which followed proved this to have been a good decision. During the first five years there was such an influx that the number of students, probationers and those newly ordained equalled those members of the WDO in appointments. Some of the new people were men, many were older candidates who brought with them a breadth of experience.

In 1990 a new and renewed order celebrated its centenary and in doing so there was recognition that the MDO had emerged from the WDO; its history, its tradition and its commitment to servant ministry were gladly owned. But questions were being asked, particularly by new people, about who they were as members of the Order and where they were going. They were questioning their training and their status in the church. They were struggling with basic questions related to diaconal ministry and the Order as a religious order. For some there was a sense of frustration at the lack of answers.

Quite independently, the Methodist Conference (the supreme governing body of the Church) decided that further work needed to be done on the theological basis and the place of diaconal ministry within the whole church. Critical attention was focussed on two basic questions. What is the nature of diaconal ministry? Is the Methodist Diaconal Order an order of ministry and/or a religious order? Some quite radical ideas emerged and gained credence, not least among ecumenical partners. Chief amongst these was that the MDO is an order of ministry in its own right alongside that of presbyteral ministry.[3] Discussions about diaconal ministry were also occurring in local churches, circuits, among presbyteral ministers and within other denominations.

II   The Need for the Order to Think for Itself

While appreciating what was happening elsewhere the Warden of the Order, Deacon (The title now given to female and male members of the Order) Christine Walters, believed that the Order needed to do its own thinking and find answers for itself. Individuals need to be clear about their personal vocation in order to exercise, as they must, their ministry independently. But, if they are to represent the order of ministry to which they belong and to work interdependently and collaboratively within it, they need to understand and to embody its collective vocation and to be caught up in it. Consequently, creative interplay between individual and collective vocations is at the heart of building both effective vocational communities and workers.

Other members of the MDO Staff Team[4] agreed with the Warden. They too wanted to know what those called and committed to diaconal ministry really felt and thought about their vocation. Also, they wanted to know how they were responding to the ideas emerging from the Faith and Order Committee of the Methodist Church appointed to report to the Conference about diaconal ministry. If the church is to think and act as one, official statements and the actualities of diaconal ministry in Christian and secular communities must inform and complement each other. Most people's understanding of diaconal ministry will come from their experience of deacons and deaconesses in the church and in the community not from official church reports. The Staff Team, along with other members of the Order, were convinced that individual members needed to think about their own ideas and feelings, to share them with others, to enter into each other's experience and to consider what was emerging in relation to the way in which, as we noted earlier, the Methodist Conference was radically reshaping the Church's understanding of diaconal ministry and its place in the Church.

III Seeking Consultancy Help

Opening up the discussion in this way was adventurous. It was quite a different approach to the more normal one of seeking to persuade people to adopt a particular attitude. The Staff Meeting realised it was a risky business. It could be unitive, but all too easily it could lead to faction. Significant differences were known to exist between the members about key issues, and some anger, hurt and insecurities led to cries for certainties. The Staff Team felt that the risks had to be taken in a calculated way because it was their absolute conviction that the integrity of the Order, its well-being and effectiveness depended upon all the members thinking through all the issues openly, freely and rigorously in an atmosphere of loving care for each other and those to whom they minister in church and society. They were prepared to take the risks providing that they could get the consultancy help from outside the Order which they felt would help them to handle the potentially contentious issues and maximise the possibilities of them achieving their objectives for diaconal ministry.

Three of them had attended Avec work consultancy courses of the kind described in pp 357-360 and Appendix III. They had been helped to see ways and means of translating their commitment to participation into practice in the Order by working *with* as well as *for* people. They felt that someone committed to the *avec* approach could help them but the other members of the Staff Team had not the experience or the knowledge to make an informed judgement for themselves. Deciding who to invite was such a critical step that the Team rightly decided to approach it circumspectly. Deacon Hilary Smith was deputed to have an exploratory conversation with me about the possibility of my providing consultancy help. (To highlight the consultant's role I will refer to myself as "the consultant".)

She spent several hours with the consultant. They conceptualised the working situation, considered the Team's objectives, modelled alternative approaches to achieving them and discussed what would be involved in the consultant being employed by the Team, including the costs. The consultant suggested that if they wanted to explore the possibility further one way would be for a self-contained twenty-four hour consultative meeting to explore what was involved in promoting the kind of participation they had in mind, and then for the Staff Team and the consultant to decide whether they wished to proceed further with the consultancy. This would mean that, whatever the decision about a consultancy arrangement, the Staff Team would have a project design.

Hilary Smith reported back to the Staff Team. Members responded positively to the suggestions about possible ways of achieving their objectives, the consultancy help that could be proffered and the idea of a meeting to get the information required to decide for or against a consultancy contract.

IV Designing, Organising and Developing a Consultative Process and Exploring Possible Consultancy Arrangements

A twenty-four hour residential meeting was arranged for April 1993 to share ideas, design a consultative process and to provide the information to make informed decisions on both sides about a consultancy contract. By way of preparation for the meeting members wrote notes on their hopes and expectations and things they thought must be taken into account. The consultant prepared a briefing paper which included a synthesis of all the points made.

This formal summary somehow stifled free flowing discussion. So at the consultant's suggestion it was put on one side and the Staff Team members discussed what they wanted the Order to be and to do, to achieve and to avoid. The discussion flowed fast and furious. Members worked in pairs on one aspect or another and summarised their findings on pieces of paper. The consultant combined these to form the collage reproduced in Figure 3:1. This displays clearly the approach of the Staff Team to the work that lay before them. Achieving such a comprehensive and clear picture of complicated issues excited and energised the Team.

A possible consultancy process was sketched out and possible ways in which the consultant could be deployed were carefully considered. The Staff Team and the Consultant agreed to establish a consultancy relationship to work together up to the 1994 Convocation.

It was decided that the Staff Team plus the consultant should be the facilitating team to the Order for the project. This meant that, whilst the consultant was the facilitator to the facilitating team and through them to the Order, he was not the facilitator to the Order: some of *the* facilitating tasks were to be undertaken by members of the Order and others by the consultant. Gradually as the project

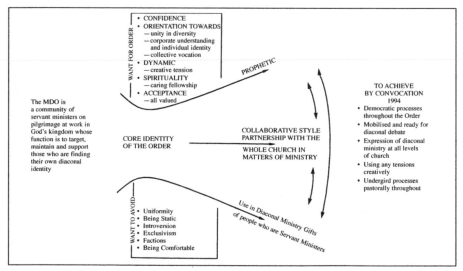

**Figure 3:1 The Facilitating Team's Thinking
at the Beginning of the Process in 1993**

proceeded an arrangement evolved by which Jane Middleton, Hilary Smith and the consultant serviced the facilitating team by doing a lot of background and preparatory work. Clarifying these working relationships was important; staying in role was vital. By common consent the arrangement proved to be creative: it combined internal and external expertise; it developed the facilitating skills of the Staff Team and other members of the Order.

V Developing the Consultative Process

Even though it was agreed, and thoroughly tested by the consultant, that the project was about members thinking things out together, during the early stages, members of the Order in the facilitating team had lingering nagging feelings that *they ought to know the answers*. These feelings persisted even though they knew that the facilitating team's job was to help all the members to find answers together and that they had to find their own answers like everyone else. The consultant got them to examine their feelings. Gradually, as their feeling caught up with their reason, they became convinced that they did not need to know *their* answers to get others thinking for themselves. Once this was sorted out the facilitating team disciplined itself to exploring the issues during their meetings only in as much as it was necessary to carry out the facilitating task; this enabled them to conserve their energies for that task and avoid developing a party line.

The consultant gave a lead in constructing a flow chart similar to that in Figure 3:2 which helped the facilitating team to conceptualise, design and manage the twin central processes: that by which the facilitating team got the members of the MDO to work at diaconal ministry; that by which the members of the MDO worked at the

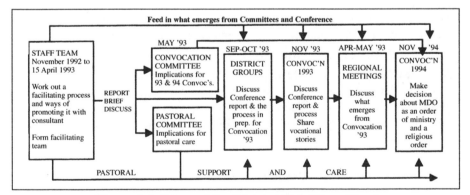

Figure 3:2 Internal Decision-making Flow Chart

subject matter and the outcome. Here we concentrate on the consultative process rather than the nature and praxis of diaconal ministry.

At one of the meetings of the facilitating team, the Warden said as an aside, that she was experiencing considerable difficulties in holding together the various things that were happening. Members expressed sympathy and the consultant encouraged her to expand on the difficulties she was experiencing. Cross referencing discussions about the Order in various courts of the Church with its everyday life, she said, was complicated. All the discussions—those within the MDO and those in the Church at large had implications for the present as well as the future. In some instances these had to be anticipated without presuming what the Conference would eventually decide about the Order. At times this complicated decision making and planning. A simple diagram, Figure 3:3, helped the Warden and the facilitating team to consider the issues. It was realised that some of the difficulties resulted from a tendency to put, at the centre of this diagram, the particular stream of activity which was in focus rather than to hold to the centrality of the essential activity. Also, there was a tendency for the Warden to feel when engaged in one stream that working it out in another was "her responsibility". Whereas, what was involved in doing so needed to be part of any of the discussions because it was part of the reality. Keeping all three in mind helped the Warden and the team to set the consultancy process in context and to work at it holistically. It also helped the Warden to do the same when

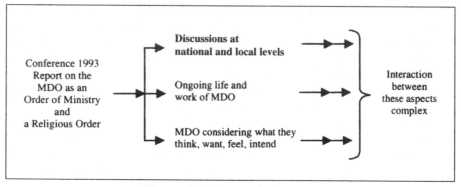

Figure 3:3 Process in Context

she was deeply embroiled in Connexional or domestic discussions. (Later the diagram helped Convocation 1994 to see things in perspective.)

VI Vocational Exploring and Sharing

The consultant and the facilitating team had to expedite three main phases of exchange between the members. The first involved telling and listening to personal stories. The second was considering in regional groups what was emerging from the collection of stories. The third was coming to a collective mind in the 1994 Convocation.

1. Sharing Personal Stories and Testimonies

Each member was encouraged to reflect personally about their own experience of diaconal ministry. Open questions were provided about: their personal calling; how they saw their own future development and that of the Order; what being a member of the Order meant to them and what it enabled them to do and be; their contribution to the Order and ways in which it sustained their ministry. Having done their own personal thinking, arrangements were made for members to share their stories in their District Groups. (These established groups enabled members living in the same area to meet three or four times a year.) In the briefing for this sharing they were encouraged to enter into each others' experience through listening undividedly to each other in turn and discouraged from a general sharing of experience which is quite a different kind of activity. The sharing was presented as a wonderful opportunity to explore their own vocational identity and that of the Order and to dream about the future of the diaconal ministry and their part in it.

Members did reflect and share. There was a small but representative response to the request that notes of what emerged be sent by individuals and District Groups to the facilitating team. Notes were collated and used to prime the next round of exchanges which was at Convocation 1993. This took place in small "mixed" groups, made up of: retired and active members; probationers and students. Now they were asked to reflect on the stories in the light of what was happening in the church locally and nationally and in the world. A person from each group acted as a facilitator and another as a scribe. Reflections of each of the groups were recorded. A summary of the records was presented to Convocation so that every member had an overview of what was emerging from all the groups in order to check that all points had been noted. (The consultant helped to prepare for and service this aspect of Convocation but was not present.)

Two members of the facilitating team and the consultant collated and classified all the points made in the group reports. Care was taken to be comprehensive and faithful to what had been said—wherever possible the phraseology of the reports was used and ambiguities were included. A copy of the paper was sent to every member to give them a picture of the range of thought in the Order. To avoid any idea that it was being offered as the collective thought of the Order it was entitled, "A Collection of Thoughts About the Methodist Diaconal Order".

2. Reflecting in Regional Groups

The next stage was to get members discussing what they felt and thought about what all members were saying about diaconal ministry. Regional meetings were organised in Birmingham, Bristol, London, Manchester and York. Anyone unable to

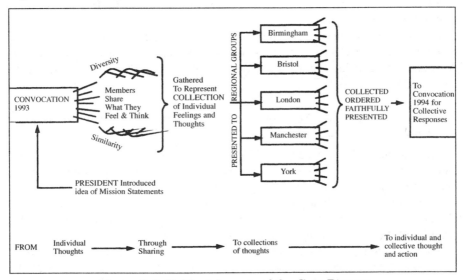

Figure 3:4 Critical Aspects of the Core Process

attend was asked to speak to someone who was, so that their voice could be heard by proxy. These groups considered the collection of thoughts about the Order.

A problem surfaced as the facilitating team prepared for the regional groups. Some facilitators felt that members of the Order could feel that they were being asked to go over the same ground *ad nauseam*. If that happened, it could spell the death of the process. The consultant encouraged the team to grapple with this possibility and the problem of maintaining the momentum of the process. The feeling was caused by revisiting the material several times in order to take manageable incremental steps from individual to collective thought. Nothing would be gained by accelerating this process to avoid the feeling of *déjà vu*. Two things emerged. The facilitating team came to a clearer understanding of the core process. Figure 3:4 shows how this was conceptualised by the consultant. Presenting such a picture of the process to the regional groups, the team realised, would not only stem any negative feelings about lack of progress but enable members to participate in more informed and active ways in the process.

The second thing that emerged was quite different. So far the discussion had been about the Order as an order of diaconal ministry in its own right alongside the presbyteral ministry. Much less attention had been given in the official papers and in the discussion, to the Diaconal Order as a religious order. The facilitating team felt it was important that both issues be considered. To stimulate further thought the consultant prepared a discussion paper, "The MDO as a Religious Order: Some Issues for Consideration".

This enabled the consultant and the facilitating team to plan the regional meetings with great care. A basic "facilitating structure" for the meetings was designed. Members of the team formed themselves into pairs of facilitators. Each pair undertook responsibility for one or two meetings. The consultant encouraged and helped each pair to make the structure their own and to prepare to act as non-directive facilitators. Problems they foresaw were discussed with the consultant and role-played in the facilitating team. Scribes were appointed. Briefing papers were sent out in advance.

By and large the meetings went well. Summaries were made by the facilitators before the meetings closed so that they could check them with the people concerned. Again they were at pains to use the language of the group. The scribes' notes made a mountain of material.

3.   From a Collection of Vocations to Commitment to a Collective Vocation at Convocation 1994

Preparation for the next stage, the 1994 Convocation, meant yet another round of gathering together and making readily accessible to the members the vast amount of material that had emerged from the regional meetings. This gargantuan task was accomplished by identifying principal themes and then clustering together similar points and phrases to get an overall structure. Cutting and pasting copies of the records filled out the structure. Editing produced a briefing paper.

What emerged was a verbal picture of how members of the Methodist Diaconal Order saw, thought, and felt about their own diaconal ministry and about the MDO as an order of ministry and as a religious order. Obtaining a reliable synopsis of the thinking of the Order was, of itself, a major achievement and development. Each member of Convocation could now engage with the thinking of all the members of the Order in ways simply not otherwise possible. And the thinking of the members of the Order could now be compared and contrasted more realistically with that of the Faith and Order Report which set out how the Church saw the ministry and organisation of the Order, the theology upon which it was based and its future. All round, better informed debate and dialogue was now possible.

Originally it had been envisaged that most of the three-day Convocation would be given up to the process of discernment. In the event there were five sessions of one and a quarter to one and a half hours' duration. The problem was how to get upwards of a hundred and fifty people to think through tricky highly charged issues with a realistic chance of them arriving at a consensus. There were several things the facilitating team felt it must do for Convocation which would help to create the optimum conditions for a good outcome.

The first of these was the preparation of objectives for the five sessions and a draft mission statement: it would be quite impossible in the time available for such a large group to produce these for themselves but it would be possible for them to adopt or adapt or reject them. The objectives related to the effective completion of a discernible stage of the process and to getting members to articulate, register and address concerns, issues and conflicts.

At an earlier stage, the idea of the Order producing a mission statement was introduced by the Revd Dr Brian Beck when he addressed Convocation during his year as President of the Methodist Conference, 1993-94. The facilitating team had not set out with the intention that the Order should formulate a mission statement. But, as the process unfolded it came to be seen as a consensus making tool: it gave the process a focus and a goal. Realistically speaking there was no way that the members of Convocation could produce for themselves in the time available the first draft of a mission statement. But, as with the objectives, they could work at a statement to make it their own. So, members of the facilitating team set out to produce a draft statement which best represented the thinking of the Order as revealed by the work done so far. From the words and phrases that had come from the regional meetings a draft mission statement was formulated by Jane Middleton and Hilary Smith with an ease that surprised them and checked out with the consultant against criteria for effective mission statements established beforehand.[5]

Then, the team, and the consultant had to prepare themselves to facilitate the five sessions of Convocation allocated to the process. First they established the overall facilitating structure and then that for each session. Facilitating the sessions was shared, two members taking primary responsibility for each session. But, to do the necessary thinking in depth small groups would be required and they too would need facilitators. These were called "base groups" and "base group facilitators" respectively. Twenty-two were recruited. They were briefed by the consultant before and during Convocation and offered ways of using and structuring the group meetings and dealing with problems they encountered. They, with the facilitating team, became an extended facilitating group. They made enormous contributions towards making the process work and as things went along they introduced important amendments to the procedures.

163

Considerable care was taken in introducing the proposed tasks to the members of Convocation and checking them for agreement. Using Figures 3: 3 and 4 they were introduced to the overall processes. Then using Figure 3:5 they were introduced to what was proposed for Convocation 1994; they already had copies of the draft objectives. Once these suggestions were presented and clarified members went into their base groups to discuss what they felt about the proposed procedures and

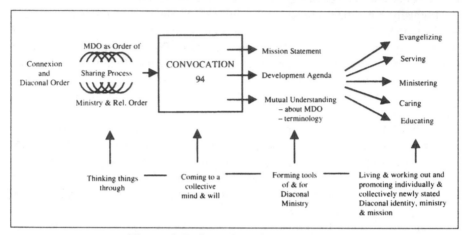

Figure 3:5 Overview, Convocation 1994

objectives and whether or not they would give themselves to the work involved. The proposals were adopted and a plethora of critical issues about the process and the outcome were tabled and dealt with to everyone's satisfaction. Convocation unanimously agreed to get on with the work with a will.

Base group facilitators worked with mixed representative groups of seven/eight people in relation to the objectives, the mission statement and all the other topics. Deciding how to feed back the thinking of the groups to all the members of Convocation was a problem. Verbal reports to plenary sessions by the base group leaders were impractical, there simply was not the time for twenty-two reports and even if there had been time they would have killed the Convocation stone dead! The way we got round this was that immediately after sessions and each evening the facilitators met the consultant. He debriefed them and summarised their reports verbally and in charts and diagrams. Then he made presentations to plenary sessions using an overhead projector and checked them out for acceptability. They did not normally take more than seven minutes. Also, groups displayed sheets summarising their discussions so that members could browse at leisure. The system worked well but it put a heavy strain upon the facilitators and the consultant, not least because the critical sessions were closely clustered.

At Convocation all the issues raised over the two years came into play as the one hundred and fifty members present discussed the mission statement. Thoughts, feelings and adrenaline flowed fast and at times furiously. This was the crucial debate. Much was at stake. A lot had been invested in the process. And members were mindful of a previous attempt to come to a common mind that had failed. They were wary and worried by the possibility of another failure and of the danger of settling for a superficial statement to avoid the appearance of having failed.

The initial presentation to a plenary session of the draft mission statement by Jane Middleton was received with acclaim. (Had it been put to the vote at this point it would undoubtedly have been adopted with a resounding majority. Subsequent difficulties to reach an agreement led some to say that advantage should have been taken of that moment.) Members were asked to consider the statement privately and then in groups, first in relation to content and then against criteria for functional mission statements (see reference 5). This primed a plenary discussion that quickly got at fundamental issues upon which people differed. The discussion became difficult and fraught. Alternative ways of wording and structuring the statement were pressed by some and resisted by others. These exchanges were interspersed with demands for a vote to be taken. There was talk of the "vocal minority" trying to impose their views and will upon the "silent majority" and of the "silent majority" trying to silence the "vocal minority". At this point it seemed that agreement would never be reached. The consultant encouraged Convocation to stay with the process, although it seemed as though there was grid lock. There was a fear that all the work could run to waste. There was a sense of crisis as the confused impasse seemed impenetrable. Anxiety grew that this would be another failed attempt at consensus. Then, providentially, there was lunch! But not for some of the members of the facilitating team and the consultant! They worked frantically to help Convocation to get a better hold on the task.

Over the lunch break they redrafted the statement to include all the suggestions that had been made. Copies were prepared so that each member had a revised text. They decided that the best way they could reopen the discussion was by:

- **summarising what had happened;**

- **offering members of Convocation the revised statement to work on;**

- **reminding them of the nature of the task;**
  (It is not to get everything I think into the statement; it is to get a statement of essentials to which we are all committed and of any issues on which we are not in agreement or undecided about. The statement must be what we think, not simply what I or a majority think. It must be inclusive rather than exclusive. Consequently taking a vote will solve little.)

- **reminding them of the nature of the participation required.**
  (Members need to be engaged in two things: ensuring that the statement adequately represents them; helping to find ways in which the statement represents others, especially those from whom they differed. This is not the time to debate points of difference nor to attempt to convert people to another point of view. Such action is not likely to be successful. This is the time to accommodate not dominate, to gather not divide, to represent not distort.)

Convocation responded very positively to this introduction which was thoroughly tested for acceptability by the consultant. There was a real desire and will to find a way forward—but not at any cost. The consultant did not share the revised statement nor reopen the discussion on it until agreement had been reached about the task and the nature of participation as stated above. As with the first draft, the revised statement was received with approbation. But, again the consultant and Jane Middleton, the co-facilitator for the session, resisted vote taking. Time was given to consider the statement in detail. New points were raised and worked through. The statement was amended until Convocation came to a common mind. Periodically it was necessary to remind people of the task and the approach to it to which they had committed themselves when exchanges deteriorated into a debate.

Quite suddenly it seemed, no more points were being made. The consultant checked out thoroughly whether there was agreement. The latest statement was read

---

DIACONAL MINISTRY:

Diaconal ministry is a way of life which expresses the servant ministry of Christ by the whole people of God to the world.

DEACONS AND DEACONESSES:

- Are men and women called by God to serve in many different ways, offering lifetime commitment, and a willingness to serve where needed.
- Their call is tested by the Church which ordains them to the Office and work of a deacon/deaconess in the Church of God.
- They share with the church in its ministry.
- They work with people in church and community. They exercise caring, pastoral, evangelistic and outreach ministries. Some are Local Preachers; all are able to be involved in the leading of worship.
- They seek to hold in balance in their ministry: worship, prayer, service and personal relationships.
- They seek to develop a lifestyle and spirituality in keeping with the calling to a servant ministry.

METHODIST DIACONAL ORDER:

- Sees itself as an order of ministry and as a religious order.
- It is a dispersed community living by a rule of life.
- It provides fellowship and encouragement, pastoral care and mutual support, prayer and discipline and opportunities for sharing God's vision.
- It trains and appoints its members to exercise diaconal ministry in partnership with presbyters and laity.
- It is a sign and a means of diaconal ministry to the church and community.
- It is a practical, prophetic and educational expression of this form of ministry which encourages and enables others in their ministry.

THROUGH GOD'S GRACE OUR OBJECTIVE IS TO SHARE IN THE CHURCH'S TASK OF WITNESS, MISSION AND SERVICE

Display 3:1 Mission Statement of the Methodist Diaconal Order

166

out two or three times (cf. Display 3:1). There was a deep quietness when we realised we had a result! Consensus had been reached. No votes had been taken. Providentially, a two-year process of exchanges rewarded Convocation 1994 with what at various stages seemed well nigh impossible, an agreed collective statement of the mission of the Order sincerely owned and joyfully embraced by everyone. Truly a high moment of vocational consensus that will be long remembered. We sang the doxology. During the communion service with which the Convocation concluded, a copy of the statement was laid on the table as a sacramental sign of what had been achieved: the Methodist Diaconal Order had a statement to which all could subscribe without any pretence that it represented the totality of their thinking.

The activity which had taken so much effort gave new energy and induced a high sense of motivation. Convocation immediately and eagerly turned its attention to establishing a development agenda and working at various other things. Progress was made on those things which need not be reported here but members had spent themselves and were not able to work with the same intensity.

Looking at this mission statement again four years later, I found myself wondering why it seemed such a great achievement to the members of the Order and to me at the time and what got us so excited. In one sense it is a minimal statement, albeit a hard won one. From the words alone it could appear that the consensus was reached through reductionism. That possibility is ruled out by the passion and emotions associated with the drafting and the collective editing of the statement, the struggling for and the achieving of consensus through it and the way in which everyone took possession of it. The important thing that had happened was that all the members had together experienced a genuine consensus around core vocational beliefs and issues and openly accepted their differences. Their mission statement was highly valued by one and all, not because they thought it was comprehensive and complete, but because it was for them a tangible expression of vital and valued existential realities they encountered separately and together which drew them together and helped them to share their vocation with the church and the world. And that is their passion.

4.   Evaluation of the Process by Members and Facilitators

Members were surveyed at the end of the 1994 Convocation through open questions about each stage of the process. There was almost 100% return. A considerable number were very carefully considered responses. The consultant made a summary of the points made and added his observations. Members of the Diaconate were deeply thankful and excited about the outcome. They placed enormous value upon the way in which, for example, the process had generated "a real feeling of wholeness in mission" and given a "greater sense of belonging together in diversity". They were greatly relieved that they had been able to reach a consensus about a mission statement and terminology to use to describe themselves (deacons and deaconesses but now they are all known as deacons) which was a contentious issue. Overwhelmingly they felt it was an inclusive collaborative consultative experience which was "as near to a consensus as we will ever get in an imperfect world". But there was far less unanimity in their responses about the processes that had been used to gain these results and especially those used during the Convocation. Generally speaking their responses fell into four main groups.

(*a*) **Enthusiasm about the processes and their wider use.** These people deeply desired to see the processes used more widely and consistently in the work of the MDO and for members to gain further experience of and training in the approaches and methods by which it is promoted. They were as excited about the process as the outcome.

(*b*) **Willing acceptance of the process** and the work it involved as a means to an end and the use of it as required.

(*c*) **Reluctant/begrudging acceptance** of the process and the work it involved. These people wish the approach to be used sparingly and then only when there is no other way.

(*d*) **Rejection of the process** in favour of other more traditional methods.

A small but significant group made the (a) kind of responses; by far the largest group variously made (b) and (c) responses; more made (b) than (c) responses; a very small minority of two or three made the (d) responses. Some of those making responses (b) and (c) seemed to be trying to straighten out inconsistencies in their thought. Such people were genuinely pleased about the outcome; not enamoured of the processes which were new to them and the work involved; felt there must be some other way which would fit them better personally; realised all the ways they knew would not have achieved the same result; accepted the outcome wholeheartedly but not the process. They were in fact faced with the challenge of transformational change in their approach to working with people and the theory and theology on which it is based. There is an example of this in a reply to a question about the members' overall feeling about the process.

It was very interesting to experience this way of working and it was a worthwhile effort—but a much smaller representative group could have produced exactly the same result and I'm not sure I would want to go through this procedure for everything, though it certainly makes me feel totally involved and that I can "own" the outcome in a way that would not have been possible otherwise.

What became very clear was that members of the Order differ significantly in their natural desire, aptitude and capacity to work at things in depth analytically and systematically. This threaded its way through the responses. Some found it very stimulating and rewarding, personally, mentally and spiritually. Others found it very hard work to be done only when absolutely necessary. They prefer to seek truth inspirationally, conversationally and devotionally. It is not difficult to see that these different approaches create tensions especially when one or other of them is dominant or in the ascendant. It follows that, whilst certain traditional and institutional functions and events associated with Convocation seem mutually acceptable to members, they differ considerably in the proportions of Convocation time they wish to see given to Bible study, prayer, meditation, worship, fellowship, business and work. The majority see the need for change, a minority are less flexible. Out of all these differences, however, a view was emerging, and gaining wide acceptance, that Convocation must be a place where fundamental issues are worked out collaboratively and openly. At the same time, there was agreement that

Convocation must not become a workshop. The discussion was about the combination of activities at Convocation which will best serve the Order and its members. Clearly the misuse of the working processes will cause all round dissatisfaction, over use will alienate one section and under use another.

All this reveals dimensions of the difficulties likely to be encountered in using this approach in an organization, the faction it can generate and the comparatively few people who are likely to become totally committed to it in contradistinction to those who will tolerate it.

Two months after Convocation the base group facilitators met for a day to evaluate their experience. Without exception they valued being facilitators even though it had been very demanding. They said it had been an "exciting adventure" and a "learning process for local needs". Major disenabling factors were the tightness of the timetable, the physical distance between meeting places and the small size and badly equipped facilitators' room. They appreciated the back-up help they had received from the team and the consultant in facilitating their groups and tackling problems they had encountered with them on the spot. In particular they found the introduction to non-directive group work skills and the questions, tasks and structures suggested for the base groups very helpful. They wanted to increase their facilitating skills and said they would be available for similar tasks in the future. A better grasp of the process, they said, would have helped them as would a preparation and training day for all the facilitators.

VII A Review of Developments and their Implications

After the Convocation the consultant presented his reflections to the Staff Team and reviewed with them the developments that had occurred and their implications. What follows is a summary of what emerged.

1.   Personal and Collective Changes

The Order now has its own mission statement. Members were amazed that they had achieved this and gained new confidence in their ability. Morale had increased. Members felt that their new understanding of the Order and of their own and each other's approach to diaconal ministry would help them to communicate what the diaconate is all about. Some time later someone who knows the Order well commented that the members were listening to each other more carefully and treating each other with more respect.

2.   Insights into the Changes in Convocation and the Order

The evaluation forms referred to earlier showed that members see Convocation variously acting as: a task group; a sentient group; a Bible study group; a spiritual retreat group; a business group; a legislating group; a bonding group; a religious order group; an association of those who belong; a group which reinforces identity through being a place of rituals; a safe place to be what they are. Members differed considerably in the importance they attached to these different facets and the ways in which they should be combined in an ideal Convocation.

Reflecting on these things led the consultant to glimmer that an inexorable transition was occurring through changes in the material upon which Convocation was being asked to work and the ways in which they were being asked to work at it. He presented what he had discerned in the diagrammatic form reproduced in Figure 3:6 (a). Discussing this led the group to clarify changes that were occurring: members were being asked to work at issues to do with the theology and praxis of diaconal ministry, for instance, which had previously been tackled by other courts of the Church; and they were being asked to decide upon them, not by democratic votes but by the much more demanding way of seeking a working consensus. Inevitably these changes led to subtle but deep secondary changes in the nature and character of Convocation. Originally it was seen as a retreat-cum-break whereas a feature of it could now be described as a hard working conference. The first formulation of this in diagrammatic form was a moment of disclosure (cf.Figure 3:6a). Identifying and conceptualising the inner nature of the transition helped to get to the source of members' feelings, to discuss the changes and to decide what response to make and action to take.

All this was symptomatic of the radical changes taking place in the way in which the Order was changing into an organisation which maximises the creative

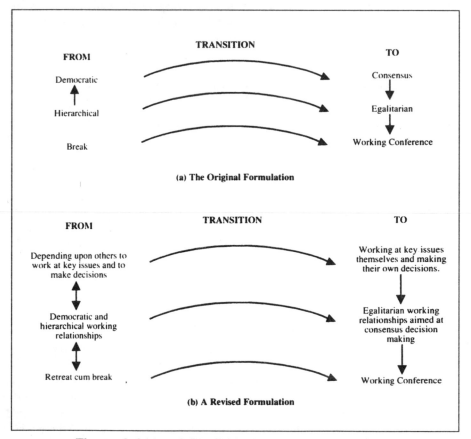

Figures 3:6 (a) and (b) Critical Interrelated Transitions

participation of all its members and groups through the leadership working *with* as well as *for* the members. The changes are all of a part: it is not possible to become egalitarian without thinking and working things through with others. These considerations led the consultant to proffer a revised formulation of the transition which is reproduced in Figure 3:6 (b).

3.   Extending the use of Internal Facilitating Resources

The consultant and the Staff Team considered the new facilitating resources resulting from the project. The Order had learnt and valued ways of using external consultancy help and of developing their own internal facilitating abilities and resources. Three ways of using and extending these resources were considered.

The first related to the facilitating team. The Staff Team felt that it had made important contributions. The consultant asked whether there was a need for such a team to be a continuing feature of the working life of the Order. It would take primary responsibility for promoting and facilitating discussions related to the overall development of the Order and its diaconal ministry. It would perform functions similar to those of a non-directive development worker. The Staff Team felt such an arrangement could be creative. They took some steps towards forming one and asked Jane Middleton, Hilary Smith and the consultant to work out the details of the proposals in a briefing paper. As they got into the task they became progressively more uneasy about what they were doing. Gradually they realised that, to be faithful to the ways of working which were fast becoming accepted practice in the Order, Convocation should have a definitive say in this innovation. So they prepared a report for the Staff Team setting out their concerns and suggestions. The Staff Team agreed. The facilitating team was disbanded and the consultancy contract concluded to eliminate the danger of the original team drifting on and in order that Convocation might have a free hand in considering this idea and any external consultancy help they might require. The idea was put on the Order's agenda.

The second resource results from the formation, preparation and training of a cadre of twenty-two group facilitators. An invaluable resource to any organisation. And these skills are those needed for some forms of diaconal ministry. This needed to be developed.

The third resource was in the evolution of a facilitating partnership, Jane Middleton and Hilary Smith. They went on to facilitate the discussions at Convocation 1995 about the implications of the decisions made at the previous Convocation.

VIII   Consultancy Arrangement Concluded

Considerable progress had been made towards achieving the Staff Team's original objectives. This can be seen quite readily by reflecting on Figure 7:1 in relation to the outcome. What the facilitating team wanted to avoid was avoided: uniformity; being static; introversion; exclusivism; faction; being comfortable. Considerable progress was made towards achieving the things they wanted for the Order: confidence; unity in diversity; corporate understanding and individual identity; a collective vocation; a dynamic creative tension; a caring fellowship; acceptance; all valued. Demonstrably one of their main objectives was realised: to be mobilised and ready for diaconal debate.

The amount of work in proceeding constructively from the articulation of individual vocations, through a shared collection to a collective consensus was enormous. Making a realistic assessment of the time taken would be difficult if not impossible. (Meetings of the Facilitating Team, for instance, took up five days. Making summaries of discussions took several people many days. Then there was the preparation.) It is of the nature of this approach that it is labour intensive. Nevertheless the consultant and facilitating team considered the time and energy was a good investment and they felt privileged to have had the experience.

Members of the Staff Meeting and the consultant felt that this was the point at which to conclude the consultancy arrangement. The Staff Team would be responsible for facilitating work on the implications of Convocation 1994 and for facilitating Convocation 1995.

IX Subsequent Developments

During the next phase the Warden and the Staff Team, in consultation with other constitutional groups took the initiative and responsibility for the facilitating process. They felt that there were several things they needed to do in order to take the facilitating process to the point where Convocation, not the Staff Team, took primary responsibility for its future. Amongst other things, they needed to get Convocation 1995 to determine the next steps to be taken in relation to: a continuing facilitating team; the nature of Convocation and the work it should do; the Methodist Diaconal Order as a religious order; the liturgical role of deacons and deaconesses.

The Team decided to use processes similar to those used for Convocation 1994. It appointed Jane Middleton and Hilary Smith to take overall responsibility for this phase of the work. They decided to draw and build upon the experience and suggestions emerging from Convocation 1994. A briefing and training day was arranged for base group facilitators, but this time they were called "task group facilitators". This proved to be a very helpful day. Facilitators were thoroughly briefed about the overall programme and provided with background information. They looked critically at proposed ways of working with Convocation on the various tasks and improved them greatly by raising issues overlooked by the team.

As in 1994, the task groups were mixed. Given the time constraints and what had been said in 1994 about the pressure of the work, it was decided that it simply was not possible for everyone to work on all the subjects. The work needed to be divided up, two group-work sessions being allocated to each task. Members were asked to indicate their first three task choices. Several groups were to work independently on the same task. Several facilitators undertook responsibility for a task and the groups so that they could work together on methods of working and the timing of sub-tasks and any problems they might encounter.

On the whole the task groups worked well. Some provided a working brief that the Warden could use and pass on to various committees. They did not need to report back to a plenary session. Some of the groups had to submit their work to the

Convocation so that it could make decisions. To use the time available to the best advantage, the facilitators of those groups working on the same task prepared a joint report which one of them presented to a plenary session inviting members to ask for clarification and to add points verbally or in writing to facilitators. Subsequently they presented amended reports for discussion and decision.

There was some dissent about Convocation nominating a new facilitating team. Somehow, members got into the "vocal minority" and "silent majority" syndrome again. After discussion, however, it was felt there should be a new team. With hindsight, the facilitators felt the time allowed and the timing was not ideal for this discussion. There were those who felt that they had been manipulated because the dissent was not handled adequately by the facilitators. The realisation deepened that to work in a collaborative way and to come to a consensus takes more time than had been allocated. Nor had the facilitating team worked out what to do if there was a negative response. Possibly they had fallen into this trap because, as the method had succeeded once, there were two unfounded assumptions: that it would work the next time; that sufficient members had grasped what it means to work towards consensus. Nevertheless, Convocation affirmed that it wished to continue to work in this new way and to develop its ability to do so even more effectively. In spite of the difficulties and partial success members had discerned the importance of the approach and methods and embraced them for themselves and the Order.

Writing in the Methodist Recorder about the 1995 Convocation a recently ordained deaconess, Judith Ashworth, said:

> There is a great sense of being on a pilgrimage as our warden, Deaconess Christine Walters, describes it.
>
> The impetus of the new life of the order is reflected in the new ways of working collaboratively to try and reach a consensus in everything we do. It's not a case of being pulled along or pushed from behind, but of moving together and feeling that we "own" what is happening.
>
> It was last year's convocation that most clearly set us on this course as we prepared a mission statement. This year, rather than focusing on one issue, we worked in small task groups on issues . . . and how we help each other to work collaboratively.
>
> But convocation was not all serious and self-analytical. Much laughter was heard . . . As always, the whole of convocation was wrapped around with worship. We were never allowed to forget who had called us to our vocation, who had called us to meet together and who calls us into the future on our pilgrim journey.[6]

X Reflections in Relation to the Seven Elements of Chapter Two

To cross reference this worked example more directly with the consultancy praxis central to this book, these reflections are presented under the titles of the seven elements of practice theory described in Chapter Two. Considering each of the elements separately illustrates their significance and shows that they are interdependent parts of a consultative system, each necessary to the others. Effectiveness depends upon an integrated consultancy performance of the seven elements: neglect of any element can flaw a consultancy even when there are outstanding performances of other elements.

Element One: Roles (cf pp 35-36).The role that the consultant had to perform was clearly enunciated at the outset. To stay in role he had not to become an advocate of a particular position nor a protagonist in the debate. This was not easy because through the papers and reports produced by members of the Faith and Order Committee and the Order, he had been convinced and excited by the biblical, theological and existential arguments in favour of the MDO being a religious order and becoming a diaconal order of ministry in its own right alongside the presbyteral ministry. Studying the concepts had been a disclosure experience: he saw that his non-directive consultancy work was a form of diaconal ministry. And sharing in the Convocation made him yearn to belong to a community of presbyters which constituted a religious order similar to that of the MDO. All this he had to contain so that his passion actually created the energy required to get members to do their own thinking. He had not to allow his own aspirations, thoughts and feelings about the nature and future of diaconal ministry to compromise in any way his ability to act as a non-directive consultant to the members of the Order: he had not to allow his own views to skew the discussion or to sway the members. Members had to come to their own conclusions independent of what the consultant thought. He had to be a facilitator and to help others to be the same.

Decision making was another tricky area. The consultant was involved with the facilitating team in making decisions about the consultative programme. Occasionally policy matters arose related to the Order in general. As the facilitating team was the Staff Team plus the consultant, it was natural for them to revert to their substantive role without acknowledging that they had done so. The consultant had to be alert to such changes, in some instances barely perceptible, because they signalled changes in his role and function. All too easily he could have acted as a member of the Staff meeting. On one or two occasions he was invited to do so. That would have confused and confounded his role. For instance, he could and did help them to make decisions but he could not and did not take decisions with them as he did in relation to the design of the consultative programme. Whenever the facilitating team reconvened itself as a Staff Meeting, the consultant drew attention to it and his change of role. This was appreciated. It avoided role drift and confusion and/or members wondering what his silence or change in behaviour meant. Vigilance was required. As working relationships became closer and the consultant was warmly accepted, it was tempting to become one of them!

Members of the Order involved in promoting facilitative processes had to resolve some role and function confusion and conflicts. Concurrently they had to come to their own conclusions about the issues and to share them *and* to get others to think for themselves and share their thoughts and feelings. So, for example, they had to share in ways which helped others to think, share and engage in creative dialogue; a very different approach from that which was normally expected of officers of the Order. Traditionally they would have been expected to reach a conclusion and, through strong, directive, charismatic and persuasive leadership, get the members to accept and adopt those conclusions. Some of the difficulties they experienced in being facilitative were noted in the account of the programme. It is highly significant that the facilitators were able to fulfil this difficult composite role, some of them outstandingly, with the remarkable success documented above. Some of the things which helped them to do this are noted in Section IV. The evaluation by the base group facilitators throws light on the enabling and disenabling factors (cf section V:4). Then there was the consultant's role model. Much of this is about how they performed the facilitative role. Less is known about how they combined the dual activities of thinking for themselves and helping others to think for themselves. It could be profitable to research how they did this: what it involved within themselves and in their interaction with others. It would be interesting to know whether women do this more naturally than men and if so how and why. (Whilst the MDO has an increasing number of male members, the membership is predominantly female.)

Element Two: Interpersonal Behaviour (cf pp 36-46). Basic aspects of interpersonal behaviour were in play. Three attributes of this element combined to make the facilitating team meeting, the regional groups and Convocation safe places in which to explore thoughts and feelings frankly and in depth: the assurance of confidentiality; empathic relating; openness and privacy.

Other attributes—the deep desire to secure the freedom of members and consultant to be their own person in interdependent relationships *and* the need to be respectful and humble in critical creative engagement—were major factors in making the interactive process creative and in reaching a consensus. A telling example of this is in the reconsideration of the draft mission statement after the lunch break (Section V:3). Getting agreement on explicit aspects of the interpersonal behaviour prior to discussing the revised draft was key to getting consensus. Even then, as already noted, in the heat of passionate exchanges members had several times to be brought back to the agreed approach to the task.

Practising another attribute throughout—paying attention through genuine interest and single minded concentration and professional curiosity—was of critical importance to the outcome. One example occurred when the consultant realised that the briefing paper into which he had put so much effort (and of which he was proud !) was not galvanising people. There was a heavy atmosphere which he felt and responded to (see Section IV). Another example is recorded towards the end of the same section. Realising that the Warden's heartfelt sharing about holding things together was important, the consultant got her and the group to explore what was happening instead of passing on to the "real business" of the meeting which they were about to do. Much would have been lost had this been treated simply as a sympathetic sharing of stress. Yet another example occurred when all the points made about the first draft of the mission statement were included in the revised draft. This had a considerable impact; up to that point some of the contributors had felt they had not been heard (cf Section V:3).

All round "controlled emotional involvement", another attribute of this element, played a vital part in the whole process. This must have made very heavy demands upon everyone as they were involved in working at issues which had the potential to profoundly affect, positively or negatively, the vocational future, happiness and satisfaction of each member and condition the efficacy and destiny of the Order.

175

Element Three: Working Relationships (cf pp 46-51). To make the programme work significantly different, working relationships had to be established for the duration of the project. Some members of the Order acted as facilitators to other members in the district and regional groups and in Convocation. Facilitators had to adopt co-consultancy relationships with the consultant. Members and facilitators became consultors. There were several desirable consequences of this: the purposes of the project were achieved through the use and development of internal and external resources; members of the Order experienced, tested and came to a judgement about the use of analytical and consultancy processes in their work and in Convocation; some members had hands on experience of facilitative and consultative skills which they now wished to use and develop; the Order increased its repertoire of operational skills; a development unit was established.

Element Four: Work-Views (cf pp 51-71). Much of the reflection and sharing was about the work-views of the members of the Order and about mission statements that properly represented their collective work-view. But the term was not used because it was only later that the consultant started to use it. Had it been available it could have been useful. It would have been interesting to see what the members would have made of it.

Element Five: Thinking Together (cf pp 71-101). All four approaches described in the exposition of this element were used in this project. The consultant was involved in:

1.   thinking things out for consultors alongside them, e.g. facilitating structures and some implications of the evaluation of the process;

2.   accompanying consultors as they thought things out , e.g. the private and group work on their experience of and ideas about diaconal ministry;

3.   promoting and facilitating consultors to think;

4.   thinking things out with consultors.

Approaches three and four were the main approaches in play throughout the project as can be seen from the description above. A number of the technical and analytical thinking aids discussed in relation to Element Five were used.

The work was done in different thinking modes: analysing and designing (particularly the process); meditating and reflecting (at all stages); praying (throughout); formulating learning (particularly through the evaluations and the subsequent discussions of findings); doing theology (the members did exercises of applied theology on their own ministry, the nature of diaconal ministry and the nature of religious life in their Order and the relationship between these things).

Careful attention was paid throughout to "interpersonal aids to interactive thinking" as can be seen from the discussions during the 1994 Convocation. The face-to-face work involved getting people of differing abilities and in varying moods thinking on subjects of vital importance to them on their own and in groups ranging from three to upwards of a hundred and fifty. This called for a range of skills including those related to purposeful non-directive group work—and to establishing and maintaining a complex of interrelated working relationships with different individuals and groups and the boundaries between them.

The backroom work played a key role in helping members to think separately and together about each other's thinking and to formulate collective thought. It involved making representative, classified collections of what people had said in small and large groups or a series of meetings. This was hard and tedious but fascinating work. (Many of these records took two days. Summarising the evaluation by the members of Convocation 1994 was the best part of a week's work.) This back-room work and reflective preparation made enormous contributions to the face-to-face work.

A common cause of failure is the neglect of the backroom and reflective work. Sometimes this occurs through facilitators assuming that *all* really creative work is done in and through face-to-face working relationships with participants. This leads some people, especially those committed to the non-directive approach and good at interpersonal relationships, to over rely on face-to-face work and neglect background work. Doing the kind of work described in this case study requires more not less backroom work.

Apart from greater all-round thinking ability, two things would have made for greater effectiveness. A better understanding by the members of the processes would have enhanced participation. To do this it would have been necessary to overcome the well-known difficulties of communicating the essence and feel of the approach to those who have not experienced it and especially those who have had bad experiences of its counterfeits. The other thing that would have helped would have been agreement in the Order about the respective uses of reaching decisions through consensus and through majority votes — and when and how to move from the one to the other. Late in the process the consultant came across the excellent schema produced by the Uniting Church in Australia.[7] Had this been available earlier it would have given all the participants in Convocation 1994 a way of dealing with the clamour for a democratic vote with more understanding.

Element Six: Systemics and Logistics (cf pp 101-122). Amongst the aspects of this element illustrated by the project are: making and concluding contracts; designing, forming and re-forming consultancy systems, phases and sequences (e.g. Figure 3:2); sculpting sessions (e.g. 24 hour residential meeting in April 1993); the evaluations of the consultancy as a whole; facilitative group work.

The logistics were difficult to manage. Time and again plans had to be revamped to take account of new factors. An example is working to the reduced time available at Convocation 1994. Coping with this stretched the ingenuity and patience of the consultant and the facilitating team almost to the limit, but with hindsight it is clear that had more time been given to this process in Convocation some people would have become disaffected and opted out and others would have found the pressure too great. These restraints were overcome by imaginative and scrupulous planning and preparation geared to the realities of the situations in which the processes were to be promoted.

Element Seven: Beliefs, Ethics, Values and Qualities (cf pp 122-145). Beliefs, ethics, values and qualities infused the subject matter and the consultancy processes in this worked example. Throughout the consultancy processes were engendered through approaches and action which:

- aim to work for the well-being, development and effectiveness of the whole and the parts of constituencies such as the MDO, so *that they are holistic;*

- work with constituencies in relation to the environment in which they are set, so *that they contextualise;*

- take seriously the interaction and interdependence of people and groups in organisations and communities through treating them as systems, so *that they are systemic;*

- promote all round egalitarian participation, so *that they are genuinely participative;*

- facilitate the opening up, sharing, gathering in and enfolding of thoughts and ideas, so *that they synthesise;*

- work for deep seated consensus between as many as possible of those involved and implicated, so *that they are consensual;*

- get people to think for themselves, critically and open mindedly, in the light of as much information as they can handle, so *that they are non-directive;*

- search out what individuals and groups believe God is urging them to be and to do, so *that they are means of theological discernment;*

- promote creative exchanges between people whose beliefs and ideas differ and conflict, so *that they are means of theological dialogue and critique;*

- build up orders of ministry and religious orders and communities so *that they are part of the methodology of pastoral theology.*

These attributes model essentials of the commitments underlying the modes of action and the processes. Combined they embody and create patterns of belief and behaviour. For instance, the processes have the potential to refine democratic processes by moving from the rule of simple majorities towards majorities and minorities working together for mutually acceptable consensual arrangements. That involves enormous changes in attitudes and procedures. A better general understanding of the approach would have helped to reduce some of the confusion surrounding it.

Another significant feature relates to the dynamic for change. Whatever the point of intervention, the interactive consultative process moves through the system in all directions, like blood flows through (and out of) living bodies. So it is not simply hierarchical, from the "top" downwards although, as in this case, the initiative came from the Warden. Neither is it a grass roots upward process. It is by intention and design systemic as is shown by Figures 2:1 and 2 and by the emphasis at the end of Chapter Two on "getting it together", that is, deploying the seven elements so that they interact harmoniously, integrate systemically and facilitate imaginative and constructive action.

Theologically speaking, the model could be described as incarnational and experiential and existential. It is based on the belief that God speaks through individuals as well as through the Church's official pronouncements and that truth is most likely to emerge from broad based open theological dialogue. It is therefore revelatory as well as salvatory and resurrectional, creational and sacramental.

ENDPIECE

Participating in this project epitomized vital aspects of my ministry in ways which for me were deeply significant, satisfying and moving. By one of those meaningful coincidences I was present at the 1978 Convocation as a guest lecturer on the non-directive approach to church and community development. I arrived early and was invited to sit in on the session which was taking place in the conference hall in which the 1994 Convocation met. The business was the future of the Order. Standing in a cluster around the microphone in commanding positions on the platform were the Warden (a Methodist minister who was the only man present apart from myself), the Associate Warden and one or two of the principal deaconesses. As I recall it the substance of what they said was that they did not know what the future of the Order should be and therefore proposed that the Church be asked to decide its future. The decision was made without discussion or vote. I was shaken to the core. I had come to talk about people, individually and collectively, being deeply involved in doing their own thinking and making and taking decisions which affect them and their destiny. Here they were, immediately before my first session, a women's order handing over critical thinking and decisions about their future to male dominated committees.What was happening contradicted everything that I held most dear. My heart bled. My whole being was deeply offended and in rebellion. It was hard not to be in a position to protest. In the next two days I sowed my non-directive seed. Some deaconesses were committed to the approach I was advocating. Over the intervening years deaconesses came on Avec courses and I had various discussions with the leaders. Then in 1992 came the invitation to share in helping the Order "to do its own thinking and find answers for itself". My heart leapt with joy. After all that time, I was given an opportunity to see done, sixteen years later, what I had yearned for in 1978. I had lived and worked through a full circle of the kind for which I continually labour.

NOTES AND REFERENCES: Chapter Three

1.   This case history is based upon and draws heavily upon a published account of the project:Lovell, George; Middleton, Jane; Smith Hilary (1996) *A Process Model for the Development of Individual and Collective Vocations* Methodist Diaconal Order Occasional Paper No. 1 (Printed for the Methodist Diaconal Order by Methodist Publishing House.) That account has been extensively edited to bring out more clearly the consultancy processes and to highlight the consultant's role. Christine Walters contributed an article entitled "To the Circuits: The Methodist Diaconal Order" to the *Epworth Review* Vol 23/1 January 1996 about the MDO as a religious order.

2.   A key document in relation to these developments was: *The Ministry of the Whole People of God*. The Revd Trevor Rowe has described the events and thinking which led to the decision to reopen the Diaconal Order: see "The Re-formation of the Diaconal Order" *Epworth Review* (Vol.24/2, April 1997) pp62-71.

3.   See Faith and Order Report to Conference 1993, *The Methodist Diaconal Order*.

4.   Members of the Staff Meeting were: Deacons Christine Walters (Warden) and Rosemary Bell (Vice-President of the Order); Revd David Blanchflower (Chaplain); Deacon Jane Middleton (Training Coordinator); Deacon Hilary Smith (Pastoral Secretary); Mrs Gill Woolf (Personal Assistant to the Warden).

5.   The criteria were that mission statements must be "portable", *i.e.:* members can carry them around in their mind and recall key features. They must give direction to the organisation and define what it is and does and for whom it exists and articulate the values and beliefs it represents. They must be readily understandable to the constituency with which the organisation wishes to communicate about itself.

6.   *Methodist Recorder* 14 December 1995.

7.   The Uniting Church of Australia has an excellent model for making decisions by consensus. The flow chart they have produced has slip roads which enable groups to take other routes when they fail to reach a consensus. When all other possibilities fail they lead to "decision by a formal majority": cf *A Manual for Meetings in the Uniting Church* (Uniting Church in Australia, 1994).

CHAPTER FOUR

From My Model to Yours

This is a bridge chapter between my experience and yours, between my approach to consultancy and yours. Up to this point, I have been concentrating on an exposition of my approach to consultancy and to being a consultor and a consultant. Throughout, the aim has been to provide information which would enable you to develop your own model of consultancy. You could find my model or elements of it helpful. I hope you do. Even if this is the case, you still have to make them your own. Undoubtedly, as you have read this book you will have been noting ideas to which you feel attracted and those which simply do not appeal to you. You may have been comparing and contrasting your approach to consultancy with mine. Suggestions are made in this chapter which could possibly help you to make the transition from studying my approach to forming and developing your own. They relate to:

- reviewing, clarifying and possibly revising basics of your approach to consultancy;
- applying your approach to a given case;
- the ongoing developing of your praxis through working at challenges and difficulties.

These sections represent complementary ways in which we shape, fashion and develop the manner in which we go about consultancy (and other things as well). On the one hand ideas and personal factors condition our choice of approach. Consciously and unconsciously we select and design ways which are a fit with our beliefs, values and understandings about how things work. We do this by learning directly and indirectly from others, by personalising approaches and methods and by coming up with ideas of our own. On the other hand, what happens when we put our preferred approach into practice can condition and modify our approach. The hard realities of the workplace quickly reveal weaknesses in our methods or in our inability to practise them skillfully enough. Amongst other things thorough going analysis of these difficulties helps us to identify what we did which contributed to the undesirable results and what we could have done to avoid or nullify the effects. Such information is vital to the shaping of approaches which are effective in the rough realities of human and spiritual interaction. So, vocational aspirations and problem solving make critical contributions towards the formation of practice theory which is consonant with the practitioner's beliefs and moral and spiritual values and operates effectively in the realities of the workplace. Effective practice theory is, in fact, a praxis bridge which can carry much two-way traffic between the ideal and the actual. Such practice theory is a made-to-measure working suit: ready-made versions fit where they touch. (Kierkegaard, the 19th century Danish philosopher and theologian, commenting on the white garments referred to in Revelation, said they were starched stiff and fitted where they touched.) This analogy has its limitations like all others. Practitioners, consultants and consultors, have key roles to play in tailoring their practice theory. Reflective practitioners soon outgrow their practice theory suits as the growth of their body of experience and knowledge requires changes in the dimensions and shape of them. Consequently, practice theory is in a continual state of evolution through new vocational insights and challenging encounters with human and spiritual factors.

All this means that what follows outlines a programme of reflective exercises for those of you who wish to develop your own consultancy practice theory and theology. It is a chapter to read and do.

I   Reviewing, Clarifying and Possibly Revising Basics of Your Approach to Consultancy

This section suggests ways in which you might:

1. review and possibly revise your own definition of, and approach to consultancy;

2. review and possibly revise your own consultancy model, and note unresolved issues;

3. articulate the basic elements of your practice theory and what needs to be strengthened;

4. draw up your own codes of good practice and annotate it for strengths and weaknesses.

1.   Your Definition and Approach to Consultancy

Form your own definition of consultancy. Do the first draft straight off out of your head and heart. Re-read the definition given earlier on pp 1, 23, 133 and 147. This could lead you to edit or revise your own. Note fundamentals of your approach in relation to:

— human and spiritual needs;

— consultancy processes;

— consultancy relationships;

— knowing and understanding;

— theological functions and responsibilities;

— theological abilities required;

— spirituality of consultant and consultors.

What emerges may be built into the descriptions of your consultancy model (point 2), your practice theory (point 3) and your codes of good practice (point 4).

2.   Your Consultancy Model(s) and Unresolved Issues

A way to get at the essential characteristics of your model(s) is as follows.

- Review the models noted and described in this book. You may possibly need to research models which interest and intrigue you but which are not fully described (see pp 27-31).

- Describe the model or models to which you yourself are attracted or use or are committed to. There are several ways in which you might depict your model (or models): by describing it in words; by representing it through the use of metaphors and images; by using diagrams and flow charts to represent the dynamics and critical paths of consultancy processes. You might try using a combination of these methods. Then consider your model(s) in relation to the non-directive consultancy model, pp 27-29.

- Consider whether your model(s) has changed through reading this book. If so, how and what influenced or caused the change?

- Describe your approach to consultancy to a potential consultor who has little or no experience of consultancy or, worse, to someone who is somewhat suspicious of it. Apart from helping you to clarify your approach, this is a useful thing to do.

- Note unresolved issues, they are items for your development agenda.

3. *Basic Elements of Your Practice Theory*

One way in which your could discover the basic elements of your practice theory is by listing every point you can think of in a brainstorming session. Having got the list you can then identify key elements and cluster other points around them. (That is how I got at the seven elements of my practice theory.) Then, very much as in relation to models (point 2 above), you could revisit Chapter Two and see whether it has anything to say to your model(s).

4. *Your Codes of Good Practice*

You could adopt the same procedure again: get out your own codes of good practice for consultors and consultants, compare them with those presented in pp 143-145, and, if necessary, revise your own codes to include further thoughts.

II Applying your Model to Given Cases

The previous section suggested you heighten your awareness of the basic principles of your own approach by comparing them with mine. A complementary follow-through exercise is to see what your approach looks like in practice and possibly compare it with mine. You could do this by considering one of your own consultancy projects. Look at the action you intend to take if it is a new project or at that which you took if it is a partially or fully completed project. The action reflects the theory and the theology of your approach. Now do a similar exercise on my approach. Work out the action that you think would have to be taken to put my approach into practice and assess the likely outcome. Compare and contrast your approach and mine to see how both could be improved. You could do this exercise from either a consultant's or consultor's point of view.

A similar exercise could be done on the worked example in Chapter Three. Establish the points at which critical decisions were/had to be made about alternative courses of action. Note the possibilities. Assess what your approach might have led *you* to do as the consultant. Compare and contrast the action you think you would have taken with what was actually done. Another exercise would be to do a similar thing from the consultor's perspective.

This is a systematic, conscious and somewhat sophisticated version of an activity in which we are continuously engaged: comparing the what, how and why of what we do with what others do.

III   The Ongoing Development of your Praxis Through Troubleshooting

No matter how well we practise the art and science of consultancy as consultors and consultants we will continually meet difficulties related to:

- the church and community work subject matter about which we are consulting;
- the consultancy relationships, procedures and processes in which we are engaged.

With respect to the first, Part Two of this book could be useful. But it is to the second group of difficulties that we now turn. By doing so we change the focus *from practice theory* (*i.e.:* that which experience shows makes consultancy effective and that which prevents it from being so) *to unresolved problems* (*i.e.:* to the issues, challenges and quandaries encountered by consultors and consultants as they pursue their practice theory tracks). Moving from practice to problem consciousness takes us into difficulties inherent in the complex human, contextual and spiritual factors associated with seeking, receiving and accepting vocational help and the proffering, providing and giving of it. Some of these difficulties could result from malpractice whilst others could indicate inadequacies in the existing practice theory itself. Thus the approach now adopted is to work from problems encountered back to practice theory whereas in Chapter Two, and to a lesser extent in the previous sections of this chapter, it was from practice theory forward to the action most likely to produce the desired results and avoid or overcome potential difficulties. The result of the complementary, combined and sustained use of these two approaches, the one deductive and the other inductive (cf p 78), deepens our understanding of consultancy processes, builds up our skill in promoting them and refines our practice theory. This section offers ways and means of working at problems yourself and with others. It also introduces the trouble shooting access charts presented in Chapter Five along with notes on some outstanding and recurring issues and problems.

1.   *The use of Standard Solutions*

A skeleton key to dealing with any problem is careful attention to its specific features and especially those which are subtly idiosyncratic. Amongst other things, this means that standard or blanket solutions are to be approached circumspectly. They might well work because similarities as well as differences do exist between a problem experienced by one person and another; but then again they might not. It is unadvisable to adopt them automatically; they need to be carefully assessed for applicability against the peculiarities of the situation. Standard solutions are, therefore, best seen as ideas and suggestions which give a potentially useful starting point in problem solving. *And that indicates the status and significance of the suggestions in this section and later in the access charts.* Undoubtedly, scanning what has helped others and thinking laterally can help, provided that the analytical focus starts and ends with the particularities of the problem being experienced.

2. *Tackling Consultancy Difficulties*

Not surprisingly, the approaches and methods used by consultors and consultants to help them to analyse and design church and community work can be used on consultancy processes to equally good effect.

(a)   Generic thinking stages. Suitably adapted, the eight stages (cf pp 79-83) in creative and imaginative thought can, for instance, help consultors and consultants examine consultancy action which has been taken and to chase out faults in processes and procedures which might be causing problems in projects and programmes.

(b)   Cases and problems. Difficulties normally present themselves in one of two forms. *Cases* are one form. A case is a sequence of events in which the consultor and/or the consultant experienced inter-personal difficulties of one kind or another which complicate, impair or undermine their ability to consult. *Problems* are another form. Problems are generally expressed in terms of "how to do this or that". Cases and problems are differentiated because they respond best to different kinds of analytical treatment. Appropriate forms of treatment are described in Display 2:3. Both are based on the eight thinking stages but formatted in quite different ways. The differences are striking.

   Cases are, of course, problems. *Specific cases and problems* arise out of particular situations and incidents. *General problems and cases* recur regularly in different situations and guises. Dealing with specific cases and problems involves focussing upon their particularities exclusively. To do this, the temptation to focus on other similar cases and problems must be resisted except, that is, to use them to help to understand those under consideration. General application of any findings follows the analysis of the particular. Dealing with general cases and problems is the reverse process. Several examples of the same kind of difficulties as possible are scanned to extract the basic common features that need to be taken into account. This information is formatted in the case or problem solving mode and given the full analytical treatment. What emerges should be generally applicable to the family of cases and problems.

   With any difficulty, therefore, it is necessary to decide whether it is amenable to treatment as a case or as a problem and whether it is best treated specifically or generally in order to use the appropriate facilitating structures. Whether analysing a case or a problem, consultors and consultants are more likely to get to the heart of the matter if they:

- write an analytical note or a record for their own reference of what has led them to be concerned (cf p 88);

- describe whatever they are feeling and thinking as accurately and honestly as possible no matter how unflattering and painful this might be;
- note and review as many explanations as possible of what is happening and any hunches (hypotheses) they might have;
- put their explanations and hunches in order of probability;
- decide precisely what they want to achieve and avoid;
- discover courses of action which are a fit for them, those with whom they work as well as all the above considerations.

The next two sections can be aids to these tasks.

(c)   Brainstorming. Brainstorming is one way of getting information of this kind out of your head and on to paper, possibly in "brain patterns" or whatever way can help you. An example of a brain pattern is given in Display 4:1. Having done this it

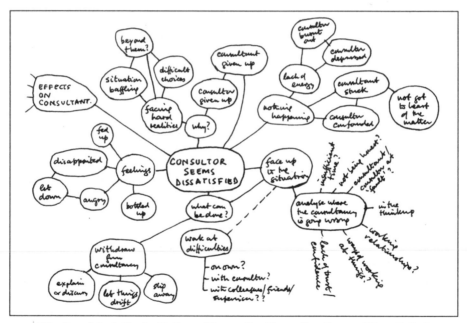

Display 4:1 A Brain Pattern Example: Consultor Seems Dissatisfied

is useful to scan any other ideas you can, either to collect those which you have not thought of or to compare and check out your own list against others.

(d)   Using troubleshooting access charts. Much information has already been provided, particularly in Chapter Two, about possible causes of problems and ideas about possible ways of dealing with them. Some of this information can be located through the extended list of contents and the indexes. That which is not easily located in this way has been made much more accessible in charts in the next chapter. They are after the style of troubleshooting charts commonly found in equipment manuals but with significant differences described in the introduction to

them. They list symptoms of unease or presenting problems, possible causes and suggestions for remedial action. They will serve you best when they help you to bring into focus as many ideas as possible and then, having scanned them, to select those to be used *in your own analysis*.

3.   *Tackling Difficulties On Your Own and With Others*

All the methods in this chapter can be used by consultors themselves on their own or with others. When working on their own they are responsible for structuring their thinking and working things out; when working with others these tasks can be divided and shared.

CHAPTER FIVE

Recurring Challenges and Problems

The first part of this chapter consists of notes on nine recurring issues and problems; the second has twenty troubleshooting charts.

NOTES ON OUTSTANDING AND RECURRING ISSUES AND PROBLEMS

This section contains notes on the following recurring issues and problems.

1. Regretting not being involved earlier
2. Questions about the experience consultants need to have and requests to visit consultants *in situ*
3. Dangers of straying beyond competencies
4. Unacceptable differences in beliefs and values
5. Taking sides
6. Encountering the surreal
7. The danger of drift from consultancy to counselling
8. Some abuses of consultancies
9. Consultancies that appear redundant

1. Regretting Not Being Involved Earlier

Some experiences of disclosure are sweet and bitter. Amongst these are those which reveal how we can achieve something we have long wanted to achieve and how we could in the the past have been more effective. Excitement and joy intertwine inextricably with regret at lost opportunities: the greater the value of the insight and the more painful, devastating, savage and possibly harmful is the regret. Times without number I have heard and voiced the plaintive cries in consultancy sessions as a consultor and a consultant: "How much more effective and useful I would have been had I known that at the beginning rather than at the middle/end of my ministry". "Oh, all this mess could have been avoided if only we had had a consultation a short time ago and all the energy required to sort it out and get back to square one, as it were, could have been used so much more profitably!" [1] Taking the downside of such discoveries seriously is essential because they are potentially harmful to consultors and consultants. Dwelling upon what could have been, squanders emotional energy needed for the present and the future. It can breed all kinds of spurious and destructive psycho-spiritual conditions: remorse, discontent, shame, self-reproach, self-castigation, being judgemental. These undesirable states are not conducive to creative thought and action. A combination of personal and

189

mental and spiritual devices help me to counter it. Brief notes on the devices follow in bullet form.

- Connote the past and future positively.

- Whatever we might now think and feel about our past in the light of new insights, it is that which has brought us to the present window of opportunity. That is the way we came. Nothing we do now can change that route. Thank God that we have been brought to this point and that there is territory still to be traversed in the light of the lessons learnt from the past.

- Our orientation must be to the present and the future: attention must be on where do we go from here and not where did I come from or how did we get here.

- Focussing on the here, now and the immediate future against the background of our evaluation of previous experience helps us to:
  — reinforce our learning;
  — redeem the past (cf pp 129-131);
  — find new vocational life;
  — engage in a new phase of creative reflective engagement;
  — connote the past positively rather than negatively.

- Regret over past actions is both a sign of our fallibility (and our need to accept it) and of our desire for infallibility (which is not an option). Rarely will we get things absolutely and totally right no matter how carefully and prayerfully we consider and consult about them because we are neither omniscient nor omnicompetent and we are prone to sin (cf pp 129-131). Several things follow from these aspects of our condition. Progress is made by refusing to aim for anything less than perfection even though we know that it will not be achieved: idealism needs to be tailored by realism. Developmental initiatives must always be followed by any necessary corrective action.

- Every human project achieves perfection only through God's salvatory work (cf pp 129-131). Our contributions are consummated not in and of themselves but in the work of Jesus Christ: "all things are held together (cohere) in him"; [2] they reach their perfection through his activity in human and divine affairs. At a particularly exciting but insecure and uncertain stage of my ministry the truth of this text, and the passage in which it is set, illuminated my whole being and released me from deep anxiety about the future. By faith and insight I had stepped out of the traditional forms of directive ministry highly favoured and protected by the Church into the non-directive approach to ministry widely unacceptable to the establishment. Where would this risky venture take me and those with whom I worked? How would it fit with the scheme of things? The insights from the Epistle to the Colossians enabled me to see clearly that redeeming and integrating all the pieces of work for human and spiritual well-being was Christ's work and not mine. Once my whole being possessed and was possessed by this article of living faith I was released to give myself without reserve to the work I believed God had given me to do. Of course, I had to trace out, examine and make as many connections as I possibly could with things in the wider setting, but without confusing my contextual and holistic tasks with those of Jesus Christ.

Each of these points has emerged from a lifetime of struggling with my propensity to dwell on aspects of the past which I now regret and to go on blaming myself and others destructively and at times masochistically. During these struggles they have been honed as I have used them to help myself and others to see the issues more clearly and to approach them more profoundly in a better state of mind and heart.

2. Questions About the Experience Consultants Need to Have and Requests to Visit Consultors *In Situ*

Two widely held assumptions about the giving are receiving of help and support run counter to the form oc consultancy described in this book. One of them is that those most likely to be able to understand, support and help you are those who have had similar experiences to yours, had the same kind of job and worked with same kind of people in similar kinds of socio-spiritual settings and have faced the same kind of problems. This assumption runs counter to what was said in the introduction to work-views about people being able to understand each other's inner and outer realities. The other assumption is that direct acquaintance with the consultor's situation is *always* an advantage if not a necessity. Those subscribing to these assumptions can find it difficult to believe that consultants who do not have similar backgrounds and have not visited them *in situ* can possibly help them through studying their work-views with them (cf pp 51-71). They can find it difficult to see how the interactive procedures can get at their realities. Not surprisingly they tend to seek consultants with whom they can identify experientially and expect them to visit their situations.

Relevant Experience

Discussing the assumption about relevant experience with would-be consultors provides opportunities to examine the essentials of consultancy processes. Amongst other things, this involves considering what is the relevant experience that consultants need to have. As we have seen, it is the experience which gives them the knowledge and skills to help consultors *anywhere and at any time* to analyse and design programmes of work with people *whether or not they have direct personal experience of the particular forms of work and the situations in which the consultors are engaged.* Consultants gain such abilities from working and consulting with a wide spectrum of people who differ from them significantly. Their essential expertise is to bring what they know about working with people in general to bear upon the particularities of consultors and the idiosyncratic features of consultors' situations through reflective engagement in detachment.

Undoubtedly, there can be considerable advantages in consultants having knowledge and experience of the kind of work in which the consultors are involved. It helps to build up initial trust and confidence in consultors because it meets the commonly held criteria for the giving and receiving of help mentioned above. It engenders vocational rapport between consultors and consultants. Consultors can feel they are more likely to get help from those who have worked in the field. Consultants are more likely to identify critical areas and know about common problems and issues. But, this kind of familiarity can inhibit penetrating analysis.

191

Consultors and consultants, for instance, can lock each other in single or second rather than in second or third loop learning. Analytical processes stop when consultants collude with statements such as, "You know what it's like".

Pursuing these themes with consultors can help them to understand and try out consultancy processes with consultants from similar and dissimilar background to theirs. For most people, however, understanding of and belief in the consultancy processes described in this book come through their own experience of it or that of trusted colleagues.

On Visiting Consultors' Situations

Generally speaking essential consultancy data is in the work-views which are deeply embedded in the minds and hearts of consultors. Visits by consultants do not generally add much of value. Nonetheless, some consultors are keen that consultants visit them *in situ* or see them at work. Very few consultors have, in fact, requested I make such a visit. But for those who have, it has been an important matter. Invariably, my first response to such a request is to explore with the consultors what they feel can be gained by such a visit and why they feel it to be necessary. Sometimes this leads to new insights and understandings of consultors and their circumstances. It involves going over critical elements of the approach to consulting about consultors' situations through their work-views, and this of itself can be useful. Such a discussion can lead consultors to decide against a visit or to put their request for one into abeyance until they have had a consultancy session or to insist that they do want one.

Should the consultor and the consultant agree on a visit, then the discussion provides a background against which they can explore what kind of a visit could be arranged and to scan the possible positive and negative outcomes. ***Helpful visits*** are those which:

(a)   give consultors more confidence in the ability of the consultants to help them; (such a relational change is facilitative—it allows the consultant's competence to come into play);

(b)   enable consultants to see significant features of the consultor's physical and affective working environment which they had not got from other discussions;

(c)   provide opportunities for consultants to see consultors engaging with those with whom they work and thus to compare and contrast what consultors say about the way in which they relate to people with the way in which they appear to do so;

(d)   lead to what emerged from (b) and (c) being checked out and explored in subsequent consultations;

(e)   cause people in the situations to trust the consultants.

In interpreting the experience it is necessary to take into account that, to a greater or lesser extent, the consultant's presence alters the situation: s/he is not experiencing things as they are when she is not present; her/his observations are those of a visitor; the value of such visits depends upon consultants experiencing or discerning something reliably approximate to "normal".

An incident illustrates some of the issues. Over a period of two or three years, as a part of a wider programme, I acted as a consultant to an Anglican Bishop's Staff Meeting. This was a group of about twelve or fourteen people who held senior posts in the diocese. I led a two-day residential retreat on "shared ministry". Then they invited me to examine the way in which they conducted their Staff Meetings suggesting that I sit in on two or three meetings like a "fly on the wall" and then share with them anything which I felt could improve their meetings. I said that I would be glad to consult with them about their meetings but the way in which they suggested we do this was not the way in which I normally operate. My preferred method was structured discussions with them about their purposes for and and the way in which they conducted meetings and any unresolved problems they might have. They agreed to have such meetings but said that they still felt more would be achieved if I sat in on some of their meetings. The structured discussions were pedestrianly productive. The bishop and the members of the meeting became quite insistent that I sit in on meetings. This I did. One of the important things that struck me was that, whilst their avowed purpose was to facilitate an holistic approach to the work and development of the diocese, the meeting always started with pastoral and vocational matters related to individual priests and churches and ended with overall diocesan matters. I noted that this meant that: individual cases were considered in relation to their own context and not that of the diocese; more energy and quality time was available for individuals than for the diocese; working on a fixed agenda structure meant that meetings were not tailor made to enable them to deal with the particular subject matter contextually in relation to their purposes for the whole diocese. They saw the significance of the points and immediately laid plans to revise the way in which the meetings were structured. Pairs of members, rather than secretaries, became responsible for designing agendas.

Once the case was put it was self-evident. In all probability a similar conclusion could have been reached by studying with the members the structure of the meetings in relation to their purposes. But it is unlikely that they would have responded so enthusiastically. I am convinced that they responded so readily because I had satisfied and proved their criterion by sitting in on some of the meetings. A discussion would have been much more economical (a consultancy session of one and a half to two hours) than sitting in on two or three four- or five-hour staff meetings.

Unhelpful Visits. Generally speaking, visits are decidedly unhelpful when they:

- **fail to achieve the desired objectives described above;**

- **break trust between any of the parties;**

- **engender or reinforce in consultors or consultants any idea that what is encountered and seen *in situ* buildings, people, meetings, events—is any more or less real than what is encountered and seen in consultancy sessions- descriptions, charts, diagrams and models which conceptualise analyses of, and insights into situations, events and designs.** These perspectives on realities are complementary. Insights into the inner dynamics and meanings of human relations and interactions, situations and events are not restricted to consultations. Practitioners can have them in intensive moments of interaction as well as in moments of reflection and in consultations. But wherever they occur their

193

generation depends upon inspired, insightful, reflective and analytical processes operating to good effect upon the relevant observations and data rather than upon physical proximity to the work situation. These processes can be induced equally well by the direct observation of events by "participant observers" (consultants) or by the examination of reliable data provided to non-observers (consultants). Some of us only see the inner pictures through consultations, most of us use consultations to sharpen our insights and models. Occasionally when I have visited a situation long after a consultancy has ended ex-consultors quip about the models and diagrams, "Now you can see what it is really like!". I cannot help feeling that beyond or within the humour they have missed something about the realities of both perspectives.

- **lead consultants (and/or consultors) to assume that they have seen consultors and their situations as they normally are.** See above. The presence of consultants modifies and possibly distorts the way in which consultors behave and the situations in which they operate.

- **lead consultors and/or consultants to give precedence or undue value to the consultant's perspective and deflect them from the central importance of the consultor's work-view.** Visitors can see things of vital importance missed by those who are regular participants. First impressions can be revealing. Nonetheless, it is important to take seriously the status and limitations of the experience and the information it provides. Observations, for instance, are those of an outsider at a particular period which may or may not be representative. Such observations can be useful when they are used to check out, develop or refine consultors' perspectives. They are not helpful if they are assumed to be more reliable and insightful than the consultor's observations.

Display 5:1 sets out some of the things which help, and those which hinder consultants making effective visits to consultors *in situ*. It is based on a discussion in a group of clergy and laity representing three denominations who had had good and bad experiences of consultants visiting them *in situ*. Questions which could help you to plan and evaluate a visit are given in Display 5:2.

3. Dangers of Straying Beyond Competences

The misuse of the non-directive consultancy model can take consultants and consultors beyond their competences. This propensity derives from the universality of this form of consultancy: it can be effectively applied to any situation in which there is, or should be, purposeful interaction between people. Consequently, as we have seen, "consultants" can be "facilitators" of analysis and design in situations of which they have no personal experience and are not conversant with apposite bodies of technical and academic knowledge. (See the discussion about consulting and facilitating). If consultors and consultants do not have these abilities and ignore the fact, the danger of working beyond their competences is ever present. Consultants are more likely to stay within their competences if consultors and consultants:

It would help if:	**It would hinder if:**
— consultants have a good reputation which goes before them	— the arrangements and preparations are chaotic
— consultants gather information carefully but lightly rather than ponderously	— there are references to private conversations between consultants and consultors which give the impression that something is being arranged behind the scenes
— consultants and consultors interact creatively	— consultants come with fixed ideas and exert pressure to get them accepted
— consultants demonstrate an understanding of the situation	— consultants give the impression that they know all about a situation
— there is real openness between consultants and consultors and honest statements of what has been discussed and done beforehand	— consultants ask "What can I do for you?" instead of indicating what they could do
— the meeting is a special not a routine one	— consultants try to sweep people along with their schemes and give the impression of listening only when what is said goes along with their ideas
— the consultant fits into the normally accepted procedures and etiquette	— consultants misunderstand and misrepresent the group and the nature of the relationship between members and insist on their explanations
	— dissonance of language

**Display 5:1 Things Which Help and Hinder Consultants
Visiting Consultors *in Situ***

Outcomes

1. What do you want to achieve through the visit?
2. What particularly do you wish to check out/observe?
3. What do you wish to avoid?

The Kind of Visit Needed

4. What kind of visit is most likely to be effective?
5. Whom do you need to meet? In what setting and circumstances?
6. What do you wish to experience?
7. What pattern of interaction do you need to observe?

Minimising Negative Effects of Your Presence

8. In what kind of a visit is your presence least likely to distort the situation?
9. How will you introduce yourself and explain your visit?
10. How can you prepare people in the situation for your visit?

Recording and Evaluating your Impressions

11. In what ways, if any, do you think your presence affected what happened? How will you compensate for distortions?
12. What struck you? Why? What meaning/significance do you attach to it?
13. Has your view of the consultor and his/her situation changed and, if so, in what ways?
14. What are the questions/issues you now need to consider with the consultor?

Display 5:2 Questions Which Could Help Consultants to Prepare for and to Evaluate Visits

- check whether between them they have the required abilities;
- discuss how the expertise that they each bring can be used most effectively so that the consultor's expertise interacts creatively with the consultant's, *e.g.:* the consultor might select and bring into play aspects which have to be considered *and* consultants might suggest suitable analytical and reflective processes and introduce relevant material about working with people in and through Christian institutions;
- build in safeguards against going beyond their competencies.

Observing such codes of good practice effectively counters the propensity for consultors and consultants to be drawn beyond their competencies by the seductive powers of the universal properties of the the non-directive approach and the momentum of consultancy processes. Consultants (and consultors) are on dangerous ground when they do not know that they do not have relevant information or that it is not in play. If, however, the consultancy subject matter has to do with ways and means of working with people individually and collectively or human relations problems, then the consultant is likely to have the necessary skills and knowledge.

Some circumstances in which consultants are in danger of being taken beyond their personal and professional competence have already been discussed:

- essential data inaccessible to consultant (pp 67-69);

- discerning lack of consultancy potential (pp 116-120).

4.   Unacceptable Differences in Beliefs and Values

Rarely, if ever, will consultants and consultors have identical systems of religious beliefs and human values. Many kinds of differences between them do not present any significant difficulties to their consulting. Discussions about them and the associated action could be informative, enriching and creative. That is all par for the course in consultancy. However, given that consultors' beliefs and values are the reference point for action outcomes, problems do arise for consultants when they find that the beliefs and values to which consultors are firmly committed are unacceptable to them because they take them beyond the boundaries of the inclusivity with which they can live and lead to action which is unacceptable to them. For instance, it is entirely against my beliefs and convictions to take any action which disenfranchises others of their legitimate human and spiritual rights and freedoms. Therefore, I could not with a good conscience offer any help at all to anyone hell-bent on overpowering others and taking away their freedom. Any opportunity to try to convince them that what they were about was wrong and to help them to accept policies of empowerment would be eagerly taken. But I would withhold consultancy help until I was sure that transformative changes had occurred in their beliefs and intentions. In the marginal cases between the acceptable and unacceptable it is desirable that consultants themselves consider:

- those things upon which they and the would-be consultor agree and those on which they differ and whether there is a basis for a consultancy;[3]

- the difficulties they are likely to experience as a direct consequence of the differences; (Differences should not be confused, nor equated with difficulties. Differences can be necessary for complementarity between practitioners, for instance. Differences may not be the cause of the difficulties: racism causes problems between black and white people not the differences in the colour of their skin. Get at the causes of the difficulties which are associated with differences in beliefs and values.)

- when/how/why the differences are likely to cause problems;

- what they think they could do in relation to these differences

197

— before they cause difficulties
— when they are causing difficulties
— when the difficulties have subsided;

- what would have to change in them and the would-be consultor for them to be able to offer consultancy services with confidence of success;
- whether they can see ways of working through the implications of their analysis with the would- be consultor;
- whether they can articulate and examine the conclusion(s) which are emerging.

If consultors find the consultant's beliefs and values lie outside those which are acceptable to them they could use this way of exploring differences and their implications from their perspective.

5. On Taking Sides

To side with or against others is a normal human activity. Like everyone else consultants and consultors have a natural tendency to do this. Generally it is part of an instinctive and involuntary response; a form of learned behaviour. It can happen in relation to any human attribute or action. Dealing with this is an important feature of consultancy work. Consultants need to understand and deal creatively with tendencies that they might have to side with or against consultors or any faction in his/her situation. Doing these things effectively influences their ability to help consultors to understand and deal creatively with their own propensities to take sides in the consultancy and in their working world.

In relation to all this consultants could find themselves in various positions and taking up different stances. Here, we explore a selection of these and their consultancy implications. Some are complementary and may come into play at different stages of consultations.

(a)   Consultants could be in the happy consultancy position of being genuinely neutral. Clearly this is a blessed state in which to find themselves.

(b)   Consultants could attempt to be neutral. This has been widely advocated. If they are not neutral they will have to feign neutrality. That means falsifying their position, living a lie, with all the negative consequences that that can have for interpersonal trust and consultancy processes.

(c)   Consultants could reserve or withhold their position when it differs from that of the consultors without inferring or feigning neutrality. This enables consultants and consultors to concentrate on the consultor's position. It also gives consultants time to consider whether their positions are congruent or incongruent with those of the consultors and the kind of interplay between them which is likely to be most constructive (cf pp 60-65 on the interplay of perceptions).

At times this approach, (c), can be adopted without explanation.Consultors and consultants can concentrate on the consultor's perspective without overt reference to where the consultants stand. At other times consultors can feel uncomfortable when consultants withhold their position: they can wonder just where they stand; they can become uneasy about exposing their thinking whilst consultants are not sharing theirs; they can become preoccupied in second-guessing what consultants are thinking or weighing up whether to ask them instead of concentrating on their own thinking. Some of these possibilities can be dealt with by consultants in various ways: by affirming consultors; by showing that they are broadly in sympathy with the consultor's position without going into detail; by indicating their position in passing so that it is known but does not become the focus of discussion; by going over the reasons for withholding their position and thus disabusing consultors of any fears they might have. But if consultors cannot go on without knowing the consultant's position in some detail and discussing it then they must be given the opportunities they want.

Sometimes when I have been pursuing this kind of approach, consultors have asked me what I think or where I stand before I felt that it would be helpful to turn to my position. Then I have said something like, "I am happy to tell you where I stand and what I feel if it is going to help you. But what is important at the end of the day is not what I think but what you think. My feeling is that we should stay with your thoughts and feelings until we get things clearer. What do you feel and think?" This kind of response can open up important discussions about taking sides and ways of proceeding in and through the consultancy.

(d)   Consultants could take the consultor's side openly when they feel at one with her/him. Professional approval is given to the consultor's praxis and theology through such a stance. Moral support is also given to them as practitioners. Such profound benefits can be of enormous help` to consultors especially when they feel they are very much on their own in situations where the people with whom they are working are in conflict and faction. They can feel justified and reinforced in whatever they are doing, thinking, and feeling. But this powerful admixture of alliance and support is not an unqualified good:

- It can create a relationship between consultors and consultants which is uncomfortably near to a coalition against those on other sides and which inhibits the formation of alliances between consultors and consultants for the common good (cf pp 118-120).
- It concentres the interaction between consultors and consultants entirely on the consultor's work-view which reduces or prevents the creative interaction of their perspectives and the possibilities of seeing things from different angles through other people's eyes).
- The independence of consultants can be compromised or lost and this can reduce their ability to perform their analytical and catalytical functions.
- It can engender polarisation and faction and insidiously infer that all the truth is on one side by promoting a one-sided approach to many-sided situations, issues and problems.
- It can make it more difficult to handle feelings and ideas as objectively as is desirable or required (cf pp 40-41).
- If consultants take sides with consultors, consultors in turn, are likely to do so with consultants and with other people in indiscriminating ways.
- It could hinder a holistic approach to taking all sides into account.

(e)   Consultants who find themselves taking up a position significantly different from that of the consultor can offer it for consideration. This is quite different from

199

consultants arguing against the consultor's position and in favour of their own. It involves consultants submitting essentials of their position for the same kind of critical scrutiny that has been given to the consultor's or anyone else's during the course of the consultation. The objective is to see what, if anything, the consultant's position has to offer to the consultor and, of course, vice versa. Any intention or suggestion of imposing ideas upon consultors must be avoided if there is to be any chance of consultors and consultants modifying their positions in the light of the other's and of them feeling that they have done so freely. Non-directivity is essential to this process which, as we have seen, precludes attack but not confrontation, challenge and being forthright.

Focussing on the *consultant's stance* helps to handle the issues creatively. A profile of the stance advocated in this book is implicit in the notes of the approach just considered and explicit in the seven elements of practice theory expounded in Chapter Two. This stance derives from commitments of consultants:[4]

- to accept the realities of similarities and differences between them and consultors and to seek to understand them and their significance;

- to work with consultors for their good and that of the situation and systems of which they are a part;

- to help consultors to remain their own person and to have good interdependent working relationships with people taking different and opposing sides in order that they are best placed to engage creatively with all parties and factions to promote the common good and to get others to do the same;

- to withhold or deploy or share their own positions (the sides to which they are naturally attracted) to achieve the objectives stated but not to deceive consultors by, for example, feigning neutrality or pretending to hold positions which they do not favour;

- to be true to themselves and their convictions and to use their perspective to promote effective consultancy processes;

- to engage in as wide a range of non-directive inclusive consultancy activity as their own beliefs, values and positions permit;

- to engage in open dialogue with those to whom they cannot in good conscience offer consultancy help.[5]

Being able to explain one's stance can help consultants (and consultors) to clarify just what they are trying to do, the role they need to take and the part they wish to play. Doing this helps them to get into the most effective working relationship with consultors (and consultants).

As problems of taking sides are a common feature of church and community work, tackling them in the ways discussed provides opportunities for experiential learning about alternative ways of approaching them as well as about facilitating consultancy.

6. Encountering the Surreal

A sense of unreality is one of the problems that can arise when the consultancy operates through the consultor's work-view for subjective and objective change.

Examples have already been considered. Consultants face aspects of the problem when what consultors communicate to them about themselves and their situations does not ring true (cf pp 67-69 and 116-118). Consultors experience aspects of the problem when consultants fail to understand, misrepresent or misunderstand how consultors experience their personal and situational realities (cf pp 230-231). Clearly, getting an agreed picture of the realities to be considered is essential to effective consultancy or to deciding that consultancy is not appropriate to the consultor's need. Possible causes for consultants and/or consultors feeling a sense of unreality are:

Miscommunications or misunderstandings between consultors and consultants. Often these can be corrected simply by checking things out.

Realities are difficult to grasp and/or understand and/or describe. Consultors and/or consultants deal with complex realities related to themselves and/or their work. Consequently they are often considering things which they do not properly comprehend or find confusing. Other possible sources of confusion may be: their opinions and understandings are in flux; the essential nature of things is eluding them; they are experiencing phenomena they find difficult to describe to their own satisfaction. Acknowledging and accepting that they are searching for descriptions and understandings which will enable them to work at the realities helps in several ways: it gives consultors and consultants the freedom to be tentative, to suggest and to examine; it reduces the danger of treating hunches which need to be explored and tested as though they were established concepts to be defended; it enables consultors and consultants to make common cause in helping each other to find words, diagrams and models which represent their realities and illuminate meaning.

Consultants are inducing confusion by using/projecting on to consultors and their situations things from similar contexts which are not applicable even though it may appear that they are. Consultors need to get consultants to work to them and to their situation. Consultants need to check inputs for applicability.

Critical aspects of the consultor's situation are outside the consultant's experience/understanding/imaginative powers or beyond his/her empathic range (cf pp 40 and 59-60). Accompanying consultors as they think things out can be a way of dealing with this group of problems (see the second approach to thinking together pp 72-73). Consultants offer moral support, encouragement and reinforcement as they accompany and gain new insights which help them to understand and empathise and if necessary to challenge (cf pp 98-101 on learning together).

Consultors and/or consultants are deceiving themselves and/or each other (cf pp 67-69).

Conceptually and emotionally the consultant may be more in touch with the consultor's realities than s/he is. Strange as it may seem this does happen! At times the spectator can see more of the game than the player. Consultors must not be too hasty in dismissing the views of consultants when they do not tally with their own. They need to examine them carefully. Even if they are not right they may well be catalysts to new insights. Consultants need to offer their ideas as hunches and to do so tentatively and humbly for critical examination.

Consultor's work-views may have no connection with realities outside themselves: they may be psychological or spiritual constructs which do not seem to correlate with the given socio-religious context. Consultants need to assist consultors to find more appropriate help.

These notes can be used as a check list to aid analysis and to help determine what action either party should take.

7.   The Danger of Drift From Consultancy to Counselling

Consultancy and counselling are in the same family of services (cf p 368). Work and personal issues can be complexly interrelated. Providing pastoral care and first-aid counselling can be a proper function of consultancy. Consequently it is all too easy to drift from an appropriate and effective consultancy or a consultancy-cum-counselling/pastoral relationship to an inappropriate and ineffective counselling relationship. Such a movement from consultancy to counselling could occur, for instance, through exploring complex personal and work relationships between a consultor and his/her spouse/partner. The focus of attention could change imperceptibly from :

(a)   practitioners and their approach to their work

   to

(b)   what their spouses and partners feel about the consultor's work and approach to it and the impact of it upon them

   to

(c)   the effects upon practitioners and their work of the attitudes of their spouses and partners

   to

(d)   marital and partnership problems between the spouses and partners.

Changing the focus from (a) to (b) and (c) is within the consultancy remit as long as consultants and consultors continue to deal with factors related to work and vocation which they need to tackle. The consultor's capacity to do his/her work can be increased or reduced or compromised through the factors indicated in (b) and (c). Consultants may well be able to help consultors to think through the causes related to (b) and (c) providing that all that is required is consultancy help or non-directive first-aid counselling. If the focus changes to (d) then the relationship between the consultor and his/her spouse or partner is the substantive issue and not the consultor and her/his work. The exchanges now relate to a different part of the system in which consultors exist. The marriage or partnership sub-system is central and the work is a significant sub-system. Whereas in (a), (b) and (c) the consultor's work sub-system is central and the partnership is a significant sub-system.[6] Moving to (d) represents a change from consultancy to counselling. A different body of knowledge and skills other than those associated with consultancy may well be required which the consultant may or may not have—and even if s/he has the skills it should not be assumed that it is necessarily right for the same person to act as both consultant and counsellor. Therefore, it is unwise to drift from (a) to (d). If a consultancy approaches a (d) position, consultants and consultors need to take stock of the situation before proceeding. Having summarised and clarified the position in which they find themselves, considering the following questions could help them to decide what action to take.

— Is it necessary to move from (a), (b) and (c) to (d) and from consulting to counselling in order to achieve the consultancy objectives?

— If it is, is the consultant capable of acting as a counsellor?

— If s/he is, is it desirable that s/he should?

— If s/he does what will be the likely effects upon, and the implications for the consultancy relationship?

— If the consultant is not capable, how should the marital or partnership problems be tackled and what are the implications for the consultancy process and contract?

Because of the similarities between consultancy and counselling there are several slip roads from one to the other. Consultancy and counselling, for instance, are both caring activities. They work systemically from different but closely connected parts of practitioners' systems in which it is all too easy to move from one focal point to another.[7] Aspects of the outcome of consultancy and counselling are similar. Through concentrating on issues related to work and vocation, consultancy contributes to consultors and their situations in relation to the healing, sustaining, guiding, reconciling, nurturing and developing functions associated with pastoral care[8] and more recently with pastoral counselling.[9] Elementary distinctions between counselling and consultancy are made in Chapter Eight (p 368). There are similarities of approach and method between consultancy and counselling when they are based on non-directive approaches and methods. As these are universal tools in human affairs which can achieve so much, consultants can be seduced into thinking because they are equipped with them they are omnicompetent. This is to be avoided. An awareness of boundaries between allied disciplines and the praxis limits to be observed must not be eclipsed by focussing upon what is common currency between them. Given the intricate connections and subtle differences, it is not surprising that consulting and counselling are sometimes confused and that dysfunctional drift between them occurs.

8. Some Abuses of Consultancies

The aim of this section is to highlight possible abuses of consultancies to which reference has already been made and their harmful effects upon people. Any kind of malpractice and misuse does, of course, have bad effects. To cover all possible forms is simply not possible as it would, for instance, involve examining the downside of all that has been said about good practice. Here our concern is with attitudes, approaches and actions which cause abuse rather than the well intentioned but incompetent or ineffectual or clumsy or unskilful use of consultancy methods.

Some Ways in Which Consultants can Abuse the Consultacy System

- *Consultants can abuse the system by trying to make consultors into something other than what they are or should be.* This can happen when consultants are trying to make consultants think, work, feel in ways which are alien to them. For a discussion of some of the issues see pp 42-45 and 121-122 and Charts I:7 and II:7.

- *Consultants can abuse the system by allowing or encouraging consultors to be unduly or chronically dependent upon them and consultancy sessions.* There could be many reasons for this happening. One may well be that consultants cannot counter or resist the consultor's desire for the security of a dependent relationship. (There is, of course, a proper form of dependence inherent in consultancy when that is a healthy dimension of the consultor's overall interdependent working relationship with the consultant.) The consultant may be encouraging the consultor to be dependent in order to satisfy his/her need to be really wanted and needed, if not indispensible. When there is any danger of this form of abuse consultants need to examine their motivation. They may need counselling help to do so. And consultors may need to do the same.

Whatever the motivation of consultants and consultors and the interpersonal dynamics, the effects of undue dependency are undesirable. Consultors are less able to be their own person. Their freedom to act independently of the consultant is compromised and eroded. They are in a subservient relationship with the consultant rather than a consultative one. Their interdependent relationships with those with whom they work are adversely affected by their dependent relationship with the consultant. Consultants have compromised themselves and their consultancy role. They have forfeited the opportunity to help the consultor to be more constructively dependent, independent and interdependent.

- *Consultants can abuse the system by thinking for consultors when they can and should be doing so for themselves.* This makes sessions into a "thinking *for* you service" instead of a means of consultancy. Of course, consultants do think *for* as well as *with* consultors (cf pp 72-73) but this is quite different from allowing consultors to misuse the thinking services they provide. Amongst the undesirable effects are: consultors can become dependent and lazy; consultants can become indulgent, superior and patronising and prone to controlling and taking over. Relationships, roles and interpersonal behaviour are a travesty of those associated with non-directive consultancy. Consultants have forfeited the opportunity to help consultors to be more constructively dependent, independent and interdependent.

- *Consultants can abuse the system by taking over.* Consultants can take over through consultors being dependent. For a survey of the problems of consultants taking over see Charts I:7 and II:7. They may seek to do so through envy, jealousy or desire for power.

- *Consultants can abuse the system by trying to exercise remote control of consultors and their work situations.* See Chart I:1.

- *Consultants can abuse the system by using consultancies for ends other than those for which they have contracted with the consultor.* See pp 118-120 and Chart I:1.

Some Ways in which Consultors can Abuse the Consultancy System

Generally speaking consultors abuse the system in the obverse way that consultants do. Thus, having noted ways in which consultants can abuse, what follows can be much briefer.

- *Consultors can abuse the system by allowing consultants to try to make them into something other than what they are or should be.*

- *Consultors can abuse the system by being unduly or chronically dependent upon consultants and consultancy sessions.*

- *Consultors can abuse the system by allowing or getting consultants to do things for them which they can and should do for themselves.*

- *Consultors can abuse the system by allowing consultants to take over or to exercise remote control over them and their situations or to use consultancies for ends other than those for which they have contracted* (cf Charts I:7 and II:7).

- *Consultors can abuse the system by using consultants and what emerges from the sessions to get their own way in the working situation and/or to absolve themselves from responsibility for things that go wrong.* They can, for instance, use sessions covertly to get the consultant to agree with their ideas and schemes so that they can use his/her authority to pressurise those in opposition to them to accept. Or they can shunt responsibility for anything that goes wrong unfairly on to consultants. Or again, they can misrepresent to their own advantage what consultants have said (cf p 37). As these things can be, and generally are, done in the absence of the consultant, s/he cannot defend herself/himself nor put the record straight.

Some Ways in Which Outside Parties can Abuse the Consultancy System

One of the ways in which outside parties can abuse consultancies is through establishing or trying to establish "denied coalitions" with consultants (cf pp 118-120). Also they can use consultants as scapegoats without the knowledge of the consultant.

9. Consultations That Appear Redundant

When consultors come to implement ideas drawn up with great care in consultancy sessions, they can find that they do not fit because things have changed or a critical factor was overlooked. This is not an uncommon experience. When this happens, consultors simply must be able and willing to re-think things on their own and/or with their colleagues in relation to the situation as they now experience it. Stubbornly holding to the original ideas and trying to force a fit is foolish and misplaced loyalty. As noted earlier, freedom to work to the new realities is utterly essential (cf pp 121-122). Participants in any consultations must aim for this; consultors must ensure that they are free agents.

Some consultors find that repeated experiences of having to abandon or revise their preparation leads them to question the value of analysing things in depth and working out plans in detail in advance. Surprisingly, a committed reflective practitioner found herself doing just that towards the end of a course on consultancy to which she had made valuable contributions. Others find that their commitment to careful forethought is challenged by those who argue that, as the experience of each human situation and problem is different, it is impossible to get to the bottom of anything with any certainty in human affairs and, therefore, why try? They see little value at all in laying plans for action because the experience of events can be so different from prior thought about them—so much so that, some times, advanced planning appears redundant if not an impediment to the action required. Everything therefore, they argue, depends upon, and must be left to the occasion and people simply have to rely upon their ability to do and say the right thing at the time. These arguments can have a strong emotional pull in church circles even amongst people who use stringent analytical processes in their work. High kudos goes to inspired action and the leading of the Spirit in many sections of the Church.

Outright denial of all this is not helpful because there is some truth in it but insufficient to make even the beginnings of a conclusive case against thinking in advance. Both spontaneous responses and planned interventions have been creative in some cases and destructive in others: both are required in work with people. And there is considerable evidence to show that the ability for creative intuitive spontaneous action in complex dynamic situations can be developed by habitually preparing, training and planning for events even though situations can/do change significantly in the period between one engagement with them and another. One situation (S2) grows out of another (S1). Therefore, even though it is not possible to foresee in advance all the nuances and contingencies of existential realities, reflective practitioners who understand S1s, have decided advantages. It helps them: to appreciate and understand S2s; to discern the changes that have occurred between S1s and S2s and what has caused them; to assess and decide how to adjust to the new situation, S2. So understanding situations at points S1, S2, S3 etc. assists consultors to work with them and the processes of change which make them dynamic entities.

Study is necessarily carried out on situations as they were at the moment when last they were observed and on projections of how they might be when next encountered. Therefore to be realistic, studies of situations must treat them as dynamic not static entities. An important part of the dynamic of change is the thought processes active within the participants and those who influence them. Consultors who have thought their way to a different position introduce new dimensions to any situation. These changes are visible when thinking is shared so the situation will never be the same again and people acknowledge that when they say things like: "You have changed your thinking", "S/he has moved her/his position". So, whatever contextual or material or logistical changes may have occurred in a situation which has been the subject matter of profound analysis, there has been a sea change in the thinking of at least one participant, the consultor, and through him/her the thinking in the situation. At any point, aspects of the thinking may have to be revised. But that is an integral part of the living dynamic of any learning practitioner, community or organisation. So any prior sequence of thought has the potential to influence change through becoming a shared part of an ongoing thinking dynamic even when it has to be altered to meet new factors. On the other hand, if the thinking has been halted and fixed in, say, a plan or proposition, consultors are trying to mesh a static entity with a dynamic one: both must be in motion to mesh. Creative collective action depends upon the thought patterns of the participants synchromeshing.

All the same, those who decide to give time to thought, analysis and planning and to working to the actualities of the changing crucibles of human existence will have to live with the feeling that some thought was redundant, or now appears to have been so. But very often such thought comes into its own later in different circumstances and in unpredictable ways.

TROUBLESHOOTING CHARTS

Notes on Their Status and Use

- These charts are aids to, not substitutes for, analytical thought by consultors and consultants about the particularities of the difficulties they are facing: they are not offered as "quick fixes".

- These charts differ from those in, say, car manuals. Generally speaking it is much more difficult in human affairs to make definitive connections between symptoms, causes appropriate treatment and solutions. Situations vary from each other significantly and subtly no matter how similar they might appear. The casual application of standard solutions is a dangerous lottery. This means that the charts need to be treated as diagnostic tools, aids to analysing a problem and deciding on the action to take: they *do not* provide ready made diagnoses and prescriptions for action. Their function is to help you to identify symptoms, to survey *possible* causes and to think of *possible* courses of action. They are to be used as an indicative check list of possibilities rather than a prescriptive list of probabilities. They will serve you best when they help you to bring into focus as many ideas as possible and then, having scanned them, to select those to be used in your own analysis.

- The charts are displays. They put on show clusters of symptoms, possible causes and courses of remedial action. So they assist people to recall and to scan potentially useful information and ideas. They can facilitate lateral thinking. They place before people material which could facilitate:
  - diagnostic reading of events and situations
  - the identification, understanding and interpretation of symptoms and their implications
  - action decision making.

- The charts would be self-defeating if they made you feel that you were being *told* what your symptoms are, what *causes* them and what *action* you should take. In some places the use of the first person can appear to be doing just that, in other places it has quite the opposite effect. The same is true of impersonal styles of address. So, to make it more likely that the charts read as open possibilities to be

207

tested for fit, the most appropriate forms of address have been used even though this is stylistically inconsistent.

- The charts are meant to prompt thought, to bring things to mind. The proliferation of question marks placed before the points are there as a reminder of this. They represent questions such as: "Is this how *you* feel?" "Could this be a cause of *your* difficulty?" "Would this help *you* to deal with the problem?"

- The charts are *not* meant to suggest simplistic connections between symptoms, causes and remedial action. A difficulty can have several symptoms and causes which are linked systemically not linearly [10] (cf pp 331-334). The columns of the charts contain alternatives; some are mutually exclusive, others are not. Consultors and consultants may well see direct connections between items in the columns in relation to their particular problem. But the charts are not constructed to show invariable linear or systemic connections between symptom, diagnosis and prescribed action. Like supermarket shelves, they are arrays of items, ideas and possibilities, to be selected and collected to be fed into the analytical processes.

- The charts are indicative rather than comprehensive. Hopefully they will trigger off other ideas and possibly get consultors and consultants themselves brainstorming.

- One way of using the charts is to mark or highlight points in all three columns (or photocopies of them) which seem to ring a bell or to be possibilities or have some relevance or challenge you. Extract, combine and edit them to be more of a fit. Reflect on what they and the pattern of connections might be saying.

- One set of charts troublshoots from the *consultor's perspective*, the other from *consultant's*. Therefore they facilitate speculative diagnostic reading of a problem from the complementary perspectives of the consultor and the consultant. (The importance of this is brought out in the discussion on the interplay of perceptions on pp 60-65.) Clearly some of the same points are made in both sets of charts and there is overlap. But there are nuances which reward careful reading of both perspectives on the same problem. Lists of the titles presented at the end of this section demonstrate this complementarity.

- Switching from the consultor's to the consultant's perspective proved to be difficult. But it was also surprisingly rewarding. I found new points emerging relevant to both perspectives. Several times charting from the consultor's perspective led me to radically revise the chart I had already done from the consultant's perspective and vice versa. Eventually I realised that, whatever value the completed charts might or might not have, *making charts of this kind is, of itself, a valuable diagnostic tool*. I found it was achieving some results in relation to tackling problems that did not emerge as readily through the use of other methods. For instance, it made me distinguish between symptoms (experiential and behavioural indicators of the problem) and causes (explanations of the roots of the problem). Therefore, constructing your own charts could help you to examine your difficulties.

THE CHARTS

To give you an overview of the charts and to enable you to find the help you might require, lists of them are given below.

I Troubleshooting Charts from a Consultant's Perspective	**II Troubleshooting Charts from a Consultor's Perspective**
1. Consultants are surreptitiously using consultors and consultancies to achieve ends other than those for which they contracted	1. Consultor's appear to be losing their freedom to explore and/or to decide upon their preferred options
2. Consultants are failing to get consultors to consider seriously ideas and information that could be important to them and their work	2. Consultors are failing to get consultants to take seriously ideas and information they consider to be critically important
3. Consultants feel that the consultancy is not going anywhere	3. Consultors feel that the consultancy is not going anywhere
4. Power failure: consultancy energy loss	4. Power failure: consultancy energy loss
5. Consultants are not keeping up with consultors	5. Consultants are not keeping up with consultors
6. Consultors are not keeping up with consultants	6. Consultors are not keeping up with consultants
7. Consultants taking over	7. Consultants taking over
8. Consultors taking over	8. Consultors taking over
9. Consultors being defensive	9. Consultors being defensive
10. Consultants being defensive	10. Consultants being defensive

I: TROUBLESHOOTING CHARTS FROM A CONSULTANT'S PERSPECTIVE

Symptoms which could be experienced by consultants: warning signals of difficulties, feelings of unease, hunches that things are not as they appear or should be in the consultancy working relationship. **References** to parts of this book which *could* be relevant.	**Possible causes** of the symptoms and **references** to parts of this book which *could* be relevant and helpful.	**Possible courses of action** open to consultants—diversionary, or protective, pre-emptive, remedial—and **references** to parts of this book which *could* be relevant and helpful.

1. Consultants are surreptitiously using Consultors and Consultancies to achieve ends other than those for which they contracted

Symptoms	Possible Causes	Possible action for consultants
? Consultants feel uncomfortable, ill at ease, apprehensive, wary, have a bad conscience.	? In the consultant's mind the outcome of the consultancy is pre-determined.	? On your own or with an independent consultant, supervisor, friend:
? The consultancy dynamic is discordant: the processes are not what they are meant to be and cannot be understood within those terms.	? The consultant is trying to run with the hare and the hounds.	? look at the situation and your diagnosis as honestly as you can.
? In relation to the overt consultancy data the consultant's performance is irrational or inconsistent or reactionary or aggressive.	? The consultant is unable to work with integrity to or through the consultor's agenda because s/he rules out some things which the consultor considers critical.	? decide, articulate, write down what are the root causes of the difficulties: — in yourself — in your relationships with the consultor and others
? The consultant feels s/he must satisfy two parties, one overtly and the other covertly, but to satisfy the one is to disappoint the other.	? The consultant's performance is being perversely influenced by factors extraneous to the consultancy e.g. by his/her commitment to his/her own agenda or that of others.	? establish what has to happen to put things right and whether it is possible and whether you want to do it.
? The consultant feels that s/he is: ? being compromised through her/his duplicity ? a false consultant and friend to consultors ? deceiving and cheating consultors ? acting as an undercover agent ? a double dealer.	? It is simply not possible to meet the expectations of the consultor and others tangential to the consultancy.	? Consider whether or not you can orientate yourself to be an effective consultant to the consultor in relation to all the issues involved and determine the implications of your conclusions.
	? The consultant is trapped in a "perverse triangle". S/he has entered into a "denied coalition" against the consultor rather than an "open alliance" (cf pp 118-120). Inter-alia this means that the consultant is working secretly to what others want him/her to achieve by trying to influence consultors in that direction regardless of their feelings and predilections.	? Examine possibility of getting covert issues into play in the consultancy in ways in which they can be handled constructively by all parties.
	? The impossibility of the working relationship and situation has de-skilled the consultant, undermined his/her self-confidence and self-respect and left him/her unable to cope with or handle the situation.	? Withdraw from consultancy with apology and a full explanation or an indication of reasons (conflict of interests).
	? By taking sides the consultant has lost the independence of thought s/he needs.	? Dismantle perverse triangles and undo denied coalitions.
		? Explain to consultor what happened if it is possible to do so without aggravation of significant relationships and discuss whether to annul or re-negotiate consultancy contract.

211

2. Consultants are failing to get Consultors to consider seriously ideas and information that could be important to them and their work

Symptoms	Possible Causes	Possible action for consultants
? Consultor listens politely to what consultant has to say and, without comment, passes on to something else.	? Consultant's ideas are not relevant or practicable. They only think they are. They are holding on to them:	? Examine your inner feelings/response to the failure to get the consultor to consider your ideas noting those which help/hinder the consultancy process. As necessary use a range of reflective methods (cf pp 86-87).
? Consultants feel/think/know intuitively that:	? because they want to be heard out and to know that they are being heard out	
? consultor is not taking what they say seriously	? stubbornly because any rejection of them hurts their pride and they feel they lose status	? Reconsider your motivation and the merit and value of the ideas and suggestions you have made in the light of the consultor's reactions.
? what they are saying does not command the attention of the consultor	? in desperation because they do not know what else to suggest	
? consultors do not see the relevance of what they say and are ignoring them	? to prove they are right.	? Decide whether or not you should revisit the ideas with the consultor with a view to learning from them and what happened rather than thinking of implementing them. Would it help:
? they are not communicating, getting through.	? Consultant fails to transfer learning (cf p 76).	
	? Consultors are simply not hearing what is being said nor seeing the significance, they are blind to it (cf Johari Window p 300, cf p 264).	? to establish with the consultor the criteria to be met by any proposed action plan
? Consultors say consultant's suggestion will not work in their situation or that they have tried it and it failed or that they themselves could not do it. But consultants are unconvinced: they feel that their suggestions have relevance and potential. Consultors have failed to convince them otherwise.	? Consultors do not acknowledge what consultants says because they are preoccupied with their own thinking.	? to ask the consultor to explain in detail what s/he has done along the same lines in order to see just how and why the ideas did not work
	? Consultors see/glimmer the relevance of the suggestion but block it off because:	? to establish criteria
	? they cannot cope with the work	? to explore the consultor's feelings and reactions and why they occurred.
? Consultants feel frustrated/angry/put down/ignored/being treated rudely or disrespectfully.	? they feel incapable/inadequate	? Raise the problem with consultors and work through it sympathetically and non-judgementally but analytically and critically. It might help if you present the difficulty in terms of, "I was unable to get you to think about this." (cf pp 96-98).
	? significant others (external reference points) would react negatively to them and to consultors even considering them (cf "group think" concept pp 323-324)	
	? they cannot handle the self-feedback induced within them by the very thought of the ideas.	? Explore areas of dissonance you have identified.

? Consultors do not feel able/confident enough to challenge the consultant's ideas so they ignore them.

? Consultants have pressed and consultors resisted to the point where they are both locked in their obduracy and their desire to win. They are arguing not exploring.

? Consultors are defensive because they feel consultants are presenting their ideas in judgemental ways (cf pp 45-46).

? There are communication blockages caused by dysfunctional:

  ? interplay of perceptions (pp 60-65)

  ? differences in preferred learning or operating styles (cf 98-101)

  ? use of approaches and technical aids (cf 73-91 and 96)

  ? differences in the respective rates of thinking and modes, methods and tempo of interaction (cf pp 93-94)

  ? mood clashes

  ? misuse of thinking modes (cf pp 86-87)

  ? use of thinking together approaches (cf pp 72-73)

  ? clashes of work views (cf pp 51-71).

? Consultors are not able to move from single to double loop learning (cf pp 77-78).

? When introducing ideas you need to:

  ? do so tentatively

  ? ask if they fit

  ? say you wish consultors to defer judgement on them until they have been fully explored

  ? ask whose backing/approval is required to make them work and examine how that might be sought.

3. Consultants feel that the consultancy is not going anywhere

Symptoms	Possible Causes	Possible action for consultants
? Consultors give no verbal or non-verbal indicators that anything of value to them is emerging from the consultation.	? The ideas that have emerged will not work.	? Face up to anything that seems outside of the power of the consultor and/or consultant to change for the better: state it, write it down.
	? The problem cannot be resolved.	
? Nothing seems to spark consultors off: their response to a wide range of suggestions is polite indifference or nonchalance; nothing seems to gel, click, galvanise them; they seem imperturbable, impervious to the consultant's inputs.	? Inappropriate thinking mood/mode being used (cf pp 86-87).	? Try to find ways of working at what is happening to and within the consultor as a result of the presenting problems and the consultancy processes as well as working at the problems themselves.
	? Emotional atmosphere not conducive to tackling given subject matter.	
? Consultors seem withdrawn:	? Consultor and/or the consultant:	? Ask consultor if it would help to discuss feelings generated by the problems and the consultancy processes.
? their participation is reluctantly reactive rather than proactive	? is suffering from reactive or referred (from some other situation) or clinical depression	? Ask consultor if s/he feels consultancy is at all useful and if so how and why. (*Note* Considering the consultant's feelings is important especially if his/her performance depends upon doing so.)
? the consultation is experienced as something done to them rather than with them	? is overstressed	
	? is unable to concentrate	
? they act as recipients of, rather than partners in the processes.	? has lost interest/hope	
	? has not the energy required for the task	? Tentatively raise your concerns.
? Sequences of thought do not mature because consultors hinder and halt them by:	? feels beaten	? Review or evaluate consultancy.
	? cannot handle feedback	
? switching to some other problem without explanation in what appears to be a random irrational manner	? is/are out of his/her/their depth.	? Summarise with the consultor the course the consultancy has taken and discuss with him/her the picture emerging and the implications (cf pp 92 and 165)
	? The exchanges are skirmishing around the outer edges of the realities or problems: they have yet to get to the heart of the matter:	
? re-presenting the problem as originally presented in a manner which ignores/disregards/ treats with indifference points made that the consultant considers to have some relevance— it is as though nothing had been said	? clues, information and ideas have yet to be discovered which will galvanise consultors and trigger off constructive analytical processes.	? Consider/discuss whether suffering from reactive, referred or clinical depression and the implications (cf pp 68, 202-203 and 368).
? consultors grass-hopping from one thing to another.	? the consultancy is at the stage of scanning and random brain storming exploration of issues and possibilities and not of constructive, systematic analysis.	? Decide which thinking mood/mode most likely to help (cf pp 86-87).
		? Try to create an approach and atmosphere more conducive to consultancy subject matter (cf pp 83-87).

? Lines of enquiry peter out in a desultory manner.

? Consultors appear to be accommodating themselves to problems which they have come to the conclusion cannot be solved and to situations that cannot be redeemed.

? Consultor is not using the consultancy to find ways of overcoming difficulties but going through the motions to:

  ? demonstrate that s/he is the victim/custodian not the cause of an intransigent unredeemable situation

  ? gain moral and spiritual sympathy and support.

? The consultor needs more time than the consultant to work through the issues and feelings because of his/her personal and emotional involvement, or vocational investment or intelligence or rate at which able to think (cf Charts I : 6 and II 6) and/or because of the risks involved for her/ him.

? The consultor is preoccupied with the inner personal work which will enable him/her to come to terms with the situation and to engage creatively with the analytical processes.

? The consultant is being diverted from the identification with the consultor and the issues which are likely to yield results through his/her being overly concerned with getting positive responses.

? Consultors are withholding positive responses because they feel acknowledgement of indebtedness leads to being beholden.

4. Power failure: consultancy energy loss

This presentation is almost identical to the one from the consultant's perspective Chart II:4.

Symptoms	Possible Causes	Possible action for consultants
? Consultant or/and consultor:	? Consultants and consultors:	? Accept the situation as gracefully as possible without being judgemental of self or others.
? not having sufficient energy for the consultancy tasks	? have spent themselves for the time being, profitably or unprofitably, used up all energy currently available	? Consultants and/or consultors need time/space to reorientate and regroup.
? drained, weary, tired rather than alert	? are experiencing inner dissonance which is absorbing energy dysfunctionally.	? Connote positively what has been achieved.
? unable to get their mind and feelings round the task; losing touch with the process as it slips away from them	? Consultants/consultors are stressed or under-stretched because:	? If consultor and consultant lose energy:
? satisfyingly tired after doing good work	? the challenge of the work is too great or too little	? soldier on in the hope that energy will return
? experiencing the weariness of being beaten	? they are overtaxed/exhausted/worn-out/burnt out/bored	? have a short break, call it a day
? unsure of self and others and judgements	? overwhelmed by the thought of all that is involved	? share feelings and possible reasons for power loss/energy failure and look at implications.
? overwhelmed, paralysed by the enormity of the task	? unmotivated.	? If consultor loses energy:
? struggling for concentration	? They have completed a cycle of work and not got the energy to start right away on the next round of work.	? consultant asks if consultor wishes to continue or not
? working at things mechanically rather than creatively	? The consultor's loss of energy could be related to the thinking tasks or to the post-consultancy action required to follow them through.	? consultant "carries" him/her until a natural break or s/he recovers energy.
? unable to face anymore	? Is the consultor the driving force behind the work under consideration or the consultor plus his/her organization. If the former, is the consultor overly responsible for finding the energy?	? If the consultant, loses energy:
? frustrated by their weakness	? Is the workforce under-powered or the work under-staffed?	? confess it
? disappointed, annoyed or angry with themselves because they have not the energy required	? Is the consultor and/or consultant losing interest in the work or the consultancy?	? continue hoping energy will return
? finding attention and energy diverted from tasks to self and tiredness.	? Is the loss of energy due to the approach and methods being adopted and the moods and modes of participation and reflective engagement (cf pp 86-87)?	? summon up as much energy and will power as possible
? Quality of engagement between consultants and consultors and with the subject matter critically reduced: it is dull rather than creative; self-confidence is depleted.		? concentrate on task rather than feelings of tiredness
? Want to give up/have a rest.		? live off consultor's energy.
		? Consider value of doing energy audit (cf pp 109-111).
		? Take a break or engage in some other activity which will hopefully revitalise consultant and/or consultor.

216

5. Consultants are not keeping up with Consultors

Symptoms	Possible Causes	Possible action for consultants
? The consultant feels:	? The consultant:	? When difficulties occur during sessions consultant can:
? s/he has not got a grasp on the situation and the essential information	? is not able to work at consultor's pace and the consultor is not able/willing to work at consultant's	? soldier on in the hope that things will become clear
? left behind by the discussion, ill at ease, out of it, insecure, not able to do his/her job, letting consultor, self and consultancy cause down	? has not done his/her home work	? seek clarification as soon as s/he feels losing grasp of the situation
? on verge of panicking at thought that this is one assignment s/he cannot pull off	? simply cannot absorb information at the rate at which it is being delivered	? reflect back what s/he is "hearing" and "seeing" and what s/he is not clear about
? deskilled, embarrassed, inclined to let things drift or to give up.	? cannot think through the material at the pace being set by the consultor	? raise with consultor concerns and problem of keeping up
? The consultant assumes/fantasizes/discerns evidence that the consultor:	? lacks confidence to ask for clarification and to check things out	? examine/evaluate what is actually happening in the consultancy session from both their perspectives and determine the implications of whatever comes to light.
? is becoming impatient and dissatisfied	? is intimidated (cf pp 93-94).	? Explore with consultor advantages and disadvantages of their different rates of thinking (cf pp 93-94).
? is confused and embarrassed	? The consultor:	? In preparing for sessions in the future consultants:
? is frustrated, irritated, let down	? not able/willing to work at the consultant's pace; on balance the rewards of adjusting to his/her pace are insufficient	? consider the kind of briefing that could help them to be more effective and sessions to be more productive and act on their conclusions
? is concerned/worried/desperate/disappointed that consultant is not going to be able to help	? is engrossed in his/her own thoughts and not properly attuned to a consultancy dialogue (cf pp 92-94, 207 on "interactive meshing")	? discuss with consultors whether prior written briefing is necessary or whether there is any background material they need to read so that they can get on top of as much information as is necessary before sessions (see p 93 and cf pp 25 and 106-107).
? is feeling that time, energy and money are being wasted	? is not presenting his situation/problem/case in a manner which enables the consultant to play his/her part (cf pp 25, 91 and 106-107 about economic input)	
? may well have to withdraw	? is trying to impress consultant	
? has written off the consultancy/consultant and is politely going through the motions.	? is trying to appear on top of things when s/he is not	
	? is trying to think through things more quickly than is realistically possible.	
	? The consultor is excitedly engrossed in describing and exploring ideas and insights which have come to them in a moment of important disclosure.	
	? There are dysfunctional differences between the consultor's and the consultant's rates of thinking and expressing, exchanging and exploring ideas which are preventing creative dialogue.	

217

6. Consultors are not keeping up with Consultants

Symptoms	Possible Causes	Possible action for consultants
? The consultant finds s/he is grappling with the issues on her/his own: the consultor is either leaving him/her to it or holding back the thinking process by making what the consultant considers to be irrelevant /inane/embarrassing contributions which s/he tends to ignore/ patronisingly acknowledge /feign to adopt them for future use without intending to do so simply to take them out of circulation.	? The consultor has got it right. ? The consultant is unaware s/he could be wrong. ? The consultant is looking for the way forward s/he would take, not the consultor's way forward: attention is on the consultant's solution, not on the consultor's nor the consultor's and the consultant's.	? Leave your own train of thought and turn to the consultor's. ? Ask consultor if s/he needs time to think privately. ? Give the consultor space to think by simply stopping talking.
? The consultant feels/knows s/he has left the consultor behind but simply does not: ? know how to enable him/her to catch up ? have the energy/patience to go back over everything again ? feel it is possible to get the consultor critically engaged.	? The consultant, consciously or unconsciously, is trying to impress the consultor. ? The consultant's thinking is sound whereas her/ his approach to the consultor is not. ? The consultant's thinking is ahead of the things that the consultor has not/cannot/will not see and/or comprehend. ? The consultant is not expressing his/her thinking coherently—possibly because s/he is not clear or because s/he is pursuing a disclosure in the flood of inspirational energy.	? Soldier on in the hope that all may eventually become clear. ? Ask the consultor's permission to complete the train of thought and then to go over it with him/her (see p 93 and cf pp 72-73). ? Ask the consultor if s/he is following—if not explain your thinking and thinking processes until the consultor understands. ? If it is not possible to enable the consultor to catch up, discuss the implications.
? The consultant has evidence/observes/feels/thinks/ assumes/fantasizes that the consultor: ? does not understand what the consultant is getting at ? does not recognise the consultant's picture/ analysis of the situation ? is not on the same wavelength ? feels left behind, out of the discussion increasingly less able to contribute and pursue what s/he considers important ? feels alienated	? The consultor does not understand the consultant's thinking because s/he does not know/ cannot discern the processes and stages of thought which have led him/her to think as s/he does. ? The speed of interchange is simply too great for the consultor to get his/her mind round the consultant's thinking and to digest and assess its value. ? The consultor is not willing/ able/ prepared to do the reflective thinking that is required or that the consultant thinks is necessary.	? Explore with the consultor any differences in their experience, knowledge and thinking patterns and yours and their implications (cf pp 91-96 and 98-101). ? Learn as much as you can from the experience of working with people generally in other situations and help the consultor to do so.
? cannot see how analyses and designs fit the situation and/or how s/he can implement action plans	? The consultor has allowed the consultant to believe that s/he is following the discussion and thinks that what the consultant says is sound/understandable/relevant/practicable.	? Check out your ideas with the consultor for fit (see pp 49-50 and cf pp 42-45 and 121-122).

218

? feels consultant is making things worse instead of better

? is more and more confused

? thinks that the consultant really understands the situation and what to do whereas s/he does not

? feels deskilled/inferior/unsure of self/losing confidence

? feels irritated/confused/resentful/defensive/angry/annoyed with self and consultant.

? The consultant is assuming an understanding of/acquaintance with the body of knowledge necessary to understand his/her contribution which the consultor does not have.

? The consultant is not paying sufficient attention to the consultor and to the interaction between them because s/he is engrossed in her/his own thoughts/confused/struggling to understand etc.

? The consultant's thinking is not sound:

  ? s/he is not thinking realistically/straight/contextually

  ? the consultant has got things wrong/out of focus, made wrong connections by thinking of things that have worked elsewhere rather than concentrating on the consultor and his/her situation.

? The consultor's contributions are:

  ? not useable

  ? useable but not seen to be so

  ? not understood by the consultant.

? There are potentially dysfunctional differences between their thinking processes to which neither consultor nor consultant have paid sufficient attention: they may, for instance, vary greatly in their abilities to think about feelings and ideas (cf pp 72. 96-98).

? The consultant is thinking on his own (cf p 72).

? Thinking together (cf p 73) is prevented by the consultant thinking at a pace with which the consultor cannot cope.

? They may not be using the right thinking mode (cf pp 86-87, 91).

? The consultant wrongly assumes that, providing the right answer is obtained, it does not matter how it is found nor whether the consultor understands how it is found: the consultor needs to understand the answer not the process.

7. Consultants taking over

Symptoms	Possible Causes	Possible action for consultants
? The consultant is behaving as though the consultor's work is his/hers.	? The consultant could be motivated to take over:	? Carefully review your role, feelings, behaviour in the light of your basic responsibilities to the consultor and yourself and take whatever action you see to be necessary (cf pp 35-36, 36-46, 49-50 and 143-146).
? S/he is confusing the consultancy partnership work with the consultor's work.	? through allowing her/his profound and healthy empathic consultancy association with the consultor and her/his work to slip over into unhealthy possessiveness	? Explore with consultors how they are feeling about the consultancy in relation to their:
? S/he talks about "our work" and "our plans" when s/he should be referring to the consultor's work and plans	? by making inappropriate responses to her/his frustrated desire to be in the consultor's position; inwardly the consultant, is taking on the consultor's role	? respective purposes for the consultancy and the contract they have made
? S/he assumes responsiblilities that properly belong to the consultor including decision making.		? roles (cf pp 35-36)
? S/he lays claim to it inspirationally, intellectually, emotionally, spiritually (cf pp 40-41, 198-200).	? through confusing his/her consultancy role with that of a colleague, partner, superior, manager	? interpersonal behaviour (cf pp 36-46)
	? because s/he thinks s/he should be directive	? working relationships (cf pp 46-51)
	? because s/he wants to be in charge	? thinking together (cf pp 71-101)
? S/he takes charge rather than enables, directs rather than accompanies.	? because s/he believes s/he must do so to safeguard the consultor	? understanding of codes of good consultancy practice (cf pp 143-145).
? Consultors:	? through her/his failure to get the consultor to consider ideas and information that could be important to their work (cf Chart I:2).	? As appropriate consider the action suggestions for Charts I:1, 2 and 6.
? are colluding with the take over		
? are pleased to have someone so closely identified with and committed to them and their work	? The consultant is surreptitiously using consultors and consultants to achieve ends other than those for which they have contracted (cf pp 118-120 and Chart I : 1).	
? are responding negatively to the "take over": it makes them feel uncomfortable, unsure, insecure, resentful, angry		
? do not know what to do about the relationship and how to put it right.		

? The consultor could be contributing to the "take over" by:

    ? colluding with it

    ? desiring and encouraging the consultant to become a colleague and encouraging him/her to take over

    ? looking for someone to direct them and their work

    ? being too passive and, for instance, failing to get consultants to consider ideas and information they consider to be critically important (cf Chart II:2)

    ? not keeping up with the consultant (cf Chart I:6 and II:6)

    ? feeling obligated to the consultant

    ? being intimidated by the consultant.

221

8. Consultors taking over

Symptoms	Possible Causes	Possible action for consultants
? Consultors: ? tend to monopolize the consultancy time, "they don't stop talking" ? answer their own questions ? contribute rather than receive: talk rather than listen ? are more open to approval than to challenge ? ignore/dismiss/parry the consultant's input ? dominate the consultancy ? appear unaware of what they are doing and the effects. ? Consultancy sessions are more of a monologue than a dialogue. ? Consultants respond positively to the consultor's energetic engagement with their work but not to the consultor's exclusive preoccupation with their own thinking. ? Consultants: ? respond negatively to the way in which the consultors monopolize and dominate ? are concerned and frustrated that they are not turning the monologue into the kind of dialogue which enables them to make their contribution ? feel their role and function has been compromised and are concerned to make their proper contribution ? are colluding with the consultors.	? Consultors: ? are so excited/absorbed/engrossed/captivated/rivetted by their work and their thoughts and feelings or so nervous about it that they just cannot stop talking ? are inveterate, garrulous extroverts ? are full of themselves ? are confusing owning their work with being possessive about it ? are out to impress the consultant, not to seek his/her consultancy help ? want the consultant's uncritical/unconditional approval and support ? have no intention of making changes to their approach and work ? do not believe/think that the consultant has anything to offer ? does not understand what consultancy is really about and has to offer ? are engaged in a form of defensive behaviour, *i.e.*: keeping the consultant at a distance (cf Charts I:9 and II:9) and in preventing her/him from taking over (cf Charts I:7 and II:7). ?	? Carefully review your role, feelings, behaviour in the light of their basic responsibilities to the consultor and themselves and then take whatever action you see to be necessary. (cf pp 35-46, 49-50, 143-145). ? Make a strong courteous bid for time to raise critical consultancy issues. ? Share and explore with consultors how you are feeling about the consultancy in relation to your: ? respective purposes for the consultancy and the contract they have made ? roles (cf pp 35-36) ? interpersonal behaviour (cf pp 36-46) ? working relationships (cf pp 46-51) ? thinking together (cf pp 71-101) ? use of consultancy time ? understanding of codes of good consultancy practice (cf pp 143-145). ? Consider the suggestions given in Charts I: 1-5, 9 and 10; II: 1-5, 9 and 10. ? Use the experience to help consultors to examine the way in which they operate beyond the consultancy as well as within it.

? feel their role and function has been compromised and are concerned to make their proper contribution

? are colluding with the consultors.

? inclined to give up/have given up.

Consultants:

? are happy with things as they are

? are allowing themselves to be intimidated/ overwhelmed by consultors

? do not want to offend the consultor

? are not able/willing to assert themselves as consultants

? are not keeping up with consultors (cf Chart 1:5)

? do not have the skills/courage/determination/ will to "take on" the consultor

? have given up to trying to make their contribution

? did not make a realistic contract with the consultors

? do not know what to do about the relationship and how to improve it.

? The consultor has a stronger personality than the consultant.

? Consultants and consultors have got fixed in a parody of the mode in which consultants accompany consultors as they, the consultors, think things out (cf pp 72-73, 86-87 and 91).

9. Consultors being defensive

Symptoms	Possible Causes	Possible action for consultants
? In relation to some aspects of their thought/feelings/beliefs/work situations, consultors: ? go on the defensive ? act as though they are under attack ? close the subject down ? indicate the topic is a "no-go area" ? are evasive, uncommunicative ? avoid answering questions, trade in elusive answers ? change the subject ? appear to be withholding things ? do not volunteer information. ? Non-verbal communication through body language and avoidance of eye contact, both of which speak of defensiveness. ? The verbal interaction does not flow in dialogue: consultant's questions/contributions are parried by consultors. ? Consultors hinder attempts to get agreed descriptions of the consultancy subject matter. They: ? are elusive ? make non-committed/indifferent responses to the consultant's attempts at clarification; there is always something not right but they do not help to correct it ? avoid acknowledging/owning/agreeing to a series of descriptions revised in attempts to meet ambiguous objections to previous ones	? The consultor is an unwilling party to the consultancy. (Defensiveness is much more likely to occur in people who have not become consultors of their own volition. When, for instance, they are in a compulsory work assessment scheme or a reluctant member of a group consultancy arrangement. ? Consultors are feeling under attack whether or not they are. ? Consultants *are* attacking, consciously or unconsciously, the consultor or his/her approach/beliefs/ideas/methods/actions. ? Consultors feel vulnerable because: ? they do not want to show themselves up ? there are issues they feel unable to explore with the consultant for fear of not being able to cope/making things worse/revealing things they do not want to ? they fear that disclosing things may adversely affect their relationships with colleagues/the consultant/significant others (cf pp 41-42) ? consultants are raising things they feel unable to consider ? they feel consultants will disapprove of their actions/ attitudes etc. ? The consultor's elusiveness reflects the way in which fundamental critical aspects of the situation elude the consultor and cause her/him to feel unsure/uncertain/ insecure/confused/ defensive. ? Consultors do not give some information because they do not wish to complicate things or because they think it will lead to another round of analysis with which they cannot cope or because they think they can take it into account themselves. ? Issues on which the consultancy is touching are difficult to access because they are buried/rooted deep in the consultor and his/her consciousness. ? Consultors are not free to explore issues freely and openly because of their commitment to a belief system/ a programme of action/ a body of people/ reference groups or people.	? Consider with consultors before a problem occurs how best to deal with: ? situations in which consultors are/feel unable for one reason or another to share relevant information ? any defensive behaviour that might overtake them. ? When consultors become defensive: ? take the pressure off them/"back off"/give them space/do not carry on with or persist with or pursue or proceed with lines of enquiry ? invite, hunt for, maintain eye contact ? give the consultor time and opportunity to return to the subject of his/her own free will ? if that fails and it is necessary to return, approach it later tentatively and humbly so that the consultor is able to decline or pursue the matter without loss of face. ? List the possible causes of the consultor's defensiveness in the order most favourable to the consultor and examine them in that order. ? Examine your thoughts/attitudes/attributes/ feelings/behaviour/verbal non-verbal communications for anything that might possibly cause the consultor to feel that s/he or her/his ideas are: ? not accepted/acceptable ? rejected ? under judgement ? being attacked.

? reject suggestions by making veiled references to their personal knowledge of things and decline to disclose their information. ("If you knew the situation like I do, you would know that that would not not work".)

? There is explosive and dangerous information which must not be disclosed but which must be taken into account by the consultor.

? Confidences are preventing consultors from providing all the information needed: they are struggling with the difficult dynamics caused by the interaction between openness and confidentiality.

? Consultors are finding it difficult to talk about others "behind their backs" (cf pp 41-42).

? The consultor lacks the interactive and verbal skills required to present/discuss/explore one or more of the above causes and their implications with the consultant constructively.

? The consultant is pressing on when the consultor needs time to digest what has emerged and to think through the implications.

? Consultors are understandably attempting to defend themselves appropriately or inappropriately against:

　? consultants surreptitiously using consultors to achieve ends other than those for which they contracted (cf Charts I:1; II:1)

　? consultants taking over (cf Chart I:7).

? The consultor's defensiveness is a cause or consequence of :

　? the consultant's failure to get him/her to consider ideas and information which could be important to them and their work (cf Chart I:2)

　? the consultor's failure to get consultants to consider information they consider important (cf Chart II:2)

　? feeling a consultancy is not getting anywhere (cf Charts I:3 and II:3)

　? power failure or consultancy energy loss (cf Charts I:4 and II:4)

　? consultants taking over (cf Charts I:7 and II:7).

? The consultor's defensiveness is a way of the consultor taking over (cf Charts I:8 and II:8).

? Decide what you can and will do to eradicate/overcome/compensate for these potential causes of defensiveness which are part of what you bring to consultancies.

? Determine what you are learning which would inform your future practice and help consultors to do the same.

10. Consultants being defensive

Symptoms	Possible Causes	Possible action for consultants
? In relation to the consultor and to other interested parties consultants find themselves: ? being defensive ? acting as though they are under attack ? being evasive ? avoiding answering questions ? withholding information ? communicating defensively through their body language and through avoiding eye contact. ? The verbal interaction between consultors and consultant does not flow in dialogue: it is stilted/convoluted/uses defensive mechanisms.	? The consultor is attacking the consultant: ? because s/he feels s/he is losing her/his freedom (cf Charts II:1 and I:1) ? because s/he is unable to get the consultant to take her/his contributions seriously (cf Chart II:2 and I:1) ? because s/he feels the consultancy isn't going anywhere (cf Charts II:3 and I:3) ? because the consultant is not keeping up with her/him (cf Charts II:5 and I:5) ? because s/he cannot keep up with the consultant (cf Charts II:6 and I:6) ? because the consultant is taking over (cf Charts II:7 and I:7) ? because s/he wants to take over (cf Charts II:8 and I:8) ? as a form of defence (cf Charts II:9 and I:9) ? because of significant differences in their approach, methods, beliefs *etc.* (cf pp 92-94, 98-101 and 197-198). ? The consultant is struggling with the difficult consultancy dynamics and the moral confusion related to openness and confidentiality because s/he has: ? entered into a coalition (cf pp 118-120) and Chart I:1and II:1) ? relevant information which s/he cannot reveal and which s/he does not know how to deal with in the consultancy	? Consider with the consultors before a problem occurs how best to deal with: ? situations in which you/they feel unable for one reason or another to share relevant information ? any defensive behaviour that might overtake either of you ? no-go areas ? *etc.* ? Should consultants become defensive they can: ? say they cannot pursue that subject at the present time ? indicate they need space/time ? ask the consultor not to press them on that point/in that way ? share how they are feeling with the consultor ? try to maintain eye contact with the consultor. ? As appropriate consider the suggestions on Charts I:1-9 and II:1-9. ? Examine any propensity you, the consultant, might have towards defensiveness. ? Under what circumstances does it occur? ? How does it manifest itself in your thoughts/attitudes/feelings/behaviour/verbal and non-verbal communications? ? Why do you think it occurs?

? explosive and dangerous information which must not be disclosed to the consultant but which must be taken into account.

? The consultant is not delivering and knows s/he is not doing so (cf Chart I:3 and II:3).

? The consultant is anxious about the possibility of the consultancy adversely affecting her/his relationships with people outside the consultancy *e.g.:* those who have commissioned the consultancy, funded it and those who are expecting to receive help through it.

? The consultant lacks the verbal and interactive skills and/or courage required to present/discuss/explore one or more of the above causes and their implications constructively with consultors and others involved.

? What helps you to overcome it?

? What could consultors do to help you to overcome it?

? Decide what you can and will do to to reduce the incidence of defensiveness when you are acting as a consultant.

II: TROUBLESHOOTING CHARTS FROM A CONSULTOR'S PERSPECTIVE

Symptoms which *could* **be experienced by consultors:** warning signals of difficulties, feelings of unease, hunches that things are not as they appear or should be in the consultancy working relationship. **References** to parts of this book which *could* be relevant.	**Possible causes** of the symptoms and references to parts of this book which *could* be relevant and helpful.	**Possible courses of action open to consultors**—diversionary, or protective, pre-emptive, remedial—and **references** to parts of this book which *could* be relevant and helpful.

1. Consultors appear to be losing their freedom to explore and/or decide upon their preferred options

Symptoms	Possible Causes	Possible action for consultors
? Consultors feeling/thinking/believing/convinced that they are being subtly:	? The consultant simply doesn't understand the consultor and his/her situation.	? Seek help.
? deflected from the course of thought or action they wish to take	? The consultor is hell-bent on a dangerous course of action and dismissive of any attempt to get him/her to reconsider what he/she plans to do.	*If you, the consultor, feel you can/want to continue the consultancy:*
? directed	? The consultant realising/believing the dangers, considers what the consultor proposes to do ill advised and is worried and:	? Discuss your feelings and/or thoughts and/or hunches with the consultant to see whether a mutually acceptable contract and modus operandi can be negotiated. (Generally speaking it is easier to open such discussions with an expression of feelings—or problems—rather than with statements about what you think is causing them or judgements about the consultant's behaviour).
? persuaded against their better judgement/ intuition		
? manoeuvre	? is trying to quietly manoeuvre consultors into what s/he considers to be a better/safer approach without making their position known	
? manipulated		? Continue the consultancy, safeguarding yourself against being deflected by:
? "used"	? does not know how to get consultors to think about alternatives.	
? losing control		? questioning and exploring with the consultant any suggestions which you feel would take you in a direction you do not wish to go
? taken over.	? The consultant is a directive practitioner not a non-directive one or s/he is committed to the non-directive approach but malpractising (see references to the non-directive approach).	
? Consultors feeling/thinking/believing/convinced that the consultants have a hidden agenda.	? The consultant believes s/he knows what should be done and is not open to any other suggestions.	? expressing your feeling of being deflected *etc.* as and when they occur and exploring them with the consultant
? Consultor's input not receiving consultant's full attention and therefore consultor not being helped to develop his/her own thinking.	? The consultant is trying to serve someone else's agenda as well as or instead of or through the consultant's. S/he may, for instance , be trapped in and acting out of a "perverse triangle" through entering into by design or default, a "denied coalition" against the consultor which prevents her/him from working with the consultor in an "open alliance" (see pp 118-120).	? asking the consultant to say what made him/her make a particular suggestion.
? Consultant seems preoccupied with other ideas.		*If you, the consultor, feel you cannot/do not want to continue:*
? Consultor feels s/he not her/his own person (cf pp 42-45).	? The consultant may be confusing her/his role with that of a tutor, supervisor, manager (see pp 35-36).	? free wheel through what remains of the contract
		? withdraw without explanation
		? withdraw after discussing with the consultant your reasons for doing so.

2. Consultors are failing to get Consultants to take seriously ideas and information they consider to be critically important

Symptoms	Possible Causes	Possible action for consultors
? Consultants listen politely to what consultors have to say and without comment pass on to something else.	? Consultant considers consultor's ideas are not relevant or practicable but does not know how to say so without adversely affecting the working relationship.	? Examine your inner feelings/responses to the failure to get the consultant to consider your ideas noting those which help/hinder the consultancy process. As necessary use a range of reflective methods (cf pp 86-87).
? Consultors feel/think/know that:		
? consultants are not taking what they say seriously even though they are complementary about it	? Consultant is simply not hearing what is being said nor seeing its significance because s/he is blind to it (cf Johari Window p 300, cf p 264).	? Reconsider the merit and value of the ideas and suggestions themselves in the light of the consultant's reaction.
? what they are saying does not command the attention of the consultant	? Consultants are not hearing/acknowledging what consultors are saying because they are preoccupied with their own thinking.	? Decide whether or not you should revisit the ideas with the consultant with a view to learning from them together about what happened rather than thinking of implementing them, if you decide to do so, would it help:
? consultants do not see the relevance of what they are saying	? Consultors are holding on to their ideas because:	
? they are not communicating, getting through.	? they want to be heard out and to know that they are heard out	? to establish beforehand with the consultant the criteria to be met by any proposed action?
? Consultants say consultors' suggestion will not work in their situation or that they have tried it and it failed or that they could not do it. But consultors are unconvinced: they feel that their suggestions have relevance and potential , consultants have failed to convince them otherwise.	? rejection of them hurts their pride	
	? those with whom they work are deeply committed to them and will not be easily persuaded to drop them	? to ask and help the consultant to articulate his/her reservations and to examine with him/her precisely how and why the ideas are likely to fail?
	? they want to prove they are right.	
? Consultors feel frustrated/angry/put down/ignored or that they are being treated rudely or disrespectfully.	? Consultants see/glimmer the relevance of the suggestion but block them off because:	? to explore the consultant's feelings and reactions and why they occurred?
	? they are wary of them instinctively but cannot say why	? Raise the problem with consultant and work through it sympathetically but analytically. It might help if consultors or consultants present the difficulty in terms of, "I was unable to get you to consider this." rather than, "You were unable to think about this" (cf pp 96-98).
	? they cannot face all that is involved in examining them thoroughly.	
	? Consultors have pressed and consultants resisted to the point where they are both locked in their obduracy and desire to win: they are arguing not exploring.	? Explore areas of dissonance you have identified.

230

? There are communication blockages caused by dysfunctional:

? interplay of perceptions (pp 60-65)

? differences in preferred learning/operating styles (cf pp 98-101)

? use of approaches and technical aids (cf pp 73-91 and 96)

? differences in the respective rates of thinking and modes, methods and tempo of interaction (cf pp 93-94)

? mood clashes

? misuse of thinking moods and modes (cf pp 86-87)

? inappropriate use of thinking together approaches (cf pp 72-73)

? clashes of work views (cf pp 51-71).

? Consultants,and possibly consultors, are unable to move from single to double loop learning (cf pp 77-78).

3. Consultors feel that the consultancy is not going anywhere

Symptoms	Possible Causes	Possible action for consultors
? The consultant does not convince the consultor that s/he understands the consultor/the situation/the issues or that s/he has a grasp upon the consultancy subject matter or processes. ? Consultants give no verbal or non-verbal indications to consultors that anything of value to them is emerging from the consultation. ? Nothing seems to spark consultants off: their response to a wide range of suggestions is polite indifference or nonchalance; nothing seems to gel, click, galvanise them; they seem imperturbable, impervious to the consultor's input. ? Consultants seem withdrawn: ? their participation is reactive rather than proactive ? the consultation appears to be something done to them rather than with them ? they act as passive rather than active partners in the processes. ? Sequences of thought do not mature because consultants hinder and halt them by: ? switching to some other problem without explanation in what appears to be a random irrational manner ? re-presenting the problem as originally presented in a manner which ignores/disregards/treats with indifference points made that the consultor considers to have some relevance—it is as though nothing had been said	? Consultant does not understand the situation/cannot get his/her mind around it/ does not retain sufficient detailed information long enough to be a creative partner in the consultative process. ? The ideas that have emerged will not work. ? Inappropriate thinking mood/mode being used (cf pp 86-87). ? The problem cannot be resolved. ? The emotional atmosphere is not conducive to tackling the given subject matter (cf pp 83-86). ? Consultant and/or the consultor: ? is suffering from reactive or referred (from some other situation) or clinical depression ? is overstressed ? is unable to concentrate ? has lost interest/hope ? has not the energy required for the task ? feels beaten ? cannot handle feedback ? is out of his/her depth ? is preoccupied with other things. ? The exchanges are skirmishing around the outer edges of the realities or problems, they have yet to get to the heart of the matter.	? Face up to anything that seems outside of the power of the consultor and/or consultant to change for the better : state it, write it down. ? Try to find ways of working at what is happening to and within the consultant's and the consultancy processes as well as at the problems themselves. ? Ask consultant if it would help to discuss any feelings generated by the problem and the consultancy processes. ? Ask consultant if s/he feels consultancy is at all useful and if so how and why. (*Note* Considering the consultant's feelings is important if his/her performance depends upon doing so.) ? Consultor tentatively raises his/her concerns. ? Review or evaluate consultancy. ? Consultor summarises with the consultant the course the consultancy has taken and discusses with him/her the picture emerging and the implications (cf pp 91-92, 165). ? Consider/discuss whether consultant is suffering from reactive, referred or clinical depression and the implications of this (cf pp 68, 202-203 and 368). ? Consider which thinking mood or mode is most likely to be helpful (cf pp 86-87, 91). ? Try to create an affective state more conducive to considering the subject matter (cf pp 83-86 and cf pp 86-87).

232

? grass hopping from one thing to another

? allowing lines of enquiry to peter out in a desultory manner.

? Consultants appear to have come to the conclusion that the problems cannot be solved and the situations cannot be redeemed and so they are encouraging consultors to accommodate themselves to them.

? Clues, information and ideas have yet to be discovered which will galvanise consultors and trigger off constructive analytical processes.

? The consultation is at the stage of scanning and brainstorming and not systematic analysis.

? The consultant does not understand the consultor's needs:

? to demonstrate s/he is the victim/custodian not the cause of an intransigent unredeemable situation

? for moral and spiritual sympathy and support.

? The consultant is not taking account of the fact that the consultor needs more time than s/he does to work through the issues and feelings because of her/his personal and emotional involvement, vocational investment and because of the risks involved for her/him.

? The consultant is preoccupied with the inner work which will enable him/her to engage creatively with the analytical tasks.

? The consultant is being diverted from the identification with the consultor and the issues which is likely to yield results through her/his being overly concerned with getting positive responses.

? The consultant's desire, need and possibly request for positive responses is inhibiting the consultor and the consulting processes and adversely affecting their relationship.

4. Power failure: consultancy energy loss

This presentation, almost identical to the one from the consultant's perspective, is included to help consultors to read it from their perspective which is, of course, different.

Symptoms	Possible Causes	Possible action for consultors
? Consultor or/and consultant:	? Consultors and/or consultants:	? Accept the situation as gracefully as possible without being judgemental of self or others.
? not having sufficient energy for the consultancy tasks	? have spent themselves for the time being, profitably or unprofitably they have used up all the energy currently available	? Consultors and/or consultant need time/space to reorientate and regroup.
? drained, weary, tired rather than alert	? are experiencing inner dissonance which is absorbing energy dysfunctionally.	? Connote positively what has been achieved.
? unable to get their minds and feelings around things; the task is slipping away from them	? Consultors/consultants are stressed or under-stretched because:	? *If consultor and consultant lose energy:*
? satisfyingly tired after doing good work	? the challenge of the work is too great or too little	? soldier on in the hope that energy will return
? experiencing the weariness of being beaten	? they are overtaxed/exhausted/worn out/burnt out or bored	? have a short break, call it a day
? unsure of self and others and their judgements	? overwhelmed by the thought of all that is involved	? share feelings and possible reasons for power loss/energy failure and look at implications.
? overwhelmed, paralysed by the enormity of the task	? unmotivated.	? *If consultant loses energy:*
? struggling for concentration	? They have completed a cycle of work and not got the energy to start right away on the next round of work.	? consultor asks if consultant wishes to continue or not
? working at things mechanically rather than creatively	? The consultor's/consultant's loss of energy could be related to the thinking tasks or to the post-consultancy action required to follow them through.	? consultor "carries" consultant until a natural break or s/he recovers energy
? unable to face anymore	? Is the consultor the driving force behind the work under consideration or the consultor plus his/her organization. If the former; is the consultor being overly responsible for finding the energy?	? live off the energy of the consultor.
? frustrated by their weakness		? *If consultor loses energy:*
? disappointed, annoyed or angry with themselves because they have not the energy required	? Is the workforce under-powered or the work under-staffed?	? confess it
? finding attention and energy diverted from tasks to self and tiredness.	? Is the consultor and/or consultant losing interest in the work or the consultancy?	? continue hoping energy will return
? Quality of engagement between consultors and consultants and with the subject matter significantly reduced: it is dull rather than creative; self-confidence is depleted.	? Is the loss of energy due to the approach and methods being adopted and the moods and modes of participation and reflective engagement (cf pp 86-87, 91)?	? summon up as much energy and will power as possible
		? concentrate on task rather than feelings of tiredness
		? live off energy of consultant.
		? Consider the value of doing an energy audit (cf pp 109-111).
		? Take a break or engage in some other activity which will hopefully revitalise consultor and/or consultant.

5. Consultants are not keeping up with consultors

Symptoms	Possible Causes	Possible action for consultors
? The consultor feels/assumes/fantasizes/discerns evidence that the consultant:	? The consultor:	? When difficulties occur during sessions you could:
? has not got a grasp on the situation and the essential information	? is not able/willing to work at consultant's pace	? soldier on in the hope of consultant getting on top of things
? has been left behind by the discussion/is (or feels) ill at ease/out of it/insecure/not able to do his/her job/letting consultor/self and consultancy cause down	? is engrossed in his/her own thoughts and not attuned to a dialogue (cf pp 91-96 and 207 on "interactive meshing")	? ask consultant if s/he has followed the points made/got a picture of the event/situation and if so ask him/her to describe things as s/he sees them
? is getting desperate/ beginning to panic	? is not presenting his/her situation/problem/case in a manner which enables the consultant to play his/her part (cf pp 25 and 106-107 on inputs)	? raise difficulties with consultant
? is deskilled, embarrassed	? has not briefed consultant in advance	? ask consultant how s/he can help you to get a working picture of the situation.
? has given up.	? is trying to impress consultant	? In preparing for sessions in the future you could:
? The consultor:	? is trying to appear on top of things when s/he is not	? consider the briefing most likely to help consultants and consultations to be more effective
? is becoming impatient and dissatisfied	? is trying to think through things more quickly than is realistically possible.	? ask consultant what kind of briefing would be helpful
? is confused and embarrassed	? The consultant:	? prepare written pre-consultancy briefing or/and verbal and possibly written briefing to be presented personally in the consultancy (cf pp 87-88 and Appendix I).
? is frustrated, irritated, let down	? is not able to work at consultor's pace and consultor not able/willing to work at consultant's	
? is concerned/worried/desperate that consultant is not going to help	? has not done his/her homework	
? is feeling that time, energy and money are being wasted	? cannot absorb information at the delivery rate	
? has written off the consultancy and is politely going through the motions	? lacks confidence to seek clarification	
? is considering withdrawing.	? is intimidated (cf p 93).	
	? There are dysfunctional differences between the consultor's and the consultant's rates of thinking, expressing themselves, exchanging and exploring ideas which, if they cannot be overcome, prevent creative dialogue.	
	? The consultor is excitedly engrossed in describing and exploring ideas.	

235

6. Consultors are not keeping up with consultants

Symptoms	Possible Causes	Possible action for consultors
? The consultant is racing ahead apparently regardless of whether the consultor is following/engaging/understanding/agreeing or not (cf pp 72 and 93).	? The consultant is:	? You, the consultor, can:
? The consultor:	? unaware s/he could be wrong	? give up
? does not understand what the consultant is saying/getting at	? looking for the way forward s/he would take, not the consultor's; attention is on the consultant's solution, not the consultor's	? soldier on in the hope that all may eventually become clear
? does not recognise the consultant's picture/analysis of his/her situation	? assuming the consultor is following	? ask the consultant to catch you up
? feels the consultant is not on the same wavelength	? not paying sufficient attention to the consultor and to their interaction	? tell the consultant what is happening and discuss implications with him/her
? feels left behind, out of the discussion, unable to contribute and pursue what s/he considers important	? engrossed in her/his own thoughts/confused/struggling to understand/out to impress the consultor	? tell the consultant when his/her thinking does not seem to fit your situation
? feels alienated	? assuming a necessary acquaintance with a body of knowledge which the consultor does not have.	? ask the consultant to explain: his/her thinking; the processes by which s/he arrived at his/her conclusions
? cannot see how s/he can implement plans	? The consultant's thinking is sound but not the approach to the consultor.	? ask the consultant for private thinking time in order to make your contribution to the consultancy
? feels consultant is making things worse instead of better	? It is ahead of the consultor's.	? discuss with the consultant how you can cope constructively with any differences in your knowledge and thinking patterns
? feels/fantasizes that the consultant understands the situation and what to do better than s/he does	? Her/his thinking is not expressed coherently.	? glean from the consultancy anything which may help you to work with people
? feeling deskilled/inferior/unsure of self/losing confidence/irritated/confused/resentful/defensive/angry and annoyed with self and consultant.	? S/he is concentrating on getting answers.	? ask the consultant to explain why particular contributions were not pursued, dropped, remain unused.
	? The consultor does not understand the consultant's thinking because s/he cannot discern the stages of thought which have led to it.	
	? The speed of interchange is too great for the consultor (cf pp 93-94).	

? The consultant does not take the consultor's contributions seriously. S/he:

  ? acknowledges them politely/patronizingly

  ? ignores them

  ? feigns to adopt them

  ? takes them out of circulation.

? The consultor:

  ? is not able/prepared to do the required reflective thinking

  ? has led the consultant to believe that s/he is following and agreeing with him/her (cf pp 72, 93, 143-144).

? The consultor's contributions:

  ? are not useable

  ? were useable but not seen to be so

  ? are not understood by the consultant.

? Thinking together (cf p 73) is prevented by the consultant thinking on his own (cf p 72) at a pace with which the consultor cannot cope and/or by not using the right thinking mode (cf pp 86-87).

? The consultant's thinking is not sound.

  ? S/he is not thinking realistically/straight/contextually.

  ? S/he has got things wrong/made wrong connections by thinking of things that have worked elsewhere rather than concentrating on the consultor's situation.

  ? The consultor has got it right.

  ? They have not paid sufficient attention to the differences in their abilities to think about feelings and ideas (cf pp 83-87, 96-98).

7. Consultants taking over

Symptoms	Possible Causes	Possible action for consultors
? The consultant is behaving as though the consultor's work is his /hers. S/he: ? confuses the consultancy partnership work with the consultor's work ? talks about "our work" when referring to the consultor's work ? assumes responsibilities that properly belong to the consultor ? lays claim to the consultor's work inspirationally, intellectually emotionally, spiritually (cf pp 40-41, 198-200) ? takes charge rather than enables, directs rather than offers services. ? The consultor's autonomy has been compromised, s/he is less free to be her/his own person (cf pp 42-45). S/he: ? is negative about the "take over" ? feels uncomfortable, unsure, insecure, resentful, angry ? does not know what to do about the relationship and how to put it right. ? The consultor favours the take over and is pleased to have someone so closely identified with and committed to them and their work.	? The consultor could be contributing to the "take over" by: ? colluding with it ? desiring and encouraging the consultant to be in charge ? looking for someone to take responsibility for them and their work ? being too passive and, for instance, failing to get consultants to consider ideas and information s/he knows to be critically important (cf Chart II:2) ? not keeping up with the consultant (cf Chart II:6 and I:6) ? feeling obligated to the consultant ? being intimidated by the consultant. ? The consultant could be led to take over: ? by allowing empathic consultancy association with the consultor and her/his work to slip over into unhealthy possessiveness ? by making inappropriate responses to her/his frustrated desire to be in the consultor's position ? by assuming the consultor's role ? through confusing his/her role with that of a colleague, partner, superior, manager ? by being inappropriately directive ? by surreptitiously using consultors and consultations to achieve ends other than those for which they have contracted. (cf pp 118-120, Chart I:1 and II:1).	? Carefully review your role, feelings and behaviour in the light of your basic responsibilities to yourself, your constituencies and the consultant and take whatever action you see to be necessary (cf pp 35-46, 49-50 and 143-145). ? Explore with consultants what you see to be happening in the consultancy and how you are feeling about it in relation to your: ? respective purposes for the consultancy and contract ? roles (cf pp 35-36) ? interpersonal behaviour (cf pp 36-46) ? working relationships (cf pp 46-51) ? thinking together (cf pp 71-101) ? use of consultancy time ? understanding of codes of good consultancy practice (cf pp 143-145). ? As appropriate consider the action suggestions in Charts II: 1, 2 and 6 and I: 1, 2 and 6.

8. Consultors taking over

Symptoms	Possible Causes	Possible action for consultors
? Consultors:	? Consultants:	? Carefully review your role, feelings, behaviour in the light of what you really need and want to get out of the consultancy and take whatever action is necessary(cf pp 35-46, 49-50 and 143-145).
? are energetically/single mindedly/obsessively engaged in their work	? are happy with things as they are	
	? have nothing to contribute	
	? are out of their depth	
? tend to monopolize the consultancy time: they contribute rather than receive; talk rather than listen; answer their own questions; sessions are more of a monologue than a dialogue	? are allowing themselves to be intimidated/overwhelmed by consultors	? Ask consultants if they have anything they wish to raise with you and, if they have, give them uninterrupted time to do so and consider what they say openly and seriously with them .
	? are not able to assert themselves—do not have the skills/courage/determination/will to take on consultor	
? are more open to approval than to challenge	? are not able to keep up with the consultor (cf Chart I:5)	? Explore with consultants how they are feeling about the consultancy in relation to their:
? ignore/dismiss/parry the input of consultants	? have given up to trying to make their contribution	
? dominate the consultancy	? did not make a realistic contract with the consultor.	? respective purposes for the consultancy and the contract they have made
? are disappointed that consultants contribute so little and wonder why they do not take a more active part—they seem to have nothing to add, agree with what is said or to be out of their depth	? The consultor has a stronger personality than the consultant.	? roles (cf pp 35-36)
	? Consultors:	
	? are so excitedly absorbed in their work and their thoughts and feelings about it that they cannot stop talking about it	? interpersonal behaviour (cf pp 36-46)
	? are confusing owning their work with being possessive about it	? working relationships (cf pp 46-51)
? do not welcome ideas from others about ways to improve the situation	? are out to impress the consultant rather than to get his/her help	? thinking together (cf pp 71-101)
	? want/need the consultant's uncritical/unconditional approval and support	? use of consultancy time
? are not entirely happy with being in the "driving seat".	? have no intention of making changes to their approach and work	? understanding of codes of good consultancy practice (cf pp 143-145).
? Consultors feel/sense/intuit/fantasize that the consultants:	? do not believe/think that the consultant has anything to offer	? As appropriate consider the suggestions given in Charts II: 1-5 and 9-10; I: 1-5 and 9-10).
? are impressed by their "performance"	? do not understand what consultancy is really about and has to offer	? Use the experience and the discussions with the consultant to examine implications of what emerges for the way in which they operate beyond the consultancy as well as within it.
? are going along with/colluding/happy with the pattern of interaction	? are engaged in a form of defensive behaviour to prevent exposure or to keep consultant at a distance (cf Charts I:9 and II:9) or to prevent consultant from taking over (cf Charts I:7 and II:7) or to keep control.	
? are irritated by them taking so much con-sultancy time.		

9. Consultors being defensive

Symptoms	Possible Causes	Possible action for consultors
? In relation to some aspect of their thought/feelings/beliefs/work consultors: ? go on the defensive ? communicate defensiveness verbally and non-verbally ? act as though they are under attack ? attack as a means of defence ? close the subject down ? indicate that a topic is " a no-go area" ? are evasive, non-communicative ? avoid eye contact ? avoid answering questions ? trade in elusive answers ? change the subject ? withhold things ? are not sharing/unable to share vital information privy to them. ? The verbal interaction is not flowing in dialogue, *e.g.*: consultant's questions/ contributions are parried by consultors. ? Consultors hinder consultant's attempts to get agreed descriptions of the consultancy subject matter by: ? being elusive and vague ? making non-committal/indifferent responses to attempts at clarification—there is always something not right but they do not help to correct it	? Consultors: ? find it difficult to talk about others "behind their backs" (cf pp 41-42) ? cannot explore issues freely and openly because of their commitment to a belief system/a programme of action/people/reference groups ? are prevented by confidences from providing all the information needed ? have information which must not be disclosed but which they must take into account; the needs for openness and confidentiality are in opposition ? experience difficulty in accessing their defensiveness because it is rooted deep in their own consciousness. ? The consultor's elusiveness reflects the way in which fundamental /critical aspects of the situation elude the consultor and cause her/him to feel unsure/uncertain/ insecure/confused/defensive. ? The consultor is an unwilling party to the consultancy. (Defensiveness is much more likely to occur in people who have not become consultors of their own volition. When, for instance, they are in a compulsory work assessment scheme or a reluctant member of a group consultancy arrangement.) ? Consultors feel vulnerable because they: ? do not want to show themselves up ? feel unable to explore some things with the consultant for fear of not being able to cope/ making things worse ? fear that disclosing things may adversely affect their relationship with colleagues/the consultant/significant others	? Consider with the consultant before a problem occurs how best to deal with: ? situations in which you are/feel unable for one reason or another to share relevant information ? any defensive behaviour that might overtake either of you ? no-go areas. ? Should you, the consultor, become defensive : ? say you cannot pursue that subject at the present time ? indicate you need space/time ? ask the consultant not to press you on that point in that way ? share your feelings with the consultant ? try to maintain eye contact with the consultant. ? Examine any propensity you might have towards defensiveness. ? When does it happen? ? In what circumstances does it occur? ? How does it manifest itself in your thoughts/attitudes/feelings/behaviour/verbal and non-verbal communications? ? Why do you think it occurs? ? What helps you to overcome it? ? What could consultants do to help you overcome it? ? Decide what you can and will do to reduce the incidence of your defensiveness.

? declining to correct/acknowledge/own/agree to descriptions revised to meet ambiguous objections to previous ones

? rejecting suggestions by making veiled references to their personal knowledge of things. ("If you knew the situation like I do, you would know that that would not work".)

? feel consultants will disapprove of their action/attitudes *etc.*

? feel under attack even if they are not.

? Consultants are, consciously or unconsciously, attacking consultors or their approaches/ideas/methods/actions (cf Charts II:10 and I:10).

? Consultors are understandably attempting to defend themselves in appropriate/inappropriate ways against:

  ? consultants surreptitiously using consultors to achieve ends other than those for which they contracted (cf Charts I:1 and II:1)

  ? consultants taking over (cf Chart I:7).

? The consultor lacks the verbal and inter-active skills required to present/discuss/explore the above causes with the consultant constructively.

? The consultor's defensiveness is a cause or consequence of :

  ? the consultant's failure to get him/her to consider ideas and information which could be important to him/her and to his/her work. (cf Chart I:2)

  ? her/his failure to get consultants to consider important information (cf Chart II:2)

  ? feeling a consultancy is not getting anywhere (cf Charts I:3 and II:3)

  ? power failure, consultancy energy loss (cf Charts I:4 and II:4)

  ? consultant's taking over (cf Charts I:7, and II:7)

  ? difference in approach, method, beliefs (cf Chart II:11 and I:11).

? The consultor's defensiveness is a way of the consultor taking over.

? As appropriate see the suggestions on Charts I:1, 2, 3, 4, 7, 8 and 10 and II:1, 2, 3, 4, 7, 8 and 10.

? Determine what you are learning which should inform your future practice.

10. Consultants being defensive

Symptoms	Possible Causes	Possible action for consultors
? Consultors find consultants: ? being defensive ? acting as though they are under attack ? being evasive ? avoiding answering questions ? withholding information ? communicating defensively through their body language and through avoiding eye contact. ? the verbal interaction between consultors and consultants does not flow in dialogue: it is stilted/convoluted through the use of defensive mechanisms.	? The consultant is struggling with the difficult consultancy dynamics and the moral confusion related to openness and confidentiality because s/he has: ? entered into a coalition (cf Chart I:1 and II:1) ? information that must be taken into account but which s/he cannot disclose to the consultor and does not know how to deal with. ? The consultant is not delivering and knows s/he is not (cf Chart I:3 and II:3). ? The consultant is anxious about the possibility of the consultancy adversely affecting her/his relationships with people outside the consultancy e.g. those who have commissioned the consultancy or funded it and those who are expecting to receive help through it. ? The consultor is attacking the consultant: ? because s/he feels s/he is losing her freedom (cf Charts II:1 and I:1) ? because s/he is unable to get her/his contributions taken seriously (cf Chart II:2 and I:1) ? because s/he feels the consultancy is not going anywhere (cf Charts II:3 and I:3) ? because the consultant is not keeping up with her/him (cf Charts II:5 and I:5) ? because s/he cannot keep up with consultant (cf Charts II:6 and I:6) ? because the consultant is taking over (cf Charts II:7 and I:7)	? Consider with the consultant before a problem occurs how best to deal with: ? situations in which you are/feel unable for one reason or another to share relevant information ? any defensive behaviour that might overtake either of you ? no-go areas ? etc. ? Examine your thoughts/attitudes/feelings/behaviour/verbal and non-verbal communications that might possibly cause the consultant to feel that s/he or her/his ideas are: ? not accepted/acceptable ? being rejected ? under judgement ? being attacked. ? Decide what you can and will do to eradicate/overcome/compensate for these potential causes of defensiveness which are part of what you bring to consultancies. ? When consultants become defensive take the pressure off them/ "back off "/give them space/ do not carry on with or persist with or pursue or proceed with lines of enquiry. ? Invite, hunt for, maintain eye contact. ? Give the consultant time and opportunity to return to the subject of his/her own free will.

? because s/he wants to take over (cf Charts II:8 and I:8)

? as a form of defence (cf Charts II:9; I:9)

? because of significant differences in their approach, methods, beliefs *etc.* (cf pp 92-94, 98-101 and 197-198).

? The consultor lacks the verbal and interactive skills amd/or courage required to present/discuss/explore constructively one or more of the above causes and their implications with the consultant and others.

? Return to the topic later tentatively and humbly so that the consultant is able to decline or pursue the matter without loss of face.

? List the possible causes of the consultant's defensiveness in the order most favourable to the consultant and work on them in that order.

? As appropriate consider the suggestions on Charts II: 1-9 and Charts I: 1-9.

? Determine what you are learning which should inform your future practice.

NOTES AND REFERENCES: Chapter Five

1.   I have written briefly about this in *Analysis and Design* pp 247f. Also in that book I refer to the way in which many problems arise from faulty initial designs and plans cf pp 159 and 173, reference 2.

2.   Colossians 1:17 R.E.B.

3.   A way of setting out differences is given in *Analysis and Design* p 236f.

4.   cf Analysis and Design pp 231ff.

5.   cf *op cit* pp 236ff

6.   This can be readily seen from a diagram in *Analysis and Design* p 218.

7.   See Campbell, Alastair V (Ed) (1987) *A Dictionary of Pastoral Care* (SPCK) p 188f, an entry by Campbell on "Pastoral Care, Nature of".

8.   *ibid* p 198f an entry by Howard Clinebell on "Pastoral Counselling".

9.   *ibid* p 189f

10.   cf *Analysis and Design* p 188f.

PART TWO

WORK AND WORKERS

Introduction

Engaging with the particularities of consultors and their situations is fundamental to the kind of consultancy work advocated in this book. By the very nature of things, this involves working with and to the idiosyncratic ways in which practitioners approach their church and community work and to the particulars of the churches, activities, communities, work, worship and organizations with which they are engaged. It also involves careful attention to their overall understanding of the nature and forms of the work and the attributes required of workers. It follows, that work-views, and the mental pictures they contain, play critical and often hidden parts in determining what consultors do and contain clues to the ways in which they can develop their work and themselves as practitioners. This is especially true of the following.

1. The consultor's work-view of the actualities of his/her situation and the work-views of those with whom they are engaged.

2. The consultor's mental picture or map of the nature of church and community work.

3. The consultor's mental picture of how the work should be done and the attributes required of workers.

4. The consultant's mental picture of the nature of church and community work.

5. The consultant's mental picture of how the work should be done and the attributes required of workers.

Starting points for consultations can be aspects of 1, 2 or 3. Briefing papers, such as those described in Appendix I, provide information about the consultor's work-view and mental pictures (1, 2 and 3). Aspects of the consultant's mental picture (4 and 5) come to mind automatically and responsively as they engage with the consultor's mental pictures (1 to 3) and inform the consultancy processes. Whether they are well or badly formed, mental pictures 2 to 5 are key players in the interchanges between consultors and consultants. They are basic reference points whether or not consultors and consultants are *au fait* with their own or each other's or are consciously referring to them .

Ideally, as I argued in the Introduction, clarity about the work situation needs to be matched by clarity about work-views: the clearer consultants and consultors are about their own and each other's mental pictures of the nature of the work and the attributes required of workers, the more efficient and effective consultations are likely to be.

Whilst practitioners in many different Christian organizations use and value the consultancy services described in this book, I restrict myself to the Christian Church at work for several reasons: the Church is the major organizational player amongst those who make critical contributions to the Christian enterprise; other organizations complement its work, generally by specializing in one aspect of Christian mission such as the well-being and development of disadvantaged people; what is said about the work of the Church and its workers is, in part, relevant to the work of other organizations; my vocational base is the Church.

In this Part I venture with some trepidation to sketch out my own mental pictures of the nature of church and community work involved in creating, maintaining, developing and deploying churches as effective missiological faith communities and instruments for the common good. This work is done by lay, religious and ordained, religious workers in private and public. Privately, they do vast amounts of thinking, studying, researching, planning, programming and praying about what needs to be done to build up and service the Christian communities they serve, to prepare for meetings and events and to run organizations to enable adults and children to pursue many different interests and activities. All this is both a consequence of and a prelude to engaging with people through casual and planned face to face contacts in all kinds of formal and informal church work and community work settings, meetings and encounters. When this work is done well, those involved become an effective work-force functioning as the Church, the body of Christ.The gifts of the spirit are freely and graciously used and people make their particular contributions. (cf I Corinthians 12). To achieve this, a lot of highly skilled and dedicated work is required. Chapter 6 explores the nature of this work and Chapter 7 describes the attributes required of those who do it. These pictures are basic aspects of my work-view (cf Element four in Chapter Two). They indicate what I bring to consultations both as a consultant and a consultor. They also give a general overall idea of the subject matter to which the consultancy processes described in Part One have to be applied. And, importantly for the purposes of this book, they could stimulate and help both consultants and consultors to clarify their own mental pictures.

Mental pictures of the work have two principal aspects: one is of the forms it takes and the other is of its essential nature. The first profiles the outward shapes it takes. The second describes the attributes and properties common to all forms of that work in any and every context. The forms of work are open to view, widely known and variously classified. Critical characteristics of the nature of the work, rooted as they are in the theology and praxis of the work and the vocational commitments of those engaged in it, are not as accessible.

The attempt to draw out general and sustainable points about the nature of the Church's work has been daunting and difficult because of the vastness, variety and complexity of that work and the danger of being superficial or obscure. It has been painful and profitable because it has shown me how I could have performed better as a consultor and consultant. That is indicative of the importance of studying the work itself. I see it as an exercise in profiling or modelling features which I find illuminate consultancy processes and not as a classification or taxonomy of church work which is a task far beyond me and the scope of this book.

In chapter seven the focus changes from my mental picture of the nature of church and community work to my picture of the attributes required of those engaged in it.

247

The sequence of the chapters underlines the importance of using the nature of the work to help to establish the attributes workers and work-forces need to have. Drawing out the attributes required of workers in this way is not meant to infer that workers are definitively formed by the work. Reciprocal formative processes are at work between workers and their work. Workers make their own personal mark upon the work and the work helps to shape them. Whatever the processes of formation might be, it is very important that the essential attributes are personalised, collectivised and become part of the work culture of the practitioners, people, churches and organizations.

Missiological and vocational confusion and deviation can recur, for instance, when activities and programmes are based simply on needs or on the gifts, skills and aptitudes of the available work-force without taking into proper account the essential nature of church and community work. This is not to say that what is done in this way is not laudable. Invariably it is. And that makes it more difficult to see that it is off course and to raise critical questions about it.

Teasing out the competencies required from somewhat idealistic descriptions of the nature of the work could appear to be a counsel of perfection ignoring widely experienced problems caused by shortage of workers. Those struggling to find people to do jobs and coping with workers who are ill-equipped for tasks they undertake could find this approach an irritant. I empathise with them. Much of my ministry has been spent struggling and juggling with situations vacant which were difficult, if not impossible, to fill and in facing the question, "What part of the work that we should be doing can we do with the workers we have?" These realities of every day life can seem a long way from working to ideals rather than messy actualities. In fact, the approach I am adopting helps us to face these problems rather than avoid them and to address them more profoundly by considering them in relation to the nature of the work and the competencies required. This helps churches and practitioners:

- to recruit, train and build up the best possible work-force that can be obtained in any situation, even the most unpromising, and to decide how it should be deployed;

- to do what they must and can do in given situations towards the Christian project, no more and no less;

- to work at the Christian project with proper respect to the limits of the capacity and competence of their work-force;

- to define and seek any additional training and resources they need to maintain and develop their work.

These things can be achieved whenever the vital reference points, nature of the "work" and attributes of "workers" are added to those of purpose and belief in designing and evaluating work programmes. Used in these ways, considering the ideal encourages rather than discourages people. It helps them to deal more adequately with the actual and the inevitable gaps between what is and what could be. This conclusion is based on experience of building up well-equipped work forces in unlikely situations. It is an example of theory helping practice.

Mental pictures of the nature of the work and the attributes required of workers, therefore, represent foundational subject matter not only for consultants and consultors but also for all those engaged in analysis and design of church and community work and in appraisal, assessment, evaluation and church review programmes.

What follows are some of the reasons why it is advisable for consultants and consultors to pay attention to both of these kinds of mental pictures.

- They contain coded information which, consciously or unconsciously and for better or worse, influence the character and qualities of the work done, the workers who do it and the people who share in it. Thus, in various ways, they shape the Church (the body of Christ) and the workers and people (members of the body of Christ).

- They are vital data bases.

- When they are in good order, creative energy flows.

- They help people to work systematically and systemically by differentiating parts of the work-views.

- They facilitate consultations about fundamentals which hold the keys to holistic development of work and workers.

- They can be used to promote creative interaction between the actual and the ideal.

- They provide overall work pictures in which to set the subject matter of consultations. (Apart from carefully prepared position papers and situation analyses, descriptions of the subject matter brought to consultancy sessions do not generally give a balanced view of the consultor's workaday world. Distortions occur because consultations tend to revolve around extraordinary opportunities and problems rather than the day to day ordinariness consultors normally experience. Indeed, frequently consultors are concerned to correct the impression that might be formed by concentrating on a problem. They say things such as: "It is not like this all the time". "A lot of good things are happening". "This is the downside of a very successful and effective church". Extracting sufficient information to work on the issues realistically during consultancy sessions is difficult enough without having to ensure it is portraying the whole accurately!)

A diagram illustrating the relationship between various aspects of work-worker systems formed in my mind as I wrote this Part. It is presented overleaf. It is an overview of this Part. Incidentally, once this pattern formed in my mind it suggested what was, for me, a quite different outline for situation analysis position papers, see Appendix I Outline Two. I was delighted to find it worked well in consultancy sessions not least because it demonstrated the usefulness of Part Two for consultancy work!

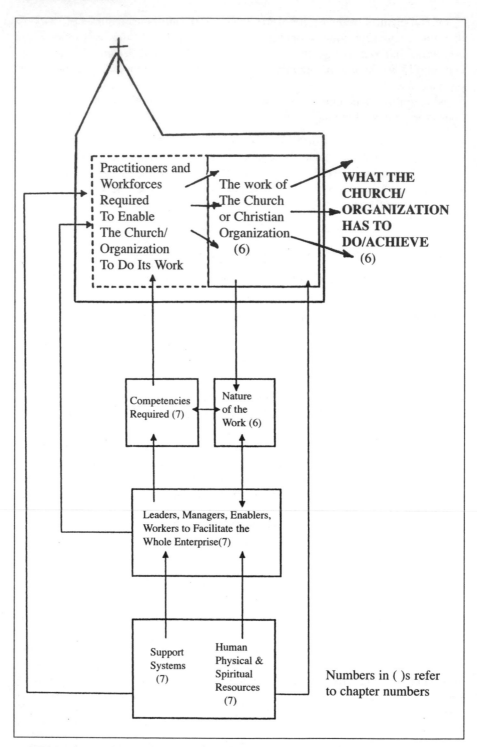

Practitioners and
Workforces
Required
To Enable
The Church/
Organization
To Do Its Work

The work of
The Church
or Christian
Organization
(6)

**WHAT THE
CHURCH/
ORGANIZATION
HAS TO
DO/ACHIEVE**
(6)

Competencies
Required (7)

Nature
of the
Work (6)

Leaders, Managers, Enablers,
Workers to Facilitate the
Whole Enterprise(7)

Support
Systems
(7)

Human
Physical &
Spiritual
Resources
(7)

Numbers in ( )s refer
to chapter numbers

A Diagrammatic Overview of Part Two: A Work/Worker Support System

CHAPTER SIX

The Nature and Properties of the Work

This chapter outlines key elements of my mental picture of the nature of church and community work. It teases out the core characteristics, the essential, inherent and interrelated properties of this work, which need to be respected if work programmes are to be theologically profound, contextually viable and purposefully effective.

An exploration of the nature of church work is not to be confused with an exposition of current practice which varies enormously. To say, for instance, that the work is collaborative does not mean that all practitioners are collaborative: by disposition and practice they may not be at all collaborative and those that are will be collaborative more appropriately and effectively in some relationships and settings than in others. What this means is that practitioners need to work collaboratively in order to contribute to the Christian project. Identifying core characteristics of the nature has more to do with work properties that should inform practice than with actual work performance. Effectiveness in all forms of work involves understanding the nature of the subject matter and reading off the implications for ways of working with it. The nature and properties of church work and the "dos and don'ts" of good practice are closely related. Respect for the nature of things human and divine is essential if Christian purposes are to be achieved through the Christian project.

Therefore, in this chapter I concentrate on identifying and defining attributes and indicating major implications. Temptations to explore their application and to speculate about how far the properties are reflected in the performance of practitioners, including my own, have been resisted!

The first major section is about the theological and operational attributes of the work. This is followed by shorter sections on: theology and values in the work; shadowy downsides; cutting the work diamond; towards a definition of church and community work.

I   THE ATTRIBUTES OF THE WORK

The attributes and properties of the work described in the first section derive from the essential nature of the Christian project. These attributes focus on the sources, ownership and purposes of the work and the participants in it. They show that the work is missiological, initiated and sustained by God and carried out through the activities of the members of the Trinity and an infinite number of divine-human vocational partnerships.

The other attributes and properties I have described result from applying and working out the Christian project in the Church and through it in the world. They consist of an admixture of attributes which practitioners need to take seriously if they are to translate the theology and theory of the work into effective action and

251

practice. They show the nature of the work which is a proper expression of the Christian project which, because they are generic qualities, operate effectively within and upon the actualities of church and community working situations generally. In the second section I have described those attributes which, broadly speaking, derive from the universals of the working context and in the third section those which derive from proven ways of approaching and doing the work effectively. (These attributes must not be confused with the personal and technical abilities and knowledge required to approach and do the work in the way the nature of the work requires. They are discussed in the next chapter.)

This is but one of many ways in which the attributes can be arranged. It is the best I can come up with. Perhaps the difficulty, and possibly even the impossibility, of getting a classification of the attributes that cannot be challenged is that the nature of the work which is essentially systemic and holistic. Notwithstanding, this description of the nature of the work enables us to consider, in relation to each attribute, the personal resources, knowledge and skills required of practitioners.

1.   Theological Attributes Which Derive From The Christian Project

This section shows that the work we are considering is:

(a)   missiological

(b)   a divine-human enterprise in creative redemptive activity

(c)   vocational, personal and collective

(d)   comprehensive and inclusive.

The discussion of these four theological attributes opens out on: the nature and scope of the Christian project; the unique contributions that God makes to it; the way in which the Church and its staff are called to work comprehensively and inclusively with and for God in human-divine partnerships through their vocations.

(a)   The Work is Missiological

An essential attribute of the work which we are considering is that it is missiological. Missiology, "the study of the theory and practice of the Christian mission"[1] has moved to centre stage through the work of people such as the late David Bosch, Kenneth Cracknell, J. Andrew Kirk and Timothy Yates.[2] Bosch, having stated that "mission means serving, healing, and reconciling a divided, wounded humanity, indicates its centrality in this way:

> Just as the church ceases to be church if it is not missionary, theology ceases to be theology if it loses its missionary character. . . . The crucial question, then, is not simply or only or largely what church is or what mission is; it is also what theology is and is about. . . . We are in need of a missiological agenda for theology rather than just a theological agenda for mission; for theology, rightly understood, has no reason to exist other than critically to accompany the *missio Dei*. So mission should be "the theme of all theology". . . .
> Missiology may be termed the "synoptic discipline" within the wider encyclopedia of theology. . . . For theology it is a matter of life and death that it should be in direct contact with mission and the missionary enterprise.

Cracknell and Lamb . . . remark that, in the first edition of their study (1980) they would not have dared to suggest that every curriculum should find some place for the study of missiology; now, however, they would insist that all theological questions should be thought about from the point of view of the theology of mission. Only in this way can a "better teaching" of every subject come about. . . . In similar vein, a curriculum revision committee of Andover Newton Theological School identified an "almost universal corporate desire to widen our perspective to one of world concern". . . . One of the committee's key recommendations was to relate "each discipline specifically to a theology of mission".[3]

He follows this with a discussion about the dual functions of missiology to other disciplines and to the praxis of mission and concludes:

Perhaps van Engelen's formulation sums it up best. He says that the challenge to missiology is "to link the always relevant Jesus event of twenty centuries ago to the future of the promised reign of God for the sake of meaningful initiatives in the present". . . . In this way, new discussions on soteriology, christology, ecclesiology, eschatology, creation, and ethics will be initiated, and missiology will be granted the opportunity to make its own unique contribution.

This remains a hazardous undertaking. Every branch of theology—including missiology—remains piecework, fragile, and preliminary. There is no such thing as missiology, period. There is only missiology in draft. . . . Only in this way can missiology become, not only . . . "the handmaiden of theology" . . . , but also . . . "handmaiden of God's world".[4]

Two things are inescapable about the nature of the work we are considering. First, the Church is intended to be an instrument, sign and sacrament of Christian mission. Precisely how people understand this in theory and in practice varies enormously and is passionately debated although there is widespread agreement that it means justice, peace and bringing in the Kingdom of God. Secondly, Church workers are, by chance or default or design, engaged in missiological activities of one kind or another. As they discuss, plan and pursue work programmes they variously encounter a range of assumptions and convictions about and approaches to the theology and praxis of the mission of the Church which lead into all kinds of issues such as: mission as a human activity and mission as God's activity, *missio Dei**; confusion between "mission" (the task for which God sends the Church into the world) and "missions" (specific activities undertaken by human decision); the meanings of "evangelism" and "evangelization";[5] the significance of conversion, personal and collective; Christian mission and people of other faiths; mission and culture; the respective value, contribution and importance in the mission of the Church of evangelism, worship, fellowship, pastoral care, altruistic services, development work. Bosch says that "the contemporary crisis as far as mission is concerned, manifests itself in three areas: the foundation, the motives and aim, and the nature of mission".[6]

---

* In a lecture on *Missio Dei* given in the early part of 1999, the Revd Dr Martyn Atkins described the concept as "theocentric aspect of mission" and commented: "Yet it must be said that if the *Missio Dei* has become a commonly accepted understanding of what *mission* is and the Kingdom of God has become a commonly agreed *purpose* of mission, then it has allowed virtually *all* understandings of mission and evangelism to be sustained. Even some appearing almost mutually exclusive."

Creative engagement with these foundational and formative issues is an essential part of the work of the Church, a characteristic of its nature. Church workers have to be able to work at them on their own and alongside people with the same and different views. In fact they have to be missiologists.

Engagement with these issues can be exciting and deeply satisfying in the work place and in free flowing speculative discussions. Agreements about the nature of mission have to be reached by individuals and groups in order to inform, underpin and underwrite programmes of work. Exploration of the issues and exchange of ideas has to be gathered in statements of belief and purpose and focussed in mission statements. As we saw in Chapter Three, that can be tricky for individual workers and for groups. Difficulties occur when people differ significantly and when they are at different stages in their intellectual, theological and emotional grasp of the issues and in their faith development. "Forced" decisions do not provide a good basis, but neither does inconclusive or confused thinking. Several things can help workers and groups to develop useful mission statements:

- positive openness to the issues and to different approaches to mission;
- tentative statements which enable people to work together in focussed ways in a given context;
- the ability and willingness to continue to reflect critically and positively on the approach to mission adopted in the light of developments and new approaches to mission and to make conceptual and practical changes as necessary.

Such an approach gives people an informed focus to their given position— however narrow or broad that might be—and an openness to learning from experience. Processes such as these enhance the quality of the work done no matter what the initial missiological stance might be. Professor Kenneth Cracknell has developed the "missiological circle", presented in Figure 6:1[7] which facilitates such a process.

(b) The Work is A Divine—Human Enterprise in Creative and Redemptive Activity

Along with other Christians, I believe that Jesus Christ and the Holy Spirit have done for us and continue to do for us what we simply cannot do for ourselves. In response, our part is, of our own free will, to appropriate what has been done for us and to stimulate and help others to do the same.[8] I also believe that God is continuously engaged in holistic creation and re-creation in every part of the universe—in personal and social lives of people, in the church, religious communities, secular institutions and the world generally. God is active in everything that makes for betterment, development, salvation and holiness. God invites us, individually and collectively, to participate in this venture. Consequently, the Christian project is a divine-human enterprise in creative and redemptive activity. That is a key characteristic of its nature and the work associated with it. Amongst other things this means that central to this enterprise there are an infinite number of partnerships and working relationships between God, the Church and members of the Christian workforce. All sides have to work hard, very hard at times, to establish these partnerships and relationships and to keep them in good repair. God has done the redemptive ground work. Those who are engaged in this work are

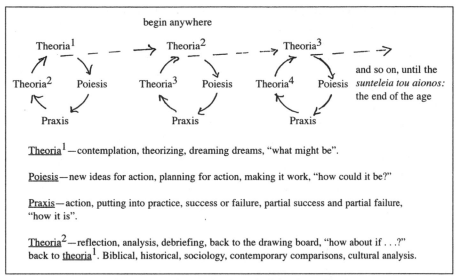

begin anywhere

Theoria[1] – – – → Theoria[2] – – – → Theoria[3] – – – →

Theoria[2]   Poiesis   Theoria[3]   Poiesis   Theoria[4]   Poiesis   *and so on, until the*

sunteleia tou aionos:

the end of the age

Praxis   Praxis   Praxis

Theoria[1] —contemplation, theorizing, dreaming dreams, "what might be".

Poiesis—new ideas for action, planning for action, making it work, "how could it be?"

Praxis—action, putting into practice, success or failure, partial success and partial failure, "how it is".

Theoria[2]—reflection, analysis, debriefing, back to the drawing board, "how about if . . .?" back to theoria[1]. Biblical, historical, sociology, contemporary comparisons, cultural analysis.

Figure 6:1 Cracknell's Missiological Circle

inspired, enabled, supported and empowered through the omnipresent Christ and the Holy Spirit and by prayer, worship, the sacraments and Christian fellowship. And, as creative and redeeming work and suffering appear inseparable, we are comforted by God, the means of grace and Christian fellowship *(koinonia)*.[9]

According to the New Testament, Christians are God's co-workers. Mark and Paul use the Greek work *sunergeo*, "to work together with", to describe this relationship.[10] The same word is used in the New Testament to describe the working relationships between apostles.[11] Collaboration, therefore, is a substantive attribute of all working relationships in the divine-human enterprise. Amongst other things this involves encouraging people to appropriate in their own lives what Christianity offers, to enter into the Christian fellowship and to co-operate in working out the implications of the Christian gospel and ethic in the world. (Collaborative practice is explored below and in the next chapter.)

Clearly it is important to differentiate and correlate the human and divine functions. It takes various forms. As we have noted God does things *for* us. He accompanies us as we do the things we have to do: nothing is done for us which we can and should do for ourselves. In all kinds of ways God, through Christ and the Holy Spirit, points us to, and stimulates and challenges us to do what we need to do as well as doing things *with* us (cf the thinking approaches pp 72-73).

One of the Biblical analogies used to indicate the nature of the working relationship is that of the servant. *Doulos* is one of the Greek words for servant which is used. Christ assumed the "form of a slave".[12] Christians are frequently called the servants, or slaves, of Christ and less frequently of God.[13] Jesus emphasises that servants are not greater than their masters.[14] But he also says "no longer do I call you servants, for a servant does not know what his master is about. I have called you friends, because I have disclosed to you everything that I heard from my Father".[15] Clearly the metaphor is used to bring out aspects of the personal and working relationships between Jesus and his disciples. Similarly for Paul, Christians, having been "bought with a price", belong to their master.[16] At the same time he insists that Christ has set them free; they are no longer slaves but sons and daughters of God.[17] Paul also says in one place that Christians must not become slaves of people[18] but in another he urges Christians to become slaves to one another in love.[19]

Clearly there are tricky nuances in our working relationships with God and each other. A story, possibly apocryphal, has helped me to understand and live out some of them. At his induction to a new church a Primitive Methodist minister said to the congregation, "I have come to be your servant. According to the New Testament that means I must be your slave. But by one of those theological paradoxes, you will not be my master no more than I, as your servant, will be your master. In fact if either of those things did happen we would be in disarray, unable to minister to each other and pursue our shared ministry, because we would have compromised ourselves. God is *our* master and *we* are his and each other's servants. To that we must be true."

Broadly speaking, Church work, a significant part of the divine-human enterprise but by no means all of it, comes under the jurisdiction of one or other of the denominations, their leaders and workers. Structures are tangible and personnel have a physical presence. In many ways denominations are organized and administered very much like secular institutions. Increasingly they are using contemporary methods of staff management. Theologically speaking, denominations are not a law unto themselves, they are under the jurisdication of God. A non-negotiable part of their ecclesiastical brief is to discern what it means for them to function as God's earthly partners, servants and co-workers. So, the divine-human enterprise is directed by the Church and by God: the one tangible through its physical presence; the other mystical, experienced through spiritual presence.

This complicated arrangement is made all the more complicated because, theoretically at least, everyone has direct access to God and can claim to know what God wants of them and the Church. Indeed, profound new challenging insights can come from anyone inside or outside of the Church.

The duality of control is illustrated by an experience of a friend of mine in theological college. As an ex-national service man he had to complete a government form. One of the questions was, "Who is your employer?" In Hebrew he wrote, "Yahweh". It was translated by a Jew in the office. When challenged, my friend refused to change it. The authorities wrote to the principal who suggested the answer should be the Methodist Church. A serious theological argument ensued, resolved only by my friend agreeing to the answer Yahweh/The Methodist Church, or was it The Methodist Church/Yahweh? This was felt at the time to be a compromise but, in fact, it is accurate, both theologically and pragmatically. Church workers are accountable to God and the Church. At best these two entities inform, complement and act as creative foils to each other; at worst, they lead to differences which can confound and be destructive. Workers can experience spiritual and practical conflicts as they grapple with significant differences between what they feel God is calling and directing them to do, their job descriptions, what the Church is actually requiring of them and the conflicting demands of different groups of powerful personalities. Such problems are commonly raised in consultancy sessions.

Doing theological, prophetic and practical exercises of the kind noted below in bullet form could help you to take seriously this aspect of the nature of the work.

- Clarify your understanding of and belief about God's overall action plan and strategy, i.e. do your missiological thinking.

- Note and reflect critically and prayerfully in relation to your working situation and areas of human and spiritual need what you discern

  — God is doing;

  — God wants people to do to appropriate the Christian gospel and promote the common good;

  — you can, should, will try to do;

  — you see to be your part generally and specifically.

  (You may find help in doing some of these things from what has been said about work-views and diagnostic reading in Chapter 2.)

- Explore imaginatively, creatively and prayerfully the nature of your working relationship with God, the Church, other religious institutions, colleagues and Christians and non-Christians, secular organizations and ways and means of improving and extending them.

- Note and reflect upon the basics of the part you play and want to play in the divine-human enterprise.

- Establish your own guide lines for working in partnership with God, the Church colleagues and people in the church and community.

Working together with God in relation to his purposes is an enormous privilege. Sharing in God's creative activity can be satisfying beyond all desert and expectation although it is frequently problematic and painful.

(c)   The Work is Vocational: Personal and Collective

Self-evidently church work is more than a job, it is vocational.* God calls people to it in all kinds of ways. Examples string their way through the Bible and Christian history: God calls; the Church, when it recognises the call, ordains and commissions. A continuing sense of vocation is a commonly accepted requirement for ordained and some forms of lay ministry. Therefore, the vocational concept is an essential characteristic of the work-force. It is written deep into the universal job description for ministry by the action of God, the response of people and the invariable practice of the Church. Over a period of two thousand years millions of people have been called to staff a vast world wide movement through this vocational

---

*I have two particular sets of meaning in mind: (a) A feeling that one is called by God to a certain career or occupation (*The Oxford Paperback Dictionary*, 1979/1983). (b) The action of God (or Christ) in calling a person to exercise some special (especially spiritual) function or to fill a certain position; divine influence or guidance towards a definite (especially religious) career; the fact of being so called or directed towards a special work in life (SOED, 1973). The first definition emphasizes the human sense of call whilst the second set of definitions emphasize divine actions.

process. This is an amazing phenomenon indicative of the ceaseless surge of spiritual energy generated by God's activity in human affairs. Here we concentrate on vocations in the church but this is in no way to deny that many more people have pursued their Christian vocations, separately and together, in the world at large.

So far the emphasis has been upon the *personal vocations* of individuals which are important building blocks in the Church's work economy. Equal attention must be given to *collective vocations*, not to be confused as they often are with *collections of vocations*. Jesus formed a group of disciples and schooled them in a common vocation which included, but was more than the sum of, their personal vocations. After his death and resurrection his disciples and followers formed a vocational community,[20] filled the apostolic vacancy, waited to be empowered and then pursued their individual and collective vocations.[21] Churches were formed each with their collective vocation. Peter spoke lyrically about the collective vocation of Christians:

> You are a chosen race, a royal priesthood, a dedicated nation, and a people claimed by God for his own, to proclaim the triumphs of him who has called you out of darkness into his marvellous light. You are now the people of God, who once were not his people; outside his mercy once, you have now received his mercy.[22]

Paul, using the analogy of the human body itemised some individual vocations and emphasized the importance of their systemic interdependence:

> And it is he (Jesus Christ) who has given some to be apostles, some prophets, some evangelists, some pastors and teachers, to equip God's people for work in his service, for the building up of the body of Christ, until we all attain to the unity inherent in our faith and in our knowledge of the Son of God to mature manhood, measured by nothing less than the full stature of Christ. . . . He is the head, and on him the whole body depends. Bonded and held together by every constituent joint, the whole frame grows through the proper functioning of each part, and builds itself up in love.[23]

And Jesus prayed ardently:

> May they all be one; as you, Father, are in me, and I in you, so also may they be in us, that the world may believe that you sent me. The glory which you gave me I have given to them, that they may be one, as we are one; I in them and you in me, may they be perfectly one. Then the world will know that you sent me, and that you loved them as you loved me.[24]

The author of the Book of Revelation indicates the correctives required in seven churches in order that they might get back on to their collective vocational tracks.[25]

Collective vocations emerge from pursuing Christian personal callings in New Testament ways. The evolution of Roman Catholic religious orders illustrate this. An order's apostolate evolves directly from its founder's vocation or "charism". Another illustration is the growth of the Methodist Church through the vocations of the Wesleys. People with strong individual vocations enable individuals and groups to find vocations, within and beyond the Church, which they would not otherwise have been able to find or pursue. The interplay between personal and collective vocations is endlessly fascinating and vitally important.

The Church is experienced and skilled at testing individual vocations and training people to pursue them personally. Generally speaking not as much attention has been paid to helping groups of people to discern their collective vocations and to training ministers and leaders to help them to do so. What I have found most helpful in doing this are the theories and practices associated with Church and community development and the non-directive approach to working with people in groups, communities and organizations. Preparing mission statements can contribute to articulating collective vocations. It has most effect when all concerned think things through together and least effect when statements drawn up by a minority are imposed upon the majority. Chapter Three describes how the Methodist Diaconal Order followed a process which enabled the members to clarify their individual vocations and define their collective vocation. During recent years Roman Catholic religious orders have been involved in similar processes. As part of their response to Vatican II they have been reviewing their apostolates through making individual and collective "discernments". This involves revisiting the "charism" of their founder, considering it openly and critically in relation to Scripture, current apostolates and their religious life style, contemporary needs and especially the "preferential option for the poor" and the resources and circumstances of their order. Such processes generally lead to a renewal of religious life for individuals, communities and congregations. Another example of defining collective vocations is to be found in the work done to define the individual and collective policies of the churches in a Methodist Circuit.[26]

When a church or an organization does not have a collective vocation it is a *collection of personal and privatised vocations*: sometimes they jell together but not always. A collection of vocations is no substitute for a collective vocation. Unthinking and uncritical general acceptance by a congregation of a charismatic or a directive leader's vocation must not be assumed to have the same properties as a hard won realisation of a collective vocation.

Much of the work of the Church is done, as it always has been, by workers pursuing their vocations with the support of Christian communities. But contemporary society demands the adoption of strategies of ministry and mission carried out by people with deep seated personal and collective vocations.[27]

Somewhat paradoxically, the sharper the definition of individual and collective vocations the more effective is the overall vocational bonding: the blurring of individual and collective vocations and the boundaries between them has no place in the processes described here; their nature and shape must be understood and respected. This is amply demonstrated in Chapter Three.

Working at vocations in this way is a theological, group and community activity; which has to do with the spiritual and the secular; it is an exercise in multi-disciplinary reflective collaboration; it involves succeeding generations taking their place in the vocational continuity pioneered and sustained by Jesus who continues to call people into the apostolic succession. Paul pleads with us to form collective vocations and indicates the graces required:

> If our life in Christ means anything to you, if love can persuade at all, or the Spirit that we have in common, or any tenderness and sympathy, then be united in your convictions and united in your love, with a common purpose and a common mind. . . . Leave no room for selfish ambition and vanity, but humbly reckon

others better than yourselves. Look to each other's interests and not merely your own.[28]

(d)   The Work is Comprehensive and Inclusive

Human diversity is a highly significant feature of church work. Theologically the Church is for all kinds and conditions of people in all kinds of circumstances and situations. In practice the range of people involved in a particular church is limited by many factors including its culture, ethos, the attitudes of its members and religious emphases, the activities and services it provides and the nature of the community in which it is set. Nevertheless, congregations can contain people with a wide and uneven spectrum of ages, intellectual ability, faith and spiritual development, gifts graces, temperaments and experience from different ethnic background and social classes. The list of variations is endless. This presents workers with enormous challenges. All age worship, the vogue that has supplanted family and community worship, is, for instance, an attempt to provide comprehensive liturgical experiences which span these differences. Alongside this, attempts are made to meet specific needs through various acts of worship, organization and activities. Exciting but difficult.

Inescapably, those with overall responsibility, lay and ordained, have to work with human diversity. In churches with a social or community work programme the diversity can be enormous.[29] Generally speaking, few churches of the main line denominations in Britain have attracted poor people in areas of deprivation: congregations mainly consist of upper working and middle class people. During the past few decades the church has had a bad conscience about this and strenuous efforts have been made to work with and minister to people who are in areas of deprivation. Large numbers of Roman Catholic religious orders have committed themselves to a "preferential option for the poor",[30] the Methodist Church has developed a "mission alongside the poor" programme[31] and the Anglicans followed the report on the church in urban priority areas, *Faith in the City*, with the Church Urban Fund. Then they produced *Faith in the Countryside*.[32]

Broadly speaking the motivation and energy for this came from two sources: the needs of poor people and the blatant injustice of their circumstances; the orientation to the poor in the Bible generally and in Jesus' ministry in particular. Combined these factors induced compassion and guilt and led to the redirection of some vocational energy and Church resources.

Examples of apostolates to people who are deprived are, of course, to be found throughout church history. Many, if not most, Roman Catholic religious orders were founded to pursue such apostolates. Protestants founded children's societies and many other charities. Whilst I am not in a position to assess the overall effect of these movements, it would seem that they added dimensions to the established and widely accepted pattern of Church work without challenging it, whereas the contemporary movement towards the poor has raised a wide ranging debate throughout the Church about the proper locus of ministry and mission.[33]

Serious questions have been raised about the Church's preoccupation with ministering to the non-poor and their place in the inauguration and economy of the kingdom of God. Amidst all the complexity of thought and action that has followed, strands can be discerned which are pertinent to our discussion. As noted, some workers and limited resources have been committed to exclusive work with people in areas of deprivation. Some local churches are developing projects alongside their other programmes. Consequently, the overall practical effect has been to broaden the spectrum in a diverse and patchy manner. Theologically, however, there is some conflict and confusion about the issues. Conceptually a tendency can be discerned towards shifting the theological spectrum from the "rich" to the "poor" with the effect of broadening it in one direction and narrowing it in another. This takes seriously Jesus' emphasis upon the poor. But I still believe it is important to take up the challenge of what Jesus thought was the most difficult problem, converting the rich and getting them through the needle's eye entrance into the kingdom.

My conviction is that the Church should work on the broadest possible human spectrum and that it should be inclusive rather than exclusive.[34] Briefly stated my reasons for holding this position fall under three headings: theological, strategical and practical. **Theologically** the Christian gospel is for all, rich and poor, and all are in need of repentance and everything that Christ has to offer. God's love embraces the whole world and his mission is directed towards it. God's salvific approach is holistic, and so must be the Church's. The rich and poor and the vast numbers between these extremes need each other, their respective and collective spiritual well-being are interdependent. **Strategically** the development and maintenance of Churches and societies which embody the Christian spirit and ethic unavoidably involves working with the poor and the rich and the in-betweens. It is essential to engage in mission alongside the poor, the rich and all the rest in order that, separately and together, they make the contributions they alone can and must make towards creating a just and sustainable society. This means working with them in their richness and poverty for their salvation in and from those states. Amongst other things this involves getting rich and poor and the rest to work with and for each other. That is a great challenge. **Practically**, it means working with and through the given constituency, and that is predominantly people who are neither rich nor poor and who are culturally and spiritually at some distance from those who are deprived. Difficult socio-religious bridge building is required. Heavy demands will be made not only upon spiritual gifts and graces but also upon the behavioural sciences and, in my experience, upon the theory and practice of church and community development.

A model of this kind of approach is to be found in Bosch's analysis of Luke's missiology in the third Gospel. He describes it in a superb section entitled, "Gospel for the poor—and the rich".[35] (I found the dash extraordinarily eloquent!) Bosch accepts that Luke had a particular interest in the poor and other marginalized people: "The first words the Lukan Jesus speaks in public (Luke 4:18f) contains a programmatic statement concerning his mission to reverse the destiny of the poor".[36] After examining the terms used for "rich" (*plousios*) and "poor" (*ptochos*) and what people in both categories have to do to respond to the gospel he concludes:

> Luke should, however, not be interpreted as if he knows of only one sin, that of wealth, and only one kind of conversion, that of giving up one's possessions. Both the poor and the rich need salvation. At the same time, each person has his or her specific sinfulness and enslavement. The patterns of enslavement differ,

which means that the specific sinfulness of the rich is different from that of the poor. Therefore, in Luke's gospel, the rich are tested on the ground of their wealth, whereas others are tested on loyalty toward their family, their people, their culture, and their work (Lk 9:59-61). . . . This means that the poor are sinners like everyone else, because ultimately sinfulness is rooted in the human heart. Just as the materially rich can be   spiritually poor, the materially poor can be spiritually poor. . . . Luke undoubtedly wishes to communicate to his readers what is today often referred to as God's preferential option for the poor, but this option cannot be interpreted in any exclusive sense. . . . It does not exclude God's concern for the rich, but, in fact, stresses it for, in both his gospel and Acts, Luke wishes his readers to know that there is hope for the rich, insofar as they act and serve in solidarity with the poor and oppressed. In their being converted to God, rich and poor are converted toward each other. The main emphasis, ultimately, is on sharing, on community. At various points in Acts, Luke highlights this "communism of love" (cf Acts 2:44ff; 4:32, 36f).[37]

Clearly, a range of factors will determine the diversity with which a local church engages and its opportunities and capacities to broaden the spectrum of its work. They include: the social setting; attitudes of the church people; the respective cultures of church and community; the intention of church leaders; the ability and willingness of lay and ordained people in the Church to engage with those who differ from them. However this may be, the nature of the work requires the thrust to be towards working with the widest manageable spectrum inclusively and not to narrowing the spectrum exclusively towards either the poor or the rich. By nature it is comprehensive and universal and therefore diverse. The personal and intellectual abilities, the knowledge and understanding, the technical skills and the spiritual resources required of workers are enormous.

2. Operational Attributes Which Derive from Basics of the Working Situation and the Christian Project

This cluster of attributes enable fundamentals of the Christian project to be worked out in the church and the world through taking seriously the realities and authority of the way things are and operate in the work place. They show that church and community work, with all kinds of people in a wide range of religious and social settings, is:

(a) relational

(b) personal, communal and organizational

(c) essentially local

(d) ecclesiastical and contextual

(e) language based

(f) voluntary

(a) The Work is Relational

Essentially the nature of the work is relational. Ministry and mission is about anything to do with shaping the complex, unpredictable inner and outer relationships between people, the world and God to conform with how Jesus related to his Father, people and things and said that we should. That is a tall order but Christians believe that it is the way to human and spiritual well-being and satisfaction. It involves particular forms of relational engagement:

— with God (indirectly through the Bible and the theological traditions of the churches and directly through spiritual experience);

— with the created order (through experiencing, studying and researching it);

— with others (individuals, formal and informal groups, communities and institutions);

— with self.[38]

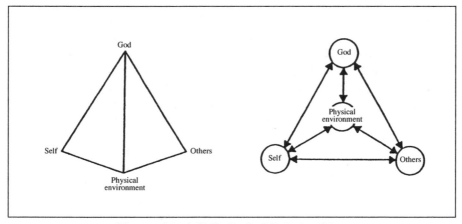

Figure 6:2 A Trihedral of Relationships

I have explored these relationships and their interaction through a trihedral model of relationships represented diagrammatically in Figure 6:2.[39] The points represent self, others, the physical environment and God; the lines represent the relationships between them. People would model these relationships differently. They might, for instance, invert it or lay it on its side to show God as the ground of all being and to avoid hierarchical inferences. Some people might substitute an ideology for God. However this might be, for me this trihedral of relationships underlies all human affairs, even though it is impossible to define with accuracy all the lines. Aspects of it may be covered and confused by institutions, churches, communities, groups or individuals, or by the way disciplines variously focus on individuals (counselling, case work, psychotherapy), on collectives (sociology, anthropology), on God (theology), or on the physical environment (physical science, technology, the work of artisans, ecology).

The shape is constantly changing. Relationships are inter-related. Change one and the others are changed. Indeed Jesus teaches us that restoring our relationship with God involves first mending our relationships with others.[40] Personal and inter-personal behaviour are influenced by, and expressions of, many different situational, personal, sociological and historical factors. At times these relationships and the factors, which can appear to have a life of their own, are dynamically balanced creatively. At other times they lock people in uncreativity or in their agitation they disturb, confuse, and confound people and their trihedral of relationships. Dissatisfaction, disillusionment or sheer frustration with vocational work, for instance, can upset our relationship with colleagues, family, friends and God.

Some workers in the Church believe in God without claiming to have a relationship with him. For others the personal experience of, and personal relationship with God are the quintessence of life and religion. They variously experience living relationships with God, Father, Son and Holy Spirit through prayer, worship and everyday human relationships and events. God calls them, Jesus is God with them, (Emmanuel) and they believe that the Holy Spirit leads and guides them. As we have seen, they feel that they work for God; they are co-workers with Christ. These relationships exercise spiritual authority in the lives of those who experience them and determine vocational choices and apostolates. When they are in good repair they engender commitment to human well-being and they enthuse and energize people. Whether in good repair or not, their influence can be far reaching and quite beyond logical deduction. But they are even more difficult to understand and analyse than human relationships—which are difficult enough.

Some aspects of these relationships and the factors that influence them are open to view because people talk about them and they are deducible from behaviour. Others are elusive. One of the difficulties in human relations work is that much of relevance is hidden from us, as Gareth Morgan says, we are always working on incomplete information.[41] Starting with what is known we have to deduce and guess what is possibly relevant in the unknown and to create opportunities for mutual sharing of those things necessary for collaborative and reflective action in ministry and mission. Such activity is an important part of working for human and spiritual development, and therefore of work consultancy.

Considering the complexities of these relationships even in a small group makes the mind boggle. Plotting the relational lines would require a powerful computer and a good programme. How incredible that, on the whole, we manage relational systems so well when so much is unknown and unknowable! Working seriously at them in a Christian context for human and spiritual development involves pursuing complementary tasks such as:

- promoting understanding about those things which according to the teaching of Christianity and the behavioural sciences build up and those which break down human and spiritual relationships between people, God and the physical universe;

- striving continuously to understand better the creative and destructive forces in human and spiritual behaviour;

- studying, researching and working to improve human relationships in specific situations and contexts within churches and communities;

- focusing on specific aspects of the relationships as required and working at them consciously in relation to the other relationships;

- working with people experientially and theologically on their needs and their concerns and interests in any aspect of their human and spiritual relationships and temporal and mystical experiences;

264

- working with people in depth to the limit of their capacity, no less and no more;
- training workers in human relations skills and providing follow up consultancy services;
- providing support and sustenance and inspiration to those engaged in human relations work through the means of grace (worship, the sacraments, prayer, fellowship), pastoral care, opportunities for biblical, theological and contextual study;
- living out what is being proclaimed in appropriate forms of personal, social and institutional behaviour.

The quality and extent of the work done by Christian organizations is inseparably and causally connected with the quality of the relationships between those who do it. Relationships, therefore, especially those between key figures in any aspect of the work, are of vital importance. Their influence suffuses the enterprise and affects it for better or worse. Good working relationships are at the heart of all effective church work. When they break down or sour, as they inevitably do at times because church workers are human beings, painful and intractable problems confuse and confound. Redeeming and rebuilding them can be one of the most difficult and unenviable jobs in church and society. But doing so illustrates the power of Christianity at work and demonstrates the efficacy of the Christian gospel. Human relations, opportunities and difficulties are at the heart of many, if not most, of the problems presented to consultants.

By the very nature of church life, working and professional relationships intermingle complexly with personal and private relationships. Ordained and lay workers are variously involved in six kinds of relationships. The first is **pastoral relationships**, *i.e.:* the relationships through which human and spiritual care, love, direction, support and assistance are offered to individuals, groups, churches and communities in relation to Christian living and faith development at any and all stages of their experience and during crises and life-determining issues.[42] The second is **liturgical relationships**.[43] These are the relationships between those who lead worship, officiate at the sacraments, weddings, funerals and other occasional offices and others involved in them. The third is what I call **ecclesiastical and collegial relationships**, *i.e.:* the many kinds of relationships through which church work is designed, organized, carried out and managed. Some of these relationships are within a particular church, others are between churches and other organizations. The fourth is what I call **latent or potential working relationships**, *i.e.:* the discovery and nurturing of relationships with other workers and organizations in the same and related fields through socializing and networking which could possibly develop into formal or informal working relationships. Then there are **extended relationships** such as those entered into through consultancy, counselling, mentoring and spiritual direction arrangements. The sixth is **personal relationships**, general and soul friendships, which can evolve from or lead into any of the other relationships.

It is of the essence of this kind of relational work that it leads to profound engagement with the realities of the human condition in church and society through active participation in many situations and events with people who differ greatly—

morally, temperamentally and spiritually. It involves working in good and bad contexts, contending with all kinds of personal and interpersonal behaviour, experiencing many different expressions and forms of love and hatred, pride and prejudice, health and suffering. Church meetings, for instance, can be sublime, deeply moving experiences of creative activity and extraordinary working relationships. On the other hand they can be awful and frightening experiences of the destructive powers of human beings and their cruelty and inhumanity. Both kinds of experience can happen when least expected. The pattern is unpredictable. All too easily those leading such meetings can respond inappropriately. Clergy and lay workers require gifts, graces and relational skills to do this work and considerable resources to cope with the pain, the emotional strain and not infrequent experiences of post-traumatic shock. Contrary to public opinion, therefore, church and neighbourhood workers do not live sheltered lives.

Threaded throughout these encounters is a search for understanding, meaning, explanation. This is particularly so in relation to destructive and painful events. At one level there is a search for insights which will enable people to understand and overcome the bad dynamics they are experiencing in, for instance, meetings or groups plagued by deep faction. Workers raid and study the behavioural sciences hoping to find clues and ways and means of researching the information they need to be able to decide how best to act. At another level theological questions are raised. Examples are: "Why should this person suffer and not that?" "What do these events mean?" "What is God saying to us through our repeated failure to do this or that?" Then there are questions about goodness and badness in human life. Should we, for instance, work on the basis of "original blessing" [44] or "original sin"? Upon what biblical and theological teaching should we base our analysing and planning in areas of deprivation and discrimination? Facing these questions is important. Simplistic answers about providence may, for instance, satisfy people during good times. They will not sustain them during bad times.

By nature, therefore, the work is demanding and difficult. So, as we shall see later, the work calls for a combination of interpersonal and intellectual abilities which help people to go deep into their experiences and to emerge better informed and equipped and more mature.

(b)   The Work is Personal, Communal and Organizational

Church work requires of those engaged in it that they work with:

- individuals and groups in their own right and as members, officers, workers of the church;
- congregations;
- churches as communities, organizations and networks.

Much has already been said about the first of these. An increasing amount of attention is focused on understanding and working with congregations. [45] Our purposes are served by concentrating on the third in this and subsequent sections.

Whilst the term community is in general use and everyone has some understanding of what it is, defining it has proved to be incredibly difficult. After two hundred years of grappling with the concept we have not found a satisfactory way of defining it or modelling it.[46] Raymond Plant said that such difficulties are to be expected when both the descriptive and evaluative dimensions of meaning come together.[47] Reference is often made to the fact that G. A. Hillery noted ninety four definitions. Roland Warren said, "My view is that the quest for a definition is a vain one". For me, a good community provides its members with both the privacy and the togetherness they require for their well-being, the relationships and resources they need to rise to the challenges of differences and faction and to work together for the common good. Propinquity is a word that helps me to understand the nature of togetherness in community. It is defined as: nearness, closeness, proximity in space (neighbourhood); in kinship or relationship; in nature, belief, similarity, affinity; in time.[48] Primarily based on feeling and a sense of belonging, it can exist without formal organization—indeed formal organization can kill it.[49]

Local secular communities perform four basic functions: economic (production, distribution and consumption of goods and services); welfare and mutual support; social, culture and moral (socialisation and social control and participation); environmental and ecological.[50] Christian communities contribute to some of these functions and to religious needs. James Fowler suggests that what he calls "communities of faith" have five functions:

(a)   the provision of a *shared core story*;

(b)   the provision of opportunities for people to participate in the *central passion* of the *shared core story*;

(c)   the formation of *affections*, and, I would add, *commitment*, in accordance with (a) and (b);

(d)   the generation of *virtues*, moral strengths and action skills;

(e)   the development and maintenance of the *practical and particular shape of worldly vocation* in each life in the community of mission, *i.e.*: an ecology of vocation.[51]

Churches, like religious orders, are formal religious voluntary organizations and institutions* as well as socio-religious communities. Invariably people first meet them as congregations or communities.

As organizations they bring something other than what is brought by communities to the performing of the functions already described. They are purposefully organized and structured for action based on the Bible, beliefs and traditions: neighbourhood communities do not normally have purposes and mission statements. Organizations have constitutions established at law, formalised procedures, rules and regulations and ways of enforcing them; they have power, organizational and administrative structures; they have members and are employers; they recruit, train and employ people; they have identities.

So, to work with churches to good effect it is sometimes essential to treat them as congregations and communities with an eye on relevant organizational features.

---

* "Organization" and "institution" are often used as interchangeable terms, almost as synonyms. It helps to differentiate them. A formal organization is "a system of consciously coordinated activities or forces of two or more persons",[52] the "structured expression of rational action".[53] Institution is used "to describe social practices that are regularly and continuously repeated,are sanctioned and maintained by social norms, and have a major significance in the social structure".[54]

At other times it is essential to treat them as organizations with an eye on the impact of what is being decided and done on congregations and community life. Only then will churches be prophetic institutions organized for mission and service pursuing their ministry from places where *koinonia* is experienced. (See Reference 9)

These distinctions are important, not pedantic, because there is a propensity towards unhelpful preoccupation with community or organization—or aspects of them. I have experienced it myself. My approach to my work as a minister was transformed by what I got from community development, community studies and related disciplines. For many years I concentrated on church as community to the neglect of church as organization. Rectifying this through drawing upon the prolific literature on organizational theory and behaviour was rewarding.

For some time now people in churches have been drawing upon practices common in the industrial and business world. It is reminiscent of what happened in the 60's and 70's in relation to community development work. An example of this is the formation of MODEM (Managerial and Organisational Disciplines for the Enhancement of Ministry) launched in 1993. It is committed to creative interaction between those engaged in the management of secular and Christian organizations based upon the mutual recognition and respect of their respective values and disciplines. Already, it has been very productive—articles; seminars; a professional critique of the Turnbull Report to the Archbishops' Advisory Group on the Organization of the Church of England, "Working as One Process";[55] and now two books have been published for MODEM. The first is *Management for Ministry—appreciating contemporary issues*. This extremely useful book is at pains to set management in two contexts: the agenda for ministry (Part one) and the agenda for organization (Part two). In his foreword Sir John Harvey Jones says, "The need for better management is ubiquitous. Churches need to be well managed, perhaps even more than private sector profit-seeking organisations do". *Leading, Managing and Ministry: challenging questions for church and society*, the second book, has just been published.[56] It considers management in relation to a cluster of issues.

Grapevines and networks, spontaneously created by people in organizations and communities, critically influence church work. They are devices which have far reaching effects for good or ill. They can be used to stimulate mistrust and unease through innuendoes, gossip and slander or to build up positive feelings between and about people; they can be used to build harmony or to cause mischief and they can be used to raise vital questions or unhelpful issues; they can be used to facilitate help and care or to cause harm and neglect. Such personal and social networks are frequently controlling factors in human, organizational and community development. They are covert, ubiquitous and elusive. They cannot be grasped or gathered together for encounter. Mapping them is always difficult and often impossible. They do not have inbuilt mechanisms for accountability or responsibility. Spin doctors are experts in using them for their purposes. What happens, for instance, on the grapevines after the arrival of a new minister powerfully influences all that follows. Important as they are in the economy of human and spiritual development, networks are much neglected in church and community work. There is much written on working with individuals, and groups, less on working with groups that interact and overlap and even less on networks. It is a subject avidly taken up by most of those to whom I have introduced this kind of subject matter because it is so pertinent to them and their work. So much of what they have attempted through formal structures has been frustrated and spoiled by the interaction on the networks whilst they stood by feeling helpless. Constructive action can be taken by addressing questions such as: what is being said on the networks about this? What can we do to correct or counter it? Before a new controversial programme is to be launched much can be gained by asking, "What do we want to be on the grapevines and what can we do to ensure that these ideas circulate?" Grapevines form a significant part of the nature of the work.[57]

(c)   The Work is Essentially Local

David J. Bosch makes and substantiates the following claims about the rediscovery of the local church:

> The church in mission is, primarily the local church everywhere in the world.

> The fundamentally innovative feature of the new development was the discovery that the universal church actively finds its true existence in the local churches; that these, and not the universal church, are the pristine expression of the church . . . ; that this was the primary understanding of the church in the New Testament . . . ; that the universal church viewed as preceding local churches was a pure abstraction since the universal church exists only where there are local churches; we now recognise that the church is both a theological and a sociological entity, an inseparable union of the divine and the dusty.[58]

> The church is, really, a family of local churches in which each should be open to the needs of the others and to sharing its spiritual and material goods with them. It is through the mutual ministry of mission that the church is realised, in communion with and as local concretization of the church universal.

> In the context of the secularized post-Christian West our witness will be credible only if it flows from a local worshipping community.[59]

> This perspective . . . was for all practical purposes ignored during much of Christian history.[60]

The proliferation of local churches makes it possible to take seriously these theological statements. Generally speaking there are local branches of several denominations deeply rooted in every community in the United Kingdom. Familiarity with this phenomenon inclines us to take it for granted. Of itself, such geographical coverage is an incredible achievement. Comparing it with the impressive but comparatively scant coverage of business empires like Sainsburys helps me to marvel that the Church is still omnipresent in contemporary society after decades of shrinkage. From the point of view of community resources alone a highly influential report said:

> The churches . . . command a network of many men and a number of women working full time and of premises suitable for communal activities unrivalled by any other voluntary body.[61]

269

Churches are, in fact, as much a part of the social fabric as schools, hospitals and social services. The amount of work done by them, in them and through them is astronomical. By any standard they make profound and incalculable contributions to human and spiritual well-being, development and happiness.

The opportunities to put the theological emphasis upon the importance of the local into practice have been taken up by people with various and quite different, and in some cases conflicting approaches to mission, evangelism and evangelization. For instance, those committed to church and community development, liberation theology and the preferential option to the poor have got local churches involved in *their* communities in new and exciting ways. Similar things have happened to those of us who from the 1960s onwards have been deeply involved in church and community development. Cliff College has changed its emphasis from conducting missions *for* local churches to helping them with *their* mission. One of their evangelists represented this when he said to the local church in a broad North Country accent, "If you think we're coming to work for you, well you'll be disappointed, we're coming to work *with* you. Do you see what I mean?" And Robert Warren has worked out in some detail from an evangelical position what is involved in being Church in mission in local churches.[62]

Paradoxically, but entirely in line with incarnational theology, local work is not done and facilitated exclusively by local workers based in local settings. It is done by the combined and collective efforts of people located in all the operational spheres of national and international church life. In fact, the *raison d'être* for regional, national and international work is local church work throughout the world. Thus, in one sense, denominational work in a region or a nation is the holistic summation of local work. Basic responsibilities of bishops, chairmen and provincials are to promote, facilitate, regulate and support local work. In most denominations local workers contribute to the work done regionally and nationally just as regional and national workers contribute to local work; regional and national people do not do all the regional and national work by any means. That does not mean to suggest that there is nothing distinctive about regional and national workers and the work they do. They work to regions and denominations like others work to local situations; theirs is a regional/national perspective. Others view the regional and national through their local perspective. The interaction of these perspectives is complex and can be creative or confusing or destructive. This all-operational-level involvement of practitioners in the life and work of their denominations is vital. It means, for instance, that local practitioners help to shape the denominational training programmes through participating in national committees, synods and conferences. Polity and theology determine that the work in every sphere is affected and effected by the separate and combined efforts of people in all spheres. Collaboration and co-operation, not stratification and competition, must be fundamentals of Christian organizations and hallmarks of their work culture, praxis and spirituality. Leaders in all operational spheres need to have the ability to work to different perspectives of the parts and the whole. Sometimes, for instance, they need to be able to work to a parish in relation to the diocese and denomination. At other times they need to work to the diocese in relation to many parishes and the denomination. Difficulties can be experienced in doing this. Parish priests, for instance, can find it difficult to act in relation to the good of their diocese when it is not in the best interest of their parish. I have worked with bishops and other diocesan officers who do find it difficult on some occasions to maintain the diocesan perspective when they are immersed in the actualities of a particular parish.[63]

The ubiquitous presence of the Church in community settings is a human counterpart to the omnipresence of Christ. It facilitates a Christian presence which is as continuous and permanent as possible. Churches that are deeply embedded in the local social fabric are long-standing neighbours. Churches in settled communities work with and minister to people in church and community throughout their lives and with one generation after another. Clergy and lay workers, in many instances the same ones, accompany and serve people over long periods of time in all the critical events they experience and as they struggle and grow from one stage of life and faith to another.[64] Thus, in succession they service life-long processes of human and spiritual development and meet changing liturgical and pastoral needs. Whereas some churches in radically changing or transitory communities serve and minister to the needs of people, often acute, over a much shorter time. Also, churches in both settled and transitory communities can continue a life-long ministry to its dispersed ex-members through prayer, occasional contacts and through welcoming those who make return visits.

Life-long involvement with people in their churches in relation to anything and everything to do with their lives is a critical aspect of the nature of this work. It is especially important when the provision of personal and community care can be fragmented and discontinuous.

(d)   The Work is Ecclesiastical and Contextual

Churches and denominations are the primary institutions through which this work is conducted, so the work is inescapably ecclesiastical. Broadly speaking, churches and denominations are used for two complementary strategies or modes of operation. One of them is the work they do with people within their own institutions and networks through a wide range of services, activities and programmes in their premises. These are intended to achieve the institution's aims through serving people and providing opportunities for them to meet some of their personal, social and spiritual needs. Participants range from deeply committed members to casual users. People enter the church from the environment, participate in its purposeful processes, bring life to it, build it up and then return to other parts of their lives hopefully better for the experience and, possibly, as ambassadors of Christ and the Church. This mode can be modelled as an "open system process" which is illustrated in Figure 6:3.[65] This model can be applied to the whole of a church's work or to aspects of it such as a service of worship, a housegroup, a night shelter for homeless people or a Christian education programme covering several years of the lives of young people. When viewed in this way, operationally speaking, churches are in the same family of institutions as schools, colleges and hospitals. They are designed and organized to achieve their purposes through their internal programmes and the relationships they engender.

The other work mode can be described as "contextual". This involves churches working as agents for change in their immediate environment or in society in general. For example, this could involve churches working with their religious and

271

secular neighbours, individuals, groups and institutions on matters of mutual concern. Equally it could involve churches acting as pressure groups and even taking direct action. Or it might involve them in evangelism or apologetics, arguing the Christian faith and presenting the Christian view on contentious moral issues.[66]

Whereas the first mode of work is within the domain of the institution this is reaching out beyond it; it is socio-religious development work in the community and society at large. The first is under the direct control of the church; the second is the church at work in open social settings in which many independent authorities variously compete and co-operate—exhilarating places in which to work but they

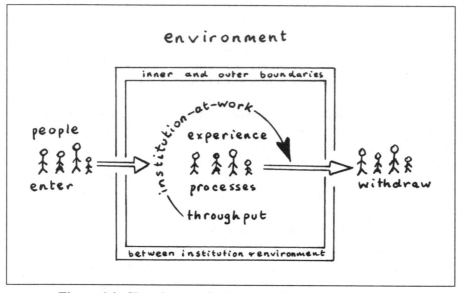

Figure 6:3 Church as an Institutional Open System Process

can intimidate.[67] The first is the church attempting to achieve its purpose domestically, the second contextually. What is important is that the "couplings" between churches and their environment are such that the effect of the one upon the other is constructive.[68]

These two modes of interrelated and overlapping work are facilitated through clergy, religious and laity operating in relation to four principal spheres of social living: local, regional, national and international.[69] Their functions and responsibilities vary enormously but, significantly, the work requires that every worker engages in a cluster of core activities, albeit, in different ways. The following classification of the core activities helps me to get my mind around them; to see them as a whole and how they relate and overlap and complement each other; to engage conceptually and practically with each of them separately and in relation to the others.

(i)   *Local Church and Neighbourhood work*

Already we have seen in the previous section that those engaged in all the four spheres contribute to local work. This section offers a three-fold classification of the nature of local church and neighbourhood work.[70]

Church work includes organizing and conducting services of worship, preaching, fellowship meetings, prayer groups and programmes of Christian education for children and adults. It includes pastoral care and counselling and the occasional offices such as services of baptism and burial. All this involves engaging and working with congregations in all kinds of different ways in order to minister to them and through them. Considerable attention is now being given to what is involved in doing this.[71] Church work also involves pursuing the mission of the church through evangelical outreach. It includes all the planning, administration, fund raising and labour necessary to design, staff, finance, organize and do this work and to operate and maintain the buildings in which it is housed. Also it has an evaluative and reflective side. Continual thought needs to be given by church leaders to all that is happening or not happening in all three areas in relation to Christian mission and local needs. Church work, therefore, refers to all that is done through prayer, thought and action to meet religious and secular needs and to promote and extend the understanding of the Christian faith and its practice and to sustain and equip people for living out their Christian lives and for all the work they do in the church, in the community and in their occupations in the world whatever they might be. (Helping people to grapple with issues arising from their working lives is as vital as helping them with those related to their personal, social and spiritual lives.) Clearly the way in which this work is done varies from denomination to denomination.

Church-community work refers to work undertaken on premises owned by the church to meet the needs of anyone without regard to their religious beliefs, practices or church affiliation. It is arranged around interests, tasks, concerns and activities not normally considered "religious" and conducted with little or no religious ceremony. Examples are: uniformed organizations; clubs and sports facilities for any age group and for people with special needs; drop-in centres; luncheon clubs for retired people; AA meetings; language study groups for immigrants; mothers' and toddlers' groups, playgroups and nurseries; social and community work agency offices; counselling services; clinics and surgeries. Examples and descriptions of this work are now commonplace.

Some churches as a matter of policy undertake all the church-community work on their premises themselves: they provide or appoint workers and leaders. Some enter into partnerships with other churches or agencies in relation to one aspect or another. Other churches make their premises available freely or let them out, to enable others to provide much needed facilities. However, no matter how open and egalitarian the working relationships with other leaders and workers, local church authorities have the final say in what is and what is not allowed. As long as they are the trustees of the premises they are the senior partners or the landlords.[72]

A limited number of churches have substantial programmes of this form of work. Increasing numbers of churches have full-time youth, community and pastoral workers. The West London Mission of the Methodist Church, for instance, has an extensive social work programme located in several centres and employing forty full-time professional workers.[73] But a programme of this scale is an exception.

Community work is work in which churches are engaged, generally with other agencies, to promote the well-being and development of people in the community. It is carried out in settings, groups, buildings and organizations not associated with

273

the Church. The Church and its members are partners with others. Examples are: the kind of things listed under church-community work; residents' associations; good neighbourhood schemes; detached youth work." Church related community work" has become a widely accepted way of referring to community work and aspects of church-community work. It is a helpful term but it does not readily make distinctions that are important here.[74]

Figure 6:4 has been widely used to express this classification diagrammatically. Whilst this classification serves our purposes it has limitations. Unfortunately I cannot improve it. For instance all three categories, not just the first, are, in my view, the work of the kingdom of God. The emphases churches, laity and clergy give to these areas will depend upon many things including: their approach to mission and ministry and their personal style and circumstances. And they will express what they wish to achieve through this work for individuals and society differently according to their theological persuasion and denominational background. However, implicit in one or other of the aspects of this work are three principal objectives:

- to initiate people into the Christian faith and Church;

- to accompany, sustain and support Christians as they mature and develop in seeking to understand Christianity, to live Christian lives, to build Christian communities, and to work out the implications of their faith in their private and working lives;

- to help non-Christians to develop by helping them to meet their personal and social needs and to build up neighbourhood communities in a disinterested way.

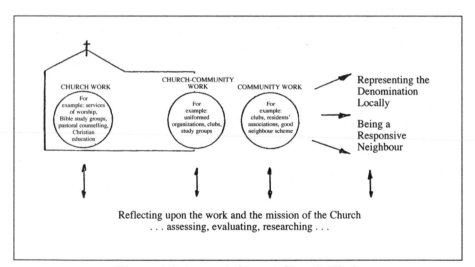

Figure 6:4 Aspects of Local Church Work

Again, theological persuasion, personal style and circumstances will lead clergy, laity and churches to weight these objectives differently. All three objectives can be pursued concurrently in *church work* and the second and third in *church-community work* and *community work*. It is however counter productive to use *church-community* and *community work* solely as a means of bringing people into the

274

Christian faith and the Church especially if overtly altruistic activities are used as a cover for attempts to evangelize or proselytize. Experience and research has demonstrated that the more genuinely altruistic church people are in *church-community* and *community* work the more effective they are. Not surprisingly, churches, clergy and laity are taken more seriously by people in the community when they show real interest in them and work with them openly.[75]

The shape and nuances that the overall programme of work of any one church depends upon many factors. Reference has been made to some of them. Another one is the geographical location. Clearly, the work of churches in villages will take on a different form from those in city centres. During the season, organizing worship and hospitality for visitors will be a priority for churches in holiday resorts. Small congregations in inner city churches and other areas of urban deprivation may well find themselves heavily involved in community work whereas churches in county, country and provincial towns and in the suburbs may find that they have a nicely balanced programme of church and church-community work with little community work.

(ii) *Promoting, Representing and Networking*

Local, regional and national workers represent the denomination to itself and to other bodies. They, acting on behalf of their denomination, network, engage and liaise with people in similar positions in other denominations and religions, Christian secular voluntary organizations and statutory bodies. They engage in all kinds of activities: they speak and argue on behalf of their denomination; they engage in conversations with others about their respective beliefs, about conflicts of interest, about possible areas of co-operation, collaboration, partnerships and possible schemes of unity; they establish joint projects. The aim is to exert religious, spiritual and political influence wherever necessary and to present Christianity. Through these activities they:

- promote Christianity
- evangelize in the church and the world
- discern and make known their own identity as Christians and that of the Church
- contextualize the work of the Church
- develop inter-organizational understanding and relationships.

(iii) *Working at Key Subject Matter*

A continuous core of hard thinking about a wide range of subject matter is required for the Church to be the Church and for it to do its work. In part, the Church's integrity depends upon it being able to do this well as does the quality of its life and its contribution to its own constituency and to society. Ideally, everyone involved in the work of the Church needs to think about and discuss the key subject matter related to Christian life and work, ministry and mission. Given the diversity of age, culture, education, occupation, intellect and training, this will be done in very different ways by individuals and churches and with different outcomes. The help most of us need to be able to do so comes from a number of sources: articles, books, courses, formal and informal discussions with all kinds of people, radio and television programmes, sermons. Fully aware of this need, and the importance of studying things in depth, a vast amount of thinking is undertaken in the Church. Some of it is initiated and facilitated by the Church, much of it by individuals and groups. This cannot be left to the experts but it cannot be done without them. They facilitate thought throughout the Church and in the world at large.

Staff members of theological colleges and universities are engaged in study, research and debate about every biblical, theological and missiological subject and a range of related disciplines and of current and political affairs. A vast number of other people positioned throughout the Church are similarly engaged. Articles and books are published. Officers are appointed and departments are in being to work at subjects such as social responsibility, education, mission and other denominations. They study and research a wide range of subjects and the disciplines to which they belong. They publish reports. They participate in various academic communities and debates and they try to work out the implications and pursue the issues in the Church, in society generally and with government, business and industry. They engage in inter-faith dialogue, apologetics, the presentation and defence of the Christian faith on theological, moral and philosophical grounds and they also help others to do so. Apologetics has taken on a new importance in this postmodern era. At a different level, but of no less value, working with people within and outside the Church involves discussions and debates about the nature of the Christian faith and the difficulties they have with it (cf pp 339-340). So, inevitably, there is a desirable and necessary apologetic element in church work.

Martyn Atkins has set out in a short, penetrating and accessible essay the nature of this apologetic task during this present period of profound cultural change. "Terms describing the change such as 'postmodern', 'late modern' or even 'New Age', are less significant", he says, "than the realisation that our world view is in a state of flux".[76] Some of the difficulties people have with Christianity are of an intellectual nature. They want answers to the big questions of faith, life and death. But, as Atkins argues, experience and research show that few people are won to Christian faith by purely academic apologetics or prevented from finding faith by purely academic questions. People want to be loved, listened to and valued. Experience of these as basics of Christianity carry their own messages and logic. As Atkins concludes, what is required is "head and heart apologetics": challenging and courteous dialogue and good experiences of Christian community. The cultivation of relational apologetics is vital to the work of the church in all its spheres. (What has been said about the praxis of consultancy resonates with this. Creative in depth analysis of vocational work which is of inestimable value and importance to consultors with minimum hurt, depends upon the quality of interpersonal behaviour and working relationships. It is not by accident that these qualities along with roles make up the first three elements of the practice theory of consultancy in Chapter Two. They precede, accompany and facilitate critical thought.)

However, all that is involved in representing Christian thinking to the world and to the Church must not be left to the experts because, important as their contribution is, they simply cannot do all that is required. Intermediaries, for instance, are needed to communicate and disseminate what they are learning from specialists. And, in any case, experts do not have a monopoly on insights, knowledge and understanding. For these and other reasons related to everyone's development, it is necessary for the whole church to engage with the subject matter and to discuss and debate it with people with whom they live and work and especially with those who differ in belief and life style. To do this most of us need the help of specialists (on appropriate subject matter and on facilitating creative dialogue) and all they produce if we, along with them, are to:

- effect the ministry and mission of the church in the academic, business, industrial and civic worlds as well as in local residential neighbourhoods
- inform and equip ourselves and the Church workforce
- help workers and members to think their way through critical contemporary issues
- contextualize the work of the Church
- equip churches to be what Peter Berger called "mediating structures"*
- develop inter-organizational understanding and relationships
- challenge and confront ideas and activities which, according to Christianity, are at variance with human and spiritual well-being and development
- help Christians to do the work of the Kingdom of God wherever they are situated in the complexities of contemporary society and their work places.

(iv) *Overseeing, Directing and Managing Allied Institutions, Agencies and Charities*

Regional, national and local workers becoming engaged in the overall administration of institutions in which their denomination has vested interests: colleges, church and public schools, local and national charities for work with children and old and handicapped people and projects of all kinds. They may act as chaplains or sit on their boards or chair their governing bodies.

(v) *Working with Other Organizations*

This work is done by a vast army of lay people who pursue their vocations in secular organizations. It is also done by an increasing number of ordained people who are seconded to work as chaplains to businesses, hospitals, prisons, schools and universities on a part- or full-time basis and as lecturers and social workers. All this helps to affect the ministry and mission of the church in the academic, business, industrial and civic worlds and to develop inter-organizational understanding and relationships. Through ministering in the work place they help Christians to do the work of the Kingdom of God in their work places amid the complexities of contemporary society. Providing them with support, spiritual sustenance, help and fellowship and opportunities to reflect on critical issues with people with similar beliefs is an important function of the Church.

(vi) *Creating and Maintaining Viable Churches and Denominations*

It follows that co-operating with God to create and use denominations and their churches and to keep them in good working order is fundamental to the work we are

---

* That is "those institutions which stand between the individual in his *(sic)* private sphere and the larger institutions of the public sphere". William Temple referred to them as "intermediate associations" and *Faith in the City* as agents of "intermediate action".[77] As such they are not political organizations but they are not apolitical. They have been described as "sub-political"[78] because they perform important functions in relation to all kinds of organizations and political structures through advocacy, apologetics, research, reports, books, lobbying, demonstrating, protesting and direct action.

considering. All else depends upon this being done well. Strangely, it has become common practice to be somewhat derogatory and dismissive about this aspect of church work. Maintenance is seen to be a poor cousin to mission and a frequent detraction from it. Inviting people to choose between them is to offer a false choice. They belong together. Theology, context, circumstances and resources inform the kind of church needed and possible; creating and maintaining such churches is clearly as much a missiological activity as using them in the service of the Kingdom of God. To be able to make churches that work, those involved require an unusual combination of: prophetic imagination, practical ability and nous; spiritual sensitivity and theological knowledge; ecclesiastical and organizational acumen; a profound understanding of the culture, intellectual environment and socio-religious context in which the churches and denominations have to exist and operate. Some tasks are common to the organization as a whole, *e.g.*: financing the denomination and building up working relationships infused with respect and trust. Others, such as preparing people for ministry, involve people located in different parts of a denomination making complementary contributions. Colleges, for instance, provide opportunities for ordinands to be students and ministerial apprentices whilst local churches provide opportunities for them to be ministerial apprentices and students: in the one situation they study theology and practice; in the other, practice and theology.

Basically this work is the human effort required to make churches of different denominations operate effectively in their own right, in relation to each other and parts of the society in which they are located. Ecclesiastical work involves several different but complementary theological, sociological and administrative activities. Here, we describe nine tasks which require sustained attention without attempting to note the many ways in which they are done or to assess current performance.

Doing theology on the nature of the Church and people's perception of it. This task involves working on the nature of the church and various perceptions of it. An exercise which can be both absorbing and tricky. Christians believe that the Church is created by God and that it is sustained and empowered in and through spiritual and mystical relationships with Father, Son and Holy Spirit and the Communion of Saints. It exists for, but is not synonymous with the Kingdom of God. These basic elements of the Church's theological and spiritual constitution are to be distinguished from ecclesiastical structures but are meant to inform them.

A proliferation of biblical models and images illuminate aspects of the nature of the Church. Avery Dulles notes that Paul Minear lists ninety-six in the New Testament. Amongst those most commonly referred to are: the house of God; the temple and tabernacle of God; God's people, flock, vine, field and city; Christ's bride and body. He makes two observations which help to find working theological models. *First*, he suggests that multi-modelling is to be preferred to mono-modelling. Each image has strengths and weaknesses. For example, the strength of the analogy of the body is that it emphasizes that the Church is a spiritual organism or a socio-spiritual system. The weakness is that it suggests that the members of the body have no personal freedom; they are controlled by other members.[79] More recently Howard Snyder has provided a more dynamic typology of church models than Dulles, as has Diane Hare.[80] As the Church is a human as well as a divine institution, secular organizational modelling can constructively complement biblical and theological modelling provided that it does not supplant it. Gareth Morgan has given us a brilliant examination of the strengths and limitations of various images of organizations as machines, organisms, brains, cultures, political systems, psychic prisons, flux and transformation and instruments of domination.[81] Each of these has, at various times, illuminated my experience of working with the Church for development. Using a cluster of models, each compensating for the weakness of others, reduces the dangers of getting it wrong which are inherent in mono-modelling. The *second* suggestion is a refinement of the first, it recommends the use of dominant models which he calls, "paradigms" to head up, as it were, clusters of models. Dulles illustrates this from the Roman Catholic Second Vatican Council. Members of the Council made use of the models but the dominant one was that of the "People of God". Dulles says, "This paradigm focussed attention on the Church as a network of interpersonal relationships, on the Church as Community".[82] This paradigm shift from the model of the Church as the "Mystical Body" resembles what Thomas Kuhn has described as a "scientific revolution".[83] (Incidentally, Hans Kung has summarised in a telling way in chart form the major paradigm shifts in the history of Christianity.)[84]

Working in and with the Church's constitution and its political power structures. Churches are working institutions in which, ideally, apposite images and models are embodied. They have legal and religious constitutions, written and unwritten codes of professional practice and moral behaviour, controlling bodies, councils, synods, conferences, chapters etc. Each denomination is structured and organized differently. They vary hierarchically, democratically and administratively. Workers have to be able to work within and through the structures of their own denomination and, with today's emphasis upon ecumenical co-operation, with those of other denominations. To do this they have to understand them sufficiently well to be able to pursue their own vocation within their denomination and to contribute towards making it an effective instrument of ministry and mission. In part this is an administrative task but it is also a political one because inevitably church workers have to engage in church politics and the formal and informal power structures. And that can be a messy business.

Analysing, evaluating, contextualising and re-designing denominational church work and organizational structures. As we have seen models and images used to conceptualize the nature of churches and organizations proliferate. Those that see them as socio-spiritual systems underline the need for them to be reflective communities staffed by reflective practitioners. Those that see them as machines to be run and maintained, value procedures and bureaucratic structures and emphasize the need to follow operational instructions. Both kinds shed light on what is involved in living and working with churches. The second points to the importance of routine; the first points to the importance of continually reflecting and periodically analysing, evaluating and assessing the work programme in relation to the context in which it has to be done and, possibly, re-designing it and the organizational structures through which it is done, in order to make churches and denominations more effective and efficient and more satisfying places in which to work.

Overall administration and organization of church and denomination. This aspect of the work relates to the administration, management, maintenance, and extension of churches and denominations. It has to do with finance, buildings, plant and the practicalities and legalities of the constitution and the organizational and administrative structures. People at all levels have responsibility for this work. They arrange meetings, conferences and synods and administer the day to day affairs between times. Overall objectives are to make the denominational institution work and to put it to work.

Recruiting, training, and validating ministers and religious. Amongst other things this involves people at all levels: testing personal vocations; accepting candidates for presbyteral and diaconal ministry, and religious life and apostolates; training, commissioning or ordaining them.

Deployment, professional and pastoral oversight, management and support of ministers and religious. The ways in which this is done varies considerably from one denomination to another as do the respective contributions made locally, regionally and nationally. Generalisations about processes and procedures are not very helpful. Vocational match making between churches and workers is a central and somewhat problematic feature of the deployment of full-time workers. Combining in one person or group, at any level of responsibility, the functions of professional oversight, management, discipline and pastoral care of workers is fraught with difficulties. Some of the issues involved are discussed in relation to the nature of church work and the competencies required in the next chapter.

Recruiting, training and deploying people in lay ministry and church and community work. Churches and denominations need a large workforce of preachers, teachers, pastoral workers, and youth workers. Building up, equipping and supporting these lay ministries, variously voluntary and salaried, is a major task to which ministers, priests and religious are required to make significant contributions.

In-service training, support and renewal of all personnel. There is a growing emphasis on life-long education and in-service training for all workers and members. All kinds of schemes from face-to-face courses and distance learning are being developed. Clergy are being given sabbaticals. Assessment schemes are being introduced. Consultants are being used by individuals and groups. People are using spiritual directors. Some Protestant clergy are following the practice of Roman Catholics and going on retreat.

Research. There is a long tradition of biblical and theological research in the Church and a growing movement to research the praxis of ministry and mission. Examples of this are to be seen in a new wave of missiological research and in a rapid multiplication of action research into all kinds of church and community work and evangelism.[85] Some of this research is systematic and sustained over long periods by individuals, working in all spheres, colleges and universities. For the main part it is ad hoc and episodic; it is not co-ordinated into holistic research programmes. This is both a strength and weakness; on balance I think it is more of a weakness.

Figure 6:5 gives an overall picture of the various aspects of the work described in this section.

(e) The Work is Language Based

Creative use of language is a central feature of the nature of the work we are considering. Every aspect of church and community work from having initial ideas

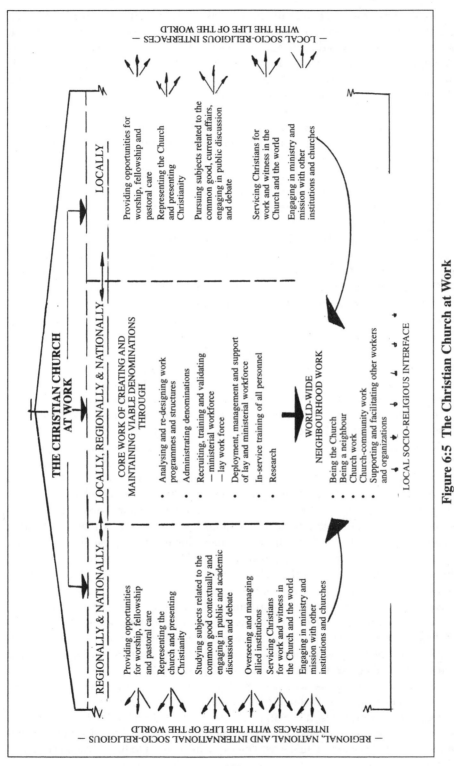

Figure 6:5 The Christian Church at Work

to evaluating the outcome of action taken is facilitated through people communicating with each other in many different ways, verbally, non-verbally and through the written word exchanged mechanically and electronically. Inescapably, therefore it is "talking work" [86] in contradistinction to manual or craft work. Words and more words are essential to conceptualising and communicating, to making things happen and to interpersonal working relationships. The quality of work depends upon the quality of talk: good talk makes for good work.

Undoubtedly it is "good to talk". It can be the elixir of life, exciting and creative. Such conversation is widespread in the church and in community organizations. In some circumstances, however, it can be extraordinarily difficult to talk lovingly, honestly and purposefully. And, sometimes talking is damaging and destructive. Noting some of the complications that arise illuminates the nature of this aspect of the work.

Linguistic complications have to be negotiated. Even people in the same church who speak the same native language can speak different biblical, theological and conceptual languages. Their life, educational and work experiences upon which they draw in discussing the work of the church vary enormously. People speak with very different spiritual dialects and the vocabularies with which they feel comfortable differ significantly. Church work has to be done in the long shadow cast by the Tower of Babel. It can be difficult to find a *lingua franca* adequate for all that is involved in talking seriously, honestly and purposefully about the work especially where differences are irritating people and causing conflict. Sometimes people simply do not know the meaning of words used by others and, confusingly, the same word can mean different things to different people. Ways in which words are said and the body language accompanying them sends messages which are sometimes clear, at other times ambiguous and confusing. And these difficulties are compounded when people in the Church are from many countries with different languages. (I counted nineteen in my local church recently.)

These difficulties are compounded by attitudes and approaches to "talking-time." Some people give value to "doing" ("getting on with things") and denigrate "talking" (which they see to be unnecessary, "we all know what has to be done"). Others will talk and talk without any intention of helping with what has to be done: they think out tasks for others. Some people talk about their work as they do it, others do not. And some talk about anything but their work as they do it. Most people fall somewhere between these extremes. Some firmly grasp that talking is a form of doing and that, in developmental work with people, doing involves talking. But people differ greatly in their ability to sustain critical thinking processes for long-term objectives and to cope with deferred satisfaction. Then again some people misuse and abuse talking time in committees and groups. Verbiage and verbosity cause some problems—as of course can the lack of communication. People abuse and squander valuable opportunities to work at things productively when they use time in meetings to gain attention, status and power; to get their own way; to settle old scores; to recite party pieces; to ride hobby-horses.

An important part of the work we are considering is, in relation to these and other complicating factors, to enable creative discussions in all kinds of circumstances, moods and environments. It is getting people to take to heart St Paul's dictum: "Do not use harmful words in talking. Use only helpful words, the kind that build up and provide what is needed, so that what you say will do good to those who hear you".[87]

And this has to be done in facing and working through significant differences of opinion, conflict and faction. Progressive movements are needed in discussions about work which sensitively but surely progress from experience through critical and imaginative thought to constructive action.[88] Endlessly working through these stages cyclically minimises the dangers of talking without doing and doing without thinking—both of which circumvent creative action and the development of workers and those with and for whom they work. When these processes pulsate through churches and organizations a culture evolves which is conducive to talking about things of importance creatively.

For faith communities there are what are commonly referred to as spiritual dimensions to all this. Christians believe that God is aware of their thoughts and that they converse in the divine presence whether or not they are conscious of it. Moreover they believe that God is one to whom they can listen, speak and pray and with whom they can dialogue. In discussions, groups, committees and councils people can have several aims: to discover what God is saying to and wants from them; to find God's will for them and how to do it; to listen to what God is saying to them through each other and events. Prayer, meditation, reflection and allowing scripture, beliefs and tradition to "speak" to particular situations and issues are critical aspects of such conversations. Sharing and talking, like the visible part of an iceberg, are only a part of the process. People are thinking their own thoughts and are in dialogue with God. So the discussion leader's job is to get people talking to each other and collectively engaging in spiritual dialogues. Interaction with self, others and the trinitarian God are critical relational aspects of this talking work. Interpersonal exchanges are combined with what Ignatius Loyola referred to as "colloquys with the Lord".

Using language in this way is different from using it in preaching and lecturing. All three modes make contributions to church work. But not all preachers and lecturers are able to facilitate the kind of dialogue described here. The nature of this work is further illuminated by examining just what is involved in promoting this kind of creative talking work. And that is what most of this book is about.

(f)   The Work is Voluntary

Voluntariness is a fundamental attribute of the Church and its work. Churches are voluntary institutions with voluntary members, heavily dependent upon voluntary workers. They are theologically committed to pursuing and promoting voluntary principles in church and society from their base in the voluntary sector of human life.

To all intents and purposes churches in the United Kingdom operate as religious voluntary organizations although some exclude them from their classification of the voluntary sector. Voluntaryism, the principle that the Churches should be supported by voluntary contributions rather than by the state, is fundamental to their constitution and practice. Churches meet other criteria by which voluntary organizations are commonly defined: they are in control of their own affairs; they are not commercial in that they are described as "non-profit distributing"—even when they raise funds through trading, as some do, they use it for their purposes or for grants, they do not disburse it as bonuses to their members or "share holders"; they are of public benefit and contribute to "the common good".[89] One of the defining factors frequently used relates to the absence of "direct" control by statutory authority. Care is taken to avoid this in contractual arrangements made with statutory authorities (and other bodies) in relation to youth, community and welfare work. With respect to this criterion the Church of England differs from the other churches because of its unique relationship to State and society through being Established.

However, whilst churches have much in common with voluntary organizations, the points made in this chapter about the nature of their work form an indicative list of their distinctiveness. Chris Baurosey in a chapter entitled, "The Church as a voluntary non-profit organization", reminds us that, "At a time when many charities and businesses are seeking to clarify and strengthen their ethos and values, the church must ensure that it does not lose its own".[90]

Various relationships have existed between the voluntary and statutory sectors including the churches. These relationships are a source of continuing discussion and revision because of the profound changes in the sectors and the contexts in which they operate.[91] They have been conceptualised in different ways: the marginal model in which the voluntary sector is on the pioneering fringes of state organized social services; the integral, plural model which gives a more central role to the voluntary sector; parallel bars and extension ladder models; partnership and contractual models. Whichever model is in play, there is a vast mixture of converging and conflicting motives, interests and goals occupying the interface between the sectors. Churches must maintain their autonomy if they are to make their proper contributions to human and spiritual welfare through service delivery, pioneering unmet needs and challenging authorities about social, moral and spiritual issues.

The essential nature of religious voluntary organizations is defined and formed from within by voluntaristic socio-spiritual communities. People enter these communities "on the basis of independent individual decisions"[92] about the Christian faith. Voluntarily they become members engaged in the life and work of churches as volunteers and voluntary workers. Moral and religious voluntaryism (or voluntarism) which emphasizes the importance of the human will in decisions about belief and conduct is a spiritual life giving source of energy which infuses the voluntary organizations and their programmes. In this regard, churches are distinctive voluntary organizations.

To make this point I have bypassed endless discussion about a range of interdependent subjects about the nature of human freedom, the influence of all kinds of personal, spiritual and social forces and pressures upon people making decisions about religious life; the moral and spiritual imperatives in play; God's part in the decision making; the place, rights and wrongs of persuasion. Amidst all these complicated issues, theological principles and precepts about human freedom in community are secured deep in the teaching and beliefs of Christianity, and in the hearts and souls of the members, and therefore in the structures, culture and ethos of churches. As those principles are fundamentals of the nature of church work—no matter how much they are neglected, denied or abused—the non-directive approach is a necessity not a matter of personal preference. (This approach is described in various parts of this book. See also pp 285-287.)

Another dimension of the voluntary nature of the Church is to be found in its workforce. Voluntary workers compose the largest group. They grossly outnumber "paid" workers. Most of them are part-time but some are more-or-less full-time workers in their "retirement". Some give professional skills freely, others become highly skilled at a wide range of things such as preaching, teaching, facilitating, working with all kinds of people, pastoral care and counselling. Presbyteral and diaconal ministers, priests and religious are the next largest group of workers. They, unlike the very much smaller, but growing, group of lay workers employed by the church, are not salaried, they are given a stipend or an allowance. The aim is to free them from earning their living in the world in order that they can whole-heartedly pursue their calling. The result is a composite work force of people—lay/ordained, unpaid/stipended/salaried extensively engaged in all kinds of social and spiritual voluntary programmes. (Some implications of staffing the work of the church in this way are considered in the next chapter.) Churches and community organizations, therefore, can make significant contributions towards maintaining and developing participatory democracy in all kinds of communities and contexts, not least through doing so in their own.

3. Operational Attributes Which Derive from Proven Ways of Approaching and Doing the Work

The nature of the work is affected by the way in which it is done as well as by the Christian project and the circumstances in which it is pursued. This section considers a group of operational attributes which derive from proven ways of approaching and doing church and community work. They show that effective work is:

(a) a particular form of creative engagement with the nature and the operation of freedom for the realization of human and spiritual development

(b) collaborative

(c) multi-disciplinary and interprofessional

(d) operational and reflective: publicly and privately; individually, collectively and collaboratively.

(a) *The work is a particular form of creative engagement with the nature and the operation of freedom for the realization of human and spiritual development*

The aim of this section is to identify this attribute which is generic to both the work we are considering and the theory and practice of consultancy. A limited aim in view of the way in which the concept of freedom opens out on to a vast area of complex subject matter which cannot be dealt with in this book.

Practitioners and participants have to work with the notion, expression, frustration and abuse of human freedom just as carpenters have to work with wood and its nature and properties. For several reasons they have to grapple with it, dialogue with it, dance with it, tango with it. The first of these is that personal and vocational responses to Christianity must of necessity be informed and freely made. The second reason is that the quality and effectiveness of church and community work depends upon practitioners and participants individually and collectively, maximising the use of whatever inner and outer freedom they might have for their own good and that of others with proper respect for other people's freedom. The resulting self-induced change is essential to development. A third reason why they have to work at it is, because there are so many things that make it difficult for people to exercise their freedom and their human rights. Individuals and groups, for instance, can experience what Erich Fromm called the "fear of freedom".[93] Opportunites for self-determined action can be neglected because of apprehension about the possible consequences and the reluctance to accept responsibilities. Even though they might grumble about it, many people prefer to be directed by others. Helping people to take action of their own free will involves working with them at these psycho-spiritual inner constraints on their freedom and the givens in their circumstances and conflicts of interest. And all this has to be done in a context where all kinds of people in the church and in society from positions of power and influence variously manipulate and persuade other people, act in an authoritarian manner and abuse the rights and freedoms of others. All this can be done with the best of intentions or out of conviction that they are doing it in the best interests of all concerned or simply to get their own way and to acquire power and control. However that might be, overriding the freedom of others is trespassing upon their rights and complicating the already difficult human and spiritual dynamics of living their lives fully and freely.

This book is, in fact, a study of what is involved in engaging with human freedom in church and community work and in non-directive consultations about it. A central theme of the work we are considering is the creation of conditions, ethos and relationships in which people are most likely to make free and creative responses. The detailed story of the developments in the Methodist Diaconal Order told in Chapter Three, for instance shows clearly just what was involved in creating circumstances in which people were, and knew that they were, free to express what they felt about their own vocation and that of the Order and to pursue them separately and together. Even a cursory glance at that study shows the nature and quality of the conceptual effort, planning and face to face work required to generate the conditions conducive to everyone involved being able to participate in the processes as freely as possible. Work of a similar kind has to be done to promote voluntary and collaborative participation in the Christian venture as can be seen from sections above. To turn to another example, there is a commonplace need for meetings in which participants have the freedom to explore constructively tricky subjects which could all too easily engender defensiveness and faction. A key attribute of church and community work is the creation of the conditions in which that is most likely to occur.

Now, having identified the attribute, it is possible to consider in a more meaningful way what is required of practitioners. They have to have a respect for freedom. They need to be able to identify the things people simply have to decide for themselves and to be consistently and determinedly non-directive in relation to them. They have to be able to grapple with the nature of freedom, theologically, theoretically and pragmatically with especial reference to promoting development through church and community work. Some of the personal attributes, knowledge and skills required to do this and to work with people freely are described in the next chapter. Fundamentally, they need to have *reverence for freedom*, to adapt Albert Schweitzer's phrase "reverence for life". A reverence, that is for their own and other people's freedom. *Basically that is what the non-directive approach is all about: a reverential way of working with people which concentrates on promoting direction from within rather than from without; the praxis of living free.*

Operationally, it is important to focus first on the nature and the reasons for the engagement with human freedom and then on ways and means of facilitating it with specific groups of people in their given circumstances. If practitioners do this, they are more likely to use directive and non-directive approaches and methods appropriately and less likely to confuse them with tasks and to be doctrinaire about their approach.

(b) The Work is Collaborative

An inescapable conclusion of any examination of church work is that collaboration is written deep into its nature. To do the work it is necessary for people to co-operate with God and with each other in relation to the realities and actualities of life. Collaboration is essential between professionals in the same and from different disciplines; between professionals, voluntary workers and the people with whom they work; between churches of the same and of different denominations; between different religious and secular agencies. Essentially it is through collaboration rather than competition that this work flourishes—providing, that is, that the collaboration is grounded in constructive engagement between people about their differences as well as their similarities.Two extended quotations about collaboration are given in Display 6:1. In the first Bishop David Jenkins, in his own inimitable way, claims that collaboration is an expression of love and a quality of the Trinity. In the second Professor R. Michael Casto, Associate Director of Practice, Ohio State University, examines the warrant for interprofessional collaboration in responding to human need. Together they show collaboration to be grounded both in theology and the human situation.

A recent report presenting collaborative ministry as a "key feature of Church life to come" is welcome as is the fact that it has attracted much interest and been applauded.[94] But that such a report is necessary and seen as innovatory, is an indictment of the Church. Not only have large sections of it neglected collaboration, some have argued against it, tried to undermine theologically those practising it and strenuously promoted non-participatory and hierarchical approaches and structures. Yet others have been calculatedly manipulative. Some clergy and laity resist it on theological grounds, arguing that leaders called by God and ordained by the Church must lead and followers must follow. Others resist it on practical and psychological grounds, *e.g.*: it takes too much time, the fear of loss of control. Promoting it involves going against the emphasis on competition in contemporary society. How to promote collaboration in all kinds of situations is a major theme in consultancy work. The need for collaborative practitioners, teams, organizations and churches is discussed in the next chapter.

(c) The Work is Multi-Disciplinary and Interprofessional

By its nature, church work involves pursuing the calling and profession of Christian ministry, drawing upon a number of related disciplines, working interjacently with other organizations and professions engaged with people in the same area. This can and does lead to interprofessional working relationships.

The Trinity thus symbolizes the discovering of love which is both transcendent and committed to being at work in history and in human beings. This is the discovery which is reflected and reported in the stories the Bible records about God and about Jesus and therefore about God, man and the world. Hence love is known to be essentially committed to collaboration in the construction of reality for eternity. Men and women are shown to be pilgrims and workers who have their own share in the creation and development of their own history. We are part of, and co-operators in, both the telling and the making of the story which will end in the community and communion of the life of God poured out into the life of men and of the whole universe.[95]

What is the warrant for interprofessional collaboration in responding to human need? Interprofessional practice by those in the helping professions finds its sanction in basic assumptions about the nature of human community and the interdependence of each of us. Whether our responsibilities as pastors and professionals lead us toward the relative isolation of academic work, the passionate response to individual crises in missionwork, or the daily routines of the pastorate, we finally discover that our work is dependent on the knowledge, benevolence, and skill of countless others. Whether the circumstances we face are hopeless or hope filled, our only real hope is in the strength that comes to us from God through those who surround us — those who came before us, those who come after us, and those who stand with us. To affirm that "our hope is in the Lord" is to affirm that the community of God's people — the ecumenical community — the community of the whole inhabited earth — is the source of our hope and our strength. It is the possibility out of which we live and to which we turn in both our joy and our pain.

We are drawn into interdependence of the human community by several dimensions of human life, among which are the anthropological, communal, technological, ethical, and educational aspects of our common humanity.[96]

Display 6:1 The Trinity, Collaboration and Interprofessional Practice

Our attempts at describing aspects of the nature of church work show that boundaries can be drawn around it. It has its own identity, ethos and culture shaped by its theoretical bases, body of knowledge, technical expertise, accepted practices, spiritual and ethical values, standards, stances and style. So, it meets some of the characteristics required of a profession.[97] Lay, religious and ordained people who pursue the work seriously share the professionalism of church work.

Church work draws upon a number of disciplines. Some have their origins deep in the profession of ministry itself, others have been developed by related professions. Examples of the first kind are biblical studies and theology, examples of the second kind are education, the social and behavioural sciences, psychology, organizational studies, community development. In fact, and increasingly so, church work and the profession of ministry are at the nexus of many disciplines. This traffic is not all one way. Over a long period of time, for instance, church work has contributed to as well as profited from educational theory and practice.

Interdisciplinary study at any depth is rewarding but difficult. New disciplinary languages have to be learnt. The literature is vast. Encountering concepts and practices which conflict with those of our own discipline can be challenging and intimidating. Discovering things which could be helpful disturbs the coherence of our own theory and practice until they are assimilated or rejected. Several things help me to explore other disciplines for things which will throw light upon stubborn problems and enhance my ability to be more effective. One of them is remaining conscious of the nature of the exercise in which I am engaged. I am foraging for anything which will help in any way. It could be any one of many things— information, techniques, ways of conceptualising things. Having discovered something it has to be assimilated into my own profession and become an integral part of the practice theory upon which I work. Describing it in this way disguises the complexities by making it appear an obvious and simple process. Many things have seduced or thrown me: getting involved in other disciplines beyond a point of economic investment through interest and excitement; being overwhelmed, confused and intimidated by the vast and expanding amount of knowledge, conflicting theories, evolutionary changes in the nature of disciplines and the growth of sub-disciplines; feeling professionally de-skilled; assuming quite unrealistically and arrogantly that I ought to master the allied discipline(s) and feeling inadequate because I know I cannot, and a charlatan because I am not doing so; using material new to me before I have assimilated it.[98] Someone with much experience of interdisciplinary work in the field of pastoral care and counselling has said:

> Interdisciplinary study at any depth is difficult, because it undermines the conservatism necessary to hold the discipline together. . . . Learning about another profession and revealing the secrets of one's own is a difficult and costly process.[99]

Given my purposes, what I have to do is to learn sufficient of an allied discipline and its language to be able to draw upon it in a professional manner and to work with people of that discipline in relation to my own. Keeping aspects of the process firmly in mind is essential: foraging in other disciplines—discovery of treasures— disturbance of coherence of professional model of ministry—affecting necessary changes—synthesizing, integrating and assimilating new insights, procedures and practices—working on the new basis. Listing elements in this way gives the process the appearance of linear tidiness, whereas it is intricately systemic and messy.

All this has to do with individual practitioners studying other disciplines in order to enhance their ability to practise their own. This is healthy providing it does not slip over into individuals themselves trying to acquire all the skills required to do all the work we are considering. That is not possible. Within the general discipline of church work there is specialisation. Teamwork is needed to bring together all the expertise required. Again, in community life, members of several professions, drawing upon a range of disciplines, make complementary contributions to the education, development and general well-being of people. Church work is interjacent to educational, medical and welfare work, serving the same constituencies. Interpersonal, interprofessional and interdisciplinary relationships are vitally important both inside and outside the Church. Their quality affects the quality of the services offered to people in the Church and in the community.

(d)   The Work is Operational and Reflective: Publicly and Privately; Individually and Collectively and Collaboratively

Work with people for development has two modes: the operational and the reflective. "Operational" has been chosen to indicate all the work that is done, publicly and privately. I have avoided "action and reflection", the more commonly used term, because reflection is an activity, sometimes deeply satisfying and exciting, at others a tortuous and tormenting one. Sometimes it is done quietly, in a leisurely way, privately by individuals or groups. At other times it has to be done publicly in the full flow of the pressure of encounters with people individually and collectively, formally and informally. Reflective action and reflection-in-action helps practitioners to keep in touch with the actualities of the ever changing human situations in which they are engaged and the deeper realities to which they are ultimately committed. This kind of an approach is essential because work with human beings cannot be standardized or mechanized.

Equating reflection exclusively with either the private or public sectors distorts the nature of the work. Relegating it to the private sector makes thinking into something of an elite activity, denies many people general and open access to the collective reflection so important to human and spiritual development, impoverishes the outcome and contributes to an unhealthy segregation of people as "thinkers" and "doers". Private reflection is, of course, essential: the quality of public thinking depends upon that of private thinking (and vice versa) and especially upon the thought given to promoting public reflection. Clearly the three pairs of contrasting variables—reflective and operational, private and public, individual and collective— are complexly related. Together, as they interact, overlap and complement one another they illustrate the subtleties of the nature of the work. This is partly illustrated in Figure 6:6.

This model presupposes that practitioners can stimulate and enable the teams, workforces, organizations and churches to be operational and reflective or that these

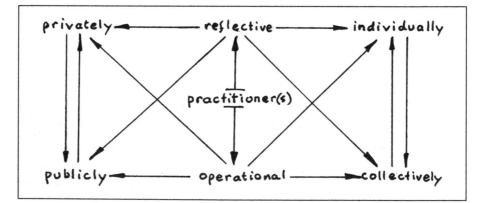

Figure 6:6   Reflective and Operational: Six Complexly Related Variables

collectives are operational and reflective. The latter case is the ideal. Promotional and reflective practitioners facilitate and reinforce each other.

Another thing about this model is that it only works when practitioners and those with whom they work are collaborative in their being, in their doing and in their reflecting. "Reflective practitioners", a term first proposed by Donald Schon,[100] need also to be "collaborative practitioners". Reflective work-forces need to be collaborative workforces. Reflection and collaboration are twin competences which need to be conjoined in practitioners and work forces. When this happens churches become developmental organizations, (see Figure 6:7) Reflection and collaboration, therefore, are both pragmatic and theological necessities.

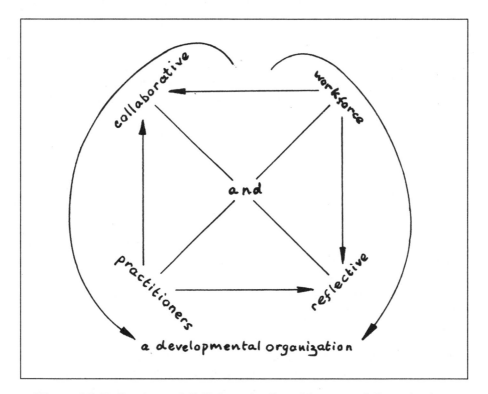

Figure 6:7 Reflective and Collaborative Practitioners and Organizations

There are significant differences between getting on with things and reflecting upon what is being done and what is happening. "Hands on" engagement is a feature of the operational side of the work; "minds and hearts on", mental detachment and distance from the action are features of reflection. Distancing of this kind is an inner disposition which can occur in quiet moments of privacy or whilst walking in the hills or around the shops or in the welter of the most intense engagements. It does not necessarily or automatically occur in any setting. But it can be induced and cultivated. Kenneth Howcroft says of reflective practitioners that they maintain a critical awareness of:

— the situations in which they find themselves;

— their thoughts, feelings, intuitive judgements, emotions, and deeper instincts;

— operative values and assumptions;

— relevant theoretical and theological understandings and knowledge.

Being reflective therefore entails a much broader range of cognitive responses than "thinking". And it is certainly a different activity from reminiscing with which it can be confused. Amongst other things, it calls for humility, insatiable curiosity, genuine interest in others, an open mind, knowledge and wisdom.[101]

Radical changes are taking place in interpersonal and working relationships between clergy, religious, lay workers and leaders and people. Collaborative action and teamwork are on the increase whilst authoritarianism is on the decrease. Equal opportunities policies and the emphasis on political correctness are eroding a wide range of unjust actions, structures and discriminatory attitudes. Inclusivism is increasingly more valued than exclusivism. Alongside all this, there is a drive for responsible accountability with all that this means for formal and rigorous work evaluation and the assessment of people. Progess is slow. Inner and outer changes in people and in their behaviour must go hand in hand to avoid insincerity and superficiality. New ways of working and new skills are required in relation to working with *and* in relation to preparing to work with people. These are discussed in the next chapter.

The subtle changes in private preparation tend to be neglected. Public behaviour is open to view and therefore readily accessible. Private preparation is hidden from view and therefore less accessible. There is much experience of the work involved in preparing for services and preaching but much less in doing the preparation work for these new ways of working with people. To complicate things, there is a common idea that the new way of working needs less preparation whereas, in fact, it requires more. The private preparation involved in deciding what people should do and how they are going to be persuaded to do it is quite different from that involved in determining how to get people to work together at critical issues, especially those they are inclined to avoid. For instance, it involves thinking things through to discern ways and means of stimulating and helping people to work through things themselves and find agreed solutions. So one of the questions for preparation is, "What has to be done beforehand in order that busy people at the fag-end of a busy day in the middle of a demanding week can work at these tricky issues to good effect and with satisfaction?" Serious consideration of such a question can really stretch the mind and imagination and make heavy demands upon the commitment to self-effacing servant ministry which undertakes backroom work to lead and empower others. It calls for many skills and much discipline especially when it is done by individuals. But it can be exhilarating, especially when it is done by groups, because of the insights it generates and the learning that occurs.

The nature of this new kind of collaborative public and private work, and what is involved in inaugurating it, is illustrated throughout this book. In the companion volume the nature of what is involved in designing and analysing church and community work, privately and in groups, is described in some detail.[102] Working privately and publicly are compared and modelled. The ways in which these two domains intersect and interact is drawn out. For instance, a telephone call can suddenly break into the middle of our private work and drag us unwillingly into the public arena in relation to the very issues which we are trying to sort out and demand responses we are not ready to give. What aids and hinders movement between the domains is considered. Consultancy illuminates the work in both domains because, whilst it is firmly located in the private domain, it is about the work of both domains.

Personal and collective reflection can perform several important functions. They can be integrative and link "private faith to public action".[103] If the reflection runs deep and true it enables people to make greater sense of the work in which they are engaged and what they are experiencing through it. Doing that enables people to tell and re-shape stories which help them to understand and handle things in their working and personal lives.[104] Many things flow from this. The raw material of experience is refined and anything of value is integrated and assimilated into the way in which individuals and groups see their work and go about it. Internalising things in these ways forms and develops creative faculties deep down in individuals, groups, communities and organizations. Operational action, therefore, is more likely to be effective because it is located in and flows from the creative centres of people[105] and churches and is embedded in the realities of the environments in which they live and work. The overall effect is that development processes are contextualised through creative cells in churches and situations.

Reflection-in-action is a way in which individuals and groups of people can increase their theoretical, theological, practical and experiential knowledge. As practice, experience, theology and theory speak to each other, new insights and connections are made. Reflecting, therefore, is vital to every aspect of doing the work we are considering, to assessing and evaluating it and to consulting about it. Rigorous reflection of this kind can facilitate a basic form of action research, *i.e.*: learning from experience, theory and theology which issues in a more effective outcome of projects and work programmes. Practitioners and those with whom they work can engage in this in several ways: by talking together; interacting and working at things in order "to find out about things" ("dialogue research"); through examining personal and shared experiences ("experiential research"); through setting out by trial and error, either on their own or in co-operation with others, to investigate things or to get to the bottom of something or other ("collaborative research").[106] In these and other ways practitioners learn to be more effective researchers of their own experience and better able to reflect in any situation.

The nature of the work requires that operation and reflection are structural aspects of church and community work. They must be integral parts of public and private and individual and collective processes. Collaborative reflective dialogues are intertwined with the action as it is planned, as it takes place and as it is reviewed. Experience and action must issue in reflection; reflective processes must be informed by experience, theology and theory.

II THEOLOGY AND VALUES IN THE WORK

The theology and moral and spiritual values of the work are written into the nature of the attributes, therefore, this section is surprisingly brief. Much of what was said about the beliefs, ethics, values and qualities of consultancy are also true of the nature of church and community work. Like consultancy processes, this work is incarnational, salvivic, revelatory, resurrectional, creational and sacramental (See Chapter 2 Element 7).

III SHADOWY DOWNSIDES

Because of its very nature the work is shot through with difficulties. Doing it is to experience shadowy downsides and the dark night of the soul as well as sublime joy and deep satisfaction. Given that the work is a partnership in Christ's ministry we can expect nothing less even when we studiously avoid the trap of equating our ministry with his. To balance the work picture that is emerging it is necessary to give a brief indicative survey of the difficulties that emanate from the nature of the work. Deliberately I am writing this in an inclusive style to indicate that I experience these problems and to avoid any inference that I am standing judgementally over and against others.

Determining just what God wants us to do in divine-human partnerships can be difficult. Assurance can evade us sometimes for long periods whilst doubt assails and debilitates. On the other hand we can get it all wrong and feel that we have got it all right. The Church might write job descriptions, God doesn't, although we do experience spiritual guidance. Self-deception in processes of spiritual discernment is sometimes difficult to identify and correct. Collective discernment can be highjacked and groups held to spiritual ransom by people who claim to know precisely what God's will is because they claim it has been revealed to them in some especial way. Consequently, personal and collective vocational uncertainty, conflict and error are commonplace. These kinds of problems add to the difficulties inherent in working out and pursuing missiological programmes which have sound biblical and theological bases and are contextually viable. Sorting out the complex missiological issues and grounding them in actual situations is a considerable undertaking. The literature is vast, the reasoning complex and the conclusions reached by scholars and church leaders vary so greatly. Kenneth Cracknell has given us an extraordinary account of some of the issues and the ways in which missionaries struggled with them during the period 1846-1914.[107] Strangely, but not surprisingly, they throw light upon our own missiological struggles.

Getting groups of people to think things through at any depth, make realistic plans, act upon them responsibly and evaluate what happens is notoriously difficult. It is also difficult on a personal basis. Consequently, thought without action and action without thought are all too common. Determining the most effective approach and method is very often far from easy. Should I be directive or non-directive or simply leave people to their own devices? When and how should I intervene and withdraw? These and similar questions are ones over which I have agonised in relation to many different situations, times without number!

Engagement with the human condition invariably means at some stage encountering personal, socio-pyschological and spiritual limitations and immaturity in myself and in and between other people. Human relationships can be difficult if not impossible. Personality clashes and disorders and interpersonal conflict can be very difficult to deal with even for people skilled in group and community work. Sin and evil can easily run riot in church as well as in society and in me. Engaging with myself and working with all kinds and conditions of people in which these things and all kinds of cultural dynamics operate is problematic.

Other difficulties occur because, as we have seen, the work opens up on so many complex aspects of human life: personal, communal, organizational, ecclesiastical. To each of these many disciplines and specialisms are dedicated. It is impossible to keep up with developments in any one of them. General practitioners of ministry are persistently out of date in most, if not all, areas and feel that they are. This is not a good feeling. It is so easy to be put at a disadvantage and feel pseudo guilt at not being on top of everything.

Working with people who are serving voluntarily, untrained and without the gifts and graces required, can be taxing and frustrating. Moreover, it can cause great difficulties when their motives are seriously askew, when, for instance, they are doing the work to gain status and attract attention rather than to serve Christ and other people.

Problems also occur through the close association of high and relatively pure vocational motivation and deep commitment with the unending amount of work to be done. Combined these things can drive us on, individually and collectively, beyond our strength and induce stress, burn out and breakdown. It is important but difficult to regulate the amount of work you do when the needs are great and you are living under the conviction that willing, costly and sacrificial giving and sharing of self is an intrinsic part of one's vocation.[108] Once overstretched, finding new energy is as difficult as it was to control the expenditure of the original energy.

Working to the whole as well as the parts can be difficult. The canvas is so big and "our part", small as it is and seems, can demand more than we have to give.

Facing and working through these and many more difficulties and being true to Christian values are vital parts of the nature of the work. To do so most of us need help and support which some get through consultancy sessions.

IV CUTTING THE "WORK DIAMOND" [109]

Diamond cutting is an image which helped me to understand and get on with describing the nature of my overall work-view/work-picture. On the one hand this was an endlessly fascinating task because of what it revealed as one face after another of the work diamond was cut, described and polished. On the other hand it was laborious beyond my expectations because of the many facets, each of which presented conceptual and descriptive challenges. But it was only when I was within sight of the end of this chapter that I saw that cutting the diamond of work was a fundamental aspect of the nature of church and community work. What I was doing in relation to my overall work-view, practitioners and churches need to do in relation to *theirs*. Analyses such as this one can help them by providing conceptual structures, distinctions and images for selection and adaptation and as stimulants to other ideas. But there is no substitute for practitioners and people, separately and together, cutting the faces of their own work diamonds. Helping consultors to do that is an aspect of work and vocational consultancy.

Strangely, it was this image that sustained me even though the systemic model is the dominant one of the many I use.[110] Throughout, I was aware of the complex systemic connections between one aspect of the nature of the work and another and noted some of them. However, I now realise that the diamond cutting image absolved and saved me from being seduced into feeling I had to trace out the tangled web of connections between the attributes and draw diagrams with double-headed arrows going in every direction! Diagrams showing the diamond faces do not have to have arrows because each face is a "side" of the substance, in this case church and community work, and it is only a side as long as it is an integral part of the work and complementary to all the other sides (see Figure 6:8).

Three interdependent shaping processes can be discerned in this description of the nature of church and community work and its basic attributes. *First* of all there is the all pervasive activity and influence of God, Jesus Christ and the Holy Spirit in human affairs and in every aspect of the work. *Second*, there is the divine-human shaping or sculpting. *Third*, there is the environmental shaping that occurs through the work being done with people *in situ*. This I refer to as existential or situational shaping. An attempt is made in Figure 6:8 to represent these distinctions diagrammatically. Basically therefore, the nature of church and community work derives from the nature and authority of God, the nature and authority of workers and the nature and authority of the situations in which the work has to be done. The actual nature and form of specific work programmes are determined by the result of the interplay of these three sources of authority.

V   TOWARDS A DEFINITION OF CHURCH WORK

An attempt can now be made to define the work we are considering. It comprises those church activities through which Christians, acting as God's co-workers variously in association with others, think and act to transform themselves and/or aspects of their physical, social, moral and spiritual worlds and help others to do the same.[111] David Deeks stated the aims of this activity in this way

> Jesus . . . makes crystal clear what God's permanent activity is all about. It's about healing and wholeness of life for individuals and communities: it's about human lives being changed, so that they are filled with the love of God and are capable of communion with God; it's about revealing a new way for human beings to live together in community, a way of life which is indestructible—eternal life, as St John calls it: not even death can block it.[112]

This work is personal and collective vocational involvement in redemptive and creative missiological activity. It is engagement in a divine-human enterprise directed by God and the Church. Its aim is to initiate, promote, foster and sustain to completion processes by which people and every aspect of their habitat become more like the Christian ideal. It involves engagement with human goodness and badness through working with and ministering to all kinds and conditions of people —personally and in all kinds of communities, socio-religious organizations and churches. This missiological work, essentially local, is a relational, personal, communal, organizational, ecclesiastical, contextual, language based, all life activity designed to meet all human, personal, social and spiritual needs through a range of religious and secular programmes which aim to be inclusive and comprehensive. By nature and circumstance the work is voluntary in principle and practice, collaborative, participatory and multi-disciplinary and inter-professional. It is operational and reflective faith and love based action. It is an application of all our faculties and an outworking of Christian values through sub-political Christian institutions. Thus, Church work is theological and mundane and holistically creative with its own culture and spirituality.

This work operates creatively on the inner and outer worlds of practitioners and those with whom they work and the complex relationships between them, their environment and God. It "begins with a feeling of something lacking, something desired . . . something to be created, something to be brought into being . . . in the environment, and in the self" and ends with the Kingdom of God.[113]

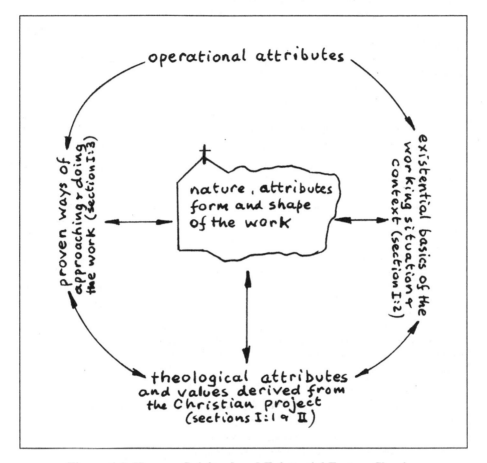

**Figure 6:8 Human, Spiritual and Existential Factors Shaping
the Nature and Properties of Church Work Discussed in Chapter Six**

NOTES AND REFERENCES: Chapter Six

1.   cf. Yates, Timothy (1994) *Christian Mission in the Twentieth Century* (Cambridge University Press) p 4.

2.   Evidence for this is to be found in the following publications and in the rapturous reviews of them from people representing a broad theological spectrum. Bosch, David J. (1991 tenth printing 1996) *Transforming Mission: Paradigm Shifts in Theology and Mission* (Orbis Books, Maryknoll); Bosch, David J. (1995) *Believing In The Future: Towards the Missiology of Western Culture* (Trinity Press International and Gracewing); Cracknell, Kenneth (1995) *Justice, Courtesy and Love: Theologians and Missionaries Encountering World Religions, 1846-1914* (Epworth Press); Kirk, J. Andrew (1997) *The Mission of Theology and Theology as Mission* (Trinity Press International, Gracewing); Yates, Timothy (1994) *op cit.*

3.   Bosch, David J. (1991 tenth printing 1996) *op cit* p 494, references not included. Kenneth Cracknell presented a paper to the World Methodist Council in 1995 entitled, *Mission and Evangelism in Methodist Theological Inquiry and Education With Special Relation to Culture and Context.* A carefully argued case for the centrality of missiology in ministerial preparation was embraced and recommendations were accepted that people and organizations be challenged to provide funds "for the teaching of missiology and evangelism . . . in Methodist seminaries throughout the world" (cf pp 18-21).

4.   Bosch, David J. (1991 tenth printing 1996) *op cit* p 498, references not included.

5.   Bosch, David J. (1991 tenth printing 1996) *op cit* pp 409ff discusses a "plethora of definitions". "Basic to my consideration", he says, "is the conviction that mission and evangelism are not synonymous but, nevertheless, indissolubly linked together and inextricably interwoven in theology and praxis" (p 411.) He then works this out through eighteen statements covering nine pages (411-420). Some people use *evangelization* to include the whole process of salvation, and evangelism to mean the proclamation of it: the preaching of the good news and calling people to repentance and conversion. Evangelization is a term more natural to Roman Catholics, evangelism to Protestants. (cf "Evangelism, Mission and Evangelization". An address by Albert Nolan to the Diocese of Cape Town's conference in June 1990 and published in the series *Southwell and Oxford Papers on Contemporary Society*, Summer 1991). Bosch, on the other hand, uses evangelism to refer to activities involved in spreading the gospel or to theological reflection on these activities and evangelization to refer to the process of spreading the gospel or to the extent to which it has been spread, p409. Kenneth Cracknell takes the same line as Bosch cf *Protestant Evangelism or Catholic Evangelization? A Study in Methodist Approaches* (The Methodist Sacramental Fellowship,1992). But William J. Abraham does not in his book *The Logic of Evangelism* (William B. Eerdmans Publishing Co. Grand Rapids, Michigan, 1989/1996).

6.   Bosch, David *op cit* p 4.

7.   A lecture handout circulated privately.

8.   cf the use of *huper*, for, on behalf of, in relation to Christ giving his life for the redemption of people; Mark 14:24; John 10:15; Acts 21:13; Romans 5:6-8.

9.   *Koinonia* has a wide range of meanings. Fellowship is the most common translation but it can also be translated as community, communion, sharing, participation, partnership and solidarity.

10.   cf Mark 16:20; 1 Corinthians 3:9; 2 Corinthians 6:1.

11.   cf 1 Corinthians 16:16; Romans 6:3 *et al*; Philippians 2:25; 4:3; Colossians 4:11; Philemon verses 1 and 24.

12.   Philippians 2:7. cf Mark 10:44.

13.   *e.g.:* Romans 1:1. In this section I am drawing upon an article by J. Y. Campbell entitled "Servant" in *A Theological Word Book of The Bible* edited by Alan Richardson (SCM Press Ltd., 1950) p 224.

14.   cf Matthew 10:24f and John 13:16.

15.   John 15:15, R.E.B.

16.   cf 1 Corinthians 6:20; 7:23.

17.   Galatians 4:7.

18.   1 Corinthians 7:23.

19.   Galatians 5:13.

20.   cf Acts 2:43. Henri J. M. Nouwen, Donald P. McNeill and Douglas A. Morrison have interesting comments on this in *Compassion: A Reflection on The Christian Life* (Darton, Longman & Todd, 1982) in chapter 4, "Community". They say, "Those who were first converted by the Apostles revealed their conversion not by feats of individual stardom but by entering a new life in community"(p 50).

21.   cf Acts chapters 1-5.

22.   I Peter 2:9-10 R.E.B.

23.   Ephesians 4:11-16 N.E.B., cf I Corinthians 12:27-31.

24.   John 17:20-23.

25.   The Revelation of St John Chapters 2 and 3.

26.   This has been written up in two Birkenhead Circuit reports: *Circuit Mission Plan: A Statement of Circuit Policy which will guide decision making and an explanation of how it is to be implemented* (January 1993) and *The Role, Function and Deployment of Ordained and Lay Circuit Staff: A Circuit Staffing Policy* (June 1983).

27.   cf *Involvement in Community: A Christian Response* (1980) A Report by the Community Development Group, William Temple Foundation in collaboration with the Community Work Advisory Group, British Council of Churches. pp 15ff.

28.   Philippians 2:1-2(a) and 3 and 4. Verses 1-2(a) from the Jerusalem Bible and verses 3 and 4 from the R.E.B.

29.   An example of this is Parchmore Methodist Church, Thornton Heath. See Grundy, Malcolm (ed) (1995) *The Parchmore Partnership: George Lovell, Garth Rogers and Peter Sharrocks*. Some of the developments facilitated through the Church Urban Fund also illustrate this, see Grundy, Malcolm (1990) *Light in The City* (The Canterbury Press) and particularly Chapter 10, "Church Growth and Renewal". See also *The Christian Action Journal: Hope in The City? The Local Impact of The Church Urban Fund* (Summer 1995).

30.   cf for instance, Gutiérrez, Gustavo (1979/1983) *The Power of the Poor in History: Selected Writings* (SCM Press).

31.   cf Holden, Tony (ed) (1989) *Mission Alongside the Poor Programme : Seeing and Hearing* (The Methodist Church Home Mission Division), and Cooper Niall (1992) *All Mapped Out?—a critical evaluation of the Methodist Mission Alongside the Poor Programme* (The William Temple Foundation Occasional Paper 22). Amongst other things this Paper notes the various reports on the Programme. Mission Alongside the Poor (MAP) is no longer regarded as a separate programme, it is "mission work in all kinds of areas— rural, urban, industrial, chaplaincy and the like" (from an official statement by the Methodist Church).

32.   *Faith in the City—A Call for Action by Church and Nation, The Report of the Archbishop of Canterbury's Commission on Urban Priority Areas* (Church House Publishing, 1985); Harvey, Anthony (ed) (1989) *Theology in the City: A Theological Response to Faith in the City* (SPCK); O'Brien, Richard, Donnison, David, Forrester, Duncan and others (1986) *Faith in the Scottish City: The Scottish Relevance of the Report of the Archbishop's Commission on Urban Priority Areas* (Centre for Theology and Public Issues, New College). *Living Faith in the City: A Progress Report by the Archbishop of Canterbury's Advisory Group on Urban Priority Areas* (General Synod of the Church of England, 1990); *Faith in the Countryside: Report of the Archbishop's Commission on Rural Areas* (ARORA Publishing , 1990); "The Country in an Urban Society: A Response to Faith in The Countryside" (*Christian Action Journal*, Spring 1991); Grundy, Malcolm (1990) cited in Ref. 29.

33.   See, for instance, the writings of Leonardo Boff, Gustavo Gutiérrez, David Sheppard, Austin Smith, John Vincent.

34.   Canon John Atherton in an address to the Methodist Wesley Deaconness Order Convocation in 1986 was reported as urging "a bias not simply to the poor but to the whole body, recognizing rights yet equally emphasizing responsibilities, passing judgement on the caring for both (poor and rich) communities", *Methodist Recorder*, 8th January 1986 p 9.

35.   Bosch, David J. (1991) *op cit* pp 98-104.

36.   *ibid* p 98. cf Vincent, John J. (1991) *Discipleship in the 90's* (Methodist Publishing House) in a section "Discipleship for the Rich" gives "Ten Commandments for suburban Christians from the point of view of a disciple in the inner city". They are: Love the people you are; Love the place you've got; Make friends with Mammon; Look for the critical edges; Do not withdraw into a Private Christianity; Face the possibility of Radical Conversion; Give away some spare time; Give away some years of your life; Give away some money; Support a missionary, pp 22-26.

37.   *ibid* p 103f.

38.   cf *The Making of Ministry: The Report of the Ministerial Training Policy Working Group to the Methodist Council* (Methodist Publishing House, Sept. 1996, Ref.PE146) p 32.

39.   Lovell, George (1994) *Analysis and Design: A Handbook for Practitioners and Consultants in Church and Community Work* (Burns & Oates) p 235.

40.   cf Matthew 5:23.

41.   Morgan, Gareth (1986) *Images of Organization* (Sage) p 81. Also, I have found "The Johari Window" (sometimes referred to as Johari's Window) a helpful device in thinking about known and unknown aspects. The basic construct is modelled as follows.

	1 OPEN	2 BLIND
Not known to others		
Not known to others	3 HIDDEN	4 UNKNOWN

This is developed in *The 1973 Annual Handbook for Group Facilitators* (2nd Edition).

42.   The Revd David Deeks1987 in *Pastoral Theology: An Inquiry* (Epworth Press), **says** there are four aims of pastoral care: to encourage people to make their own sense of their own experience; to disclose Christian meaning in life; to stimulate men and women to engage in their own conversation with Christian tradition; to encourage holiness, pp 80-94. Alistair V. Campbell suggests four main pastoral functions: healing; guiding; sustaining and reconciling. cf Campbell, Alistair V. (ed) (1987) *A Dictionary of Pastoral Care* (SPCK) p 188 cf 188. He differentiates it from pastoral counselling (although it may include it) and pastoral and practical theology which he sees as "theoretical counterparts". I would add to the list of functions: supporting, accompanying and challenging. cf John Nelson (ed). (1996) *Management and Ministry: appreciating contemporary issues* (Canterbury Press), Chapter 2 "Pastoral theology re-defined: Correspondence between Gillian Stamp and Norman Todd" for an interesting exploration with especial reference to care of practitioners.

43.   The idea for this term came from a distinction made by Argyle, Michael and Henderson, Monika (1985) *The Anatomy of Relationships and The Rules and Skills to Manage Them Successfully* (Heinemann) between "professional and service relationships" pp 267ff. Examples of the former are teacher and pupils, doctors and patients. Examples of the latter are customer-salesman p 274. It struck me that it is a useful term for those who provide Christian services not least because it is a double entendre. Chapter 10 in this book, "Social Relationships at Work", is useful even though it does not have a section on church workers. I was particularly interested in the way in which they plot work relationships

on two four quadrant graphs (p 240) and the rules for co-workers, superiors etc. Earlier in the book I found the relationship scales helpful (p 4) and the high, moderate and low intimacy relationship clusters (54f) and the intimacy rules (42 *et al*). Cf also Argyle, Michael (1972, 1981 reprint) *The Social Psychology of Work* (Penguin Books) and Argyle, Michael (1964, reprinted in 1967) *Psychology and Social Problems* (Social Science Paperbacks in Association with Methuen & Co Ltd.) especially Chapter 14 "Behaviour in Small Organizations".

44.　cf Fox, Matthew (1983) *Original Blessing* (Bear & Co Inc.).

45.　Examples are: Hopewell, James F. (1988) *Congregation: Stories and Structures* (SCM Press); Grundy, Malcolm (1998) *Understanding Congregations: A New Shape for the Local Church* (Mowbray); Harris, Margaret (1998) *Organizing God's Work: Challenges for Churches and Synagogues* (Macmillan Press).

46.　cf Bright, Laurence (ed) (1971) *The Christian Community: Essays on the Role of the Church in the World* (Sheed and Ward) p 47.

47.　Plant, Raymond (1974) *Community: An Essay in Applied Social Philosophy* (Routledge and Kegan Paul) p 12.

48.　cf *The Shorter Oxford English Dictionary*.

49.　Roland L. Warren　(1963, third edition 1978 reprint 1987) *The Community in America* (University Press) has a penetrating look into this possibility in the following quotation in which he discusses *gemeinschaft* (community) and *gesellschaft* (association):

> Community development, seen as a process of converting the community or parts of it into a formal organization for problem-solving and action purposes, is an attempt to achieve a substitute for *gemeinschaft* through *gesellschaft*-like structures and methods, . . . This raises an interesting question, to paraphrase a popular song from a few years back, "Where Has All the *Gemeinschaft* Gone?" The answer, it would seem, is that it is very much still here and always will be. p 419.

50.　cf. Warren, Roland L. *op cit* pp 21-551; Thomas, David N. (1983) *The Making of Community Work* (George Allen & Unwin) p 300.

51.　cf Fowler, James W. (1984) *Becoming Adult, Becoming Christian* (Harper & Row) p 114ff and (1981) *Stages of Faith: The Psychology of Human Development and the Quest for Meaning* (Harper Row) p 98.

52.　C. I. Barnard quoted by P. Selzwick p 301 in Emery, F. E. (ed) (1970 Revised Edition 1981) *Systems Thinking Volume I* (Penguin).

53.　Emery, F.E.. *op cit* p 301.

54.　Abercrombie, N., Hill, Stephen and Turner, Bryan S. (1984) *Dictionary of Sociology* (Penguin) p 110f.

55.　*Working As One Process: MODEM's Submission on The Turnbull Report to the Archbishops' Advisory Group* (MODEM Occasional Paper, May 1996).

56.　Both books are edited by John Nelson and published by The Canterbury Press in 1996 and 1999 respectively.

57.　I have been greatly helped in my work by a publication long out of print. It is an *Automomous Groups Bulletin* which was edited by Maria Rogers and Ralph B. Spencer (Vol. VII No. 4-Vol. VIII No. 1, Summer-Autumn 1952) and it is entitled "Leadership and Authority in the Local Community: A Report to the Fourth International Congress on Mental Health by The Preparatory Commission on Autonomous Groups and Mental Health". It was this publication which helped me to realise just how influential networks are in relation to development and counter-development.

58.　Bosch, David J. (1991, Tenth Printing 1996) *Transforming Mission: Paradigm Shifts in Theology of Mission* pp 378 and 389.

59.　Bosch, David J. (1995) *Believing in the Future: Towards a Missiology of Western Culture* p 59.

60.　p 378 of reference 58.

61.   *Community Work and Social Change: The Report of a Study Group on Training Set Up by the Calouste Gulbenkian Foundation* (1968) p 25.

62.   There is a vast amount of literature on liberation theology and the preferential option for the poor as there is on church and community development. Some of the latter is referred to at various points in this book. Interestingly, the Rev. Howard Mellor drew upon his experience of Avec and the non-directive approach when he introduced the revised approach to mission and missioners cf *Telling Experiences: Stories about a Transforming Way of Working with People* (Chester House Publications, 1996). The quotes are from pp 49-51. Robert Warren's book is *Being Human, Being Church: Spirituality and Mission in the Local Church* (Marshall Pickering , 1995).

63.   cf *Analysis and Design* p 78.

64.   cf The work of James W. Fowler *et al* and particularly Fowler, James W., Nipkow, Karl Erust and Schweitzer, Friedrich (eds) (1992) *Stages of Faith and Religious Development: Implications for Church, Education and Society* (SCM Press) and Fowler, James W. (1981) *Stages of Faith—The Psychology of Human Development and the Quest for Meaning* (Harper & Row).

65.   cf. Reed, Bruce (1979) *The Dynamics of Religion: Process Movement in Christian Churches* (Darton, Longman & Todd) p 147 and a chapter he contributed to Mitton, C.L. (1972) *The Social Sciences and The Cultures* (T & T Clark) entitled "The Local Church as Institution" pp 44ff. The diagram is based on, but not identical with, those by Bruce Reed in the books referred to on pp 148 and 46 respectively.

66.   In *The Church and Community Development: An Introduction* (Grail Publications & Chester House Publications, 1972 revised 1980, Avec Publication 1992 reprint) I offer several models of the church at work in the community, cf Chapter 8.

67.   In Lovell, George 1994 *Analysis and Design: A Handbook for Practitioners and Consultants in Church and Community Work* (Burns & Oates) there is a section entitled "Coping with Contextual Intimidation" pp 149ff.

68.   McKelvey, Bill (1982) *Organizational Systematics:Taxonomy, Evolution, Classification* (University of California Press) contrasts, compares and synthesises two organizational models "allogenic" (directed from without) and "autogenic" (directed from within). He discusses the kinds of "couplings" between organization and environment which produces these different organizational forms. cf pp 75ff.

69.   Professor Gillian Stamp suggests five spheres of social living: the immediate home area, the neighbourhood, the extended community, the district, the region. She relates these to sub-parish units, the parish, group deaneries, district deaneries, dioceses. *Spheres of Social Living* (Brunel Institute of Organization and Social Studies, An undated occasional paper).

70.   This classification evolved from a six-year programme of action research with sixteen churches of seven denominations. The research is reported in Lovell, George and Widdicombe, Catherine (1978 Reprinted 1986) *Churches and Communities: An Approach to Development in the Local Church*. See also Grundy, Malcolm (ed) (1995). *The Parchmore Partnership: George Lovell, Garth Rogers and Peter Sharrocks* (Chester House Publictiobns) for an analysis of the work done in a Methodist Church, Youth and Community Centre over a period of twenty five years based on this classification. Work areas are modelled in these publications.

71.   See for instance, Hopewell, James F. (1988) *Congregation*; Luscombe, Philip an article entitled "Churches and Congregations" in the *Epworth Review*, Volume Eighteen Number One January 1991. (Luscombe helpfully examines the relationship between church and congregation.); Tisdale, Leonara Tubbs (1997) *Preaching as Local Theology and Folk Art* (Fortress Press, Minneapolis); (There is a very helpful chapter on "Exegeting the Congregation which is referred to later.) Grundy, Malcolm (1998) *Understanding Congregations* (Mowbray). (This is a practical and popular approach to the subject.)

72.   There is an unusual if not a unique example of a united Anglican/United Reformed Church handing over its premises to a trust to form a centre and becoming one of the users of it. It is the Copleston Centre in Peckham, in the Inner London Borough of Southwark. Richard Bainbridge did a study of it entitled, *Church and Centre: An Examination of Church Centre Relationships in a Shared Church and Community Centre in South London*. It is an unpublished Diploma Dissertation. There is a copy in the Avec Archives, Westminster Institute of Education, Oxford.

73.   A book has been written about this by Philip S. Bagwell, (1987) *Outcast London: A Christian Response: The West London Mission of the Methodist Church* 1887-1987 (Epworth Press).

74.   For accounts of church related community work see: Ballard, Paul (ed) (1990) *Issues in Church Related Community Work* (Holi 6, Pastoral Studies, University of Wales College of Cardiff in association with The Community Resource Unit, B.C.F.). Grundy, Malcolm (1995) *Community Work: A Handbook for Volunteer Groups and Local Churches* (Mowbray).

75.   This was a conclusion of the research described earlier cf *Churches and Communities* p 196f.

76.   The essay forms a chapter entitled "More than Words? Christian Apologetics for the Third Millennium" in *A Charge to Keep: Methodist Reflections on the Eve of the Third Millennium* compiled by Thornton, Brian (1999) (Methodist Publishing House) pp 68-75.

77.   See: Berger, P. (1977) *Facing up to Modernity* (New York Basic Books) I owe the reference to Willmott, Peter with David Thomas (1984) *Community in Social Policy* (Policy Studies Institute) p l0; and *Faith in the City—A Call for Action by Church and Nation: The Report of the Archbishop of Canterbury's Commission on Urban Priority Areas* (Church House Publishing) pp 57f.

78.   I owe the term to Professor Hywell Griffiths through an address given to South Region Conference 21st March 1981 entitled: *Community Work in the 80's: Paid and Voluntary Action* (1981) p 9. There is an extract in *Analysis and Design op cit* p l52.

79.   cf Dulles, Avery (1976) *Models of The Church: A Critical Assessment of The Church in All Its Aspects* (Gill & Macmillan) see particularly pp 17 and 26.

80.   See Snyder, Howard (1991) *Models of the Kingdom* (Abingdon Press). Hare, Diane M. (1993) *A Critical Examination of the Nature and Scope of Community in an Ex-Mining Valley in South Wales, and Its Impact on Church, Ministry and Mission* (An unpublished dissertation submitted for the Diploma in Church and Community Development in the Roehampton Institute of Higher Education for a course of study at Avec, an Associated Institution of RIHE) produced the following chart to help her to understand the models of church and ministry, local people in churches to which she ministered in the South Wales Valleys and their implications (p 41). They demonstrate just how useful church modelling can be to local ministry.

Model of Church	Minister	Members	Theology
Family of God/ society/club	Servant/ caretaker	Owners/ masters	Ownership/control. A "contained"and customised God
Pillar of the establishment	Law and order figure	Obedient subjects	Conformity/loyalty Maintains status quo
Vineyard	Nurturer Gardener	Tender plants Branches	Spiritual (and also numerical growth) Unity/holding on ?Pruning/harvesting
Community of faith	Holy person Theological resource	Disciples Thinkers Prayers	Fellowship/support Acting/reflecting Doing theology
Body of Christ	Limbs/organs/co-workers Ideally non-hierarchical		Mutual value. Interdependence Teamwork
Community resource (baptisms, weddings, funerals)	Community resource	Supportive pastoral follow-up	Presence ministry. Rites as pastoral opportunities
Community conscience	Prophetic voice	Prophetic witness/action	Faith and lifestyle. Standards/values. Danger of being judgemental
Community and social care centre	Community worker	Supportive? Involved?	Social concern. Mission
Business concern	Manager	Money-maker	Stewardship
Base for mission	Sender Encourager	Evangelists Witnesses	Mission/outreach

Holy people Pilgrim people	Leader or Guide	Separate Dedicated Shared aims	Journey/promise. Pilgrimage/search. Dynamic/moving
God's army	Captain	Soldiers or followers	Militant crusade Triumphalism
God's workforce	Overseer	Workers	Task-oriented, not place-oriented
Holy place	Priest or intermediary	Worshippers (passive?)	Liturgy and ritual. Priestly autocracy
Worship theatre	Performer Preacher Orator	Audience (passive or Participative)	Entertainment. Drama. Emotionalism
Circus Ring	Ringmaster or Clown	Performers Participants	Openness/surprise. Untidiness/action. Fun/involvement
Museum	Curator	Keepers of tradition	"Our fathers' God" Historical/ancestral
Place of education	Teacher	Students	Self-improvement
Place of healing	Healer or counsellor	Patients/ suffer	Faith and prayer, miracles and hope
Place of encounter with God	Challenger	Strugglers	Making links between heaven and earth
Place of refuge	Shepherd/ "Minder"	Sheep/ victims	Safety and comfort. Peace and escapism
Preparation for heaven (hospice)	Comforter/ nurse	Patients/ suffers	Heavenly reward. Escape to joy

81.   Morgan, Gareth (1986) *Images of Organization* (Sage Publications).

82.   Dulles, Avery *op cit* p 26 and 27. Following Thomas S. Kuhn he defines paradigms as "concrete-puzzle-solutions which, employed as models or examples can replicate explicit rules as a basis for the solution of remaining puzzles of normal science".

83.   Dulles, Avery *op cit* p 28.

84.   cf Kung, H. (1986) *Church and Change: The Irish Experience* (Gill & Macmillan) pp 70f. And (1991) *Judaism: The Religious Situation of Our Time* (SCM Press) on the front and rear inside covers.

85.   See refs. 1 to 4 for books and papers on missiological research by Bosch, Cracknell and Yates. Action research into mission and evangelism is a part of the new MA in Evangelism Studies Course at Cliff College. A note of the action-research undertaken over the past thirty years into church and community development is to be found in my book *Avec : Agency and Approach* (An Avec Publication, 1996) pp 135ff.

86.   The phrase "talking work" I owe to Argyle, Michael (1972) *The Social Psychology of Work* (Harmsworth, Penguin) pp129f. In *Analysis and Design op cit*. I discuss "words spoken and written" as basic equipment in analysis and design, pp 176ff. Smail, David (1984) *Illusion and Reality: The Meaning of Anxiety* (J. M. Dent & Sons) has two extremely useful chapters on language: "The Domination of Words" (4) and "The Language of Anxiety" (5).

87.   Ephesians 4:29 as translated in *The Divine Office: The Liturgy of the Hours According to the Roman Rite* Volume III (Colins, E. J. Dwyer & Talbot, 1974) p [114].

88.   This process is described more fully in Chapter Two and *Analysis and Design, op cit*.

89.   Wilson, U. and Butler, R. (1985) *Voluntary Organisations in Action: Strategy in The Voluntary Sector* (Journal of Management Studies 23) (5) p 521, define the key elements of a voluntary organization as follows:

(1) A considerable proportion of the labour force is voluntary and, hence, unpaid. A voluntary organization does not lose its title, however, if some of its members are paid, or if it receives financial aid from government agencies. Membership of a voluntary organization is not inherited through familial or societal connections. Neither is membership specifically aimed at securing economic benefit for its individuals.

(2) Such organizations are engaged in the non-commercial provision of goods or services. Voluntary organizations do not specifically seek profit from the selling of goods or services in the market although, as we shall see, many voluntary organizations set up profit-seeking subsidiary trading companies, but with the purpose of providing funds for that voluntary organization.

I owe this quotation to Sr Catherine Ryan.

With reference to the phrase "the common good" , Professor Ronald H. Preston, in the Hartley Lecture 1995, having critically examined challenges to this concept by John Atherton, André Dumas and postmodernist thinkers express my own feelings about the term in his conclusion:

I think the concept of the common good is fundamental to Christian social theology and that there should be no question of abandoning it. Especially it is a call to each Christian and to the Churches to take civic responsibility seriously. We cannot think that God is concerned only with the well-being of Christians. We are born into this world as human beings, made in his image, not as Christians. We are globally involved with those of other faiths and philosophies, cheek by jowl with them. We must assume God wants us all to flourish and not to destroy ourselves in conflicts. A common good must continually be sought. What contribution can Christians make today to that search? (cf the *Epworth Review* 24/1 Jan. 1997).

For other discussions of the common good see: Kennedy, John "Machiavelli and The Good Republic", The Beckly Social Service Lecture, (1997) published in the *Epworth Review* 24/3, July 1997 and *The Common good and the Catholic Church's Social Teaching, A statement by the Catholic Bishops' Conference of England and Wales* (1996).

90.   Nelson, John (ed) (1996) *Management and Ministry—Appreciating Contemporary Issues* Chapter 9, p 117.

91.   Brenton, Maria (1985) in *The Voluntary Sector in British Social Services* (Longman) maps the development and growth of voluntary agencies in the spheres of social welfare and social focussing on the new era from 1979 to the mid eighties. She identifies and discusses the main issues. Unfortunately she does not include the Church in this study. The current issues were fully examined by The Commission on the Future of the Voluntary Sector. The National Council of Voluntary Organizations published three volumes on the Commission's Report under the titles: *Meeting The Challenge: Voluntary Action into the Twenty-first Century* (NCVO, 1996). Handy, Charles (1988) *Understanding Voluntary Organizations* (Penguin).Batten, T. R. and Dickson, A.G. (1959) *Voluntary Action and Social Progress* (The British Council). These I still find useful.

92.   I owe these two phrases to Bonino, José Miguez (1983) *Towards a Christian Political Ethics* (SCM Press) p 60.

93.   Fromm, Erich (1942/1960) *The Fear of Freedom* (Routledge and Kegan Paul).

94.   cf. *The Sign We Give: Report from the Working Party on Collaborative Ministry* Bishops' Conference of England and Wales (Roman Catholic) 1995.

95.   Jenkins, David E. (1976) T*he Contradiction of Christianity: The 1974 Edward Cadbury Lectures in the University of Birmingham* (SCM Press) p 155.

96.   An article by Casto, Michael R. entitled "Towards Theology for Pastoral Care: Ministry with Persons in Pain" in Jones, Richard G. (ed) *Epworth Review* Vol. 16/2 May 1989.

97.   Russell, Anthony (1980) *The Clerical Profession* (SPCK) is a carefully researched book which studies the history of the professionalization of the Church of England clergyman's role from the late eighteenth century to the late 1970s. Of particular interest to us is the detailed exposition of the roles and functions of the clergy and the way in which they have evolved and changed in relation to the emergence of the professions in English society. A contemporary view would see "professions as socially prestigious avocations that control their own training, recruitment and practice and which apply specialized

knowledge, under the guidance of an ethical code in individual and social problems". A Robertson in an article on "Professionalism" in Campbell, Allistair V (1987) *A Dictionary of Pastoral Care* (SPCK) p 220. I consider the Christian ministry meets these criteria.

98.   There is a good example of this in Lovell, George (ed) (1996) *Telling Experiences: Stories About a Transforming Way of Working With People* pp 163 ff.

99.   Norman H. Todd, in a contribution to *A Dictionary of Pastoral Care, op. cit.*, under the entry "Interprofessional Relationships", p 136.

100.   See: Schon, Donald A. (1990) *Educating the Reflective Practitioner: Towards a New Design for Teaching and Learning in the Professions* (Jossey-Bass Publishers). It has already been indicated that this is a major emphasis in *The Making of Ministry* (see next reference).

101.   From an unpublished paper, "Ministerial Competence", dated 22nd February 1996. cf *The Making of Ministry: The Report of the Ministerial Training Policy Working Group the Methodist Church* (The Methodist Publishing House, Ref PE 146, September 1996) pp 66ff.

102.   Lovell, George (1994) *Analysis and Design, op cit.*

103.   I owe this phrase to Ann Morisy. It is the sub-title of an article in *Crucible* (January/March 1993) "Community Ministry: Linking Private Faith to Public Action."

104   David Smail (1984) in his book *Illusion and Reality: The Meaning of Anxiety* argues persuasively that, "For everyday purposes, it seems, that reality is the best description I am able to give myself of it". (p 64 cf 172). People tell themselves stories which they believe and which enable them to live with events and happenings. As they work through experiences they revise their stories.

105.   This kind of action is what Eric Fromm calls "non-alienated activity". He writes:

> In alienated activity I do not experience myself as the acting subject of my activity; rather, I experience the **outcome** of my activity—and that is something "over there", separated from me and standing above and against me. In alienated activity I do not really act; I am **acted upon** by external or internal forces. I have become separated from the result of my activity. . . . In non-alienated activity I experience **myself** as the **subject** of my activity. Non-alienated activity is a process of giving birth to something, of producing something and remaining related to what I produce. This also implies that my activity is a manifestation of my powers, that I and my activity are one. I call this non-alienated activity **productive activity**. . . . Productiveness is a character orientation all human beings are capable of, to the extent that they are not emotionally crippled. Productive persons animate whatever they touch. They give birth to their own faculties and bring life to other persons and to things.

To Have or To Be (Jonathan Cape, 1978) pp 90ff.

106.   I owe these titles to Ian Cunningham from a chapter entitled, "Interactive Holistic Research: Researching Self-Managed Learning" in Reason, Peter (ed) (1988) *Human Inquiry in Action: Developments in New Paradigm Research* (Sage Publications) pp 164f. I was particularly helped by diagrams he uses which are reproduced opposite. The first he entitles "testing and evolving theory" and the second "contextual locating" pp 167ff.

Dialogic research: two or three people talking and interacting as a way of "finding out".

Collaborative research: a group of people together investigate their own experience or experience outside the group.

Experiential research: research which focuses upon the direct experience of the person(s)/researcher(s).

Action research: action areas of the practitioners are the source of research material. Other "modes do not necessarily assume active 'doing' as central to the process".

107.   Cracknell, Kenneth (1995) *Justice, Courtesy and Love: Theologians and Missionaries Encountering World Religions* (Epworth Press).

108.   This is discussed further in *Analysis and Design*, p 126f.

109.   Long after I had written this section I discovered through the Revd Geoff Cornell that Jackson W. Carroll had also used the same metaphor for similar purposes in *As One With Authority: Reflective Leadership in Ministry* (Wesminster /John Knox Press) p 99.

110.   As the text makes clear I am committed to multi- rather than mono-modelling. cf Chapter 3, II.4.

111.   cf Jacques, Elliott (1976 reprinted 1981) *A General Theory of Bureaucracy* (Heinemann Educational) p 99.

112.   Sermon given by The Revd David Deeks at The Annual Service of "Church At Work In London" on 17th May 1993, p 1 of published version.

113.   Jacques, Elliott, *op cit* p 101 cf *Analysis and Design* pp 215ff and 226.

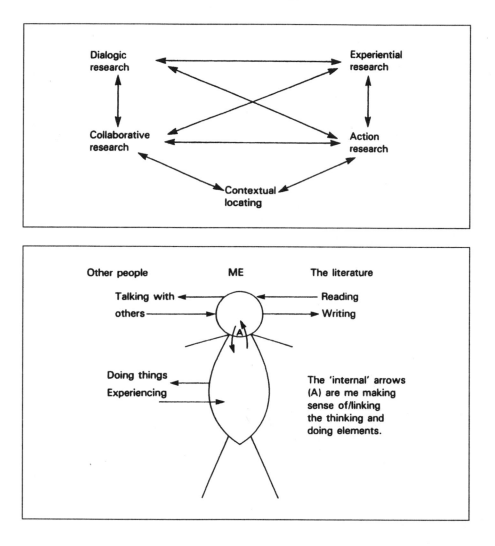

CHAPTER SEVEN

Attributes of Workers

Our attention now focuses on three kinds of interrelated attributes which enable practitioners to do the work described in the previous chapter. The first is the personal characteristics of workers and has to do with their being and behaviour. The second is the body of knowledge they require and has to do with knowing and understanding. The third kind is the technical and human relations skills required and has to do with doing and making. Combined these attributes integrate what practitioners need *to be* with what they need *to know* and what they need to be able *to do*.

An example chosen at random illustrates the distinctions. Being a vocational team player by conviction and commitment rather than a solo worker or prima donna is what I am referring to as a *personal attribute*. Understanding the theology and practice theory of teamwork in religious organizations and secular communities is an aspect of the *body of knowledge*. The ability to work with people interdependently is one of a cluster of *abilities and skills* required of a team player. Properly equipped practitioners are endowed with apposite personal characteristics, the relevant knowledge and appropriate abilities and skills.

Attributes of all three kinds are required. They complement each other but, whilst the strength of one might compensate for the weakness of another, they must not be treated as substitutes. The commitment to be a team player, to continue the illustration, essential as it is, does not of itself equip a practitioner to be one. Lack of knowledge and skills prevent the full expression of any personal characteristics. On the other hand, attempts to act as a team player without personal commitment to the concept will lack conviction and credibility no matter how much knowledge and skill practitioners might have. At any level of competence it is essential that there is unitive interplay between personal characteristics, knowledge and skills. They are complexly and inextricably tied up with each other in the practitioner's being, reflecting and doing. Each of them is a sub-system, intricately connected to the others and to the whole human system in which they have their existence. Assimilated and made a personal fit, they make for the development of work and practitioners.

Nevertheless, the attributes can be expressed and experienced separately. Sometimes it might be one or other of the practitioner's personal attributes, at another aspects of his/her knowledge or skills. At times appropriately and at other times inappropriately. When they are assimilated and correlated, all attributes are present and active in one way or another in a natural unity, even though one is in the forefront. Each aspect is experienced, known and reinforced through the others: they are all of a piece in genuine encounters. Attitudes, the way in which things are done and the explanations are all expressions of the personal characteristics which they embody; there is three way traffic through the interconnecting routes between them. Some of this I have attempted to portray diagrammatically in Figure 7:1.

Using this broad threefold classification I describe the things I believe equip people to be church and community work practitioners Much can be learnt by examining the attributes separately provided that that does not lead to them being treated as separate entities or simplistically connected in a mechanical or linear manner.

These attributes can develop and change, for better or worse, through various external and internal stimuli. Identifying and examining them, as we have done here, contributes to the knowledge about them and the practice theory associated with them. That could enhance practitioner's skills. It could also help people to decide what action they wish to take, to acquire or develop their attributes—or it might lead them to compile their own list of desirable attributes.

I have concentrated on attributes required to engage creatively with people and the nature of the work. Abilities, gifts and skills associated with important functions such as liturgy, preaching and Christian education and accountancy are beyond the range of this study and in any case there is a vast amount of literature on them. The kind of consultancy in which I am normally involved is about their place in the scheme of things and the work with people involved in promoting and organizing them rather than the technicalities of doing them.

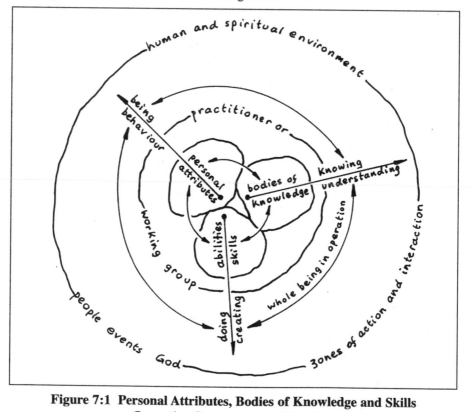

**Figure 7:1 Personal Attributes, Bodies of Knowledge and Skills
Operating Separately and Together**

I PERSONAL ATTRIBUTES: What Practitioners Need To Be

The ideal nature of the work is downloaded into the actualities of church and community work through practitioners willingly accepting and embracing its human and spiritual characteristics, allowing them to be embodied in their being and their work-views and by working at the actual in relation to the ideal. When this happens the nature of the work is a reality in practitioners, in what they do and how they do it and, therefore, in the work done and what is created through it.

An attempt is now made to define personal characteristics which play such a vital part in bringing theory and theology to life in the workplace. They correlate with those of the nature of the work which have been described fully in the previous chapter. Attributes are so closely connected with skills that in some instances the description of the one runs into that of the other. Ideally practitioners are:

- in love with their work
- workforce persons
- team players and leader-enablers
- reflective workforce members
- committed to widely based developmental, collaborative participation
- instruments and subjects of human and spiritual development
- situationally committed and contextually engaged
- personally, professionally and spiritually disciplined disciples.

1. Practitioners are in Love with their Work

Ideally practitioners need to be in love with the nature of the work, to believe in it passionately and to have an affinity with it. For them it is an affair of the soul. They need to love God and people and to be able to relate to and engage with both. They need to be committed to the pursuit and evolution of their own vocation and to those of others. These are missiological, vocational and existential features of the work as set out in the previous chapter. They need to engage vigorously with its theological, theoretical and practical implications. They need to be committed to, relate to and to work with and for God, people generally and workers in allied disciplines. These positive psycho-spiritual relationships and their affective, intellectual and faith content are at the top end of a spectrum of characteristics which shades off until it enters the negatives of these positives. They have a dynamic which generates and develops personal characteristics. For those who have them the work becomes a spiritual and professional way of life.

When these attributes are present in individuals and groups they make unique contributions to the quality of the work. In almost any context and company attributes of this kind make them infectious workers. They bring the work to life because it has brought them to life and this shows in all they are and do. They spark off interest, enthusiasm, anticipation and hope. Other people get caught up in the work and fall in love with the theory and practice of it. All kinds of things happen because, through being endowed with these attributes, key aspects of the nature of the work are embodied in the very soul of practitioners—not only in their minds or in how they do things. This gives added meaning, significance, value and status to

311

anything they do or say. It makes them creative in ways in which knowledge and skills alone could never make them. Such attributes are the heart of the body of knowledge and the corpus of skills. This does not mean that the attributes always operate at a high level of performance. They do not. Performance is influenced by such things as mood, interpersonal relationships, circumstances and energy levels. In this they are not dissimilar to any other human or spiritual attribute.

People acquire these kinds of characteristics in many different ways. Some people seem naturally endowed with one or other of them. They can come through moments of disclosure or evaluated human and spiritual experience, study or training practice through taking on challenges or through experiencing them in other people, events, experiences, study and research, conversation and many other and often unpredictable ways. They can be formed by becoming committed to ideas and by using or experiencing the methods associated with them. But, as they are more and other than learned behaviour, they have to become consistent and integral parts of the essential character and being of practitioners.

2.   Practitioners are Workforce Persons

This is one of the personal attributes formed by the perspective practitioners have of a collaborative workforce and their part in it. As Church workers have to use all their faculties they require many skills. That, an unavoidable conclusion of our analysis, is reflected in a recent denominational report, *The Making of Ministry*,[1] in a section about competencies and expectations of ministers as reflective practitioners. Display 7:1 summarises the points made.[2] Skilled as individual practitioners might be, nothing less than a workforce, balanced and finely tuned, can bring together all the abilities necessary for the work. Every aspect of the form, nature, complexity and size of the work require it.

Basically what is required to do this work is a workforce composed of practitioners with aptitudes and skills for particular jobs who can work on their own and with others in groups and teams. A way of thinking about this work I find helpful is to determine the "pool of competences" required of the workers and members of a church to make it collectively competent.[3] Apart from doing their own work practitioners contribute towards making task groups and workforces jell together, function effectively and economically.

It is common for churches to look for, and exult in, polymathic practitioners, individualistic and directive solo performers. Clearly this militates against building up collaborative workforces and teamwork. Everything must be done to change this approach so that proper emphasis is given to polymathic workforces.

A primary personal attribute of practitioners, therefore, is that they are by conviction, not simply fashion or necessity, inwardly committed to forming and taking their place in collaborative workforces of vocational practitioners committed, motivated, disciplined and directed by their collective vocations. Anything less is second best.

3.   Practitioners are Team Players and Leader-Enablers

Lay and ordained church work practitioners can make significant contributions towards building up workforces through being team players and leader-enablers in

A Methodist Minister (presbyteral or diaconal) will be a **Reflective Practioner**. This means that he or she

1) engages with God, with the created order, with others (individuals, communities and institutions) and with self
   —directly through personal encounter and the exercise of basic skills and through
   a) knowledge and understanding of biblical, theological and other appropriate theoretical material
   b) imagination, vision, empathy and self-awareness

2) rehearses the integration of the skills, knowledge, understanding, imagination, vision, empathy and self-awareness into creative performance

3) reflects on the experience, process and outcome of particular acts of ministry
   a) personally
   b) with others (*e.g.*: Circuit Staff, Leadership Team, Support or Reference Group),

   takes the necessary steps suggested by that reflection of
   —studying
   —practising basic skills or acquiring new ones
   —praying
   and as a consequence improves his or her performance on the next occasion

4) receives regular supervision for what he or she does in ministry

5) exercises accountability to others for his or her ministry, articulating it to them in appropriate ways

In general he or she

6) understands the basic content and nature of biblical and theological material and of particular pastoral contexts, relates them to each other with discernment and, where appropriate, preaches effectively about them

7) discerns the imperatives of the Gospel and the needs of contemporary society, relates them to each other articulately and prophetically; and, as a consequence, enables people to engage in appropriate forms of Mission in response to both

8) knows the liturgical traditions of the Church and of Methodism in particular; understands the principles underlying worship, participates in it creatively and, where appropriate, plans, organises and leads it in different contexts and for different kinds of congregation

9) understands the dynamics affecting the life-cycles of communities, groups and individuals, discerns where they are operating in particular situations, addresses them with pastoral sensitivity and, where appropriate, helps devise and preside at suitable rites of passage and sacramental activities for them

10) knows the Constitutional Practice and Discipline of the Methodist Church, understands its underlying principles and the dynamics that affect the life of groups, and assists them to make effective decisions, taking the chair where appropriate

11) discerns how issues of power affect the way people work together and handles authority effectively, both acting under that of others and, where appropriate, exercising it over them

12) understands the nature and role of the different forms of ministry, collaborates with them effectively, and maintains that quality of relationship with others which is essential for effective pastoral work, discerning his or her own strengths and weaknesses in dealing faithfully with administrative matters and knowing when to call for help

13) knows the spiritual traditions of the church, discerns both the public and private aspects of his or her life of prayer, and persists in the discipline and development of his or her own spiritual life so that all that he or she does retains its freshness

14) makes use of accompanied self-appraisal, knows how to give and receive help and is able to deal creatively with his or her areas of incompetency.

In particular he or she may specialise in some of particular areas of ministry, *e.g.*: Christian Worship; Social Justice and Peace; Pastoral care; Church Administration; Christian Education; Evangelism; Professional and Personal Nurture.

Display 7:1 Competencies of Ministers as Reflective Practitioners

313

their own organizations and in the wider socio-religious context in which they operate. As team players they differentiate their part and place and are living models of what it means to participate in this way.

As leader-enablers their primary functions are: to get the theory and practice of workforces thoroughly considered in relation to the work as a whole and/or to aspects of it and projects; to work with others to develop and deploy workforces in their own organizations and, where necessary, with other institutions. The leadership can be enthusiastic, vigorous and even charismatic, indeed it often has to be, but, as informed, free and willing participation is a condition of effective collaborative teamwork in a workforce, it must be essentially non-directive. These leadership roles and functions are not the exclusive prerogative of a few individuals. All concerned have opportunities and responsibilities to build up the collective leadership. However, there is simply no way in which churches can or will operate in the ways being considered without principal team players who are leader-enablers. Their services are required in every grouping and meeting point of the workforce from the staff of a parish to international consultations for the routine round of activities, the development of new approaches and programmes and when there is a spontaneous surge of thought and action. As primary workers they play key, but not exclusive, roles in making things work and getting all concerned to make their contributions towards making them do so: if leadership is left to anyone and everyone the chances of purposeful co-ordinated effort are remote; on the other hand if leadership is left entirely to the "leader" undesirable things can and do happen.

The facilitative functions performed by enabler-leaders are key to helping people to develop working relationships and practices which enable them and their organizations to work systemically. But the ability to enable people to do things must not be confused or equated with the ability to do those things: enablers may or may not be able to do them and even when they can it may not be appropriate for them to do so. No one person in a complex organization can do everything. They should not expect nor be expected to do so; they cannot possibly possess all the skills or time required to do the work. That is why workforces are required.

4.   Practitioners are Reflective Workforce Members

Practitioners need to engage in creative reflection, on their own and with others, on what they experience as they pursue their vocation. By their example and by stimulating and enabling others to do the same, they promote and induce collaborative reflection throughout the churches and organizations in which they are involved.

Critical reflective engagement is an expression of an approach to life and work rather than a technique used periodically. It is a vital force deeply rooted in practitioners and work-forces which pulsates through everything they do from face to face work through prayer and meditation to academic study. Moments of deep inner engagement with those with whom they are working can, for instance, occur when they are writing up notes of events in the privacy of their study. The quality of academic engagement is invariably reflected in task group work and vice versa. In fact critical reflective engagement is holistic: it is a reflexive and systemic

314

activity; engagement in one part can suffuse the whole. All this is reflected in the aids to engagement. Respect for people affects the way in which practitioners behave towards them and the ways in which they think about them in preparation and planning. Conceptual abilities facilitate every aspect of engagement with ideas, people and events.

5. Practitioners are Committed to Widely Based Developmental Collaborative Participation

Another personal attribute is the deep seated yearning for widely based participation in anything and everything that relates to the human and spiritual well-being of people, individually and collectively. No one form of participation is invariably right: the form it takes will be determined by purpose, people and circumstances.[4] These factors will lead people to participate in many different appropriate ways from giving their opinions to working in egalitarian partnerships. Two modes of intervention and engagement are necessary to promote such pluriform participation. One is directive. This approach involves thinking, deciding, planning, organizing, administering and providing *for* people. The other is non-directive. This approach involves working *with* people in order that they think, decide etc. for themselves.[5] It facilitates working with people interpersonally in depth which is a distinctive feature of the nature of the work we are considering. It enables practitioners to get very close to the inner places at the very heart of being and living in individuals, groups, communities, religious and secular organizations. That is where human and divine activities and work and ministry interact and fuse. Therefore, it is very important that practitioners should be able to engage with people participatively.

Both approaches require practitioners to be forthright, responsible, loving, caring compassionate and close. Directive action can all too easily become impersonal, arrogant, autocratic and dictatorial: non-directive action can all too easily appear clinically cold, distant and laissz-faire. Neither directive nor non-directive action is *ipso facto* right or wrong: doing too much or too little *for* or *with* people can inhibit development. Both approaches are necessary because, if we are to live and develop, some things must be done *for us*, some things must be left for us to do *for ourselves* and *with others* and some things we will only be able to do if someone works *with us*, alongside us. Therefore, choices have to be made continually between approaches in relation to key reference points such as purposes and circumstances.[6] What worked in one situation may be inappropriate or dysfunctional or disastrous in another. Requests for a fixed formula for choice of approach must be resisted. Questions that help me to decide on appropriate directive or non-directive action are:

What must I do *for* these people at this time and in this situation?

What must I do alongside them, *with them*?

What must we do *together*?

What must I leave them to do *for themselves* and with *each other*?

Should I decide the approach to be adopted without consulting or should I negotiate it?

315

When and how must I withdraw so that my waiting and returning promote processes of development?

The questions are universally relevant; the answers, and therefore the action to be taken and the leads to be given, vary enormously as people grow and from one situation to another.[7] This indicates that this approach is much more complex than this brief introduction might suggest. Critical elements are charted in Appendix II. Many have come to refer to it as the *"avec approach"* (from the French for "with" chosen to represent the central concept of working *with* people for human and spiritual development which was promoted by "Avec", an ecumenical training and consultancy agency for church and community work, 1976-1994).

6. Practitioners are Instruments and Subjects of Human and Spiritual Development

Undoubtedly practitioners can make contributions, possibly significant ones, to the development of others and their work, without experiencing comparable changes in themselves. But it is difficult to imagine how anyone can give themselves wholeheartedly to the work we are discussing without themselves being changed in various ways. For many years, using methods similar to those we are considering, Dr. T. R. Batten ran courses which enabled small groups of practitioners to reflect on and analyse the theory and practice of their work. He often said, "I do the course with the members", meaning that he was learning and changing as he facilitated their development. He could not describe himself as a catalyst as some do because of the first meaning of that word, "a substance that, without itself undergoing permanent chemical change, increased the rate of a reaction" (*The Concise Oxford Dictionary*, Ninth Edition, 1997). He was an instrument and a subject of change. There is a healthy and wholesome feel about this which is absent from those who operate on people and things without being changed or expecting to be so themselves. Profound all round human and spiritual development occurs when reciprocal formative processes are at work which causes change for the better in practitioners, those with whom they are engaged and the work they are doing. Practitioners engaged in these forms of interchange are instruments and subjects of human and spiritual development throughout their lives.

7. Practitioners are Situationally Committed and Contextually Engaged

Generally speaking practitioners are most effective when they are situationally committed and contextually engaged. That is, they are dedicated to the situations and jobs to which they are appointed, be it in a local church or a denominational office. From that base they are involved in contextualising their work in its ecclesiastical, secular and academic worlds and settings. They can do this through sharing in the corporate life of their own denomination or religious order[8] the overall organization and administration of their denomination, ecumenical affairs and secular bodies and by participating in their workforces.

Practitioners can be active members of a community of scholarship sharing in conferences and training events. Workers who are thus engaged can, through using imaginative approaches, get members of local churches thinking about anything that is of interest and value to them and in this way help them to set their work in a wider context.[9] At the same time they are able to share with others what is happening in their situation and that can be an extension of their particular ministry. Apart from this there are all round benefits from this interaction as workers grow and develop and are therefore increasing their potential. The more they take from their own situations to their other relationships, the more they can bring back to them.

Paradoxically, the nearer workers are to those with whom they work the more important it is for them to distance themselves in the ways described and through meditation, reflection and prayer. Situational workers are, generally speaking, better workers when they are contextually engaged. Getting a creative balance between situational involvement and contextual engagement is clearly vital. There are real dangers of one or the other taking over. Denominational jobs, academic study, ecumenical fellowship and community involvement, for instance, can provide attractive and respectable escape routes from facing tough situational realities. They can become an alternative, absorbing time and energy that should be given to situational ministry. On the other hand workers can give themselves exclusively to their "own" situation to the neglect of the wider scene, their studies and their vocational development. More work may be done in their own situation, although this does not necessarily follow because contextual engagement can give added momentum and value to practitioners in all their activities. Isolationism can be injurious to workers and situations. It can produce "group think", see section III:1.

Timetabling situational and contextual work can help to get the right balance. That generally works even though there are times when it is essential to drop everything in order to concentrate totally and exclusively on one's situation over short or long periods. General studies have to be suspended in order to grapple with extraordinary events. On the other hand, it may be necessary to do the absolute minimum in relation to one's job in order to reflect, study or research. This is quite different from neglecting things for trivial pursuits. It is synchronising working rhythms with those of the situation and context so that they are developmentally in harmony and neither damages the other. Achieving this kind of dynamic balance is critical to creative reflective engagement. This is not to be confused with everything being in flux and open ended. Routine standard procedures and programmes are amongst the many things which can contribute to rhythmic work flow and dynamic balance. Rigid adherence to them, however, is to give priority to the equilibrium of the practitioner's work programme rather than to that of the whole work system in which s/he is engaged. The result is a static or dead weight balance rather than a dynamic one.

Practitioners most likely to promote and enjoy dynamic balance are oriented contextually to their situations, dedicated to their job, sensitive to events and open to change, purposefully flexible but not malleable, organized and disciplined.

8. Practitioners are Personally, Professionally and Spiritually Disciplined Disciples

> To sum up, the minister is a reflective practitioner in that s/he
> is a *prayerful person*, a *collaborative colleague* and a *member*
> *of a community of scholarship and interpretation* which
> exercises *mutual accountability*.[10]

This is the way in which the report on the making of ministry quoted earlier summed up the marks of a minister (cf Display 7:2 for an extended quotation). Discipleship of this kind requires discipline, "training that produces obedience, self-control, or a particular skill".[11] Inner personal discipline and accountability help to convert the freedom of thought, expression and association, which is fundamental to the approach advocated in this book, into creative reflective engagement. Freedom and discipline must go together with commitment and ability. Gordon Wakefield ends a dictionary note on discipline in this way:

> What must be generally conceded is (a) that the way must not be narrower than Jesus made it, and (b) just as poetry is a "desperate discipline" (Richard Church) so the Christian life cannot be one of "uncharted freedom", and the very generosity of the divine love demands an absolute dedication in return.[12]

To be an active member of a professional discipline related to ministry and church work, a community of scholarship, is to be self- and other- disciplined by the rigour of study, research and academic standards and codes of practice. To be personally disciplined is to work assiduously at the core of one's calling and its application to the situations in which practitioners find themselves. To be spiritually disciplined takes many forms in relation to private prayer and meditation, "attendance upon the 'means of grace' ", sharing in Christian fellowship (*koinonia*), studying the bible and literature about the Christian life and being open to "spiritual direction". What makes people into practitioners of church work is the combination into an integrated whole of personal, professional and spiritual disciplines. Practitioners who practise these disciplines concurrently as a threefold core of ministry pursue a developmental path. They become lifelong learners, disciples, attempting to master and practice their disciplines.[13]

The values implicit in these personal attributes can be made explicit through a brief indicative list of the commitments associated with them. They are the commitment to:

- work at the Christian missiological project with and for God and Christians and non-Christian people;
- work at theory and theology, situationally and academically;
- active purposeful involvement in church and community rather than to a spectator or commentator role;
- work with, through and in the Church for overall betterment of people in church and society as a whole rather than any one part of it;
- the responsible and accountable empowerment of people;
- cultivate human and spiritual working relationships and to engage in action which generates well-being, happiness, joy, satisfaction, socio-religious communities and *koinonia*;
- supportive non-threatening working relationships which enable, for instance, people to stand by, empathize with and help each other without attempting to take over one another or to take each other's place;
- approaches and methods which promote creative consensus by revealing and working constructively at differences, factions and conflicts;

Ministers, Deaconesses and Deacons have a commitment to a particular form of engagement
— with God (through the Bible and the theological traditions of the churches and through spiritual experience)
— with the created order
— with others (individuals, communities and institutions)
— with self.

Training for this life involves a rigorous and prayerful process of
— acquiring, understanding and applying theoretical knowledge
— developing practical skills
— analysing situations and experience
— discerning, understanding and applying appropriate value systems
— developing a critical awareness of situations so as to maintain a prophetic stance towards them
— developing self-awareness whilst undergoing affective change.

This process is a particular form of being a "reflective practitioner". Ministers Deaconesses and Deacons form corporate bodies of such reflective practitioners which on the one hand enable the church to become a community of reflective practice, and on the other are nurtured by it. The Convocation of the Methodist Diaconal Order, and Ministerial Session of Synod and Conference are focal points of these corporate bodies. We would urge that these be developed further to ensure that provision is made for mutual and communal experiences of spirituality, worship and theological reflection on mission and church life. The training for this process of becoming a reflective practitioner therefore best occurs within particular communities of scholarship, interpretation, collaboration and mutual accountability.

To sum up, the Minister is a reflective practitioner in that she or he is a *prayerful person*, a *collaborative colleague* and a *member of a community of scholarship and interpretation* which exercises *mutual accountability*.

Display 7:2 Marks of a Minister as a Reflective Practitioner

- work primarily with all people for self-induced change rather than to provide services for them;
- get people, including those who differ from each other significantly to work with and for each other for the common good;
- collaborate rather than compete;
- promote those processes of change in others, ourselves and structures that facilitate human and spiritual betterment;
- work at actual situations, no matter how small or large, and to do so in context;
- work with churches, communities and organizations as systems,not simply as collections of individuals or congregations;

- use verbal skills, status and resources *for* and not *against* people;

- open processes of educational dialogue within which people freely articulate their needs in their own way through their own cultural norms;

- get people thinking and thinking again;

- be inclusive rather than exclusive;

- respect people and their needs for privacy, interdependence, autonomy and dependence;

- creating equal opportunities for all people to participate and especially those who are disadvantaged, discriminated against, marginalised, victims of injustice and cruelty.[14]

II BODIES OF KNOWLEDGE: What Practitioners Need to Know

Various attempts have been made to describe the bodies of knowledge that are fundamental to the practice of the profession of ministry. One attempt is summarised in points 6-13 of Display 7:1. Professor Kenneth Cracknell's conceptual map of related bodies of knowledge I find enormously helpful. It is presented with his permission in Display 7: 3 [15] (cf the earlier discussion on missiology). It gives a focal discipline, (theoria). Then it presents five other disciplines: bible and tradition; practical theology; mission (praxis and poesis); practical disciplines; human sciences. Each of these disciplines and their sub-disciplines have their bodies of knowledge. The diagram is important because it shows how the disciplines are systemically interrelated. This is much more helpful than lists which give linear connections. For me the diagram shows that missiology is the hub of a wheel of which the disciplines are the spokes and the bodies of knowledge are conjoined to form the rim which is the means of engagement and missiological and developmental traction.

But the debate about appropriate bodies of knowledge continues. New bodies of knowledge are identified. Earlier sections indicate how the bodies of knowledge expand exponentially. This raises some basic questions for practitioners: what are the most appropriate bodies of knowledge for me? Which is/are fundamental and how do other disciplines and bodies of knowledge relate to it/them? How do I build up my understanding of them? (Aspects of the third question are discussed in various places.)

III ABILITIES AND SKILLS : What Practitioners Need to be Able To Do

Now we turn from what practitioners and work-forces need to be and what they need to *know* to what they need to be able *to do, i.e.:* to the abilities and skills required.

The ten points noted are indicative rather than comprehensive. Separating and listing them is something of a distortion of reality. Each characteristic is a part of a system of competence: the skills, like tools, are used in relation to various tasks often in combinations. Practitioners, therefore, need the ability to use them separately and together as appropriate to tasks, situations and people. When they are

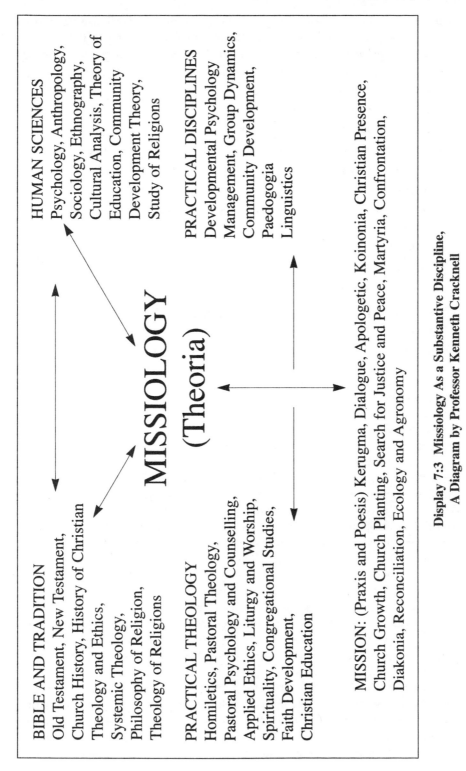

HUMAN SCIENCES
Psychology, Anthropology, Sociology, Ethnography, Cultural Analysis, Theory of Education, Community Development Theory, Study of Religions

PRACTICAL DISCIPLINES
Developmental Psychology Management, Group Dynamics, Community Development, Paedogogia
Linguistics

MISSIOLOGY
(Theoria)

BIBLE AND TRADITION
Old Testament, New Testament, Church History, History of Christian Theology and Ethics, Systemic Theology, Philosophy of Religion, Theology of Religions

PRACTICAL THEOLOGY
Homiletics, Pastoral Theology, Pastoral Psychology and Counselling, Applied Ethics, Liturgy and Worship, Spirituality, Congregational Studies, Faith Development, Christian Education

MISSION: (Praxis and Poesis) Kerugma, Dialogue, Apologetic, Koinonia, Christian Presence, Church Growth, Church Planting, Search for Justice and Peace, Martyria, Confrontation, Diakonia, Reconciliation, Ecology and Agronomy

Display 7:3 Missiology As a Substantive Discipline, A Diagram by Professor Kenneth Cracknell

used well they do not obtrude, they are integral, natural, subordinate parts of the aspects of the practitioner's person and the dynamic and rhythms of their working engagement with people and things. For this to happen practitioners need to be able:

- to relate to God and work with people inclusively and interdependently through sentient task groups

- to promote vocational involvement

- to use all human and spiritual facilities

- to access and put to effective use appropriate bodies of knowledge

- to form and re-form work views

- to discuss constructively issues of life and faith

- to cope with the psycho-spiritual ups and downs of creative reflective engagement

- to deal with their own incompetence and that of others

- to use and provide support systems

- to disengage creatively.

1. Practitioners Need to be Able to Relate to God and Work With People Inclusively and Interdependently Through Sentient Task Groups

The human and spiritual relationships required for this work were discussed in the previous chapter (cf pp 262-266). Here we concentrate on maintaining and deploying sentient task groups to work inclusively with all kinds of people interdependently for Christian ends and the common good. An undertaking calling for considerable skills.

Christian workforces are task groups, that is they have jobs to do. They are also sentient groups.[16] Without some positive sentience a workforce cannot do its job: deep mutual feelings help to galvanise workers, individually and collectively; "we" feelings strengthen groups and provide security in vulnerability; empathy and loving care and concern provide support. Creating a particular form of sentience, *koinonia*, is, as we have seen, a feature of church work. However, if sentience takes priority over task, a workforce betrays its *raison d'être*.[17] This can happen in several ways. For instance close relationships between members of teams can make others feel outsiders. On several occasions I have seen teams of workers become so preoccupied with their interpersonal dynamics that they have seriously neglected and impaired the tasks they were appointed to perform in the church and community. On the other hand the workforce is impaired if the approach to the tasks engenders negative feelings because, for instance, it is too businesslike. And what is true of the workforce is true of other groups and of churches themselves. Workforces are required which are sentient task groups able to promote developmental sentient activity.

Many things make it difficult to form such groups. Some people wish to be businesslike and eschew close personal relationships in working groups. Others value the sentience above the tasks. Sometimes they can be possessive about their workforce and make it difficult for others to belong or feel they belong: they introduce a tendency towards sentient exclusivism. Similarly some people are

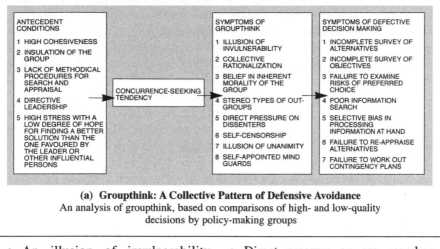

ANTECEDENT CONDITIONS		SYMPTOMS OF GROUPTHINK	SYMPTOMS OF DEFECTIVE DECISION MAKING
1 HIGH COHESIVENESS		1 ILLUSION OF INVULNERABILITY	1 INCOMPLETE SURVEY OF ALTERNATIVES
2 INSULATION OF THE GROUP		2 COLLECTIVE RATIONALIZATION	2 INCOMPLETE SURVEY OF OBJECTIVES
3 LACK OF METHODICAL PROCEDURES FOR SEARCH AND APPRAISAL	CONCURRENCE-SEEKING TENDENCY	3 BELIEF IN INHERENT MORALITY OF THE GROUP	3 FAILURE TO EXAMINE RISKS OF PREFERRED CHOICE
4 DIRECTIVE LEADERSHIP		4 STEREO TYPES OF OUT-GROUPS	4 POOR INFORMATION SEARCH
5 HIGH STRESS WITH A LOW DEGREE OF HOPE FOR FINDING A BETTER SOLUTION THAN THE ONE FAVOURED BY THE LEADER OR OTHER INFLUENTIAL PERSONS		5 DIRECT PRESSURE ON DISSENTERS	5 SELECTIVE BIAS IN PROCESSING INFORMATION AT HAND
		6 SELF-CENSORSHIP	6 FAILURE TO RE-APPRAISE ALTERNATIVES
		7 ILLUSION OF UNANIMITY	7 FAILURE TO WORK OUT CONTINGENCY PLANS
		8 SELF-APPOINTED MIND GUARDS	

(a) Groupthink: A Collective Pattern of Defensive Avoidance
An analysis of groupthink, based on comparisons of high- and low-quality
decisions by policy-making groups

a. An illusion of invulnerability, shared by most or all of the members, which creates excessive optimism and encourages taking extreme risks.

b. Collective efforts to rationalise in order to discount warnings which might lead the members to reconsider their assumptions before they recommit themselves to their past policy decisions.

c. An unquestioned belief in the group's inherent morality, inclining the members to ignore the ethical or moral consequences of their decisions.

d. Stereotyped views of rivals and enemies as too evil to warrant genuine attempts to negotiate, or as too weak or stupid to counter whatever risky attempts are made to defeat their purposes.

e. Direct pressure on any member who expresses strong arguments against any of the groups stereotypes, illusions, or commitments, making clear that such dissent is contrary to what is expected of all loyal members.

f. Self-censorship of deviants from the apparent group consensus, reflecting each member's inclination to minimise to himself (*sic*) the importance of his doubts and counter-arguments.

g. A shared illusion of unanimity, party resulting from this self-censorship and augmented by the false assumption that silence implies consent.

h. The emergence of self-appointed "mindguards', members who protect the group from adverse information that might shatter their shared complacency about the effectiveness and morality of their decisions.

(b) An Exposition of the Symptoms

Display 7:4 Groupthink

possessive about the work and keep others at bay. An extreme form of these dangers of seeking to preserve oneself through self-isolation, exclusivism, possessiveness and sentient indulgence is known as "group think". Characteristics of this phenomenon are presented in Display 7:4.[18] This analysis has helped me to identify, understand and get people thinking creatively about forms of the phenomenon which differ in degree.

One of the antidotes to these dangers is the ability to get right alongside people and to talk with them, not at them, about anything and everything to do with working together including the dangers described above. Another is to emphasize building up teamwork throughout organizations rather than teams. Yet another is building up a sense of identity and destiny which enhances the ability and confidence of the members of a workforce to pursue their purposes consistently whilst working inclusively with people, within and beyond their own organization, when there are some significant differences between all parties. Through experience of doing this people come to know that in the wider encounters they will find rather than lose themselves. Consequently they enter upon such encounters with expectation and excitement and find greater fulfilment in being inclusive rather than in being exclusive.

Doing this involves practitioners and participants working interdependently with God and a wide range of people inclusively. Interdependency takes many forms. J. D. Thompson[19] has identified three in relation to work in factories. Adapted, I find they help me to understand modes of interdependency in church and community work. *Pooled interdependency* occurs when different people work separately on things that come together in some event or creation. Most acts of worship illustrate this mode. Separately, ministers write sermons, organists select and practise music, caretakers and stewards make the necessary arrangements etc. Then at the appointed time their independent preparations are brought together. *Sequential interdependency* occurs when the success of one step in a process depends upon the satisfactory completion of a prior step. Programmes of Christian education illustrate this mode. *Reciprocal interdependency* occurs when people have to work together because their inputs and outputs feed each other. Working groups, committees, study groups teamwork and some acts of worship are examples of this mode. Many activities involve the first and the third (worship and committee meetings for example) and some all three (a building project for example). Thompson also suggested that three kinds of co-ordination are necessary to facilitate these three kinds of interdependency. Pooled interdependency requires what he calls *standardization i.e.:* procedures, structures, rules and regulations. Sequential interdependency needs what he refers to as plans *i.e.:* programmes, critical paths and task sequences. Reciprocal interdependency requires *mutual adjustment* which in church work I take to mean the ability of people to act collaboratively.

Those engaged in interdependent action are variously: in dependent relationships with each other; deployed interdependently; acting in concert. Promoting creative interdependency in church and community work, a key function of pastoral leaders and managers, involves connoting each mode of activity positively, facilitating them and bringing them together organically. Thompson's classification shows that being dependent upon others and independent action are as necessary to interdependency as doing things together.

2. Practitioners Need to be Able to Promote Vocational Involvement

Earlier it was established that personal and collective vocations are important aspects of the nature of church work. Generally speaking practitioners have to pursue their own vocation as they work with people whose sense of vocation and understanding of mission differ significantly. Vital aspects of their vocation are to help individuals to develop their own sense of vocation and to facilitate the processes by which groups form cohesive collective vocations and programmes and pursue them. This calls for advanced group work skills and the ability to "do theology" with people whose spirituality and theological knowledge varies enormously. Much is said in various parts of this book about ways and means of doing this. Here we concentrate on voluntary accountability.

Promoting vocational participation involves, inter alia, generating disciplined, accountable, sustainable involvement of all the members of the workforce, regardless of whether they are paid or unpaid, ordained or lay. This can be problematic. Some people, ordained and lay, welcome the increasing practice of workers having job descriptions, contracts and assessment procedures to follow which enable them to be publicly accountable. Many do not want to work under such conditions. And, as we have seen, most church and community work is undertaken voluntarily and in many instances sacrificially by very busy people. Some want to learn how to do their job well and to be accountable to the Church for what they do. By and large, however, demands for disciplined accountability of the kind associated with paid employment would be seen or felt as an affront to the voluntary sector of church life. It would be culturally abrasive. It runs counter to a widespread attitude that in the voluntary labour market you take what is given with gratitude, fulsomely acknowledge it and do not attempt to apply conditions other than those which are essential. (Training is of course required for some jobs and rightly there are strict procedures to follow in the deployment of those working with children and young people.) In practice this can mean that voluntary workers themselves determine the conditions of service and in some instances hold off attempts to challenge them by threats of withdrawing their labour ("I'm doing my best. If it is not satisfactory, find someone else.") when they know there is no-one else. This is no basis for collaborative work and personal development.

When finding people to do necessary jobs is desperately difficult, taking peoples' offers on their terms is natural and understandable. Contract making is difficult in such one-sided contests but in as much as progress is made in doing so, however small that might be, personal working relationships are enhanced. Strange as it may seem the ability to establish the theological basis for working vocationally for God through the church, whether it be in a paid or voluntary capacity, is a key to the solution of many of the problems. To do this effectively, ways and means have to be found of discussing with all kinds of people before they accept jobs, some basic issues. For instance, in relation to the voluntary giving of self and time, some points for discussion could be: giving time to church work involves sharing control and ownership of that time with the Church and God just as the control of the time of paid employees is shared with the employer; time that is given belongs to the

325

Church and God who must have a say in the use of it just as do secular employers. When this is accepted, time has been truly given by a worker to God and the church. A vocational transaction has been made. Ideally this should be done with people before they accept jobs through language with which they are familiar and in ways in which they can handle. In some cases the discussion could be short, low key and tentative; in others it could be extended, deep and binding. However this might be, any progress contributes to shared, if not mutual, understanding of the nature of the work. That is a good basis for working relationships and the continuing exploration of the spiritual and pragmatic nature of doing the work together.

Ideally such discussions should be made through joint reflective collaboration. Not everyone has a strong personal call but behind most offers of help are inner promptings and some desire to do something for God, the church and the community. Helping people to articulate and understand their promptings and to see how the work they do for the church relates to the collective vocation is an important part of making and renewing contracts. Without such an understanding paid and unpaid workers can act as though they have acquired and privatised part of the work of the church through taking it on. That is a travesty of vocational involvement. I am not suggesting the Church dictate how workers and their time should be used. That is as undesirable as a worker dictating how they should be used. What is needed is a proper basis for collaboration.

Open exploration and discussion of these theological issues when there is not a case in point can help to form vocational learning communities. When these theological principles are integral to the work culture it is much easier to discuss them openly, naturally and simply, and to establish vocational contracts with individuals and teams of the kind required for the work of Christian mission. Establishing, communicating and reinforcing them is part of the education for work and can be done through preaching, bible study discussion groups, in-service training and general conversation. Contracts based upon mutual understanding of the spiritual and practical nature of jobs enable everyone to feel relaxed with one another and provide a sound basis for tackling problems as they arise.

3. Practitioners Need to be Able to Use all Human and Spiritual Faculties

Church work is the product of all faculties faith and love based action.[20] In a sense the phrase says it all. It draws upon natural and acquired human and spiritual faculties and feelings, hunches, intuition, inspiration, insights, action-learning, reflections, ideas, theories, thoughts. . . . (Church work is not unique in this regard. Other occupations have similar characteristics including scientific work.) It is no more the exclusive work of the intellect than it is of the intuitive faculties. It is hard rigorous thinking combined with Christ-like loving: it is neither cold and clinical nor abstract thought nor is it thoughtless emotional and spiritual action. But at times it does involve taking conviction based action which logically does not make sense. Ideally there is a creative interplay of the faculties in a faith framework. This can occur in individuals as it can in partnerships, teams and groups where different members, possibly on different occasions, are operating on different faculties.[21]

In any case it is highly desirable that people think, and at times think very hard, about feelings, hunches, experiences interpreted as divine inspiration in the same way as they do about thoughts, ideas, concepts—and research them. All this accords with Jesus' commandments."you must love the Lord your god with all your heart, with all your soul, with all your mind, and with all your strength" and "you must love your neighbour as yourself".[22] Charles Elliott caught some of the meaning of this when he described the work of the Kingdom as that of the mind, the heart/soul, the hands and the feet.[23]

4. Practitioners Need to be Able to Access and Put to Effective Use Appropriate Bodies of Knowledge

Practitioners need to be able to access appropriate bodies of knowledge and to put what they find to appropriate use. As we saw in the discussion about the multi-discipline and interprofessional nature of Church work this does not necessarily involve becoming well versed in one or more additional disciplines, although it might lead to that. (It did so in my case. Having found help in community development for problems I was facing in local church work, I went on to study the subject seriously.) It can however involve learning enough of the language of other disciplines to be able to forage in the most economic manner because, for most practitioners, the time and energy available for such activities is at a premium. This is akin to searching manuals for information in relation to particular problems or to scanning them to see what help they could possibly give should certain contingencies arise. As such it is an important way of self-training. Any form of serious academic and experiential study of the human and spiritual condition has the potential to enhance the quality and efficacy of situational and academic engagement with church work. Earlier we discussed some of the things which help to do this in such a way that what is discovered is used and integrated into the basic profession of ministry (cf the section "multi-disciplinary and interprofessional", pp 287-290).

5. Practitioners Need to be Able to Form and Re-form Their Mental Pictures or Maps of Work Situations

Work performance and professional development of practitioners depend upon their mental maps of work situations and of their attributes being in good repair. (cf Chapter Two, Element Four.) Unexpected experiences and problems, studies and moments of disclosure are amongst the things that can lead practitioners to reconsider them, sometimes radically. Therefore, they need to be able to form and re-form their mental pictures and maps so that they are reliable aids to thinking and doing. Practitioners are helped to this when they are able:

(a) to approach knowing and not knowing reverentially

(b) to reflect and think again

(c) to think and operate systematically and systemically

(d) to "listen" to and to "read" and "dialogue" with work situations

(e) to act as a "participant observer" in work situations and to gather and use data

(f) to use other people's ideas and research critically and creatively

(g) to portray work situations.

Each of these abilities enhances all the others. In fact they operate in concert. Figure 7:2 represents the processes in operation. For instance, the approach to knowing is generic and the ability to listen to work situations is key to participant observation.Generally speaking, abilities (e) and (f) help practitioners to gather information and material whilst (a) to (d) help them to study it and (g) helps them to make conceptual sense of it and to communicate it. They could, of course, have been listed in reverse order, starting with collecting data and then processing it. The given order was chosen because (a) to (d) are abilities which facilitate every stage of forming work-views and reflecting on them privately, or with colleagues and consultants or in appraisal sessions. Consequently, some of the subject matter discussed in this section correlates and overlaps with that considered in Element 5, "thinking together", in Chapter Two. The difference between the two sections is that the one in Chapter Two is primarily about consultors and consultants reflecting and thinking in consultancy sessions whilst this is about practitioners doing so on their own and with others in any situation.

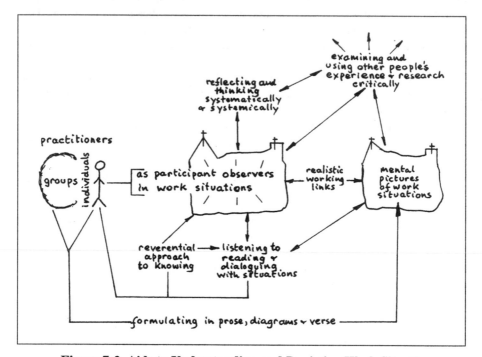

Figure 7:2 Aids to Understanding and Depicting Work Situations

This section is reminiscent of an outline for a training manual even though all that can be attempted within the scope of this book is to describe briefly the competencies and some sources of further information about how to acquire them. *(a) The Ability to Approach Knowing and Not Knowing Reverentially.* Some things practitioners need to know can only be known from the people themselves through voluntary disclosure. Reference was made to this in the previous chapter and to the usefulness of Johari's Window (see pp 212, 230, 300). Much in this book is about creating the conditions in which people can safely share, information and the responsible and constructive use of it by all concerned.

People are most likely to share their knowledge, thoughts and feelings when they: trust those with whom they are sharing, identify with their purposes and are at ease with them, feel they are contributing to something that is important to them; know that they and their privacy are being respected; feel that there is a genuine interest in them and their opinions—and that cannot be feigned in face to face work; they know that they are not being "used" by others.[24] They need to feel that the balance of advantage for them is in sharing and that the risks are worth taking. For example during the opening session of a consultation I led in Zimbabwe just after the new state had been formed in 1980, the black African church leaders said to me, "You have come at a good time. Before liberation we would have told you what we thought you would like to hear. Now we will tell you what we think and feel and just how it is with us". The quality and reliability of information depends upon factors such as these.

Those acting as workers and facilitators need to do all they can to see that these conditions of free exchange are met. They can all too easily prevent the kind of sharing required and damage personal and working relationships by pressing for information about thoughts or feelings which people feel reluctant or unable to provide.[25] Information must always be collected respectfully and with economy. Moments of openness must not be used to pursue idle curiosity. Sensitivity is required which enables practitioners to identify no-go areas and to stop short of trying to probe them. Trespassers will be prosecuted!

With religious knowing, it is always necessary to find a middle way:

— it requires seriousness of purpose, but lightness of touch;
— it cannot thrive either when people's emotions are uninvolved or when they are unrestrained;
— it requires a sense of relatedness to God that is neither one of identification with Him nor of alienation from Him;
— it is a matter neither of pure faith nor of pure reason;
— it is not independent of observation, but neither does it follow straightforwardly from it;
— it inhabits the realms, neither of private fantasy nor of external reality, but a space between;
— it is a creative act, that goes beyond the "given" but must be faithful to it;
— it shows a capacity, in myth and sacrament, to make connections that are more than merely symbolic representations of literal truths, but without going so far as to confound the symbol with the symbolised;
— it depends on the combination of both genuine personal experience and the effort to articulate it, for neither alone can lead to knowing;
— it requires the intellectual effort and clear-headedness to reach towards religious knowing wherever possible, but also the recognition that there is a time for silence and not-knowing.

Display 7:5 The Middle Way of Religious Knowing

Fraser Watts and Mark Williams have helped me to understand this through what they call the "middle way" of religious knowing. Display 7:5 reproduces a summary description of this which occurs at the end of an enormously helpful book.[26] Good practice requires gathering and gleaning as much information as is necessary and possible and being aware of what is not known. Considerable progress can be made within the constraints noted. But, as we observed in various places (cf pp 264 and 300), there will always be the unknown and the unpredictable in the hidden depths of ourselves, others and God. Church work is always an act of faith based upon what is known and upon assumptions, hunches, hypotheses, intuitions, guesses, suppositions about the unknown. Thus, whilst it can never be an exact science, it can be based on the best possible intelligence.

(b)   Practitioners Need to have the Ability to Reflect and Think Again. Earlier we explored the need to reflect and the forms it takes. Now we consider the capacity of practitioners to do so.

Practitioners have to be able to respond and to deal with the unexpected because any kind of work with people for development is punctuated by surprises, good and bad; the unexpected of people and of God. These events cannot be foreseen in planning because the future is shrouded by the unpredictable acts of God and people. One of the implications of this is that practitioners cannot depend entirely upon set procedures. They have to continually reflect about their work especially at the critical stages. The quality of the work depends upon it, as does their own development as reflective practitioners and that of their colleagues. The capacity to reflect is an important personal attribute. What then is the nature of this activity?

Reflecting about things is a normal part of human behaviour. It is a cerebral and affective activity. Often it is spontaneous, things just come into our mind either casually or persistently. Sometimes it is pleasurable, often it is painful. The issues and implications can be clear or vague and bemusing. Some thoughts crowd in on us and stay with us or we stay with them. On some occasions we make progress as we think about them, at others we go round in circles. From some thoughts we try to escape, some we repress but others haunt us. The reflective capacity required of church and community workers is the ability to get to grips with this raw material, to take hold of it, and to process it through their beings (not simply their minds) in such ways that work-wise progress is made and everyone concerned grows and experiences satisfaction. For me this is the central hard creative core of reflective practice. It is dynamic. It is adventurous and explorative and therefore both exciting and frightening.

Reflection can take place either during or after action in a whole range of formal and informal settings. "Reflection-in-action", is a term Donald Schon uses to describe "the thinking what they (practitioners) are doing while they are doing it [the action]".[27] They can do this in relation to any and every aspect of their experience. This can lead to "knowing-in-action".[28] Sometimes people reflect on their own and other people's reflections as one stage of reflection gives way to another. Schon describes these as rungs on a "ladder of reflection".[29]

The capacity to reflect is made up of several parts which can be expressed as a formula: the intellectual ability, attitude, courage, will and stickability to face up to and to think about the realities encountered in relation to work and work-views *plus* the personal and particularly the emotional ability, to work through any negative or positive feedback encountered through facing up to whatever the process reveals *plus* the will, determination and stamina to initiate and sustain the reflective processes to their conclusion *plus* the requisite knowledge and insights *plus* the technical skills which enable practitioners to conceptualise, analyse, research and design church and community work.

The capacity to do this varies enormously from person to person and in the same person from circumstance to circumstance. Practitioners, for instance, who are intellectually able can be emotionally weak and vice versa. Amongst other things the ability to reflect depends upon there being a match between the practitioner's capacity and the complexities upon which they need to reflect. It also depends upon the moral, personal and technical support that they receive from others. That underlines the importance of consultancy.

For people schooled in the traditional ways of doing church work, creative reflective engagement can be a work paradigm shift and a culture shock. Making the transition is a risky business, an act of faith requiring courage. Developing reflective practice for Christian ministry and mission involves educating and training practitioners, forming church workforces which promote reflection within their own organization and creating an action-reflection work culture.

Displays 7:1 and 2 illustrate how one denomination understands what makes a reflective practitioner.

From the 1960s I have worked to promote action-reflection and action research in communities and between them. I was taken by surprise by the amount of work that had to be done with church leaders for them to be sufficiently committed to and equipped for the promotion of reflective and collaborative practice in their own organization and with others. Substantial progress was made through using non-directive reflective processes to help people explore the practical, theological and missiological implications of such an approach. This approach combined experiential learning with critical study of the concepts and methods.

My experience suggests that to remain reflective, practitioners need reflective groups and organizations just as organizations need reflective practitioners to become and remain reflective. But research is needed into the processes and factors which help practitioners, churches and allied organizations to become more reflective and collaborative and into the dynamics between the private and public modes of reflection and collaboration in practitioners and organizations and how they affect one another.

People reflect generally and critically in many different ways. Part One describes how it can be done through consultancy. This section describes aids which can help practitioners to reflect on their own and with others. It is cross referenced with sections of Part One to which it is closely related.

(c)   The Ability to Think and Operate Systematically and Systemically. Systematic thinking is the ability to put order and shape into subject matter and to examine things through analytical sequences. This was discussed and illustrated in Chapter Two in relation to problems, the study of cases and the analysis of work situations (cf pp 73-83). Aids and guides for systematic analysis and thought are formed by formulating a series of questions or discrete tasks which break down complex processes of analysis, design and planning into manageable stages. By working through these stages in some orderly, but not irreversible or dogmatic way, the process is completed. These facilitating structures can help people think about systems systematically and systemically. But there are other ways and aids.

According to one definition, "A system is an organized whole made up of interdependent elements that can be defined only with reference to each other and in terms of their positions in the whole".[30] A more colloquial or user friendly definition is: "A system is a perceived whole whose elements 'hang together' because they continually affect each other over time and operate towards a common purpose"[31] Checkland and Scholes suggest that "all (definitions of systems) take as given the notion of a set of elements mutually related such that the set constitutes a whole having properties as an entity".[32] Organizations, communities and churches are examples of social and socio-religious systems.

"Systems thinking" has become a technical term. Checkland and Scholes differentiate between "hard systems thinking" which "takes the world to be systemic" and "soft systems thinking" which treats the world as if it were a system by creating "the process of enquiry as a system." [33] There is a tendency to use the hard and soft approaches indiscriminately, I have done so. Practice theory is clearly improved by distinguishing between them.

A wide range of methods is used in systems thinking.[34] Two of them are described briefly in Display 7:6. David Campbell and Rosalind Draper,[35] drawing heavily on the work of the Tavistock and Grubb Institutes, have edited an extraordinarily useful "systems thinking and practice" series on family therapy and work with

---

Two of a wide range of methods used in systems thinking are noted in this display.

In the U K Professor Peter Checkland and his colleagues at Lancaster University have developed what they call a "soft systems methodology" (SSM) for use in organization analysis and design. Central to their system is a sequence of operations indicated by the mnemonic CATWOE: customers; actors, transformation process: weltanschauung (worldview); owner(s); environmental constraints. Widespread use is made of "rich pictures" to depict the "rich moving pageant of relationships".[36]

In the U S A Professor Peter M Senge and his colleagues have worked out in great detail an approach to systems thinking for the management and development of learning organizations. They call it the "fifth discipline" (the other four are: personal mastery; mental models; building shared vision; team learning). Their approach builds upon "system dynamics" developed by Professor Jay Forrester and his colleagues at Massachusetts Institute of Technology over the past forty years. The tools and methods are: "links and loops", archetypes; stock-and-flow modelling.[37]

Display 7:6 Two Approaches to Systems Thinking

---

organizations. (Their work was referred to earlier in relation to their systemic approach to consultancy, see pp 35-36.)

What follows in bullet format are notes of some of the things which I personally have found helped me to think and work systemically. Some have already been mentioned but they are noted here for completeness.

- **Diagrams** aid systems thinking because they provide opportunities to represent pictorially and symbolically key people, groups, events in a situation and to position them spatially in ways which bring out the relationships, interactive patterns and dynamics between them and the ebb and flow of cause and effect. As they represent how things function and malfunction they provide diagrammatic "scale" or "disclosure" models.[38] They help us to understand aspects of work situations and to design developmental programmes. Consequently, as diagrams portray elements of systems in an orderly way, they help practitioners to work at things systemically and systematically and to express what they think. Checkland and Scholes use them extensively as I do, and have coined a most telling phrase for them, "rich pictures" because, they say, they are a better means for reading the rich moving pageant of relationships and connections than linear prose.[39] (I was amazed to find how similar their pictures are to the ones I have used quite independently.[40]

- **Images and metaphors** bring into play holistic concepts and, therefore, are aids to thinking systemically about churches, communities and organizations (see pp 74-75).

- **Charts and spread sheets** can also help people to think systemically and systematically. An outstanding example is the way in which Professor Gillian Stamp has used this method to do what she describes as "workscaping" in relation to the Anglican Church. Each horizontal line of "boxes" in a large spreadsheet represents a particular level of the life of the church from that of the parish to that of the international Anglican communion. In these boxes she notes things like: scale of community, object of work, what has to be left behind by those who move from one level to another, responsibilities, creativity, vulnerability, what causes disintegration. The result is a most revealing detailed systematic and systemic picture of the work structure of the parts and the whole of the Church of England. Then symbols are used to represent the systemic nature of the work at each level.[41]

- **Loop analysis** is an effective way of tracing out positive and negative feedback in complex systems of mutual causality. Aspects of an organization or a programme are set out and connected with lines indicating positive and negative effects. An example is given in Display 7:7.[42] There are similarities with Buzan's method of "brain patterning" which can help with this process.[43]

- **Circularity** a somewhat misleading term for a way of tracing out the interaction between people living and working in a socio-religious system from as many perspectives as possible which has already been described (pp 65-66).

- **Systemic hypotheses**, also mentioned earlier, help to work to systems and to multiple rather than linear causation (cf p 75).

- **Lateral thinking**, a well-known process popularised by Edward de Bono, involves switching to something radically different in an attempt to tackle problems in a "non-vertical" way.[44]

- **Parallel thinking** [45] is another of de Bono's concepts which I have found extraordinarily helpful in thinking systemically. It involves: accepting alternative possibilities or both sides of a contradiction without judging them; laying them down in parallel; designing forward from alternative or parallel possibilities. These processes enable all those involved to focus in the same direction and to think co-operatively in parallel. All ideas are drawn into the process so people do not have to try to squeeze in an idea or to jump on one as soon as it is presented. He claims that "the method provides a means of talking about thinking and for organizing thinking". Parallel thinking is particularly useful in understanding and practising the art of designing which is a systemic and holistic activity. "We have become obsessed", says de Bono, "with analysis and spend far too much time on analysis and far too little on design". Possibly that is because it is easier to dismantle systems than to put them together.

- **Community studies and community development** help through their respective emphases upon researching and working with communities as communities and, therefore, systemically.[46]

These methods are ways and means of helping practitioners to approach, conceptualise and engage with things systemically. It helps them to engage conceptually with the whole in relation to the parts and vice versa. It also helps them when they are working face to face with individuals or groups or meetings to do so in relation to the whole. Whilst it is possible to engage conceptually with the whole and the parts and to consider things systemically from this perspective and that or from this sub-system and that, it is possible to engage practically with the whole only through working with a particular part at specific periods of time. A key to positively affecting the part and the whole, the sub-system and the system, is to pay careful attention to the positive and negative connections and dynamics between them. Systemic thinking is potentially creative, as is systematic thinking. Combined, their potential increases exponentially.

(d) The Ability to Listen to and to Read and Dialogue with Work Situations. Much of the time and energy of practitioners and participants goes into writing their developmental programmes and scripts into working situations. They will do this perfectly legitimate purposeful activity more effectively if they learn how to listen to [47] and to read and dialogue with work situations. This can be done through concentrating on a situation, working at it from this angle and that and focussing on anything that strikes you, rather than your thoughts about and plans for it, musing and reflecting on it until it starts to speak to you, says things to you. Jackson W Carroll, in a book on reflective leadership in ministry urges practitioners to "attend to talkback from the situation."[48] Gareth Morgan gets near to what I am trying to articulate with the following sentences with which he ends a book on images that help people to get to grips with organizations:

> . . . the trick is to learn how to engage in a kind of conversation with the situation one is trying to understand. Rather than impose a viewpoint on a situation, one should allow the situation to reveal how it can be understood from other vantage points. In a way we can say that one should always be sensitive to the fact that a situation "has its own opinion" in that it invites understanding through a frame of reference other than the one being applied. The art of analysis described above allows one to probe a situation through the reading process, gradually moving to some judgement or critical evaluation of the situation at hand.[49]

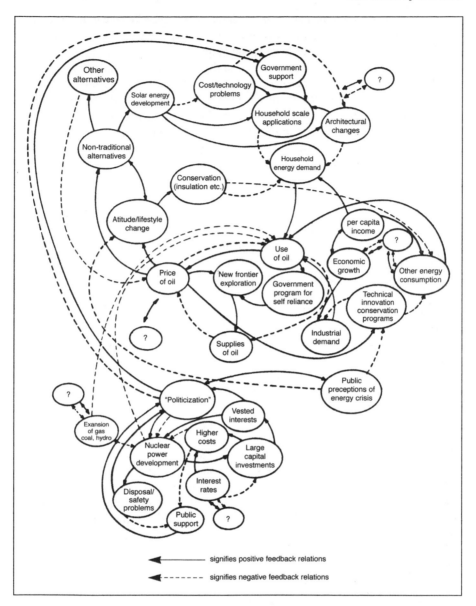

Display 7:7 Positive and Negative Feedback in the Power Industry [50]

Earlier, reference was made to Morgan's telling phrase "diagnostic reading" which he uses to describe attempts to "discern the character of a situation" (pp 74-75). This is quite a different approach from those in which people are preoccupied with talking to or at a situation, dictating to it, doing things to it, modelling it on some pre-determined design. It is, in fact, working *with* and *to* situations and all we find in them in relation to what we bring to them and want for and from them.

Enough, then, about the nature of this important ability. What can help people to address situations in this way whatever their natural aptitude might be? I will restrict myself to those things which I have found helpful.

Inner orientation is key. Situations reveal their nature to practitioners who attend to them, who wait upon them (cf pp 86, 334), and who approach them with eager expectation and willingly accept the discipline and challenge of doing so. (Compare the way in which consultants attend to consultors, pp 37-40.) And this is possible because people, not things, comprise the most important aspect of any working situation. Patient perseverance is necessary because, whilst situations sometimes speak to us clearly and unambiguously, they do not normally talk to us through carefully sculpted sentences and edited texts. They can speak to us with many voices and in different languages. Messages and meanings can be garbled and unclear. Listening to, reading and dialoguing with situations can be difficult and at times impossible especially when they overwhelm us. Assuming they can be read like books is dangerous. The truth of the matter is that it is simply not possible to completely understand work situations and some of the things we feel most certain about may not be correct. This enhances not diminishes the importance of attending to what situations have to say. It underlines the importance of having a reverential approach to knowing and being humble before the realities with which we are engaged. If we are to be able to act on what we know and learn from situations as we do so two things need to be held in tension: being clear about what is seen, understood and believed; holding to and using the knowledge confidently whilst remaining alert and open to new insights which indicate that it needs to be rethought, revised or corrected. Being able to hold these things together is an important skill.

I-Thou rather than *I-It* relations between practitioners and situations, to use Martin Buber's telling phrases, are a central feature of these reflective processes. They induce inner dialogues about practical, intellectual, emotional and theological issues. The experience is akin to a combination of praying and doing mental exercises. The human ability to sort out a complex of confusing information, thoughts and insights is incredible but not infallible. Our minds and hearts have ways of their own for doing this. The unconscious can perform miracles in sorting out chaos and confusion if given time to do so before its findings are suppressed by imposed interpretations.

Several things I find help these inner processes. One of these is through getting things on paper. This can be done by using Buzan's method (cf p 186) or loop analysis (cf pp 333, 335) or through simply writing down everything that is going through our minds without trying to organise it and then to try to get some meaning and order out of it as we read off what it is saying to us. One way of doing this is by preparing *records* which are structured accounts of meetings or events which describe purposes, processes and implications. They are different from minutes or diary entries.[50] "Journalling"[51], another method of dialoguing with situations and events on paper, is a structured way of writing reflectively about things from different perspectives. Another way is the preparation of work and position papers by using outlines. Examples of such outlines are given in Appendix I. Practitioners have been amazed at the increased understanding of themselves as workers and of their situation that comes from simply assembling information and thoughts in this way. Other outlines help people to write about cases and problems.[52] "Profiling", in these and other ways, is another creative process.[53] Drawing diagrams is yet another way (cf pp 90-91).[54] When people simply cannot put pen to paper they can provide the information verbally whilst someone else listens attentively and takes it down.

Projecting what is in the mind onto paper presents the broad picture of the inner thinking. Objectifying it in this way means that practitioners can engage with what is on the paper rather than chasing thoughts and feelings around their heads. Others can also engage with what is in the practitioner's mind through what is in writing. This brings us to another aid. Informed and structured conversations and consultations with other people, as we have seen in Part One, can contribute enormously to reflective processes.

The social and behavioural sciences offer a wide range of tools and information which help practitioners to know and understand the realities of churches and communities. They have made available, for instance, a vast amount of information about the ways in which people act in all kinds of social and religious contexts and settings and many different theories and hypotheses. These can help us to interpret and understand situations. They have also provided tools by which to explore and research human situations through asking questions, interviewing, surveying and observing. (The second of these methods is considered in the next section.) One fascinating development is the study of signs and symbols ("semiotics") in church and congregational life.[55] Research into symbolic boundaries I found particularly helpful.[56]

Any and all of these activities can induce "double loop learning."[57]

(e) ***The Ability to Act as "Participant Observers".*** This ability and the previous one facilitate each other: The ability to participate and observe depends upon the ability to listen to and to read and dialogue with situations and vice versa.

Clearly, by the very nature of their vocation all ordained and lay leaders have wide ranging access to church, community and family life in their formal and informal settings. Thus, through participating and observing, they have much information, many perspectives and insights into what is happening and why. By and large they are not trained in the skills necessary to do this professionally,[58] but that is not to say some of them are not good at it; they are. For those who wish to develop these vitally important skills there is a wealth of readily available highly relevant experience and knowledge about the theory and practice of "participant observation", the principal field work method of ethnography used by anthropologists and those who carried out the community studies noted earlier.[59] James P. Spradley says that ethnography means *learning from people rather than studying people.*[60]

Clergy and lay leaders are ideally placed to use these methods because, unlike anthropologists and other researchers of community who have to feign an acceptable role such as that of an author, they have an ascribed and accepted place in church and society. Moreover, as ministers and priests belong and yet do not belong to local churches and are therefore insiders and outsiders of the congregational culture, they stand in a unique position to meet two of the necessary conditions of those who want to be effective participant observers: personal

337

involvement, passive or active, and detachment.[61] Experience has proven that help of various kinds is available to practitioners of church and community work from the practice theory of participant observation. Basically what this help does is to sharpen up the use of opportunities to participate and observe so that they are more creatively deployed in developmental use. This practice theory will help practitioners to:

- clarify their roles and functions as participant observers and pastor-workers and the ground rules necessary for such involvement;

- clarify the nature and significance of the data that they obtain; (For instance, it provides inner pictures of action meanings and cause and effect which cannot be obtained from external observation survey methods.)

- take into account the effect that the nature of their participation (active, passive, interested or disinterested, directive or non-directive) might have on their observations and vice versa;

- make general, focussed and selected observations and describe them;

- identify taken-for-granted feelings and meanings and things which lead to self-deception in practitioners and themselves;

- recognise misinformation "evasions", "lies", "fronts" and ways of dealing with them or taking them into account;

- collect data and assess it for bias and distortion;

- make an ethnographical analysis of churches and communities;

- make better informed judgements about what they have done and seen;

- record and write up their observations and findings;

- stand back and reflect and sharpen the pictures of what they have experienced and observed.

I have used these methods extensively in work with people in churches and communities and in research and training programmes.[62] A telling example of the use of them by a group of ordinary people to solve an acute problem of violence in a youth centre has been written up.[63]

Some ministers I have worked with have been uncomfortable with the idea of using anything that smacks of scientific research methods. They felt that doing so leads to using people for research and spying upon them. Such outcomes are as unacceptable to them as they are to me because it can have adverse effects upon how we see people and our relationships with them. Two things I have found reduce the danger of these things happening. The first relates to the use being made of the methods. They are being used to study *the work* and the human factors which help and hinder it, *not the people*. As noted above ethnography is about learning from people rather than studying them. Clearly this involves looking at what people do and how they do it. However, this is quite different from studying parishioners and participants *per se*. Observing carefully and thinking deeply about vocational work and our personal and working relationships adds value to them if our motives and purposes are honourable; it demeans and diminishes them if our intentions are not. The second thing is, that whilst thinking about some of our observations is of necessity a private activity which influences the ways in which we go about things, the sharing of observations and working together at their implications is central to the approach advocated in this book. And when all is said and done we do observe and think our thoughts. What is being suggested here is that we do it more carefully and scrupulously in relation to Christian purposes and beliefs and the common good. Apart from its usefulness, it can refine and redeem inner human and spiritual processes, understandings, attitudes and approaches.

(f)   The Ability to use Other People's Ideas and Research Critically and Creatively. Up to this point the emphasis has been upon practitioners gathering their own data and doing their own research. A complementary approach is to use the ideas and researches of others. All my work has been informed and enriched through a wide range of research and thinking which I simply could not have done for myself, this book makes that apparent. Generally speaking other people's work has helped me to understand: the nature of the constituency with which I am engaged (through, for example, biblical, theological, community and organizational studies); the processes of intellectual, moral and faith development (through, for example, the work of Piaget, Kohlberg and Fowler); the functioning of people in groups, teams, communities, secular and religious organizations; ways of working with people and modes of leadership (through a vast number of social and behavioural science scholars). Some ideas about what was involved in drawing upon various disciplines were discussed earlier, cf pp 288-290.

One of the many people upon whose work I have drawn is that of Professor Michael Argyle. He is highly skilled at drawing together the findings of research in relation to the socio-psychology of a range of human activities. Of itself the way in which he does this is an education about the way in which practitioners in church and community work can use other people's research. Moreover, research findings are presented in user friendly ways.[64]

Other people's research findings, for instance, can greatly help practitioners to formulate working hypotheses and to establish assumptions. Community studies and profiles can be used as templates to explore the actualities of a local community. Examining dissonance between general research findings and the evaluated experience and researches of practitioners can be rewarding. Effective use depends upon practitioners thoroughly testing out the research in relation to their own experience and the actualities of their working context: unthinking, uncritical acceptance and application of independent research findings is dangerous no matter how prestigious the source and is contrary to the way of working described in this book. It is essential that practitioners have confidence in their own evaluated experience and their ability to test that of others.

(g)   The ability to Portray Work Situations. Drawing upon all their information, insights, beliefs and aspirations, practitioners need to be able to conceptualize and portray how they see and understand their work situations. This can be done in prose or in diagrams through position papers of one kind or another (cf p 87 and Appendix I). What is involved in this activity is discussed in Chapter Two.

6.   Able to Discuss Constructively Issues of Life and Faith.

Inevitably and naturally, as we noted earlier, engagement in church and community work leads to exchanges and discussions about life and faith between people of similar and different beliefs and approaches to religion. As trust and respect grows between practitioners and those with whom they work they are able to explore the questions that concern them. The subjects and the slants on old and new agendas are legion. The literature is varied and vast. It would be interesting to have a survey of the topics that arise, but to the best of my knowledge that is not available. What is important is that the approach to these questions is entirely consistent with the approach to working with people advocated in this book and a natural extension of it. So, for instance, anyone and everyone who participates needs to be free to express just what they feel and think and to be helped to do so, to think about each other's ideas beliefs and fears, to question and challenge each other critically but graciously, to point each other to important sources and to learn from each other. Above all they need to be able to help each other to think more effectively and satisfyingly and to struggle together with issues that concern them rather than to strive against each other. Many of the skills we have already discussed such as conceptualising and analysing can be used in relation to these matters. Practitioners need to be able to participate in such discussions and to facilitate them. This means that Christians participate on the same terms as anyone else and they help others and especially those who differ from them to do the same: there is no place here for religious group think (cf pp 212, 323-324). This activity is not about winning theological arguments or scoring spiritual points. It is not preaching to others. It will involve sharing beliefs and religious experiences and exploring their meanings with humility.

Quite commonly practitioners feel that they should have all the "answers". At times it is an advantage to have some or the ability to find them through exploring the literature or consulting specialists. Generally speaking, however, admitting ignorance and setting out with others to see what can be discovered is much more creative than providing answers. But it must be a genuine search. This can draw people together. It can cause them to learn how to explore and research a subject for themselves. Answers apart, all this can promote human and spiritual development.

What practitioners need to be able to do is to engage in, promote and facilitate conversations of a reflective kind which enable people to learn from one another, grow together and build up communities capable of working together and doing theology and exploring faith together.

7. Practitioners Need to be Equipped and Resourced for the Psycho-Spiritual Ups and Downs of Creative Reflective Engagement

The inner lives of practitioners and other participants engaged in creative reflective engagement are pivotal points of the whole process. Essentials of the whole drama of engagement are played out over and again in their heads, hearts and souls. Their inner world is alive. They could, for instance, be trying out this idea or that, or speculating about how others might respond to particular courses of action, or rehearsing and re-rehearsing how they might go public with their thoughts. After events they could be re-enacting, re-living, re-working things that have happened and the emotions associated with them, from the most wonderful and sublime to the most debilitating and painful such as pride, shame, fear, panic, angst.

Some of my most searing and unpleasant experiences have occurred during the overnight interval between working sessions when things had got into an intellectual or emotional or interpersonal mess to which I had contributed. Trying to get at causes, sort out complex issues on my own and decide what action to take whilst struggling with tiredness, emotional flash backs and my raw feelings were enormously difficult things to do. At times panic was hard to keep at bay especially when the stakes were high. The quality of the subsequent engagement with others depended to a large extent, but not entirely, upon my ability to turn my debilitating reactivity into constructive proactivity overnight. These experiences are by no means limited to times of privacy, similar ones occur in public. Inner and outer engagement reciprocate and intersect. All this illustrates that the inner lives of practitioners are base workshops which produce critical elements of creative reflective engagement: practitioners are, as we have noted, the subjects and instruments of the engagement. The open system process we considered earlier is another way of looking at what happens (cf pp 271-272). The currents and effects of the engagement flow into and through practitioners who, at their most effective, act creatively upon them through their inner activities and, at their worst, are beaten, mauled and hurt by them. Clearly, the well-being and development of practitioners and their work are strongly influenced by the quality of their inner life. So, what are the abilities and resources which experience has proved help practitioners to live and endure this inner working life?

Many have already been considered. Topics still to be considered in this chapter are highly relevant: discipline, dealing with our incompetence, support systems, disengagement and prayer. In this section I concentrate on the nature of the abilities and resources rather than on how to acquire them. Listing points distorts the reality that at any one time is an interdependent cluster of things which helps practitioners to deal with the ups and downs of engagement.

Accepting, knowing and trusting yourself as an instrument of engagement and analysis (cf p 71). Self-knowledge and acceptance of oneself as an instrument of engagement and analysis is vitally important. Understanding, which emerges quite naturally, can be sharpened by listing strengths and weaknesses or by getting a psychological profile.[65] I was greatly helped to understand and use myself as an instrument of research by some simple methods for determining my response to sensory experience and how strongly I feel.[66] Acceptance is as important to current practice, as the desire to improve is to future development.

Understanding and acceptance are most productive when they are combined with the confidence to trust yourself.[67] Take, for instance, an incident of the kind described earlier, an overnight interval between sessions when things have gone seriously wrong. There is a pattern in my experience of such events: working hard to try to sort things out; reluctance to go to bed before I do so; getting more and more tired; ending up with what I know to be a somewhat forced and unconvincing plan of action; going to bed; wakening three or four hours later with everything more-or-less sorted out in my mind in a way with which I immediately feel comfortable; relief! Given the knowledge that this happens more often than not, the sensible thing to do is to conserve my energy by gathering the material and resting whilst at some deeper level of consciousness things are sorted out. But I will keep worrying at it when I know I should leave it. Three things are needed to stop work at a strategic point: the ability to discern when I have done sufficient thinking,

341

working and worrying for my unconscious to take over and do its job; the confidence that my mind can and will operate constructively analytically when I am not conscious of it doing so; the discipline to overcome my desire to complete things in a tidy order and my impatience with the slowness of the process. At my best I instruct my unconscious to get on with it without disturbing my sleep!

Of itself, developing such self-knowledge and the confidence to use it enhances performance.

The ability and resources to think clearly under pressure and to access appropriate bodies of knowledge. Much has already been said about facilitating structures that, when assimilated, come into play automatically to help to order thinking and feelings and reduce emotional dissonance.[68]

The ability to bond with people emotionally at levels and depths appropriate to the nature of their working relationships. Practitioners need to be able to control their emotional involvement. Given the nature of the engagement, cool clinical involvement is ineffectual and spiritually unacceptable. At the other extreme, to be out of emotional control is neither desirable nor useful. As with "knowing", there is a middle personal and professional way for practitioners. Emotion must be a constituent part of a practitioner's involvement with people but it must not control relationships nor work programmes.

Ability to respond constructively to complicating events in face-to-face work. An event could be an unexpected acrimonious breakdown of working relationships in a group at a critical moment over a point of principle or policy. Some such events can be anticipated, others cannot. Speculative anticipation about the worst and best eventualities gets people thinking about a range of possibilities and preparing for them. This overcomes the tendency for preoccupation with the desired critical path. Important as it is, foresight cannot by definition deal with that which is unpredictable and unimaginable. Therefore, what practitioners need are the skills to deal with the ever present possibility of a visit from the unexpected. Many of the things already mentioned help. Amongst the many other things that people find helpful a few can be named by way of illustration: the confidence and personal discipline to allow events to unfold and to face up to the issues and get others to do the same; the ability to describe the event in ways which enable everyone to see it more objectively, to talk about it and to work at it; the wisdom and discipline not to take sides whilst trying to facilitate creative discussion between all parties; the ability to get people working together at the event constructively. Amongst other things, this means that leaders must refuse to pander to or be intimidated by any misplaced expectations they or others may have of them, for example, that if they are worth their salt they must be able to save the situation by immediate and definitive responses. What practitioners need to be able to do is to know themselves, the strengths and weaknesses of their attitudes, approaches and skills and to assiduously work at improving them in and through learning from past experiences, study, role play, mental exercises, and any other means in preparation for the unexpected. Anticipation, preparation and training is a sound trinitarian formula!

The Ability to handle positive and negative feedback constructively.[69] There are two main kinds of feedback, the inner self feedback which comes unbidden and that which comes from others. Getting feedback is one thing, handling it is another. Individuals and groups need the ability to process it constructively through their personal and interpersonal systems. Doing this can make heavy demands upon the intellect, the emotions, and spiritual resources whether the feedback is negative or positive. Both forms of feedback have good or bad potential: for instance, acclamation can lead to conceit and strident criticism to depression or loss of self-worth if they are not properly processed through the human psyche. Developing the ability to handle any and all forms of feedback is especially important at a time

---

Personal Preparation for Feedback

Some questions help to prepare to receive and work on feedback that comes in all ways:

- What kind of good and bad inner responses and reactions do you customarily make when you receive feedback that is positive/negative?

- What responses do those with whom you work often make and what effects do they have upon you?

- What would you have to do in order to improve the way in which you process and use feedback?

- What kind(s) of feedback do you need from whom or from what?

- Why do you need it?

- Are there any dangers in trying to get it?

- How can you get and receive it?

Guidelines to Processing Feedback

Remain critically open to negative and positive feedback; don't dismiss or quench it by denigrating the sources. In relation to feedback, however, the source may be wrong and you may be right. Several things can help:

- Make it usable and manageable by:
  - collating and condensing it to avoid the problems of feedback overload;
  - try to de-personalize and objectify it possibly by writing it down, or talking to someone else about it. Look at it from different perspective. Feelings are facts but try to avoid being preoccupied with them. Delay reaction when possible.

- Determine quite specifically to what the feedback properly relates: to you? your work? your beliefs/purposes/your organization? Or is it a projection of a problem that others have?

- Decide whether or not anything can be done about it and whether it is worthy of serious attention.

- Try to keep things in proportion by counter-balancing positive with negative feedback and vice versa.

- Avoid confusing qualitative with quantative feedback: one person may be right and the rest wrong and vice versa; the person who makes most noise may or may not be right!

- Evaluate feedback and determine its implications in relation to beliefs, purposes, needs, resources and your personal performance (not only in relation to yourself) *and* in relation to what you know of its source.

- Whenever possible seek help and support, not just one or the other.

- Think, feel and pray things through.

Display 7:8 Some Guidelines for Preparing for Processing Feedback

when evaluation, assessment and accountability are being stressed. Display 7:8, guidelines for preparing for and processing feedback, indicates the skills and resources required.

Getting the work flow right. As noted earlier, Professor Gillian Stamp has discovered that "flow" is widely used to describe the state of well-being at work. "People in flow", she says, "feel alert, energetic, competent and creative . . . they feel good about themselves . . . sound judgements 'just happen' and because they are more often than not correct, flow feeds on itself and confidence grows accordingly".[70] This is described as a state of "well-being". It occurs for each person when challenges and capabilities are matched: stress occurs when challenges are more than or less than capabilities (cf pp 109, 150, 376, 388 and 391). A state of well-being and flow is both an agent and a consequence of creative reflective engagement. They are reciprocals of each other. Consequently practitioners with a deep seated state of well-being and in flow with rhythm and momentum are well endowed to ride the ups of creative reflective engagement and to cope with and correct the downs.

One of the many practical things that help practitioners to find and maintain this flow is to work within or just beyond the work capacity with which they are most comfortable. Another is organizing themselves realistically in relation to four repetitive sequences in church work: planning; doing; follow-through; reflecting. When practitioners allocate time realistically for each element they are, as one would expect, more effective and fulfilled. Strange as it may seem this is far from normative in my experience. There is, for instance, a propensity in compiling work diaries to enter events and meetings without entering time for the other work associated with them.

8. Practitioners Need to be Able to Deal With Their Own Incompetence and That of Others

Recently there has been much concern in my denomination about ministerial and diaconal incompetence. Reports[71] have been presented to the Methodist Council and Conference and carefully considered. New procedures have been adopted for responding to complaints in professional and pastoral ways. Generally speaking such complaints are made when the incompetence is long-standing and chronic and therefore extremely difficult to deal with effectively. Clearly, corrective action by practitioners themselves and those to whom they are accountable is essential at a much earlier stage. Much is being done to this end by way of making contracts to which practitioners are held accountable through assessment programmes and by the emphasis on reflective practice and lifelong training. Many of the things advocated in this book can assist people to become more competent and to correct incompetence at an early stage. Personal resources and skills are required which enable practitioners and people to confront and challenge each other and together to work out the implications constructively. Much of what was said about dealing with feedback is relevant here.

Significant changes in attitude and approach can occur when the focus of attention is changed from the incompetence of particular practitioners and how to deal with it, to the incompetence to deal with incompetence. When a group of people are asked to consider the incompetence of others there is a tendency for them to think of themselves as amongst the competent, whereas in fact they are to a greater or lesser sense incompetent. A result is a "them" (incompetent)-"us" (competent) attitude. (I experienced this in the annual Methodist Conference discussion on the Report and only faced it when reflecting on my unease.) That is very unhealthy. Admittedly the range of competence and incompetence is wide. What is required is a levelling sense of our common incompetence and especially that related to dealing with it, and a solidarity in finding ways of dealing with our own incompetence and that of others. Confession and remedial action need to go together.

Pursuing this shift in focus can lead to a systemic approach to incompetence which is more likely to treat the problem "holistically". Such an approach looks for the causes of incompetence in any and all parts or members of the system, in a church for instance, rather than in the individual who is showing the symptoms. An illustration of this is in treating "burn-out" and stress as a function of the whole system of which the particular person is a part. The person who has burnt out may be acting as the "fuse" of the work system (cf pp 109 and 151).[72] The ability to deal with incompetence systemically is essential to enhancing the competence of workforce systems and practitioners.

9. Practitioners Need to be Able to Use and Provide Support Systems

From time immemorial there have been those engaged in lay and ordained ministry who have supported each other. However, the practice has never been universal. Sadly, there have also been those who have withheld support from each other and even undermined and attacked each other. New impetus has been given to the provision of support through the emphasis upon collaborative ministry and the increasing practice of the use of support systems.[73] The latter take many forms of spiritual direction, counselling and consultancy, support groups and appraisal procedures. Formal and informal systems variously offer technical assistance and personal, moral and spiritual support. Great progress has been made in the theory and practice of providing help. This is reflected in the enhanced quality of formal and informal support. This is not the place to survey these systems as our purpose is simply to note some of the basic abilities required of those who wish to give and receive support. Part One examined in detail what is required of those who wish to give and receive work and vocational consultancy help.

Fundamentally, support must enhance the ability of those receiving it for creative reflective engagement in their work and situation. To do this, the interaction between supported and supporter needs to be a form of creative reflective engagement. Consequently the basic attitudes, approaches and skills required are the same as those for creative reflective engagement. Essentially and substantively supporters must be non-directive towards those seeking their support and the situations in which they work. Thus, they must not presume to "take over", supervise, control, direct. Suspicion that outsiders are covertly controlling people and their situation through supposedly providing support to their primary workers seriously complicates and confounds their creative reflective engagement.

I know from bitter experience just how easy it is to fall foul of these dangers. They are insidious. Apart from lack of skill they derive from undesirable propensities on all sides. Those seeking support may be looking for direction from supporters or the false security of unhealthy dependency or wanting someone else to take or share their responsibility. Those offering support may be wanting to influence and control or to indulge in a feeling of being indispensable or to have power without responsibility (cf references to consultants taking over). When some of these propensities meet, match and mate, collusion leads to unholy alliances.

Thus, the onus of avoiding the dangers does not rest entirely and exclusively upon supporters. Those seeking support need to be aware of the dangers, to be able to resist their temptation and to take corrective action should things start to go wrong. Ways in which consultors can do this have already been considered.

10. Practitioners Need to be Able to Disengage Creatively

One of the important rhythmic movements in working with people in the way we are considering is: intervening, engaging, withdrawing, waiting and returning.[74] Another is the movement from action to reflection. Yet another is the progression from the various aspects of creative reflective engagement to creative disengagement and the return journey. The ability to do this is vital and for some, hard to acquire. (I am experiencing it now as I come to the end of weeks of work on this section!) Practitioners will differ greatly in doing this. Each needs to find and cultivate his/her way.

_____

Consultors can and do seek vocational and work consultancy help on any and every aspect of the work described in this PART. Thus, the list of contents. when used as a "map", helps consultants and consultors to locate and cross reference subject matter under consideration. Therefore, it is an aid to thinking about wholes and parts systemically and systematically from any and all perspectives.

NOTES AND REFERENCES: Chapter Seven

1.   *The Making of Ministry: The Report of the Ministerial Policy Working Group to the Methodist Council. September 1996* (Methodist Publishing House) pp 66ff, as revised.

2.   *op cit* p 67f.

3.   McKelvey, Bill (1982) *Organizational Systematics: Taxonomy, Evaluation, Classification* (University of California Press) has helped me greatly in relation to this with his ideas of "compools" which he defines as "the total pool of competence elements (comps) making up the dominant competencies of all members of an organizational population". "Comps", or "competence elements", he defines as "elements of knowledge and skill that in total comprise the dominant competence of an organization". pp 454 and 193-210.

4.   cf Lovell, George (1994) *Analysis and Design: A Handbook for Practitioners and Consultants in Church and Community Work* (Burns & Oates) pp 255-258, 260 and 270f for a discussion of the promotion of creative forms of participation and sharing and egalitarian working relationships.

5.   For an exposition of the approaches see Batten, T. R and M., *The Non-Directive Approach* (Oxford University Press, 1967; 4th impression 1978; Avec Publication of an abridged version 1988), and Lovell, George, *The Church and Community Development—An Introduction* (Grail Publications/Chester House Publications, 1972, revised 1980, Avec Publications 1992 reprint).

6.   The Battens, *op cit,* have a useful chapter on "Factors Affecting Choice".

7.   There is a fuller discussion of this approach in Lovell, George (1994) *Analysis and Design, op cit,* pp 197ff *et al.*

8.   The Methodist Church produced an interesting report as a basis for discussion, *The Corporate Life of the Presbyteral Ministry,* (presented to the President's Council in February 1992). It argues that

presbyters "belong to an order" (paragraph 1.7). See Chapter Three of this book for a discussion about the Methodist Diaconal Order as an order of ministry and a religious order.

9.   cf Charles New's assessment of the value of being engaged in national training and local church and circuit work in Lovell, George (Editor, 1996) *Telling Experiences: Stories About A Transforming Way of Working With People* pp 35 and 196f.

10.   *The Making of Ministry* (see Reference 1) p 66, as revised.

11.   cf *The Oxford Paperback Dictionary.*

12.   Wakefield, Gordon S. (1986) *A Dictionary of Christian Spirituality* (SCM Press) p 118.

13.   cf Senge, Peter M. (1990) *The Fifth Discipline: The Art and Practice of the Learning Organization, op cit* p 10f.

14.   This is a revised version of a list which first appeared in *Analysis and Design* p 232.

15.   This diagram was in a paper by Cracknell, Kenneth (1996) *Mission and Evangelism in Methodist Theological Inquiry and Education with SpeciaL Relation to Culture and Context*, presented to the World Methodist Council Theological Education Committee with two practical requests that funds be found (a) for the teaching in Methodist seminaries throughout the world of missiology and evangelism which acknowledges culture diversity (b) for programmes in which theological teachers and students may experience what it is to do theology in cultures other than their own.

16.   In writing this and in much of the work I have done I am indebted to an article by B. W. M. Palmer which first appeared in the *Expository Times* and was later published in Mitton, C. L. (ed) (1972) *The Social Sciences and The Churches* (T & T Clark) pp 11-26. It was entitled "Work and Fellowship in Groups and Organizations". At the time Palmer was Director of Studies, The Grubb Institute of Behavioural Studies, London.

17.   cf Palmer *op cit* p 20.

18.   cf Janis, Irving L. and Mann, Leon (1977) *Decision Making: A Psychological Analysis of Conflict, Choice and Commitment* (Free Press, Collier Macmillan) p 132, cf pp 129ff, cf Morgan, Gareth (1989) *Creative Organization Theory: A Resource Book* (Sage Publications) pp 224-228 and A summary of the symptoms by Dr. Frank Heller in *The Guardian*, 31st January 1983 issue, in an article entitled "The Danger of Group Think".

19.   I owe this to McKelvey, Bill (1982) *Organizational Systematics: Taxonomy, Evolution and Classification* pp 183ff.

20.   In part the phrase is borrowed but regrettably I cannot recall the source.

21.   Much thought has gone into the interaction between people with different personalities. See, for example, the work of Isabel Briggs Myers and Katherine C. Briggs on the Myers Briggs Type Indicator (MBTI). See an article in *The Way* Supplement 69, Autumn 1990 by Robert J. Thesing entitled "The Myers-Briggs, Enneagram, and Spirituality" pp 50-60. (There is a scholarly assessment of this indicator in an article by Professor Leslie J. Francis in *Movement* Autumn, 1996, see reference 65.) Another example is Belbin, R. Meredith (1981 reprinted 1985) *Management Teams—Why They Succeed or Fail* (Heinemann), it describes experiments into the personal characteristics required of different members of teams to make them effective.

22.   Mark 12:30f R.E.B. The parallel account in Matthew, 23:37ff does not include "strength".

23.   Elliott, Charles (1987) *Comfortable Compassion: Poverty, Power and The Church* (London: Hodder & Stoughton) p182f.

24.   An example of the importance of this is given in Lovell, George and Widdicombe, Catherine (1978) *Churches and Communities: An Approach to Development in the Local Church* p.37.

25.   I faced this problem when researching the work that I was doing as a local Methodist Minister to learn how to do it better and writing a doctoral thesis on it in order to submit the methods I was using to the test of academic rigour. I knew the examiners would be looking for "hard" information which could have been obtained but only by compromising working relationships. The following statement indicates how I resolved the dilemma.

By conscious decision the worker made no attempt to quantify these reactions and views (to the non-directive approach). To do so would have meant conducting a survey and could have had serious adverse effects on the relationships between the worker and the people. It could, for example, have caused people to hold to their views more dogmatically. This would have made it more difficult for the worker to achieve his purposes. The ways in which the worker responded did in fact facilitate changes in people's attitudes to the non-directive approach which were in accord with his purposes. A similar point is made in Chapter 10 "Records and Recording", where it is argued that even if there had been people who could record "interaction sociograms" and "discussion direction diagrams" it would have been more than the people could have taken.

Lovell, George *An Action Research Project to Test the Applicability of the Non-Directive Concept in a Church, Youth and Community Centre Setting* (University of London, 1973) p 344.

26.   Watts, Fraser and Williams, Mark (1988) *The Psychology of Religious Knowing* (Cambridge University Press) p 153. Watts and Williams argue that religious knowing involves not so much coming to know a separate religious world as coming to know the religious dimensions of the everyday world (151). Religious knowing is concerned with a world in which religion and material interact (152). Religious knowing is, "a highly personal process that is both similar to, and intertwined with, knowledge of ourselves" (152).

I have also found great help from Smail, David (1984) *Illusion of Reality: The Meaning of Anxiety* (J. M. Dent and Sons). He argues that immediate knowledge of interpersonal truth is transmitted through "intuitive sensibility". This faculty is acquired through being an "embodied subject in a difficult and often cruel world".

27.   Schon, Donald A. (1990) *Educating the Reflective Practitioner: Towards a New Design for Teaching and Learning in the Professions* (Jossey-Bass Publishers) p xi.

28.   *op cit* pp 22ff.

29.   *op cit* pp 114ff.

30.   Palazzoli, Mara Selvini *et al* (1986) *The Hidden Games of Organizations* (Pantheon Books, New York) p 175 Note 2.

31.   Senge, Peter; Kleiner, Art; Roberts, Charlotte; Ross, Richard B.; Smith, Bryan J. (1994, reprinted with corrections 1997) *The Fifth Discipline:Strategies and Tools for Building a Learning Organization* (Nicholas Brealey) p 90.

32.   Checkland, Peter; Scholes, Jim (1990, 1993 reprint) *Soft Systems Methodology in Action* (John Wiley and Sons) p 4.

33.   Checkland, Peter *et al, op cit* p 25, cf p 22.

34.   Senge, Peter *et al, op cit* includes cybernetics, chaos theory, gestalt therapy and the work of people like Gregory Bateson.

35.   They are published by "Karnac Books", London. Reference is made to those of particular interest to people engaged in work consultancy in Part Two and listed in the Bibliography.

36.   cf. Checkland, Peter, *et al, op cit*.

37.   cf Senge, Peter *et al* (*op cit*) and Senge, Peter (1990, reprint 1993) *The Fifth Discipline: The Art and Practice of the Learning Organization* (Century Business).

38.   Lovell, George (1980/1991) *Diagrammatic Modelling: An Aid to Theological Reflection in Church and Community Development Work* (An Avec Publication) p 16.

39.   cf, Checkland, Peter *op cit* p 45.

40.   I have described my use of them in *Diagrammatic Modelling* (see reference 35) and *Analysis and Design* pp 181-184.

41.   See Stamp, Gillian (1988) *Well-Being and Stress at Work* (A Brunel Institute of Organisation and Social Studies, BIOSS, Paper) and Stamp, Gillian (1988) *A Confusion Owned is a Change Begun* (A Brunel Institute of Organisation and Social Studies, BIOSS Paper; and a chapter entitled "The hidden depths of organizations: people in working relationships: correspondence between Norman Todd and Gillian Stamp" in Nelson, John (ed) (1999) *Leading, Managing and Ministering: challenging questions for church and society* (Canterbury Press) pp 263-311.

42.   This diagram is given by Morgan, Gareth *Images of Organization* (Sage Publications 1986) p 251 in a very helpful section on loop analysis. cf Senge, Peter (1994) *op cit* Chapter 17 and *et al.*

43.   cf. Buzan, Tony *Use Your Head* (BBC 1974). See also Widdicombe, Catherine, (2000) *Meetings that Work: A practical guide to teamworking in groups* (The Lutterworth Press) pp 50f.

44.   cf de Bono, Edward (1967) *The Use of Lateral Thinking* (Penguin Books, Ltd.) and numerous other publications.

45.   de Bono, Edward (1994) *Parallel Thinking: From Socratic to de Bono Thinking* (Viking).

46.   The books on this are numerous but see Bell, Colin and Newby, Howard (1971) *Community Studies* (Studies in Sociology: 5, George Allen and Unwin) and especially the discussion on community as open and closed systems, 57-60. Margaret Stacey made a breakthrough in community studies by drawing diagrams on the connections made by individuals between the various civic, sports and religious institutions in Banbury. cf Frankenberg, Ronald (1966) *Communities in Britain: Social Life in Town and Country* (Penguin Books) pp 154ff. F. W. Boal used a similar method in a chapter "Territoriality in Belfast" in Bell, Colin and Newby, Howard (ed) (1974) *Sociology of Community: A Selection of Readings* (New Sociology Library, Frank Cass and Co. Ltd.) p 191f. Warren, Roland L. (1963/1987) *The Community in America* (University Press of America) wrote about the American community as a social system.

47.   cf Fiumara, Gemma Corradi (Translated by Charles Lambert) (1990) T*he Other Side of Language: A Philosophy of Listening* (Routledge) I am reminded of the "I-Thou" rather than the "I-It" relationships Martin Buber wrote about.

48.   Carroll, Jackson W. (1991) *As One with Authority: Reflective Leadership in Ministry* (Westminster/John Knox Press) p 129.

49.   Morgan, Gareth (1986) *Images of Organizations* (Sage Publications) p 337.

50.   Records and recording are described in *Analysis and Design* pp 178f.

51.   Catherine Widdicombe, my colleague, uses this method. She mentions it in her book *Meetings that Work, op cit* In a note on p 82 she says, "Ira Progaff, after studying with Jung, developed journalling as 'a tool for life'. See *At a Journal Workshop and Process Meditation* (Dialogue House Library NY). Information about Progoff Intensive Journal Workshops can be obtained from William Hewitt SJ, Campion Hall, Oxford OX1 1QS.

52.   Many different structures are offered by different authors. Catherine Widdicombe describes several in *Meetings that Work, op cit*. The ones I use are described in *Analysis and Design*.

53.   cf for instance, Hawtin, Murray, Hughes, Geraint and Percy-Smith, Janie with Foreman, Anne (1994, 1996 reprint) *Community Profiling: Auditing Social Needs* (Open University Press).

54.   I discuss diagrams and their use in *Analysis and Design* pp 105, 175, 179-184.

55.   Two examples illustrate this movement. The work of James F. Hopewell is an example of this approach to understanding churches and their culture. In his book *Congregation: Stories and Structures* (SCM Press, 1987) he differentiates and analyses different world-views through using what he refers to as the "semiotic square" which has four sections representing four world-view categories: authoritative, gnostic, charismatic, empiric. Leonora Tubbs Tisdale shows how to go about the semiotic analysis of a congregation in *Preaching as Local Theology and Folk Art* (Fortress Press, 1997). In a chapter entitled "Exegeting the Congregation" she discusses the symbolic approach to cultural analysis, argues that pastors need to be "amateur ethnographers" skilled in observing and describing the subcultural signs and symbols of the congregations they serve. She suggests guidelines for identifying symbols for study. Then, she discusses seven symbols for congregational exegesis: stories and interviews; archival materials; demographic information; architecture and visual arts; rituals; events and activities; people themselves. Clearly all this helps pastors to listen to and to read and dialogue with churches and congregations.

56.   The following research on symbolic boundaries and constructs I have found very helpful: Cohen, Anthony P. (ed) (1982) *Belonging: Identity and Social Organization in British Rural Cultures* and Cohen, Anthony (ed) (1986) *Symbolising Boundaries: Identity and Diversity in British Cultures* (both published by Manchester University Press). See also Cohen, Anthony (1989) *The Symbolic Construction of Community* (London, Routledge).

57.   "Double loop Learning depends upon being able to take a 'double look' at the situation by questioning the relevance of operating norms". "Single loop learning rests in an ability to detect and correct error in relation to a set of operating norms". Morgan, Gareth (1986) *Images of Organization* (Sage) p 88. He uses the following diagrams to illustrate the processes.

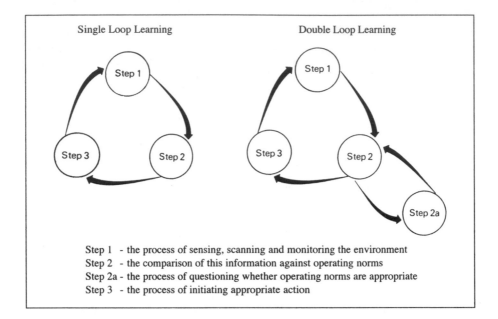

Single Loop Learning

Step 1
Step 3
Step 2

Double Loop Learning

Step 1
Step 3
Step 2
Step 2a

Step 1 - the process of sensing, scanning and monitoring the environment
Step 2 - the comparison of this information against operating norms
Step 2a - the process of questioning whether operating norms are appropriate
Step 3 - the process of initiating appropriate action

58.   An exception to this is referred to by Leonara Tubb Tisdale (*op cit* see ref. 55) p 60. A Christian educator, Denham Grierson, has apparently developed a participant observer approach to congregational studies for Australian theological students. He has produced the following very useful guidelines.

1. The participant-observer shares in the activities and sentiments of the people. This involves face-to-face relationships, and direct contact with their shared life.

2. The role of the participant-observer requires both a necessary detachment and personal involvement.

3. The participant-observer is a normal part of the culture and the life of the people under observation. He or she does not come as an expert, but rather as a learner who, in order to learn, participates in the life of the people.

4. The role of the participant-observer is consistent within the congregation, so that no confusion is created by unexpected changes of behaviour or alternating of roles.

5. The participant-observer has as a target a symbolic level of meaning in the life of the congregation which cannot be gained from observing external behaviour alone, as would be the case for a detached observer.

59.   There are many books and articles and chapters in books on social research on participant observation. Books I have found particularly helpful are: Spradley, James P. (1980) *Participant Observation* (Holt, Rinehart and Winston); Kane, Eileen (1983) *Doing Your Own Research* (Marion Boyars). In my doctoral thesis I made a comparative analysis of the advantage and disadvantages of survey and active and passive participant observation methods and a section on the relationships between the nature of my active participation and my observations.

60.   *op cit* (in ref. 54) p 3.

61.   cf Leonara Tubb Tisdale (*op cit*, ref 52) p 59ff for an interesting piece on "The Pastor as Ethnographer".

62.   I first used them in Parchmore Methodist Church and Youth and Community Centre from 1966 to 1972 both to do and research the work in which I was engaged. It was the principal research method for my doctoral thesis on that work. A short account is contained in Grundy, Malcolm (ed) (1995) *The Parchmore Partnership* (Chester House Publications). Then it was used on a major action research programme, Project 70-75 and on the work of Avec, a Service Agency for Church and Community Work. The first was written up in *Churches and Communities* and the second in *Avec: Agency and Approach*.

63.   cf Grundy, Malcolm *op cit* in ref.58 pp 52-60.

64.   cf for instance: Argyle, Michael (1964/1967) *Psychology and Social Problems* (Social Science Paperback in association with Methuen and Company Ltd.); *The Psychology of Interpersonal Behaviour* (Penguin, 1967); *The Social Psychology of Work* (Penguin, 1972). And Argyle, Michael and Henderson, Monika *The Anatomy of Relationships—and the rules and skills to manage them successfully* (Heinemann, 1985).

65.   "The Myers Briggs Type Indicator" (MBTI) is now, for instance, widely used in the churches to profile people psychologically. Prof. Leslie Francis, in an excellent one-page article, "Hi, I'm ESFJ—who are you?" concludes his assessment in this way:

> Christians who take the psychological and theological challenges of the MBTI seriously are enriched. Those who accept the MBTI uncritically, however, are as impoverished as those who reject it out of hand (*Movement* 1996 p 6).

I accept his judgement. Three things have concerned me about the use to which I have seen people putting this method: the tendency to treat it as more scientific and accurate than it is; using it to excuse rather than to explain weaknesses in competence; treating the analysis as definitive instead of as a base and marker for development; using it to classify people. It is important to distinguish between a personality profile and a description of character which can never be complete. (I owe this last point to Margaret O'Connor.)

66.   It is a fact of common experience and knowledge that individuals vary in the ways in which they see, feel and recount their experiences. Some people embellish, exaggerate and romanticise their experiences whilst others under-state them. Most people, however, fall between these extremes. The ways in which people consistently see, feel and describe their experiences is of critical importance in assessing the meaning and value of observation data. A general acknowledgment of these differences does not provide an adequate basis for making corrections to observations. I was helped by work by James Reason in a *New Society* article entitled "How Strongly Do You Feel?" (No. 395, April 1970 pp 680-682). His basic thesis is that the brain appears to contain a kind of 'volume control' for sensations. This determines how vividly we perceive the world. Following Asenath Petrie he divides people into three groups according to the way they typically deal with sensory stimulation. There are: *augmenters i.e.:* those who automatically amplify the strength of their sensations; *reducers i.e.:* those who have a built-in tendency to damp down or decrease the intensity of their sensory experience; *moderates i.e.:* those who are in an intermediate category on the continuum. Reason says that 'the variation in the way people intensify or damp down their sensory experiences remain much the same irrespective of the type of sensation involved, so it is reasonable to suppose that we are dealing with a general function of the brain, rather than with the efficiency of any particular sensory mode'. He has devised physical tests to determine into which category people fall. This work suggests:

- there is a consistency in the ways in which people feel, interpret, and react to describe their experiences;
- for some 'the world is a brighter, smellier, louder, tastier, heavier, faster, more painful, altogether more vivid place than it is for others'.

Most people consciously and unconsciously take into account whether the person they are talking to is an augmenter, reducer or moderate in interpreting and evaluating what s/he says. Successful personal, business or social intercourse depends upon the native or acquired skill in making these assessments. A similar device can be used in assessing observation data if it is known what type of persons (augmenter etc.) the observers and the observed are. I have been helped in my work by knowing that I am a 'moderate augmenter' *i.e.:* on the top of the 'moderate' or the bottom of the 'augmenter' scale.

67.   An earlier reference to the work of Professor Gillian Stamp shows that a practitioner is more likely to trust their own judgement when their church trusts their judgement and entrusts them with the purposes of the Church. God does this to us.

351

68.   cf *Analysis and Design* p 47f.

69.   I discuss this in some detail in *Analysis and Design* pp 139-141.

70.   Stamp, Gillian (Sept. 1988) *Well-Being and Stress at Work* (Brunel Institute of Organisation and Social Studies, BIOSS, Occasional Paper).

71.   *Ministerial and Diaconal Incompetence: The Methodist Council Report to Conference 1995.*

72.   Friedman, Edwin H. (1985) *Generation to Generation: Family Process in Church and Synagogue* (The Guildford Press) pp 216-219, compares two approaches to burnout: "burnout and the individual model" and " a systems view of burnout". The first sees "burnout as a symptom of the enervated person". In the second the burnt-out person is "seen as the 'identified burnout', and the focus will be the overloading system". The systemic approach to family therapy takes a similar approach to a malfunctioning member of the family system of which they are an integral part, cf the work of Mara Selvini Palazzoli.

73.   cf Caplan, Gerald and Killiea, Marie (eds) (1976) *Support Systems and Mutual Help: Multidisciplinary Explorations* (Grune and Stratton, 1976 pp 325) *etc.:* The SPCK "New Library of Pastoral Care" and especially Coate, Mary Anne (1989) *Clergy Stress* (SPCK) pp 213; Jacobs, Michael (1989) *Holding in Trust—The Appraisal of Ministry* (SPCK) pp 187;Waldrond-Skinner, Sue (1988) *Family Matters—The Pastoral Care of Personal Relationships* (SPCK) pp 179 and reports such as that produced by the United Reformed Church Stress in *Ministry* (1978).

74.   I have discussed this process in some detail in *Analysis and Design* pp 197ff cf pp 45 and 122 of this book.

PART THREE

TOWARDS MAKING CONSULTANCY PROVISION

Introduction

In this Part the focus changes from the nature of consultancy (Part One) and the nature of the work and the attributes required to do it (Part Two) to ways and means of providing it in the working context through considering:

- different ways in which consultancy services are provided through personal consultancy and co-consultancy arrangements, courses, conferences and projects (Chapter Eight);

- significant members of the family of associated activities (Chapter Eight);

- a picture, howbeit a partial one, of the take-up of these kind of consultancy services, through an analysis of the actual use made of Avec, a consultancy service agency, and the needs addressed over a period of some twenty years (Chapter Nine);

- a strategy by which to achieve comprehensive consultancy provision provided by local and specialist consultancy services (Chapter Ten).

CHAPTER EIGHT

Forms and Modes of Consultancy

Essentially consultancy is a form of private activity which provides consultors with opportunities to explore things openly with impunity in preparation for working with people individually and collectively, in private and in public. Part One is about the ways and means by which consultants and consultors do this consultancy work and the problems they can encounter. Consultancy arrangements and relationships vary enormously as do the nature, duration, frequency and degree of formality of consultations. Here I describe and discuss some modes of consultancy and a representative range of the forms they take in relation to work studies and vocational development. Finally, I consider the place of consultancy in the family of activities of which it is a member.

I   MODES OF CONSULTANCY

There are three basic modes of consultancy. In the first of these the initiative is with consultors. They decide when they wish to consult and what they wish to consult about and make contact with their consultants. They may brief consultants in advance or, as is quite common, brief them when they meet. The contract is an open one. In the second mode, consultors and consultants establish a programme of consultations. Sessions are fixed well in advance to cover a contracted period, say a year. Consultors may brief consultants when they meet. Or, consultors and consultants may confer in advance about the next consultation and decide how best to prepare for it. The third mode is similar to the first or the second except that consultants receive copies of minutes and any other relevant documents.

An advantage of the first is that consultations are restricted to the felt needs of consultors and their initiatives. An advantage of the second and third modes overcomes a limitation of the first, it provides opportunities for consultants to identify issues requiring attention of which consultors are unaware. In the first mode consultants are cast in a responsive, re-active role; in the second and third they can be pro-active. The third mode enables consultants to monitor developments and multiplies their opportunities to take initiatives but it involves them in taking on much more work and responsibility. Most of my work has been done in the first two modes.

II   SOME FORMS OF CONSULTANCY PROVISION

In this section we note some of the many ways in which consultancy services are provided.

1.   Consultancies With Individuals and Groups

A private arrangement between a consultor and a consultant forms the basic relational unit. Larger units are formed by multiplying the numbers of consultors

355

and/or consultants. This occurs when groups, teams, councils, organizations and churches are the consultors. Occasionally when consultants are acting for groups such as teams they also act with their permission or knowledge, for individual members of the group. Such an arrangement can be helpful all round, but only when the work of the individual is considered with respect to that of the whole group and when any conflict of interest is managed through the careful maintenance of the boundaries between the group and the individual consultancies (cf p 48).

External contributions to the consultancy relationships modify the dynamics. This occurs when consultants have supervisors and get help from specialists. It also occurs when members or groups of the organization employing consultors are active parties to the consultancy contract. As we have seen, it is of vital importance that all concerned should be clear about the nature of the consultancy contract, the contracting and sub-contracting parties and the respective responsibilities of all participants to each other.

2.   Co-consultancy Arrangements

A co-consultancy arrangement is one in which two or more people offer each other consultancy help by adopting in turn the roles of consultor and consultant. Practitioners who can offer this service to each other in the work place make vital contributions towards the provision of comprehensive consultancy cover (cf Chapter Ten).

One way of developing effective co-consultancies is through a consultant working with two or more consultors. Consultations focus first on one consultor's work, then on the other and on any work they might be doing together. When they are concentrating exclusively on one of the consultor's work, the other consultor acts as a co-consultant. (Consultancy contributions are enhanced because they draw upon the knowledge and experience of two people acting as consultants. Triads can be much more creative than dyads especially when two people cannot see a way forward or are locked in conflict.) This enables them to develop skills and confidence in providing consultancy services to peers and colleagues, the facility to engage in role reversal and the understanding and experience to offer each other help without the assistance of the consultant. Thoroughgoing co-consultancies between two people and members of groups lead to egalitarian consultancy relationships and avoid the ever present potential for patronage in one person helping another.

A co-consultancy arrangement in which I am currently engaged is proving extremely productive. It is with two co-consultors/consultants and is based on the second mode, viz, a programme of consultations fixed in advance for a period of one year at a time to be reviewed and terminated or re-negotiated at the end of that time.[1]

3.   Self-consultancy

Practitioners can act as consultors to themselves. I find I can do this by describing to/for myself what I need to consult myself about. Sometimes I do this in the first person but I find that it helps to objectify things and to induce the consultancy dynamic if I use the third person singular: "George said . . ." or "Lovell did . . ." or "The minister/chair/worker felt . . .". The form of address depends upon how good or bad am feeling about myself, things that have happened and what I have done.

Then I submit the situation, subject matter, myself and my actions to appropriate consultancy procedures.[2]

4.   Consultancy Courses

Work and vocational consultancy courses were developed by Avec (cf p 6 *et al*) and widely used over a period of twenty years. These courses had certain basic elements in common but each was tailored to the particular work consultancy needs of its members. They were generally held in two periods of five days separated by a month or so. Ideally they comprised a group of twelve people with two or three staff members. All participants had to undertake to be present throughout because the sessions were progressively interrelated and they had to promise to treat discussions on work situations as confidential. These conditions were essential to the consultancy process at the heart of these courses.

The subject matter for these courses came from three sources. Beforehand members were required by way of guided preparation to write a paper on their work, either that in which they were currently engaged or that which they were contemplating. These papers, similar to outline one in Appendix I, were circulated to all participants in advance of the course but only after they had presented one and had committed themselves to treat them as confidential. After studying these papers staff members decided the initial input required to prime the co-consultancy and consultancy processes and facilitate collaborative learning. That provided the second subject matter input. The third was the basics of the practice theory upon which the course and the approach to church and community work and to consultancy was based. This material formed the initial syllabus which inaugurated two-way consultancy process between members and staff: members presented their situations for work analysis in relation to the experience of the group in general and the staff's approaches to church and community development work in particular; the staff presented their ideas and approaches for analysis in relation to the members' work and situations. Staff acted as lead consultants whilst members acted as co-consultants to each other and the staff.

During the first week members and staff established their collective objectives and checked the programme presented by the staff against them. Towards the end of the week members and staff together determined the core curriculum for the second week, methods to be used and emphases in the approach. Between weeks, staff members prepared a programme and sessions. Members did the preparation necessary for further sessions on their work situations.

These courses provided consultors with opportunities to experience consultancy processes in four settings. The **first** setting was preparing in private. Before the course they wrote a paper designed to present themselves as practitioners and their work situation so that people who did not know them or their situation could grasp the essentials quickly and engage in constructive discussion with them. Then, after the first week they had to work out the implications of the discussion in preparation for the next round of consultation and action in the second week. Privately they had also to prepare themselves to act as co-consultants to other members by studying their position papers. Guidance was given about approaches to diagnostic reading. Thus the courses presented rich opportunities for learning about the private preparation which helps people to be most effective as consultors and consultants.

357

The **second** setting was in comparatively short tutorials of twenty to thirty minutes with a member of staff. These sessions were used for preparation for group consultancy sessions and afterwards for discussing how to follow them through. Preparatory discussions dealt with things such as how to introduce the group consultation, how to make the best use of the time, no-go areas and how to cope with their emotions and challenges or criticisms. Follow-through tutorials concentrated on implications of the group consultancy and any feelings consultors were finding difficult to handle. In short these tutorials were consultations about promoting the consultancy process and handling the outcome. They facilitated both the process and the learning about it.

The **third** setting was in a sub-group of six members with one or two staff members. Each member had two consultancy sessions in the first week and two in the second. In both weeks the first was about 90 minutes. The second, about 20-30 minutes two or three days later, enabled consultors and members of the group to share their subsequent thinking. The sessions in the first week were dedicated to analysis and helping the consultor to decide what s/he needed to concentrate on in the second week. Those in the second week were dedicated to designing and planning work programmes and projects. This consultancy sequence for each member is charted in Display 8:1. These became known as "work paper groups".

To picture the group sessions imagine six or seven people sitting at a round table four feet in diameter on which were placed sheets of newsprint for drawing diagrams and writing working notes or lists. It could be a group of ministers or priests of any denomination, equally it could be an ecumenical group—a monk, a nun, two priests, a deaconess and lay workers or a group of Anglican and Roman Catholic bishops, provincials and Methodist chairmen (now known as "chairs'). One member is the consultor. Attention is focused exclusively upon him/her and his/her situation. In order to maximise concentration on the given situation no anecdotes or yarn swapping are allowed. (Initially this was a hard discipline for clergy but one in which they eventually rejoiced.) One of them is taking notes, they do this for each other in turn. (Sometimes note takers were required to write up the session as a service to the consultor, and to enable them to study the consultancy session and the situation in greater depth and to acquire skill in writing up consultancy records. At other times they handed their notes to the consultor to write up the session for himself/herself. They then grappled with whatever had emerged and shaped it in ways most meaningful to them. This meant they got the understanding and insights that come only through doing the structuring and writing for themselves.) One person is acting as an observer. Generally s/he is seated outside the consultancy circle. After the session observers had an opportunity to discuss with the group what they had noted about subject matter and process. Other members acted as co-consultants under the leadership of the staff member/consultant. In this setting consultors had opportunities:

- to examine their work in detail;
- to experience one or two staff members acting as a consultant to the group and the other members acting as co-consultants, observers and note takers;
- to have supervised experiences of acting as a consultor, co-consultant, observer and recorder.

PREPARATION		**WEEK ONE**		
Members Prepare Position Papers	Staff and Members study papers privately	Private consultation with a staff member	First co-consultancy session with group	Consultations with staff member privately and then with the group
Stage 1	Stage 2	Stage 3	Stage 4	Stage 5
Presenting self as practitioner and his/her perceptions of his/her situation	Preparing to act as co-consultants to other members	Each member prepares to act as consultor, decides on how session should be introduced, establishes "no-go areas"	Group members seek to understand consultor and his/her situation, analyse it and establish possible areas for development	Establishing development agenda and deciding what to work on during the second week

GAP BETWEEN WEEKS ONE AND TWO
Members write consultancy briefing papers for circulation to members of consultancy groups so that they can prepare to act as co-consultors

WEEK TWO

Private consultation with a staff member	Co-consultancy session with group	Private consultation with a staff member	Final co-consultancy session with the group
Stage 7	Stage 8	Stage 9	Stage 10
Preparing to act as consultor Deciding — what want to achieve and avoid — how session should be introduced	Working at the development agenda: designing and planning	Discussing what has emerged from session 8 and the implications	Sharing and discussing what consultor has decided to do

Display 8:1 Ten-day Consultancy Courses: Consultancy Sequence for Each Member

The **fourth** setting in which members experienced consultancy processes was in the full group of twelve members and two or three staff members. This group worked at an agenda which had three interrelated aspects:

- the subjects of common interest to them as church and community work practitioners; (Display 8:2 lists the subjects covered *in toto*. Most courses majored on four or five of these which were decided by careful consultation between staff and members towards the end of the first week.)

- the approaches and methods staff considered relevant to the participants as practitioners and to their situations;

- the examination of the experiences during the course of the non-directive approaches to church and community work, to analysis and design and to consultancy.

All this provided opportunities for medium sized group consultancy in which staff and members variously acted as leading consultants, co-consultants and consultors. In these sessions there were opportunities to engage in general and specific discussions of subjects and problems. General discussion allows people to draw upon all their experiences without majoring on any one of them. Specific discussion compels people to concentrate exclusively upon a particular example. Acquiring skills to do both is essential to consultancy.

Clearly these courses constituted variegated intensive experiences of consultancy which helped participants with their work and enabled them to learn experientially about analysis, design and consultancy. In these courses private preparation and full group, sub-group and tutorial consultations were interwoven into a rich consultancy tapestry. I never ceased to be amazed at the rapid development of reflective skills and consultancy expertise which practitioners acquired after participating in this process. A more technical presentation of the structure of these courses is presented in Appendix III.

Subsequently, some course members set up local "work paper groups". One ran for several years.[3]

5.   Consultancy Projects

Consultancy projects involve consultants working alongside officers and members of churches or agencies or organizations on agreed tasks related to aspects of *their* work. It can involve consultants working with a council or a team or the archdeacons of a diocese or the members of a church.[4] The tasks can vary enormously. It may be to review their work, design new projects or tackle long standing problems. Project work invariably involves consultancy sessions but it is more than a private consultancy service. In project work consultants are actively involved publicly in decision making about the programme and in carrying out what has to be done: they have responsibility, sometimes primary responsibility, for the action as well as the planning. This is not so in straight consultancy work. Consequently, consultancy projects are jointly "owned" by consultants and their agency and the organization which commissioned them. Chapter Three presents a worked example of a consultancy project.

The primary purpose is to provide consultancy help which assists others in their work. Generally speaking those involved gain experience of ways of working new

Anger and Aggression	Inducting People into New Ways of Thinking and Working
Assimilation	
Authority and Status	Leadership
Belief, Purpose, Objectives etc.	Learning from Experience
Bible Studies	Management: Theory and Practice
Case Study Method and Cases	Ministry: Aspects of
Change, Social Conflict and Faction	Mission of the Church
Church and Community Work: Its Overall Context	Models
	Motivation and Motivating
Church Growth	Personal and Working Relationships
Classifying Work	Planning
Committees	Practice Theory
Communications	Primary Reference Points
Communities and their Development	Problem Solving
Community Work, Direct Action, Group Work	Promoting Participation
	Psychological and Theological Variables
Conceptualising	
Decision Making	Putting Ideas into Practice
Devotions	Questions
Diagrams	Recording
Directive and Non-Directive Approach: The Concepts, Practising them, Training in them	Role and Function
	Skills Practice
	Stance
Disabled People	Structures
Educating People for Change	Teams
Evaluating	Theological Reflection
Evangelism	Theory and Theories
General and Specific Discussion	Time: having
Groups and Group Work, including affective content (compare communities and their development)	Training
	Work Consultancy

Display 8:2 Subjects Covered on Ten-Day Courses

to them especially those related to analysis, design and consultancy. And some projects offer training to those involved. Quite commonly, for instance, people are trained and prepared for sub-group work which is essential to carrying out the project.

The Avec experience proved that consultancy projects were most effective when some of the consultors had attended courses of the kind described in the previous section.[5]

6. Consultancy Conferences

Consultancy conferences are similar to consultancy projects. They could be a part of a project. They are noted separately because, generally speaking they do not involve consultants in as much responsibility as do projects. A typical contract is to facilitate a conference and act as a consultant to the members and staff. Their responsibility begins and ends with the preparation for and the conduct of the conference however long or short it might be.

A spin on this is acting as a consultant to those who are running a conference. This involves assisting them to establish objectives, consider difficulties they might foresee, assess different ways of running the conference, tease out the one which best suits the situation and people and which they feel able to manage, deciding who is going to do what and plotting out the critical path from the preparation through the conference to the follow-through.

Consultancies of this kind have been effective in helping people to put on good conferences for themselves, in developing their own resources, in building up their self-confidence, extending their autonomy and in saving them from outside ineffectual and destructive facilitators and the costs they incur. Apprehension about these latter possibilities is often present when churches seek external help.

I provided this kind of consultancy service to a church with a very mixed racial congregation in an inner city area. I spent an evening with the stewards. They used the work we did to design an exciting, novel and very creative consultative conference which fitted the people. Had I remained a member of the planning group I fear that that creative approach might not have emerged because it was not something which I would have been comfortable in implementing. On the other hand, without the work I did with them it would not have emerged, at least so they said!

Consequently, whenever I am approached to facilitate a consultative conference I ask them to consider which is best for them in the long run, to do it themselves with consultative help or to share in the design and leadership with a facilitator or to get someone to design and facilitate it for them. Getting people to think of these and other options is an important consultative service whatever the outcome might be.[6]

7. Consultancy Combined With Training

Consultancy helps consultors to learn how to do things differently and to acquire new insights and skills. Some of this is through processes of osmosis. However, some of the abilities required by consultors to do their work effectively can only be acquired through training programmes of one kind or another. Consultancy of itself is helpful but insufficient. Some of the most effective consultancy work done through Avec was achieved through working out arrangements and contracts based on realistic assessments of the kind of consultancy services and training programmes and, in some cases, the research, which were required in order to help people do their jobs more effectively. Consultancy plus training proved to be a powerful formula.

Display 8:3 is a chart which helps to sort out training requirements and consultancy agendas. It is an adaptation of one which T. R. Batten devised.[7] Frequently the consultancy help required is to help practitioners to work through this chart in order that they can establish their own training, study and research programmes. The ability to do this as required by practitioners in the course of their work is part of the basic equipment they require.

III CONSULTATIONS ON WORK AND VOCATION

Consultations generally focus on work issues with which consultors are preoccupied because action is required in the immediate or near future. Often they are urgent. Some, however, as we have noted, are about longer term concerns related to work or the development of a practitioner's skills and/or vocation. This comes out clearly in the overview of need and usage of consultancy services in the next chapter. These two consultancy tracks are illustrated in Display 8:4 which is based on Display 8:3, an aid to establishing development programmes and consultancy agendas. Both consultancy tracks emerge from an analysis of a consultor's felt needs. Each consists of three strands, theology, praxis and theory. One moves inexorably towards what consultors can and need to do now with the skills and resources that they have in order to make progress in relation to their purposes in the given situation. The other explores what consultors can and need to do in the longer term to equip themselves to be more effective practitioners and to develop their capacity to pursue their vocations. The tracks can feed each other: analysing particular pressing issues can indicate the kinds of development which would help consultors to equip themselves more adequately for such circumstances; identifying and pursuing programmes of development can have a positive effect on current work praxis and programmes. So, for instance, through consultancy help on specific concerns on an ad hoc basis, consultors can find that their understanding of the work (cf Chapter Six) and the attributes required to do it (cf Chapter Seven) is growing and that they are better resourced practitioners.

IV CONSULTANCY AND ASSOCIATED ACTIVITIES

So far, apart from a short section in Chapter One on other consultancy models, we have been considering a particular approach to consultancy by describing, discussing and defining it in relation to itself and the nature of the work upon which it operates. This approach to consultancy is a compatible member of a family of associated activities. Significant members of this family are described briefly here under the following headings:

>enabling and facilitating;
>undertaking work reviews and assessments;
>mentoring;
>proffering spiritual direction;
>pastoral counselling;
>facilitating spiritual exercises.

The felt need and desire to be able to do something you cannot do to your satisfaction and to become a better worker

Articulate purposes, beliefs, assumptions and

what it is that is prodding and motivating you to do something about the situation(s)

the needs(s) and problem(s) feelings and hunches

what you want to:
— be, become
— be able to do (better)
— know
— understand

Pool, edit, prune, list and decide what is key

This could lead to several training, study, research, personal development needs

Towards Establishing
Study/Research Programmes
The breaking down of the subject matter in this way is far more important than the categories and classifications; they are neither comprehensive nor sacrosanct

Needs for human relations skills in working with people

?Spiritual direction
?Therapy/sensitivity groups
?Consultancy/counselling

Knowledge about
—the human situation
—social and behavioural sciences
—Christianity and the Church
—Theology
—Bible
—Specific work situations

?Structured discussion
?Instruction
?Study/research

Personal development as a Christian and worker

Consultancy Agenda

Needs for technical skills *e.g.*: computers language, etc.

?Instruction

Needs for information

Analysing and identifying the needs

Categories of need

Possible ways and means of meeting them

Display 8:3 An Aid to Establishing Study, Research and Development Programmes and Consultancy Agendas

364

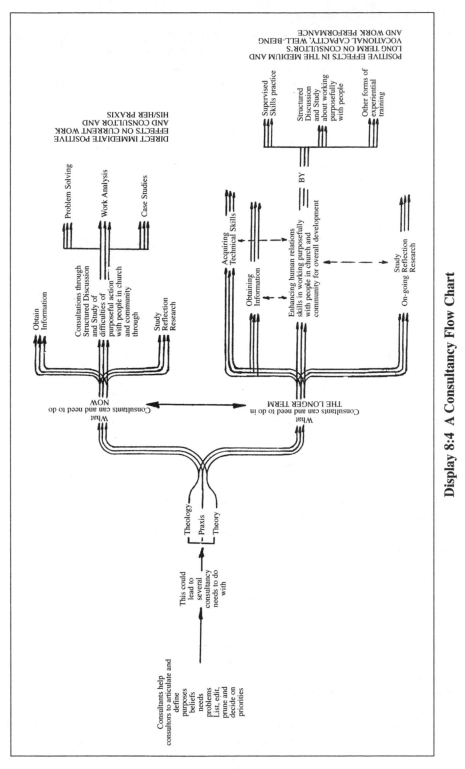

Display 8:4 A Consultancy Flow Chart

a) Enabling and Facilitating

Enabling activities include those through which people "facilitate" large and small groups or act as "catalysts" to them. They help members of such groups to think through complicated and sometimes potentially divisive issues. The number of facilitators (that is the title most commonly used) is growing fast but there are not sufficient of them to meet the growing demand particularly amongst Roman Catholic religious.[8]

A basic difference between facilitating and consulting is that consultants have technical knowledge of the subject matter under discussion which facilitators may or may not have. I acted as a facilitator when I helped a group of Benedictines to examine critically their monastic life and the theology and praxis on which it is based. My expertise was in the process, not in the subject matter. I would have acted as a consultant if I had helped the same group to design a church and community development project, because that is a field in which I have some expertise. This distinction helped a recent consultation of facilitators and consultants to see that sometimes with the same group they find themselves changing from one role to the other and that it is essential to be clear about this and to negotiate role changes as necessary.[9] The overlap of these roles can obscure differences of considerable importance between them.

Both consultants and facilitators have knowledge of group processes. Their style, approach and methods are dependent upon the various and different theories of groups to which they are committed. Those which focus on personal interaction have a high risk factor for task groups such as teams. I have experienced incidents where they have rendered relationships seemingly irreparable. Work consultants and most facilitators use a task group approach which takes serious account of interpersonal factors and feelings but is not a sensitivity or group dynamics approach.

(b)   Undertaking Work Reviews and Assessments

Work reviews take many different forms and are variously described as "appraisals", "assessments", "audits", and "evaluations". As Michael Jacobs[10] shows, the terminology is not used in a consistent way. "Assessment" is widely used to indicate schemes formally structured into the organisation by which people with the help of second parties (sometimes their immediate superiors) assess their performance at set intervals, say annually, and record the outcome in the worker's file. "Appraisal", whilst it is sometimes used as a synonym for assessment, is generally used to indicate the appraisal of self by the self as a private activity even when helped to do so by others. There is overlap between these activities and work consultancy. Work consultancy does involve helping people to evaluate their work; evaluative schemes and audits are of themselves discussions about work. Whether or not the parties proceed from assessment to work consultancy will depend upon whether or not they are able to analyse situations and design action programmes in ways similar to those described in this book.

The potential of institutionalised evaluative schemes and of work consultancy sessions can be seen by considering their principal features. Both aim for better and more satisfying work and for better workers and have considerable potential to achieve these things. However the activities must not be confused. They have different focuses: the one focuses on evaluation and the other on work development. Workers are required to participate in the first whereas they normally participate freely in the other. Information about the one is recorded and can affect job prospects positively or negatively; the other is entirely confidential and is normally serviced by people without ascribed power over consultors. A reasonable inference is that participants in work consultancy sessions are much more likely to be open and undefensive than in evaluative assessments when they will naturally and prudently have in mind the effects of the exchanges upon their working relationships, their current work and their future careers. Therefore those with power, or those who are likely to acquire power over practitioners can be handicapped when attempting to act as work consultants. If they are thoroughly competent consultants and trusted as people of integrity they will, of course, be able to act in that capacity with the most confident, secure and committed workers. They are less likely to be able to do so with those who are insecure and those who are unhealthily ambitious. Clearly one of the advantages of assessments is that they provide opportunities to attempt to discuss work critically with people who would not do so if it were not required of them by their organisation. It follows that, for assessment and consultancy schemes to be complementary, they need to be seen to be so separated that there cannot be leaks or links between them apart, that is, from those made voluntarily by those being assessed and those acting as consultors.

(c) Mentoring

The third kind of activity is training people as they do the job through a process known as mentoring: non-directive help offered by an experienced expert to a novice working in the same field of work but independent of the mentor. These relationships are established so that some people can help others to learn their job. Mentoring is quite different from being supervised or being an apprentice. In these relationships those who instruct and teach have some control over their student workers, they observe them at work and intervene quite freely and directly. There are significant differences between working relationships associated with consulting and mentoring partners although the aims are similar, to help practitioners to learn how to do their job better.[11]

(d) Proffering Spiritual Direction

Kenneth Leech introduces an amazing study of the many schools of spiritual direction in the Christian tradition and the relationships between spiritual direction, counselling and therapy in this way:

> The term "spiritual direction" is usually applied to the cure of souls when it involves the specific needs of one individual. Max Thurian's definition is a useful starting point. "Spiritual direction, or the cure of souls, is seeking after the leading of the Holy Spirit in a given psychological and spiritual situation". Here the stress is on seeking and the seeking is mutual. The director, and he *(sic)* who is being directed, are both seekers; they are both parts of a spiritual relationship. "Spirituality" and "spiritual life" are not religious departments, walled-off areas of life. Rather the spiritual life is the life of the whole person directed towards God.[12]

Spiritual direction understood in this way is anything but a form of religious authoritarianism[13]. The stress on seeking resonates positively with the approach to consultancy discussed in this book. Spiritual directors, according to Leech, are helping people to direct or redirect their whole being towards God. Earlier we saw that the Ignatian method of spiritual direction aims to facilitate coloquys with the Lord (see pp 87 and 128). The method is different from that of consultancy but the coloquys with the Lord properly complement the dialogues between consultors and consultants.

(e)   Pastoral Counselling

Counselling has to be distinguished from guiding, advising and directing. It is a positive way of helping people to tackle problems and difficulties. Counsellors work with people, individually and in groups, to create environments in which they can tackle their problems, grow, develop and become more effective and satisfied human beings. Paul Halmos identifies three main values of the "counselling ideology": a non-judgemental and non-condemnatory attitude, humble and accepting; a mutually honest and intimate I-thou relationship; an opposition to all forms of self-deception, dishonesty, false righteousness and anger. Carl Rogers' stress on the non-directive approach and the unqualified acceptance that goes with it have become widely accepted aspects of the counselling relationship.[14] Halmos says, "to some extent all counselling procedures share a method: they are all "talking cures", semantic exercises, they all attempt treatment through clarification of subjective experiences and meanings".[15] Large numbers of clergy have looked to counselling as a way of finding help with their ministries.

Approaches and processes in counselling and consultancy have much in common.[16] They differ in focus and subject matter: the one focuses on a person and his/her life, the other on the person as a practitioner and his/her work and vocation. Effective counselling and effective consultancy affect every aspect of a person's life. Changes for the better in any one aspect, the person or their work, reverberate through the whole system of their being, doing and relating. They can both be therapeutic and enhance vocational satisfaction and performance. They complement each other and they do so most powerfully when they remain within the boundaries of their respective disciplines and hold to their orientation (person and life/ practitioner and work). (See pp 68-69 about consultants acting as first aid counsellors.)

(f)   Facilitating Spiritual Exercises

Other members of the family of activities are those modes of prayer, meditation, liturgy and preaching which combine with the guiding and prompting of the Holy Spirit to stimulate self-awareness and self-examination and the reconsideration of vocation and stewardship. In this sense they should not be seen as disparate from consultancy. Each member of the family of activities we are considering seeks to promote creative inner dialogue about any and every aspect of Christian life and work. Robin Green, for instance, in a remarkable book which claims that liturgy is a mode of pastoral care says:

> *Liturgy, which is the vehicle through which worship is expressed creates an environment in which human beings confront those sides of themselves which under normal circumstances they dare not face.* (Italics are Green's.)[17]

Worship and prayer gives the environment and support which hold people in loving care as they face and work through something of importance in deep privacy with themselves and God. Every aspect of the act of worship and the setting in which it occurs can contribute to such experiences. Sermons are one of the elements that can play a part.

Willem Berger, a Roman Catholic priest who was at one-time professor of pastoral psychology at Nymegen University in Holland, identified a clear parallel between preaching and counselling.[18] Through his researches into the psychological processes induced by listening to sermons he discovered that when preachers were in "true communication" with their own "personal spiritual experiences" members of their congregation invariably had a conversation with themselves: sermons set in motion personal interior dialogues. Berger does not speculate about whether these inner dialogues involve communicating with God: he rigorously restricts himself to that for which he can produce evidence. Counsellors and consultants also aim to stimulate critical inner dialogues. There is much evidence that, like preachers, they help people to be in deep and honest communication with themselves — their feelings, thoughts and beliefs — and possibly to have colloquy with the Lord and encounters with the Triune God. Such inner experiences are the source of the most profound change and development.

A common trait of this family of activities stands out from these basic notes about their nature. Each member's activity seeks to stimulate and facilitate within people themselves creative engagement with their inner selves about things to do with their being and personal and vocational doing which at the time is of critical importance to their well-being, effectiveness and destiny. They all concentrate on this. Those who practice the various associated disciplines stimulate people to move inwards and outwards. They promote contextual introspection. The interface between the inside and outside worlds of human and spiritual experience is charged with creative potential: it is a fulcrum for development. Overall effectiveness is closely related to getting human and spiritual dynamics working well in relation to the inner and outer worlds of people and the interaction between them. This kind of existential engagement is of the essence of creative Christian living. This book explores in some detail just what is involved in achieving engagements of this kind through working *with* practitioners on their work and vocation. Similar explorations have been made of the other disciplines and the relationships between them. Kenneth Leech, for example, has done a superb job on the relation between spiritual direction, counselling and therapy.[19] Studying these different disciplines reveals much about the nature form, mechanics and dynamics of inner human activities in relation to various aspects of life and work and about what is involved in engaging with them from within and influencing them from without.

This brief excursion into allied and complementary disciplines illustrates the potential of such exercises. To do a comparative analysis of the different disciplines is beyond the scope of this book as it is beyond most practitioners. However, readers may find it useful to set work consultancy in the context of allied disciplines known to and valued by them.

Formalised processes of reflection do not operate in an analytical and evaluative vacuum. They actually emerge from, and the results of them return to, continuous processes of thought and action. Practitioners and those with whom they work are mulling over their experience in their own ways and time—formally and informally, systematically and discursively, seriously and casually—and trying to make sense of it in relation to their beliefs and theories about how things work. Best overall effects are obtained when people are able to gather up and integrate the insights and understandings emerging from these different activities. Practitioners of each reflective discipline and process need to be respectfully cognizant of those of others and open to their influence and findings.

NOTES AND REFERENCES: Chapter Eight

1.   There is a reflective article by Copley, David, Lovell, George and New, Charles entitled "Take Three Presbyters . . . The Role of Co-Consultancy " in the *Epworth Review*, July 2000, Vol 27 Number 3.

2.   This is illustrated in relation to using the case study method in self- and co-consultancy see *Analysis and Design: A Handbook for Practitioners and Consultants in Church and Community Work*, (Burns & Oates) p 44.

3.   Stories about the effects of these courses are to be found in *Telling Experiences*, see particularly Section II: 1, 2 and 4; III: 4; IV: 1, 3 and 4.

4.   Examples of consultancy projects are to be found in many books including the following: Bradford, Leland P. (1976) *Making Meetings Work: A Guide for Leaders and Group Members* (University Associates); Checkland, Peter and Scholes, Jim (1990) *Soft Systems Methodology in Action* (John Wiley and Sons); Kubr, Milan (ed) (1996) *Management Consulting* (International Labour Office Geneva); Lovell, George and Widdicombe, Catherine (1978) *Churches and Communities: An Approach to Development in the Local Church* (Search Press); Lovell, George, (1994) *Analysis and Design*; Lovell, George (1996) *Avec: Agency and Approach*, gives a list of all the project work undertaken, cf pp 151-153; (1996) *Telling Experiences* (Chester House Publications) pp 103-137; Palazzoli, Mara Selvini *et al*, (1986) *The Hidden Games of Organizations* (Pantheon Books); Schein, Edgar H. (1988) *Process Consultations Vol.1—Its Role in Organization Development* (Addison Wesley Publishing Co.); Schein, Edgar H (1987) *Process Consultations Vol II—Lessons for Managers and Consultants* (Addison Wesley); Widdicombe, Catherine (2000) *Small Communities in Religious Life* (Lutterworth Press).

5.   cf *Avec: Agency and Approach* p 62.

6.   Catherine Widdicombe's books can greatly help people to run consultancy conferences: (2000) *Meetings That Work: a practical guide to team working in groups* (Lutterworth Press); (2000) *Small Communities in Religious Life op cit.*

7.   The original was presented to members of the "Community Development and Extension Work" courses in the University of London, Institute of Education in the 1960s.

8.   This need was fully explored in a series of consultations and conferences between Religious and Avec staff and documented in the following reports: *Religious Orders and the Need for Work Consultancy: A Report of a Seminar in January 1985; Consultants and Facilitators for Religious: A Brief Report of a Consultation Jointly Organised by the CMRS (Conference of Major Religious Superiors) and Avec on the 26th and 27th November 1991; Facilitator's Conference, Ireland 8th and 9th September, 1992.*

9.   cf the first Report quoted in reference 8, *Consultants and Facilitators for Religious*. The relationships between consulting and facilitating was a major concern of this consultation. See also Lippit, Gordon and Lippit, Ronald (1986) *The Consulting Process in Action* (University Associates, Inc.) p 59. The distinction they make between the consultant as process facilitator and as technical expert is helpful although I have some hesitation about the following diagram for two reasons. First, it reads as though the consultants give up their facilitator role to take up their technical expert role. If they do this they become advisers. Consultants are responsible for facilitating critical considerations of their technical input or for seeing that such consideration is facilitated. Second, the diagram gives the impression of a

graduation between the roles when in fact there is disjunction between them.

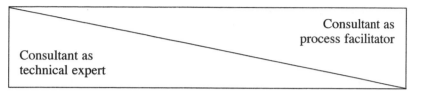

Consultant as
process facilitator

Consultant as
technical expert

10.   Jacobs, Michael (1989) *Holding in Trust: The Appraisal of Ministry* (SPCK) See pp 19 and 21. At the request of the Methodist Executive a Working Party produced a comparative analysis and review of nine schemes of review and appraisal variously used in the Methodist Church. Their findings were presented in a Report to the Methodist Council at its October 1995 meeting.

11.   Although it is not described as such, an interesting and early programme of mentoring is reported by David E. Richards in a chapter entitled "Peer Consultation Among Clergy: A Resource for Professional Development" in Caplan. Gerald and Killilea, Marie (1981) *Support Systems and Mutual Help: Multidisciplinary Explorations* (Grune and Stratton) pp 263-271. Richards reports that over a period of 5 years 70 bishop dyads have been formed to engage in peer consultation (p 264). Dyadic consultation he describes as "a process of borrowing and lending" (p 270) It has the following characteristics:

> *The important point is that for the first year or two of a new bishop's career he has an experienced colleague outside his own immediate system to whom he can turn in complete confidence for help, guidance, support, and the opportunity to explore the broadest possible range of options with regard to any problem or dilemma he may face. This makes available to him a reservoir of professional experience and is a major step toward reducing the professional and social isolation that sometimes besets persons who are promoted to positions of greatly increased responsibility and prestige (p 264).*

Richards notes ten qualities of these consultations:

1.   They are free of judgementalism.
2.   Problems can be dealt with at the time they are pressing.
3.   The learned disciplined form of interaction keeps the focus on the problems not the feelings.
4.   The style of consultation can be used with others.
5.   Dyadic consultation does not open up issues that cannot be dealt with.
6.   Systematic reflection dissipates worry.
7.   Regular peer consultation helps to overcome professional and personal isolation.
8.   Options increased.
9.   It affirms that consultees are not helpless, simply temporarily stuck.
10.   Peer consultation places high value on mutuality and thus reduces the importance of personal status (pp 266-270).

I question the accuracy of point 5.

12.   Leech, Kenneth (1977, seventh impression 1985) *Soul Friend: A Study of Spirituality* (Sheldon Press) p 34.

13.   N. W. Goodacre in an entry entitled "Direction, Spiritual" in Wakefield, Gordon (ed) (1983) *A Dictionary of Christian Spirituality* (SCM Press) claims:

> There is no authoritarianism in spiritual direction. It should not be followed blindly; guidance of every kind should be checked against conscience, holy scripture, church teaching, the dictates of common sense, and relevant circumstances. It is a sign of deterioration in spiritual direction if force of any kind is used (pp 114f).

14.   I owe these references to Paul Halmos and Carl Rogers to Leech Kenneth *op cit* p 94f.

15.   Halmos, Paul (1965, second revised edition 1978) *The Faith of the Counsellors* p 3.

16.   I considered some of the similarities and differences in *The Youth Worker as First-Aid Counsellor in Impromptu Situations* (Chester House Publications, 1971 revised in 1975 and reprinted in 1979).

17.   Green, Robin (1987) *Only Connect: Worship and Liturgy from the Perspective of Pastoral Care* (Darton, Longman, Todd) p 8.

18.   The Revd Dr W Berger wrote a brief article on his research entitled, "Preaching and Counselling" in *Tydschrift voor Pastorale Psychologie*, June 1972 Vol IV No 2. It was made available to me through a private translation I believe by members of The Grail.

19.   cf Kenneth Leech's book quoted in reference 8 above.

CHAPTER NINE

An Overview of Need and Usage

To the best of my knowledge the way in which consultants are used by those engaged in church and community work has not been comprehensively researched. A useful picture can, however, be obtained from the experience of Avec (cf p 6 *et al*) because it provided a wide range of consultancy services. Full records were kept, services were evaluated by consultors and consultants, MARC Europe carried out a postal survey of participants which was supplemented by structured interviews with a selection of participants. Essential information and data about the services have been published.[1]

These consultancy services were provided by an ecumenical team of which I was a member. It had two full-time members, one or two part-time and a group of associates. Over a period of fifteen years there were eighty associates representative of six denominations and various Roman Catholic religious orders. They came from various parts of Britain and Ireland. Between them they had experience of most kinds of church and community work both in the U.K. and overseas.[2] At any one time there would be roughly twenty of them active. By drawing upon this accumulated experience an attempt is made in the first part of this chapter to profile the things about which practitioners sought consultancy help through Avec and to describe what they valued. The second part examines an extended consultancy relationship with Dr. T. R. Batten which was fully recorded. Part three is a note about the limitations and dangers of consultancy services.

I   THOSE WHO CONSULTED THROUGH AVEC

A brief overview of those who used the Avec consultancy services helps to contextualise the information about the consultancy subject matter. From 1976 to 1991, the period from which the information in this chapter is drawn, Avec staff had conducted 357 work consultancy courses of one kind or another. These ranged from half-day conferences to a two-year part-time post-graduate diploma in church and community development, with ten-day work and theory courses as the central core of the programme. They had also provided consultancy services to or worked on 139 projects, mostly in the U.K., though some were in Africa and Ireland. All this means that Avec had worked with over 7,500 people of ten denominations, including almost 4,000 Roman Catholics, 2,000 Methodists and 1,500 Anglicans.[3]

These services were used by people at all levels (5,000 at local and 2,500 at regional and national levels) by clergy (2,800), religious, deaconesses and church workers (3,800) and lay people (1,000). The subject matter was varied: it included most forms of local church and community work and specialist work with, for example, the profoundly deaf and travellers. There were courses for specific groups such as missionaries (on furlough and returning to work in the UK), religious (for

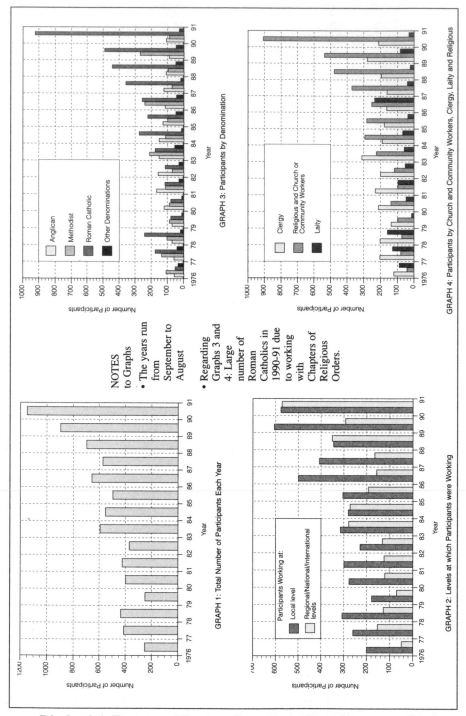

NOTES to Graphs

• The years run from September to August

• Regarding Graphs 3 and 4: Large number of Roman Catholics in 1990-91 due to working with Chapters of Religious Orders.

GRAPH 1: Total Number of Participants Each Year

GRAPH 2: Levels at which Participants were Working

GRAPH 3: Participants by Denomination

GRAPH 4: Participants by Church and Community Workers, Clergy, Laity and Religious

Display 9:1 Features of the Avec Consultancy Programme as a Whole

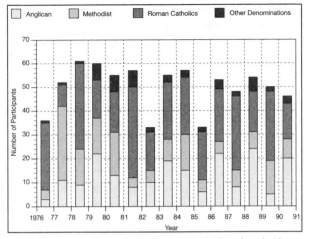

**Display 9:2 Participation by Denomination in Avec
Ten-day Work Consultancy Courses**

superiors and provincials), people working regionally and nationally.[4] The graphs
and charts in Displays 9:1 and 2 give a break down of these bald statistics.[5] Those
who participated were widely representative of church and community work in
every part of the British Isles (including Northern Ireland), The Republic of Ireland,
and some fifteen other countries.

1. Feelings and Needs

Those who used Avec's consultancy services were healthy practitioners who came
in many different emotional states. They were variously excited about new projects
and ideas, happy with things but wanting to develop and improve themselves and
their work, bemused by events, concerned and worried about dysfunctional working
and personal relationships, depressed by their performance, stressed out by what
they experienced as intractable problems. They wanted and needed consultancy
help, not counselling. Several felt needs were dominant and recurring.

One was the deep desire to get their minds around their situation, what was
happening to them as practitioners and positive and negative events they were
experiencing. They wanted to get on top of things intellectually, emotionally and
spiritually; they wanted to get to the heart of whatever matter was concerning them.
Time and again, bishops and chairmen of districts, for instance, said that they
desperately needed to discern the central thrust of their job. All kinds of practitioners
wanted mental maps and working models which put things into better conceptual
order and enabled them to work with the whole and all the parts more effectively.

A second felt need was to check things out. They wanted to test their plans and
the ideas and beliefs underlying them against the knowledge and experience of
others and to contextualise them. This was closely associated with a third need,
confidence building. They needed help and moral, spiritual, technical and academic
support for themselves and their work programme. Help and support in decision
making was a fourth need. And the fifth was help with specific situations and
problems. This aspect is discussed in the next section.

375

Some fundamental needs suffused all the others and turned them into wants. All those seeking consultancy help deeply desired the inner assurance that they were being faithful to their calling and effective whether things appeared to be going well or badly. It was this assurance that gave them the inner disposition—a sense of vocational integrity and of well-being—which enabled them to apply themselves energetically, happily and creatively to their work and ministry and to gain satisfaction from it. Life and work lost their lustre without this assurance.

Professor Stamp's insights about the importance of "flow" in relation to the state of well-being at work[6] has helped me to understand and work at these needs. (This concept is referred to earlier also on p 388.) This psychological and spiritual state can be experienced in any and all kinds of work and working environments. It is not to be associated exclusively with work programmes that are or appear to be successful, although generally it is. Vocational unease can be experienced by those whose ministry and work seem to be flourishing. This inner state of well-being and the work and vocational flow that goes with it, is experienced in all kinds of good and bad circumstances and working relationships and in conflict as well as in collaboration. When it is profound it engenders a sense of vocational fulfilment, satisfaction and harmony. Purposeful engagement is one of its key characteristics: positive engagement, that is, with everything and everyone to do with one's work, with self and with God. Words to describe this wonderful experience are difficult to find. It is accompanied by a sense of rightness and fulfilling one's vocational destiny, the feeling of being in the right place and doing the right thing at the right time in the right way. "This is where I ought to be and this is what I am meant to do". This state is not without doubt, particularly the feeling that it is all too good to be true. Counterfeits of this state are dangerous.

Naturally, this state of well-being has its ups and downs. When it is dislocated, consultors and consultants must do all they can to reinstate it on the bedrock of vocational, personal and contextual realism. Well-being is the antithesis to being under dysfunctional stress. People in stress, says Professor Stamp, are "tired rather than alert, dull rather than creative, prone to poor judgements which deplete self-confidence and increase self-consciousness, ill at ease with the work as it progresses, constantly questioning self and others as the work proceeds".

Work and vocational consultancy can help people to move out of the stress-work-mode and enter into the well-being-work-mode *or* establish themselves more firmly in the well-being mode.[7] It has this potential because it concentrates upon what makes for well-being and development of people at work *and* the well-being and development of their work. It is firmly based upon a body of knowledge and praxis derived from thoroughly researched experience of what helps workers for human and spiritual betterment to get into the well-being mode in all the different contexts they are likely to meet.

The MARC Europe survey records what consultors said they wanted from the Avec services. It is by no means a comprehensive picture because of the limitations of the questionnaire and the response rate: 45% from the ten-day courses, 85% from missionary courses and low for the project work because of difficulties encountered in contacting people. Nonetheless the survey gives some useful pointers which tally with the staff's experience.[8]

The survey of the ten-day courses (described in Chapter Seven) showed that people attended them because of a felt need to extend their skills in human relationships, in communication, in thinking with others and in church and community development work. Display 9:3 shows what respondents felt they needed for their jobs and those things in which they felt strong, and where they felt weak.[9] (MARC Europe also surveyed what people got from these courses—see Section 4 of this chapter.) Responses from those in the project work added the following to this list: to improve group work, to clarify objectives, to prepare for chapters of religious orders.[10]

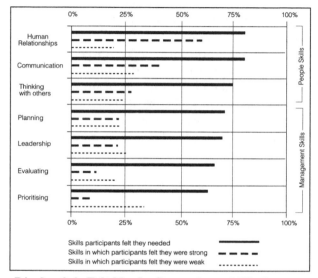

Display 9:3 Felt Needs, Strengths and Weaknesses

Missionaries on furlough said they attended consultancy courses to evaluate the work in which they were engaged overseas and to get guidance on specific issues and problems. Interestingly these consultancy sessions worked admirably even though the missionaries had quite diverse jobs. About a third of them were in pastoral ministry of one kind or another, but the others were variously involved in administration, agriculture, basic communities, education, engineering, medicine, social development, theological training and theological education by extension.[11] What they had in common was working with people on equal terms in countries and cultures other than their own in the ministry and mission of the Christian Church.

Missionaries returning to work in Britain and Ireland said that they attended courses and consultancy sessions to help them to adapt to U.K. culture and church and community work and to discuss key problems they experienced: materialism, pace of life; indifference to the Third World.

2. Consultancy Subject Matter

The more detailed picture of the consultancy subject matter which follows has been obtained by reviewing the experience of Avec in general and my own in particular. It covers the main categories without claiming to be exhaustive. Much more detailed work could be done when it is possible to research the vast number of papers in the Avec Archives.[12] For example, it would be useful to examine differences in felt needs between practitioners of different denominations working in different socio-religious contexts locally, regionally and nationally. But it is not possible for me to undertake or organize the research necessary to correlate and compare these factors.

The subject matter experienced by Avec staff and associates takes five forms. First, there is that which relates to living, current work issues of one kind or another. Then there is that which has to do with consultors as practitioners and their skills. Third, there is that which has to do with consultors' vocation and their development. Fourth, there is that which has to do with the reflection, study and research of phenomena underlying extended and diverse programmes of work. Finally there are the underlying approaches to working with and for people. But, by the very nature of consultancy, starting with a particular subject invariably leads to others. For instance, any discussion about current work situations and issues invariably involves considering the nature of the worker's involvement, aspects of his/her vocation and other experiences of similar phenomena. When the subject matter is vocational development, all other areas are in play.

Generally speaking there is an immediacy, if not an urgency about the subject matter. Certainly, this is so in the first three areas. Decisions have to be made. Action is called for. Events and circumstances are pressing. Inaction could incur heavy penalties. These are the kind of situations in which people can learn fast; in fact consultancy can be a form of emergency learning and training.

(a) Current Work

Aspects of current work for which consultancy help was sought were legion. They are organised here under the following headings:

- reviewing and analysing situations
- designing and planning projects
- examining problems and cases
- working with people who differ significantly
- promoting creative participation and sharing
- conflict and faction
- decision making and taking
- preparation for significant events
- event management
- ethical issues and decisions
- making radical work transitions
- expressing and examining feelings.

Reviewing and Analysing Work Situations. In this category the totality of a consultor's work situation was the subject matter of the consultations. Typical examples of work situations over which consultancy help was sought were: local churches and parishes; circuits, dioceses, districts; communities and provinces of religious orders; national and international organizations related to aspects of the work of the church such as mission or social responsibility; Christian charitable agencies focusing on children and people with handicaps.

This mode of consultancy involves conceptualising and examining the parts and the whole of the consultor's organization, the people involved in it, its culture, ethos and context and its structures and infra-structures. Aims of the organization have to be defined. It is necessary to discover how the parts and the whole are functioning and malfunctioning and what energizes and de-energizes the systems and those engaged in them. Significant patterns in the way in which things are proceeding have to be conceptualised in order to assess what is evolving satisfactorily and to determine what is blocking progress and/or is ripe for development. Doing this inevitably involves considering what consultors think and feel, the purposes that motivate them and the beliefs and spirituality which galvanize them.

Then, as we have seen, the processes must change from the analytic to the design mode: from conceptualising what is happening to figuring out what could possibly work better. In turn that can lead to modifying or re-shaping programmes and/or organizations. A systematic presentation of the stages and sequences of these analytical processes is given earlier, cf pp 79-83.

People came to need and want this kind of consultancy help in different ways. Some simply felt the need to review and develop their work although they were not aware of pressing problems or possible openings for development. Frequently they said, "I want to take a step back and take an objective look at things". Others were vaguely dissatisfied about things without being able to put their finger on the source of their unease. Yet others were facing difficulties ranging in severity from that which irritated to that which profoundly affected them and the whole of their work.

Designing and Planning Projects. Consultations about projects were quite common. Examples are: establishing a base for a Roman Catholic religious order to work ecumenically in Portadown;[13] a local church project to meet the needs of handicapped people in the local neighbourhood; a project to strengthen interdependent working relationships between the Methodist Church in Britain and those of three countries in West Africa[14]; a project to promote shared ministry in an Anglican diocese.

With projects, the ethos is generally one of enthusiasm and hope associated with new ventures in relation to things of great importance to those involved: generally they have far reaching implications for the existing organizational programmes.

Examining Problems and Cases. Problems and cases formed a significant part of Avec's consultancy work. They came in all kinds of shapes and sizes and varied greatly in complexity and in their resistance to resolution. One set of problems was the things that prevented consultors from doing what they needed to do to achieve their purposes and to translate their ideas into creative action. They derived, not from past mistakes, but from future hopes. They were the "how to do something we cannot do" problems. How, for instance, to establish working relationships with people who differ from us significantly? How to make contact? How to say "no" to attractive opportunities for which I simply have not got time? Another set of problems related to things that had gone wrong either through events that could not have been anticipated or through human error or sin. They are "the how to put something right" problems. How to sort out snarled up relationships in a church or a team? How to stop or prevent a person or group dominating an organization?

Generally speaking cases were about a sequence of inter-personal events which led to a deterioration or breakdown of human relationships with serious consequences for all concerned. They covered any and every possible combination of working relationships to be found in church and community work. One case went something like this: a vicar started a group for young people belonging to the church; he handed over leadership to a young schoolteacher who, to extend the influence of the group and with the backing of the church council, opened it to non-church young people who became integrated into the club but not the church; the vicar got a new curate who showed interest in the young people's group; the curate argued that the club should be for church young people only, others should be expelled and he got the vicar to side with him; the leader resigned and, with ninety per cent of the members, set up an independent club in much inferior accommodation. The distressed vicar sought consultancy help.

Major topics of problems and cases were: authority; communication: committees; friction conflict and faction; work-overload; establishing and keeping to priorities; self-management; pastoral management of church and community work and paid and voluntary workers; conflicting and confusing expectations about role and function; decision making and taking; promoting egalitarian participation; getting people to take responsibility; leadership and using the non-directive approach. They also related to major issues such as: authoritarianism. clericalism, racism, sexism, deprivation and injustice.

Working With People Who Differ Significantly. This was a recurrent theme. Sometimes it was colleagues who differed from the consultors in their ideas, approaches and orientations. At other times it was differences between people in church and community work programmes. In some instances, such as Ireland, the differences caused acute problems and were frequently associated with violence.

Promoting Creative Participation and Sharing. Another common subject was participation and sharing. Consultors really wanted to see more people participating and sharing creatively in all kinds of ways. But very often they were concerned about, and sometimes fearful of losing control.[15] Influenced by what was increasingly seen to be politically correct, there was a tendency to think exclusively and unrealistically of one mode of sharing through egalitarian partnerships,[16] whereas, as noted earlier, sharing and participating can and must take many different modes and forms in church and community work. Consequently they had a propensity to over use totally open forms and under use other forms. This had generated unnecessary difficulties, with some of which they were struggling. They needed help with the praxis of participation, the many modes it could take and the practicalities of engendering constructive sharing.

Conflict and Faction. Consultancy help was sought in relation to infinitely varied forms of conflict and faction between people and in and between groups, churches, organizations and communities. Conflict and faction are noted separately because, whilst they occur under other headings, they were frequent presenting themes. Deciding how best to examine the conflict and faction is part of the consultancy process: should it be through one method (situational analysis, studying cases, treating it as a problem) or a combination of these and, if so, in what order?

Decision Making and Taking. Decision making (involvement in processes which contribute to decision taking) and decision taking (acts of deciding) were common consultancy subjects. There were the decisions that consultors themselves had to take, and there were the collective decisions that they had to help others to make and take or to make and take with them. Common problems were: what part should consultors play and what contributions should they make towards making and taking decisions? Which decisions should they themselves take and how should they communicate them? Who should participate and how to get them to do so qualitatively? How to maximise egalitarian participation? How to get groups of people with conflicting ideas and interests and significant differences of approach to make good decisions ideally by consensus? Such questions arise under other headings. Again, they are listed separately because they were often presenting problems under the heading of "decisions".

Preparation for Significant Events. Significant events are common features of church and organizational life. One form that they take is people assembling locally, regionally, nationally or internationally to discuss, debate, argue and decide about things of importance. Examples of these assemblies are: meetings; conferences; consultations; councils; synods; workshops; chapters (meetings of people in a religious order which review community life, ministry and work). Consultors who had key roles to play in such events sought help with difficulties they had foreseen or encountered in planning, organizing or leading them. They found consultancy services helped them: to define purposes; to determine how to get the most effective kind of egalitarian participation through plenary and sub-group work; to form groups and to prepare people to staff and service them; to determine the input required.

Common features of these consultancy sessions were: considering carefully who would be participating; speculating about the inter-personal dynamics of the event; deciding whether to invite those assembled to work out their own purpose and programme or to present possibilities for them to adopt or adapt; constructing detailed flow charts of the stages and steps by which the purposes of the assembly would be most likely achieved; deciding the criteria for subgroups, working out viable tasks and the questions which would generate discussion; selecting and preparing sub-group leaders; gathering the findings of the groups and getting them considered in plenary sessions; establishing decision making procedures either by consensus and/or by majority votes;[17] and composing introductions to conferences and sessions. Doing this thoroughly is demanding and time consuming. Most people find it absorbing, animating and constructive.

However, there are situations in which clergy and laity involved in these events feel they cannot lead them for various reasons: they have a vested interest in the outcome; they are not equally acceptable to all the parties in conflict; they cannot acquire the skills required in time; interpersonal relationships are too tricky. In such circumstances the growing practice is to invite people to "facilitate" the event (cf p 366). On occasions such an arrangement is the best way to proceed. However, as noted earlier (p 362) before consultors accept such a role they should check out with the consultors if it is the best arrangement and, if it is, how to avoid any disadvantages it might have. Inter alia, this involves looking at alternatives, such as them doing it themselves with or without consultancy help.

Another example of consultancy about significant events is that of preparing individuals or groups to meet other individuals and groups to discuss things of import. Apart from the standard things—establishing purposes and formulating opening gambits—this involves speculating about the thoughts, feelings, hopes and fears of other parties: standing in their shoes; seeing things from their perspective. Doing just this through role playing dramatically affected the outcome of a historic first ever meeting between members of the Conference of Religious and the Roman Catholic Bishops' Conference. Through role playing bishops the religious realised they were in danger of relating to the hierarchy of today as though they were the hierarchy of yesterday. Such an approach would have been catastrophic whereas the one they adopted as a consequence of this insight was highly productive.

Event Management. [18] "Event management", a term borrowed from organizational praxis, catches the essence of an aspect of consultancy subject matter. It is about the action required by leaders in organizations and communities when the members have been perturbed by events and there are significant differences of opinion and conflict about the action to be taken. Such events could be the collapse of valued projects, a tragic death, a local or national scandal, an act of vandalism or terrorism, confusing or divisive statements about beliefs, the threat of the closure of a church, school or community service agency. Whatever it is, the event is high on the agenda of informal networks or grapevines; public statements are being made; people may be forming action and pressure groups. What action should a leader take? That is another frequent consultancy subject.

Ethical Issues and Decisions. Ethical issues were raised frequently by consultors working overseas in different cultures. Difficult moral predicaments were experienced, for instance, in societies where bribery and corruption were commonly practised. Missionaries found themselves in situations where the only way to get desperately needed supplies such as medicine was to bribe people. They agonised over their decisions as they grappled with conflicting human, moral and spiritual demands and tried to establish when they should go with prevailing practices, "work the system", and when and how they should challenge them. [19]

Making Radical Work Transitions. Voluntary work and vocational transitions, especially those that are deeply desired, induce the excitement and anxiety of new beginnings and opportunities. However, leaving the old can be traumatic. Involuntary transitions are painful and can be debilitating and soul destroying. Consultancy processes which enable people to examine transitions of both kinds and the emotions associated with them have proved to be extremely creative. Defining the nature of the transition is one aspect of that process. Of itself this is invariably helpful. One person I helped to do this was a man in training for diaconal ministry. Before he entered college he had been unemployed for some time. Getting to the underlying nature of the transition led him to articulate for the first time that the transition that he had found/was finding most problematic had to do with the control over the use of his time: as an unemployed person he had almost total freedom to use this time as he liked; as a student he had to fit into a highly structured timetable;

as a deacon he himself would have to structure large parts of his time constructively. Seeing the nature of those changes enabled him to work more creatively at things which had niggled him during the two years he had been in training but which he had never been able to get a purchase on.

Consultancy sessions for missionaries (now known as "mission partners") soon after they returned from overseas and before they started work in the United Kingdom, have proved to be particularly helpful.[20] Such sessions were designed to help ex-missionaries in transition to work at their feelings, to evaluate their experience, to articulate what they had learned and to determine its value for their new work. To do this they had to overcome the tendency to devalue or over value their missionary experience. It also helped them to determine their initial objectives for the new phase of their working lives, including changes they might wish to make in the way they related to their spouses or families, and the ways in which they worked. Following these sessions a year later with consultancy sessions on the work in which they were actually engaged did help people to make better work and personal transitions than they would otherwise have done. By this time the subject matter was very much the same as that on which other people in the U.K. wanted to work, apart that is from reviewing the transition they were making. The effectiveness was even greater when spouses shared in the process through residential courses and when their children accompanied them and pursued appropriate exercises about their transition.

What was learnt from working with mission partners was widely used to good effect in consultancy sessions with people making all kinds of transitions such as those:

- from being a theological student to a curate or probationer minister, a curate to a vicar, a vicar to a bishop, a minister to being a superintendent or a chairman, etc.;

- from being a religious in a teaching order with its own school to a religious social worker/pastoral worker in a community of many apostolates;

- from living religious life in large communities to living in small ones;[21]

- from being a member of a religious order to being a provincial and from being a provincial to being a member;

- from work to retirement.

Expressing and Examining Feelings. An important aspect of the subject matter of consultations is the feelings that consultors have about their work and the effects it has upon their family and friends, the church and their socio-religious context (cf pp 83-86). As we have seen, it is of the utmost importance to treat these as a proper part of work analysis and design and to demonstrate that at one level they can be examined and studied in the same way that ideas can. Therefore, whenever necessary and possible, consultations provided opportunities for consultors to express and examine their emotions related to their work and vocation.

Consultors frequently needed help in handling positive and negative feedback (cf pp 342-343). This is an increasing need in these days of greater openness, egalitarian participation and accountability through evaluation and assessment.

Missionaries needed opportunities to express and explore their feelings. Most of them were intellectually and factually quite well informed about what was happening in Britain. Their unease was on the emotional level. They were often bewildered by the pace of life, confused and incensed by the variety of goods in the supermarket which seemed obscene in the light of the poverty they had experienced and angered by the attitudes they found to international affairs, racial questions, use of money and wastage of resources. It was particularly disturbing when these attitudes were within their own family circles.[22]

(b)   The Consultor as Practitioner

Consultors often needed and wanted to focus on themselves as practitioners. The emphasis shifted from the work and the consultor to the consultor their vocation and the work. Consequently there were many circumstances when consultors themselves became the primary and proper subject matter of consultations. Amongst them were the following: when, for one reason or another, consultors were dissatisfied with their performance and wanted/needed to adopt different approaches or to develop new skills; when they felt under- or over-used, under- or over-stretched; when they were experiencing a crisis of confidence; when they were simply unhappy without apparent cause; when things were not working out for them. Consultancy sessions on these things were often about the consultor's spirituality, beliefs, purposes, convictions, approaches, theories, ideas, calling, that is, upon the infra structure of the consultor's working life. Discussing them called for sensitivity because they were part of the soul of a consultor. At the same time they were often about the interaction between that which motivated and energized and the actualities of the work in which the consultor was engaged. All this was examined through consultancy unless and until it proved to be ineffective, which rarely happened, and then it could be a good and safe gateway into counselling or whatever else was needed.

(c)   Vocations, Their Maintenance and Development

Closely related consultations were about the state and maintenance or development of the consultor's vocation. Such consultations differed from those described in the previous section which were about particular episodes in the consultor's vocational journey. These were about the past, present and future of a consultor's vocation. Quite commonly a wide range of positive and negative work experiences were analysed, evaluated, reflected upon and prayed about in relation to spiritual experiences and newly emerging convictions about what needs to be done and achieved in church and society. Vocational journeys were teased out to help consultors discern what they were being called to do in the future. New vocational trajectories were extrapolated. A vivid example of this occurred in a co-consultancy session with a group of missionaries on furlough. Little progress was being made in attempts to help a consultor discern what she was being called to do next. Probing the alternatives and assessing their potential locked us in the impasse she was experiencing. Something then led me to suggest that she trace out the main stages of the critical path of her vocational career. That she did, there and then, with help from the group. Plotting the various future possibilities as trajectories of the past path threw new light upon them and the way ahead became clear surprisingly quickly. By the next morning all the members of the group had plotted out their vocational paths and started to review the next phase of their ministry and mission! Dianne Clutterbuck expressed aspects of this in a different way:

> I have to go on making sure that the work and the vocation are in harmony ... the vocation is not the work but I've got to make sure that the work is the vocation. It's very easy to get out of that. In the position I'm in now I could start thinking, "Well, you know, this is OK. I like being a church bureaucrat. What could I do next? What other office could I hold within the Church?" I'm sure it would be quite possible to continue along that line. But I don't think it's the right way. I think it's rather going back to the vocation and saying, "Where is it leading me now? What work fits with it? What should I be doing?" Which isn't the same as looking for the next thing.[23]

Consultations of the kind described in (b) and in this section often overlapped or flowed in and out of each other. The analytical and technical work study element in vocational consultancy means that, whilst it is akin and complementary to vocational counselling and spiritual direction and appraisal, it differs significantly from them.

Consultancies which span both work and vocation have proved to be rich in potential. There can be creative interaction between consultations about work and vocation.[24] Helping consultors to analyse and design their work enables consultants to get to know them as workers, reflective practitioners, and gives them insights into their sense of vocation. This informs in a profound manner consultations about their vocation and its development. In turn, consultations about vocations inform subsequent consultations about specific aspects of their work, consultors themselves and experiences of pursuing their vocation.

(d) Long Term Evaluation, Study and Research

Consultations about long term evaluation, study and research were other ways in which consultancy services were used. This aspect can be closely associated with vocational review. From time to time practitioners felt the need to do more study or acquire more skills. When they felt like this they were generally open to help in working hard at what they needed to study and research and what skills they needed to acquire in order to do the work better, make themselves into more effective practitioners and equip themselves more fully for their vocation in the present and the future. A way of helping them to do this was through assisting them to formulate their own "study, training and research proposals". (cf Display 8:3) Another way was through helping practitioners to plan, evaluate and write up their sabbaticals. Yet another way was through consultations about proposals for and the conduct of action research projects, sometimes for further degrees. This is complementary to the job of a research supervisor and not to be confused with it. I have experienced this as a consultor and as a consultant.[25] Doing these things meant practitioners/consultors were taking charge of their own developmental programme. Consultors valued what emerged and the processes by which they themselves could do this periodically for themselves and with others.

(e) The Non-directive Approach

Through consultations, consultors had personal experience of the non-directive approach, often for the first time. Generally speaking it was accepted and valued,

385

not least because consultors got help through its use that they had not got through directive and advice giving approaches. Periodically this approach was discussed in relation to the consultancy process. But it was in considering the consultancy subject matter that consultors and consultants had to grapple with it because designing projects and work programmes involved deciding what directive and non-directive action the consultor should take, with whom, in what way. As most consultors had more experience of acting directively or permissively than non-directively, they were in especial need of help with the praxis of the non-directive approach. Interestingly, in considering just what action to take in specific situations the terms were not usually used. Invariably the kind of action to be taken was described and discussed in ordinary language as were the ways and means of taking it rather than in technical terms which described its form and nature. Consultors were inclined to talk about taking directive and non-directive action when they first got hold of the ideas. This was not encouraged and soon wore off. The terms got in the way and clouded the issues not least because they obscured the subtle nuances of the way in which particular people in specific situations should be or not be approached, directively or non-directively. Concentrating on details of the appropriate action and ways of taking it, took consultors and consultants deep into the differences between the approaches and the various combinations of doing things *with* and *for* people and leaving them to do things *for themselves* (cf pp 315-316). Nevertheless, whether defined as such or not, non-directivity was a common denominator to all the subject matter. Its neglect was an invariable cause of the difficulties that led consultors to seek consultancy help. And it was invariably a key feature of future action.

3. Things Valued

Drawing upon the consultancy experiences described above and my memory of them, the top ten things that were valued by consultors can be summarised as follows.

• Consultors valued opportunities to explore their work in the strictest confidence with people who had no power over them and no ulterior motives regarding the outcome.

• Consultors valued consultants taking them and their work very seriously and giving them undivided attention and the quality time required to do so. Frequently consultors were surprised and moved by the experience of a consultant or a group of co-consultants concentrating exclusively for an hour and a quarter on them and their work. Leslie Griffiths, reflecting in 1995 on co-consultancy sessions he had on a course in 1977 when he was preparing for a second period as a missionary in Haiti, said:

> Certainly nobody had listened to me for that long ever about my work. And that is a great sign of our poverty when you realise that we don't have time to think about our work in the way that the course made us think about it. We are more and more conscious of interpersonal listening at the level of counselling and therapy and all that kind of stuff. But we don't apply those skills or those insights to the work we do.[26]

With the growth of consultancy services and assessment schemes such experiences would not now be quite as novel, but they are still highly valued.

- Consultors valued gaining information and insights which helped them to understand themselves as workers and their work better and therefore to engage more critically and creatively with:
  —themselves as practitioners
  —their vocation
  —their situations and churches
  —their socio-religious contexts
  —climates of thought
  —decision making and taking.

- Consultors valued a model of leadership which integrated directive and non-directive approaches.

- Consultors valued the emphasis upon and the discovery of things, always practicable and often simple, that they themselves could do and needed to do to:
  —develop their ability
  —improve their performance
  —be more effective
  —experience greater job satisfaction
  —help others to do the same.

- Consultors valued conceptual re-modelling and re-shaping in ways which helped them to see more clearly the essential design of projects, programmes and the various religious entities with which they were engaged (churches, organizations, communities, etc). This was all part of what was described earlier as "cutting the work diamond" (see pp 295-296).

- Consultors valued consultations because they were encounters with the theory and theology as well as with practice and existential realities of church and community work and of consultancy. Opportunities for interaction between their theory and theology and those of consultants were greatly appreciated. Many were looking for a rationale which gave coherence to an eclectic collection of approaches, methods and practices which they used. Some found it through consultations about their approaches. Others found it in the *avec* approach. They said that it was precisely what they had been reaching out for and that they had been intuitively practising it in one way or another but, because they had not got a sufficiently clear conceptual and theoretical base for what they were doing, their efforts were not as effective and conceptually satisfying as they might otherwise have been.[27]

- Consultors valued the ways in which technical help went together with moral, pastoral and spiritual support and they appreciated the way in which they were offered through warm relationships by people who were genuinely interested in them and believed in them and their work.

- Consultors who participated in co-consultancy sessions valued learning about the experiences of other practitioners and studying their work. Two benefits were regularly acknowledged. The first was the realisation that other people had similar problems. This they found reassuring not least because it broke down the sense of isolation felt through struggling on their own with difficulties they felt were peculiarly their own. The second was that frequently they saw things about themselves and their situation through entering into the experience of others that they had not seen through concentrating on themselves and their situations: that is they had experiences of a kind of lateral disclosure or revelation.

- Consultors valued the momentum in consultations which helped them to make progress from a "stress-work-mode" to a "well-being-in-flow-mode" with all that meant for changes in attitude, mood and creativity (cf pp 344 and reference 6). This momentum was variously generated by one or other of the other nine factors noted above or different combinations of them.

- Consultors valued being treated in an adult way, as normal, healthy practitioners in need of work consultancy help and not as patients in need of counselling.

II CONSULTATIONS WITH T. R. BATTEN, 1974 TO 1991

Throughout the time that Avec was offering the work consultancy courses and services described in this chapter, the two full-time staff members, Catherine Widdicombe and myself received consultancy help from the late Dr. T. R. Batten.Separately we had attended courses run by the Battens in 1967 and 1970. T. R. Batten supervised our research for further degrees and was the consultant to Project 70-75 from 1969 to 1976. His consultancy to Avec started in 1974 and concluded in 1991. For a few years afterwards both of us had consultations with him. Detailed notes were kept of all these consultations. An analysis of them reveals the kind of consultancy help and supervision we required to make our best contribution towards developing and running a consultancy agency and the provision of consultancy services. We determined the initial and presenting agenda for the consultations. During the consultations other subjects emerged as being important. The subject matter of these consultations covered the following topics.

1. The founding, organization, development and funding of Avec

At various times there were consultations about: the structure and status of the organization, working relationships between full-time, part-time and associate staff members and trustees; external working relationships with churches and agencies; management; funding; promoting the agency and its work; becoming an affiliated unit of Roehampton Institute of Higher Education.

2. Shaping the Avec work programme

This aspect of the of the consultancy included: allocation of staff time to courses and consultancy sessions, preparation, study, research and administration; how to start a programme; confidentiality; areas of work: design and structure of courses and programmes; working in selected areas; in-house in-service training of staff and associates; promotion and recruitment; designing and developing a two-year diploma; periodic reviews and evaluations of Avec and its work.

3. Consultancy, project and field work

This covered a large number of consultancy commissions with The Young Women's Christian Association; an ecumenical body in Northern Ireland; a project with the Methodist Church in Rhodesia at the point where the country became Zimbabwe; a development programme in the Anglican Diocese of Sheffield; and many more.

4. Staff members

This aspect variously involved: recruiting and deploying staff; working relationships between staff members; the development of their skills and extension of their experience and their abilities to conduct courses; their studies, research and writing programmes; sabbaticals.[28]

Subjects from these four areas were interwoven. A consultation, normally three and a half hours, would cover three or four main topics. Some emphases can be discerned in this overall pattern. From 1974-76 consultations were predominantly about implementing the findings of the action research programme Project 70-75 and the ideas which eventually led to the formation of Avec. During the next three years consultations concentrated on designing, shaping and organizing the training and consultancy programme. From 1979 to the late 1980s, when the formal consultancy arrangement with Batten was beginning to tail off due to his age, the consultations were equally about the work programme, the future of Avec and researching the work and writing it up.

Catherine Widdicombe and I valued consultations with T. R. Batten for many reasons. At a practical level he always made himself available when needed, even at short notice. He gave himself completely to the discussions, his powers of concentration even in his eighties were phenomenal, almost total. He always helped us to see things more clearly and opened up possibilities we had not identified. Subjectively he was totally for us and unstintingly gave us personal and moral support as well as technical and academic help. At the same time he always saw points of view of others and enabled us to face up to them even when it was painful to do so. More objectively Batten helped us to:

- create, maintain, establish, monitor and develop Avec as a viable autonomous service agency;
- design, re-design and adapt the overall work programme in relation to developments that occurred and the changing pattern of needs;
- implement the work programme which involved, inter-alia;
  - designing, planning, carrying out and evaluating courses, consultancy and project work
  - learning how to do the work and training others to do it
  - staffing courses and projects
  - recruiting for courses
  - identifying crucial issues and key subject matter;
- develop creative working relationships throughout the Agency and between Avec and supporting organizations and clients;
- engage in long-term staff preparation, training and education;

- write things up;
- research Avec and its work;
- develop as practitioners, consultors, consultants and as people.

III LIMITATIONS, FRUSTRATIONS AND DANGERS

Human and spiritual inscrutability and unpredictability impose limitations upon work analysis and consultancy as they do with all attempts at thoughtful action with people. Work analysis and consultancy are not exact sciences.Many things consultors and consultants would like to know are simply unknown or unknowable. Consultors and consultants can deceive themselves and each other. Not all problems can be solved. Analyses and designs are never perfect, generally they are good enough. Forgotten or ignored these limitations undermine analytical and consultancy processes; understood, remembered, respected and accepted they become challenging and intriguing aspects of the processes. Taking them into account and treating them as existential friends stretches the mind, wit, imagination and the intuitive senses of consultors and consultants alike as they grapple with human and spiritual realities. To dream, design and plan to influence the unknown future purposefully calls for faith and insight as well as logic and knowledge. These activities also call for candour about the status of the outcome of the processes. And that requires intellectual and spiritual honesty, humility and courage.

The limitations indicated are part of the nature of things. Alongside them are the limitations inherent in the capacities and capabilities of the participants and their fallibility. The boundaries of these limitations are traced out by the abilities consultors and consultants have or lack. The limitations in the nature of things and those in the capabilities of the participants interact dialectically. Sometimes this interaction is creative, at others it is not. Differentiating the two sources makes for positive interaction, confusing them confounds them.

Other limitations are to be found in the ever present danger of the abuse and misuse of consultancy relationships and processes. These possibilities are considered in pp 203-205. Yet another form of limitation can be experienced when, during the time between consultations and the consultors taking action, situations so change that analyses are invalid and plans inappropriate. This does not mean the work done is necessarily wasted but it does mean things have to be re-worked, often on the spot, prior to action. This is discussed earlier, see pp 205-207. Many of these dangers and limitations have been examined in some detail in Chapters Two and Five.

Clearly, whilst there are very definite limits to and hazards in consultancy processes and to what any person can do to help others to think things through, considerable benefits can accrue to consultors and their work through good consultancy relationships and practice. Sadly, all too often and sometimes tragically, practitioners experiencing work stress who need technical help are referred for counselling when they need consultancy, a more appropriate and safer first port of call.

NOTES AND REFERENCES: Chapter Nine

1.   See Lovell, George (1996) *Avec: Agency and Approach* (An Avec Publication) and *Viva L'Avec, A Service Agency for Church and Community Work: An Evaluation on Avec's Training (and Consultancy) Ministry* by MARC Europe (A MARC Europe Report, 1991) pp 237. A series of in-depth interviews followed up this survey. They were published in *Telling Experiences*. Three Avec internal reports give useful information about consultancy needs: *Religious Orders and the Need for Work Consultancy*: A report of a seminar in January 1985 at which some thirty religious from men's and women's orders carefully considered eight year's experience of Avec staff working with 330 religious of 50 orders. *Consultants and Facilitators for Religious*: A Report of a consultation organised jointly by the CMRS and Avec on 26th and 27th November 1991; Facilitator's Conference: Ireland 8th and 9th September, 1992.

2.   Full details are given in *Avec: Agency and Approach*, pp 62-73 and 155-157.

3.   *op cit.*

4.   *cf op cit* p 19f.

5.   *cf op cit* pp 144f and 147 respectively from which these graphs have been extracted.

6.   Stamp, Gillian (September 1988) *Well-Being and Stress at Work* (Brunel Institute of Organisation and Social Studies, BIOSS) p 3. Quotations from this paper help to contextualise her thinking:

> In the course of the past fifteen years I have had the privilege of listening to more than a thousand men and women, of different ages and levels of education in different countries, from different cultures and at all levels of capability, as they talked to me in depth about their working lives. They were employed by, or belonged to, a wide variety of commercial, military, religious, educational and voluntary organisations. This rich and diverse experience has given me a unique opportunity to learn about well-being and stress at work, both from the point of view of the individual and of the organisation (p 1).

> More tends to be written about the experience and consequences of stress than about well-being. In the course of my interviews I have had the opportunity to hear much of both, and my findings echo those of others who have set out to understand the psychologically healthy individual. Our shared conclusion is (a) that well-being occurs when what there is to do is in balance with what the person feels able to do, and (b) that continuing personal development happens only when what the person feels able to do is matched by growth in what there is to do (p 3).

> A word that is very widely used to describe the state of well-being is "flow". People in flow feel alert, energetic, motivated, competent and creative . . . (p 6) (people in stress) are tired rather than alert, dull rather than creative, prone to poor judgements which deplete self-confidence and increase self-consciousness, ill at ease with the work as it progresses, constantly questioning self and others as the work proceeds (p 7).

7.   MARC Europe in their report of their survey of Avec's consultancy and project work said that the main effect of courses and consultations on respondents was to give them more confidence. This greater confidence, the survey shows,came through improving their ability to lead, to work with groups and to plan and evaluate purposefully thus helping to find ways by which they themselves could do things. *op cit* p 4 section 5.5, pp 97ff.

8.   A summary and analysis of the survey by Peter Brierly is given in *Avec: Agency and Approach* pp 158-171.

9.   *op cit* p 160.

10.   *op cit* p 165.

11.   cf Russell, Peter W and Lovell, George (1988) *Furlough Work Study* (An Avec Internal Paper) p 31.

12.   These are to be housed at Westminster Institute of Education, Oxford.

13.   This is described in detail in Lovell, George (1994) *Analysis and Design* (Burns & Oates) pp 93-106.

14.   This is described in detail in an article by Leslie Griffiths, "Relationships in Mission" in *Epworth Review* (Vol 15. No 2 May 11988) pp 85-94.

15.   cf Lovell, George (1994) *Analysis and Design* pp 253-259.

16.   *cf op cit* pp 255ff.

17.   The Uniting Church of Australia has an excellent model for making decisions by consensus. The flow chart they have produced has slip roads which enable groups to take other routes when they fail to reach a consensus. When all other possibilities fail they lead to "decision by a formal majority", cf *A Manual for Meetings in the Uniting Church* (Uniting Church of Australia, 1994).

18.   On this subject see: Chapter 6, "A Model of Event Management" in Smith, Peter, B. and Peterson, Mark, E. (1988) *Leadership, Organizations and Culture* (Sage Publications) pp 79-93.

19.   cf *Furlough Work Study* referred to in ref 11, pp 11ff.

20.   cf *Avec: Agency and Approach* pp 168ff.

21.   Catherine Widdicombe has made a detailed study of this transition: see *Small Communities in Religious Life: making them work* (The Lutterworth Press, 2000).

22.   cf *Furlough Work Study* pp 14f.

23.   Lovell, George (ed) (1996 *Telling Experiences: Stories About a Transforming Way of Working with People* (Chester House Publication) p 159f.

24.   There are examples of this in *Telling Experiences* cf Charles New's story pp 29ff, and Howard Mellor's p 52.

25.   cf Lovell, George and Widdicombe, Catherine (1978) *Churches and Communities: An Approach to Development in the Local Church* (Search Press) pp 209ff and *Avec: Agency and Approach* p 77.

26.   *Telling Experiences* p 19.

27.   *Avec: Agency and Approach* p 37.

28.   What this involved is discussed in *Avec :Agency and Approach* pp 62-73.

CHAPTER TEN

Towards Developing Consultancy Resources and Services

The first part of this chapter argues for a form of comprehensive consultancy provision and describes a way of achieving it which emerges from my experience and that of my colleagues in Avec. The second part indicates where effort needs to be concentrated in the next phase of development.

I   AN EMERGING STRATEGY FOR COMPREHENSIVE PROVISION

An inescapable conclusion of this book is that it is imperative that consultancy services be made readily available to all members of the church and community workforce when they are wanted and needed in accessible forms. Such provision would greatly enhance the effectiveness and well-being of the church in general and its practitioners in particular. Yet the total unmet consultancy need towers over that which is being met. The climate of opinion is only now turning slowly in favour of making consultancy provision. How can the enormous task of providing comprehensive consultancy coverage be tackled realistically and seriously in the present context? To address this question it is necessary to turn from considering the details of consultancy praxis, to plotting out elements of a strategy by which it would be possible to move steadily and surely from the present situation towards better provision. That is attempted in this section.

Fortunately, there is now a good base upon which to build a strategy: much work has already been done and experience gained. First there is a bald bulleted list of separate but interrelated aspects of the strategy. Then some of its more subtle nuances are discussed. Gradual and purposeful progress could be made towards convincing the Church constituency about the need for consultancy help and getting the administrators to make the resources available to provide it:

- by getting Christian leaders, workers and people to see that consultancy is an efficient and economic way of improving the effectiveness of the Church;

- by getting people to see that work and vocational consultancy is a profound professional and practical form of pastoral care for practitioners — it ministers to workers' souls as well as to their praxis;

- by getting the idea so widely accepted that consultancy help can be received from colleagues as well as from specialist consultants;

- by promoting the conviction that the consultancy help needed can only be provided through a combination of specialist consultancy services and practitioners giving and receiving consultancy help from each other in the workplace;

- by those who can providing, informally and formally, consultancy services to anyone open to receive them of such a quality and apparent value that even the most sceptical become convinced;

- by multiplying endlessly and continuously evaluated experiences of work and vocational consultancy and supervised opportunities to practise it for people in all spheres of church and community work, lay, religious and ordained;

- by getting both those who offer consultancy and those who receive it to study the theory, theology and practice of it;

- by helping church workers (lay, religious and ordained) at an early stage in their preparatory training to begin to learn how to be effective consultors and encouraging and assisting them to develop their skills throughout their working life through in-service and vocational consultancy programmes;

- by getting people to think of work consultancy as a normal healthy service needed by all at times, and not as a pathological activity;

- by creating an environment of thought conducive to the finding of comprehensive consultancy provision;

- by establishing as an element of good practice the budgeting of fees for consultancy services and support for workers (lay and ordained) and for projects;

- by developing a cadre of specialist regional/national/international consultants who are committed to building up the kind of provision described here, rather than developing an elitist consultancy service;

- by developing ecumenical, inter-church and inter-organisational collaboration in making overall provision and particularly in providing consultancy services for one another; (People in one denomination or diocese, for example, can provide consultancy help for some practitioners in another who cannot receive it from would-be consultants in their own denomination or diocese.)

- by researching the experience of providing and receiving consultancy help and its theology;

- by providing more literature and by producing tapes and videos on consultancy practice and processes.

This strategy is designed to affect the consultancy praxis of Christian institutions through key members of their workforce. The aim is to promote change from within through changes in the practice of people located in complementary parts of the overall work-systems: members and officers, administrators, educationalists, general practitioners, pastoral managers and trainers and through them the members generally. Thus it is a strategy of holistic gradualism developing from many nuclei of good practice and research. Approach-wise, therefore, the strategy is in harmony with the practice theory of work and vocational consultancy itself. That is precisely how it ought to be because it is about an aspect of the work culture of Christiain institutions as a whole.

Overall, the principal advantages of this strategy are: it provides consultancy help as it develops it; it holds together praxis, theory, training and research; it affects practice working relationships and work culture at the same time; it builds up the self-confidence of all implicated and of organizations themselves; it provides updating feedback from the actualities of work situations to training programmes; it is a consultancy instrument to the whole church; it is most likely to get to the heart of the consultancy matter.

Much of the detail of this programme is self-evident and illustrated in the earlier parts of this book. But it is necessary to explore further the ideas of meeting more of the needs for consultancy help through increasing the number of people who can provide specialist consultancy services and by building up the practice of workers giving to and receiving from each other consultancy help in their work places. It is imperative that these two modes of provision are developed concurrently as interdependent aspects of consultancy services: combined they represent the principle of subsidiarity and facilitate its practice. This is the ideal way to meet the need, to ensure that practitioners are as self-sufficient and independent as possible, that their autonomy and working relationships with colleagues are not undermined or compromised, that they are affirmed and challenged; that good consultancy help of one kind or another is available to them when they need and want it; that consultancy practice, theory, theology and culture develop together. This strategy minimises the real dangers of the establishment of exclusivist professional consultancy services and ensures that meeting these needs is, of itself, a programme of church and community development.

Interestingly, having adopted this approach I discovered that a similar conclusion had been reached through a research programme commissioned by the Department of the Environment into the management training needs of Urban Programme Project Managers. One of their conclusions was that inexperienced managers need two types of support: a local generalist and a national specialist.[1] Experienced managers also need such support.

Without any doubt there is a need for specialist consultancy services within the denominations and independent of them. Certain consultancy needs can be met only by consultants who are autonomous and quite independent of any of the consultors, those with whom they work and their organizations, and are seen to be so. The Avec experience proved that beyond any doubt. However, no matter how proficient and readily available such a service becomes it could never meet all the consultancy needs that church and community development practitioners have and especially those that need immediate first-aid help. Some of those needs can only be met by people on the spot, by colleagues or by others in their organization including those in senior positions. And, in any case, a proficient and readily available specialist service could, through its very proficiency and availability, prevent other important needs being met.

One such need is that nothing is done at a distance from the workplace that can be done in it. That is an application of subsidiarity. The health of an organization and the well-being of its staff and members depends upon it. For effectiveness and their integrity and satisfaction practitioners need to be as self-sufficient as possible. Another need is for workers to build up their working and personal relationships by giving and receiving help from each other. One of the sad things about the evolution of social work is that, in some circumstances, it stripped neighbours of the confidence to counsel and care for each other. They began to feel that they were not qualified to do so because they were not "experts'[2] whereas in fact they were *the* local experts. Should this happen through the provision of consultancy services for church and community development practitioners it would be a travesty of the purpose of the whole enterprise because it would diminish rather than enhance workers and local resources, it would not be an exercise in vocational or organizational development. Building up co-consultancy infrastructures of the kind described reduces this danger and also minimises other dangers inherent in specialist consultancy relationships. Dangers, for instance, of workers becoming unhealthily dependent upon consultants, insecure in their own judgements, hesitant or unable to act without having consulted. These things impair workers and their relationships with any who resent the procrastination that ensues and what could appear to be the undesirable influence of an absentee consultant in their affairs. Consultants must take action to avoid these and other problems but, as we have seen in relation to consultancy in general, so must consultors. They need to be aware of these dangers and how to avoid and counter them. They will be best able to do so through being helped and trained to be as self-sufficient as possible in thinking through their own work. They need to be able to use the analytical and design tools used in consultancies in a dialogue with themselves, in other words, to be a self-consultant. Having got as far as they can on their own they then need to be able to turn for help to those working alongside them with confidence that they will get consultancy help rather than advice. In these ways workers act as first-aid consultants to each other and build up their own D.I.Y. consultancy services.

So we are forced back again to the need for both specialist and local consultancy provision. Combined, they strengthen the work force of any church or organization and enhance its power through creating highly desirable work consultancy infrastructures.

Avec and its training and consultancy programme researched, modelled and facilitated a comprehensive approach of this kind. Staff members provided specialist consultancy services whilst getting practitioners to offer to and receive consultancy help from each other. The way in which this was done through ten-day courses is described in some detail in Chapter Eight (cf pp 357-360 and Appendix III). This led some practitioners to organize consultancy conferences and projects and to establish co-consultancy arrangements, dyads and small groups (cf pp 356). This was a modest contribution to comprehensive consultancy provision.

The comprehensive approach is as theologically sound as it is pragmatically and developmentally necessary. It contributes to the ministry of the Church being and becoming what it should be, collaborative and collective (cf pp 290-291). Paul spelt this out quite unmistakably in Romans 12 and in 1 Corinthians 12. People who genuinely and selflessly help other people with their work become less egotistical and operate as colleagues and co-workers rather than as solo workers and prima donnas. Over and again I have seen this happening to members of the Avec work consultancy courses. For this reason alone it is highly desirable that as many clergy, religious and laity as possible have opportunities to act as consultants and co-consultants to each other. Building one another up through genuine sharing and investing in each other's ministry is an enormous privilege and an extension of our own vocation. It contributes to the realisation of the church as the covenanted body of Christ and the priesthood of all believers and helps people to be workers who need not be ashamed.[3] When practitioners from different denominations and faiths and secular disciplines offer to and receive consultancy help from each other, consultancy becomes an instrument of ecumenical and social development, missiology and inter-faith dialogue. When this happens consultancy develops deep relationships and mutual understanding between those who differ significantly in religious conviction and belief but who find they face common work problems and that they can help each other with them.

Therefore, the kind of consultancy provision advocated contributes towards achieving ultimate purposes. For me these purposes are about a dynamic pattern of interdependent human and spiritual relationships through which all are loved and cared for and by which all are developing as they go about the day to day work of the church in the church and in the world.

II GENERATIVE ELEMENTS

Progress has and is being made towards the provision of consultancy services. As this book shows Avec (cf pp 6 and 373-388) has made various kinds of contributions. At best, appraisal schemes are gateways to consultancy help and they are legion. And there is a growing number of technical publications for consultors and consultants, some are introductory, whilst others are handbooks and text books like this one. However, a critical point has been reached in the evolution of consultancy services in the Church. Avec has ceased to trade and, although some in-service training courses incorporate aspects of its approach, the extensive programme of consultancy services it provided is simply not available. Some services are available through individuals and agencies but to the best of my knowledge no other organization is offering services comparable to those provided by Avec.[4] And this at a time when a paradigm shift is occurring in the work culture of churches and allied organizations in the U.K. Egalitarian, participative and non-authoritarian working relationships are becoming more widely accepted. Increasingly more clergy, religious and laity are using methods of social analysis and being urged to become accountable, reflective practitioners and to form accountable reflective communities. As we saw in the introduction, work and vocational consultancy services are important features of this emerging work culture and, along with in-service training, they are needed to help practitioners to enter and grow into it. Work consultancy services having proved their value are increasingly in demand. As appraisal schemes become more effective the demand will grow. But there is a serious shortage of consultants and affordable courses for training them.

Meeting the need for consultants is frustrated by factors other than the shortage. There is considerable confusion about the precise nature of consultancy and bewilderment about the different forms it takes. There is an absence of generally recognised practising qualifications and registers of accredited consultants for church and community work to help would-be consultors to vet consultants. In fact, most people offering services, including myself, are self-elected and self-trained consultants. This means that there is an over reliance on personal recommendations and finding helpful consultants by trial and error. This is serious, because, as we have seen, those acting as consultants can hinder and harm as well as help consultors. It had been assumed that the church generally and appraisal schemes in particular could readily make use of consultants from the business world. But experience is showing that the transfer of consultancy skills from business and industry to the church is more complicated and problematic than was previously thought, not least for theological reasons.

At this critical point, emphasis upon orientation, promotion and training could give impetus to the strategy described in the previous section. Four modes of orientation and training could be generative. Urgent action is required along the following lines.

1.   Promotion, Orientation and Education of the Church Constituency

The church generally needs to be much better informed about the nature and value of consultancy: those with power and influence in the body politic as well as those who are practitioners. Work consultancy is an off-the-stage, back-room activity. For the most part it has to be done confidentially and therefore privately and hidden from sight (although, of course, the same approaches and methods can be and are used publicly). Results are rarely attributed. In many cases to succeed consultants must avoid publicity. It is an expensive labour intensive activity: for the most part one or two consultants work with individuals or small groups. One of the major disadvantages of these essential conditions of providing these services is that it does not get the attention and the funding that is given to more dramatic activities to meet extreme needs or the routine work of the church—all of which can benefit from consultancy. Yet the quality of all kinds of work depends now, and will do so even more in the future, upon building and maintaining an adequate and comprehensive consultancy infrastructure properly serviced and funded so that it can provide essential services. Time and again, a few hours consultancy has saved or salvaged or greatly enhanced the effectiveness of projects in which salaries of the workers alone have run into £100,000 per annum, to say nothing of the capital and running costs, for as little as £500 in consultancy fees. The economic value of consultancy is known by those who have experienced and practised it but it is normally hidden from view and its quality and value are difficult, if not impossible, to quantify.

Opportunities for an all-round sharing of ideas about and experiences of consultancy in the Church could be valuable. One way of doing this would be through a conference similar to one organised in 1994 by the South Bank University, London under the generic title, "What makes consultancy work—understanding the dynamics". Some excellent papers were produced and subsequently published, mainly but not exclusively from the secular experience of consultancy.[5] Such consultancy conferences would enable the sharing and gathering of different experiences. There were some rich exchanges on consultancy at an ecumenical conference at Westminster College (now Westminster Institute of Education), Oxford in 1996 on, "Reflective and Collaborative Practitioners in Ministry".

2.   Preparing Trainees and Practitioners to be Consultors

A case has already been made for the importance of making all future church workers at an early stage in their pre-service training aware of different forms of consultancy and their respective merits. Ideally, they should have evaluated experiences of consultancy (some through tutorial relationships) and instruction into what is involved in acting as consultors.

One way of giving introductory training to practitioners to act as consultors, consultants and co-consultants in one fair swoop has been described (cf pp 357-360 and Appendix III). Codes of good practice for consultors and consultants have been offered (cf pp 143-145). Emphasis has been placed upon the value of entering into the practice theory of consultancy through being a consultor. In this way practitioners get a real understanding of what it is like to be on the receiving end of consultancy before they attempt to offer it. Talks, lectures, articles, case studies, evaluated experiences, personal testimonies and demonstrations can help to inform people and to contribute towards the comprehensive provision outlined earlier.[6]

3. Apprenticeships and Mentoring

For those who wish to build up their experience and expertise in order to act as local or specialist consultants, mentoring, apprenticeships and supervised practice complement introductory training, as does the study of the growing body of literature and case study material.

4. Extended Training for Consultants

Large numbers of people have developed consultancy skills through the kinds of induction and training described earlier. But disappointingly, comparatively few have emerged capable, willing and free to act as specialist or professional consultants. Consequently Avec found it difficult to recruit sufficient full- and part-time staff members. The Conference of Religious experienced difficulty in recruiting consultants to staff a consultancy unit to serve religious congregations and members. Westminster College, encountered the same difficulty when it researched the possibility of setting up a consultancy unit in applied theology. When the staff faced up to this difficulty they decided to put the development of the unit on hold and concentrate on designing and providing a training course in work and vocational consultancy. A course is now being offered through a partnership between Cliff and Westminster Colleges and The Urban Theology Unit.[7]

Validated consultancy courses will indicate that those who have successfully completed them have some knowledge of the theory and practice of work and vocational consultancy. Whilst these qualifications would give some idea of knowledge and ability they will not be a professional qualification nor will they necessarily guarantee the competence of people to act as consultants. A professional association is needed to do that. Consultancy courses could, however, contribute to the research into ways and means of training people to act as work and vocational consultants. They could also be a means of identifying and equipping people who might help to provide more and better consultancy services in and for people in the Church. Training programmes would, in turn, provide evaluated feedback which would help to make pre-and in-service training increasingly more relevant to the actualities experienced by practitioners. Consequently all engaged in the learning/practice system would benefit from these educational feedback loops: students, consultors, consultants, staff training institutions and the Christian and secular constituencies they serve.

Pursuing these elements purposefully could prove to have a generative effect on every aspect of the outlined strategy. It could give momentum to the wide ranging effort that is going into making comprehensive provision, set up new working partnerships, provide new resource material for practitioners and researchers and establish work and vocational consultancy as the priority that it ought to be in the Church.

III IN CONCLUSION

Individuals, of their own volition, are actively promoting and providing consultancy services through pursuing one or more aspects of this strategy. Whilst some churches say that they are convinced of the value of consultancy, they seem to give a low priority rating to making adequate provision for it. An inescapable conclusion is that the greatest hope of significant progress still lies in highly motivated individuals, centres of excellence and agencies or units which can provide specialist help and training. For the foreseeable future it is they who will provide limited resources and will be the conscience of the consultancy need, the custodian of the vision, the source of inspiration and they will maintain the pressure upon the churches and allied organizations to take the institutional action that is so clearly required.

NOTES AND REFERENCES: Chapter Ten

1. *Managing Urban Change: A Report on the Management Training Needs of Urban Programme Project Managers* prepared for the Department of the Environment by URBED (Urban and Economic Development) Ltd (HMSO) 1988 section 6.1 p 41f.

2. cf for example Seabrook, Jeremy (1978) *What Went Wrong? Working People and the Ideals of the Labour Movement* (Victor Gollancz Ltd). Writing of working people in Bradford, Seabrook says, "Human skills (no less than work skills) absorbed unselfconsciously by the family have been taken away from them without effort and laboriously invested in professional social workers who have to be taught them, an act of human plunder." p 116f, see also pp 100, 211, 214.

3. cf 2 Timothy 2:15.

4. Amongst consultancy services on offer a few known to me can be mentioned by way of illustration. I have not surveyed or classified them. Approaches and methods vary considerably. The Oxford Diocese of the Church of England provides training in consultancy and is developing a course with Brookes University, Oxford. The Bible Society has developed a programme of consultancy services to help local churches to be missionary communities. These services were designed and organised by the Revd Barrie Cooke, whilst he was the Senior Consultant at the Bible Society. He is currently researching the work done over several years. Information can be obtained from Bible Society, Stonehill Green, Westlea, Swindon, SN5 7DG. The Conference of Religious (Roman Catholic) has done much to build up the consultancy facilities available to members of religious orders. MODEM, Managerial and Organizational Disciplines for the Enhancement of Ministry, was founded in 1993 "to set the agenda for management/ministry issues so that by the year 2000 the value and disciplines of those engaged in the management of secular and church organizations will be mutually recognised and respected." Information about MODEM can be obtained from Suite 503, Premier House, 10 Greycoat Place, London, SE1P 1SB. Amongst other things, MODEM has produced an annotated membership directory giving details of the people offering various kinds of consultancy services. The listed areas of the members' interests and expertise include: investment consultancy, management consultancy services, ministry consultancy, personnel consultancy. At best, appraisal schemes are gateways to consultancy help and they

are legion. And there is a growing number of technical publications for consultors and consultants, some are introductory, whilst others are handbooks and text books.

5. The papers were published in Casemore, Roger *(et al)* (1994) *What makes Consultancy Work— understanding the dynamics* International Consulting Conference 1994 (South Bank University Press). Unfortunately out of print.

6. *Telling Experiences* is an example.

7. A course is now being developed and offered through a partnership between Westminster College Oxford, Cliff College, Calver and The Urban Theology Unit, Sheffield. *Westminster College*, founded by the Methodist Church, has recently amalgamated with Brookes University, Oxford. It has pioneered an international distance learning programme in applied theology. *Cliff College* is a Methodist Institution situated between Sheffield and Chesterfield. It has an ecumenical and international student body. It is a mission training centre preparing laity and ministers for evangelism and Christian service. It has open educational access for its basic college courses. Graduate and post-graduate courses are validated by the University of Sheffield. It has a research programme. This is now acting as the lead institution to the course. *The Urban Theology Unit* is a Methodist Foundation which operates ecumenically. It has a pre-service training programme for ministers and a range of first and further degrees validated by the University of Sheffield. These colleges have a range of interests in consultancy for mission and ministry in contemporary society. They have quite different theological stances. Consequently the interaction between staff, students and colleges will of itself provide profound all round opportunities for learning. Details from Cliff College, Calver, Hope Valley, Derbyshire, S32 3XG. The course is a postgraduate two-year part-time course leading to a diploma or an MA in work and vocational consultancy for mission and ministry. It will be delivered through a combination of distance learning units, residential study and structured reflection upon practical consultancy engagement. Course members will study the theory and the theology of work consultancy. They will engage in the practice of consultancy as consultors, consultants and co-consultants to each other through various supported exercises based on their own studies and work. They will engage in assessed consultancy project work. A significant feature of the course is that it will contextualise work and vocational consultancy theory, practice and theology. Critical aspects of contemporary thought about the nature and the theology of church and community work, ministry and mission and the culture of organizations and communities will be studied.

APPENDIX I

Aids to Describing and Profiling
Work-Views and Situations

The outlines in this Appendix are designed to help people to write notes or position papers about themselves as practitioners and the situations in which they work or are about to work. They can be used to produce notes or position papers:

- which portray work views of practitioners and work situations
- for private use or to share with others
- as aids to analysis and design and personal and private reflecting
- to prime consultancy sessions
- for co-consultancy courses
- as aids to appraisal and self-appraisal.

This Appendix contains six outlines. You may choose the one which best suits your situation and with which you feel most comfortable. Or you may wish to pick and mix or simply pick out questions or sections.

Outline one has been extensively used to good effect by several thousand people working at all levels of seven denominations in the UK and many other countries. It is illustrated and described in *Analysis and Design* pp 71-106 and 301-303. Its use in relation to co-consultancy courses is discussed in Chapter Eight (see pp 357-360). An "energy audit" section has been added to include a sequence of questions which have proved to be useful in consultancies (cf pp 109-111).

Outline two is a new outline which has been pilot tested to good effect. It is based upon Part One of this book.

Outlines three, four and five are designed for consultors who have been appointed to work in posts and situations which are new to them. The first part of Outline five helps people to establish what they are learning from their past experience. This could have many uses.

Outline six is designed to help consultors prepare for consultations about projects. (*Analysis and Design* pp 93-106).

OUTLINE ONE: Your Present Work Situation

Guidelines are given below as writing prompts. Your own reflections are most important. Follow the suggestions where they are helpful. Supplement these to add things that are important to you and which you would like to include in your writing. Use the opportunity to write as fully and freely as you wish but 2000 words is a useful guide. For the sake of balance, normally no more than a quarter of the paper should be given to Part 1. This is not a questionnaire: the questions are meant to stimulate reflection, not to be answered one by one. Deliberately they come at things from different perspectives and can give the impression of repetition.

Part 1—My working life, journey and story

The first part invites you to reflect and write about your vocational story up to now and to assess your present position. The following headings may help you to do so.

The major landmarks in my vocational journey to the present.

People and ideas that have influenced me and my ministry.

Ways in which my present work fits into the story or my journey or seems a misfit.

The aspects of my ministry/work that I find enjoyable and fulfilling; difficult and frustrating; and those that occupy most of my time and thought.

Dimensions of my work/ministry that I would like to develop.

No more than a quarter of the paper should be given to Part 1.

Part 2—My beliefs, purposes and approaches

This part is for you to indicate the beliefs, principles, concepts, assumptions, ideas and purposes that are and have been fundamental to your life and work. Also indicate what you have learnt about working with and ministering to people that now informs the ways in which you work and minister (cf Outline five, Part one).

Part 3—The section of the organization, church (parish, circuit, diocese, district etc.) for which I am responsible.

My present job or appointment

Note how long you have been in the job and how long you hope/expect to remain in it. Describe the principal aspects of your present job, the overall context in which you have to do it and how they relate.

Features

Describe the features of the church or organization in which you work and the geographical area within which it operates, the activities in which it is engaged and the people for whom you work.

Describe the way you see the different church, organizational and community entities with which you work and the relationships between them.

Tasks and Purposes

Describe and rank in order of importance as you perceive them the main tasks and purposes of the part of the church or organization in which you work and the way it is organized to carry out its tasks.

Who is responsible for what areas of work?

Who makes decisions and carries them out?

The process by which decisions are made.

Ways in which people are accountable for the effectiveness and well-being of your church or organization and staff.

Relationships in theory and practice between national, regional and local levels.

Your views of these aspects.

My place in my church and organization

The way you see the place and role that you occupy in your church or organization.

The primary responsibilities and tasks that you undertake within your church or organization.

The ways in which you are supported from above and below.

Aspects of the church's or organization's life and structure which you find helpful and those which hinder.

How would you describe the primary working and personal relationships you have? For example, with colleagues, with other churches and religious orders or organizations, with others working professionally with you.

The Context

Can you state the positive and negative factors for you in the contemporary Christian, ecclesiastical and social contexts?

Change and Development

Describe any significant patterns you discern in the way in which things are proceeding and developing in your work. Note the things you consider to be sound, to be evolving satisfactorily, to need considering, to be ripe for change or assessment, to be problematic.

What has to change to make you and your church/organization significantly more effective and your work more satisfying?

Can you do a similar exercise on the way in which you are developing in your vocation/profession?

Feelings

Describe what you feel about yourself as a worker in the situation, the situation, your future participation.

Part 4—Energy Audits (cf pp 109-111)

This part provides you with an opportunity to audit and profile your experiences of the flux and flow of energy in yourself and in your working situation. Clearly, understanding these important aspects of the picture of your work dynamic could help you to become a better and more effective practitioner.

One way in which you can carry out the audits is by simply reflecting on questions given below. Another way is by keeping an "energy diary or journal" for specific periods in which notes are made, with or without reflective comment, about anything that happens energy wise. Then, the questions given below can be explored by examining and reflecting upon the recorded information and recollected experiences.

1. *A Personal energy audit* (cf p 110)

From where and in what ways do you find the emotional intellectual, moral and spiritual energy for your work?

How do you draw upon them?

What is the present quality of your energy here and now?

What does "energy" mean to you?

What metaphors and concepts do you use to think about it?

Do you experience positive/negative surges of energy?
When?
What causes them?

What good and bad effects do they have upon you and others?

What consumes most energy? Why?

What saps your energy and vitality?

What galvanises you?

What renews your energy? How?

What restricts/blocks your energy flow? Why?

What are the implications of your observations for you?

2. *A Situational energy audit* (cf p110)

Whom or what are the main sources of emotional, intellectual, moral and spiritual energy in your working situation/church/ organization?
    How do individuals and groups draw upon them?

What is the quality of this energy?
    How is it renewed and developed?

What importance do people attach to it?

What metaphors and concepts do the people use to discuss their energy and that of the organization/church?

Are there positive/negative surges of energy?
    When?
    What causes them?
    What good and bad effect do they have?

What consumes most energy? why? when?

What saps energy and vitality in your situation/church/organization?

What restricts energy flow? How? Why? When?

What galvanises people collectively?

What are the implications of your observations for you?

Part 5—Consultancy Need

Indicate what you wish/need to consult about and why.

OUTLINE TWO : Your Present Work Situation

Introduction

As in Outline One

Part 1—My Working life, journey and story

As in Outline One

Part 2—My beliefs, purposes and approaches

As in Outline One

Part 3—My working situation

This section correlates with Part Two of this book. It differentiates between:

    — *the work in which a church or organization engages in order to achieve its purposes. (There are two interrelated aspects of this: the work done to maintain the organization as a vital and viable operational institution for mission and ministry;*

the work done by the institution with and for its own members and with and for others in other churches, allied institutions and society.)

— *the work done by the workforce to enable the church to do its work;*

— *the work done by you in your own right and that which you do to facilitate the work of the whole organization and its workforce.*

The diagrammatic overview on p 250 might further elucidate the distinctions being made.

The work of "your" church or organization

This section is about the work of "your" church or organization
in contradistinction to the work that you do in it and with and for it.
The following questions point to the kind of information which could
help to get a picture and grasp on this.

- What kind(s) of work does your organization do? (Here "work" includes all purposeful activities including things such as worship and pastoral care.)

- What are the:
  — intended/desired outcomes of this work?
  — actual outcomes of this work?

  How would you describe the nature of the work?

- What is your assessment of the effectiveness of the work done?
  What is going well?
  What is not working as well as you would like?
  What is problematic?
  What needs attention?

- What new work would you like to see developed?

The work-force

- Apart from yourself who does this work?

- What work do they do, individually and collectively and independently and interdependently?

- What is your assessment of them as workers?

- How effective are they?

- How are they "managed" and to whom are they accountable?

- What resources, support, training are available to them?

- What attributes and new skills do they need to make them more effective?

- How amenable are they to staff develoment programmes?

- What do you feel about the workforce?

- Are there issues that need attention?

Your work

Describe briefly what is involved in:

    (a)   the work you do in your own right in the pursuit of your vocation within and beyond the situation/job to which you are appointed;

    (b)   the work you do to make the church/organization to which you are appointed function and that which you do to support and help others to do their jobs and pursue their vocations.

Clearly some of the work done in (b) facilitates that which you do in (a).

In relation to (a) and (b):

>What is key?
>
>How much of what you need to do are you able/expected/allowed to do?
>
>What would help you to be more effective?

Your context

Can you state the positive and negative factors for you in the contemporary Christian ecclesiastical and social contexts? If you can, have a go at doing so.

Change and development

As in Outline One.

Do you discern any implications in all this for you?

Feelings

Describe what you feel about yourself as a worker in the situation, the situation, your future participation.

Part 4—Energy Audits

As in Outline One.

Part 5—Consultancy Needs

Indicate what you wish/need to consult about and why.

OUTLINE THREE: A Prospective View of a New Post and Work Situation

This outline is a variant of Outline One.

Introduction

As in Outline One.

Part 1—My Working life, journey and story

As in Outline One.

Part 2—My beliefs, purposes and approaches

As in Outline One.

Part 3—The section of the organization, church (parish, circuit, diocese, district etc) for which I will be responsible

The job or appointment

Describe the principal aspects of the new job and the overall context in which you will be working.

Features

Note anything you know about the features of the church or organization in which you will work and the geographical area within which it operates, the activities in which it is engaged and the people for whom you will work.

Describe the way you see the things.

Describe how you feel about the new appointment and the hopes you have for it.

Your place in the church/organization in which you will work. How do you see:

— your primary responsibilities;

— the future of the church/organization.

The context

Can you state the positive and negative factors for you in the contemporary Christian, ecclesiastical and social contexts? If you can, have a go at doing so.

Change and Development

As in Outline One.

Do you discern any implications in all this for you?

Initial Hopes and Objectives

Describe your hopes and objectives for the new appointment.

Note the considerations, approaches and things which will guide:
— your entry into the new situation;
— the initial period.

Part 4—Energy Audits

As in Outline One.

Note particularly the energy you seem to have for the new appointment and what thinking about it does for your energy levels.

Part 5—Consultancy Needs

Indicate what you need to consult about and why.

OUTLINE FOUR: Prospective View of a New Post and Work Situation

This outline is a variant of Outline Two.

Part 1—My working life, journey and story

As in Outline One

Part 2—My beliefs, purposes and approaches

As Outline One.

Part 3—My working situation

Preamble

As in Outline Two.

The work of "your" new church or organization

This section is about the work of "your" new church or organization in contradistinction to the work that you will do in it and with and for it. The questions in Outline Two could help you articulate the picture you have of it.

The workforce in your new church or organization

The questions in Outline Two could help you to gather together what you know of the workforce.

Your work in the new post

Describe briefly what you think and feel about:

(a)   the work you will do in your own right in the pursuit of your vocation within and beyond the situation/job to which you are appointed.

(b)   the work you will do to make the church/organization to which you are appointed function and that which you do to support and help others to do their jobs and pursue their vocations.

Clearly some of the work done in (b) facilitates that which you do in (a).

In relation to (a) and (b):
- — What do you see to be key?
- — How much of what you need to do, do you expect to be able to do?
- — What hopes or concerns or fears do you have?

Your context

As in Outline Two.

Change and development

As in Outline One.

Do you discern any implications in all this for you?

Feelings

Describe what you feel about yourself as a worker and your participation in the new situation.

Part 4—Energy Audits

As in Outline One.

Part 5—Consultancy Needs

Indicate what you wish/need to consult about and why.

OUTLINE FIVE : Retrospect and Prospect in Transition Between Posts

This outline is designed to help consultors to update what they are learning from their previous experience and to carry it forward into the next phase of their work. Also, it suggests ways of looking forward.

Part 1—What is being learnt from the past

Much can be learnt from past experience if we make a conscious effort to use it constructively. Starting a new job can be a time to capitalise on our past experience, an opportunity to make a new start and to introduce change.

Looking back over your career, establish the main things you have learned from your previous experience that you really want to affect how you go about things in the future. The following questions and incomplete sentences may help you to review your past experience.

> I'll never do that again . . .
> Next time I'll make sure that . . .
> That's something worth remembering . . .
> That changed my approach to people/work/things . . .
> What do you want to avoid?
> What do you want to develop and build on?

Part 2—Looking forward

Drawing upon what you are learning from the past and what you know about your new appointment, make notes on the following topics.

Your new situation

> Note what you know/believe/hope/think/feel about the following aspects
> of your new situation.
>
> > The church, organization or institution by which you will be employed.
> >
> > The activities in which your church/organization is engaged. Classify
> > them if you can. For instance you could differentiate between:

the activities undertaken by the church; the activities undertaken by the church and other organizations; the activities on church premises undertaken by other agencies *e.g.:* clinics, playgroups.

The people who work in the church/organization.

Relationships with other local church, agencies, organizations and neighbourhood groups.

Approaching and Facing your new Situation
Describe :

Your feelings about and your reactions to the new situation.

What you must avoid, especially as a newcomer.

Opportunities, difficulties and ideas
Describe:

What are the main opportunities you see in being a newcomer and in your new appointment.

Problems you already know about or foresee.

Ideas you have for your new work and how can you test out whether or not they will fit the people and the situation.

Initial objectives

Describe what you want to achieve in the first few hours/days/weeks/months of your new job. (First impressions can be very important.)

Your home base

Assess how your new job will affect your home life and others close to you.

Will it affect, positively or negatively, other aspects of your life, leisure, study etc?

Your aims

Describe:

The beliefs, principles, concepts, assumptions, ideas and purposes that are and have been fundamental in your life and work.

What you want to help Christians and non-Christians in your new appointment to achieve in their lives.

All the questions may not fit your situation, but they may suggest others you should consider.

OUTLINE SIX : A Project Proposal
Part 1—The Project
Describe

— how the idea for the project originated.
— the stage of its development.
— the part you have played in its evolution.
— the church, organizational and community settings.

Part 2—Aspirations, Motivation, and Rationale

Make notes on the following.

What are the motivating beliefs and convictions about the project?

Why is the project needed?

411

The official purposes and objectives for the project.

Your purposes and objectives.

Official hopes and dreams for the project.

Your hopes and dreams.

Things to be avoided.

Part 3—Approaches and Methods

Describe the approaches to be adopted and the methods to be used.

Part 4—Critical Conditions and Factors

Features of the design and the working out of the project which in your opinion are necessary for its success/effectiveness.

Things which will impair the project or cause it to fail.

Critical contextual/environmental factors.

Part 5—Commitment

How do you rate your commitment to the project and that of others who are involved in it or able to affect it positively or negatively?

Part 6—Risk Factors

Note the risks.

Aspects of the project about which
   — you feel uneasy or unsure
   — you worry
   — you are afraid.

Things which would
   — allay your fears and misgivings
   — ameliorate the disadvantages
   — reduce the dangers and risks.

Part 7—Viability

How confident are you in the project?
What do you think are the chances of it coming off?
What snags, problems, difficulties do you foresee?

Part 8—Evaluation

How will the project be monitored?
How will the effectiveness of the project be evaluated?
What will have to happen for the project to be adjudged a success by
   — those with overall responsibility?
   — key individuals or groups associated with it?
   — you?

Part 9—Consultancy Need

Indicate what you wish/need to work at and to consult about and why.

APPENDIX II

Nature of the Non-Directive or *Avec* Approach to Church and Community Development Work

The nature of the core process (from experience through critical and imaginative thought to creative action) is fascinatingly complex; discovering some of its facets has been one of the exciting privileges of living and working with it. I can best summarise it in the following way.

In its application it is:

- a human and spiritual activity;
- focused and centred on workers and their work, however mundane it is;
- proactive, and stimulates and facilitates others to be proactive;
- outwardly directed to wider socio-religious contexts and issues;
- interventionist, provocative and perturbing but respects the autonomy and privacy of others;
- structured and systematic — not to impose order and shape but to enable others to order and shape their working world as they need to;
- logical, affective and intuitive, giving equal attention to thoughts, feelings and hunches;
- specific but systemic and holistic, concentrating on people, situations and issues;
- practical because it is theoretical and theological;
- collaborative and mutual accountability in action;
- both a private and a public activity;
- reflection-in-action, and, when used rigorously, a form of action research;
- hard but rewarding work!

In its effects it:

- uses and promotes theological understanding;
- engenders interdependency which properly respects independence and dependence;
- distributes power;
- empowers people;
- mandates equal opportunities to participate;
- promotes creative consensus by revealing and working constructively at differences, factions and conflicts;
- promotes self-induced and interrelated human and spiritual development in secular and religious contexts;
- is educational without being didactic — it leads to perceptive ways of "knowing" about the human and the divine;
- helps build socio-religious learning communities that can live and work for human well-being and the glory of God;
- equips people to work for development with each other and to be co-workers with Christ in the church and in the world;

- is ecumenical, bringing together in common endeavour all kinds of people;
- makes contributions to all stages of human and spiritual development;
- is challenging and stretching but deeply satisfying!

In its intention, orientation and approach it:

- starts with people where they are, accepting them and their situations as they are;
- stands by people without attempting to take their place;
- works to the rhythms of people;
- stimulates people to do all they can for the common good;
- is both inductive and deductive;
- is an act of faith in the abilities and willingness of others to pursue their own well-being and development and to work for the common good;
- is non-directive—religiously so in relation to the decisions people need to make for themselves;
- is complementary and integral to that which is done for us by God and other people;
- is inclusive rather than exclusive;
- contributes to all aspects of the ministry and mission of the church;
- makes unique and essential contributions to the work economy of the kingdom of God.

It can be embodied in people (individuals and collectives) and their work through their:

- love of people and God;
- inner commitments, human graces and technical skills.

Unfortunately there is no word or phrase that points to the richly endowed nature of this approach. What a travesty it is, for want of a better word, to have to call it "non-directive".

APPENDIX III

The Critical Consultancy Path of Avec Ten-Day Co-consultancy Work and Theory Courses

This Appendix models the essential design of co-consultancy courses described in Chapter Ten (pp 357-360). It is based on a critical examination by a group of people who had staffed a large number of the Avec ten-day co-consultancy courses. The model gathers together what has been learnt about conducting these courses. It draws upon the accumulated experience of conducting a large number of courses over a period of twenty years (cf *Avec: Agency and Approach* especially pp 41ff and 140). It is a well-tested and well-used model which has been useful to course staff members. The version presented here weaves together the various consultancy elements described earlier and illustrates stages in the creative consultancy process and the critical consultancy path. The following notes may help people to read and use the model which is charted separately.

- The chart could give the impression that the process is mechanical and invariable, a rigid rather than a human system. It is anything but that. It provides guidance and rubrics for those who wish to make each co-consultancy course a unique existential event. It helps staff and members of such groups to examine things openly, freely and constructively within agreed parameters.

- Working at content is a living process. The forms that creative participation takes varies from one group to another because each group is unique and moments of disclosure and transformation cannot be planned or foreseen, much less contrived. However, attention to attitude, approach, process and procedures can create atmospheres and circumstances most likely to engender creative participation. Attention to individual participants, the group and what is actually taking place is most likely to bring people, issues and content alive with a life that will outlive the group and the course.

- The chart shows the path by which members and staff find and work at the essential content. This is one cross section, as it were, of a complex pattern of interaction operating at many levels of consciousness and unconsciousness.

- Pursuing the stages of the critical path normally produces a good working dynamic between the members. Members of courses often said that they were "fortunate to be in a group that jelled and got on so well". Chance and providential factors are ever present but this phenomenon happened so often and in the most unlikely groups—in, for instance, ecumenical groups formed from four main denominations without selection processes in Northern Ireland during the height of the Troubles—for it to be simply a matter of chance or providence. It is best explained by approach and process.

- Theology, theory and practice provide a triple plaited core to the process from beginning to end but it is too confusing to show them running through the process on the chart.

- During the first week, broadly speaking, the essential movement is one of opening up and exploring ideas, issues, interests, concerns, problems and situations and identifying possibilities. The time between the two weeks is one of assimilation and preparing for the second week. Essentially this second week involves closing down on options and focusing on ways and means of working out the implications within the actualities of the lives and situations of the members.

415

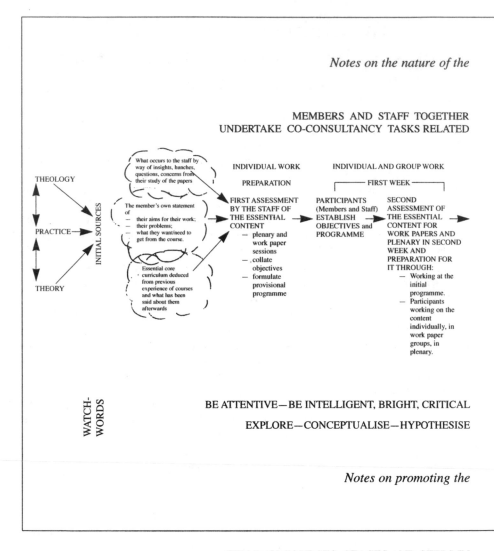

Notes on the nature of the

MEMBERS AND STAFF TOGETHER
UNDERTAKE CO-CONSULTANCY TASKS RELATED

THEOLOGY

INITIAL SOURCES

PRACTICE

THEORY

What occurs to the staff by way of insights, hunches, questions, concerns from their study of the papers

The member's own statement of
— their aims for their work;
— their problems;
— what they want/need to get from the course.

Essential core curriculum deduced from previous experience of courses and what has been said about them afterwards

INDIVIDUAL WORK
PREPARATION

FIRST ASSESSMENT BY THE STAFF OF THE ESSENTIAL CONTENT
— plenary and work paper sessions
— collate objectives
— formulate provisional programme

INDIVIDUAL AND GROUP WORK
FIRST WEEK

PARTICIPANTS (Members and Staff) ESTABLISH OBJECTIVES and PROGRAMME

SECOND ASSESSMENT OF THE ESSENTIAL CONTENT FOR WORK PAPERS AND PLENARY IN SECOND WEEK AND PREPARATION FOR IT THROUGH:
— Working at the initial programme.
— Participants working on the content individually, in work paper groups, in plenary.

WATCH-WORDS

BE ATTENTIVE—BE INTELLIGENT, BRIGHT, CRITICAL
EXPLORE—CONCEPTUALISE—HYPOTHESISE

Notes on promoting the

TEN-DAY COURSES: STAGES AND STEPS IN
AND WORKING AT ESSENTIALS RELATED

co-consultancy process on next page

SHAPE THE COURSE AND
TO ANALYSIS AND DESIGN IN PLENARY AND SUB-GROUP SESSIONS

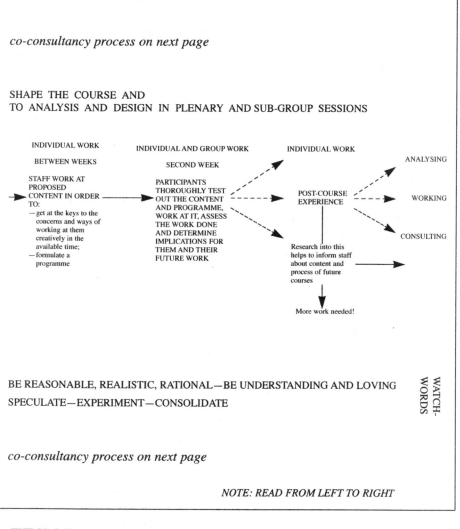

BE REASONABLE, REALISTIC, RATIONAL—BE UNDERSTANDING AND LOVING

SPECULATE—EXPERIMENT—CONSOLIDATE

WATCH-WORDS

co-consultancy process on next page

NOTE: READ FROM LEFT TO RIGHT

THE PROCESSES OF FINDING, CONSULTING
TO CONSULTORS AND THEIR WORK

Notes on the Co-Consultancy Processes in Ten-Day Work and Theory Courses

1. The content Process as a Whole

(a) It is a process fed by many streams of thought and therefore it variously flows smoothly, turbulently, slowly, rapidly.

(b) It is a process which opens up wide areas of work and then centres down on critical content.

(c) When functioning it is alive. It has existential moments and events which are frequently occasions of disclosure. These cannot be planned, programmed or anticipated. They happen and they are key.

(d) However, the sequence of events can be planned; the process often loops back on itself going over previous discussions and ideas until the core is reached.

(e) Tidiness and the desire to get on can inhibit what is indicated in (c) and (d).

2. Promoting the Process as a Whole

• You cannot produce the process but you can make significant contributions towards creating the conditions and circumstances most conducive to it happening and you can live it out.

• Work to people, their work and the subject matter. Check:
  — are we doing this or working to our own agenda?
  — periodically reflect on how things seem to be going with the group and each person in turn and follow up your conclusions;
  — are there any clues you have not taken seriously?

• Given that it is highly desirable that people are able to promote this process should you make overt the essential process and if so when?

• What kind of changes are necessary to bridge any gaps there might be between their work as it is and as it could/should be?

• See this book and *Analysis and Design* about promoting participation and structuring content.

• Work with the parts *and* with the whole: working with a part can facilitate a holistic approach.

• Present your thinking succinctly and clearly in words and/or diagrams and/or charts.

• Mobilise the group to work with you on promoting the processes and especially when you are stuck or lost—but think things through yourself independently as well as you possibly can.

• Check that you are doing *for* participants what needs to be done *for* them, doing *with* them what must be done *with* them and leaving them to do *with* each other and *for themselves* what they must do *with* each other *for* themselves.

3. Aids to Promoting the Process Stage by Stage

Prior to Co-Consultancy Sessions

• Explore the material, scan it and search it out; let your mind and attention move around it.

• Immerse yourself in the material, empathise and suspend critical judgement until you feel you have got inside the worker and his/her situation.

• Note key issues that are emerging, cluster and group them, assess which will be best dealt with in work paper groups and which in plenary sessions.

- Note what the position/work papers are saying to you. e.g.: their problems may not seem to you to be *the* problems; their ideas and statements may not be consistent or coherent.
- Mull things over assimilate them and note what occurs to you;.
- Extract list of their problems and issues for ease of reference.
- In forming and establishing position/work paper co-consultancy groups take care to:
  — list criteria for groups;
  — list characteristics of members;
  — form provisional groups;
  — check with criteria;
  — check when meet people;
  — publish groups.

Preparing for plenary sessions

- Assemble data so that people can look at it in various ways (with left and right brain) which could mean using charts, diagrams and pictures as well as words.

At Initial Session

- Present the initial programme and possibly a list of the provisional aims so that people can grasp them and consider them. Check before the session:
  — will members be able to test out the objectives and programme critically?
  — what more can you do to help them to do so?
- After the session check:
  — did they really test things?
  — if not what should you do?

During the course

- Enable as many people as possible to work with as many as possible in pairs and small groups—keep a record of the pairs and the membership of the sub-groups and use it as a check list.

Getting out agenda items, approaches and emphases for the second week

- Take great care when getting out ideas for the second week with the members, to get clear precisely what subject matter they want/need to work at, do not assume anything. Do all that is possible to get all the essentials by pruning and clarifying. It saves a lot of time later.

Preparing the second week programme

- Do not make an automatic transfer of the suggestions to a programme for the second week—scan them, explore them, work at them, shape them in this way and that until you get the essence of things. Then programme it, it will be easier to work at.
- Work through subject matter privately and then go back over it to find ways and means of helping the members and the group to work at it creatively, separately and together.

Bibliography

This short bibliography is restricted to books related to the main themes of this book, work and vocational consultancy. It is a guide to authors whose approaches to consultancy are similar to or which resonate with or illuminate the approach described in this book. In one way or another they have helped me to understand, form and develop my own approach. They could help readers to do the same as they formulate their own practice theory.

Books marked with an * contain case study material.

Milan Kubr's book is the most systematic, comprehensive and professional exposition of consultancy that I have found. The latest edition is 850 plus xvi pp!

Argyle, Michael, and Henderson, Monika (1985), *The Anatomy of Relationships and the Rules and Skills to Manage them Successfully* (Heinemann, London).

Batten, T. R. in collaboration with Batten, Madge (1967), *The Non-Directive Approach in Group and Community Work* (Oxford University Press). This book is now out of print but the first two parts have been reprinted as, Batten, T. R. and Batten, M. (1988), *The Non-Directive Approach* (An Avec Publication)*.

Batten, T. R. with the collaboration of Madge Batten (1965), *The Human Factor in Community Work* (Oxford University Press)*.

Batten, T. R. with the collaboration of Madge Batten (1970), *The Human Factor in Youth Work* (Oxford University Press).

Bellman, Geoffrey, M. (1990), *The Consultant's Calling, Bringing Who you are to What you do* (San Francisco, Jossey-Bass).

Block, Peter (1981), *Flawless Consulting, A Guide to Getting your Expertise used* (San Diego, Pfeiffer & Company).

Bradford, Leland P. (1976), *Making Meetings Work: A Guide for Leaders and Group Members* (University Associates)*.

Briscoe, Catherine and Thomas, David (1977), *Community Work: Learning and Supervision* (George Allen and Unwin).

Brown, Rob and Brown, Margaret (1994), *Empowerment: A Practical Guide to Leadership in the Liberated Organization* (Nicholas Brealey, Publishing).

Campbell, D. (1995), *Learning Consultation*, (Karnac Books).

Campbell, D., Coldicott, T. and Kinsella, K. (1994), *Systemic Work with Organizations: A New Model for Managers and Change Agents* (Karnac Books).

Campbell, D., Draper, R. and Huffington, C. (1992), *Teaching Systemic Thinking* (Karnac Books).

Campbell, D., Draper, R. and Huffington, C. (1992), *A Systemic Approach to Consultation* (Karnac Books).

Caplan, Gerald and Killilea, Marie (eds) (1976), *Support Systems and Mutual Help* (Grune and Stratton)*.

Casemore, Roger, Dyos, Gail, Eden, Angela, Kellner, Kamil, McKauley, John, Moss, Stephen (eds) (1994), *What Makes Consultancy Work: International Consulting Conference* (South Bank University Press).

Chawla, S. and Renesch, J. (eds) (1994), *Learning Organizations: Developing Cultures for Tomorrow's Workplace* (Productivity Press).

Checkland, Peter and Scholes, Jim (1990), *Soft Systems Methodology in Action* (John Wiley & Sons)*.

Cockman, Peter, Evans, Bill, Reynolds, Peter (1992), *Client Centred Consulting, A Practical Guide for Internal Advisers and Trainers* (London, McGraw-Hill Book Company).

Craig, Adolf Guggenbuhl (1982), *Power in the Helping Professions* (Spring Books).

Eastell, Kevin (ed) (1994), *Appointed for Growth: A Handbook for Ministry Development and Appraisal* (Mowbray).

Friedman, Edwin H. (1985), *Generation to Generation: Family Process in Church and Synagogue* (Guildford Press).

Friumara, Gemma Corradi (1980), *The Other Side of Language: A Philosophy of Listening* (Routledge).

General Synod Board for Mission and Unity (1984), *Mission Audit* (Church House Publishing).

Gordon, Judith (1993) *Organizational Behaviour: A Diagnostic Approach* (Allyn & Baker).

Grundy, Malcolm (1998), *Understanding Congregations* (Mowbray).

Handy, Charles (1976), *Understanding Organizations* (Penguin).

Handy, Charles (1988), *Understanding Voluntary Organizations* (Penguin).

Harris, Margaret (1998), *Organizing God's Work* (Macmillan Press Ltd).

Huffington, C. and Brunning, H. (1994) *Internal Consultancy in the Public Sector: Case Studies* (Karnac Books).

Inger, I. and Inger, J,. (1992), *Co-Constructing Therapeutic Conversations: A Consultation of Restraint* (Karnac Books).

Jacobs, Michael (1989). Holding in Trust—*The Appraisal of Ministry* (SPCK).

Kubr, Milan (ed) (1996 Third [revised] edition), *Management Consulting: A Guide to the Profession* (International Labour Office, Geneva).

Leech, Kenneth (1977, Seventh impression 1985), *Soul Friend: A Study of Spirituality* (Sheldon Press).

Lippett, Gordon and Lippett, Ronald (1986) *The Consulting Process* (University Associates Inc.)*.

Lovell, G. (1994), *Analysis and Design: A Handbook for Practitioners and Consultants in Church and Community Work* (Burns & Oates).

Lovell, G. (ed) (1996) *Telling Experiences: Stories About a Transforming Way of Working with People* (Chester House).

Lovell, George and Widdicombe, Catherine (1978), *Churches and Communities: An Approach to Development in the Local Church* (Search Press)*.

Lyon, David (1994), *Postmodernity* (Open University).

McCaughan, N. and Palmer, B. (1994), *Systems Thinking for Harassed Managers* (Karnac Books).

Margerison, Charles J. (1988), *Managerial Consulting Skills* (Gower Publishing Aldershot).

Mills, John and Nelson, John (1983) *Explorations into Parish Ministry: A Guide to Joint Work Consultation* (Liverpool Diocese).

Morgan, Gareth (1986), *Images of Organizations* (Sage) *.

Morgan, Gareth (1989), *Creative Organizations Theory, A Resource Book* (Sage).

Nelson, John (ed) (1996), *Management and Ministry: Appreciating Contemporary Issues* (The Canterbury Press).

Nelson, John (ed) (1999), *Leading, Managing, Ministering: challenging questions for church and society* (The Canterbury Press).

Palazzoli, Mara Selvini *et al* (1986), *The Hidden Games of Organizations* (Pantheon Books)*.

Russell, Anthony (1980), *The Clerical Profession* (SPCK).

Schein, Edgar H. (1985), *Organizational Culture and Leadership* (Jossey-Bass, San Francisco).

Schein, Edgar H. (1988), *Process Consultation Vol. I—Its Role in Organization Development* (Addison Wesley Publishing Co.)*.

Schein, Edgar H. (1987), *Process Consultation Vol. II—Lessons for Managers and Consultants* (Addison Wesley Publishing Co.)*.

Torrington, Derek and Hall, Laura (1995), *Personnel Management* (Prentice Hall).

Waring, Marilyn (1989), *If Women Counted: A New Feminist Economics* (Macmillan).

Widdicombe, C. (2000), *Meetings that Work: A practical guide to teamworking Groups* (The Lutterworth Press) .

Widdicombe, C. (2000), *Small Communities in Religious Life: making them work* (The Lutterworth Press) .

Wynne, Lyman, McDaniel, Susan and Weber, Timothy (eds) (1985), *Systems Consultation* (Guildford)*.

Index of Subjects

Index of Names

Index of Bible Passages